THE ILLUSTRATED ENCYCLOPEDIA OF THE
UNIVERSE

THE ILLUSTRATED ENCYCLOPEDIA OF THE

UNIVERSE

Exploring and Understanding the Cosmos

Principal Author
Richard S. Lewis

HARMONY BOOKS

NEW YORK

A Salamander Book

Published by Harmony Books, a division of Crown Publishers, Inc., One Park Avenue, New York, New York 10016 and simultaneously in Canada by General Publishing Company Limited

HARMONY and colophon are trademarks of Crown Publishers, Inc.

Manufactured in Belgium.

Library of Congress Cataloging in Publication Data

Lewis, Richard S.,1916—
    The illustrated encyclopedia of the universe.

    1. Solar system—Popular works. 2. Space probes—Popular works. I. Title.

QB501.2.L48   1983   523   83-10730
ISBN 0-517-55109-8

10 9 8 7 6 5 4 3 2 1

First American Edition

This book may not be sold outside the United States of America and Canada.

Credits

Editor:
Philip de Ste. Croix
Editorial consultant:
Dr. S.A. Briggs,
Queen Mary College, University of London
Contributing author (captions):
Heather Couper

Designers:
Nick Buzzard
Roger Hyde
Carol Warren

Color cutaway artwork:
Michael Badrocke
© Salamander Books Ltd
Color planetary artwork:
Tudor Art Studios
Ross Wardle
Bernard Robinson
©.Salamander Books Ltd

Diagrams:
Michael Badrocke
Alan Hollingbery
TIGA
© Salamander Books Ltd

Filmset:
Modern Text Typesetting Ltd, England
Color and monochrome reproduction:
Culver Graphics Ltd
Rodney Howe Ltd, England

Printed in Belgium:
Henri Proost et Cie, Turnhout

Acknowledgments

In the course of preparing this book for publication, I have been fortunate to receive advice and assistance from a host of people. I would like to take this opportunity of thanking them all. Apart from the exceptional support that I received from Richard Lewis and his team of contributing authors, I would like to mention the valuable consultancy work undertaken by Dr Stephen Briggs who advised on the selection of pictures and diagrams for the first five chapters, and who also captioned them; and thank Heather Couper who wrote most of the captions for Part II.

The pictures that appear in this encyclopedia come from many sources, and in this connection I would like to thank all the contributing artists, and the many aerospace manufacturers, space research institutes and astronomical observatories that have supplied photographs, and whose pictures are credited on page 320. In particular, I must mention the excellent co-operation I received from NASA personnel, both at Headquarters in Washington D.C., and the many research centres that were contacted. The help of several individuals in providing pictures was also invaluable. They include: David Skinner; Theo Pirard; David Allen and David Malin of the Anglo-Australian Telescope; M.C. Sandford and E. Dunford of the Rutherford Appleton Laboratory; Peter Hingley at the Royal Astronomical Society; Dr Robert Hutchison, Department of Mineralogy, British Museum (Natural History); Dr Rupert Haydn of the University of Munich; Dr Raymond Davis of Brookhaven National Laboratory; Margaret Weems at the National Radio Astronomy Observatory; Charles Veillet of CERGA; Jurrie van der Woude at JPL; Rice Sumner Wagner; Jack Bateman and Renate Scheb at Hughes Aircraft Company.

I gratefully acknowledge permission to quote copyright material: from W. H. Auden's poem *Nocturne* in his *Collected Poems*—courtesy Faber and Faber Ltd and Random House Inc. (US edition edited by Edward Mendelson); the excerpt from T. S. Eliot's *Four Quartets*—courtesy Faber and Faber Ltd; from *For the 1956 Opposition of Mars*—courtesy Robert Conquest.

Finally, I would like to thank Roger Chesneau for his editorial assistance, Harry Coussins for reading the proofs, and Stuart Craik for compiling the index.

Philip de Ste. Croix

Contents

J.R. Arnold

Professor James R. Arnold was born in New Jersey in 1923 and was educated at Princeton University, where he gained an AB, an MA and a PhD in chemistry. He was awarded a Fellowship at the Institute of Nuclear Studies, University of Chicago, in 1946, where from 1948 until 1955 he was Assistant Professor. He was Assistant Professor of Chemistry at Princeton for two years from 1955 and Associate Professor in 1957-58. Associate Professor of Chemistry at the University of California, San Diego, from 1958 until 1960, he was Chairman of the UCSD's Department of Chemistry 1959-62, becoming Professor of Chemistry in 1960. In 1964 he was elected to the National Academy of Sciences. In 1980 Professor Arnold became the First Director of the California Space Institute, the University's newly established Statewide Research Organisation.

Among the many honours and awards conferred on him have been the Ernest Orlando Lawrence Award (Atomic Energy Commission, 1968), a Guggenheim Fellowship (1972), the Meteoritical Society's Leonard Medal (1976), an Honorary Lectureship by the American Astronomical Society's Division of Planetary Sciences (1974) and the James B. Macelwayne Award (American Geophysical Union, 1976). He was Contributing Editor to "Comments on Astrophysics and Space Physics" from 1974 to 1976, and from 1980 has been an editorial board member of *Icarus*, the International Journal of Solar System Studies.

M.J.S. Belton

Dr Michael J.S. Belton holds a PhD and is currently an astronomer at the Kitt Peak National Observatory in Tucson, Arizona. He is a specialist in spectroscopy and planetary atmospheres and has contributed more than eighty research papers on these topics. He is at present the team leader for the Imaging Science

(Television) Experiment on NASA's Project Galileo which is to be launched in 1986 to orbit Jupiter.

E.G. Chipman

Dr Eric Chipman, born in 1944, was educated at Harvard University, where he gained a BA and subsequently a PhD in Astronomy. From 1972 until 1978 he was a Research Associate at the Laboratory for Atmospheric and Space Physics at the University of Colorado, where he worked on the design, the operation and analysis of data from one of the experiments on board NASA's Orbiting Solar Observatory-8 (OSO-8) satellite.

Since 1978 Dr Chipman has been Program Scientist in the Solar and Heliospheric Physics Office at NASA Headquarters in Washington, D.C.; this office is responsible for the planning of NASA's space missions for the study of the Sun and the solar wind, and his duties include arranging reviews and making funding recommendations for research and analysis programmes, headquarters co-ordination of the science programme for the Solar Maximum Mission, the Solar Optical Telescope and the OSS-1 mission, the management of the selection process for science instruments on board the Solar Optical Telescope, the presentation of research results, and the detailed planning of future solar physics programmes.

D. Dooling

Dave Dooling is Science Editor of *The Huntsville (Alabama) Times*, Editor-in-Chief of *Space World* magazine (published in co-operation with the National Space Institute) and Managing Editor and chief writer of *Canopus* (published by the American Institute of Aeronautics and Astronautics). He has contributed articles for *Spaceflight*, *Astronautics & Aeronautics*, *Astronomy* magazine, Funk & Wagnall's *Yearbook*, the *World Topics* annual, *Odyssey* magazine

and Salamander's *Encyclopedia of Sp* has edited *Shuttle Space Age*, and is c *Huntsville: A Picto*

His work has bee by the bestowal of such as the Nation Goddard History E the NSC's Press Av Aerospace Writer's Award and the Ala Professional Engin Journalism Award. associate fellow of Interplanetary Soc member of the Ame of Aeronautics and of the Aerospace V Association, of the Association of Scie and of the Nationa

K.W. Gatland

Kenneth W. Gatlan President of the Br planetary Society– beginning of the Sp first book, *Develop Guided Missile* (19 immediately transl republished in Mos known many of the and astronauts pers own contributions are recorded in the programme. (Notab studies for small m satellite launchers, rendezvous and do techniques for land lunar module on th orbiting mothership

Mr Gatland was f member of the desi Hawker Aircraft Lt past 25 years he ha himself to space stu writing about space He has been a mem Council since 1945, years edited the Soc publication *Spacefl* currently works for Aerospace at Kings Thames. In additior technical writing, h contributes as Spac Correspondent to T

Contributors

S. Lewis

...orn in 1941 at Trenton, New ...ersey. John S. Lewis is Professor ...t the University of Arizona's ...unar and Planetary Laboratory, ...epartment of Planetary Sciences, ...ucson, Arizona. His scholastic ...ualifications include an AB in ...hemistry from Princeton ...niversity, an MA in Organic ...hemistry from Dartmouth College ...nd a PhD in Geochemistry and ...hysical Chemistry from the ...niversity of California at San ...iego. Among his honours and ...wards have been an Honorary ...ectureship conferred by the ...merican Astronomical Society ...Division of Planetary Sciences) in ...974 and the James B. Macelwayne ...ward of the American ...Geophysical Union in 1976, while ...e was also Guggenheim Lecturer ...t the US National Air and Space ...Museum, Smithsonian Institution, ...n 1974.

From 1974 until 1976 he was ...Contributing Editor to "Comments ...n Astrophysics and Space ...Physics" and since 1980 has been ...n editorial board member of ...carus, the International Journal ...f Solar System Studies. Since ...970, Professor Lewis has also ...erved on numerous advisory ...ommittees sponsored by NASA ...nd by the US National Academy ...f Sciences/Space Science Board.

R.S. Lewis

...Richard S. Lewis, a journalist ...pecialising in science and ...echnology, has covered US space ...rogrammes since Project ...Mercury. A former Science Editor ...f *The Chicago Sun-Times* and ...Editor of the *Bulletin of the Atomic ...Scientists*, Mr Lewis has recently ...completed a history of the Space ...Shuttle; his earlier books include ...*Appointment on the Moon*, a ...history of the US space programme ...rom Explorer 1 to Apollo 11; and ...*From Vinland to Mars*, an analysis ...f exploration over the last one ...housand years. He is also the ...author of a history of US Antarctic ...exploration—*A Continent for ...Science*—and a work describing

the beginnings of the anti-nuclear movement in the USA, *The Nuclear Power Rebellion*. He contributed two chapters to Salamander's *The Illustrated Encyclopedia of Space Technology*: "Man on the Moon" and "The Space Shuttle". In other fields, he has written books on special education for children with learning disabilities and management of the brain-injured child. He is a graduate of Pennsylvania State University, and a member of the US National Press Club and of the British Inter-planetary Society. He was, until recently, the vice-mayor, and a Town Council Member, of his home town, Indialantic, Florida.

S.P. Maran

Dr Stephen P. Maran is Senior Staff Scientist at the Laboratory for Astronomy and Solar Physics at the NASA-Goddard Space Flight Center, researching into nebulae and stars, comets and observational ground-based and space astronomy. Born in 1938, he obtained a BS Physics degree at Brooklyn College and an MA in Astronomy and a PhD in Astronomy at the University of Michigan. His current work includes a number of programmes associated with the Space Telescope; he has previously been responsible for the 50in automated telescope programme at Kitt Peak National Observatory and been Senior Lecturer in Astronomy at the University of California, Los Angeles and part-time Visiting Lecturer in Astronomy at the University of Maryland; he has worked at the Goddard Center since 1969, where he was Project Scientist for Orbiting Solar Observatories, Manager of Operation Kohoutek and Head of the Advanced Systems and Ground Observations Branch.

Dr Maran is co-author of a number of books, including *New Horizons in Astronomy* and *A Meeting with the Universe*, while he is the Astronomy columnist for *Natural History* magazine and contributes to such publications

as *Scientific American, Popular Science, Physics Today* and *Sky & Telescope*. He is the Associate Editor of *Astrophysical Letters* and is currently editing a new work entitled *The Encyclopedia of Astronomy and Astrophysics*.

T.L. Page

Dr Thornton L. Page was born in New Haven, Connecticut, in 1913. Educated at Yale, where he obtained a BS degree in Physics and Maths, he was a Rhodes Scholar from 1934 to 1937 and then took up a position as Chief Assistant at Oxford Observatory. For twelve years from 1938 he was at the University of Chicago and from 1950 was Deputy Director at the Operations Research Office, during which time he acted as Science Advisor to the HQ US Army in Europe. In 1958 he became Professor of Astronomy at Wesleyan University; from 1971 to 1976 he was an Astrophysicist at the Naval Research Laboratory; and he subsequently joined the NASA-Johnson Space Center as Research Astrophysicist.

Among Dr Page's highly regarded contributions in the field of space science have been the design and production of two fast spectro-graphs, one with an image tube, and the compilation of research papers on the spectra of nebulae and comets, on nuclear warfare, on communications, on the masses of galaxies and on clusters of galaxies. He has also written and edited a large number of publications, many in association with his wife Lou. He was awarded the NASA Medal for Exceptional Scientific Achievement in 1975.

T. Pirard

Theo Pirard was born in Belgium in 1947 and graduated from the Catholic University in Louvain with a degree in Modern History. He is currently Director of the Centre d'Information Spatiale (Space Information Centre) in Belgium, contributing articles to several specialised periodicals including *Space Age Review*,

Avianews International, Spaceflight and *Satellite Week*. He contributed the sections on European, Japanese, Indian, Italian and private launch centres to Salamander's *The Illustrated Encyclopedia of Space Technology*. He is a member of many organisations, including the British Interplanetary Society, the L-5 Society, the Planetary Society, the National Space Institute and the American Institute of Aeronautics and Astronautics. He is especially interested in the future of Man in space.

S.E. Strom

Stephen E. Strom, born in 1942 at Bronx, NY, gained AB, AM and PhD degrees at Harvard University in 1962-64 and since then has held a number of important positions in the field of space science, including that of Professor of Astronomy at SUNY, Stony Brook, and of Visiting Professor of Astronomy at the University of California at Berkeley; today he is Adjunct Professor of Astronomy at the University of Arizona and an Astronomer at the Kitt Peak National Observatory. His particular interest is the study of the evolution of stars and galaxies. He has served on a number of committees, including the Review Committee for Astronomy Proposals (Office of Naval Research), the Greenstein Committee's Optical Astronomy and Theoretical Panels and the NASA Spacelab II Experiments Review Panel; he was a member, and subsequently Chairman, of the Committee on Space Astronomy and Astrophysics and has been a member of the Space Science Board and a Councillor of the American Astronomical Society. Currently, he is Associate Editor of the influential *Astrophysical Journal*. Among his honours have been the award of a Woodrow Wilson fellowship (1963), the 1971 Bok Prize (Harvard University) and the 1976 Warner Prize of the American Astro-nomical Society.

We have been privileged to live and participate in one of the most exhilarating periods in human history.

During the past quarter century, only about one-third of a normal human lifespan, we have begun to expand our environment beyond the Earth. In the process, we have advanced our knowledge of mankind's place in the Universe further than in all previous eras.

We have visited the Moon. We have explored the planets in some detail. We have lived and worked in space for an extended time, breaking away from the pull of gravity that bound us to Earth until the last half of this century. Our spacecraft have landed on Mars and Venus and explored them in great detail. And by the end of this decade we will have observed at close range all of the planets of our Solar System, except Pluto.

Hundreds of scientific spacecraft are giving us new insights into the immensity and beauty of the Universe and expanded knowledge of its origins and ultimate destiny. This great adventure into the unknown is only beginning. But we are learning how we came to be and, equally important, what we can become in the future, as civilization expands inevitably into space.

From man's earliest days on Earth, we gazed at the stars. We wondered at those flickering points of light in the heavens and dreamed that some day we would wander among them. Today we know that those dreams will be realized some day in the not-too-distant future.

The basic human urge to know the unknown is firmly rooted in the human spirit. Indeed, it is one of the common elements in the forward march of all great civilizations. This is especially true for Americans, who in 300 years or so, have demonstrated a restless and inquiring psyche and natural bent toward discovery.

The exploration of space, however, is not the job of any one nation, or any group of nations. Nor should it be. Rather, it is the job of all peace-loving peoples on Earth. For space exploration can be the catalyst for a great human adventure which could give mankind access to the infinite resources of the Universe and its potential to enrich knowledge and the human spirit.

We, in the United States, are now at a pivotal period in space exploration. With the Space Shuttle we are making dramatic and rapid progress in learning to live and work in space. Ultimately, perhaps within a decade, we will be operating a long-duration manned facility, or space station, in low Earth orbit. The station would not only increase our capabilities for scientific investigations, but it will hasten the advent of the truly commercial era in space that we have been dreaming of for the past quarter century. The most important commercial developments are ones we have not yet dreamed of, simply because we have not been operating long enough in space to realize its infinite potential.

A space station lends itself uniquely to extended and extensive international co-operation. If the United States can attract partners in such a venture, there would be benefits for all involved. And we would have a highly visible symbol of what free people, working together, can accomplish.

With such a station, we would have an essential stepping stone to the future. With the use of an orbital transfer vehicle, to be developed to move us into geosynchronous orbit, we would be able to operate routinely some 22,000 miles above the Earth. From there, perhaps, we will begin to take the next step—the realization of Wernher von Braun's great dream to return to the Moon to build a base, and from there, to mount a manned expedition to Mars.

As a species, human beings are unique. We have the ability not only to steer our own evolution, but to forge our own destiny. Indeed, the only limits imposed on us are those of our imaginations.

We are only beginning to gain a real perspective on our own potential as we learn more about our place in the scheme of the Cosmos. Four and a half centuries after Copernicus liberated the human race from the notion that the Earth was the centre of the Universe, we have learned much. But we have come to realize how much more there is to know.

As we continue to expand our knowledge of who we are and how we came to be, we can expect to realize the full potential of the human spirit to develop and progress.

Our rendezvous with the Cosmos is just beginning. We have set sail on an endless sea. And it is quite possible that our voyage will continue far longer than we can even imagine. As the great Norwegian scholar-statesman Fridtjof Nansen once said,

"The history of the human race is a continuous struggle from darkness toward light. It is, therefore, of no purpose to discuss the use of knowledge—man wants to know. And when he ceases to do so, he is no longer man."

What we have done and what we have learned has brought a new sense of pride to the human race.

It has refreshed our spirits and heightened our awareness of the human potential and of our options as a species.

It has brought us new knowledge and an infinite capacity for astonishment about how much more there is to know.

It has given us a new field of commercial and scientific opportunity.

It has provided us with a renewed confidence in the human potential.

And it is beginning to bring the world's people closer to one another. For space exploration ignites human hopes and expectations and reminds us of our common heritage and common destiny.

Indeed, as the focus of the collective vision and boldness of free and imaginative people, it is at the core of our common humanity.

Foreword

James M. Beggs

Administrator,
National Aeronautics and Space Administration
August 1983

"We shall not cease from exploration
And the end of all our exploring
Will be to arrive where we started
And know the place for the first time."

T.S. Eliot *Little Gidding, Four Quartets*

How will history account for the onset of space exploration in our time? Having been conceptualized in modern terms in the late 19th century, the space age opened in this century as soon as technology made it possible. Why?

Was it the logical outgrowth of the development of rocket technology during the Second World War and the rivalry of the Cold War? Or is its motivation more fundamental than the economic, political and military competition that induced the advanced societies to invest in it?

In terms of cause and effect, the exploration of space may be considered an inevitable reaction to the techno-scientific revolution. This idea was succinctly expressed in a remark attributed to Mark Twain:

"When it's steamboat time, you steam."

We do, but why? From a biological view, space exploration may be a response to the limits of growth imposed by the finite resources of one planet. Philosophically, it may be said to express the intellectual drive to understand the nature of the Universe and the processes of its origin and evolution. It may be the techno-scientific means by which man seeks to identify his role and divine his purpose in the design of the cosmos.

The search for genesis, indeed, is as old as the human species. It has taken many paths throughout history. In the space age, it remains a magnificent adventure.

Yet, even as an aspect of techno-scientific development, space exploration seems to derive its impetus from a characteristic of the human species. This is an imperative which is deeply ingrained in the human psyche. It functions as a compulsion to extend the range of human experience, to cross rivers, oceans and continents; to conquer Everest, reach the South Pole, be first on the Moon.

This imperative may be rationalized as an aspect of political and economic aggrandizement or of survival, but it goes beyond ordinary motives. It impels man not only to know the natural world but to assert mastery over it and control it. Space technology extends this drive beyond the Earth, into the Solar System, the Galaxy, the Universe.

Historically, space exploration appears to be a continuation of a process of expansion initiated by western people a thousand years ago with the Norse voyages to Greenland and Canada. Five hundred years after Eric the Red colonized Greenland, Columbus and Magellan transformed the Ptolemaic view of the world to one which more closely corresponds with the world we know now. And 500 years later, the exploration of the Moon and planets has transformed man's perception of the nature of the Solar System. From the vast unknown has emerged a comonwealth of new worlds, open to mankind.

The Exploration Imperative has been a force throughout history. It has functioned as a mode of adaptation in which the human species, having spread over the Earth even before the dawn of history, now stands on the verge of expanding beyond its terrestrial habitat.

We who live at the beginning of the space age have been privileged to witness an event of evolutionary scale. Long after many other events of the 20th century have faded from memory, the onset of space exploration will remain as a benchmark in the record of mankind.

In this belief, the authors and editors of this volume have sought to present a review of this experience in the context of its scientific and technological background.

As we view the development of space travel in the last 25 years, there is the suggestion that the Exploration Imperative is leading us to become a space-faring species. If so, it compels us to wonder whether we are the first, or whether there are, or have been, others.

Introduction

Glossary

A

Ablation The process whereby heat is dissipated by the flaking off of material on the outer layer of a surface exposed to high heating.
Absolute magnitude The magnitude a star would have at a distance of 10 parsecs.
Absolute zero A theoretical temperature at which heat emission ceases (0 Kelvin, −273° Celsius, −459·4° Fahrenheit).
Absorption lines Dark lines marking absorption and scattering of certain wavelengths of light.
Accretion The process of planetary formation by the accumulation of mass by gravitational attraction.
Achondrite A stony meteorite without chondrules.
Albedo The ratio of light reflected by an object to the total light it receives.
Alpha particle A helium nucleus.
Altitude The angular distance above the horizon.
Ambient Surrounding environmental conditions.
Angle of incidence The angle between a light ray striking the surface of a reflecting or refracting material and a line perpendicular to the material.
Ångström (Å) A unit of length in measuring wavelength; 1cm equals 100 million ångströms.
Angular momentum A quantity of motion due to rotation.
Anorthosite A silicate rock rich in aluminium; found on the Moon.
Anti-matter A hypothetical form of matter composed of particles with electrical charges opposite to those of ordinary matter.
Aphelion The point in a solar orbit most distant from the Sun.
Apoapsis The point in an orbit most distant from the primary.
Apoastron The point in a stellar orbit most distant from the star.
Apocynthian The point in a lunar orbit most distant from the Moon.
Apogee The point in an Earth orbit most distant from the Earth.
Apollo A US three-man spacecraft developed for lunar exploration.
Apollo group A group of asteroids whose orbits cross that of the Earth.
Asteroid A small planetoid or large fragment in solar orbit.
Asteroid Belt The region between Mars and Jupiter.
Astronomical Unit (AU) The mean distance between the Earth and the Sun: 92·96 million miles (149·6 million km).
Attitude The position of a flight vehicle relative to the ground.
Azimuth The angular position of an object on the plane of the horizon.

B

Barred spirals Spiral galaxies with bar-like formations passing through the centre; arms emanate from the ends of the bar.
Barycentre The common centre of two bodies revolving about each other.
Binary Two close stars revolving around a common centre.
Big Bang In theory, the primeval explosion from which the Universe evolved.
Bipropellant Fuel and oxidizer in the same liquid state stored in separate containers.
Black hole A very dense object with such high surface gravity that light cannot escape from it.
Blue giant A bright, hot star shining by contraction of its centre while the outer parts are expanding.
Bode's Law A supposed numerical relationship among the positions of the planets purporting to show an orderly sequence of distance from the Sun in astronomical units.
Bok globules Spherical clouds of gas identified by Bart Bok, a Dutch-American astronomer.
Bow shock A region where the solar wind impacts the geomagnetic field.
Bremsstrahlung Radiation emitted by decelerating or accelerating electrical charges in a hot gas.

C

Caldera A bowl-shaped volcanic vent.
Calorie The amount of heat energy required to raise 1 gram of water 1°C.
Candle A unit of light intensity (the amount of light emitted by incandescent platinum through an aperture 1/60 of a square centimetre in size).
Carbonaceous chondrite A type of chondritic meteorite containing carbon compounds.
Carbon cycle A process transforming hydrogen to helium in massive stars.
Cassegrain reflector A reflecting telescope using a convex secondary mirror to bring the light to a focus through a hole in the primary mirror.
Cassini's Division The gap between the A and B rings of Saturn.
Celestial equator The projection of the terrestrial equator upon the celestial sphere.
Celestial pole Points on the celestial sphere projecting the Earth's north and south poles.
Celestial sphere An imaginary sphere of infinite radius beyond the Earth in which all celestial objects are seen.
Cepheid variable A class of stars of variable brightness which are used as distance indicators; named for the prototype, Delta Cephei.
Chondrite A type of meteorite composed of small spherical bodies called chondrules.
Chromosphere The atmospheric layer of the Sun immediately above the photosphere.
Cislunar space The region between the Earth and the Moon.
Clast A component of an aggregate rock.
Collimator A lens which aligns light rays in parallel.
Coma The fuzzy region around the head of a comet.
Comet A fuzzy-bright body with a small nucleus of rock and ice characterised by an extensive gaseous tail in elongated solar orbit.
Conjunction The apparent alignment of the Earth, the Sun and another planet; inferior conjunction is the apparent alignment when the other planet is between the Earth and the Sun, superior conjunction when the other planet is on the opposite side of the Sun from Earth.
Constellation A group of stars which seem to form a figure or pattern; about 88 are commonly recognised, and many are named for mythological figures or animals.
Copernican system Referring to the thesis proposed by the Polish astronomer Nicolaus Copernicus (AD 1473-1543) that the planets revolve around the Sun.
Core The central mass of a planet or star; a region of highest density.
Corona A faint haze and stream which appear around the Sun during total eclipse.
Cosmic rays Energetic particles (ions) in space emitted by the Sun and other stars.
Cosmogony A branch of cosmology dealing with the origin and evolution of matter.
Cosmology The study of the origin, design and structure of the Universe.
Crater A cone or bowl-shaped depression on the surface of a body created by the impact of a smaller body or by volcanic eruption.
Crepe ring The inner ring of Saturn.
Crust The outer region of a differentiated body, such as a planet or large moon.
Cryogenic The super-cold liquid state of a gas which liquifies at very low temperatures.

D

Decay In spaceflight, the loss of altitude by a vehicle in orbit as a result of a reduction in kinetic energy caused by atmospheric friction.
Declination The angular distance of an object north or south of the celestial equator (in degrees).
Diastrophism The process by which the crust of a planet is deformed by internal forces.
Differentiation The separation of light and heavy elements in a body as the result of internal heating which allows heavier elements to settle to the centre and lighter elements to float to the surface. Bodies undergoing episodes of heating and cooling become differentiated into regions of varying density called the crust, the mantle and the core.
Diffraction The bending or deflection of light rays as they pass through narrow apertures or slits in a grating or are reflected from a finely etched surface. The process is a means of producing and analysing spectra and measuring the wave length of spectral lines.
Dispersion The separation of light into its component wavelengths.
Docking The mechanical linkage of two space vehicles.
Doppler effect The change in frequency of electromagnetic or sound waves resulting from relative motions between the observer and the source.
Drag Air resistance to the motion of a vehicle.

E

Eccentricity The degree of displacement from a centre; the degree of flatness of an ellipse or its departure from a circle; the ratio of the distance between the foci of an ellipse and the length of its major axis.
Eclipse The interposition of a body between a luminous object and the observer.
Ecliptic The great circle on the celestial sphere formed by its intersection with the plane of the Earth's orbit.
Electron A negatively charged particle in motion around the nucleus of an atom.
Elevation The angular position of an object above mean sea level (terrestrial); its position above the horizon (celestial).
Ellipse A closed plane curve in the shape of an oval.
Ellipticals Galaxies in the shape of an ellipse.
Emission lines Colours in a spectrum produced by hot gas indicating the chemical composition of the gas.
Elongation The angular distance on the celestial sphere between the Sun and a planet as seen from Earth.
Encke's Division The gap in the A ring of Saturn.
Ephemeris A timetable showing the computed daily positions of celestial objects.
Epicycles Small circles describing the motion of the planets as they move around the larger circle of their orbit; epicycles were invented by early astronomers to account for the motion of planets.
Equinox One of the points of intersection between the ecliptic and the celestial equator; the Sun crosses the equator and day and night are of equal length.
Escape velocity The velocity required for a space vehicle to leave a celestial body without falling into orbit about it (see **Orbital velocity**).
Ether An imaginary substance believed to permeate space and through which light is propagated.

F

Faculae Areas of the Sun's surface that appear brighter than their surroundings.
Fission Energy released by splitting the atom.
Fluorescence The property of emitting light from the impact of radiation or particle bombardment.
Fly-by An encounter with a planet by reconnaissance spacecraft in solar orbit.
Fraunhofer lines The most prominent absorption lines in the spectrum of sunlight or starlight.
Fusion The union of nuclei of light elements to form nuclei of heavier elements; the fusion of hydrogen nuclei to create helium nuclei with vast energy release.

G

Gamma ray A photon emitted spontaneously by the decay of radioactive elements.
Gauss A unit of magnetic induction equal to magnetic flux density.
Gegenschein The counterglow; light reflected by cosmic dust opposite the Sun.
Gemini A two-man spacecraft, manoeuvrable in orbit, developed by the United States as an intermediate manned spacecraft between the one-man Mercury and the three-man Apollo.
Geodesic The shortest line between two points (on a mathematically constructed surface).
Geodetic Pertaining to the geoid or surface measurement of the Earth.
Geoid The shape of the Earth at mean sea level.
Geomagnetic Referring to the effect of the Earth's magnetic field.
Geomagnetic tail The anti-solar extension of the geomagnetic field which is blown beyond the sunward side of the Earth by the solar wind.
Geostationary Referring to an orbit 22,300 miles (35,880km) above the Earth's equator; in this orbit, a satellite revolves around the Earth at the same rate as the Earth's rotation and thus appears to remain stationary in longitude.
Geosynchronous See **Geostationary.**
Gimbal Referring to the motion of a rocket nozzle to change the direction of flight.
Globular cluster A compact, spherical system of thousands of stars.
Granules The smallest units visible on the Sun's surface.
Gravitation The force of attraction between two bodies.
Gravitational collapse The effect of gravitation in condensing matter to form galaxies, stars, planets and (in theory) black holes.
Greenhouse effect Atmosphere heating by trapped infra-red radiation.
GTO: Geostationary Transfer Orbit.
Gyroscope A wheel which spins rapidly about its axis; in spaceflight, the device is used to resist torque that would change the axis of spin of a spin-stabilised satellite.

H

H I region A region of neutral interstellar hydrogen.
H II region A region of ionized interstellar hydrogen.
Halo A luminous, gaseous cloud around a celestial object.
Halo orbit Satellite motion around a point between two celestial bodies (Sun and Earth) where gravitational forces are in equilibrium.
Herbig-Haro object A star which is not visible directly from Earth but which is detected by its illumination of a nearby cloud (named for two astronomers).
Hertzsprung-Russell diagram A diagram showing the distribution of stars according to their luminosity and temperature.
Hubble constant The ratio of the velocity of recession of a galaxy to its distance from the Earth; the ratio is expressed as 100km/second per million parsecs.
Hyperbolic orbit An orbit following an open-ended curve (hyperbola) which approaches infinity.
Hypergolic Referring to a propellant mixture which ignites when the oxidant is brought into contact with the fuel.

I

IGY The International Geophysical Year, 1957–58.
Inclination The angle of an orbit around the Earth with the equator; the angle of the equator of a planet with the orbital plane.
Infra-red (IR) radiation Electromagnetic radiation with a wavelength slightly longer than that of visible light; radiation sensed as heat.
Io flux tube The powerful electric current flowing between Jupiter's ionosphere and the moon Io.
Ion A nuclear particle with an electron missing or added, thus giving it an electrical charge.
Ion drive An electric propulsion system which expels ions to create thrust.
Ionization The process by which atoms become electrically charged by the removal of an electron.
Ionosphere The region of the upper atmosphere where atoms have been ionized by solar radiation.
Isostasy The shifting of mass within the Earth to maintain equilibrium of mass distribution.
IUS An Inertial Upper Stage rocket used to boost satellites into geostationary orbit or interplanetary trajectories.

J

Jovian Referring to Jupiter, to its system of satellites or to any of the major planets.

L

Lagrangian point A point in space where the gravitational effects of two bodies are neutralised.
Laser The acronym for Light Amplification by Stimulated Emission of Radiation; a device for producing a coherent, monochromatic beam of light.
Launch window The interval during which a spacecraft must be launched to achieve a desired orbit under optimum conditions or a targeted interplanetary flight path.
Libration The apparent rocking or wobbling from side to side of a celestial body such as the Moon.
Light year The distance light travels in one year (186,282·39 miles, 299,792·45km, per second) a total of about 4·95 trillion miles (9·45 trillion km).
Line of apsides A line joining the periapsis and apoapsis of an orbit.
Luminosity The ratio of light emitted by a celestial body to the total light of the Sun; the total energy emitted by a star per second.
Luna A class of Soviet spacecraft developed for exploring the Moon.
Lunar module (LM) A two-man US vehicle developed to ferry astronauts between orbiting Apollo spacecraft and the surface of the Moon.

M

Mach The ratio of the speed of a vehicle to the speed of sound in the atmosphere.
Magellanic clouds Two nearby galaxies of irregular shape which are visible from the southern hemisphere; named for the Portuguese explorer Ferdinand Magellan.
Magnetic storm The effect of the disruption of the Earth's magnetic field by energetic particles from the Sun.
Magnetometer An instrument which measures the strength of a magnetic field.

Magnetopause The boundary region where the solar wind impacts the Earth's magnetic field.
Magnitude The apparent brightness of a star expressed in numerical terms (bright stars have low numbers, dim stars high numbers).
Main sequence A band of stars on the Hertzsprung-Russell diagram in which energy is generated by thermonuclear reactions in the core; most stars, including the Sun, are classified as main sequence stars.
Mantle The region of an evolved planet between the crust and the core.
Mare The Latin term for sea, applied in antiquity to the dark basins on the Moon (pl. = maria).
Mariner A class of 3-axis stabilised spacecraft developed by the US for planetary reconnaissance.
Mascon A concentration of mass in the crust of the Moon.
Mass-luminosity relationship The proportionality of luminosity to mass of stars of mass less than or more than the mass of the Sun on the main sequence.
Mean solar day The time between successive meridian passages of the Sun; on Earth, the 24-hour day.
Meridian A great circle on the Earth passing through the poles; a circle on the celestial sphere passing through the zenith and the north and south poles of the sphere.
Meteor A meteoroid emitting light as it passes through the atmosphere.
Meteorite A meteor that has survived the heat of atmospheric friction and reached the surface of the Earth.
Meteoroid A piece of rock or space boulder, usually a fragment of a larger body, moving through interplanetary space.
Microgravity A preferred term used by space scientists for the "zero" gravity of orbital free fall.
Micrometeoroid A grain of space dust.
Milky Way The part of our Galaxy that we see.
Mohorovicic discontinuity (MOHO) The boundary between the Earth's crust and mantle as indicated by seismic waves.
Molecular cloud A cloud of gas and dust at low temperature in space containing molecules of carbon monoxide, formaldehyde and other compounds.

N

Nebula A cloud of gas and dust in deep space.
Nebular hypothesis The theory of Laplace that the planets condensed from the solar nebula.
Neutron star The collapsed core of a star following a supernova event.
Newton The unit of force that accelerates 2·2lb (1kg) of mass 3·28ft (1m) per second.
Noctilucent clouds Faintly luminous clouds seen at night at high altitudes.
Node One of two points (ascending and descending) where the orbit of a celestial body crosses the ecliptic; a point where the orbit of a spacecraft crosses the Earth's equator.
Nova A star that suddenly increases dramatically in brightness and then returns to its original luminosity.
Nutation The nodding of a celestial body such as the Moon.

O

Oblateness Characteristic of an oblate spheroid which bulges at the equator and is flattened at the poles.
Occultation The interposition of a large body between the observer and a body being observed; the blockage of radio signals from a spacecraft by the planet ball as the vehicle passes behind the planet relative to the Earth.
Olbers' paradox If the Universe is infinite and stars are distributed uniformly and are stationary, the night sky should be bright instead of dark.
Opposition A planet in opposition is opposite the Sun from Earth.
Orbit The path of a satellite around its primary; in spaceflight, an orbit is computed from one ascending crossing of the equator to another (see **Revolution**).
Orbital velocity The velocity required for a vehicle to go into orbit about a celestial body; to reach Earth orbit, a velocity of 5 miles per second (8·1km/sec) is required.

P

PAM Payload Assist Module; an upper stage rocket used to raise the orbit of satellites delivered to low Earth orbit by expendable boosters or by the Shuttle.
Parabola A bowl-shaped curve; the trajectory followed by a projectile; an open curve generated by a point moving so that it remains equidistant from a fixed point and a fixed line; the pathway of comets which leave the Solar System.
Parallax The apparent shift in the position of an object caused by a shift in the position of the observer.
Parallax second (parsec) A celestial measure of distance equal to 3·26 light years; the distance of an object which shows a parallax of one second of arc.
Penumbra The outer and lighter part of a shadow cast by a body eclipsing a star.
Periapsis The point in an orbit nearest the primary.
Periastron The point in a stellar orbit nearest the star.
Pericynthian The point in a lunar orbit nearest the Moon.
Perigee The point in an Earth orbit nearest the Earth.
Perihelion The point in a solar orbit nearest the Sun.
Perilune See **Pericynthian.**
Period The time of one orbit, or of one rotation of a body on its axis, or of a cycle of change such as the pulsed emission of electromagnetic energy.
Perturbation The disturbance of a celestial body in its normal orbit by the influence of other bodies.
Photometer An instrument designed to measure light.
Photon A quantum of light.
Photosphere The visible surface of the Sun or of a star.
Photovoltaic cell A crystalline wafer (solar cell), commonly silicon, which transforms sunlight into direct electrical current.
Pioneer A class of spin-stabilised spacecraft developed by the United States for observing the interplanetary medium and the reconnaissance of planets.
Planck's Constant The constant (h) in Max Planck's formula for the black body radiation spectrum which relates the energy of a photon to its frequency.
Planet An evolved, non-luminous body orbiting a star.
Planetary nebula A nebula resembling a planet.
Planetesimal A clump of matter which aggregates with myriad other clumps to form a planet.
Planetoid A small, asteroidal body in space.
Plasma Ionized gas flowing out from the Sun.
Polarimeter An instrument designed to measure the amount of polarisation of light or the proportion of polarised light in a ray.
Population I and II stars Types of stars distinguished by age, colour and location in the galaxy; Population I stars are blue and confined to the galactic plane, Population II stars are red and fairly widespread throughout the galaxy.
Precession A slow change in the direction of the Earth's axis caused by the gravitational pull of the Moon on the equatorial bulge; the axis moves in a slow circle like the axis of a spinning top.
Prominence A luminous extrusion of gas from the Sun's corona along the edge of the solar disc.
Proper motion The angular velocity of a star in a direction perpendicular to the observer's line of sight.
Proton-proton reaction The nuclear process which transforms hydrogen to helium in the interior of some main sequence stars.
Protostar The portion of a nebula condensing into a star.
Ptolemaic system The representation by Ptolemy of the geocentric universe of Aristotle.
Pulsar A neutron star emitting pulses of radio energy.
Pulsating stars Stars that vary in brightness, presumably from periodic changes in volume.
Pyrheliometer An instrument used to measure the radiant energy of the Sun.

Q

Quadrature The position of a superior planet 90° east or west of the Sun; the configuration in which two celestial bodies are separated by 90°.
Quantum A unit, packet or amount of energy.
Quasar A quasistellar object of great luminosity believed to be at vast distance.

R

Radial velocity The motion of a star or galaxy along the observer's line of sight.
Radioactive decay Spontaneous nuclear reactions that continue at a predictable rate.
Radioastronomy The branch of astronomy dealing with radio waves emitted by celestial bodies.
Radiometer An instrument which detects and measures emissions or reflections of radiation.
Radius vector A line joining any point of an orbit with the focus.
Ranger A lunar photographic impact probe launched to the Moon by the United States to relay close-up pictures of the surface.
Red giant A member of the "giant" sequence of stars in the Hertzsprung-Russell diagram with radii 15 to 30 times that of the Sun and luminosities 100 times greater; a stage of stellar evolution where helium is burning in the core and hydrogen in an outer shell. Red giants are luminous and relatively cool.
Redshift The shift of spectral lines towards longer wavelengths (towards the red) as galaxies recede.
Red spot A reddish eye-shaped feature in the atmosphere of Jupiter's southern hemisphere, supposed to be a semi-permanent hurricane.
Refraction The change in the direction of light as it passes through a different medium such as glass or water.
Regolith The powdery, clumpy topsoil of the Moon.
Relativity A theory in physics developed by Albert Einstein which views time and space as relative to moving systems or frames of reference rather than as absolute quantities.
Resolving power The ability of a telescope to separate close points into distinct units.
Retrograde motion The apparent backward or westward motion of a planet through a star field or of a satellite orbiting a planet.
Revolution In spaceflight, an orbital circuit of the Earth which is completed when the spacecraft passes the longitude of the launch site; the orbital circuit of a satellite around its primary or of a planet around the Sun.
Rille A narrow valley or canyon on the Moon.
Right ascension The angular distance from the prime meridian to a celestial body measured eastwards along the celestial equator from 0° to 360°.
RR Lyrae stars Stars that appear to change in brightness like Cepheid variables.

S

Schmidt telescope A reflecting telescope which uses a spherical mirror with a correcting lens in front of it.
Seismometer An instrument that measures and records quakes and impacts imparting seismic energy in solid bodies, such as earthquakes or moonquakes.
Semi-major axis One half of the longest dimension of an ellipse.
Sensor A device which detects releases of energy.
Seyfert galaxy A galaxy with a prominent energy source at the centre.
Shield volcano A volcano which has accumulated successive layers of lava on its slopes.
Sidereal period One revolution by a planet of the Sun as seen from one of the fixed stars.
Siderite A nickel-iron meteorite.
Solar constant The quantity of radiant energy from the Sun falling on the top of the atmosphere at 1·94 calories a minute per square centimetre.
Solar flare A sudden brightening of a region on the Sun signalling the emission of high-speed jets of plasma.
Solar wind Protons and electrons (plasma) streaming from the Sun through interplanetary space; the extended atmosphere of the Sun; the heliosphere.
Solstice The point of maximum declination of the Earth on the ecliptic.
Specific impulse The ratio of pounds of thrust per pound of fuel in a rocket engine.
Spectral bands Lines in a spectrum caused by the absorption or emission of light by molecules.
Spectrograph An instrument that collimates (makes parallel) light rays and disperses them through a prism or grating into a spectrum which is photographed.
Spiral galaxies Galaxies with arms extending from a central bulge.
Spokes Radial, spoke-like structures in the rings of Saturn.
Standard candles Stars which indicate distance.
Star A globe of gas shining by means of its own energy production.
Steady state The theory that the density of the Universe remains the same and its extent is constant because new stars form as old ones are extinguished.
Sunspots Dark patches that appear from time to time (in a cycle) on the photosphere of the Sun.
Supernova A star that suddenly increases in brightness up to a million times and does not return to its original state.
Surveyor A US unmanned, soft-landing reconnaissance vehicle that made soil tests and took landscape photos on the Moon.
Synchrotron radiation Electromagnetic energy emitted at radio wavelengths by electrons spiralling in a magnetic field.
Synodic period One revolution of a planet around the Sun as seen from Earth.
Synthetic aperture radar (SAR) A satellite radar imaging system in which the aperture (antenna extent) is greatly increased by satellite motion.
Syzygy An alignment of three celestial bodies.

T

Tektite A button-shaped, glassy object showing signs of aerodynamic shaping from a molten state and found in several parts of the Earth. Tektites were once considered to be of lunar origin, but it is probable that they originated as blobs of melt in volcanoes.
Telemetry The radio transmission of instrument data from spacecraft.
Terrae Light-coloured regions of the Moon generally higher in elevation than the dark basins (maria); ancient observers believed that the terrae were land masses and the dark basins seas.
Terminator The boundary between the illuminated and dark portions of a celestial body; the line between day and night on the Earth and Moon as seen from space.
Thermal protection system (TPS) A heat shield applied to a manned spacecraft.
Transit The motion of a smaller body across the face of a larger one, such as the passage of Venus across the Sun as viewed from Earth.
Transponder A radio that receives a signal, modulates it and re-transmits it at a different frequency.
Tropical year The common year.
Tropopause The region of the atmosphere between the troposphere and the stratosphere.
T-Tauri stars Stars that vary irregularly in brightness and appear to lose mass; named for the prototype in Taurus.

U

Ultraviolet (UV) radiation The radiation of wavelengths shorter than those of visible light and longer than those of X-rays.
Umbra The dark shadow cast by a planet or a satellite.
Universal time (UT) Mean solar time at the 0° meridian, Greenwich, England; Greenwich Mean Time.

V

Van Allen zones Zones or belts of electrified particles trapped in the Earth's magnetic field at high altitudes.
Venera A class of large, Soviet reconnaissance vehicles (including orbiters and landers) used to explore Venus.
Viking A US dual interplanetary spacecraft (consisting of an orbiter and a lander) used to explore Mars.
Voyager An advanced, Mariner class reconnaissance spacecraft used to reconnoitre the outer planets and their moons.

X

X-rays The radiation of extremely short wavelengths.

Z

Zenith The point in the celestial sphere directly overhead.
Zero-g The supposed absence of gravity in orbital free fall; microgravity.
Zodiac A band of the celestial sphere 8° wide on each side of the ecliptic, divided into 12 equal sections of 30° each.
Zodiacal light A faint glow in the west just after sunset and in the east just before dawn appearing along the Zodiac.

Abbreviations

Å Ångström
AU Astronomical unit
b Brightness or galactic latitude
B Blue magnitude
c Velocity of light ($\sim$186,000 miles per second or 3×10^{10}cm/sec)
D Distance from Earth
δ Declination
Δ λ Change in wavelength
eV Electron volt
E Elliptical galaxy
f Frequency
G Gravitational constant
H Hydrogen
Hz Hertz (1 cycle per second)
k Boltzmann constant
°K Degrees Kelvin
l Galactic longitude
L Intrinsic luminosity
λ Wavelength
Λ Cosmological constant
m Apparent magnitude
M Absolute magnitude
r Radius
S Spiral galaxy
SB Barred spiral galaxy
t Time
T Temperature
V Visual magnitude
z Redshift ($\Delta\lambda / \lambda$)

The modern view of the nature of the Universe has been evolving over the last four centuries in step with the development of observational technology. Until the beginning of the 17th century, the established view in the West held that the Earth was the centre of the Universe and that fixed stars were mere points of light in the celestial sphere. With the invention of the telescope, Galileo's observations confirmed the Copernican revolution which altered the Earth-centred cosmos to a Sun-centred one.

Advances in observational technology have been steadily dispelling the illusions of antiquity and of the Middle Ages. This process continues. The Earth has been displaced not only from the centre of the Solar System but from the centre of the Milky Way galaxy to a position more than 30,000 light years from that centre. In this century, other patches of nebulous luminosity, such as the Clouds of Magellan, have been recognized as other island universes and these now seem to extend without disminishing in number beyond the farthest reach of ground and space observatories.

By the middle of this century, we found ourselves inhabiting a rather small planet orbiting an average star in a Galaxy among millions of galaxies. We can only imagine the magnitude of this cosmic environment; we have no perceptual reference for it. One of the last of the old illusions left to us is that the Earth is unique as the abode of life. But as new and improved instruments allow us to peer more deeply into the cosmos and detect cosmochemical processes in clouds of interstellar dust and gas, this illusion becomes intellectually untenable.

Among the billions of suns and millions of galaxies, it seems reasonable to suppose that there are many abodes life. Chemical compounds from which life evolves have been detected in the clouds where stars are formed. It thus also seems reasonable to suppose that life arises where conditions allow it as an aspect of stellar and planetary evolution.

This supposition has become so acceptable to the space science community that plaques depicting the galactic location of the Earth and the nature of life upon it have been attached to outer planet reconnaissance spacecraft. One of them, Pioneer 10, has already left the Solar System and entered the interstellar medium.

The advent of space technology has enabled scientists to look into the celestial sphere beyond the narrow window of visible light and observe energy processes in stars and galaxies which could not be seen from the ground because their radiations could not pass through the atmosphere. Orbital observatories have opened up the electromagnetic spectrum from the radio and infra-red bands to ultraviolet, X-ray and gamma ray radiation.

Such observing instruments as those aboard the International Ultraviolet Explorer (IUE), the Infra-red Astronomical Satellite (IRAS) and Exosat have revealed processes of star formation and of supernova explosion at wavelengths undetectable from the ground. Beyond these space age instruments looms the most powerful of all, the Space Telescope. Hundreds of astronomers are depending on it to resolve specific questions when it is put into orbit circa 1986.

The instruments of the space age have facilitated the task of subjecting theory to experimental evidence. The evidence so far points to the origin of the Universe in a cosmic explosion of a primeval nucleus. The effects of it are perceived by the apparent recession of galaxies and the discovery of the 3° Kelvin radiation coming from all directions which is interpreted as the residue of the "Big Bang".

In the last quarter century, the processes of cosmic evolution have been observed and seem to be continuous throughout time and space. Star systems which formed thousands of millions of years ago can be assumed to have arisen in the same way as stars that can be seen forming now.

The space observatories see protostars forming within the gas clouds of the Milky Way. Thus, the birth of stars as well as their deaths in supernova explosions are observed as a continuing process.

From a cosmochemical view, we and all other life forms are descended from the stars, insofar as the chemical elements that comprise our being are created by nucleo-synthesis in the core of stars which explode and release the elements to be recycled into newly forming stars.

As in the time of Copernicus and Galileo, observation continues to confirm, refute or modify theory. Evidence for the existence of neutron stars is seen as confirming theory of stellar evolution. The supposed nature of Black Holes is seen as supporting one of the predictions of Einstein's General Theory of Relativity.

Current views, as expressed in the following pages, may change with the deployment of new instruments in space, such as the Space Telescope, the Advanced X-Ray Astrophysics Facility and new Gamma Ray Observatories. But the main challenge is likely to persist into the next century and beyond. It is the resolution of the structure of the Universe and of the question whether it is open or closed.

Will the Universe continue to expand forever? In that case, it is open. Or will expansion stop as gravitational forces overcome the energy of the Big Bang and cause the Universe to collapse into the primeval nucleus from which it emerged? In that case, the Universe is closed.

In the 2,400 years since Aristotle propounded his theory of cosmology, science has discerned the beginning, but not the end.

I

The Origin and Evolution of the Universe

The scientists' view of the Universe has evolved from the Earth-centred cosmos accepted by Astronomers of antiquity and the Middle Ages, to the Sun-centred Universe of the Renaissance and thence to a Universe of receding galaxies without a discernible centre in the twentieth century. This current view is the result of the invention of the telescope in the sixteenth century and the discovery of methods of measuring the distances of stars in the twentieth. It relies evidentially on Hubble's law of redshifts which shows that the galaxies are moving away from each other and that therefore, the Universe is expanding, and intellectually on Einstein's General Theory of Relativity. The concept of an expanding Universe requires a beginning and the prevailing theory is that the Universe began expanding with a cosmic explosion—the Big Bang—10 to 20 billion years ago. A more precise date lacks a consensus because of a dispute among scientists about the value of the Hubble constant which specifies the velocity-distance relationship. This view reflects the predominant state of cosmology in the early 1980s. It may change. Myriad problems are associated with it. Astronomers and astrophysicists are counting on NASA's Space Telescope to resolve some of them.

Early Cosmology

Our understanding of the Universe has developed over many centuries, from religious speculation more than 2,000 years ago, through later reasoning based on the motions of stars and planets in the sky, to highly mathematical modern theories of cosmology. It may well be said that most systems of religion, and our knowledge of the physical sciences, have come about as a result of the thought devoted to the origin and evolution of the Universe. Space exploration has provided the most recent and rapid development, but we start with the early ideas, in order to give the background against which space exploration is to be assessed.

In biblical times "heaven" was the Universe, and God created it. What does "Universe" mean? All that is. But during the last 20 centuries, "Universe" has had several meanings. To Ptolemy and the early Greeks, Egyptians, and Romans, it meant the planets—the Solar System—with a thin sphere of stars around it, and Earth at the centre. Ptolemy (Claudius Ptolemaeus, dates unknown) published the *Almagest* in circa AD 150. His was *the* theory of the Universe up to 1543, when the Polish monk, Nicolaus Copernicus (1473-1543), proposed a Sun-centred system which he considered simpler, although he still used Ptolemy's epicycles.

Ptolemy explained all motions in the sky by uniform motions in circles. The sphere of stars, still used by astronomers today as the Celestial Sphere, rotated around the Earth once in 23hr 56min, and inside that were other transparent spheres carrying the planets (from the Greek word for "wanderers") Saturn, Jupiter, Mars, Venus, Mercury, Sun, and Moon. Because none of these move uniformly around the Earth, Ptolemy devised a set of "epicycles". Each epicycle centre moved uniformly in a circle around the Earth and the planet moved in a circle around the epicycle centre.

As the measurement of planetary positions became more accurate, it was necessary to add epicycles upon epicycles and "equants" (off-centre circles) until, in the 13th century, the Ptolemaic system became so complex that King Alfonso X of Spain exclaimed, "If the Lord Almighty had consulted me before the creation, I would have suggested something simpler!"

Below: *The Ptolemaic view of an Earth-centred Universe held sway for some 1,400 years. This representation of it is from William Cuningham's "The Cosmographical Glasse", published in London in 1559.*

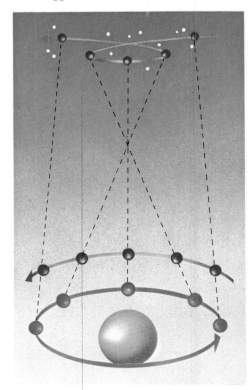

Proof that the Earth moves, and is not the centre of the Universe was finally given in 1838 by Friedrich Bessel (1784-1846), who measured the minute change in direction of stars due to a change in the Earth's position. Earlier, Tycho Brahe (1546-1601) and Johannes Kepler (1571-1630) had shown that the planets move in *ellipses* around the Sun (not circles), Galileo Galilei (1564-1642) was prosecuted for "suspicion of heresy" and was placed under house arrest for trying to convince Pope Urban VIII that the Earth moves, and Sir Isaac Newton (1643-1727) formulated the laws of motion and gravitation that explained the elliptical orbits very accurately.

Bessel's discovery that the "fixed stars" move, led to many more: stars move in orbits around the centre of the Milky Way Galaxy, outside galaxies are all moving away from us, and these motions started when the Universe began expanding 10 or 20 billion years ago. Indeed, accurate measurement of the distance of stars is the key to perceiving the evolution of the Universe.

Bessel started measurements with telescopes which showed that the stars on the celestial sphere are at greatly different distances from the Earth, from 1·31 parsecs (4·3 light years) for the nearest outward. A parsec is the distance from the Earth at which the parallax of a star is one arc second; this is equal to 3·26 light years, 3·086 x 10^{13}km.

Parallaxes of stars are measured by taking photographs of a star field every six months, and observing the shift of nearby stars with respect to more distant (fainter) stars in the photographs.[1]

Such observations carry distance measurements out to about 300 parsecs (980 light years) within which multitudes of stars are found, but there are many more distant ones. To measure their distances, astronomers use star brightness which decreases with the square of the distance. That is, if the Sun were moved twice as far from us, it would appear one quarter as bright. However, the stars at distances measured by parallax proved to have wildly different intrinsic brightness, or candle power—some 1,000 times that of the Sun, others 1/100.

Standard Candles

In 1912, Henrietta Leavitt (1868-1921) at the Harvard College Observatory studied scores of stars that vary in brightness in the Large and Small Magellanic Clouds. (They are called Cepheid Variables, each varying in brightness or magnitude in a regular cycle which can last from a few days to several weeks).[2]

Miss Leavitt, working with Harlow Shapley (1885-1972) who became director of the Harvard College Observatory, found that the periods of Cepheid Variables in the Large Magellanic Cloud are correlated with their brightness or magnitude (m). Since all the Cepheids in the Large Magellanic Cloud are at about the same distance from us, this means that the candle power, or *absolute magnitude* of a Cepheid Variable, is related to its period of waxing and waning in brightness. The longer the period, Miss Leavitt found, the brighter the star. The brightness-period correlation of the Cepheid Variables provided a means of determining

1 With the best telescopes, such as the US Naval Observatory's 61-inch at Flagstaff, Arizona, an accuracy of 0·003 arc-second can be achieved. The Space Telescope, to be launched from Space Shuttle in 1986, can get the same accuracy in three observations with its Fine Guidance Sensor.

2 A Cepheid Variable (Constellation of Cepheus) is a giant star which undergoes periodic changes in luminosity and size. The longer its period of waxing and waning, the greater is its absolute magnitude. Because the length of the period and apparent magnitude are readily observable, the distance of a Cepheid can always be found.

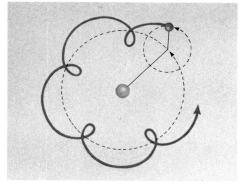

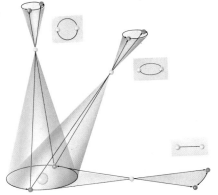

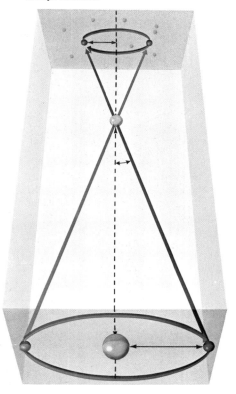

Planetary Motions
As a superior planet (ie one further from the Sun than is the Earth) passes through opposition, its apparent path in the sky executes a loop (**left**). This is easily explained in the Copernican system: as the Earth, which has a higher orbital speed, passes between the Sun and the planet, it overtakes the planet which consequently seems to move backwards in the sky, contrary to its true direction of motion. This phenomenon is thus a result of the motion of both planets around the Sun. Ptolemy attempted to explain this apparently anomalous behaviour while maintaining the ancient philosophical axioms of a geocentric Universe and circular motion of celestial bodies. He devised a system whereby the planets, the Sun and the Moon moved in circular orbits, known as epicycles, whose centres themselves moved uniformly about the Earth in a circle known as the deferent (**above**).

Trigonometric Parallax
The position of a nearby star will appear to change with respect to a distant stellar background as the Earth orbits the Sun. If the star is near the pole of the Earth's orbit, its path will be almost circular, reflecting the shape of the Earth's orbit. Stars of lower inclination seem to move in increasingly elliptical paths until, in the case of a star in the plane of the orbit, the path is a straight line (**above**). One half the angle of apparent variation is termed the parallax of the star and is measured in units of seconds of arc. This is also the angle subtended by the Earth's distance from the Sun as seen from the star (**right**). Since the Earth-Sun distance is well-known, measurement of the star's apparent motion enables us to work out its distance from us. A parsec is the distance at which the measured parallax is 1 arc-second. The nearest star to the Earth, Proxima Centauri, has a parallax of 0·76 arc-seconds and is thus 1·31 parsecs away.

absolute magnitude which, in turn, provides an indication of distance.

Absolute magnitude, M, is defined as the magnitude a star would have if it were just 10 parsecs—32·6 light years—away. If it is actually twice that far, in clear space, its brightness would be only 1/4 of the brightness, B, at 10 parsecs because its light is spread out over a sphere twice as large, with four times the surface area. Astronomers chose 10 parsecs as a standard base for a scale of absolute magnitude. Distance is indicated by the difference between apparent magnitude (m) and absolute magnitude (M). The calculation is expressed by m − M = D. This is the "distance modulus," the indication of how far a star of known absolute magnitude is from us (D) in parsecs.[3,4]

So the Cepheid Variables became "standard candles" from which large distances could be determined. Other types of stars also became standard candles, with less accuracy. The spectra of stars were classified according to lines in their spectra from O (hot) through the sequence B, A, F, G, K, to M stars (cool). It was found that stars of spectral type O have M=−10 (a million times the candlepower of the Sun for which M= +5). Since they have so high candlepower, O stars can be seen to very great distances, much greater than G-type stars like the Sun, or Cepheids with an absolute magnitude of −1 to −6.

The Milky Way

Using these distance indicators, and others, astronomers plotted the locations of stars—noting distance as well as position in the sky—and mapped out the Milky Way Galaxy. As its name implies, the Milky Way is a faint band of light that extends completely around the sky in a great circle around the celestial sphere. Telescopes show that it is made up of billions of faint stars and the mapping in the early 1900s showed that they are spread out in a thin pancake-shaped universe around the Sun, very different from Ptolemy's thin celestial sphere. Two questions arose. How far does the pancake extend? Is the Sun at the centre? These questions were answered in two essentially different ways: one by taking much larger distance measures, the other by studying the motions of stars.

In 1917, Harlow Shapley, then at Mt Wilson Observatory, used the globular clusters as distance indicators.[5] He found that about 100 globular clusters form a huge spherical array centred about 10,000 parsecs (32,000 light years) from the Sun in a bright part of the Milky Way in the constellation Sagittarius, and assumed, reasonably, that this, not the Sun, is the centre of the Milky Way system.[6]

Absolute magnitude

Type I Cepheids

Type II Cepheids

RR Lyrae

Period (days)

Period/Luminosity Relations
A key step in determining extragalactic distance scales was the discovery of relationships between the period and intrinsic brightness of certain types of regularly variable stars. Relations for RR Lyrae stars, Type I and Type II Cepheids are shown here. Their discovery meant that once the period of a variable star was known its intrinsic brightness and hence distance from us could be calculated.

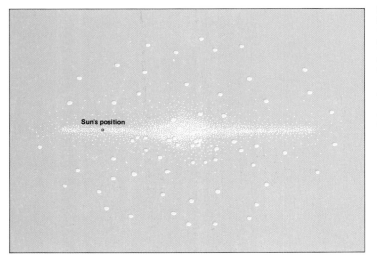

Above: *The globular cluster Messier 13 in the constellation of Hercules. It is about 35 light years in diameter and 27,000 light years distant. It contains c500,000 stars and is 10,000 million years old.*

The Rotating Galaxy

This "Island Universe", our Galaxy, would collapse due to gravitational attraction if its components were not in motion, and the natural assumption is that it is *rotating*, so that stars, clusters, and interstellar material are in orbit around the centre, just as the planets orbit around the Sun. Study of stellar motions confirmed this, and provided an important number—the *mass* of the Galaxy.

Motion of a star is measured in two ways: by Doppler shift of lines in its spectrum, giving the radial velocity, and by a continuing change in its position in the sky—so-called "proper motion". Radial

Sun's position

Distribution of Globular Clusters
Early observations of the structure of the Galaxy, based on star counts in different regions of the sky, suggested that the Sun was centrally located, Shapley, however, found the globular clusters were symmetrically distributed about a centre some 32,000 light years from the Sun. He concluded that the clusters were arranged about the true centre of the Galaxy, and that the Sun, far from being central, actually lay about two-thirds of the way to the edge of the Galaxy. Previous star counts had not revealed this, as interstellar absorption prevented us from seeing the true stellar distribution.

---

3 Magnitude is an inverse logarithmic scale of brightness used by astronomers. First magnitude is the average of the brightest stars in the sky. Stars brighter than this are assigned zero or minus apparent magnitude numbers. The Sun's apparent magnitude is −27. (Its absolute magnitude, M, is +5.) Sixth magnitude, 100 times fainter than first magnitude, is the limit of unaided visual observation on a clear, dark night. Eleventh-magnitude stars are 100 times fainter still, and 21st-magnitude stars, near the limit of large Earth-based telescopes, are 10^8 times

fainter than first-magnitude stars. The Space Telescope will be able to detect 28th-magnitude stars and galaxies, $6·3 \times 10^{10}$ times fainter than first-magnitude stars.

4 For a distance of D parsecs, the brightness $b=B(10/D)^2$ Using m−M=2·5 log (B/b), we find m−M=5 log (D/10). For example, if D=100 parsecs, m−M=5 log10=5. If D=1,000 parsecs, m−M=5 log100=10. So m − M, the "distance modulus," indicates how far a star of known absolute magnitude is from us, in parsecs, when its measured brightness is m. The formula for changing brightness, b,

to magnitude, m, is $m_1 − m_2 = 2·5 \log(b_2/b_1)$ where m_1 and b_1 are the magnitude and brightness of star 1, m_2 and b_2 for star 2.

5 These spherical collections of 50,000 to 100,000 stars have M= −5 to −10, and Shapley found Cepheid Variables in a few of them. He also used the angular sizes to estimate their distances and mapped their locations.

6 Our Galaxy (the Milky Way) contains many types of objects. In addition to stars and globular clusters, there are open clusters of stars, bright gaseous nebulae, dark interstellar

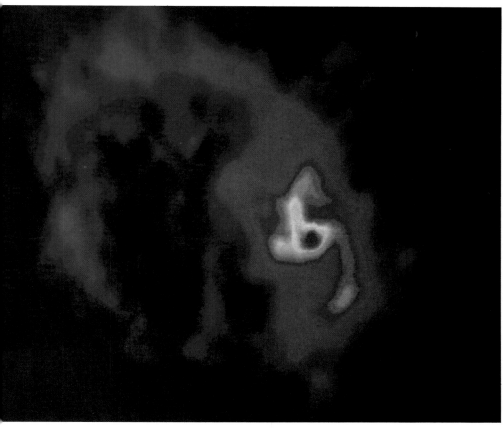

are moving slower than the Sun, and have proper motions "backward".

In the mid 1920s, in Holland, Jan H. Oort (1900-) used the average radial velocities of stars in different directions to demonstrate the rotation of the Galaxy and derive the Sun's orbital speed—about 155 miles/sec (250km/sec). From the Sun's orbital speed, we can calculate the mass of all stars, clusters, and interstellar material closer to the centre, using Newton's laws, as 2×10^{11} solar masses. (1 solar mass or "sun" is 1.99×10^{33}gm, the unit of mass used by astronomers.) Of course, this calculation omits the mass *outside* the orbits of the outermost stars and assumes that the Galaxy's interior mass acts like that of a single body at the centre.[7]

The Universe of Galaxies

Of course, the model of our island Universe was not prepared without reference to other external galaxies. One of the nearer ones, M31 or NGC 224 with its spiral arms, globular clusters, Cepheid Variables, and lanes of interstellar dust provides a good prototype for our Galaxy.[8]

Beginning in about 1920, Edwin Hubble (1889-1953) put some order into the studies of galaxies. First, he noted the "zone of avoidance" along the Milky Way, where few or no galaxies appear in the sky. He rightly interpreted this as the obscuration of the external galaxies by interstellar dust in our Milky Way Galaxy.[9]

Hubble went on to classify the many different types of galaxies, from loosely wound spirals (Sc) and barred spirals (SBc) (about one third of all spirals have prominent bars running through their nuclei, hence the term), through tightly wound Sa and SBa to armless ellipticals of types E5 (lenticular) to E0 (circular). (The lower case letters distinguish variations of the general types —see also pages 31-32 for a diagram illustrating the classification of galaxies.) He showed that all of these galaxies are composed of stars, with more gas and dust in the spirals, almost no dust in the ellipticals.

Age of the Universe

Perhaps the most important of Hubble's contributions was the velocity-distance relation, now called the Hubble Law. He noticed that fainter and fainter galaxies have larger and larger Doppler redshifts or velocities of recession. After observing Cepheid Variables in a few spiral galaxies, Hubble estimated the absolute magnitude of an elliptical as $M = -20$, and could then measure distances to fainter ellipticals from their apparent magnitudes, m, corrected for obscuration in the Milky Way. The Hubble Law states that recession velocity $(V) = HD$, where D is the galaxy's distance and H is the

---

velocity is the rate at which stars and galaxies are moving away from us. Proper motion refers to the orbital movement of stars, including our Sun, around the centre of the Galaxy. Proper motion can be measured only for relatively nearby stars, but it shows the systematic effects expected of stellar orbits around the Galaxy's centre.

As in the Solar System, the speed of bodies in orbit decreases with the square root of the orbit's size, so stars closer to the

Above: *The centre of our Galaxy as seen by the Very Large Array radio telescope in New Mexico. The red spot is a point source thought to be the actual Galactic nucleus; it is surrounded by hot gas.*

Galaxy's centre (toward the constellation Sagittarius) are moving faster than the Sun, and have proper motions directed in the forward direction. Stars farther from the centre (toward the constellation Auriga)

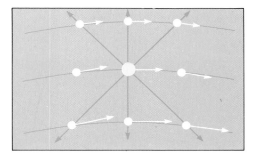

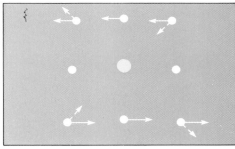

Differential Rotation and Stellar Motions
A static observer situated outside our Galaxy and looking down on the Galactic disc would see a rotation pattern among the stars as shown above left. Stars travel around the centre of the Galaxy in

almost circular orbits with orbital speed decreasing with radius, just as in the Solar System planets farther from the Sun have lower orbital speeds than those which are closer. This effect produces a "shearing" motion in the Galactic plane, called

differential galactic rotation. Stars farther from the Galactic centre are thus overtaken by the Sun, which is itself overtaken by stars at smaller radii. The net motions of stars seen by an observer travelling with the Sun are hence as

shown at right. Dashed arrows are the observed radial velocities i.e. the component of stellar motion towards or away from the Sun. Analysis of the motions of stars allows the solar orbital speed and local shear rate to be measured.

---

dust and invisible interstellar gas (discovered by radio telescopes after 1935).
7   Recent investigations show that the sphere of globular clusters may be filled with low-luminosity matter called the "dark halo" of the Galaxy, and that the total mass of the Galaxy is 5 to 10 times larger than 2×10^{11} suns. Moreover, the structure of the Milky Way Galaxy is further complicated by spiral arms in the disc, which have been clearly mapped from observations. The reason for these arms, which contain young stars, nebulae, and most of the interstellar gas, is obscure. One theory

predicts spiral "density waves" that may account for them.
8   The "M" number and "NGC" (New General Catalogue) number are from early catalogues made by Charles Messier (1730-1817) in France, and William and John Herschel (1738-1822 and 1792-1871) (revised by J.L.E. Dreyer [1852-1926] in England in 1888). In those early days, telescopes did not have the fine resolving power that they have today, and photography was in its infancy. Hence, both Messier and the Herschels lumped galaxies with gaseous nebulae, and classed M31-NGC

224 as a "spiral nebula". Until the early years of this century, spiral nebulae and all the M-NGC objects were thought to be part of our Milky Way System. Then better photographs and early spectrograms cast doubt on this.
9   Hubble went further to show that the average number of catalogued galaxies per square degree is proportional to the secant of the angle from the Galactic poles (the points 90° away from the Milky Way great circle of Galactic latitude 0°.) This secant law is what one would expect if we were in the centre of a flat disc of interstellar dust.

CHARACTERISTICS OF DIFFERENT GALAXY TYPES				
	ELLIPTICALS	**SPIRALS**	**IRREGULARS**	**QUASARS**
Mass in Suns	$(6\pm3) \times 10^{11}$	$(2\pm1) \times 10^{10}$	$(2\pm1) \times 10^{10}$	10^8 (black hole?)
Luminosity in Suns	$(7\pm6) \times 10^9$	$(5\pm3) \times 10^9$	$(4\pm3) \times 10^9$	10^{12} to 10^{14}
Ratio of Mass to Luminosity	90 ± 37	4 ± 2	5 ± 3	
Absolute magnitude, M	-17 to -20	-18 to -20	-17 to -19	-25 to -30
Spectral type	G to K	A to K	A to F	Broad-line, peculiar
Interstellar matter	Very little	Lots of gas and dust	Lots of gas, both dust and no dust	Lots of gas

Hubble constant.[10] At present (1983) the Hubble constant seems to be between 50 and 100km/sec per million parsecs (mega-parsecs or Mpc.) This number is important because it gives an approximate age of the Universe, t_0.[11]

Because the galaxies are all moving away from us, it may seem that this place in our Milky Way Galaxy is the centre of the Universe—an unpopular place. Since Copernicus shifted the centre of the Solar System from Earth to Sun, scientists have not been happy with our being at the centre of anything (Galaxy, local group of galaxies, or Universe). The Hubble Law does *not* imply that we are at the centre—every other galaxy has the same view, and people there might think that they are at the centre.

The masses of outside galaxies have been estimated from measurement of their rotation and from measurement of orbital motion in pairs. These estimates show that giant ellipticals are much more massive than our Milky Way Galaxy, and spirals are of about the same mass. Ignoring "dark halos", the average characteristics of the different galaxy types are given in the table, assuming that H = 100km/sec/Mpc.

Clusters of Galaxies

After Hubble's work, he and other astronomers then found that *clusters* of galaxies were even larger groupings of matter in the Universe. The 48-inch Schmidt telescope on Palomar Mountain was used to survey the northern sky and George O. Abell (1927-) catalogued on the Palomar plates 2,712 clusters of galaxies. These

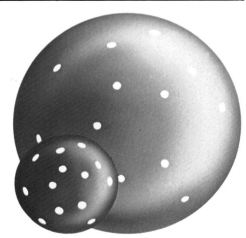

Expansion of the Universe Imagine an observer on a dot on the surface of a balloon. As the balloon is inflated, the other dots appear to recede from him, with a speed of recession proportional to the distance from his dot. He might thus deduce his own version of Hubble's Law. Note that the same effect is experienced by every dot on the surface.

clusters range from small (100 galaxies within 1°) to large (2,500 for the 12° cluster in the constellation Virgo).

The interest in clusters of galaxies grew, as estimates showed that cluster masses are several times larger than the sum of the individual galaxy masses in the cluster. In 1965 Page showed that "hidden mass" increases from that in single and binary galaxies, through groups of galaxies to the largest clusters.

Some astronomers believe that a fraction of this hidden mass is in an intergalactic medium, gas between galaxies in a cluster. It cannot be dust, because the space

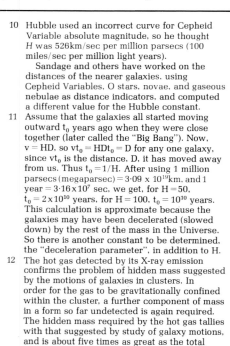

between galaxies in a cluster seems to be very transparent. Radio astronomers find no atomic hydrogen in clusters, but X-ray astronomers detect hot gas at 10 million degrees Kelvin.[12]

Abell's 2,712 clusters are seen in every direction (except the zone of avoidance in the Milky Way). They seem to indicate that clusters of galaxies are spread evenly through space out to about 1,200 million parsecs or 4·8 billion light years (much farther than individual galaxies). That is, there is no evidence of any thinning out at

Below: *HEAO-2 X-ray images of the Perseus cluster containing the giant galaxy NGC 1275, and the cluster Abell 2199. Both clusters show X-ray emission from hot gas with, in Perseus' case, a superimposed spike due to the X-ray source in NGC 1275.*

10 Hubble used an incorrect curve for Cepheid Variable absolute magnitude, so he thought *H* was 526km/sec per million parsecs (100 miles/sec per million light years).
  Sandage and others have worked on the distances of the nearer galaxies, using Cepheid Variables, O stars, novae, and gaseous nebulae as distance indicators, and computed a different value for the Hubble constant.

11 Assume that the galaxies all started moving outward t_0 years ago when they were close together (later called the "Big Bang"). Now, $v = HD$, so $vt_0 = HDt_0 = D$ for any one galaxy, since vt_0 is the distance, D, it has moved away from us. Thus $t_0 = 1/H$. After using 1 million parsecs (megaparsec) = $3·09 \times 10^{19}$km, and 1 year = $3·16 \times 10^7$ sec, we get, for H = 50, $t_0 = 2 \times 10^{10}$ years, for H = 100, $t_0 = 10^{10}$ years. This calculation is approximate because the galaxies may have been decelerated (slowed down) by the rest of the mass in the Universe. So there is another constant to be determined, the "deceleration parameter", in addition to H.

12 The hot gas detected by its X-ray emission confirms the problem of hidden mass suggested by the motions of galaxies in clusters. In order for the gas to be gravitationally confined within the cluster, a further component of mass in a form so far undetected is again required. The hidden mass required by the hot gas tallies with that suggested by study of galaxy motions, and is about five times as great as the total mass of galaxies and hot gas combined.

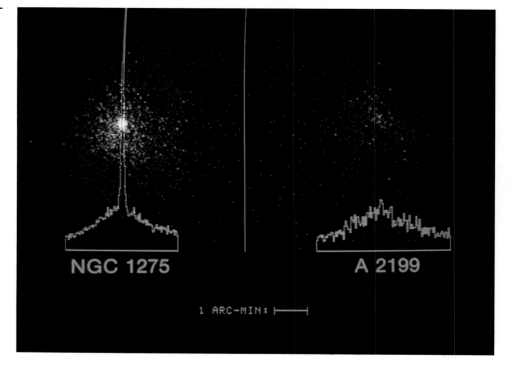

NGC 1275   A 2199

1 ARC-MIN:

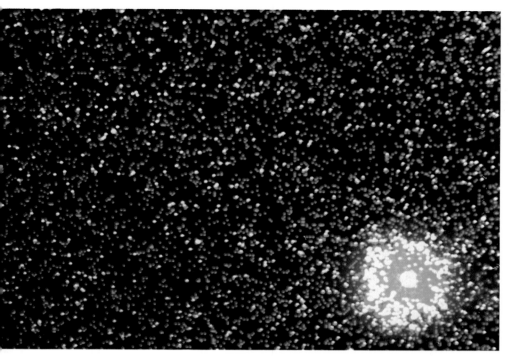

Relativity provides a different formula, such that v never exceeds c.[14]

Several thousand quasars have been studied. They are linked with Seyfert galaxies that have bright nuclei and emission-line spectra. No one has yet detected with certainty the spiral galaxy around a quasar, but that is suspected. The Space Telescope must surely be used for this purpose in 1986–87.

There are other peculiarities of quasars including their short-term brightness variations, their age, and their energy source. Theorists consider the energy source in both Seyfert galaxies and quasars to be a large black hole of 10^6 to 10^9 suns, into which stars and other material are falling, providing the variations in energy.

According to the General Relativity theory of Albert Einstein (1879-1955), a black hole is formed when matter condenses to such high density that the escape velocity exceeds the velocity of light. A black hole is believed to be the final stage in the evolution of massive stars (i.e., stars exceeding 5 solar masses). At this stage, the energy processes of the star are exhausted and it collapses inward by the force of its own gravity. Matter becomes so compressed that a star the size of our Sun (with a radius of 432,500 miles, 696,000km) would be compacted to a ball 1·5 miles (2·5km) in radius. At that size, the star's gravitation would be strong enough to

large distances, although there *are* clumps of clusters. On the large scale, clusters are uniformly distributed, so that one part of the Universe is occupied by the same number of clusters as any other part.

This homogeneity, and the Hubble Law, are important observational facts for cosmology, the theory of the origin and evolution of the Universe. Another important observational fact is the mean density, about 3×10^{-30} grams per cubic centimetre (gm/cm³), among the galaxies out to 17 million parsecs (Mpc), not including the nearest cluster in Virgo. However, this may be too low by a factor of 10 or more because of the hidden mass in groups and clusters of galaxies, or in dark halos omitted from the measurement of individual galaxy masses.

Some astrophysicists challenge one or more of these "facts". Geoffrey Burbidge (1925–) at Kitt Peak Observatory in Arizona is not convinced that the Hubble Law holds (remains linear) at the large distances at which quasars (see below) have been detected and D. W. Sciama (1926-) of Cambridge University has assumed that intergalactic space is filled with ionized hydrogen (protons and electrons) at a density of 10^{-28}gm/cm³, but this has not been detected. (One might also assume intergalactic space is filled with 1-metre boulders at that mean density; boulders would be more difficult to detect than ionized hydrogen.)

Quasars and Black Holes

Discovered by radio astronomers, chiefly Sir Martin Ryle (1918-) at Cambridge University in the 1950s, quasars (quasi-stellar objects) were identified by Maarten Schmidt (1929-) at Mt. Wilson Observatory in 1963. He recognized that emission lines in their visible spectra are redshifted far-ultraviolet (short λ) lines[13]. The Doppler shifts, $\Delta\lambda/\lambda = z$, range from 0·5 to over 3, which would seem to imply from the Doppler effect formula that quasars are receding from us faster than the velocity of light (c). For such high speeds (v comparable to c) Einstein's Special

The Bending of Starlight by the Sun
As light from distant stars passes a massive body like the Sun, it is deflected from a Euclidean straight line, as predicted by the General Theory of Relativity. This can be shown by measuring (at a time of total eclipse) the apparent positions on the sky of two stars whose light just grazes the obscured solar disc. They then appear to subtend a larger angle on the sky than when the Sun is in a different part of the sky. For optical observations one must wait for a total eclipse so that the starlight is not obscured; however radio observations of quasistellar radio sources can be made at any time, and they show the same effect.

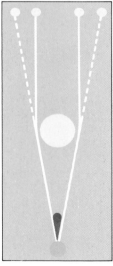

[13] In a spectrograph, light is spread out into a rainbow of colours from red (longer wavelength λ) to blue (shorter λ) by a glass prism or a diffraction grating. λ is the Greek letter, lambda, the symbol for wavelength. Most stars show dark absorption lines in their spectra, wavelengths that have been absorbed by gases in the star's atmosphere. Gaseous nebulae have bright emission lines in their spectra, emitted by gases excited by ultraviolet light (very short λ) or beams of high-speed particles (electrons and ions). The pattern of these lines identifies the gases; for instance, hydrogen has a series of lines from Hα in the red to Hβ in the yellow, Hγ green, Hδ blue, etc. The Doppler shift (Δλ in wavelength) is the difference (Δλ) between the "correct" λ and observed λ, and the radial velocity of recession, and is calculated by $v = c\Delta\lambda/\lambda$ where c is the velocity of light and Δ, the Greek delta, is velocity change. Doppler shifts in the spectra of some spiral nebulae showed recession of hundreds of kilometres per second (km/sec), which would carry them out of the Galaxy. The Doppler effect is named for Christian Doppler (1803-1853), an Austrian physicist who discovered that the frequency of light (and sound) waves varies with the motion of their source.

[14] The formula is—
$$v = \frac{cz(2 + z)}{2 + 2z + z^2}$$
For $z = \Delta\lambda/\lambda = 3$, $v/c = 0·88$ or $v = 2·64 \times 10^5$km/sec. Using the Hubble Law, $D = V/H$, we find $D = 2,640$Mpc (8,500 million light years) if $H = 100$. At such an extreme distance, the quasar, which appears as a fuzzy faint star, about 17th magnitude, in the largest telescopes, must have enormous luminosity, as indicated in the table. Of course, the light left the quasar 8·5 billion years ago when the Universe was only 1·5 to 11·5 billion years old.

Doppler Shifts of Spectral Lines
Spectral lines in stellar sources receding from us at high velocity are observed not at their laboratory wavelengths, but at longer wavelengths ie shifted towards the red end of the visible spectrum. The amount of this redshift is proportional to the velocity of recession of the source and to the original wavelength of the line. The *ratios* of wavelengths of any pair of lines is thus constant and line patterns, while becoming more spread out with greater recession velocity, still maintain their characteristic appearance. This means that gases can be identified by these lines even though they appear at different points in the spectrum.

Ultraviolet   Visible light   Infra-red

prevent light from escaping and it would disappear—become a black hole.

There are many sizes of black holes; some small ones may have been formed in the Big Bang, and are now "evaporating". Stellar-size black holes have masses from 3 to 50 Suns and form when high-mass stars "blow up" in a supernova, leaving a black hole with a "singularity" at its centre. That is, the 3-50 solar masses are packed within a point. It is estimated that such supernova

Right: *The primary mirror for the Space Telescope at the Perkin-Elmer Corporation plant in Connecticut after the reflective aluminium layer had been applied.*

Technical Data
Length: 43ft (13·1m).
Diameter: 14ft (4·26m).
Weight: 24,200lb (11,000kg).
Solar panels: 43ft (13·1m) x 14ft (4·26m); output 2400 watts.
Orbit: 90mins (6 nickel-cadmium rechargeable batteries provide power on night side of orbit).
Telescope: 94in (2·4m) reflecting Cassegrain type; 94in (2·4m) primary mirror, 12in (0·3m) secondary mirror.
Prime contractors: Lockheed Missiles & Space Co; Perkin-Elmer Corp.

Wide Field/Planetary Camera
1 Pick-off mirror.
2 Fold mirrors.
3 Pyramidal mirror.
4 Charge-coupled device (CCD) assembly.
5 External radiator.
6 Filter carousel (50 filters).

Designed principally to carry out observation of planets within our own Solar System (except Mercury) and, in a second mode, to survey wide areas of space and thus assist in the calculation of spatial relationships between distant objects, this instrument is a complex camera in which a system of mirrors and other equipment can split the field of view into four distinct parts. Light levels of low intensity are recorded and trans-mitted to Earth for analysis.

Faint Object Camera
1 Refocus mirrors.
2 f/48 filter wheels.
3 f/96 filter wheels.
4 Removable Cassegrain for f/288.
5 Calibration source.
6 Removable shutter and mirrors.
7 f/96 aperture with coronagraphic mask.
8 f/48 aperture with spectrographic slit.
9 f/96 detector.
10 f/48 detector.
11 Photocathodes.
12 Removable mirror.
13 Fixed grating.

This instrument, which is being designed and con-structed under the supervision of the European Space Agency (ESA), is tasked with the detection of objects up to 50 times dimmer than any now visible; it will be able to image objects of the 28th magnitude, as compared to the limit of 24th magnitude imposed on ground observatories.

Among its functions, for example, are the location of extrasolar planets, the observation of extra-galactic supergiant stars, the study of condensing gas clouds and the gathering of information about variable-brightness stars. With a focal ratio of f/96 and equipped with four filter wheels, the camera focuses starlight on to an electronic intensifier, the output being scanned by a 250,000-pixel vidicon tube. In the spectro-graphic mode, at an f/48 focal ratio,—in which exposure time may be as great as 10 hours— galactic centres, and the black holes which are supposed to exist within them, can be studied.

Faint Object Spectrograph
1 Digicon detectors.
2 Off-axis paraboloid collimating mirror.
3 Grating and filter wheel.
4 Light baffles.
5 Grazing mirror.
6 Polarizer.
7 Entrance aperture.

Chemical elements emit or absorb light according to temperature and elemental abundance, and the Space Telescope's Faint Object Spectrograph will study the spectra of very faint light sources and hence disclose information concerning their mass, temperature and composition; moreover, it can determine their distance and their velocity through space. A digicon detector fitted to the spectro-graph records a star's image after it has been converted from a point of light into a wide beam by means of mirrors and gratings, counting photons and transmitting the information, via a spectrogram, to Earth.

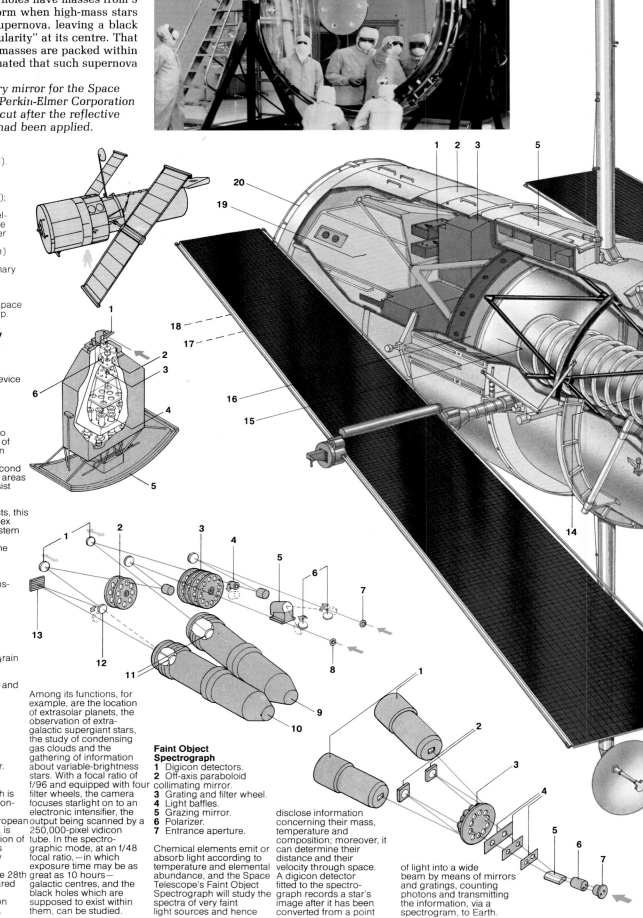

explosions, and smaller nova explosions, have left over a billion black holes in the Milky Way Galaxy.

Much larger black holes of 100 billion solar masses, a mass like that of our Galaxy, have much lower density. All black holes have only three measurable characteristics: mass, angular momentum or spin, and electric charge. This means that an isolated black hole would be almost undetectable. Fortunately, black holes are unlikely to be completely isolated in space, and their interactions with surrounding matter should lead to luminous signatures by which they can be identified. The primary source of this signature would be from gas or dust around

the hole falling in. This accreting matter is expected to form a fairly flat disc of material spiralling in around the hole. In the strong gravitational field, impacts are so energetic that they generate X-rays, as well as visible light.

The highly luminous nuclei of certain spiral galaxies called Seyfert galaxies, and the even higher luminosity quasars, may be powered by black holes. That is, matter may be falling into galaxy-size black holes to provide their enormous radiation output. These galaxy-size black holes may be the cause of the increase in mass/luminosity ratio with size of group or cluster of galaxies.

Stellar-size black holes will be most easily detected if they have a normal star as a companion in orbit around the black hole, supplying gas to fall in. In fact, candidates for two or three black holes have already been discovered this way, the most famous being Cyg X-1, a strong X-ray source in Cygnus.

There are individual stars of about 1/10 the Sun's luminosity which show continuous spectra with no absorption lines. A few dozen such stars, known as DC white dwarfs, may be black holes into which interstellar gas and dust are falling. If so, they should fluctuate in brightness at very short intervals—about 100 microseconds.

Space Telescope
1 Electronic boxes for fine guidance optical control.
2 Optical Telescope Assembly (OTA) module.
3 Fine guidance sensor (3).
4 High-gain antenna.
5 Support System Module (SSM), includes main command, communications and data handling electronics, and stabilization system.
6 Double roll-out solar array.
7 Magnetic torquer (4).
8 Crew handrail.
9 Aluminium main baffle.
10 Aperture door.
11 12in (0·3m) secondary mirror assembly.
12 Secondary baffle.
13 Graphite epoxy metering truss.
14 Central baffle.
15 94in (2·4m) Ultra Low Expansion Glass primary mirror (reflective coating: aluminium; protective coating: magnesium fluoride).
16 Main ring.
17 Radial scientific instrument module (beneath axial modules).
18 Fine head star tracker (3) and rate gyro assembly (beneath radial SI module).
19 Axial scientific instrument module (4).
20 Rear of aft shroud (houses low-gain antenna, 3 tip docking probes, coarse Sun sensor and vent).

To be orbited by the Space Shuttle, NASA's Space Telescope (ST) will dramatically extend the range of astronomical observation in terms of distance and "look-back" time: it is expected to resolve questions concerning the birth and death of stars, the evolution of galaxies and the nature of quasars and black holes; and it will also play an important role in Man's attempt to locate hitherto undiscovered planetary systems. The ST has three major elements: the telescope proper (Optical Telescope Assembly, OTA), protected by a meteoroid shield and sunshade; scientific instruments, comprising two cameras, two spectrometers and a photometer which convert the image produced by the OTA to electronic signals for transmission, via the Telescope's antennas, to Earth for reconstruction; and a Support Systems Module (SSM) containing pointing and stabilization controls, communications equipment and thermal control and electric power systems, and which interfaces with attachments in the Orbiter's payload bay for launch and recovery via the Shuttle's manipulator arm. Orbit-to-ground transmission is effected in association with the Tracking and Data Relay Satellite System (TDRSS), the Shuttle, and the White Sands, New Mexico, ground station. The Telescope's attitude in space is controlled by four reaction wheels in the SSM which respond to torquers, aligning the entire spacecraft with the Earth's magnetic field; precision pointing is achieved by means of six rate gyros and two fine guidance sensors. The "brain" of this complex instrument is the central computer and Data Management Subsystem: the computer receives, stores, processes and controls all data for spacecraft operation, while the Data Management Subsystem, using its own computer, decodes and assembles data relating to the scientific instruments.

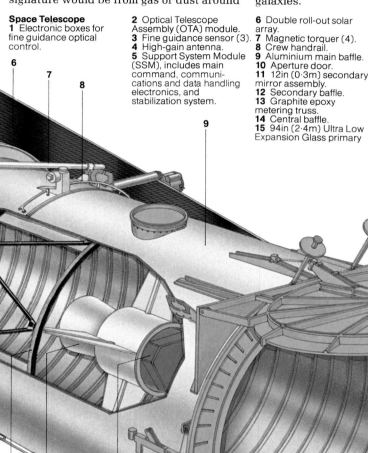

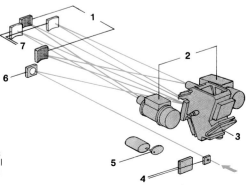

High Resolution Spectrograph
1 Concave cross-disperser gratings.
2 Digicon sensors.
3 Grating and camera mirror carousel.
4 Entrance slits.
5 Shutter for large slit.
6 Collimator off-axis paraboloid.
7 Concave camera mirrors.

Similar in concept to the Faint Object Spectrograph but operating only in the ultraviolet band, this instrument will explore in much greater detail the sorts of objects previously only detectable by extra-atmospheric instruments like those carried by spacecraft such as the International Ultraviolet Explorer. It will be capable of resolving optically inseparable bodies such as binary stars, study the composition of comets, the structure of planetary atmospheres and gas clouds, and investigate supernovae, active galaxies and quasars. Resolution will be 1,000 times greater than hitherto achieved.

High Speed Photometer
1 Ellipsoidal relay mirrors.
2 Image dissector tubes for relay light rays.
3 Straight-through image dissector tube.
4 Aperture plate assembly.
5 Filter plate assembly.
6 Photomultiplier tube.

The High Speed Photometer is the least complex instrument carried by the Space Telescope, and is charged with the task of observing fluctuations in the brightness of an object in space and of detecting fine shapes or structures associated with it. The photometer has no moving parts: it simply registers a light source and measures its intensity over a wide spectral range, from visible to ultraviolet. Its ability to measure brightness in fine detail will enable stellar distances to be ascertained with greater accuracy than hitherto, resolution being achieved over time scales as short as 16 microseconds. Rapidly spinning neutron stars and their flare structure may also be detected.

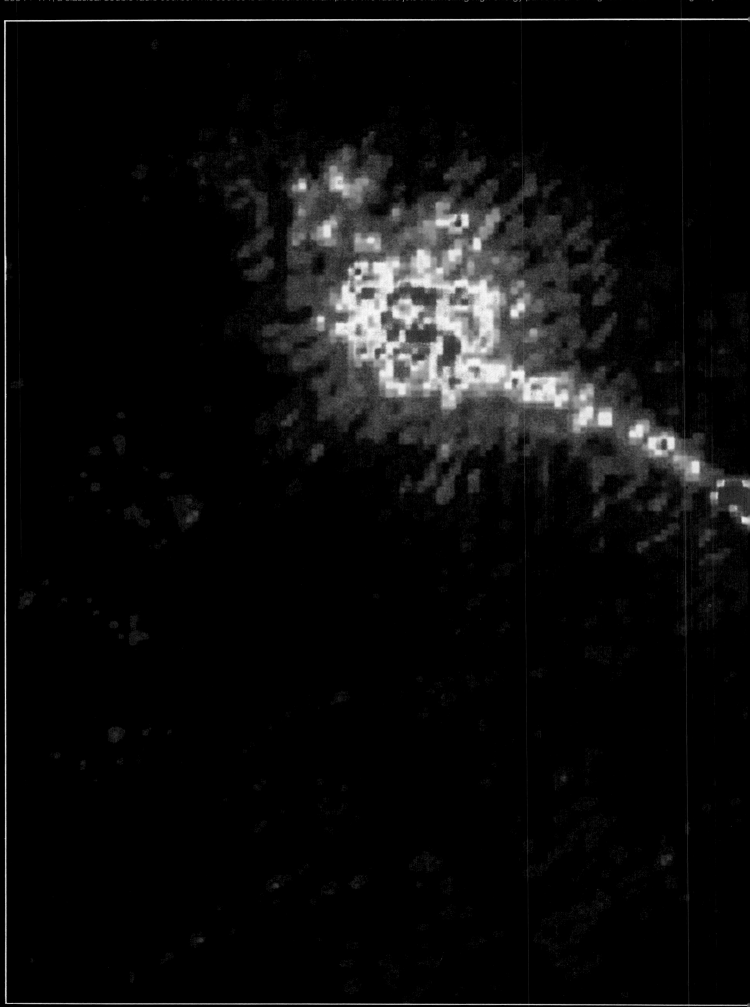

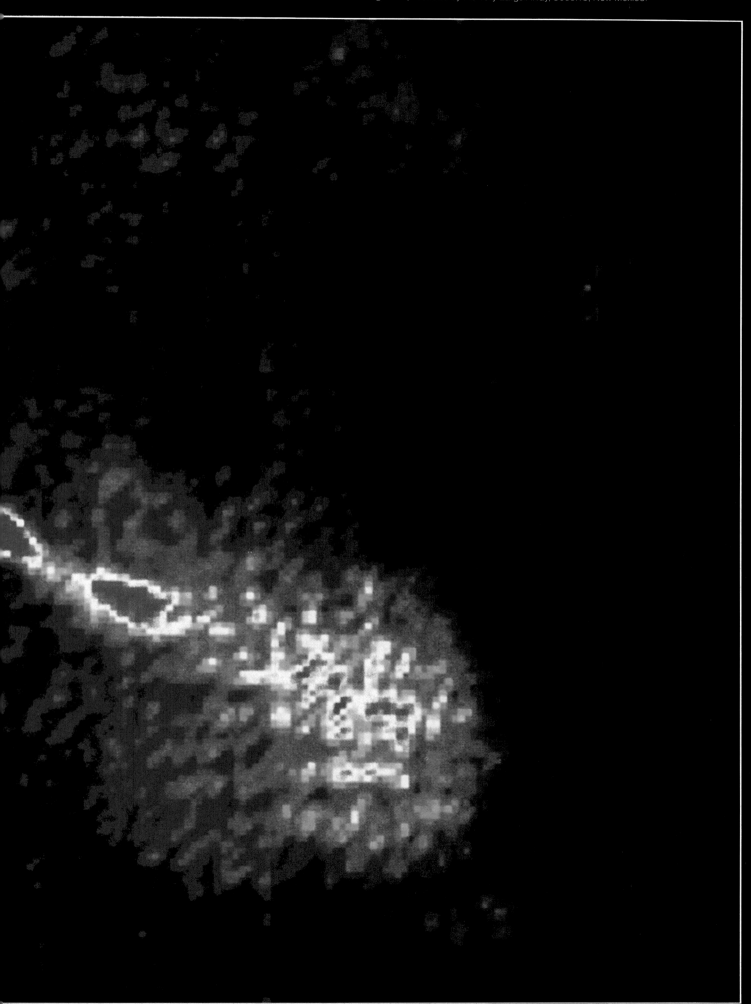

Right: *IUE image of the globular cluster NGC 6752. The two lines are ultraviolet spectra of sources in the cluster, suggesting the presence of unexpected hot stellar objects, and perhaps implying the presence of a massive black hole.*

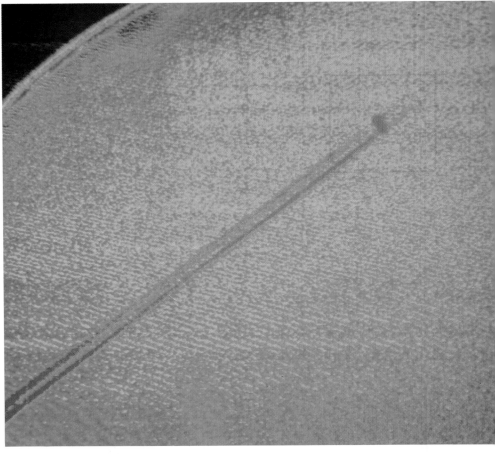

Also, some globular clusters and nuclei of galaxies that are X-ray sources may have large black holes at their centres.

The Echo of Big Bang

In 1965, A.A. Penzias and R.W. Wilson of the Bell Telephone Laboratories, Holmdel, New Jersey, discovered cosmic background radio noise with a high frequency radio receiver at wavelength $\lambda = 7 \cdot 3$ centimetres (cm). This noise spectrum has since been confirmed at shorter wavelengths, and measured to be isotropic (coming equally from all directions). It is explained by cosmologists as the remains of the "fireball" (1,000 billion degrees Kelvin) shortly after the Universe exploded into being in the "Big Bang". Since then, the radiation cooled because of the expansion of the Universe. At 7·3cm wavelength, its intensity corresponded to a black body temperature of 3 degrees Kelvin. The radiation was as intense as it would be if the whole Universe were emitting radiation like a cold, black body at 3 degrees Kelvin (3°C above absolute zero).

Other background radiation is at much shorter wavelengths, $1-10A^\circ$ X-rays ($1A^\circ$ or Angstrom $= 10^{-8}$cm) and 200MeV gamma rays. The X-ray background is due to many individual X-ray sources, including quasars, but it is still uncertain as to whether the gamma-ray background comes from individual sources, or something more uniform in the sky.

For thousands of years people have been thinking about the beginning and end of the Universe, generally in religious terms. About two centuries ago, astronomers began reasoning about the Universe of stars and how far it could extend. As they built larger telescopes to see farther, they saw more and more stars, apparently without end.

Heinrich Olbers (1758-1840) of Bremen then cited his famous paradox: "If there is an infinite number of stars, how can the sky be dark at night?" With a truly infinite number, even though spread out to infinite distance on all sides, each star's brightness is reduced by $1/D^2$ (the square of the distance) but the number at distance D goes up with D^2, so the whole sky should be as bright as the surface of a star—as bright as the Sun!

We now know that the stars in our Milky Way Galaxy are not infinite in number, but the same paradox applies to galaxies and clusters of galaxies, which seem to extend at roughly constant space density as far as we can see.

Before Hubble's Law, cosmology based on Newton's laws of motion and gravitation would have considered galaxies fixed in space and extending out to infinity. (At any "edge" of the Universe, the outer galaxies would be pulled in by the whole mass of the others.) With Hubble's Law, a Newtonian cosmologist could assume that the galaxies and clusters were thrown out into

Olbers' Paradox
If stars were uniformly spread throughout an infinite static Universe, every line of sight would eventually intercept the surface of a star and the night sky would appear uniformly as bright as the surface of an average star. This dilemma is not resolved by the grouping of stars into galaxies, as the same argument then applies to them. As explained below, Einstein's theories provide a solution to the paradox.

infinite space by a giant explosion, but he would be left with an "edge" beyond which there would be no galaxies—something not observed—and the Universe would have a centre, implying more galaxies in that direction than in others—also not confirmed by observation.

Einstein's General Relativity theory provides the solution to Olbers' paradox and avoids the "edge effects" by introducing the curvature of space-time to explain Newton's Law of Gravitation. This allows a finite but unbounded volume of the Universe (no edge or centre) and a finite number of galaxies (no bright night sky). It is impossible to visualize finite but unbounded curved space; an analogy is the finite but unbounded *surface* of the spherical Earth, a surface which has no geometric centre. Einstein and others developed a whole new mathematical technique (tensor calculus) to deal with curved space, and cosmologists have enshrined the *Cosmological Principle* to guide their efforts with mathematical models of the Universe. It states, "Regardless of his location, any observer in the Universe must get the same large-scale view of the Universe as any other observer at the same time." More specifically, it is assumed that the Universe is isotropic and homogeneous on the large scale, and the laws of physics are the same everywhere. Of course, the observers must correct for peculiar motions, such as the Earth's revolution about the Sun, and the Sun's orbit around the centre of the Galaxy—they are "co-moving" observers in a galaxy, equipped with accurate clocks, telescopes, etc.

In his General Relativity, Einstein assumed that every free-moving mass moves along a "geodesic", a line defined by the local geometry in curved space-time. This sounds complicated, but it simply means (among other things) that a planet follows an elliptical path around the Sun. In general, the deviations from Newton's laws are minute. The main differences from Newton's dynamics relate to very large masses and very large distances.[15]

Other Models

In addition to Einstein, many others applied General Relativity to cosmology, including Hermann Minkowski (1864-1909) in Germany, Willem de Sitter (1872-1934) in Holland, Georges Lemaître (1894-1966) in France, Alexander Friedmann (1888-1925) in Russia, and H. P. Robertson (1903-1961) in California. Each of these cosmologists produced one or more models of the Universe based on the "field equation" which relates the Einstein tensor to the stress-energy tensor and an adjustable constant. Using different values of this "cosmological constant" and different assumptions leads to different models.

The equations of cosmology apply to a smoothed-out Universe with a continuous density (no concentrations of matter in galaxies or clusters depending on time). By integrating from present conditions at time (t_0) back to $t=0$, conditions in a given model can be computed for various times. Not all the proposed models agree on these conditions; in fact, the early Minkowski models are static (no Big Bang).

In the early 1960s, the English theorists Hermann Bondi (1919–), Thomas Gold (1919–), and Fred Hoyle (1915–) extended the cosmological principle, assuming that the Universe is the same at all times as well as at all places, that it had no beginning, and will have no end. In order to maintain a constant density during expansion, Bondi, Gold, and Hoyle had to assume that matter is being created everywhere at a slow constant rate of about one hydrogen atom per year per cubic mile. This "Steady State Theory" has since been contradicted by the detection of the cosmic 3°K background radio noise, clear evidence of the "Big Bang".

Among the accepted models of the Universe there are, in general, three types expanding with positive curvature parameter, expanding with negative curvature parameter, and oscillating; the first two expand to infinity. More accurate observations of the Hubble Law may determine the deceleration parameter and rule out one or two of these three types.

Evolution

For 5.6×10^{12} seconds (177,000 years) after the Big Bang, radiation dominated the Universe. During that time helium (He) was formed in the expanding gas cloud. Then matter took over, atoms were formed. At 2×10^{17} sec (8×10^9 yr) galaxies started forming, and stars, which are still forming today. At least one star (our Sun) has a family of planets, and on at least one planet (Earth) life developed, starting 3·3 billion years ago.

All this looks very neat—the history of the Universe in the few square inches of a diagram—but it conceals a few uncertainties. The major one is how the galaxies formed. The theory deals with a continuum of radiation and matter, uniformly distributed throughout three-dimensional space. No one has yet shown how the gas, about 75 per cent hydrogen and 25 per cent helium, broke up into discrete clouds that condensed into galaxies of roughly the same size.

On the positive side, the Cosmic 3°K background radio noise confirms the fireball, and astrophysicists and geophysicists have confirmed the tail end of this universal history. The evolution of stars has been developed into a nearly complete theory of the workings inside stars of various sizes from 1/10 the mass of the Sun to 10 Suns and more (see also Chapter 3, "Stellar Evolution", for further information).

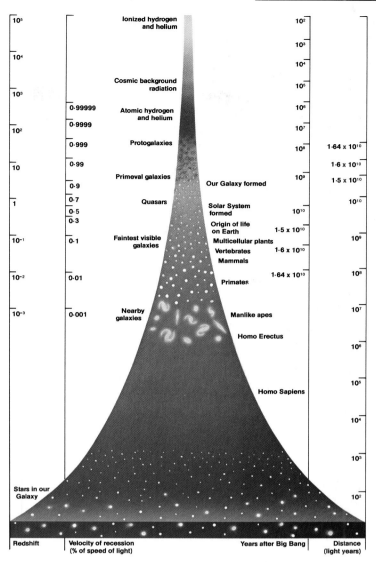

| Redshift | Velocity of recession (% of speed of light) | | Years after Big Bang | Distance (light years) |

Theory predicts that massive stars "burn" up their nuclear fuel rapidly, and thus evolve rapidly in a time as short as 50 million years.

Less massive stars like the Sun evolve much more slowly, and spend most of their lifetimes on the "main sequence", the evolutionary stage in the life of a star when it generates energy by thermonuclear reactions in its core which convert hydrogen to helium.

Evolution starts with the condensation of a cloud of cold gas and dust moving for about a million years to the main sequence. There the star stays for 10 billion years or more, until most of its hydrogen is gone.

Major Events in the History of the Universe
Reading downwards, the figure at left shows the sequence of the most significant stages in the evolution of the Universe as envisaged by astronomers today. Our chart begins at a cosmic age of 100 years, when after a rather more exotic period the Universe has settled down as a mixture of protons, helium nuclei and electrons bathed in a sea of photons. The temperature of the whole is about 300,000°K at this point. The Universe cools as it expands until, at a cosmic age of about 300,000 years, the electrons combine with the protons and helium nuclei to form hydrogen and helium atoms. The radiation emitted in this process, initially with a characteristic temperature of 3,000°K, will cool as the Universe continues to expand to be observed by us as the 3°K micro-wave background. The atomic material then coalesces to form the first protogalaxies, then galaxies like our own and quasars, the most distant objects observed. Looking upwards from the bottom of the figure we see the Universe as it appears to us. Within a few thousand light years are the stars in our own Galaxy; there then lies a gap to the nearest external galaxies at a distance of several million light years. The light which we are now receiving from these began its journey as the first manlike apes walked the Earth. The faintest galaxies are seen at redshifts up to z~1: beyond this all we can see are the quasars, up to a present limit of z~4.

Then, the solar-size star reddens and brightens to become a huge, red giant, "burning" helium. The next stage is more uncertain. It involves variable, unstable phases, possibly an explosion, which may form a planetary, shell-like nebula.

In the end, the star degenerates to a dense, white dwarf, about the size of the Earth, with no power source. It cools slowly, possibly to become an even smaller neutron star or, for larger stars, a black hole.

The tendency of black holes to gobble up matter near them is like the reversal of the Big Bang, the cosmic explosion which started from a black hole at $t = 0$, the origin of the Universe.

15 There were three confirmations of General Relativity shortly after its publication in 1916. First, Mercury, the planet closest to the Sun, changes the position of its perihelion (closest approach to the Sun) more than Newton's laws predict by the very small amount of 43 arc-sec per century. (Mercury had been doing that ever since astronomers started accurate observations of its position.) Second, light rays passing close to the Sun are deflected from a straight line by 1·75 arc-sec (following a geodesic in the curved space near the Sun), and this was measured on photographs taken a few months before, during, and after, the total solar eclipse of 1918—and for other eclipses through 1952. Third, General Relativity predicted a wavelength redshift in radiation from high-density objects. Spectra of dense white-dwarf stars (where the shift is about 20 A°) confirm this.

RECOMMENDED READING

Abell, George O., *Exploration of the Universe*, 4th Ed., Saunders, Philadelphia, 1982.
Hubble, Edwin, *The Realm of the Nebulae*, Yale University Press, New Haven, 1936.
Page, Thornton and Lou (Eds), *Beyond the Milky Way*, Macmillan, N.Y., 1969.
Page, Thornton and Lou (Eds), *Space Science and Astronomy*, Macmillan, N.Y., 1976.
Robertson, H. P. and Noonan, T. W., *Relativity and Cosmology*, Saunders, Philadelphia, 1968.
Sciama, D. W. *Modern Cosmology*, Cambridge University Press, 1971.
Shu, Frank H., *The Physical Universe*, University Science Books, Mill Valley, CA, 1982.
Weinberg, Stephen, *The First Three Minutes*, Basic Books, 1976.

The Formation and Evolution of Galaxies

I n this century, man has learned that the
Earth, the Sun and the planets are part
of a vast assemblage of 100 billion stars
in an island universe, the Milky Way
Galaxy. Other galaxies, island universes,
with their billions of stars and clusters of
galaxies have been identified also in this
century. Now, the Space Age has made it
possible to place cameras and other sensing

Below: *A hand-drawn panoramic view of
the Milky Way. The dark rift in
Cygnus/Aquila appears to the left of the
Galactic centre which lies in the direction
of Sagittarius. At lower right we see the
Magellanic clouds. The original map,
drawn by astronomers at the Lund
Observatory, Sweden, has more than 7,000
star positions marked.*

devices above the atmosphere to perceive
the structure of the Universe beyond the
power of ground-based telescopes. Soon, a
large telescope is to be placed in orbit
around the Earth with the power to see
farther than man has been able to see
before.

One of the triumphs of early 20th century
astronomy was the recognition that the
Earth, Sun and Solar System were located
at a distance of 32 thousand light years
from the centre of an aggregate of 100
billion stars, in the disc of the Galaxy we
call the Milky Way. It has been only 60
years since other patches of nebulosity,
galaxies, were first recognized as analogues
of the Milky Way—island universes—located
millions of light years from our home
Galaxy.

It is therefore not surprising that despite
intensive studies, our present understanding
of their origin and evolution is relatively
primitive. Yet the collective efforts of three
generations of scientists have brought us to
a point where we believe, perhaps arrogantly,
that our questions are becoming sharply
focused and that major breakthroughs in
understanding are within the grasp of the
next generation.

The ability of men to place their mechanical
and electronic "eyes" above the Earth's
atmosphere represents a qualitative step
forward in our ability to look back in time
and to exploit the expansion of the Universe
as a tool to probe the origin and evolution of
its denizens. By carefully charting the
formation and evolution of galaxies, we will
better be able to use these systems as a

PHOTOGRAPHIC MAGNITUDES

-1 0 1 2 3 4 5 6 7 8

means of determining the scale and structure of the Universe itself, and to learn its fate and perhaps the destiny of intelligent life.

Nearby Galaxies

From photographs of any patch of sky well away from the relatively opaque plane of the Milky Way, we can observe and classify galaxies on the basis of their appearance. Two main classes are discernible: elliptical and disc systems. Elliptical galaxies are smooth systems whose light distributions —deriving from the superposition of unresolvable starlight along the line of sight—fall off monotonically from their bright centres and whose shape, in projection on the plane of the sky is an ellipse. They come in a variety of flattenings, from circular or E0 galaxies to E5 systems in which the long axis of the

ellipse is twice the length of the short axis. (Initially, the classification recognized seven types of E system but E5 systems are now regarded as showing maximum flattening.)

Disc galaxies are in general composed of two parts—a thin disc of stars analogous to the disc of our Milky Way and a bulge, similar in appearance to an elliptical galaxy. The ratio of bulge to disc sizes can vary from zero (pure disc) to values in excess of 10, where the disc is barely discerned.

Although all bulges at first appear featureless, the range of disc characteristics is great. In some galaxies, the disc is relatively smooth; these are called S0 galaxies. In others, bright clusters of stars appear to map out spiral "arms". By comparison with similar regions in our Milky Way we know that these bright clusters contain "young"

(a mere 10 million years old!) newly-formed stars, luminous and hot enough to ionize hydrogen gas, causing it to glow like a cosmic fluorescent lamp.

The spiral patterns traced by these young stars differ from galaxy to galaxy. Some are "tightly wound" while others are more "open". Edwin Hubble, a pioneering investigator of galactic evolution, divided these spiral systems into three major types—*Sa* ("early" Hubble type) with tightly wound arms, *Sb* with arms of intermediate pitch and *Sc* ("late" Hubble type) in which the arm pattern is most open. In some spiral galaxies, the arm pattern appears to emanate from a straight, bar-like region passing through the centre of the galaxy. Spiral galaxies with this feature are called "barred spirals". Their arm patterns are classified in the same way as those of non-barred spiral galaxies. Still other disc galaxies contain regions of newly formed stars apparently arranged at random across the disc. These "irregular" galaxies are found primarily among galaxies of low intrinsic brightness.

Galaxy Types

While on very large scales the Universe as mapped by the distribution of galaxies appears to look everywhere the same, this is not the case on a small scale (hundreds of millions of light years). We find evidence for galaxy "clustering"—from small, scraggly groups of a few tens of systems to well organized, gravitationally-bound structures of many hundreds to perhaps thousands of galaxies.

Elliptical and S0 galaxies dominate the population of great clusters; few galaxies

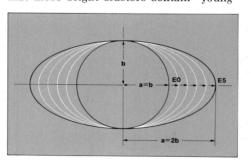

Classification of Elliptical Galaxies
The numerical suffix n in the En classification is a measure of the apparent flattening of elliptical galaxies. If a and b are the semi-axes of the elliptical image then n is given by $n = 10 (a-b)/a$. Thus if the galactic image is circular,

$a = b$ and so $n = 0$. The galaxy is thus an E0. In the extreme case where $a = 2b$, $n = 10 (2b-b)/2b$ i.e. $n = 5$ and such a galaxy is hence an E5. Intermediate classes have axial ratios a/b between 1 and 2 giving values of n that range between 0 and 5.

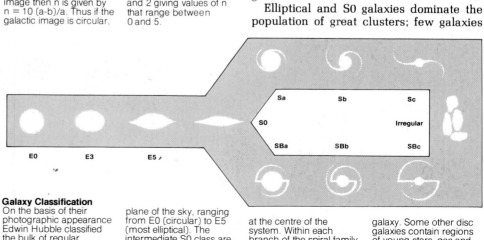

Galaxy Classification
On the basis of their photographic appearance Edwin Hubble classified the bulk of regular galaxies as either elliptical or spiral systems. Elliptical galaxies show a smooth light distribution and are subclassified by their projected shape on the plane of the sky, ranging from E0 (circular) to E5 (most elliptical). The intermediate S0 class are, like the spirals, disc systems but show no evidence of spiral arms. Two series of spirals are defined, depending on whether there exists a bar at the centre of the system. Within each branch of the spiral family further subclasses exist which are defined by how tightly wound are the spiral arms and the degree to which the nucleus dominates the galaxy. Some other disc galaxies contain regions of young stars, gas and dust but show no apparent structure: these are termed irregular. The figure above is known as Hubble's "tuning-fork" diagram.

making young stars are found within their borders. In loose, low population groups, spirals and irregulars dominate.

Recent X-ray observations have revealed the presence of hot (T $> 10^8$ °K), low density gas pervading rich clusters of galaxies. Galaxies may be the source of the intra-cluster gas which may control star formation in cluster galaxies. The environment of a galaxy plainly affects its present observed morphology. Is it also the driving influence on galaxy formation and evolution?

Distances to Galaxies

In examining the properties of individual galaxies it is crucial to determine their distance from us. Unless we know how far away a galaxy is, its angular extent on the plane of the sky cannot be translated into a true physical size;[1] we cannot infer masses or luminosities nor can we quantitatively compare dark clouds, nebulae and other structures in external galaxies with similar appearing entities in the Milky Way. Establishing the distance scale to the galaxies has been an heroic enterprise demanding ingenuity in concept and technique from some of the most talented astronomers of three generations.

In theory, establishing the distance scale is simple: locate *standard candles* (objects of known intrinsic luminosity) or standard "meter sticks" (objects of known size) in distant galaxies and compare the apparent brightness and sizes of these candles or meter sticks with the known brightness and sizes of the "standards" in nearby galaxies (see also pages 17-20). The distance can then be deduced either because the apparent brightness of a standard candle decreases with the square of its distance, or since the apparent angular size of a "meter stick" will decrease linearly with increasing distance.[2]

Checks on the distance derived from Cepheids are provided by other pulsating stars—RR Lyraes—and by novae. Other objects—luminous blue and red super-giants—are also used as standard candles. We can use these standard candles only in galaxies out to 10 million light years. After that, we must depend on less reliable indicators. The sizes of ionized hydrogen regions—the glowing gas surrounding clusters of young stars—appear to be rough but reliable standard meter sticks in the most luminous Sc galaxies. Measurement of their apparent angular sizes allows the distance scale to be extended to 50 to 100 million light years.[3]

The calibration of the meter stick is of course dependent on the calibration of the standard candles! The absolute calibration is a tenuous house of cards and real improvements have come slowly and painfully over the past 60 years.

One of the major discoveries of 20th century science was Hubble's compilation of the apparent brightness of galaxies and their motions relative to the Earth. The motion of galaxies perpendicular to our line of sight (ie proper motion) cannot be discerned by comparing the position of a galaxy from one time to another.

However, measurement of a galaxy's velocity along the line of sight (radial motion) can be determined by measuring

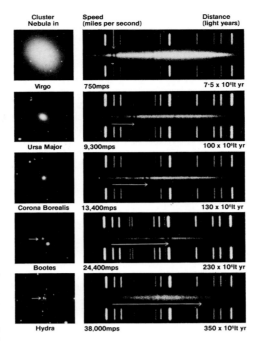

Cluster Nebula in	Speed (miles per second)	Distance (light years)
Virgo	750mps	7·5 x 10⁶lt yr
Ursa Major	9,300mps	100 x 10⁶lt yr
Corona Borealis	13,400mps	130 x 10⁶lt yr
Bootes	24,400mps	230 x 10⁶lt yr
Hydra	38,000mps	350 x 10⁶lt yr

the spectra of stars and gas in the galaxy and comparing them with laboratory spectra. The Doppler shifts towards red in observed wavelength were found to increase as apparent luminosity of a galaxy decreased, indicating that the galaxy was receding from us. The relationship between redshift (or velocity of recession) and apparent brightness is called the Hubble law. Since the intrinsic brightness of a galaxy dims with increasing redshift, the Hubble law expresses a relation between redshift and distance: the greater its distance, the greater a galaxy's redshift. Hence, at least for galaxies within a billion light years, the relative redshifts of two galaxies provide a good estimate of their relative distances.

At vast distances, the light emanating from a galaxy may take billions of years to reach us. Hence, by identifying galaxies of large redshifts, we may hope to discover evidence of change in galactic properties with time. Sadly, from the surface of the Earth, we cannot resolve distant galaxies with sufficient clarity to compare their detailed appearance with those of nearby systems. Thus far, comparisons have been restricted to quantities such as size, brightness and colour.

Luminosities and Colours

Quantitative measurements of brightness, colour and size offer important clues regarding the constituents and internal dynamics of galaxies.

Apparent luminosities are typically obtained by observing a galaxy's light through a coloured filter using photometers which record the flux received through a series of circular apertures of different size. By plotting apparent brightness against aperture size, it is possible to deduce the "total" luminosity of a galaxy by extrapolation. If a galaxy's distance is known, the apparent luminosity can be converted to absolute units. Observed luminosities range from $\sim 10^{12} L_\odot$ at the brightest to $\sim 10^6 L_\odot$ for the faintest dwarf galaxies. ($L_\odot$ is a unit of solar luminosity = 3.9×10^{26} watts.)

By using a series of filters which isolate different spectral regions, differences in

Redshifts and Distances of Galaxies
The montage at left shows the spectra of several galaxies in clusters at different distances away from us. In each case the displacement $\Delta\lambda$ of the prominent H and K absorption lines of calcium from their laboratory wavelength λ_0 is shown and the redshift z expressed as a velocity $v = c\Delta\lambda/\lambda_0$. Comparison of the redshift and distance to each galaxy shows that the Universe is expanding uniformly, with the velocity of recession in each case proportional to the distance of the galaxy from us (compare with the balloon analogy on p22). The constant of proportionality between velocity and distance is Hubble's constant, H. The accurate determination of the value of H remains one of the most important tasks in modern-day astronomy. One light year equals about 6 trillion miles or 6 x 10¹² miles.

galaxy colour can be assessed. Colour measurements of E-galaxies of differing luminosity reveal a definite trend: brighter ellipticals are red while fainter ones are blue. In the early 1970s the apparent cause for this effect was found by Sandra Faber. By making a series of measurements which isolated spectral features arising from absorption due to metals such as magnesium, calcium or iron, she determined that the metal feature strengths in low luminosity ellipticals were weaker than in the high luminosity systems. Because the absorption features arise in the atmospheres of stars whose composite contribution dominates the visual light of a galaxy, her result means that the stars in low luminosity galaxies contain, on average, fewer "metals" (i.e. elements heavier than helium) than do the stars in high luminosity systems. High luminosity ellipticals also have the highest mass. The cause of this relationship between luminosity, mass and metallicity may be a

---

1 Angular size refers to the angle of the sky subtended by the object. The smaller the angle, the greater is the distance of the object from the observer.

2 To be a useful Standard Candle, an object must be luminous enough to be seen at a great distance. Hence, efforts have been concentrated on calibrating the distances to the most luminous stars in our own Galaxy. Among them is a class of pulsating stars of varying brightness, the Cepheid Variables (see Chapter 1). The discovery of a relationship between the luminosity of these stars and their periods of variation in luminosity in the Magellanic Clouds has made it possible to establish a scale of extragalactic distance. If the distance to a Cepheid of known period in our own Galaxy can be observed, the relationship can be placed on an absolute luminosity scale and the distance to any galaxy with observable Cepheids can be obtained. Accurate distances to a few Milky Way Cepheids have been measured and the period-luminosity relation is now believed to be well calibrated.

3 Sizes of galaxies are estimated by measuring their angular size as far as some fixed brightness level (usually taken to be the level at which the galaxy brightness drops to 1 per cent of the intrinsic brightness of the sky as seen from Earth on the darkest nights). For galaxies of known distance, the angular size can be converted to linear dimensions.

Surface temperature

25,000°K   10,000°K   5,000°K   3,000°K

Luminosity

Wavelength (Angstroms)   2,000   4,000   6,000   8,000   10,000

Stellar Temperatures
The apparent colour of a star depends on its surface temperature. The intensity of light from any star as a function of wavelength closely follows theoretical Planck curves, some examples of which are illustrated above for stars of different surface temperatures. The light from hot stars, above about 10,000°K, falls mainly in the blue and ultraviolet regions of the spectrum and the stars hence appear blue in colour. Stars with a surface temperature of 5,000°K are yellow-orange while still cooler stars peak in the red or infra-red.

Above: *NGC 3115, a luminous disc (S0) galaxy viewed nearly edge-on. In this colour-coded intensity map the system displays a smooth virtually featureless disc without spiral structure (see also below, top left picture).*

clue to understanding the formation and evolution of these systems.

Disc systems also show a colour—luminosity effect. Does this suggest a metallicity/luminosity trend as well? Most astronomers think not. Disc systems show different levels of star-forming activity. In photographic images of galaxies, low luminosity systems *appear* to exhibit spectacular episodes of star-formation, as evidenced by the brightness of newly-formed stellar clusters. When a cluster of stars is young, light from the high mass cluster members dominates. Such stars have surface temperatures of 15,000 to 50,000°K and their light is very blue. As the cluster ages, high mass stars evolve and eventually turn into extremely dim stellar remnants. The light from such older stellar groups is much redder since it is dominated by the light of dwarfs and giants of lower mass stars whose temperatures range from 4,000° to 6,000°K. Hence, a large admixture of young stars will cause the composite colour of a galaxy to be blue.

The colour-luminosity relation for disc galaxies thus may reflect differences in the ratio of new-to-old stellar population; bluer, low luminosity galaxies may contain a greater admixture of young stars.

If this interpretation is correct, then the colour of a disc galaxy provides an indirect indication of its relative evolutionary state. High luminosity systems may have produced most of their stars early in their history. During their initial burst of activity they might have been 100 to 1000 times as bright as they are now. The remnants of that burst of star-forming activity (billions of years in the past) are billions of cool stars of mass close to that of the Sun. Lower luminosity disc galaxies, on the other hand, appear to form stars more steadily at a rate not much different than in the past.

Disc galaxies of lower mass make new stars at a nearly steady rate during their history while higher mass systems make most of their stars at an early epoch. Hence the mass of a disc galaxy appears to control its star-forming history.

How big are galaxies? We know from measuring the distance of stars of known brightness in the Milky Way that the diameter of our Galactic disc is about 200,000 light years. The largest systems have diameters of about 500,000 light years; the smallest of a few thousand light years.

There is a close relationship between a galaxy's luminosity and its size: the most luminous galaxies are also the largest. The size-luminosity relationship for discs and ellipticals appears to be the same everywhere, except in the central regions of dense clusters of galaxies. Here, galaxies of a fixed luminosity are smaller, again demonstrating that environment appears to play an important role in determining the present day appearance of a galaxy.

For nearby galaxies, we can measure brightness as a function of position. Elliptical galaxies are brightest at the centre and grow fainter at greater distances from the galaxy's centre. The fall-off in measured surface brightness depends roughly on the square of the projected distance from the galaxy's centre.

The bulges of disc galaxies show a similar effect. However, their discs exhibit an exponential fall-off in light with distance from the centre. The structure of ellipticals and disc galaxies inferred from their light distributions contains evolutionary clues as vivid as stratigraphic distribution of flora and fauna on Earth. These clues indicate the kinds of stars formed, when they were formed and in what quantity. Decoding this information requires modelling of the dynamical history of the gas and stars in a galaxy (which is analogous to understanding the geological history of the strata).

NGC 3115

NGC 7332

NGC 4762

NGC 4594

NGC 4565

NGC 5907

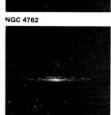

NGC 4274

NGC 4622

NGC 628

Galaxy Types
This matrix contains examples of both actively star-forming and inactive disc galaxies. It provides examples of the range in bulge/disc ratio (decreasing from left to right) found in both types of disc systems. The discs in the top panel are forming no stars at present and are classified as S0 systems. Actively star-forming systems of similar bulge/disc, viewed edge-on, are shown in the middle panel. The bottom row depicts the nearly face-on appearance of some actively star-forming spirals. The bright knots in the spiral arms represent complexes of newly-formed stars which ionize nearby hydrogen gas. When the electrons (stripped by the star's ultraviolet ionizing radiation) recombine with protons, they produce the fluorescent spectra which characterize these bright regions. The strongest of these emission lines, the Balmer alpha line of hydrogen, occurs at a wavelength of 6563 Angstrom units.

The Gas Content of Galaxies

Regions forming young stars in the Milky Way appear rich in gas, mainly atomic and molecular hydrogen. Stars are believed to form from a blob of gas which cools and then collapses as the internal pressure of the condensing gas can no longer support the blob against its own gravity.

After World War II, the technology which brought radar to the Allies was applied to scanning the heavens, and the radio signature of hydrogen gas emission at 21cm wavelength was observed. Astronomers mapped the Milky Way, whose plane was found to contain more than a billion solar masses of hydrogen. New stars are formed from this gas at a rate of a few solar masses per year.

When receivers improved in sensitivity, the search began for hydrogen in galaxies beyond the Milky Way. From careful surveys we now know that most elliptical and S0s contain no hydrogen gas while spirals contain an amount which, relative to the mass in stars, increases from early (Sa) to late (Sc) Hubble types. Low luminosity irregular galaxies contain the most hydrogen compared with their stellar mass.

These conclusions are fundamental to a study of galaxy evolution because they suggest that the rate at which gas is turned into stars differs from system to system, being highest for Es and S0s and lowest for the irregulars.

The absence of many star-forming systems in rich clusters of galaxies suggests that gas poverty might characterize the discs in such clusters—an hypothesis which just now is being checked. If such systems are gas poor, how did they become so? Were more stars induced to form by some characteristic of the high galaxy density environment or does such an environment lead somehow to the removal of gas?

Masses of Galaxies

It is important to know how much galaxies weigh, to assess their relative evolutionary state and to see whether galaxy mass plays a role in dictating evolution. That possibility is strongly suggested by colour, luminosity and gas-content relations. Galaxies can be weighed in two ways—either by observing the motions of stars and gas within the system, or indirectly, by observing their motions in gravitationally-bound groups.

We know that the Earth revolves about the Sun once a year in a nearly circular orbit of radius of nearly 150 million km. It is clearly in an equilibrium orbit, neither falling into the Sun, nor flying away from its gravitational pull. We know that the Sun, at a galactocentric distance of 3×10^{17}km completes an orbit around the centre of the Milky Way in 200 million years (called a "cosmic year"). Since the mass necessary to hold a body in an equilibrium circular orbit is proportional to the square of the velocity times the radius of the orbit, we deduce that the mass interior to the Sun's orbit about the Galactic centre is $\sim 10^{11}$ (100 billion) solar masses. Although we cannot resolve individual stars in other galaxies and chart their motions directly, we can detect motions of gas and stars by obtaining optical or radio spectra. Here the motion of gas or stars is signified by a shift in the wavelength of a spectral feature—an

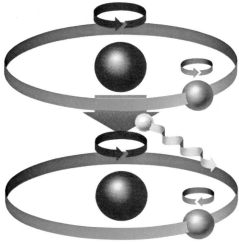

Origin of 21cm Radiation In interstellar space the hydrogen atom can exist with the electron in its lowest orbit spinning either in the same or the opposite direction to the spin of the proton which forms the nucleus of the hydrogen atom. The former of these two configurations has a slightly higher energy than the latter. A spontaneous transition between the two states will lead to the emission of a photon with an energy equal to the difference in energy between the two states. The wavelength of such a photon is 21 centimetres.

emission or absorption line. The magnitude of the shift in wavelength gives the velocity in units of the speed of light.

By charting stellar and gas motions we find that the mass of galaxies ranges from $\sim 10^{12} M_\odot$ for a few, to $\sim 10^{6} M_\odot$ typical of numerous faint dwarf galaxies (where $M_\odot$ is one solar mass or $1 \cdot 989 \times 10^{27}$ tonnes). The most massive galaxies are also the brightest and, approximately, the ratio of mass to light is constant over this range in mass.

Weighing galaxies in clusters involves a similar procedure.[4] In rich clusters, the mass of cluster galaxies has been calculated as actually being 10 times the mass inferred from the luminosities of individual galaxies and typical values of mass/luminosity for isolated galaxies. This discrepancy is one of the factors which has led many astronomers to believe that galaxies are surrounded by large halos of optically invisible material extending perhaps to 10 times the size of the photographic image of a galaxy and weighing 10 times as much as the luminous mass. In other words, we may be "seeing" only 10 per cent of the matter of the Universe (see page 22, note 12). It is of fundamental importance to identify the constituents of galactic halos and to determine the role they play in the evolution of galaxies.

Formation and Evolution

Most astronomers believe that galaxies were formed soon after the "Big Bang" (see Chapter 1), the cosmic fireball in which the Universe began. All matter in the Universe was at first compressed in a singularity of incredible density and temperature; "in the beginning" the Universe was born in an explosion of this primordial matter. When expansion of the exploding material had gone on sufficiently long for radiation and

gaseous matter to begin to decouple, density inhomogeneities in the gas developed.

Nearly all protogalaxies must have formed at this early time, since the continuing expansion of matter in the Universe makes it more and more difficult to "grow" blobs of protogalactic mass; the mean matter density is decreasing with time. Some density enhancements in this expanding cosmic "soup" were sufficiently great so that the self-gravity of these gaseous blobs was able to overcome the effects of expansion.

The expansion in these regions was locally halted and such blobs of protogalactic gas began to contract under the influence of their self-gravity. We know from studies of our own Galaxy that the possibility of forming stars depends on the gas density: high density means higher star-forming likelihood. Hence, in the densest of these blobs, star formation takes place rapidly, consuming most of the gas before collision between gaseous blobs within the protogalaxy dissipates much kinetic energy. These systems become elliptical galaxies whose characteristic round shapes suggest a minimum of gas dissipation.

The first massive stars formed during the collapse of the protogalaxy evolve quickly—perhaps within a few million years as compared to the gravitational collapse or "free fall" times of several hundred million years characteristic of the protogalaxy. The first atomic species more complex than the hydrogen and helium produced in the "Big Bang" are assembled by fusion reactions in the hot, dense cores of these first-generation massive stars.

These heavy elements or "metals" are then ejected into the collapsing gas in giant stellar explosions—supernovae. The protogalactic gas, inexorably contracting under its own gravitational pull, is contaminated by these stellar ejecta and simultaneously heated by the stellar explosion.

Those galaxies massive enough to hold onto their heated, metal-enriched gas continue the star-forming process through multiple generation of stars. The gas and

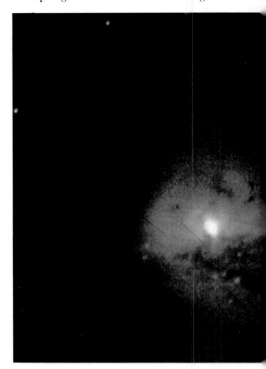

---

4 If an aggregate of galaxies is in equilibrium, then the mass of the group is proportional to the mean value of $R \times (V - V_{avg})^2$ where $(V - V_{avg})$ is the difference between the velocity of an individual galaxy and the average velocity of the cluster and R is the distance of the galaxy from the centre of the cluster.

the stars formed from it become ever more metal rich as such galaxies continue to contract. Less massive galaxies, with weaker gravitational pull, lose their gas at a stage during their early evolution, when the velocity of gas atoms induced by supernovae and collisions during contraction, becomes so great that all the remnant gas escapes.

This picture has the virtue of predicting the observed round shape of elliptical galaxies and the important relation between metal content of the surviving stars and the total mass of the system. It also predicts "strata" of stars of differing metal abundance — those nearest the galactic centre should be most metal rich. This has been confirmed by observations of systematic colour and line strength variations in many (though not all) ellipticals.

The gas ejected by lower mass ellipticals may be the source for the hot gas recently observed at X-ray wavelengths. In rich clusters, the gravitational pull of the clusters is high enough to retain the gas lost by individual galaxies. Collisions between clouds ejected from different galaxies heats the gas to a temperature corresponding to the velocity dispersion of the cluster $T \sim 10^8$ K.

Until a few yars ago, it was thought that this picture of E (elliptical)-galaxy formation could predict the observed range of galaxy flattenings as well, by assuming that gravitational "torques" exerted by neighbouring protogalaxies induced varying degrees of rotation in each protogalaxy. Flattening took place along the axis of rotation since dissipative gas blob collisions within the protogalaxies occur more frequently along this axis rather than perpendicular to it.

Since the distribution of stars follows that of the parent gas, such flattenings seemed a natural consequence of rotation induced by tidal torques. Astronomers were surprised to learn a few years ago that the systems expected to show signs of high rotation — the flattened E5s — show far too little rotation to explain their shape. This critical observation has sent theorists back to the drawing board to see how ellipticals of different shape form. The most radical suggestion at present is that elliptical galaxies do not represent a special class of galaxy but rather are the end products of multiple collisions among disc galaxies. Stellar discs can be "re-arranged" into elliptical shapes during a collision between disc galaxies; the disc gas is lost to the system during the collision.

Perhaps the greatest attraction of such galaxy mergers is that they may explain the high frequency of Es in galaxy clusters where the frequency of collision among galaxies is highest.

Star Formation

Most models of disc galaxy evolution start with the assumption that they began their lives as protogalactic blobs of lower density than those giving birth to ellipticals. The blobs are assumed to rotate as a consequence of tidal interactions with nearby protogalaxies. When the proto-disc system begins to collapse, the collapse proceeds most rapidly at the denser centre of the giant gas cloud. As with ellipticals, we assume that high density produces more rapid star formation. Thus in the central, dense regions of a proto-disc galaxy, gas is consumed rapidly in star-forming events thereby creating the elliptical-like nuclear bulge found at the centre of many discs. In the outer, lower-density regions, the collapse proceeds more slowly and the density is low enough so that fewer stars are formed.

Blobs of gas within the protogalaxy collide with one another, heating the gas; the energy is lost in such collisions because the gas radiates. Hence, through dissipation of energy, the gas settles into a thin disc rotating about the nuclear bulge of stars.

What happens to the disc gas? As it cools, individual blobs begin to contract and star-formation then proceeds at random throughout the disc. When enough disc stars are formed, the disc becomes susceptible to the growth of wave disturbances. The wave modes tend to be spiral in shape and produce spiral-shaped density enhancements which have a profound effect on the remaining disc gas. The gas rotates about the galactic centre faster than the spiral density pattern changes with time. When the gas encounters a spiral arm a shock wave in the gas is induced. Gas is compressed and star-formation is supposed to ensue.

Evidence in support of such a picture is found in galaxies having well-developed spiral arms. Gas compression and star formation take place on the inner edges of the underlying spiral density wave.

Star formation, triggered by galactic shocks, is supposed to proceed most vigorously in regions where the gas is compressed to very high density. High compression occurs when the velocity of encounter between gas and arm is greatest — that is, in systems where the circular velocity

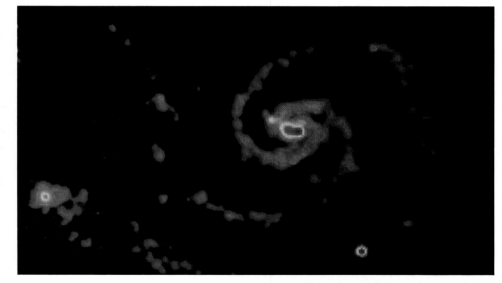

Left: *NGC 5194/5 (the "Whirlpool Galaxy" and its companion) are one of the touchstones for the density-wave theory of spiral structure. Comparison of radio (**upper**) and optical (**lower**) spiral structure shows that the radio arms lie inside the optical arms along the dust lanes as predicted by the density-wave theory. The radio observations, made with the Very Large Array (see page 42), present a picture of the spiral arms that qualitatively closely resembles the optical "beads on a string" image.*

of the gas is highest. Since circular velocities are highest in massive galaxies, compression and hence star-forming efficiency is predicted to be highest in such systems as well.

However attractive the galactic shock picture may be, it cannot account for all star-forming events in disc galaxies. The initial disc stars supporting the density wave are believed to arise from random star-forming events occuring in the cold disc gas. In low mass systems where characteristic circular velocities are low, galactic shocks cannot occur. These systems are not likely to produce stars efficiently and it is not surprising that they contain more gas and more new stars currently.

Unseen Halos

Galactic shock models predict that star formation proceeds most rapidly in systems showing the greatest differential rotation. They exhibit greater concentration of mass toward the galactic centre and massive central bulges. Hence, such systems should consume their disc gas in star-forming events most rapidly. Observation of the systematics of gas content and colour for early and late Hubble type galaxies at fixed luminosities suggests such a trend. Moreover, the disc galaxies (S0s) showing no star-forming activity at present have the biggest bulges. Were these systems once actively star-forming galaxies which have consumed their gas in star-forming activity?

Perhaps the greatest uncertainty surrounding galactic evolution studies at present, is the role played by unseen halos of dark matter. How and when did they form? What is their prime constituent? Did the embryos of optically visible galaxies form within these cosmic eggs?[5]

Though the advance in photon gathering power and spatial resolution from Galileo's telescope to the 200-inch has been enormous, our current powers of observation have raised more questions than can be answered even with the most diligent thought.

A variety of new instruments and approaches are needed. We must be able to discern detail in galaxies located at far greater distances from us and hence at much earlier stages in their evolution. To press our study to the earliest evolutionary stages we must observe galaxies not only at optical wavelengths but in the infra-red (at wavelengths longer than 1 micrometre), since the light from these most distant and earliest of galaxies is redshifted by Hubble

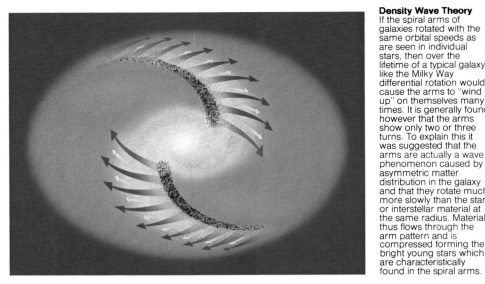

Density Wave Theory
If the spiral arms of galaxies rotated with the same orbital speeds as are seen in individual stars, then over the lifetime of a typical galaxy like the Milky Way differential rotation would cause the arms to "wind up" on themselves many times. It is generally found however that the arms show only two or three turns. To explain this it was suggested that the arms are actually a wave phenomenon caused by asymmetric matter distribution in the galaxy and that they rotate much more slowly than the stars or interstellar material at the same radius. Material thus flows through the arm pattern and is compressed forming the bright young stars which are characteristically found in the spiral arms.

recession. To obtain critical information about galaxy environments and the role of intracluster gas on evolution, further X-ray observations of galaxies and the medium between them are mandatory.

Fortunately, our ability to launch sophisticated instruments into space promises a revolution in our understanding of galactic evolution. At optical and ultraviolet wavelengths we will be able to resolve much finer detail with optical/UV telescopes located outside the Earth's turbulent atmosphere. We can then observe bright, young stellar complexes and ionized hydrogen regions in much more distant galaxies, whose discs and bulges are blurred even on the best ground-based photographs. We may also be able to launch a permanent X-ray observatory, which, free from the obscuring effects of the atmosphere, will provide images and spectroscopic studies on the Universe in the 1-100 thousand electron volts energy window. Freedom from the atmosphere, combined with cryogenically-cooled optical elements will provide the necessary conditions for IR observations of sufficient sensitivity for the galactic evolution problem.

The Space Telescope

In 1986, NASA will launch the Space Telescope (ST)—a 94in (2·4m) diameter telescope equipped with a photometer, high and low resolution spectrographs, a wide-field camera and a long focal length camera (see pages 24-25 for illustration and further details).

The advantages of ST's pinpoint images are twofold: first, we can resolve objects of fixed angular size in systems ten times farther away than we can at present; second, by concentrating the light from point sources into a much smaller blue circle, objects 100 times fainter can be observed against the "sky" background. Another important advantage of ST will be its ability to image the sky at ultraviolet wavelengths. The implications of these advances in imaging quality and wavelengths for the study of galactic evolution are enormous.

Perhaps the most dramatic gains will be in our ability to define the distances to galaxies with far greater precision and to identify galaxy types at distances ten times as great as we can now.

The ability to image galaxies in the ultraviolet will also be of major importance.

Below: *The Andromeda galaxy (M31) as seen by the 200in optical telescope at the Palomar Observatory. Like the Milky Way, M31 is a spiral galaxy orbited by two companion galaxies seen here as bright spots above and below Andromeda.*

5 Some astronomers believe that the tendency to find S0 galaxies in clumps results from relatively recent "stripping" of gas. In one such model the discs of star-forming galaxies are "fed" fresh gas from "reservoirs" of gas still found in roughly spherical halos surrounding the galaxies. When galaxies are assembled through gravitational interaction into denser groups, the probability of a collision between these halos increases dramatically. In such collisions, the gas in the two systems will be left behind as the stellar subcomponents of the systems move past one another. At first the gas will be heated to temperatures of tens to hundreds of millions of degrees as the kinetic energy of relative galaxy motion (100-1,000km/s^{-1}) is converted to heat. The heated gas will radiate and eventually cool unless it is kept hot by collisions with the other stripped gas. However, it can no longer participate in star-forming events in either of the original colliding systems.

High Energy Astronomy Observatory 2 (Einstein)
1 Solar panels.
2 Spacecraft equipment module.
3 High-resolution imaging detectors.
4 Focal-plane crystal spectrometer.
5 Solid-state spectrometer.
6 Imaging proportional counters.
7 Central electronics.
8 Broad band filter and objective grating spectrometer.
9 X-ray telescope mirror.
10 Monitor proportional counters.
11 Sunshade.
12 Star trackers.
13 Thermal precollimator.
14 Forward antenna.

Second in a series of three High Energy Astronomy Observatory satellites, HEAO 2 was launched in November 1978 into a 333 miles (537km) circular orbit inclined 23·5° to the equator. Its task was to further the study of X-ray astronomy, in particular to observe X-rays emitted by stars, pulsars, quasars, black holes and galaxies. The heart of the satellite was a 23·2in (58cm) grazing incidence X-ray telescope, and there were five major instruments. The high resolution imager was an X-ray camera which recorded images to a resolution of 1-2 arc seconds. The study of X-ray spectra was carried out by the focal plane crystal spectrometer, which could distinguish emission lines

and hence analyze a star's chemical composition. The imaging proportion counter produced images of 1 arc minute (i.e. over a wider field of view than that achieved by the high resolution imager, though with reduced resolution), and the solid state spectrometer was equipped with silicon-germanium crystals which, when struck by photons, enabled their wavelength and energy to

be measured. The fifth item was a non-analytical monitor proportional counter (MPC): functioning independently of the telescope, it studied X-ray radiation over a wider

energy range and examined time variations within the sources detected. Attitude control was effected by rate gyroscopes and reaction

jets. Data were transmitted via STDN to NASA at 128,000 bits per second for

relay to the Goddard Space Flight Center. Financed by NASA, the craft was built by TRW Inc. Launch weight was 7,000lb (3,175kg).

Telescope Mirrors
The mirrors of the Einstein Observatory's X-ray telescope were not flat dishes, but four concentric glass tubes whose inside surfaces were polished to high precision. A slight curve in each of the

cylinders ensured that the X-rays struck the mirrors at a grazing angle, and were concentrated at a common focus. The mirrors were made of special glass of fused quartz coated with a layer of nickel.

Technical Data
Length: 22ft (6·7m).
Diameter: 7·7ft (2·35m).
Weight of instruments: 3,000lb ((1,360kg).
Length of telescope assembly: 15ft (4.6m).
Focal length of telescope: 11·25ft (3·43m).

First, hot blue stars will stand out even more prominently against the background of old, red stars. With the advantage provided by greater contrast, we will be able to discern evidence of star-formation even at very low levels of activity. Second, observing the ultraviolet colours of nearby galaxies is essential to detecting evolutionary effects.

Below: *This wide-field composite X-ray view of the Andromeda galaxy obtained by HEAO 2 reveals over a dozen bright X-ray emitting regions. Unlike the centre of our Galaxy, the nucleus of Andromeda is related to a very strong X-ray source.*

Of greatest immediate value will be the ability to compare pictures of galaxies at Z (redshift) = 0·5 (lookback times of ⁓ 5 billion years) with those of nearby galaxies. From the ground, photographs of clusters this distant are sufficient only to distinguish galaxies from stellar images; no detail is seen within the galaxy image.

Hence, we cannot directly compare the properties of distant Sc's and nearby Sc's, for example, to check our predictions regarding present and past star-forming activity. By imaging distant isolated and cluster galaxies, we can judge, again empirically, the effects of environment on galaxy evolution.

AXAF

One of the unexpected discoveries of late 20th century astrophysics was the richness of the X-ray sky, first glimpsed from early rocket and satellite flights but only fully grasped from the work of the Einstein satellite (HEAO 2). After the initial great success of X-ray explorations, astronomers proposed a permanent observatory in space. AXAF (Advanced X-ray Astrophysics Facility) is that observatory. It will be blessed with an X-ray telescope of unprecedented power to image and carry out spectroscopic studies. .Virtually every class of object we can observe at optical wavelengths—from white dwarf stars to clusters of galaxies—will be accessible to observation at X-ray wavelengths.

Charting the temperature, gas distribution and chemical composition of hot intracluster gas as a function of lookback time (by observing clusters at differing redshifts) is a primary initial goal of the AXAF observatory. Combined with the images of distant clusters obtained with ST, we can hope better to understand the relationship between the environment revealed to us from X-ray observations and galaxy evolution, perhaps best revealed by ST.

X-ray observations of galaxies with the Einstein High Energy Astronomy Observatory show that many contain bright X-ray sources within their nuclei. Often these are associated with strong optical and radio nuclear emission as well. The Einstein survey suggested that X-ray maps would be of enormous value in selecting the most distant galaxies containing bright or "active" nuclei. The source of

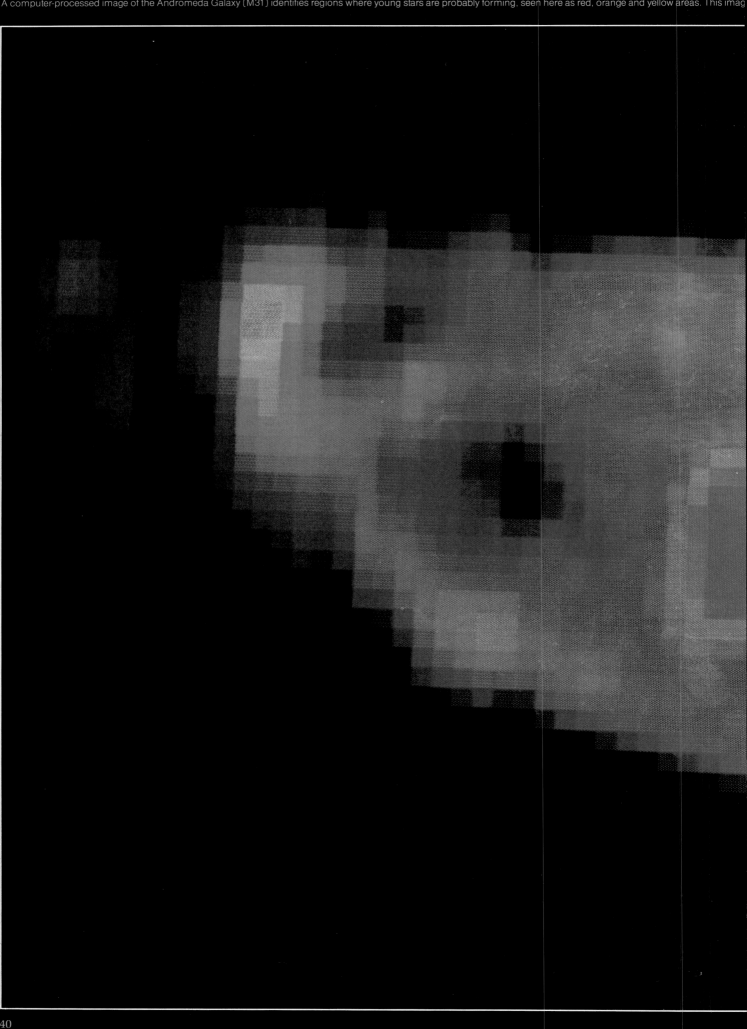

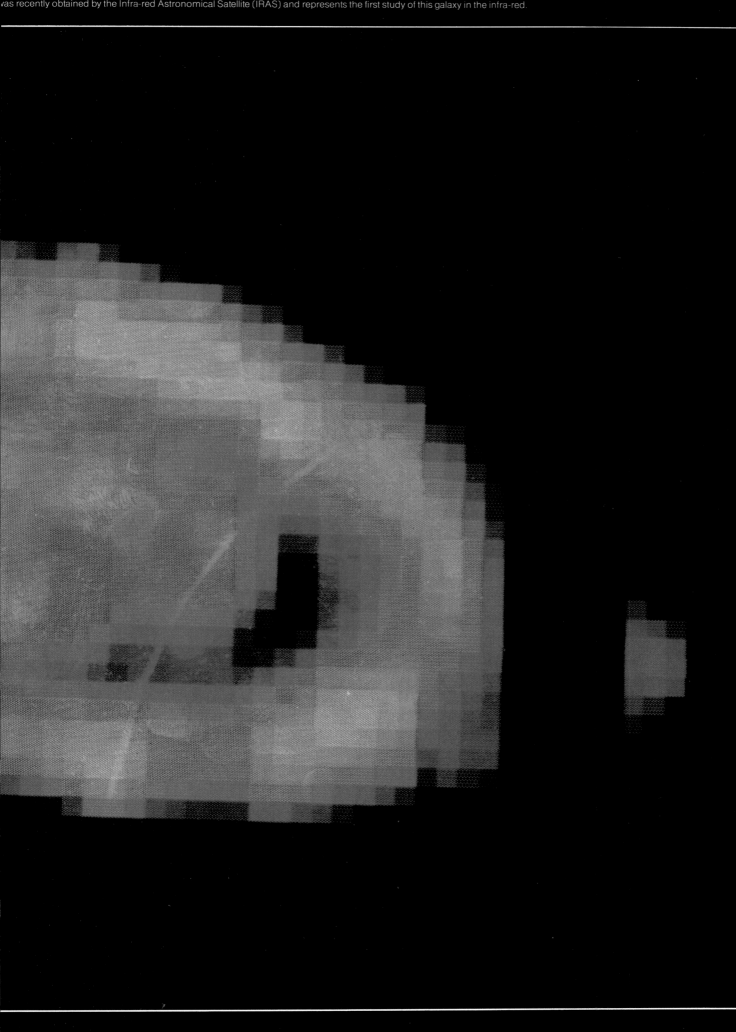

Above: *Twenty-seven identical antennas operating together near Socorro, N.M., form the Very Large Array (VLA). The Y-shaped array has the resolving power of a single receiver 21 miles (34km) in diameter.*

optical, radio and X-ray nuclear emission and their role in galaxy evolution is not known. Many suspect that the enormous amounts of energy produced in galactic cores, within volumes less than a light year on a side, can only be produced by accretion of gas onto a supermassive $(10^7-10^9 M_\odot)$ black hole. By combining radio, X-ray and optical observations we can observe in detail regions of vastly differing temperatures and densities — to map the gas entering and leaving the black hole — and possibly to unlock the secrets of the energy engines at galactic centres.

The higher spatial resolutions afforded by Space Telescope, AXAF and ground-based radio interferometers such as the Very Large Array (VLA) will be critical in modelling these sources. The frequency of nuclear activity apparently increases with increasing lookback time, at least if our interpretation of distribution of quasar counts (quasars contain the most energetic of active nuclei) with redshift are correct.

IR Observations from Space

Because the most distant, and earliest galaxies are also receding from us at high velocities, study of the early stages and possibly the formation of galaxies is ultimately the province of infra-red astronomy.

Already, ground-based IR observations have proved to be an invaluable tool for studying galaxies. The luminosity even of some nearby galaxies at wavelengths longer than 1 micron exceeds the luminosity at optical frequencies. The source or sources of this IR luminosity have not been identified with certainty, although in many cases, huge bursts of star-forming activity, shrouded from optical view by dust clouds, may account for this IR brightness.

By going to space to make IR observations, two advantages accrue. First and most obvious, the absorption and emission of the Earth's atmosphere can be avoided. Second, the telescope itself can be shielded and

cooled to temperatures ($\sim 10°K$) near that of liquid helium. By cooling a telescope and placing it in space, the IR background can be reduced by a million fold. This enormous gain, compared to ground-based facilities has made it attractive to design a new breed of "cryogenic" telescope. In January 1983, the US, UK and Holland launched the first of these cooled telescopes — IRAS or Infra-red Astronomical Satellite — which will provide a complete survey of the sky in the wavelength range from 8 microns to 120 microns. Toward the end of the decade, astronomers hope to launch a Shuttle-based Infra-red Telescope (SIRTF) with good pointing rather than primarily survey capability. IRAS and SIRTF offer the possibility of detecting and then studying

1 Protogalaxies: highly redshifted galaxies visible only in the infra-red, which are undergoing their first bursts of star-formation.

2 Galaxies whose emission is dominated by IR emission; our understanding of star-forming activity in disc galaxies will be woefully incomplete without an IR census of optically obscured star-forming regions.

3 Halos of galaxies whose light might be dominated by very low luminosity, cool dwarfs. Such studies would allow us to learn whether such objects account in part or in total for the "missing mass" in galaxies.

To study processes critical to understanding the star-forming history of galaxies, we need an instrument capable of producing images of galaxies with one arc second resolution at a wavelength of 100 microns and big enough to permit measurements of velocities with a discrimination of 0·12 miles/sec (0·2km/sec). This requires a dish 65·6ft (20m) in diameter — over eight times the size of the ST mirror and four times the size of the Palomar telescope. To operate in the wavelength range from 50 microns to 1mm, such a telescope must be placed in space since the Earth's atmosphere is nearly opaque at such wavelengths.

The challenge of designing and building such a unique telescope, which may have to be assembled in orbit, has begun to attract the attention of the world's astronomers. Building the LDR or Large Deployable Reflector is one of the major projects under discussion for funding by NASA in the late 1980s and launch in the mid 1990s. Its power to study galaxy formation and evolution will be immense.

The LDR has the capability to study the most striking example of cosmic expansion — the highly redshifted relic radiation from

Below: *Artist's impression of the Shuttle Infra-red Telescope Facility being deployed in space from the Shuttle cargo bay. Various instruments will be mounted on the SIRTF on missions of up to 14 days.*

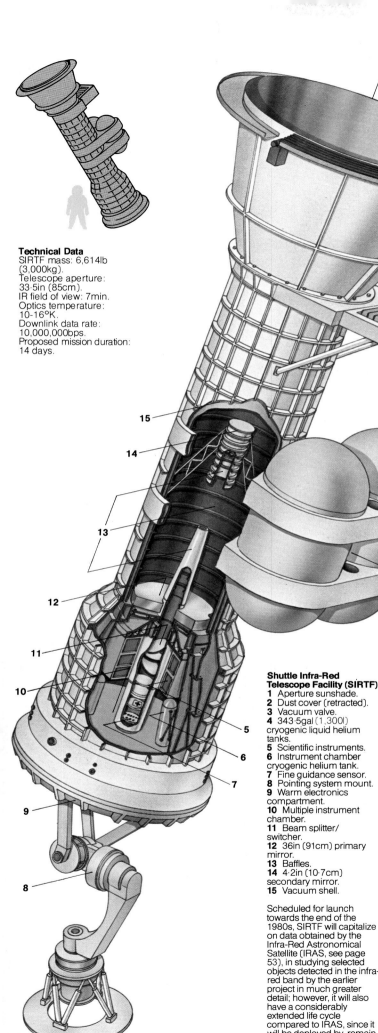

Technical Data
SIRTF mass: 6,614lb
(3,000kg).
Telescope aperture:
33·5in (85cm).
IR field of view: 7min.
Optics temperature:
10-16°K.
Downlink data rate:
10,000,000bps.
Proposed mission duration:
14 days.

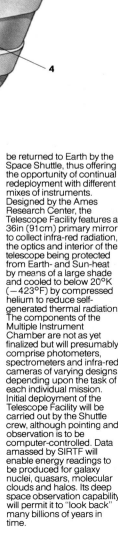

**Shuttle Infra-Red
Telescope Facility (SIRTF)**
1 Aperture sunshade.
2 Dust cover (retracted).
3 Vacuum valve.
4 343·5gal (1,300l)
cryogenic liquid helium
tanks.
5 Scientific instruments.
6 Instrument chamber
cryogenic helium tank.
7 Fine guidance sensor.
8 Pointing system mount.
9 Warm electronics
compartment.
10 Multiple instrument
chamber.
11 Beam splitter/
switcher.
12 36in (91cm) primary
mirror.
13 Baffles.
14 4·2in (10·7cm)
secondary mirror.
15 Vacuum shell.

Scheduled for launch
towards the end of the
1980s, SIRTF will capitalize
on data obtained by the
Infra-Red Astronomical
Satellite (IRAS, see page
53), in studying selected
objects detected in the infra-
red band by the earlier
project in much greater
detail; however, it will also
have a considerably
extended life cycle
compared to IRAS, since it
will be deployed by, remain
in physical contact with, and

be returned to Earth by the
Space Shuttle, thus offering
the opportunity of continual
redeployment with different
mixes of instruments.
Designed by the Ames
Research Center, the
Telescope Facility features a
36in (91cm) primary mirror
to collect infra-red radiation,
the optics and interior of the
telescope being protected
from Earth- and Sun-heat
by means of a large shade
and cooled to below 20°K
(−423°F) by compressed
helium to reduce self-
generated thermal radiation.
The components of the
Multiple Instrument
Chamber are not as yet
finalized but will presumably
comprise photometers,
spectrometers and infra-red
cameras of varying designs,
depending upon the task of
each individual mission.
Initial deployment of the
Telescope Facility will be
carried out by the Shuttle
crew, although pointing and
observation is to be
computer-controlled. Data
amassed by SIRTF will
enable energy readings to
be produced for galaxy
nuclei, quasars, molecular
clouds and halos. Its deep
space observation capability
will permit it to "look back"
many billions of years in
time.

the primordial fireball—the cauldron which gave birth to the Universe. By studying this radiation, we can probe the Universe at a time when it was but 1/1,000th its current size and 1/10,000th of its current age (estimated to be at least 10 billion years). The radiation from the "Big Bang" bathes the Universe nearly uniformly in radiation with a characteristic temperature of 3°K (see also page 28). A radiating body at 3°K has its peak emission at a wavelength of 1mm. Hence, studies of the cosmic background must be made in the far IR/sub-mm wavelength band.

The homogeneity of the cosmic background on large-scales has been the object of intensive study from the ground. In 1988 NASA will launch COBE, the Cosmic Background Explorer, which will perform extraordinarily accurate measurements of the large-scale homogeneity of the background. COBE will provide an essential check on our assumption regarding the large scale uniformity of the Universe as well as a measure of the Earth's motion relative to the background.

LDR *can* make observations with high angular resolution (∼10″ at 1mm) and this is critical. For encoded in small-scale variations of the background may be information regarding the sizes of the first condensations of matter to achieve coherent form in the Universe.

Through LDR's ability to image galaxies in the infra-red with resolutions of 1″, we will be able to take a complete census of star-forming activity in galaxies. We can observe clusters of stars condensing within optically opaque complexes of gas and dust and trace the star-forming process from its inception to the appearance of optically visible stars.

The launch of the ST, AXAF and LDR represent three stages in NASA's long-term goal to place in space orbiting observatories sensitive over the full range of the electro-magnetic spectrum. The contribution of these observatories will be instrumental not only to unravelling the galactic evolution problems recounted above, but to a wide range of complex and important astrophysical problems. If we can commit the resources to complete this triad of observatories, mankind will, by the end of this century have placed in space instruments of a potential significance virtually unparalleled in the history of science.

RECOMMENDED READING

Abell, G., *Exploration of the Universe*, Holt, Rinehart & Winston, 3rd ed. New York, 1975.

Baker, R.H., *Astronomy*, Van Nostrand, Princeton, 1964.

Hawkins, G. D., *Splendor in the Sky*, Harper & Row, New York, 1961.

Hoyle, Fred, *Astronomy*, Doubleday, New York, 1962.

Hynek, J. A. and Anderson, N. D., *Challenge of the Universe*, McGraw Hill, New York, 1962.

Lovell, Sir Bernard, *Our Present Knowledge of the Universe*, University of Manchester Press, Manchester, 1967.

Mihalas, D., *Galactic Astronomy*, Freeman, San Francisco, 1968.

Page, T. and Page, L. W., *Beyond the Milky Way*, Macmillan, New York, 1969.

Vaucoulers, Gerard de, *Discovery of the Universe*, Macmillan, New York, 1957.

Stellar Evolution

The evolution of stars through stages of energy production and dissipation has been inferred from their mass, luminosity, chemical composition and location in the galaxy, There are blue giant stars, red giants, white dwarfs and invisible objects known as black holes.

Born in interstellar clouds, stars evolve by thermonuclear conversion of their primordial hydrogen to helium; of helium to carbon and oxygen and of these substances to heavier elements. The oldest stars, including the red giants, tend to be concentrated in the central bulge of our Galaxy. Younger stars, such as our Sun, reside far from the centre, in the spiral arms.

If the processes of thermonuclear conversion in stars have been correctly identified, the fate of stars like our Sun on the main sequence of energy production is known. They become red giants.

What is a Star?

A star is a luminous object in space, composed of gas and held together by its own gravity. The study of how stars are born, live, and die makes use of astronomical observations, physical theories, and elaborate computer calculations. These determine the nature of events that have transpired over the estimated 15 thousand million year lifetime of our Milky Way Galaxy.[1]

At one time, the stars were thought to be eternal and unchanging. Contrary views sometimes were regarded as heresy. However, two simple facts, ascertained long before telescopes and computers were invented, show that stars must change in dramatic ways: the occurrence of Guest Stars, and the circumstance that our star, the Sun, is shining.

Guest Stars, as the ancient Chinese called them, were bright stars seen with the naked eye in places in the sky where no such stars had been seen before. Today we call them novae and supernovae and recognize them as powerful explosions in stars so far away that they were invisible prior to the brilliant outbursts. The most famous Guest Star was seen in AD 1054 and recorded in Oriental and Middle Eastern chronicles. In the place

---

1   The reader should not confuse the estimated age of the Galaxy with that of the Universe. Elsewhere in this section, the estimated age of the Universe is given as 10 to 20 thousand million years. Obviously the Galaxy cannot be older than the Universe, yet certain measurements allow an age as low as 10 thousand million years. The author believes that 15 thousand million years is reasonable for the Galaxy. (Ed.)

"Furthest, fairest things, stars, free of our humbug, each his own, the longer known the more alone, wrapt in emphatic fire roaring out to a black flue."

Basil Bunting,*Briggflatts*

where that Guest Star briefly shone, astronomers today observe the Crab Nebula, the violently expanding remains of the cosmic explosion.

Because a star such as the Sun is shining, we can deduce that one day the star will die. To generate its heat and light, the Sun must have a source of energy. Unless that souce is replenished, it will eventually be exhausted and the Sun will fade away. Physicists realized this in the 19th Century as they puzzled over the source of solar energy. Now we know that the Sun and most other observed stars shine due to nuclear energy generation in their interiors. When their

Left: *An aerial view of the Kitt Peak National Observatory in Arizona. The large dome in the foreground houses the Mayall 4-metre telescope, the third largest in the world.*

nuclear fuel is spent, stars like the Sun begin to fade and die.

However, more massive stars instead of fading, die explosively, like the progenitor of the Crab Nebula. Along the way, an evolving star passes through several distinct stages. The study of stellar evolution is pursued to identify these stages among known stars. It seeks to determine the sequence in which the stages occur, and to relate the findings to the larger picture of the origin and fate of our Galaxy and to the vital questions of how our Sun and its planets were formed and what eventually will become of them.

Stars much less massive than the Sun, called red dwarfs, glow so weakly and burn so slowly that trillions of years must pass before their fuel stores are gone. As a result, no red dwarf has evolved beyond the stable, slowly-burning state since the Universe began. Smaller than the red dwarfs, the very

Left: *The Eta Carinae Nebula, the brightest portion of the Milky Way as seen by the unaided eye. The region contains an unusually high number of hot, young stars, many of which were formed within the nebula. The brightest of these, Eta Carinae, is the most luminous star known.*

Below: *The Crab Nebula, the result of a supernova observed by astronomers in AD 1054. At the centre of the nebula is a rapidly-rotating neutron star, first detected by radio astronomers as a pulsar. This relic of the original massive star was formed when the outer layers were blown away.*

low mass "brown dwarfs", predicted by theory, are incapable of igniting and sustaining nuclear reactions. The brown dwarfs are so dim that none has been found; searching for them is an important task of the future Space Telescope.

Telescopes and Satellites

The observational evidence for stellar evolution comes from space and ground-based observatories. Conventional ground-based telescopes, such as the 200-inch reflector at Palomar Observatory in southern California, are sensitive to the visible wavelengths of light, and provide basic data on most kinds of stars. Radio telescopes, notably the Very Large Array (VLA) in New Mexico, are used to observe nebulae associated with stars and to measure radio emissions from pulsars, flare stars and other unusual stars.

X-ray observatory satellites, such as Einstein (High Energy Astronomy Observatory 2), are the prime sources of information on two end states of stellar evolution, namely neutron stars and black holes; on coronas (the hot outer atmospheres of stars); and on the accretion discs through which matter is transferred from one star to the other in some binary star systems. Ultraviolet observatory satellites, especially the International Ultraviolet Explorer (IUE), obtain key data on hot stars, including white dwarfs and the central stars of planetary nebulae, and are used to gauge stellar winds. (These evolutionary stages are fully explained later in the chapter.)

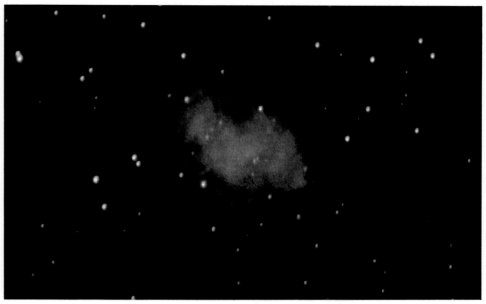

Specialized telescopes, such as the United Kingdom Infra-red Telescope in Hawaii, gather valuable information on infra-red radiation from stars, especially the proto-stars, with their cocoons of interstellar dust that cut off visible light, but allow infra-red rays to pass.

Space infra-red observatories such as IRAS (Infra-red Astronomical Satellite), launched on 25 January 1983 and SIRTF (Shuttle Infra-red Telescope Facility), to be launched in 1989, will carry this work much farther by providing higher sensitivity and the capability to measure light at many infra-red wavelengths that are absorbed in the Earth's atmosphere.

Populations and Properties

The nature of stellar evolution is inferred from observations of the different kinds of stars, their properties, relative numbers, and the places in the Galaxy in which they occur. In the Milky Way, a spiral galaxy resembling a huge flat pinwheel, stars are found in a dense bulge at the centre of the disc and in its spiral arms, which are the disc's most striking feature.

The Sun is located in the disc of the Milky Way about 30,000 light years from the centre or three-fifths of the way to the rim. Stars of various types tend to be found in groups in one part of the Galaxy or another. The youngest stars, newly formed from clouds of interstellar gas and dust (microscopic solid particles of rock and carbon), occur in the spiral arms, often in loose groupings ("associations") and in tighter bunches, the "open star clusters". Older stars, including many red giants, are found throughout the Galaxy but are markedly concentrated in the central bulge and in the closely-packed, spheroidal-shaped globular star clusters. The open clusters and associations are confined to the disc, but the globular clusters, most abundant in the bulge, extend out into a vast spherical region where isolated stars also occur, the galactic halo.

There are systematic differences in the chemical compositions of the stars in the various regions of the Galaxy, suggesting differences in evolutionary history. The young stars of the galactic disc tend to have more "metals" (astronomers' jargon for the elements heavier than helium) than the older stars found in the galactic bulge, the galactic halo, and the globular clusters.[2]

The disc stars are termed *Population I;* the others in the bulge, the halo, and in clusters compose *Population II.* Among disc stars, those actually located in the spiral arms tend to be younger and perhaps more metal-rich. The first stars that formed in our Galaxy, presumably made from pure Big Bang material (exclusively, or almost exclusively hydrogen, helium, and deuterium) are called *Population III.* Their properties are hypothetical, since none has been identified among existing stars.

Most stars are members of binary or multiple star systems; the Sun, as a single

---

2 Metals are produced by nuclear processes in stars and by supernova explosions. Stellar winds and explosions eject these nucleosynthesized metals into the interstellar medium from which new generations of stars form.

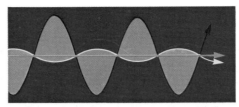

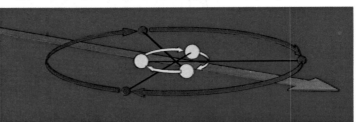

star, is atypical in this respect. It is not known whether the existence of planets is common or rare. The only known planets are those of our own Solar System, although there are tantalizing indications (slight wiggles in a star's motion) that some nearby objects such as Barnard's Star may have planets of their own.

The basic properties of the Sun have been adopted as dimensions for astrophysical discussions. Thus, the masses of stars are described in units of the solar mass ($1 M_\odot$), ranging from about 150 $M_\odot$ to perhaps 1/100th of 1 $M_\odot$. There are unconfirmed reports that R136a, a brilliant object in the Large Magellanic Cloud galaxy, is a star with 3,000 to 5,000 times the Sun's mass. Most stars are less massive than the Sun.

Unseen Companions
The presence of a faint companion star or planet around a nearby star can sometimes be inferred from close study of the motion of the primary star. The primary (yellow) and secondary (red) components of the stellar sytem both orbit about their common centre of mass (orange), in the same way that the Sun and other elements of the Solar System orbit about the centre of mass of the entire system. Hence if only the primary is seen, its motion over a period of years will not be rectilinear but will show "wobbles" due to orbital motion. Astronomer Peter Van de Kamp has interpreted observations of Barnard's star taken from 1937 on to indicate the presence of either a single giant planet, larger than Jupiter, in a highly elliptical orbit or (a better fit to the data) two giant planets in orbits which are more nearly circular.

Giants, Dwarfs and H-R Diagrams

The Hertzsprung-Russell Diagram, named after the Danish astronomer Ejnar Hertzsprung (1873–1967) and the American astronomer Henry Norris Russell (1877–1957), is the principal way in which astronomers organize observational data for comparison with theories of stellar evolution. It displays data on the brightness and temperatures of stars. The brightest stars are at the top of the H-R Diagram, the dimmest at the bottom, the hottest at the left, and the coolest at the right. The most striking feature of the diagram is the presence of a diagonal band, running from upper left to lower right, that is occupied by the largest number of observed stars. Called the *Main Sequence,* this band is identified as the region of the

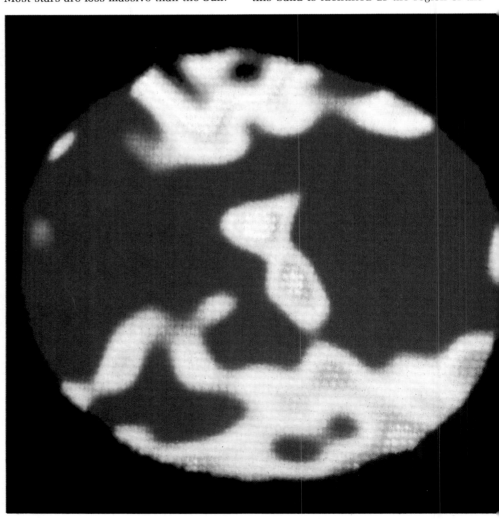

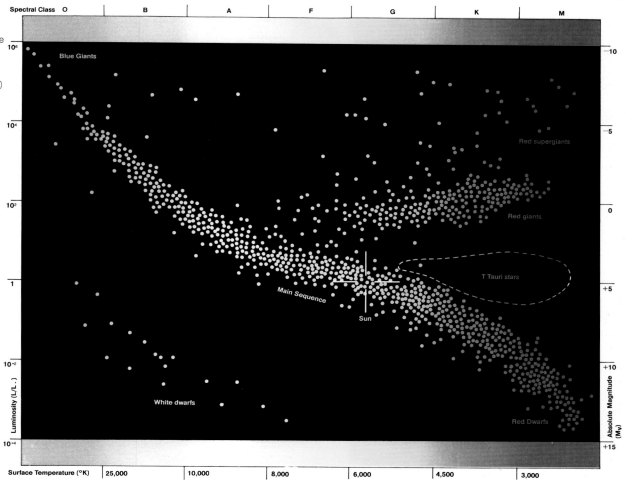

The Hertzsprung-Russell Diagram
The principal means by which astronomers organize data on the luminosity (brightness) and surface temperatures of stars is by the construction of a Hertzsprung-Russell (H-R) diagram. In this figure the hottest, brightest stars are at top left while the coolest, faintest stars are at bottom right. The diagonal band of stars running from upper left to lower right is known as the Main Sequence and comprises those stars which are converting hydrogen to helium in their cores under stable conditions. The point on the Main Sequence at which a given star is found during this evolutionary stage depends on the star's mass, with the blue giants being the most massive and the red dwarfs the least massive of Main Sequence stars. Stars in other stages of their life are found elsewhere in the H-R diagram, for example as a red giant (upper right) or as a white dwarf (lower left). The spectral class of a star (top) depends on the excitation and ionization level of the atoms present in the stellar atmosphere; these in turn depend primarily on the atmospheric temperature. The spectral class of a star is thus closely linked to its surface temperature, as seen here.

stars, such as the Sun, that are converting hydrogen to helium by nuclear reactions in their cores.

Stars found off the Main Sequence on the H-R Diagram shine from some other cause, such as hydrogen burning in regions outside the core, burning of other elements, gravitational contraction or radiation of residual heat into space. Stellar evolution theory provides the explanation in each case.

Some kinds of stars which are observed to be in or beyond the Main Sequence are:
Red dwarfs: small cool stars with masses much less than that of the Sun; they are Main Sequence stars. Their colours range from orange to red. Proxima Centauri, the nearest star beyond the Sun, is a red dwarf.
Red giants: large cool stars, with masses that may be less than that of the Sun, or slightly greater than the solar mass. They are stars that have already passed through the Main Sequence stage; the hydrogen in their cores has all been converted to helium and the stars are now burning hydrogen in a shell just outside the core. Arcturus in constellation Bootes is a red gaint.
Red supergiants: very large cool stars, with masses several times greater than that of the Sun. Nuclear reactions form elements heavier than carbon within these stars, which are evolved well beyond the Main Sequence stage and are on the road to exploding as type II supernovae. Betelgeuse,

Left: Hot and cool areas or "starspots" are shown as different colours in this 1974 photograph of the surface of Betelgeuse or α Orionis. This is a cool, supergiant star 1,200 times larger than the Sun.

the bright red star in constellation Orion, is a red supergiant.
Blue giants and blue supergiants: large, hot blue-white stars, with masses many times greater than that of the Sun. The term "blue giant" is used both for Main Sequence stars, still burning hydrogen in their cores, and for more evolved stars that, like the blue supergiants, have left the Main Sequence. The supergiants are brighter than the giants. Rigel, the brightest blue-white star in constellation Orion, is a blue supergiant, while Alkaid, the star at the end of the handle of the Big Dipper, is a blue giant.
White dwarfs: small, dense stars with up to 1·4 times the mass of the Sun. They are in the last stage of their evolution; no nuclear reactions are underway to release energy and instead the stars are just slowly cooling; as they cool, their surfaces grow dim and eventually they become unobservable. "The Pup", the dim companion of Sirius, the Dog Star, is a white dwarf.

Red dwarfs, with low masses, make up the bottom end of the Main Sequence, while massive blue stars comprise the upper end.

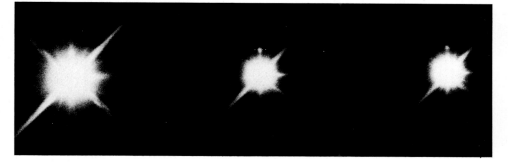

Above: Three exposures of Sirius taken with the 3-metre reflector of the Lick Observatory, California. Its companion star, a white dwarf known as Sirius B, can be seen just above the primary star. The "spikes" on the image of Sirius A are an artifact of the telescope system.

Thus, the location of a star on the Main Sequence tells theorists its mass as well as its energy generation process. Red giants and red supergiants are above the Main Sequence on the right side of the H-R Diagram and blue supergiants are above at the left, while white dwarfs are to the left and below. For these non-Main Sequence stars, position on the H-R Diagram is not necessarily an indicator of mass.

Some regions of the H-R Diagram are bare, with few if any observed stars. This does not mean that no stars occur there with observable brightness and temperature. Instead, stars may exist with these values of observed brightness and surface temperature for only brief periods, so that observers have little chance to glimpse them.

Normal stars, which shine from nuclear energy generation in their interiors, range in temperature from less than 2000°K among the red dwarfs, giants and supergiants to about 50,000°K among the blue giants. White dwarfs and the compact central stars of planetary nebulae (so called because they resemble faint planets as seen in small telescopes) are generally hotter, with temperatures of up to 100,000°K or slightly more. All these terms refer to stars in varying stages of evolution (see page 47). Hottest known (at an estimated 200,000°K) is a star in the planetary nebula LT 5; its temperature was measured in 1982 by the International Ultraviolet Explorer satellite.

White dwarfs are cooling steadily. Although observed examples are hot, there may be many of them which have already reached temperatures lower than that of the Sun (6000°K) and are unobservable by present methods.

Neutron stars begin with temperatures measured in the millions of degrees and then cool off, but are so small that even when they are hot, they glow almost imperceptibly as seen from the distance of Earth. They are detected thanks to pulsar activity (directional beaming of radiation from high-energy particles) in their surrounding magnetic fields, or due to energy released by matter streaming down from a companion.

Neutron stars may be only a few tens of miles in diameter, and white dwarfs may be as small as the Earth. However, red giants are far larger than the Sun, and a red supergiant, if placed at the Sun's position, would actually engulf the Earth orbiting at a distance of 92,960,000 miles (149,600,000 km). Stellar evolution theory provides a physical explanation for the typical diameter of each kind of star.

Stars and Nebulae

Many stars are associated with interstellar matter that takes the form of bright or dark nebulae. Each type of cloud or nebula is connected with a distinct stage in the evolution of stars. Dark nebulae occur in the form of Bok globules (round, thick and compact clouds of dust, named after the astronomer Bart J. Bok), as larger dark clouds such as the Horsehead Nebula, and as so-called giant molecular clouds, which are the largest objects in the Galaxy.

Bok globules contain no stars, but may be sites of future star formation. Bright stars, sometimes found near dark clouds, may illuminate them, so that the clouds shine by reflection. The giant molecular clouds, such as OMC-1 (Orion Molecular Cloud No. 1) are the locations where stars-in-the-making, the *protostars*, are found. OMC-1, located behind the Orion Nebula as seen from Earth, is a good example. Infra-red telescopes reveal protostars in OMC-1.

H II Regions and Planetary Nebulae

The most conspicuous bright nebulae are the *H II regions* ("H II" stands for ionized hydrogen) such as the Orion Nebula. They are the sites of hot, bright young stars, which heat and ionize the nebulae, causing them to glow. Without the energizing ultraviolet radiation of the stars, H II regions would be just dark clouds of dust and neutral gas.

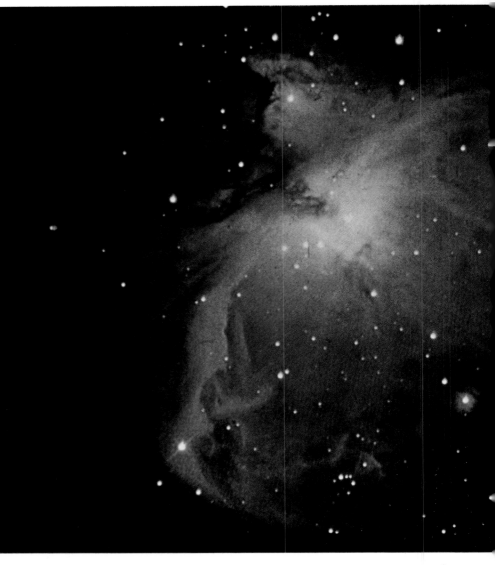

Above: *High energy photons from the hot young stars in the Orion nebula strip electrons from the (mainly hydrogen) gas: when the electrons and protons recombine, lower energy photons are emitted, giving rise to its characteristic red colour.*

Right: *Strong stellar winds from associations of hot, young stars can sweep up the surrounding gas and dust to form a stellar bubble. An example of such a bubble is the Rosette Nebula in the constellation Monoceros.*

Below: *The Ring Nebula in Lyra, a classic example of a planetary nebula. Late in its lifetime a star may blow off its outer layers to form such an expanding shell of material.*

Below right: *The Veil Nebula, an ancient supernova remnant in Cygnus. The shock wave from the original explosion compresses and sweeps up the surrounding gas: collisions cause it to heat up and radiate.*

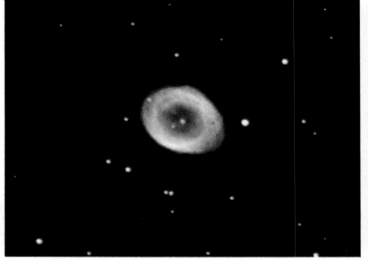

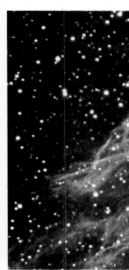

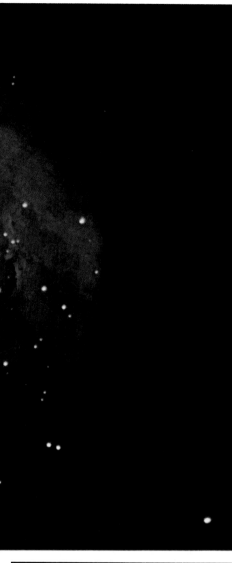

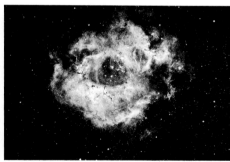

Planetary nebulae, which have nothing to do with planets, are the cast-off shells of what once were red giant stars. At the centre of each, the small, hot star is all that remains of the once huge and cool giant. The most famous planetary is M57, the Ring Nebula.

Thus, H II regions are associated with the early stages of stellar life, while planetary nebulae correspond to an advanced stage. A typical H II region is many times more massive than the Sun and is the home of many stars; a planetary nebula, usually less massive than the Sun, is the product of a single star.

Stellar bubbles are another class of nebulae, formed around stars and star clusters by the action of outward-blowing stellar winds. The Rosette Nebula, which surrounds a cluster in Monoceros, is a prominent example.

Supernova remnants are still another type of nebula, one intimately connected with the death of stars. Some, such as the Crab Nebula, are wholly composed of debris from an exploded star, while other, older supernova remnants consist mostly of interstellar matter swept up by the blast wave from the stellar explosion. In the latter case, the swept-up gas may have many times the mass of the exploded star, so that it is impossible to distinguish the explosion debris. The Cygnus Loop is an example of an older supernova remnant that consists primarily of swept-up matter.

The Theory of Stellar Evolution

The diameter and internal structure of an isolated star (i.e., one free from the disturbing effects of a companion star), the processes by which it generates energy and manufactures chemical elements, and the way in which it evolves with time are all determined by the initial mass and chemical composition of the star. This remarkable circumstance underlies the modern theory of stellar evolution and enables astrophysicists to calculate the properties and time histories of a wide variety of stars. In close binary stars, tidal forces and the transfer of matter from one star to the other can affect the evolution of either member of the binary system.

Within a star, energy is produced by nuclear fusion or by gravitational contraction (which compresses the stellar gas, making it hotter). Nuclear reactions affect the chemical composition in the region of the star where they occur, changing hydrogen to helium ("hydrogen burning") and transforming helium to carbon and oxygen ("helium burning") or building even heavier elements, depending on the mass and evolutionary state of the star.

Sometimes a large region within a star seethes with turbulent motions as huge blobs of hot gas rise and cooler gas falls. This process, convection, may bring the newly-made elements to the surface of the star, where they can be detected by astronomical spectroscopy. The bright red stars called carbon stars (such as R Coronae Borealis) are good examples: the relatively abundant carbon observed in their surface layers was mostly made deep within the stars themselves and later convected upward to the surface.

Energy travels outward within a star by means of radiation (in the form of X-rays, gamma rays and other kinds of light) and through convective motions in the stellar gas. In the core of the Sun, for example, energy is generated by the fusion of hydrogen to helium. The energy then travels outward from the core as X-rays and other forms of light through a radiative zone, then is transported partly by bulk motions of the gas in a convection zone (some energy does travel as light even in this zone).

Atop the convection zone, the visible surface region, or photosphere, is spotted with bright granules, rising blobs of hot gas that hint at the intense convection which takes place just below. From the photosphere, energy travels to the Earth as light.

In the newborn protostars, energy comes from gravitational contraction; even their centres are too cool for nuclear reactions to ignite. Red dwarf stars, it is believed, are wholly convective, boiling from centre to surface. Thus each kind of star, each stage in a star's life, has a characteristic internal structure.

Astronomers are limited, for the most part, to studying the exterior properties of stars, although the theory of stellar evolution deals mostly with stellar interiors. The observable properties of a star include the temperature, luminosity, and chemical composition of the surface layer, and the mass loss rate. The luminosity is the rate at which energy is released from the surface of the star, while the mass loss rate measures the amount of matter that flows into space with the stellar wind.

By comparing the theory of stellar evolution with the results of observation, astrophysicists can estimate the ages and original conditions of known kinds of stars and star clusters, and anticipate future trends.

Onset of Convection in Outer Stellar Layers
The main reason for the existence of a convection zone in the outer regions of some stars is an outward increase in the stellar opacity i.e. the resistance of the stellar material to transport of energy by radiation. We can see how this occurs by comparison with a water-wheel analogy shown below. If the paddles have large holes in them (low opacity) the water (heat energy) flows freely without disturbing the wheel. As the holes are made smaller (increasing opacity) the force of the water rotates the wheel and it again flows freely downstream. The transport of water by the wheel is then analogous to the transport of energy through the star by convection. Similarly, as in the convection process there is no net transfer of stellar material: only the energy is transported outwards.

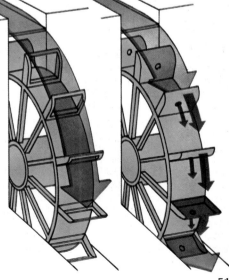

Hydrostatic Equilibrium

What determines the size of a star? A star such as the Sun has a finite measurable diameter, although it is composed of gas that, one might suppose, can expand indefinitely into space. The solution to this seeming paradox is that a balance of forces called hydrostatic equilibrium exists in the Sun. Gravity attracts the solar gases toward the Sun's centre, while a force due to pressure ("the pressure force") pushes them outward. The pressure force in a star is comparable to the force exerted by the gas in a balloon against the balloon's inside surface.

In a star, the outward-directed pressure force has two sources, gas pressure (as in a balloon) and radiation pressure, the pressure due to the photons of light streaming outward in a star. Radiation pressure repels stellar gases just as the pressure of sunlight acts to push the dust in a comet's tail in a direction away from the Sun.

The fact that most stars are neither noticeably shrinking nor expanding means that the stars (or at least their outer, observable layers) are in hydrostatic equilibrium — the forces are in balance. If the pull of gravity on a star's surface layer exceeded the repulsion by pressure, the star would be forced to contract. On the other hand, if the pressure force were stronger than the pull of gravity, the pressure would force the star to expand. The lack of observed shrinking and expanding among most stars proves that they, or at least their outer layers, are so close to being in hydrostatic equilibrium that any slight force imbalance, should one exist, will require a very long period of time to produce visible consequences.

Thermal Equilibrium

If the rate at which energy is produced within a star is balanced by the release of energy at an equal rate from the stellar surface, the star is in thermal equilibrium. Otherwise, the star would soon change. For example, if nuclear fusion in the Sun suddenly produced energy at a rate ten times greater than normal the excess energy would rapidly cause the Sun to expand. The fact that the Sun and most stars clearly are not expanding rapidly means that they satisfy the conditions of both thermal equilibrium and hydrostatic equilibrium.

Within a star, the energy flowing into any given layer must be balanced by energy flowing out from the layer at an equal rate. Otherwise the layer would heat and expand, or cool and contract, until a balance were achieved or disruption occurred. Thus, thermal equilibrium is a condition that applies both to a stable star as a whole and to each layer within the star.

Within the star, the central core and each successive layer around it, as well as the surface, must be in hydrostatic equilibrium, or else that region will contract or expand. When a layer contracts, its constituent gas is compressed and therefore gets hotter; when a layer expands, the gas cools.

The rate at which nuclear energy is generated increases steeply with the temperature. Thus, if the region where fusion is taking place contracts and rises in temperature it will generate more energy.

The increased gas and radiation pressures produced in this way will act to counteract the contraction and produce a new state of hydrostatic equilibrium. These basic principles of stellar structure, namely hydrostatic equilibrium, thermal equilibrium, and the temperature sensitivity of nuclear reaction rates enable astrophysicists to calculate the physical nature and evolutionary trends of stars.

Star Birth: the Cosmic Trigger

A star is literally born in the dark, then brings forth light. In our Galaxy at the present time, star formation occurs in the cold, dark, giant molecular clouds of the spiral arms. Key stages in star formation are the collapse of a small cloud or cloud fragment, followed by the development of a protostar with a core and surrounding thick envelope, then envelope dissolution and nuclear ignition. For the more massive stars, ignition may precede the loss of the envelope.

Within a giant cloud, a small clump of interstellar gas and dust begins to contract under the force of its own gravitation, triggered by a push from an external agent. Theorists have suggested several possible agents, and observations indicate that each of them may be at work at various places in the Galaxy.

One likely trigger is the shock wave from a supernova explosion, which can squeeze a cloud as the wave passes — as blast waves from nuclear explosions have imploded buildings instead of blowing them apart. A possible case of supernova-induced star formation is found in the OriGem Loop, an old supernova remnant that straddles the Orion-Gemini boundary. Several young stars are found on the loop.

The impact of an expanding ionization front, the boundary between the ionized gas

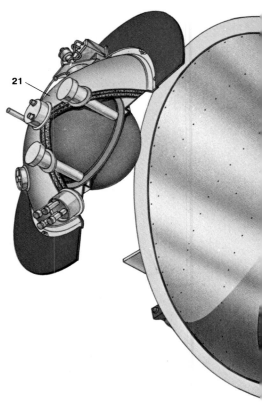

21

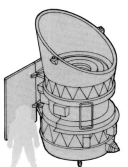

Technical Data
Height: 11·8ft (3·6m).
Diameter: 7·09ft (2·13m).
Width with solar panels deployed: 10·6ft (3·24m).
Launch weight: 2,372lb (1,076kg).
Weight of telescope: 1,785lb (810kg).
Weight of spacecraft bus: 586lb (266kg).
Telescope operating temperature: 2°K (−455°F).
Orbit: 560 miles (900km); near polar.

Stellar Generations
Observations of age gradients across stellar associations prompted the recent idea that massive stars form in successive generations throughout clouds of interstellar material. An external shock wave strikes one edge of a molecular cloud, induces a gravitational instability and causes a layer of gas to collapse and form into stars. Their expanding H II regions (pink) generate new shock waves which penetrate through the cloud, sweeping up matter behind them. The density in this layer rises until it becomes gravitationally unstable, fragments and collapses to form a second generation of stars. These new stars eventually also create H II regions which expand, forming shock waves of their own which travel through the cloud forming the next group of stars. The cycle continues, with star formation progressing upwards in our diagram. The older generations at bottom continue to evolve to maturity. In such a cloud one thus sees an evolutionary sequence of star formation across the cloud, with stars at all various stages of their existence.

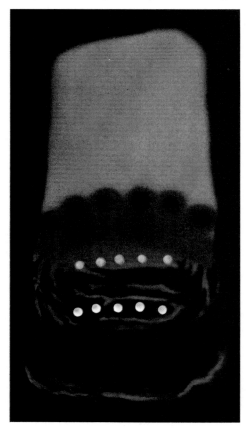

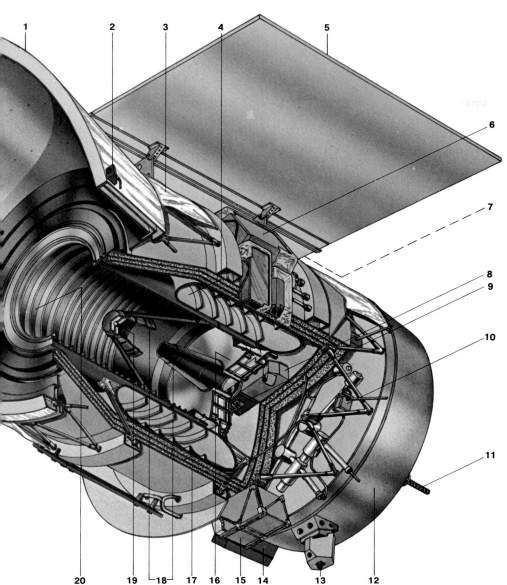

1 Gold-plated sunshade (to reflect solar and Earth IR radiation).
2 Coarse Sun sensor (6).
3 Evacuated main shell.
4 125gal (475l) superfluid helium tank (for telescope cooling).
5 Deployable solar panel.
6 Experiment electronics.
7 Fine Sun sensor (2). (behind solar panels).
8 Dutch Additional Experiment (DAX).
9 Focal plane assembly: 62 rectangular detectors.
10 Cryogenic valves and manifold.
11 S-band antenna.
12 Spacecraft telemetry, attitude control and command module.
13 Horizon sensor (60° field of view).
14 Nickel-cadmium battery.
15 DAX electronics.
16 22·4in (57cm) beryllium primary mirror.
17 Mylar and Dacron net insulation.
18 Baffles.
19 Secondary mirror.
20 Baffle.
21 Helium-cooled telescope aperture cover (ejected after IRAS check-out in orbit).

Infra-Red Astronomical Satellite (IRAS)

Launched on 25 January 1983, IRAS was designed to perform the first all-sky survey in the infra-red portion of the electromagnetic spectrum, and so detect the emission of infra-red radiation from stars that cannot be seen by telescopes limited to observations in the visible light wavelengths. Thus it has proved possible to detect protostars (newly coalescing stars), which means that scientists will be able to study new data concerning the formation of stars, and even of solar systems. IRAS is a joint US-Dutch-British venture: JPL designed and built the telescope, provided the Delta launcher, and processes the data; Fokker and Hollandse Signaalapparaten, under Dutch National Aerospace Laboratory management, designed and produced the spacecraft; and the British Rutherford Appleton Laboratory provides tracking and data acquisition systems. An Additional Experiment, a spectrometer and two photometers for measuring the spectra of bright objects at very high resolution, was designed by the Dutch Groningen University and was also carried. The principal IRAS component is a 1,785lb (810kg) Ritchey-Chrétien design telescope with a 22·4in (57cm) aperture beryllium primary mirror. The equipment has to be maintained at 2°K (−271°C) by means of a superfluid helium-filled shroud in order to keep detected IR radiation above temperature levels experienced by the craft itself: the rate of helium exhaustion, indeed, will determine the lifespan of the spacecraft. Solar cell panels provide 250 watts of power at 28 volts, and there are a total of 62 detectors, operating in four wavelengths of the infra-red band. Attitude control is critical, in order to keep the telescope aperture pointed away from the Sun, the Moon and the Earth. Pointing accuracy of 30 arc seconds has been achieved. Data are computer-controlled, recorded and received by the Rutherford Appleton Laboratory, commands being directed by NASA through the Satellite Tracking and Data Network stations operated by the Goddard Space Flight Center in Maryland.

---

of an H II region and the surrounding neutral interstellar medium, is another triggering agent for cloud collapse. As the Orion Nebula expands, it is thought, new stars are formed at its outskirts, in Cloud OMC-1 that extends beyond the nebula in the direction opposite the Earth. Sequential star formation thus occurs, with the youngest stars near the expanding ionization front and those formed earlier located behind the front, in the direction whence it came. Other agents thought to trigger star formation are galactic density waves and collisions of small interstellar cloud units within a giant molecular cloud. Density waves are travelling gravitational disturbances which cause piling up of interstellar gas and produce the spiral arms of the galaxy.

Radio and infra-red telescope observations indicate that a chain of new stars may have been produced by the collision of two smaller dust clouds within the NGC 1333 molecular cloud. Still another possible trigger: the powerful stellar winds from blue giant stars, which blow so fiercely that they may impel nearby clouds to contract. This

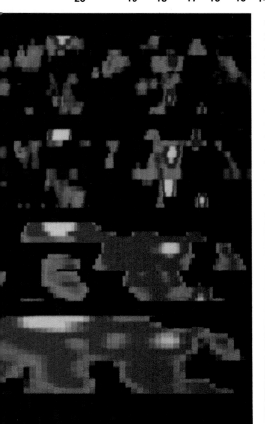

Left: *False-colour IRAS image of the Large Magellanic Cloud revealing many infra-red sources invisible from Earth. Some of these are new stars forming in clouds of dust which re-radiate in the infra-red.*

process seems to be at work in the H II region IC 1805, where an infra-red star sits on the edge of a stellar bubble blown by the winds from a group of hot young stars.

Life Begins for a Protostar

However it begins, contraction draws a clump inexorably together, heating the gas as it gets denser at the centre. Now warmed, the once cold clump emits infra-red rays; it has become a protostar. Collapse often fragments a large clump into several smaller units, each itself contracting; thus multiple births are common and protostars tend to be observed in groups. Because infra-red radiation penetrates the thick shroud of protostar dust that blocks almost all visible light, astronomers use infra-red telescopes to locate forming stars that they cannot see. With the great sensitivity and incredible sharpness of view of the future Space Telescope (see pages 24–25), it may be possible to detect infalling blobs of matter at a protostar.

As the protostar evolves, two structural components develop, the core and the envelope. The core shrinks faster and faster, rapidly going from the density of a thick cloud to the density of a star, and warming as it does so. In effect, it separates from the envelope, which constitutes a cocoon of dust and gas around the glowing core.

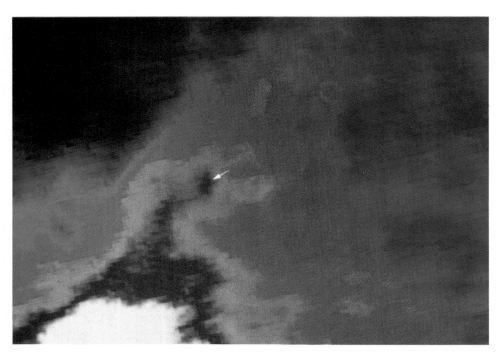

Some of the cold envelope material, perhaps in the form of small condensations, plunges toward the core, like comets smashing into the Sun. A powerful stellar wind begins to flow from the core and push through the envelope. It reveals the newborn star to direct visual observation, although the star is dimmed by dust in the large surrounding cloud of which the protostar's birth clump was just a tiny fragment. The core continues to shrink and its temperature rises.

Approaching Starhood

Eventually, at the centre of the core, the temperature reaches about 10 million degrees K, and nuclear burning of hydrogen commences. Now the protostar is approaching the Main Sequence and true starhood. When the hydrogen burning is sufficiently intense, gas and radiation pressures halt the contraction of the core itself. Hydrostatic equilibrium has been achieved; a star is born.

In low mass stars (those with less than a few solar masses), the protostar envelopes are dissipated while nuclear fusion is still turning on and the stars pass through several pre-Main Sequence stages that have been studied intensively by astronomers. Stars in these formative stages are called young stellar objects (YSOs) and are recognized by their spectra, which include unusual emission lines as well as the ordinary stellar absorption lines. The emission lines signal the presence of chromospheres much brighter than that of the Sun and powerful stellar winds as well. YSOs include Herbig-Haro objects, in which the envelopes may still be partly present, and T Tauri stars.

In a Herbig-Haro object, named after the two astronomers who pioneered its study,[3] the star itself may be invisible, yet its light, perhaps shining through a gap in the envelope away from the Earth, illuminates a small adjacent dust cloud. Accordingly, Herbig-Haro objects have the appearance of nebular clumps, but the spectra of young stars with emission lines.

T Tauri stars,[4] in contrast, have dissipated most of their envelopes, except, in some cases, for a residual, flattened halo of dust. They have powerful stellar winds, and sometimes inflowing material as well. The flattened dust clouds of T Tauri stars may resemble the disc of the protosolar nebula in which the Earth and other planets formed. It is likely that when the young Sun went through this stage, its powerful T Tauri wind swept away the original atmosphere of the Earth. The nature of the T Tauri stage, thus, may be crucial to understanding the development of planetary atmospheres, and (in consequence) the origin of life.

In higher mass stars, hydrogen burning sets in so rapidly that the stars may attain nuclear ignition and reach temperatures and luminosities close to those of the Main Sequence before the massive envelopes dissipate. They are not observed as Main Sequence stars in this stage, however, because the envelopes block their visible light. However, infra-red spectroscopy can reveal the presence of ionized hydrogen gas around such stars, behind the shrouding material. The ionized gas is the tell-tale clue that the stars have attained high temper-

Above: *A recently discovered newborn star (arrowed) is seen embedded in a cloud of dust and gas in this IRAS image. The young protostar, called B5-IRS 1, is no more than 100,000 years old and is one of possibly several protostars coalescing out of the cloud known as Barnard 5.*

Below: *False-colour infra-red image of the Orion nebula superimposed on a black-and-white photograph. North-west of the central bright star complex (The Trapezium) lies a cluster of pre-stellar infra-red sources enshrouded by dust. New stars are being formed throughout the whole region.*

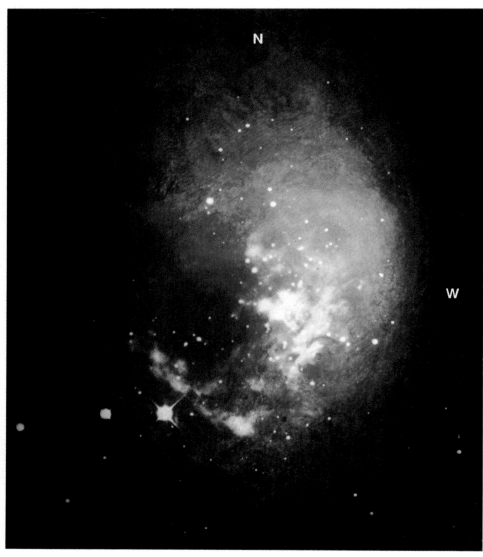

atures and substantial luminosity. The Becklin-Neugebauer object, a bright infrared source in molecular cloud OMC-1, may be in or near this state.[5]

While some patterns of nebulae and newborn stars are consistent with theories of collapse-triggering agents, as mentioned above, some evidence conflicts with theories of sequential star formation. In particular, T Tauri stars are observed scattered throughout dark clouds, with no obvious pattern of age-related-to-position. This suggests that a moving external agent is not required to initiate the collapse of a clump that eventually becomes a T Tauri star. Perhaps the more massive stars are formed predominantly by sequential processes triggered by an external force, while smaller stars, including those like the Sun, do it on their own.

Born Together or Born Free

Most stars are members of binary or multiple star systems. In binary systems, two stars revolve around one another. The stars in some binaries were formed together, true stellar twins, while others were born free, then were taken captive to form wide binary systems. Support for this proposition comes from the observation that the members of close binaries tend to have similar masses (that of the smaller star averaging 70 per cent of the large star's mass), while those of wide pairs do not.

The smaller or "secondary" stars in wide binary systems (defined as systems in which the orbital period is at least one century) have masses that occur in the same relative proportions as those of randomly chosen single stars, supporting the theory that the binaries formed by random capture.

"Capture" is more easily said than done, for two stars passing in space should perturb each other's motion but not lock themselves into closed orbits. If a third star were in the neighbourhood, its gravity might help two passing stars to form a stable system, but a three-way meeting of stars is highly improbable. Two protostars that happened to form in adjacent parts of a molecular cloud might, however, form a wide binary. Or, protostars passing each other within a resisting medium, the larger cloud from which they condensed, could capture each other. Such a pair-formation process could explain the circumstance that the masses of companion stars in wide binaries appear random.

Other theories attempt to explain the formation of close binary stars, in which similar masses and close proximity suggest that the member stars were born together. A spinning protostar might split, for example, producing two smaller protostars by cosmic mitosis.

3 The astronomers are George H. Herbig of the Lick Observatory, University of California, Santa Cruz and Guillermo Haro, National Institute for Astrophysics, Optics and Electronics, Puebla, Mexico.

4 The term, T Tauri, refers to a class of stars named after the first known star of the class, namely the star T Tauri in the constellation Taurus.

5 This object was named after Eric E. Becklin, Institute of Astronomy, Hawaii, and Gerry Neugebauer, Palomar Observatory, California Institute of Technology.

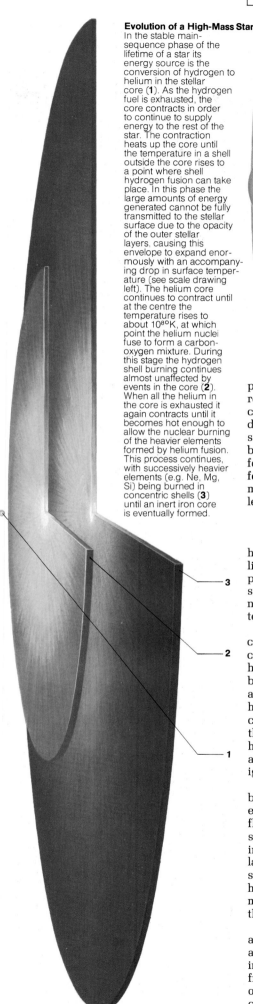

Evolution of a High-Mass Star
In the stable main-sequence phase of the lifetime of a star its energy source is the conversion of hydrogen to helium in the stellar core (**1**). As the hydrogen fuel is exhausted, the core contracts in order to continue to supply energy to the rest of the star. The contraction heats up the core until the temperature in a shell outside the core rises to a point where shell hydrogen fusion can take place. In this phase the large amounts of energy generated cannot be fully transmitted to the stellar surface due to the opacity of the outer stellar layers, causing this envelope to expand enormously with an accompanying drop in surface temperature (see scale drawing left). The helium core continues to contract until at the centre the temperature rises to about 10^8°K, at which point the helium nuclei fuse to form a carbon-oxygen mixture. During this stage the hydrogen shell burning continues almost unaffected by events in the core (**2**). When all the helium in the core is exhausted it again contracts until it becomes hot enough to allow the nuclear burning of the heavier elements formed by helium fusion. This process continues, with successively heavier elements (e.g. Ne, Mg, Si) being burned in concentric shells (**3**) until an inert iron core is eventually formed.

According to the fragmentation theory, a protostar might first take the form of a great rotating doughnut, rather than a centrally condensed core-envelope combination. The doughnut then breaks up, and two or more smaller protostars are produced to form a binary or multiple star system. The cluster formation theory asserts that protostars form in small clusters, the faster-moving members escape, and the remaining few are left as a binary or multiple star system.

Towards the Death of Stars

On the Main Sequence, a star burns hydrogen, fusing this most abundant and lightest element to form helium and in the process releasing energy that makes the star shine. Fusion takes place in the core but not in the outer layers because the necessary temperature is reached only near the centre.

Eventually, however, the hydrogen in the core is entirely converted to helium; the central region of the star has become a helium core. Since there is now no hydrogen burning in the core, there is not enough gas and radiation pressure to keep the core in hydrostatic equilibrium. Gravity now exceeds the repulsive force of pressure, and the core must contract. As compression heats the core the layer just above the core also is heated and the hydrogen in that layer ignites. Now there is fresh fuel for fusion.

The layer just above the core thus becomes a hydrogen-burning shell. Stellar energy production increases and this greater flow of radiation puffs up the outer layers, swelling the star to giant size. Since expanding a gas (in this case, the star's outer layers) cools it, and a cool stellar atmosphere shines with a red or orange colour, the star has become a *red giant*. About five thousand million years from now, the Sun will reach that state.

A red giant is dense in the centre, tenuous and turbulent throughout most of its interior, and steadily expelling its own substance into space. The furious outpouring of energy from the hydrogen-burning shell keeps the outer part of the giant star in seething, convective motion. The convection layer, or

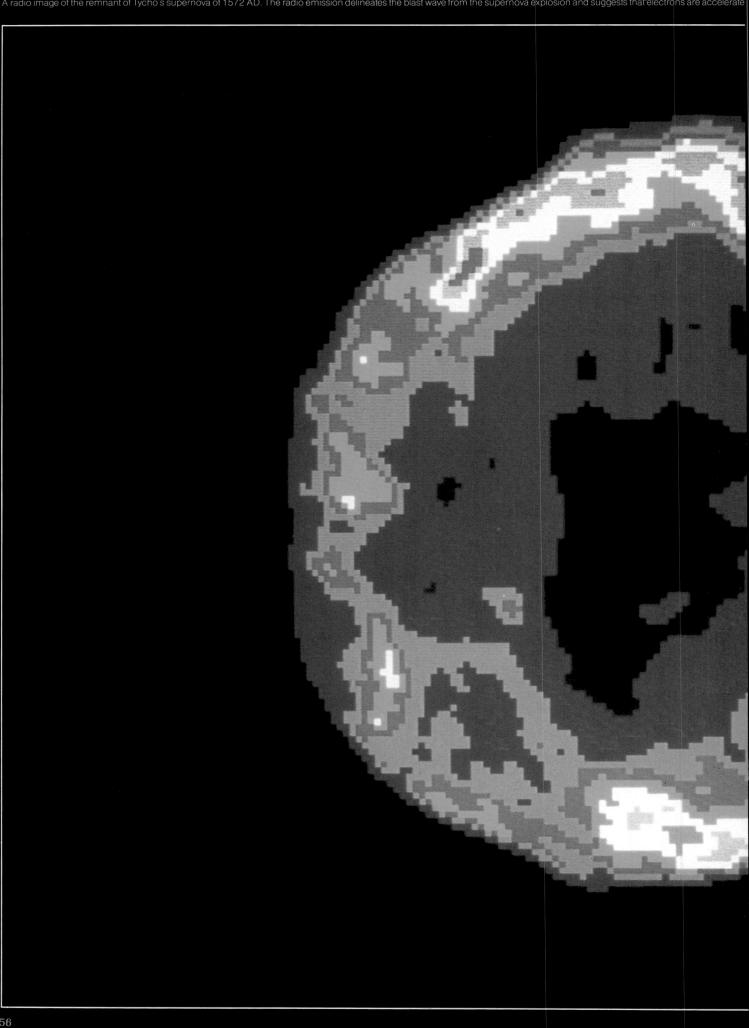

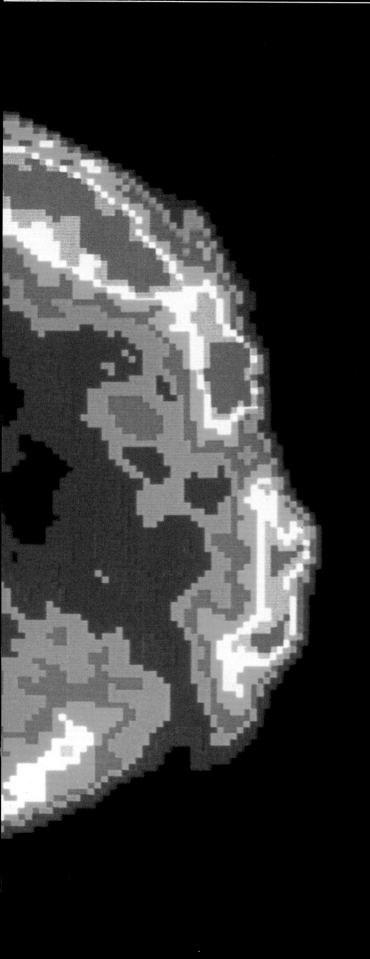

envelope, fills most of the star's volume: the envelope of a typical red giant may have a diameter 100 times that of the Sun, yet contain only half the mass of the red giant.

By contrast, the tightly packed helium core is only about the size of the Earth, yet contains the other half of the stellar mass. In this stage, no nuclear reactions occur in the core, and thus there is not enough gas and radiation pressure to maintain hydrostatic equilibrium in the core. Therefore, the core continues to contract under gravity, getting hotter as it is compressed. Eventually, the core reaches 100 million degrees K, hot enough so that nuclear burning of helium begins.

At this point, two regions of the star are releasing nuclear energy: the helium-burning core and hydrogen-burning shell. Fusion makes carbon and oxygen from helium and more helium from hydrogen. The surface temperature of the star increases, so that the point which represents the star in the H-R Diagram moves to the left. As the surface temperature increases, the star's colour becomes yellow or white. no longer a red giant, it is called a *horizontal-branch star* from its roughly horizontal H-R track.

Spectroscopic observations reveal that red giants have strong stellar winds, which may strip away most of their envelopes, so that the stars lose as much as 50 per cent of their mass into space. For example, Arcturus, the bright red giant in the constellation Bootes, is found to be shedding mass in its stellar wind at the rate of one-hundred-millionth of a solar mass per year. At this rate, it will expel a mass equal to that of the Sun in just 100 million years, or a fraction of the time (tens to hundreds of millions of

Above: *The nebula NGC 2359 is the result of a single Wolf-Rayet star, HD 56925, shedding its outer layers. The stellar ejecta interact with the surrounding gas and dust to produce the type of cosmic bubble seen here.*

International Ultraviolet Explorer (IUE)
1 Sunlight baffle.
2 Secondary mirror mounting.
3 Strong ring.
4 Primary mirror.
5 Fine error sensor.
6 Long wavelength redundant camera.
7 Short wavelength echelle housing.
8 Solar array stowage locks.
9 Long wavelength spectrograph collimating mirror.
10 Long wavelength spectrograph camera mirror.
11 Short wavelength spectrograph collimating mirror.
12 IRA electronics.
13 Camera electronics.
14 Shear panel (5).
15 Hydrazine tanks.
16 Hydrazine auxiliary propulsion system (HAPS).
17 HAPS reaction engine.
18 Apogee motor adapter ring.
19 Lower cone structure.
20 VHF antenna (4).
21 Apogee boost motor.
22 Upper cone structure.
23 Main platform (includes command, control, data handling and communications subsystems, and electronics).
24 Thermal louvres.
25 Panoramic attitude scanners.
26 Solar array deployment mechanism.
27 Solar array.
28 Short wavelength spectrograph camera mirror.
29 Upper platform.
30 Inertial reference assembly (IRA).
31 Ejectable telescope cover.

The International Ultraviolet Explorer (IUE) is a highly successful orbiting observatory, developed jointly by NASA, ESA and the UK's Science Research Council (SRC, now SERC) and designed to investigate stars, quasars and galaxies in the ultraviolet band between 1,150 and 3,200A. It was launched on 26 January 1978 and has been continuously in view from the Goddard Center and for 10 hours a day from the Villafranca (Madrid) ground station. The IUE comprises an octagonal bus from which a 51in (130cm) long telescope with a 17·5in (45cm) aperture protrudes at the top; electronic equipment is carried on a heat-regulated platform, and a hydrazine propulsion system enables the entire craft to manoeuvre. In detail, the tasks of the satellite are to obtain high-resolution stellar spectra and low-resolution spectra of faint objects; study gas streams around certain binary star systems; to make regular observations of objects known to show features that vary with time; and to report on the way gas and dust affect visible starlight. The telescope has a Cassegrain-type optical system, light being directed to one of a pair of spectrographs to analyze UV components in short or long wavelengths. Sensors provide a real-time image for display at the ground station; guide and target stars thus identified are then imaged by the spectrographs for UV conversion and transmission.

Technical Data
Dimensions: 13·8ft (4·22m) high, 4·66ft (1·42m) body diameter.
Solar panels: 14ft (4·3m) span.
Weight: 1,479lb (671kg).
Orbit: Eccentric geosynchronous, 28,600 miles by 15,535 miles (46,000 x 25,000km), inclined 28·6° to the equator.
Optical system: 17·5in (45cm) diameter Cassegrain telescope; focal ratio: f/15; focal length: 266in (675cm).

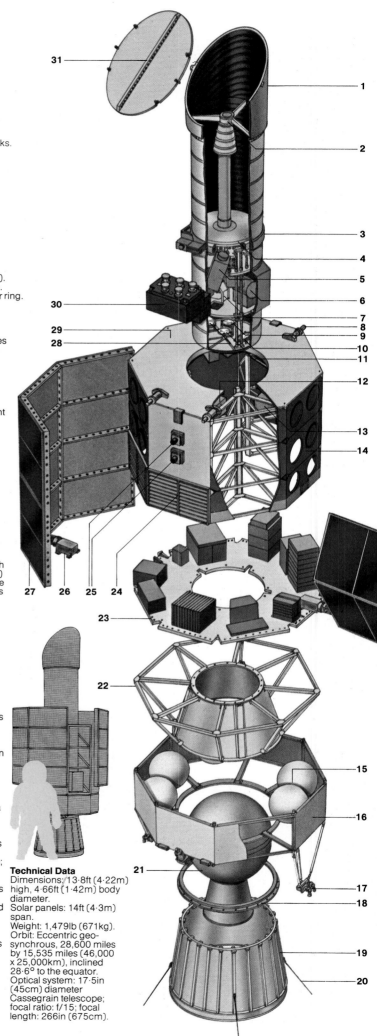

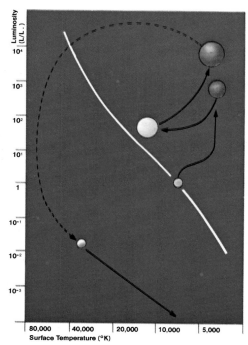

Luminosity (L/L☉)

80,000	40,000	20,000	10,000	5,000

Surface Temperature (°K)

Late Evolution of a One Solar Mass Star

Stars like the Sun do not follow the scheme of nucleosynthesis of successively heavier elements undergone by stars of greater mass. During the shell hydrogen burning phase the star moves to the right off the main sequence. Due to the lower mass of the star, helium burning does not begin until the core has become degenerate. Helium burning thus occurs in conditions where the normal "safety valve" of

stellar equilibrium on the main sequence does not operate. For this reason the onset of helium burning is known as the "helium flash". The star then descends to the left in the H-R diagram: at this point the core becomes non-degenerate again and the star is once more stable. At the end of core helium burning it again ascends the red giant branch, finally passing through poorly-understood unstable phases (dashed line) to become a faint white dwarf.

years) that the average star spends in the red giant stage.[6]

Just as hydrogen burning eventually turned the core to helium, helium burning turns the core to carbon and oxygen. When the helium of the core is exhausted, the core contracts and heats itself, as it did earlier after exhausting its hydrogen. The new contraction warms the shell around the core, where hydrogen burning earlier created helium. Helium now ignites at the bottom of the layer. The bottom portion becomes a helium burning shell while the upper part of the layer consists of unignited or inert helium. Just above the inert helium, hydrogen remains and is ignited. Fusion is under way because the temperature is high enough for hydrogen burning but not for helium burning. Thus, the star has an inert carbon-oxygen core but two shells in which nuclear energy is released. Inert though it may be, the core is not static. Instead, it grows as fusion in the surrounding shell deposits fresh-made carbon and oxygen.

The two nuclear-burning shells which form at the end of the horizontal-branch stage release so much energy that the star swells and becomes a red giant again. However, inside the reborn red giant, convective motions have taken newly-made matter from the deep interior and brought it to the stellar surface. As a result, the red giant's spectrum is marked by prominent lines of carbon and its compounds: it is now a *carbon star*. Events in the carbon star

---

6 The most rapid example of mass loss so far discovered is the case of Zeta Ophiuci, which is losing mass via a stellar wind at a rate of 5×10^6 solar masses per year.

stage are poorly understood, but it seems that the star somehow sheds its vast convective envelope, enriched with the products of hydrogen and helium burning. The expulsion may occur in a great pulsation, by means of an especially powerful stellar wind, or perhaps when solid particles of carbon form and are pushed outward by radiation pressure.

At first, the expelled matter may be dense and opaque; as such it may glow strongly in the infra-red. The Egg Nebula and the Red Rectangle, two opaque nebulae discovered by US Air Force infra-red sounding rockets, may be proto-planetary nebulae formed in this way.

In any case, the expelled envelope, flying into space at about 45,000mph (72,000km/h), eventually thins and forms a *planetary nebula*, like the Ring Nebula in Lyra. No longer opaque, it is heated, ionized, and made to glow by ultraviolet radiation from a small blue star at the centre. The little star is all that remains in one piece from the progenitor red giant.

The small star seems dim in visible light, but produces so much ultraviolet radiation that its total or bolometric luminosity (total luminosity in all wavelengths of light) equals that of the vanished giant star. In fact, the planetary nebula central star consists of the core and immediately surrounding layers of the red giant, and fusion continues to release nuclear energy. Only the huge envelope is gone.

Convective Dredge-Up

As a transparent, glowing nebula, the expelled stellar envelope is more susceptible to study than when it lay beneath the red giant's photosphere. Thus, astronomers measure chemical abundances in planetary nebulae in order to determine the composition of the carbon star red giants that gave rise to them. Such studies reveal the efficiency of convective dredge-up, the process that brings freshly synthesized atoms from the layers where nuclear burning occurs to the red giant envelope where it does not.

Recent observations with the International Ultraviolet Explorer have made possible a galaxy-to-galaxy comparison of the efficiency of convective dredge-up. The investigators compared planetary nebulae in three galaxies —the Milky Way, the Large Magellanic Cloud (LMC), and the Small Magellanic Cloud (SMC)—with the interstellar gas of the three galaxies.

Above: *Astronomer George H. Herbig with IUE telescope operator William Hathaway (seated) in the control room at NASA's Goddard Space Flight Center, Maryland. Technical data referring to the satellite are displayed on the monitors in front of the*

operator who is in constant radio communication with the IUE telescope. The large screen on the wall displays the astronomical data, in this case a high dispersion spectrum of a stellar object. Each "stripe" is a section of the spectrum.

Above: *A false-colour image of Eta Ursae Majoris, the first star to be observed by IUE, received from the Fine Error Sensor on board the satellite. The FES is used principally to locate and track the astronomical objects to be studied.*

Stars form from the interstellar gas and must retain its chemical composition unless nuclear reactions generate fresh material. The interstellar gas of the Milky Way contains about six times as much carbon as that of the LMC and about 40 times that of the SMC. Yet the IUE observations revealed that planetary nebulae in the three galaxies have roughly equal abundances of carbon, more in each case than the interstellar medium of the Milky Way. Thus, the net result of nuclear reactions and convective dredge-up within stars is to produce comparable amounts of new carbon, regardless of the chemical composition with which the stars are born.

Stellar Endings

After perhaps 30,000 years, a planetary nebula dissipates into space. Meanwhile, nuclear burning has run down in the central star. Gravitational contraction cannot produce more energy, for electrons in the star generate enough pressure to resist further compression. The star is now a *white dwarf*, like Sirius B, companion to the bright star Sirius. A white dwarf has no source of new energy but simply glows because it is hot. Over thousands of years, the white dwarf will radiate its heat energy into space until finally it is cool and dark.

Stars with less than about four to six solar masses (estimates vary) follow the above scenario. Through stellar winds and the expulsion of planetary nebulae, they shed mass. Finally, they end up as white dwarfs with only a fraction of the Sun's radius and only 1·4 solar masses or less.

Stars with more than four to six solar masses suffer a different fate. They erupt as supernovae in violent explosions that sometimes outshine a whole galaxy of stars.

How a Supernova Occurs

In massive stars, nuclear reactions continue until the core of the star is transformed to iron. No further reactions will generate additional energy. Lacking energy to support itself through radiation and gas pressure, the core of the star collapses catastrophically. This implosion sets off an explosion that hurls the outer layers of the star apart and into space; the core of the star may remain as a condensed object—a neutron star or a black hole—or it too may be torn apart. This process, a *type II supernova*, produced the Crab Nebula and Cassiopeia A supernova remnants. Another explosive phenomenon, the *type I supernova*, occurs in binary stars when mass transferred from one star to a second condensed object (probably a white dwarf star) compresses and heats the stellar surface to the point that a nuclear explosion is set off. These supernovae occur in relatively low-mass stars, unlike type II supernovae. Tycho's Star, the supernova of 1572 AD, was a type I supernova.

Such an explosion ejects most of a star's matter, creating a rapidly expanding *supernova remnant* such as the Crab Nebula.

Right: Supernova remnant in Cassiopeia as it appears in three wavelength bands: radio (blue), optical (red) and X-ray (green). In contrast to the Crab Nebula, no pulsar relic of the original star has been found at the centre of Cas A.

Some supernova stars, believed to be among the most massive stars, and also those with less than eight but more than four to six solar masses, apparently shatter wholly. They leave remnant nebulae but not remnant stars. Cassiopeia A, the remains of a star of perhaps 20 solar masses which exploded in the 17th Century (probably unseen from Earth at the time), may be the remains of such a supernova in which the massive star was totally disrupted. Other supernova stars, with perhaps 8 to 10 solar masses, do leave a dense remnant core, a *neutron star*.

In a white dwarf star, matter is so dense as a result of core contraction in the red giant that one cubic inch would weigh one ton on earth; the white dwarf may have been compressed to the size of the Earth. Although a neutron star may be only 6 to 12 miles (10-20km) in diameter, one cubic inch of it

Above: An electronic "Pulsar Hunter" camera was used by H.Y. Chiu, R. Lynds and S.P. Maran of KPNO to record the Crab pulsar as it blinks on and off twice in each pulse period of 1/30th of a second. The pulsar is seen at various phases of the period in the photographs above.

would weigh thousands of millions of tons on Earth. According to theory, neutron stars can form with masses of 1·4 to perhaps 4 solar masses. However, in every case of an observed neutron star where the mass can be estimated, it seems likely that the mass is in fact 1·4 to 1·5 solar masses.

Like a white dwarf, a neutron star has no remaining internal source of nuclear energy and can only cool with time. However, if either kind of star is located in a binary system, it may accrete gas shed by a larger companion star. In such a case, the accreting

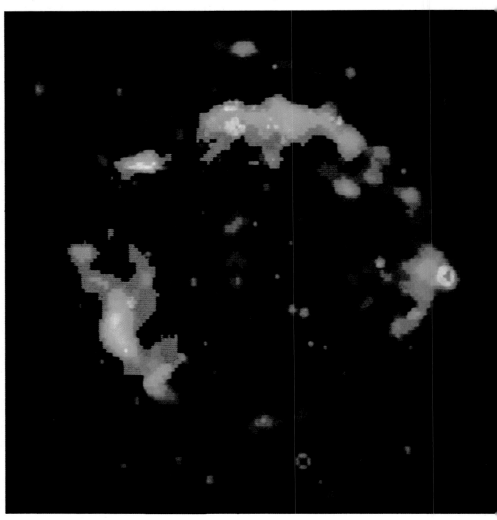

matter is compressed by the powerful gravity of the white dwarf or neutron star and made to glow brightly in X-rays.

In some cases, nuclear reactions may be induced in the accreted matter at the surface of a compact star. Possessed of powerful magnetic fields, neutron stars also produce searchlight-beamed radio emissions, which seem like intermittent pulses as they sweep by the earth. Over 300 such stars, called *radio pulsars*, have been found with radio telescopes.

A few dozen binary systems studied by Uhuru (Explorer 42, Small Astronomy Satellite 1) and Einstein (HEAO-2) X-ray observatory satellites appear to consist of a neutron star and a larger companion. However, in a few cases, it appears that the mass of the compact star in an X-ray binary system is more than the roughly 4-solar-mass theoretical limit to the mass of a neutron star.

In these cases, the compact objects are believed to be the long-sought black holes, collapsed stars with gravity so powerful that nothing, not even a ray of light, can escape from within. A famous and well-established case of a black hole is the compact member of the binary system Cygnus X-1. A more recently established case is the compact member of the LMC X-3, a binary star in the Large Magellanic Cloud.

Although a black hole must form by the collapse of a star, it is not known for certain how provisionally-identified black holes such as that in Cygnus X-1 were actually formed. One possibility is that supergiant stars, with more than 10 solar masses,

sometimes form black holes when nuclear fuel is exhausted and the stars collapse (a process that causes the supernova explosion).

Perhaps the inner portion of such a star reaches so high a density that it becomes a black hole, while the exterior part is ejected in the supernova event. Another mechanism that may form a black hole consists of the accretion of matter onto the surface of a neutron star. If not explosively ejected, a few solar masses deposited on a neutron star surface might cause the star to collapse as a black hole.

A general rule of stellar evolution is that the more massive the star, the more rapidly it evolves. The lowest mass stars, with a few per cent or less of a solar mass, hardly evolve at all over thousands of millions of years. In contrast, the most massive stars may survive only a few million years before blowing themselves apart, first by stellar winds and then, the *coup de grâce*, by supernova eruptions. Some may survive the eruptions as black holes, but if so there is little that we can learn of them.

However they form, black holes have effectively left the Universe. We can detect their presence through the effects of their gravity on companion stars and adjacent matter, but matter that falls within a black hole is lost forever and no radiation can emerge to reveal its condition. Therefore there is very little that we can learn about the collapsed star. The boundary or event horizon of a black hole is a natural limit to studies of stellar evolution.

RECOMMENDED READING

Gehrels, Tom, (Ed.), *Protostars and Planets*, The University of Arizona Press, Tucson, Arizona, 1978.

Giacconi, Riccardo, (Ed.), *X-Ray Astronomy with the Einstein Satellite*, D. Reidel Publishing Co, Dordrecht, Holland, 1981.

Maran, Stephen P., "Strung-out Stars" in *Natural History*, Vol. 87, No. 2, 1982.

Maran, Stephen P., "Telescope in Space" in *Natural History*, Vol. 89, No. 7, 1980.

Maran, Stephen P., "A Nonconforming Supernova" in *Natural History*, Vol. 90, No. 5, 1981.

Maran, Stephen P., "Stellar Togetherness" in *Natural History*, Vol. 90, No. 12, 1981.

Maran, Stephen P., "Origin of the Crab Nebula" in *Natural History*, Vol. 91, No. 10, 1982.

Shipman, Harry L., *Black Holes, Quasars and the Universe*, 2nd edn, Houghton Mifflin, Boston, Massachusetts, 1980.

Shu, Frank H., *The Physical Universe*, University Science Books, Mill Valley, California, 1982.

Sugimoto, Daiichiro, Lamb, Donald Q., and Schramm, David N., (Eds.), *Fundamental Problems in the Theory of Stellar Evolution*, D. Reidel Publishing Co, Dordrecht, Holland, 1981.

Below: *False-colour X-ray image of Cygnus X-1 obtained by the Einstein Observatory satellite. This is essentially a point source with the brightest part of the image a few arcseconds in diameter: its apparently greater extent is due to scattering of X-rays by the telescope. Cyg X-1 is a good candidate for a black hole remnant of a collapsed supermassive star.*

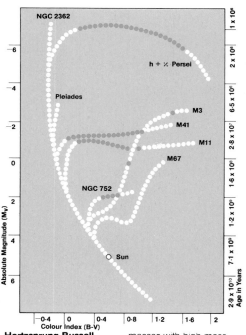

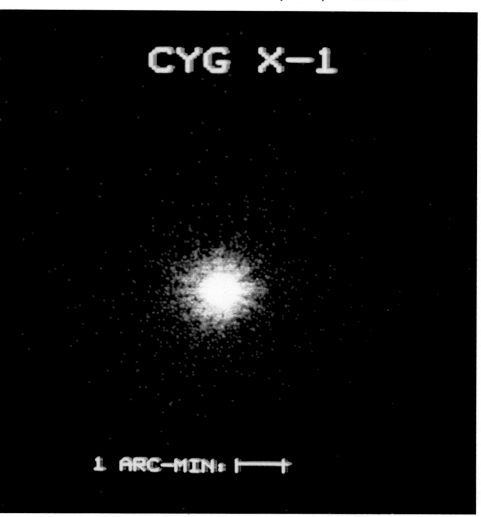

Hertzsprung-Russell Diagrams of Star Clusters

By constructing H-R diagrams for the stars in any cluster the age of the cluster can be deduced. Shown above are such plots for several different clusters, plotted in terms of absolute magnitude against the B-V colour (~) index, the difference between the absolute magnitude of a star in the blue and visual wavebands and a measure of stellar temperature. A standard main sequence represents a distribution of stellar masses with high mass stars at top left and low mass stars at bottom right. We also know that high mass stars evolve more rapidly than low mass stars. Thus in the cluster NGC 2362, even the most massive stars are still in or near their main sequence phase and the cluster must be young. In contrast, in M67, stars only slightly more massive than the Sun have evolved substantially during the age of the cluster. The turn-off point from the zero-age main sequence gives the cluster age.

The Sun

By the 1920s, solar physicists knew that neither the energy of chemical burning nor that of gravitational contraction was sufficient to fuel the Sun over its lifetime up till then of 4·5 thousand million years. The development of nuclear physics showed which nuclear reactions could be expected in the Sun and their energy release. The centre of the Sun is a gigantic, continuous hydrogen bomb explosion where hydrogen is being converted into helium at the rate of 700 million tons a second. So far, the Sun has used up about half of its hydrogen fuel; it is predicted to continue burning much as it does today for another 5 thousand million years.

Our Daytime Star

Although there are billions of stars visible through telescopes, there is only one that can be studied in great detail by man, where we can see individual surface features and watch the evolution of spots as they rotate across the star's disc. This star, our Sun, has always been used by astronomers as a guide to stellar physics, for we cannot hope to understand the more distant stars until we first know what is happening closer to home. Interest in our Sun is by no means entirely academic. The Sun is the source of virtually all light and heat which maintain life here on Earth. Even a relatively small rise or fall in the energy output of the Sun would have disastrous consequences for us.

Of course, the fossil record shows that life on Earth has survived continuously now for over 3×10^9 years, which is evidence for some degree of long-term stability of the Sun. On the other hand, it is likely that some of the changes in the variety and distribution of life forms over geological time may be due to temperature changes caused by solar variability.

The Sun has also had a powerful influence on mankind's ideas about our place in the Universe. Copernicus' claim that the Sun is far larger than the Earth and is the true centre of our Solar System implied that we do not reside at a special place in the centre of the Universe, but are residents of one planet of several orbiting the Sun. This was a major blow to the old Aristotelian cosmology which prevailed through the Middle Ages. Later, in 1610 when Galileo developed the telescope as an instrument of astronomical observation, one of the first objects he looked at was the Sun. He immediately saw sunspots moving across the Sun's disc and could measure its rotation period (about 27 days). The undeniable existence of sunspots shattered yet another tenet of the

THE SUN:BASIC DATA	
Spectral Type	G2 ("yellow" star)
Luminosity Class	V ("dwarf" star)
Stellar Population	I (characteristic of stars in the spiral arms, or disc, of the Galaxy, as opposed to Population II or halo stars which are thought to be older)
Position in Galaxy	In a spiral arm about 30,000 light years from the Galactic centre
Age	4·5 x 10⁹ years
Radius	432,500 miles (696,000km) (109 x Earth's radius)
Mass	1·99 x 10³³g (333,000 x Earth's mass)
Density (average) (at centre)	0·81oz/in³ (1·41g/cm³) 92·5oz/in³ (160g/cm³)
Distance from Earth (average)	92,960,000 miles (149,600,000km)
Surface Temperature	6,050°K
Interior Temperature (centre)	15,000,000°K
Energy Output (whole Sun)	3·83 x 10²³kW
Energy received at Earth	1,373W/m²
Rotation Period* (at equator) (at 60°latitude)	26·8 days 30·8 days
*Relative to Earth	

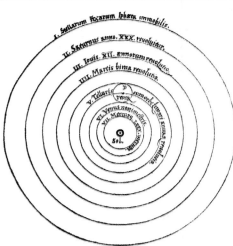

Above: *Copernicus' view of the Universe, as expounded by him in* De Revolutionibus Orbium Coelestium, *published shortly before his death in 1543.*

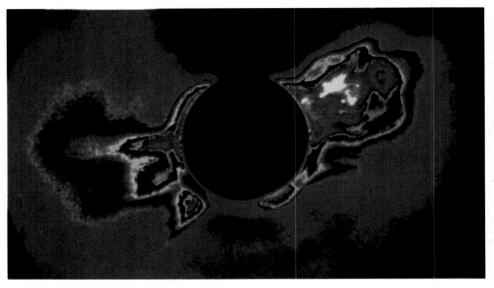

Above: *This false-colour image of the solar corona was take by the coronagraph on the Skylab mission in 1973. The very elongated shape is typical during times close to sunspot minimum.*

ancient cosmology, which held that the objects in the heavens are perfect and unchanging, moving across the sky driven by a celestial clockwork of circular cycles and epicycles (see page 17).

When the basic mechanics of planetary orbits were finally worked out in 1666 by Isaac Newton, there still remained the difficult problem of determining the actual distances of the Earth from the Sun and planets. Newton's theory of gravitation can be used, along with observations of the planets' apparent paths through the sky, to work out very accurately the *relative* sizes of the orbits of the different planets, but this

does not tell us the *absolute* distance (in kilometres, say) to any celestial bodies.

The only methods available until very recently for such distance determinations were based on the principle of triangulation or parallax (commonly used in surveying) with the Earth's diameter limiting the maximum possible separation between two observers in measuring the planets' posi-

"So sinks the day-star in the ocean bed,
And yet anon repairs his drooping head,
And tricks his beams, and with new spangled ore,
Flames in the forehead of the morning sky."

John Milton, *Lycidas*

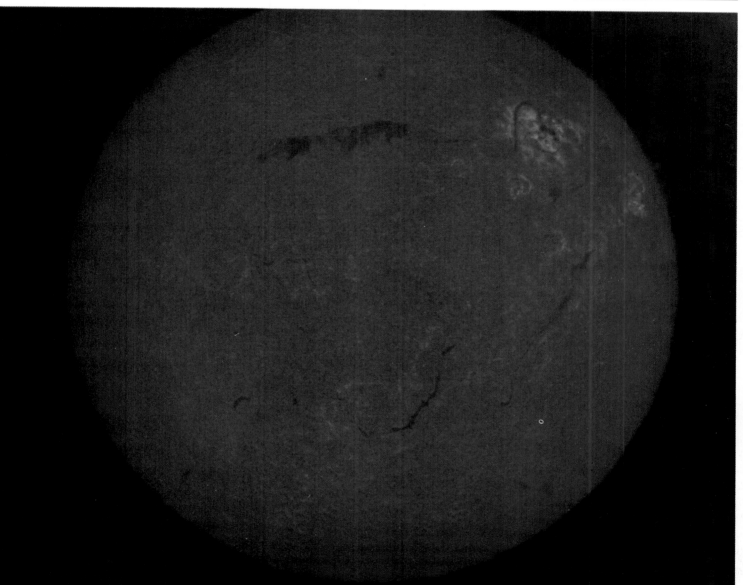

Above: *A sun storm region, upper right, covering an area 100,000 miles (161,000km) across. This storm, the most intense in several years, was first detected by sensors on NASA's OSO-7.*

tions. But since the planets are all very far away relative to the diameter of the Earth, the measurements are difficult and the ultimate value obtained is only accurate to within about one per cent. The famous method of observing the transits of Venus when it passes between the Earth and the Sun is a variation on the triangulation idea. In this century, use has been made of the peculiar orbit of the asteroid Eros, which occasionally passes very close to the Earth and thus has a large parallax for a few hours. In this way a much improved accuracy of 0·01 per cent can be reached.

All of these triangulation methods have now been rendered obsolete, however, since the advent of a capability for bouncing radar signals off the planets Venus and Mars and for exchanging radio signals with space probes in orbit around these planets or actually sitting on the planetary surfaces. Direct timing of the flight of these signals yields distances accurate to about one part in 10^8, or approximately one kilometre, which is more precise than our ability to define the location of the surface of the Sun, a cloudy layer 62 miles (100km) thick. This short history of the measurement of one solar parameter shows the tremendous influence of new techniques in astronomy within the past few years, while at the same time showing the continuity over the centuries of some research objectives.

Solar physics clearly has a long and illustrious history. Here we will give a concise account of our present understanding of the Sun, including its interior make-up, surface activity, and upper atmospheric layers. Finally, we will investigate

The Proton-Proton Chain

The interior of the Sun is like a huge power station which is running continuously. It works by means of a reaction called nuclear fusion in which light nuclei fuse together to form heavier nuclei, during which process energy is released. There are various ways in which this fusion may occur. This diagram illustrates the possible chain of nuclear reaction for fusing hydrogen into helium that is thought to be the main source of energy production in the Sun. In nearly all instances two protons combine to form a nucleus of deuterium which emits a positron and a neutrino (**1**). In 0·25% of cases, two protons and an electron combine to yield a nucleus of deuterium and a neutrino (**2**). The deuterium then combines with a proton to produce a nucleus of helium-3 and a photon (**3**). Usually two helium-3 nuclei then fuse to form a nucleus of helium-4 and two protons (**4**). The proton-proton chain may follow a different route: a helium-3 nucleus can combine with a helium-4 nucleus so yielding a beryllium-7 nucleus and a photon (**5**). This nucleus then usually gathers an electron to make a lithium-7 nucleus and a neutrino. A proton then links with the lithium-7 and the nucleus splits into two helium-4 nuclei (**6**). In certain circumstances the beryllium-7 nucleus absorbs a proton so becoming boron-8 and emitting a photon. The boron-8 nucleus then decays into a nucleus of beryllium-8, a positron and a neutrino. The beryllium-8 will then divide into two nuclei of helium-4 (**7**). The neutrino emitted during the last reaction is thought to possess sufficient energy to make it detectable on Earth. It can be trapped in perchloroethylene—dry cleaning fluid—where it will transform an atom of chlorine-37 into the radioactive argon-37. So far, experiments to detect these neutrinos have been disappointing, which implies that either the chain reaction is not operating at present or that our theories may have to be reconsidered.

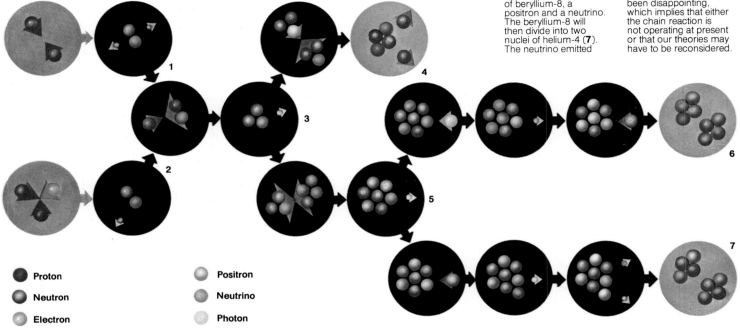

- ● Proton
- ● Neutron
- ○ Electron
- ○ Positron
- ○ Neutrino
- ○ Photon

how changes in the solar emissions are thought to affect activities here on Earth.

The Nuclear Furnace

A coherent picture of our star begins with an examination of the solar core, where the energy that fuels the Sun's fires is generated, and continues outward as photons gradually travel toward the surface and eventually escape into space. Since, except by use of one specialized technique, we cannot see directly into the solar interior, our knowledge of the processes going on deep inside the Sun is derived by application of known physical laws to those facts which we do know about the Sun as a whole: its mass, radius, surface chemical composition, rate of energy output, and age. Using these facts and the laws of physics as starting points, we can create mathematical "models" of the temperature, density and other physical parameters at all depths in the solar interior and can look for a model which will satisfy all the constraints we impose. It turns out that models meeting the criteria we have listed here can be constructed quite easily, so, until recently, it was believed that we had a relatively good picture of what the solar interior is really like.

The first question to be answered is: what is the origin of the Sun's energy? By the 1920s, solar physicists knew that neither the energy of chemical burning nor the energy that could be derived from gravitational contraction was sufficient to fuel the Sun over its known lifetime of $4·5 \times 10^9$ years. Even though atomic energy had not yet been discovered, it was widely hypothesized that the Sun's energy arose from some type of subatomic process. The development of nuclear physics in the 1930s and 1940s later showed which actual nuclear reactions could be expected to occur in the Sun, and what energy each one releases.

Basically, the centre of the Sun is a gigantic, continuous, hydrogen bomb explosion, where hydrogen atoms are being converted into helium atoms at the rate of 700 million tons per second. Through a series of nuclear reactions four hydrogen atoms are fused together into one helium atom. However, a helium atom has a mass of only 4·003 atomic mass units, while four hydrogen atoms together total 4·032 atomic mass units. The difference is released as energy, or photons, according to Einstein's formula $E = mc^2$.

In each second's nuclear burning the Sun drops in mass by 4 million metric tons, the mass equivalent of the solar energy output. The chemical composition of the original

Below: *Skylab spectroheliogram of a solar eruption. The solid disc shows gas at 50,000°K; the image at right, due to much hotter gas, shows bright emission from a magnetic region in the lower corona.*

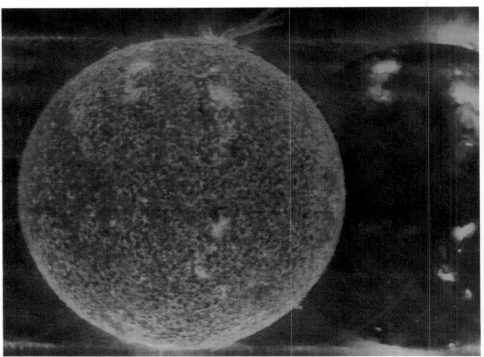

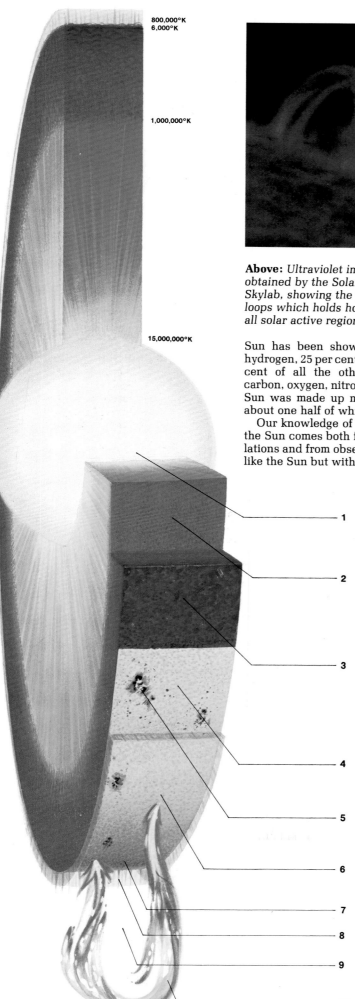

800,000°K
6,000°K

1,000,000°K

15,000,000°K

Above: *Ultraviolet image of the Sun obtained by the Solar Telescope on Skylab, showing the pattern of magnetic loops which holds hot, ionized gas above all solar active regions.*

Sun has been shown to be 73 per cent hydrogen, 25 per cent helium, and only 2 per cent of all the other elements such as carbon, oxygen, nitrogen and iron. Thus the Sun was made up mostly of nuclear fuel, about one half of which still remains.

Our knowledge of the past and future of the Sun comes both from theoretical calculations and from observations of other stars like the Sun but with different ages. Obser-

The Structure of the Sun
1 Solar core.
2 Radiative interior.
3 Convective zone.
4 Photosphere.
5 Sunspot.
6 Chromosphere.
7 Granular appearance of surface of photosphere.
8 Spicule.
9 Corona.
10 Solar flare.

As the proton-proton chain diagram (left) shows, the energy of the Sun is generated in its core where hydrogen nuclei are converted to helium nuclei and energy is released. Temperatures here approach 15 million °K. The heat is transferred through the radiative interior and convective zone to the visible surface of the Sun—the photosphere. This has a granular appearance. Sunspots occur on the photosphere: they are cooler areas and are associated with strong magnetic fields. A region known as the chromosphere rises above the photosphere, and this is penetrated by hot gaseous jets called spicules. The solar wind originates here. Other features of the chromosphere are prominences, which may be quiescent or eruptive, and solar flares, violent eruptions from the solar surface which emit UV radiation and charged particles. The outer part of the Sun's atmosphere is known as the corona. Temperatures in it are very high and it is a source of strong radio waves; however it is visible to the eye only during a total eclipse.

vations in the far infra-red part of the spectrum have now shown us what has been suspected for years: that stars condense inside giant clouds of gas and dust, so we can never see their birth in visible light.

The planets of our Solar System formed out of the solar nebula, or cloud, and then eventually the Sun moved out of the nebula into open space. In the course of the 4.5×10^9 years of its life so far the Sun has used up almost half of its available hydrogen fuel, so it is predicted to continue burning much as it does today for another 5×10^9 years.

Although theory says that the Sun has increased in luminosity by about 10 per cent over the past 3×10^9 years, the fossil record indicates that the Earth's climate has become cooler, if anything, over this period. This might mean that the Sun has not behaved as theory suggests, but a more likely explanation is that the Earth's atmosphere has changed its composition and has lost much of its "greenhouse effect" or insulating capacity over the millennia.

In any case, we are certain that toward the end of its lifetime, as the nuclear fuel is running out, the Sun will become a so-called *red giant*, dropping in surface temperature from 6,000°K to 3,000°K and increasing so much in size as completely to engulf Mercury and Venus. The Sun will then be so bright that the oceans of the Earth will boil and all life on Earth will surely end.

Then, very soon (on a cosmological time scale) after reaching the red giant stage, all its fuel will be exhausted and the Sun will shrink and decrease in luminosity to become a white dwarf star which gradually cools to invisibility, collapsing ultimately to a sphere the size of the Earth with a density so incredibly great that one teaspoonful would weigh 5 tons.

The Interior

Other aspects of the solar interior are also predicted by our models. The outer 20 per cent of the Sun is found to be unstable and to develop a "boiling" or convective action to transport heat efficiently from the inside toward the surface. This result of the models is at least partially confirmed by pictures of the Sun's surface which show convective bubbles rising up and flowing back down almost everywhere on the Sun. Surprisingly, however, the Sun turns out to have two quite different types of convection, with typical bubble sizes of 620 miles (1,000km) and 18,640 miles (30,000km), a feature not predicted at all by the computer models.

The inner 80 per cent of the Sun's interior is known as the radiative zone. In this region the gas does not show any convection or flows, and energy is transported outward by radiative processes, mostly by X-rays which are absorbed and re-emitted many millions of times by the atoms of gas in the radiative zone. The X-ray photons gradually work their way outward from the hotter interior to the cooler surface, travelling in an almost random track with a slow outward motion that takes on the average 50 million years to reach the surface. The slowness of this energy flow means that if the nuclear burning were suddenly to stop it would still take tens of millions of years for the Sun's luminosity to drop noticeably.

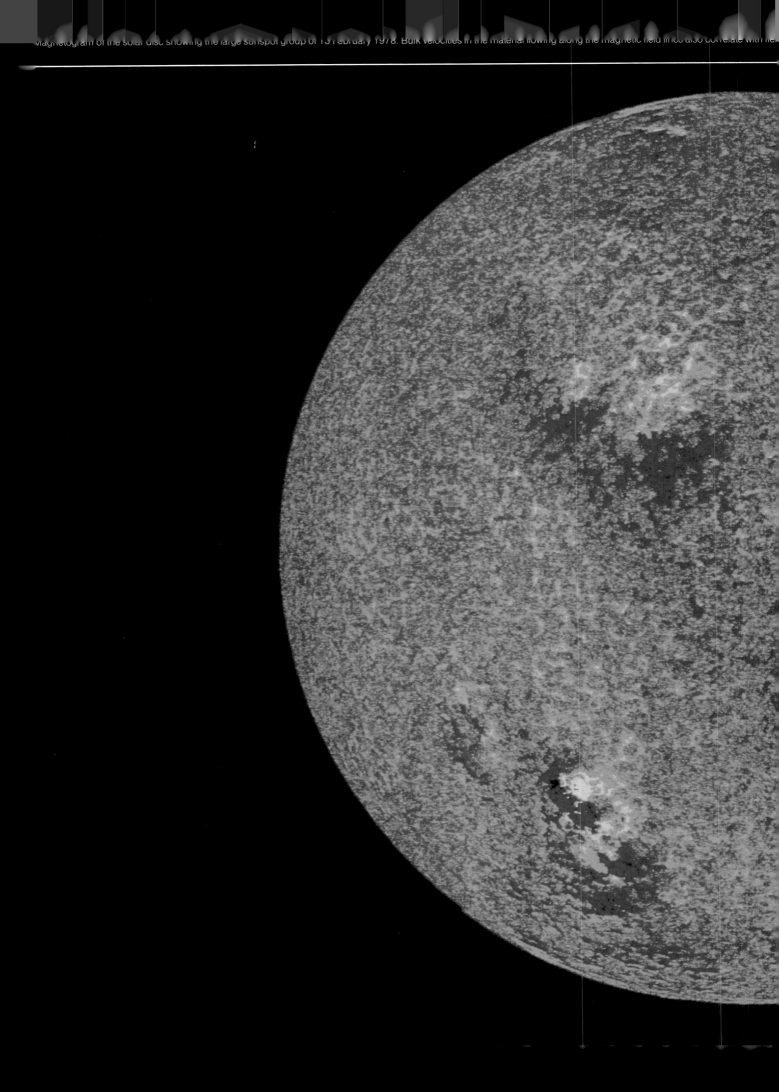

Magnetogram of the solar disc showing the large sunspot group of 13 February 1978. Bulk velocities in the material flowing along the magnetic field lines also correlate with hel...

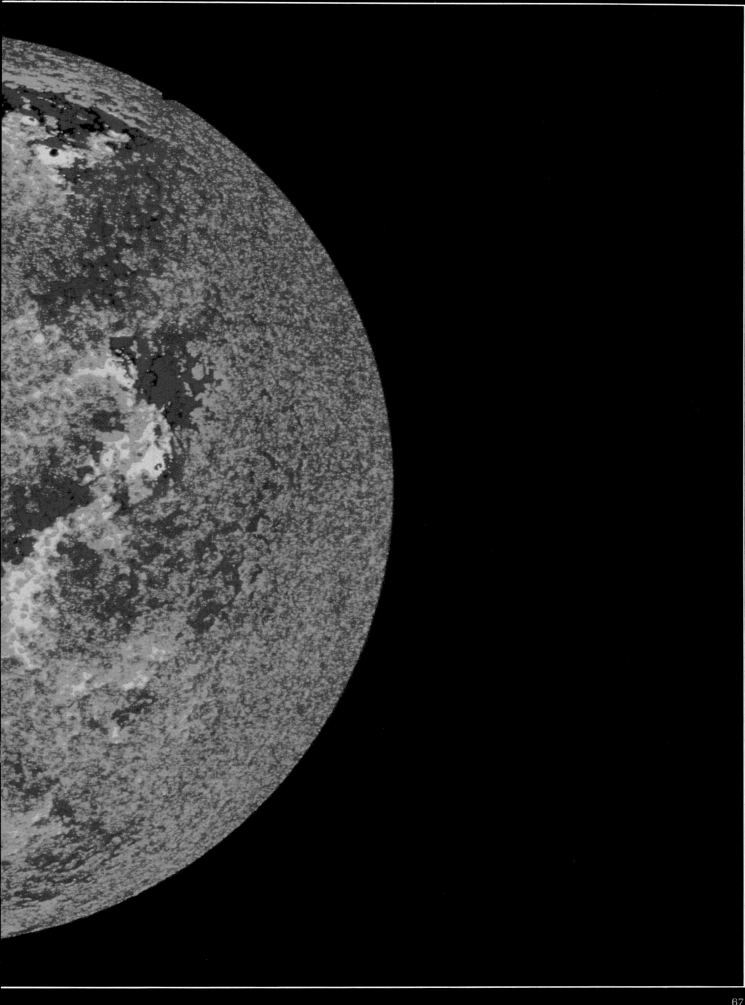

The Neutrino Question

This fact brings up an extremely important puzzle about the solar interior that remains unsolved today. In the burning of hydrogen to helium, a small amount of the energy is released in the form of subatomic particles called neutrinos. Neutrinos interact so seldom with matter that over 99 per cent of those emitted pass directly through the Sun and escape into space. Using the methods of experimental nuclear physics it is possible to detect these solar neutrinos, and in this way we can actually "see" the centre of the Sun. In 1968, a special neutrino detector was built deep underground in the Homestake gold mine at Lead, South Dakota to perform this experiment free from interference from cosmic rays. It consisted of a tank of c.100,000 gallons (400,000l) of dry cleaning fluid (perchloroethylene) which contains chlorine-37. The elusive neutrino would betray its presence by changing a chlorine atom to argon-37 which is radioactive and thus easily detectable. Raymond Davis, the scientist in charge, found an unexpected result: only about one third of the predicted number of neutrinos seem to be emerging from the Sun.

Various theories have been proposed to explain this paradox, including errors in our basic theory of what the neutrino is, or other errors in the atomic physics used to calculate

the expected rates of emission or detection of neutrinos. If current neutrino theory is correct, however, we must consider the possibility that our mathematical model of conditions at the centre of the Sun is incorrect. For example, if the Sun's nuclear burning were to turn "on" and "off" every few thousand years this would strongly affect the measured neutrino emission while leaving the surface luminosity essentially constant.

Other modifications to our solar models have been proposed as well, but thus far no final solution to the neutrino problem has

been accepted by a majority of scientists. In the meantime, yet another technique for studying the Sun's interior has been developed. For many years terrestrial seismologists have been studying the ways in which the Earth "rings" like a bell when a great shock such as an earthquake occurs. In the same way it has been found that the Sun rings, or oscillates, when driven by the sound waves given off by huge convective bubbles as they push through the solar atmosphere. And just as a bell rings with many overtone notes sounding simultaneously, the Sun has hundreds of different "notes" of oscillations vibrating continuously. Two basic differences between the phenomena observed in the Sun and more familiar bells are that the Sun's ringing occurs mostly at frequencies near 1/300 cycle per second, which is about 10,000 times lower in pitch than the largest earthly bells; and since sound does not travel through space we cannot hear the

The Active Surface of the Sun

The energy generated deep inside the Sun travels slowly outward until it eventually reaches the surface and escapes into space. This surface layer that we see with the naked eye and through our telescopes is called the *photosphere*. Lying above the photosphere are other layers of the Sun's atmosphere called the *chromosphere* and *corona* which are much fainter than the photosphere, and hence are only visible with special instruments or during a solar eclipse when the moon blocks the intense glare of the photosphere.

Through a telescope the photosphere may at first appear quiet and inactive, but techniques such as time-lapse photography show a very different picture. Convection cells erupt and then fade away, with the smallest cells changing their pattern every 15 minutes or so. Sunspots appear and evolve, sometimes giving birth to the violent explosions called solar flares. Other dense clouds known as solar prominences hang suspended in the corona high above the surface of the Sun, sometimes erupting suddenly as giant, glowing sheets of gas.

What causes the gases of the Sun's surface to assume so many different shapes and to produce so many different active phenomena? The answer is that, with the exception of convection, all of the Sun's activity is due to the existence of magnetic fields. In 1912, George Ellery Hale found that sunspots contain magnetic fields thousands of times stronger than the Earth's natural field. It had been known since 1848 that the average number of sunspots visible at any one time rises and falls with an 11-year period, so Hale's discovery clearly meant that the Sun has a varying magnetic field. Hale also found that sunspots usually occur in pairs of opposite magnetic polarity, with the western spot of each pair being of north polarity (like the Earth's north pole) in odd-numbered cycles and south polarity in even cycles. Thus the true magnetic period of the sunspot cycle is 22 years rather than 11 years (see diagram left).

The conclusion from these facts is that there is a giant magnetic dynamo located deep inside the Sun. This dynamo generates magnetic fields which emerge through the photosphere as sunspots and other features, and which reverse their direction every 22 years. It is believed that the dynamo action is due to interactions between the convective flows in the solar interior, the rotational forces in the Sun, and the magnetic fields left over from the previous cycle, but the precise mechanism is not yet understood.

When we look at a sunspot, we do not see the magnetic fields themselves, but their effects on gases. The magnetic fields change the ways in which energy is transported into or out of these gases, so the gases in magnetic field regions can be denser or cooler than the surrounding material and can outline the magnetic fields visibly. In a sunspot, the strong fields prevent convection from carrying energy into the gas of the sunspot, and sunspots have typical temperatures of about 4,200°K. Sunspots are quite hot, but when compared with the 6,000°K of the photosphere they are cool enough to appear almost black in photographs taken of the Sun's surface.

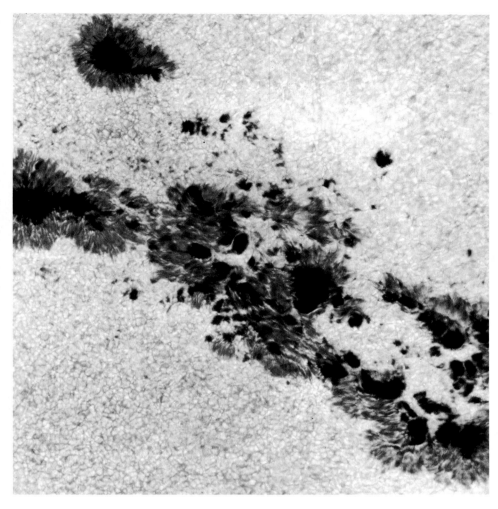

Above: *An enormous group of sunspots stretching across the solar disc. The pattern of granulation representing the tops of convection cells is seen over most of the solar disc, but is inhibited by the strong magnetic fields near sunspots. The prevention of energy supply to these regions by convection means that they are some 1,800°K cooler than the surrounding photosphere and they appear dark.*

Variation of Sunspot Latitudes with Time

At the beginning of each 11-year cycle sunspots appear at high solar latitudes (about ±30°). As the cycle progresses new spots appear at lower latitudes until by the end of each cycle the last spots are seen near the solar equator as the first of the new cycle begin to appear at high latitudes. (Note however that the latitude of any given sunspot or sunspot group remains constant throughout its life.) Sunspots are usually seen in pairs of opposite magnetic polarity: the polarity of the leading spot reverses from one cycle to the next.

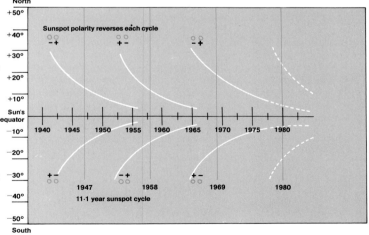

Sun directly, but must measure the vibration of the solar surface by means of light waves, as if we were to watch a bell's ringing by measuring the motions of its surface.

Since the solar oscillations which we see consist of sound waves which have been travelling through the Sun's interior, their frequency or pitch depends on the density and temperature of the gases they have travelled through. Thus, comparison between measured and theoretically calculated frequencies can serve as a check on our model of the Sun.

Study of these oscillations has already paid several dividends. It now seems that the convection zone is deeper than had been believed. In addition, those oscillations which extend all the way to the centre of the Sun do not occur at exactly the expected frequencies, providing additional evidence that our picture of events at the Sun's core is not as precise as we would like. Nevertheless, the basic features of our picture of the Sun's interior are undoubtedly correct. These new observing techniques are helping us to clarify details of the picture, rather than calling into question our notions of underlying design.

Prominences and Flares

Another way in which magnetic fields can affect the appearance of atmospheric gases is by inhibiting the conduction of heat from hot regions to cooler regions. When a region of high magnetic field occurs inside the corona thousands of kilometres above the chromosphere, it is often possible for a cool cloud of gas to be isolated inside this field so it does not disappear due to conduction of heat from the much hotter corona. This explains the existence of solar prominences, some of which can last for weeks before they gradually fade away. Other prominences, such as one that was seen during the Skylab space mission of 1973, suddenly become buoyant and soar upward in a gigantic arch and out into space.

This type of erupting prominence is closely related to the most important and in many ways the most spectacular form of solar activity, the solar flare. During a solar flare, a small region on the surface of the Sun releases a tremendous amount of energy, the equivalent of up to 10 million hydrogen bombs, all within a space of only 30 seconds. The flare energy comes from the destruction of chromospheric magnetic fields, usually in the vicinity of sunspots, and solar physicists believe that most of the flare energy is initially released by the acceleration of powerful beams of subatomic particles such as protons and electrons to very high velocities, much as we do in our giant particle accelerators here on Earth. These particle beams then interact with each other, with the remaining magnetic fields, and with the chromospheric and coronal material to produce a great variety of radiations in the radio, visible, ultraviolet and X-ray parts of the spectrum, and to create shock waves and clouds of solar protons which can travel all the way to the Earth in a few hours. Powerful flares are rare, occuring only a few times per year even during the peak of the sunspot cycle. During the minimum years of the cycle there are almost no flares, because flares depend on the magnetic fields associated with sunspots for their energy.

One of the rarest types of flare is so strong that it can be seen through a normal white-light solar telescope, with no special filters. The first flare ever reported was such a white light flare seen by Richard Carrington in England in 1859. At that early date he was aware of the significance of the fact that the flare was followed a few hours later by variations in the Earth's magnetic field (a geomagnetic storm) and by a bright display of the aurora borealis.

We now know that these effects are caused by clouds of protons from the Sun which hit the Earth's magnetic field. The old theory that the solar particles directly strike the gases in the upper atmosphere causing the auroral glows has been disproved by observations from spacecraft located inside and just above the auroral zones. Instead, perturbations in the Earth's magnetic field caused by the solar particles accelerate protons within the Earth's upper atmosphere, and these protons subsequently produce the aurora.

The photosphere has a temperature of 6,000°K, which is much cooler than the 15

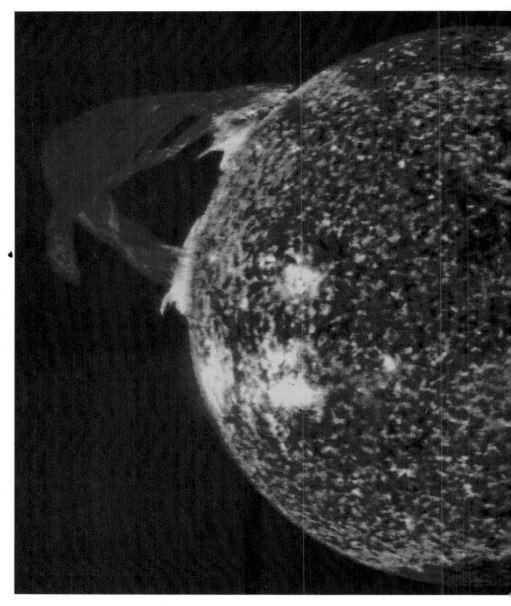

Above: *This giant, twisted prominence was caught in the act of erupting by Skylab's extreme ultraviolet spectroheliograph in 1973. The image was taken in the far ultraviolet light of ionized helium, which occurs over a relatively narrow temperature range near 50,000°K.*

Below: *A brilliant flare near a sunspot throws out gas into space. This picture was taken through a filter which isolates the red spectral line of hydrogen and shows only the chromosphere, the normally invisible region above the solar photospheric disc.*

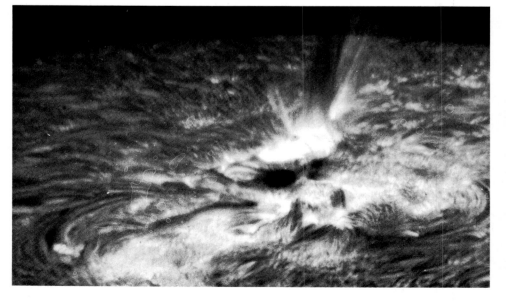

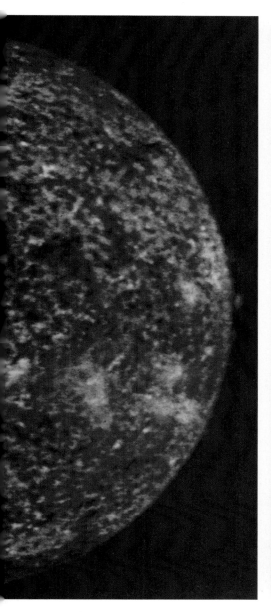

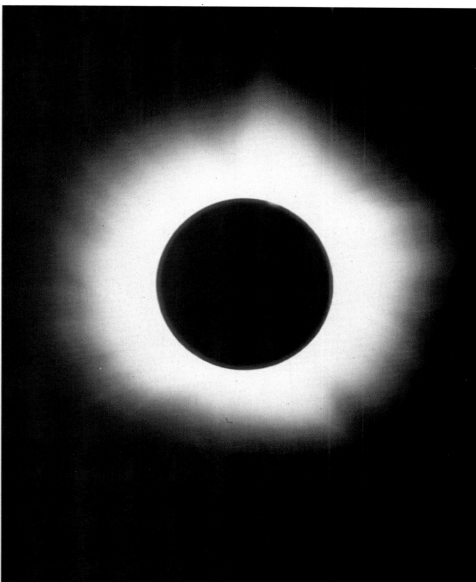

million°K at the Sun's centre, but is still hot enough that no solid particles can exist and all materials are present in their gaseous forms. In addition, almost all molecules are broken up into their constituent atoms, with only a few molecules of carbon monoxide, molecular hydrogen and some exotic species such as cyanogen (CN) present.

Moving upward from the photosphere one would expect that the temperature of the Sun's atmosphere would gradually decline as it has up to this point, but we find that the temperature passes through a minimum of about 4,400°K and then begins to rise.

A layer of gas even hotter than the photosphere lies above the temperature minimum with a predominant temperature close to 7,000°K. This layer is seen during solar eclipses as bright pink in colour due to strong emission from hydrogen gas, and is called the chromosphere from the Greek "chromos", meaning colour. Above the chromosphere is an even hotter region, the solar corona, which extends far out into space.

The Solar Corona

A total eclipse of the Sun is one of the most beautiful and spectacular of all natural phenomena. Observers in the narrow path of totality of an eclipse can, for a few minutes, see the feathery pearly-white glow of the solar corona and the brighter pink layer of the chromosphere shining around the Moon's disc.

In spite of the great impression that an eclipse leaves on the observer, it was not until the early 1800s that any reliable descriptions of the appearance of the corona were recorded, and it was not until 1942 that the true nature of the corona was understood. Before 1942, it was known that the corona emits light in several spectral lines, but none of them matched any of the thousands of lines measured from all the known elements in laboratory spectra up to that time. A common hypothesis was that the corona was made up of an element, "coronium", not found on Earth. This idea may sound far-fetched, but in fact a similar hypothesis had worked well in the case of the element helium. The spectral lines of helium had been seen in the chromosphere during the eclipse of 1868, so the element helium was identified on the Sun and named long before it was found on Earth.

In 1942, however, Bengt Edlen, a Swedish spectroscopist, showed that the spectral lines of the corona came from high temper-

Above: *The solar corona, photographed during a total eclipse at Miahuatlan, Mexico on 7 March 1970. This outstanding phenomenon of nature occurs so rarely that expeditions comprising astronomers from all over the world trek to the eclipse site for its observation.*

ature forms of familiar elements such as iron, calcium and sulphur, where ten or more of the electrons normally surrounding each nucleus had been stripped away by collisions with other electrons. The corona was found to have a temperature of 2 million°K, far higher than the photosphere or chromosphere.

Edlen's discovery immediately posed the question of how such a high temperature could exist in the corona of a star with a surface temperature of only 6,000°. This question and the related problem of the temperature of the chromosphere have inspired much of the research in solar physics during the past 40 years. In the course of this work two principal theories have emerged, which could be called the acoustic hypothesis and the magnetic hypothesis; there are also a few intermediate theories which have both acoustic and magnetic components.

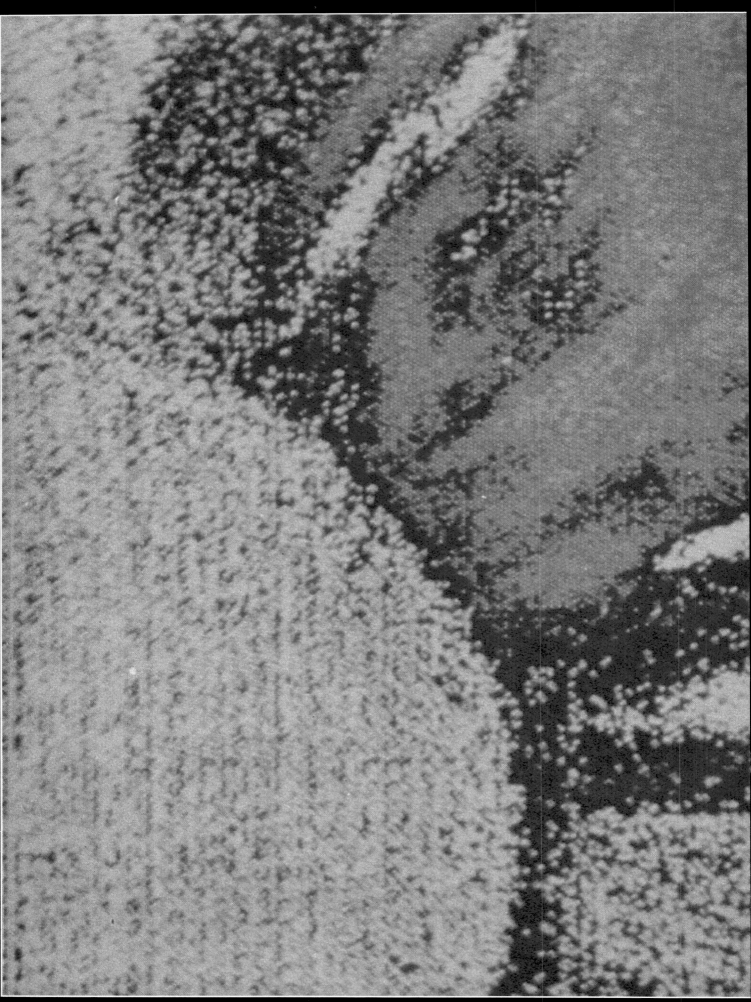

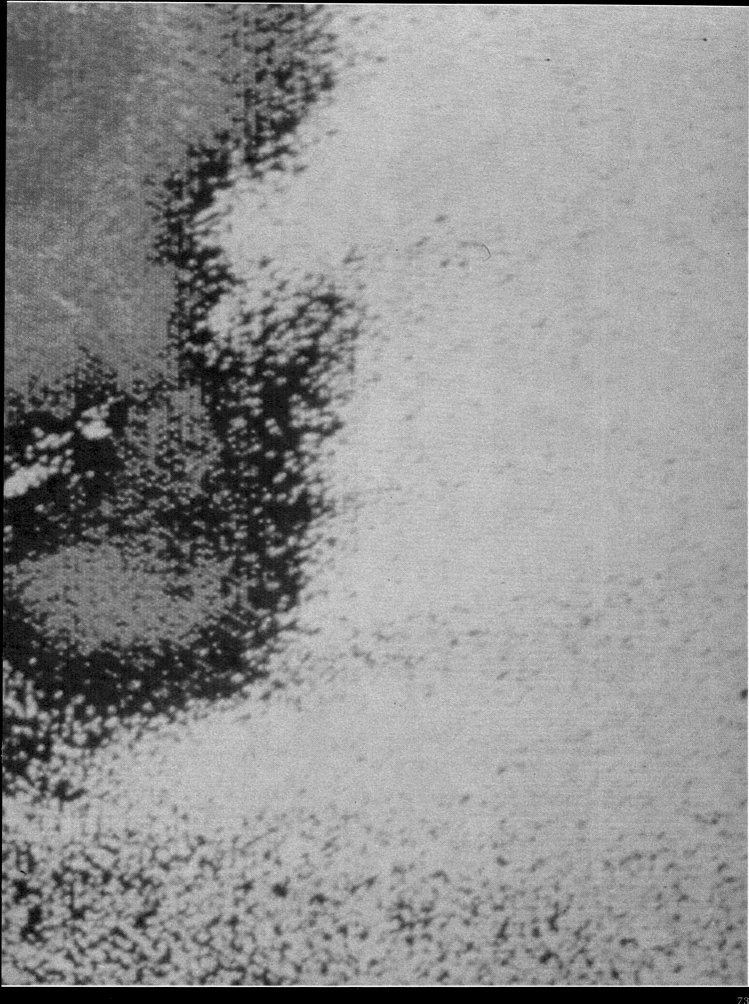

Apollo Telescope Mount (exploded view)
1 Dual X-ray telescope aperture door.
2 Sun-end work station foot restraint.
3 XUV coronal spectro-heliograph aperture door.
4 X-ray spectrographic telescope aperture door.
5 Hydrogen alpha telescope aperture door.
6 Sun-end film tree stowage.
7 Handrail.
8 Clothsline support boom (for EVA transport).
9 Command antenna.
10 Experiment canister.
11 Girth ring.
12 Foot restraints.

13 Astronaut work station.
14 Charger-battery-regulator modules.
15 Film retrieval door.
16 Control moment gyro.
17 Thermal shield.
18 Rack assembly (octagonal structural frame).
19 Command antenna.
20 Telemetry antenna.
21 Solar array wing 1.
22 Radiator.
23 Solar shield.
24 UV scanning poly-chromator/spectro-heliometer aperture door.
25 As 5.
26 White light corona-graph aperture door.
27 Temporary camera storage.

28 As 3.
29 As 3.
30 Fine Sun sensor aperture door.

The Apollo Telescope Mount (ATM), a component of the Skylab space station launched on 14 May 1973, was the first manned astronomical observatory in Earth orbit. Carrying telescopic instruments for solar studies, ATM comprised five main components: a cylindrical experiment canister containing solar astronomy experiments; an attitude pointing and control system (three-axis stabilization and manoeuvring); four solar arrays to convert sunlight into electrical power; an aluminium rack assembly for attaching solar/thermal shields, outriggers, etc; the experiment pointing control system; and a control and display console, located in the Multiple Docking Adapter from which the Skylab astronauts operated the ATM instruments. In addition to ATM solar physics experiments, Skylab was equipped with five for Earth observation, nine in astrophysics, 18 in material science, 12 in

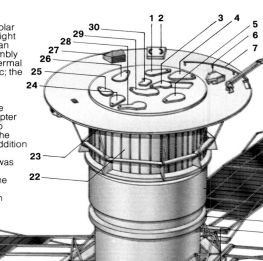
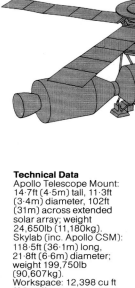

Technical Data
Apollo Telescope Mount:
14·7ft (4·5m) tall, 11·3ft (3·4m) diameter, 102ft (31m) across extended solar array; weight 24,650lb (11,180kg).
Skylab (inc. Apollo CSM): 118·5ft (36·1m) long, 21·8ft (6·6m) diameter; weight 199,750lb (90,607kg).
Workspace: 12,398 cu ft (351m³).
Liftime: 6 years 58 days.

Right: *The solar corona, as seen by the X-ray telescope on Skylab. Sunspot regions show up as bright white, while a large coronal hole (dark) extends from the north polar region past the equator. This was associated with geomagnetic storms.*

Acoustic and Magnetic Theories

The acoustic model of coronal heating is based on the idea that sound waves generated beneath the visible surface of the Sun can propagate upward into the corona and die away there, depositing their wave energy far from the region of wave generation. This idea is especially plausible because one can see abundant evidence of sound waves in the photosphere. For example, the solar oscillations described earlier are themselves sound waves, and it is obvious that the convective bubbles in the photosphere are sources of strong sound waves. Since the solar corona is extremely tenuous (it is actually a better vacuum than any we can create in laboratories on Earth) only a miniscule fraction of the Sun's energy output need be diverted into sound to heat the corona. Unfortunately, attempts to measure the actual upward transport of this wave energy have not been successful. Recent measurements by space instruments have shown that the sound waves do not display the progressive increase in amplitude, or loudness, with increasing height in the chromosphere that the theory predicts.

As an alternative to the acoustic hypothesis, the magnetic hypothesis would have energy released directly inside the corona in the form of miniature solar flares powered by the magnetic fields which permeate the corona everywhere. These "flarelets" are supposed to be so small that they are not individually detectable, so we see only their cumulative heating effect. This theory is attractive because we do see that regions of high magnetic field show elevated coronal temperatures, and it is known that on other stars there is a strong correlation between stellar magnetic fields and coronal emissions. However, our inability directly to observe magnetic energy release makes this theory hard to prove.

The Solar Wind

As mentioned earlier, solar flares emit clouds of particles, mainly protons, which can reach beyond the orbit of the Earth. Even when there are no flares, it has been known for decades that the tails of comets always point away from the Sun, as if they are being pushed backward by some force emanating from the Sun. The very high temperature of the corona provides a natural explanation for this force on comets' tails, since a corona as hot as two million degrees cannot be held down by the Sun's gravity, but will tend to "evaporate" and flow out into space in the form of a *solar wind*.

Mariner 2, the first spacecraft to cross interplanetary space, detected a continuous flow of gas en route to Venus in 1962. The gas was the wind from the Sun which had been theoretically predicted. The flow velocity is high, varying between 250 and 750km/sec, and the density is only about 10 atoms per cm³, or a million times less than the already tenuous lower corona.

In visible light, the corona is far fainter than the underlying photosphere. However, a telescope which can make images in X-rays will show the 2-million-degree corona as much brighter than the far cooler photosphere, and will enable us to see that part of the corona in front of the Sun's disc. Such a telescope was carried on the Skylab space mission in 1973–74 and took many thousands of pictures. These pictures revealed that the corona is not a layer of the Sun's atmosphere, since its shape is completely outlined by magnetic fields which project out of the Sun's surface and which contain the coronal gas within arches, loops, and streamers. Instead the corona consists primarily of hundreds of magnetically confined arches arranged in arcades covering over 90 per cent of the solar surface.

In some regions, however, and usually near the north and south poles of the Sun,

engineering/technology, 19 in the life sciences and 19 proposed by students. X-ray and ultraviolet solar photography, carried out in an airlock on the sunlit side of the Orbital Workshop, provided high-resolution data concerning both the solar disc and corona, and also obtained information on the Comet Kohoutek and the surface of Mercury. The other major solar experiments, housed in the ATM itself, comprised a white light coronagraph, for recording corona activity; an X-ray spectrographic telescope, for photo-graphing solar flares; a UV scanning polychromator spectroheliometer, for recording changes in UV radiation; an X-ray events analyzer/X-ray telescope to chart physical processes in the solar atmosphere; and an extreme ultraviolet spectro-graph-spectroheliograph, for photographing the Sun in UV wavelengths. (Two hydrogen alpha telescopes provided the means for boresight pointing the ATM.) Lastly, there was a magnetospheric particle composition experiment, which by means of a foil collection technique measured the fluxes and composition of magnetospheric ions. The ATM's solar array provided 10·5kW at 55°C for equipment loads and battery-recharging, the average output capacity of the complete system being 3,700W per orbit. A self-contained VHF data system was complemented by a UHF system for ground command. Film used in the ATM was retrieved and replaced by astronauts based in Skylab itself, who performed EVAs outside the station in order to accomplish this.

the X-ray images show virtually no emission from the corona. These regions have been called coronal holes. Close examination of the X-ray images show that coronal holes occur where the lines of magnetic force emerging from the Sun's surface do not form into loops or arches and return into the Sun close by, but instead move directly outward into interplanetary space.

We now believe that much of the gas which eventually leaves the Sun as solar wind comes out through coronal holes, and, in particular, coronal holes are definitely the sources of the highest speed streams in the solar wind, where velocities upwards of 500km/sec are found. A large coronal hole can sometimes persist over several 28-day solar rotations, and can create recurrent disruptions of the geomagnetic field and auroral displays at 28-day intervals as its corresponding high speed solar wind stream strikes the Earth's magnetic field.

Spacecraft Observations

Since 1962, the US National Aeronautics & Space Administration and the European Space Agency have successfully placed in orbit 14 major satellites dedicated to observing the Sun.

The largest was the Solar Observatory aboard the Skylab space station. Its eight solar telescopes, housed in the Apollo Telescope Mount, were full-sized observatory instruments 9·84ft (3m) long, with a total mass of 1,984lb (900 kg).

The Skylab observatory instruments consisted of two X-ray telescopes, an extreme ultraviolet spectroheliograph, a visible light coronagraph, an ultraviolet spectroheliometer and ultraviolet spectrograph and two telescopes which continuously photographed the Sun in the red light of hydrogen and displayed the pictures on a television screen in the Skylab Workshop for the crew. A total of 150,000 exposures were made successfully by this unprecedented array of solar

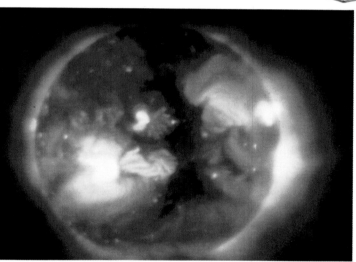

The Inner Solar System
This diagram shows the complex interaction of fields and particles in the inner Solar System. The Earth's magnetosphere (**1**) is blown into a teardrop shape by the solar wind (**3**), a stream of electrically charged particles, which creates a bow wave (**2**). Various phenomena visible are sunspots (**4**), long filaments (**5**) and the corona (**6**). Corona matter is retained in arches (**7**) and streamers (**8**) by magnetic loops extending between areas of opposite polarity. The arches may run into boundary regions (**9**) in the interplanetary magnetic field (**10**). The magnetic field is agitated by many disturbances including Alfven waves (**11**) and shock waves (**12**) produced by flares (**13**). Propagation of solar cosmic radiation occurs in spiral paths in the IMF (**14**). Galactic cosmic radiation (**15**) must penetrate in a similar way. Zodiacal light (**17**) may be regarded as a continuation of the low-intensity corona made by the scattering of light on small dust particles (**16**) that occur in space.

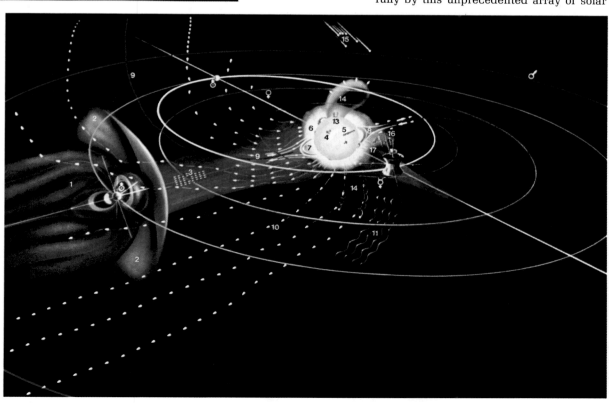

telescopes in space. They were returned to the ground on film by astronaut crews and thus provided more coherent data than satellite imagery sent to ground stations by radio telemetry.

The most recent Sun observer is NASA's Solar Maximum Mission (Solar Max) satellite. With a launch weight of 5,104lb (2,315kg), it is the heaviest of individual solar satellites. It was launched into a 352 mile (566km) equatorial orbit on 14 February 1980 to observe solar flares near the peak of the Sun's 11-year activity cycle. Solar Max was the first spacecraft designed specifically as a flare monitor. It also was the first to be equipped with latches so that it can be retrieved for repair by the Shuttle.

Solar Max carries seven instruments to record flares in the X-ray, ultraviolet and gamma ray as well as the visible light portions of the electromagnetic spectrum. It has sent back pictures and data showing the structure of hundreds of flares. Temperatures up to 1 billion degrees K have been recorded in flares by the satellite which made detailed observations of colliding magnetic fields. The collisions are thought to trigger a flare.

Solar Max found hard X-rays emanating from the footpoints of loop structures in flares, instead of from their prominent arches. The discovery has a bearing on the question of whether the X-rays and the intense energy of solar flares are generated by thermal or non-thermal energy in the form of electron beams at the foot of the loops.

Below: *Two spectrometers aboard the Orbiting Solar Observatory satellite, OSO-8, are checked by an engineer during testing. The satellite was launched on 21 June 1975 from Kennedy Space Center.*

Both Skylab and Solar Max data have shown that prominences which are condensed streams of ionized hydrogen appear to have their source in sunspot groups. The loop configuration suggests that they are controlled by strong magnetic fields.

In addition to looking at the Sun, Solar Max was equipped to measure changes in the intensity of sunlight falling on the top of Earth's atmosphere. Historically, the intensity has been considered unchanging (1,373 watts per square metre) and for that reason the amount reaching the top of the atmosphere has been called the solar constant. However, Solar Max detected minor variations in the solar constant. Whether they are large enough to affect weather and climate on Earth is speculative.

Other discoveries, about the Sun have been made by NASA's seven successful Orbiting Solar Observatories (OSO) between 1962 and 1975. OSO 1, the first dedicated solar monitor, was launched 7 March 1962 with a mass of 595lb (270kg) into a 348 mile (560km) orbit. It and its successor machines have observed solar flares, scanned the solar disc, measured fluctuations in the corona, noted changes in radiation intensities and provided data from which scientists have attempted to define solar-terrestrial relationships.

Comparatively cool polar areas (some observers called them caps) were discovered by the OSOs and confirmed by Skylab's solar telescope. Goddard Space Flight Center reported that the smallest caps were seen at

Below right: *Helios 1, the first of two Sun-observing satellites launched by NASA for West Germany. They monitored the solar wind, interplanetary dust, the IMF and Galactic cosmic rays.*

Solar Maximum Mission
1 Flat crystal spectrometer.
2 Bent crystal spectrometer (**1** and **2** comprise the X-ray polychromator.)
3 Total solar irradiance monitor.
4 Coarse Sun sensor.
5 Hard X-ray imaging spectrometer.
6 White-light coronagraph polarimeter.
7 Fine pointing Sun sensor.
8 Hard X-ray burst spectrometer.
9 Solar gamma ray scintillator.
10 High resolution UV spectrometer and polarimeter.
11 Thermal enclosure.
12 Electronics enclosure.
13 Instruments.
14 Instrument support plate.
15 Transition adapter.
16 Shuttle grapple point.
17 Communications and data handling module.
18 Signal control and conditioning unit.
19 High gain antenna system.
20 Module support structure.
21 Power module.
22 Attitude control subsystem module.
23 Base structure assembly.
24 Solar array.
25 Experiment instrument module.

The Solar Maximum Mission spacecraft (SMM) was launched by NASA on 14 February 1980. It was designed to study solar flares during a peak in the flare cycle. SMM provided the first complete picture of flare build-up. free from the obscuring screen of our atmosphere. It examined solar activity in six different portions of the electromagnetic spectrum from visible light, through UV and X-rays to high-energy gamma rays. Returned data made it clear that flares are related to sunspots, cooler areas that signal the eruption of a local magnetic flux which suppresses heat transport. Flares occur about 5,000 miles (8,000km) above the Sun's surface, and seem to be triggered by the collision of powerful magnetic fields. An eruption creates a dense shock wave in the solar wind. Other scientific data have advanced studies of how solar magnetic fields can contain the super-heated matter of thermonuclear explosions, and provided accurate measurement of the total solar energy "constant". Changes in this value are thought to have a significant effect on the Earth's climate. After about a year in operation, a fuse failure in SMM's attitude control system prevented it from maintaining its fine-pointing mission. A repair mission is due to be flown on the Shuttle flight STS-13 in Summer 1984.

24

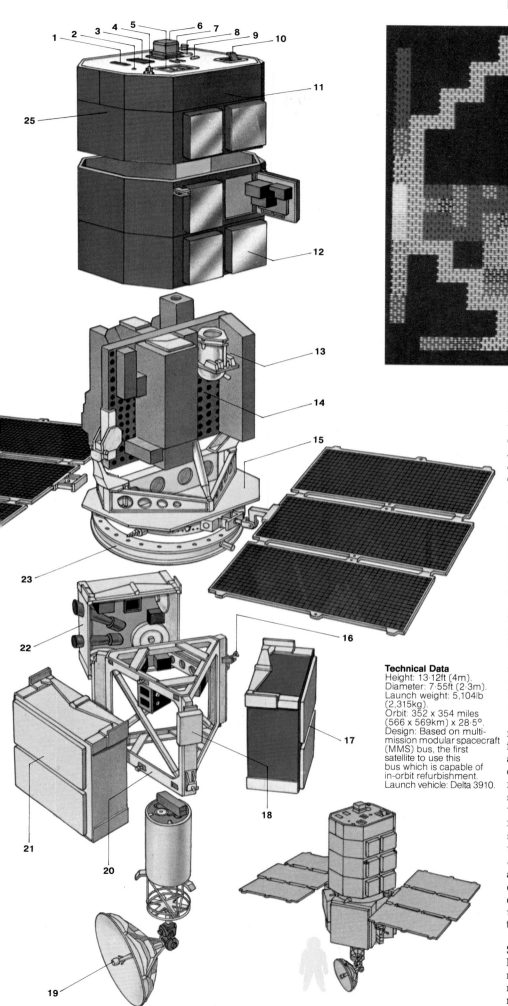

Above: *An image of a solar flare returned by SMM's Hard X-ray Imaging Spectrometer. The Sun is at the top of the picture while the lighter hues indicate hard X-ray emissions from the flare which is bursting 25,000 miles (40,000km) outwards from the Sun. Each picture element (pixel) corresponds to 3,630 sq miles (9,400km²).*

the peak of the solar cycle.

An international programme of solar observation was started in 1977 with the launch of two International Sun–Earth Explorers. ISEE 1, a 750lb (340kg) spacecraft equipped by NASA, and ISEE 2, a 366lb (166kg) spacecraft built by ESA, were launched together by a Delta rocket on 22 October into a highly elliptical orbit around the Earth. The third vehicle in this programme ISEE 3, a 1,034lb (469kg) observer, was launched on 12 August 1978 into a "halo" orbit at a point on the Earth–Sun line at 0·99 million miles (1·6 million km) from Earth, where it was stabilized by the gravitational balance of the Sun and the Earth–Moon system.

The ISEE satellites were instrumented to measure the solar wind, solar magnetic fields and the Earth's magnetic field (ISEE 1 and 2 only), low, medium and high energy cosmic rays, nuclear particles and electromagnetic radiation. Sunward of its sister satellites, ISEE 3, equipped by Goddard, transmitted an early warning of solar magnetic storms during intense episodes of solar flares. The inner satellites measured the intensity of proton and electron fluxes as they swept past the orbits of ISEE 1 and 2, and recorded the effect of the storm on the geomagnetic field. ISEE 1 and 2 carried out continuous measurements of the transient boundaries and discontinuities of the magnetosphere and the solar wind.

In 1974, NASA launched the first of two Sun-observing satellites for West Germany, Helios 1, into a solar orbit at 0·31 Astronomical Units. The 816lb (370kg) machine monitored the solar wind, the interplanetary magnetic field, interplanetary dust and

Technical Data
Height: 13·12ft (4m).
Diameter: 7·55ft (2·3m).
Launch weight: 5,104lb (2,315kg).
Orbit: 352 x 354 miles (566 x 569km) x 28·5°.
Design: Based on multi-mission modular spacecraft (MMS) bus, the first satellite to use this bus which is capable of in-orbit refurbishment.
Launch vehicle: Delta 3910.

Zones of differing density in the solar corona are mapped in false colours in this image generated by Solar Maximum Mission's coronagraph/polarimeter, which is used to study th

Galactic cosmic rays. Helios 2 was launched on 15 January 1976 on a similar mission at 0·29 AU.

In addition to the dedicated solar observatories, other satellites and interplanetary probes have observed the Sun and monitored its particle and electromagnetic emissions. Among them are NASA's Orbiting Geophysical Observatories and advanced TIROS weather satellites which look at the Sun as well as the Earth.

More than 100 satellites including NASA and Soviet lunar and planetary probes have returned data on solar electromagnetic radiation, the solar wind and solar cosmic (high-energy) particle radiation. The most distant report has come from NASA's Pioneer 10 which continued to observe the solar wind as it crossed the great gulf between Uranus and Neptune in the outer reaches of the Solar System.

Solar Effects

The Sun's emissions of atomic particles, of X-rays and of ultraviolet light can change by orders of magnitude during the course of the sunspot cycle, and especially during solar flares. Inasmuch as these emissions affect man's activities on Earth in many ways, an ability to predict flares and other types of solar activity can have considerable economic and military value. At present our predictions are based almost entirely on statistics of past solar behaviour rather than on mathematical calculations of how solar conditions will develop. This situation is similar to that of terrestrial meteorology about 20 years ago, and although solar "meteorology" is undoubtedly more difficult to practise than the terrestrial variety, solar physicists hope that eventually it will be possible to make accurate predictions of solar activity.

What are the terrestrial effects of solar activity? For our purposes they can be conveniently classified as: ionospheric disturbance, particle storms, and weather; each of these categories in turn covers many different phenomena.

Anyone who has listened to distant stations at night on AM radio has been taking advantage of the absorption of solar ultraviolet light in the ionosphere of the Earth. During the day the Sun's radiation causes the ejection of electrons from the atoms in the upper levels of our atmosphere creating ions, and hence the ionosphere. At night most of the ions recombine into atoms, but a layer is left very high in the atmosphere which can reflect radio waves over great distances. At times of strong solar activity the ionosphere can be disturbed, sometimes absorbing radio waves rather than reflecting them, sometimes showing erratic long-distance propagation which fades in and out, and sometimes not reflecting certain waves at all, but allowing them to pass out into space. Many of our communications and radar systems use frequencies which are strongly affected by the ionosphere, and therefore by the Sun.

We have already described how flares can send out sprays of high speed particles which impinge on the Earth's magnetic field, causing geomagnetic storms. Surprisingly, these relatively small variations in the geomagnetic field can have some signi-

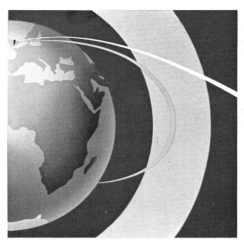

Disruption of Earth Communications by Solar Activity
Long wavelength (low frequency) radio waves can be reflected around the surface of the Earth by charged particles in the ionosphere. Increased solar activity can affect the structure of the ionosphere, destroying its reflective property and disrupting communications.

ficant economic consequences. For example, in several instances field variations have been sufficient to induce large undesired voltages in power lines in northern Canada and have caused power outages over large areas. Due to this experience, the Alaskan pipeline has been designed with a special protective system to ground harmlessly any induced currents. Magnetic naval mines, designed to detect ships by their magnetic disturbances, can sometimes be detonated by naturally occurring magnetic variations; it is reported that during the Vietnam war a large number of mines placed in Haiphong harbour exploded spontaneously after a large solar flare.

Another and potentially far more dangerous aspect of solar flares is the potentially harmful effect of high-speed particles on astronauts in space. Outside the region of protection of the Earth's magnetic field, such as in a geostationary orbit or near the Moon, the particles given off by one flare can sometimes approach or exceed the allowable radiation limits for an unprotected man. Some protection can be provided by the space vehicles, but the dangers must be taken into consideration and the total working times for a whole lifetime for men in the affected high-altitude orbits may have to be limited for safety reasons.

Solar Cycles and our Climate

Sun-weather effects are of course the most interesting type of possible solar-terrestrial interaction to most of us. We now believe that the major ice ages and climate variations on time scales of 40,000 years or longer are due to changes in the Earth's orbital parameters, so these weather influences are not connected with solar activity. On shorter time scales of a thousand years down to a few days, however, evidence has been put forth for many different types of Sun-weather interaction. Some of these claimed correlations are quite convincing, while many others are best considered as only speculation.

Three of the more plausible Sun-weather effects range in time scale from centuries to mere days. Historical records indicate that there were practically no sunspots visible on the Sun between the years 1650 and 1715. It would appear that the solar cycle essentially ceased to exist for this period of 65 years. John Eddy of the High Altitude Observatory in Boulder, Colorado has

Annual Mean Sunspot Number

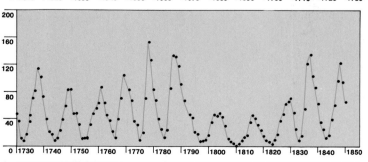

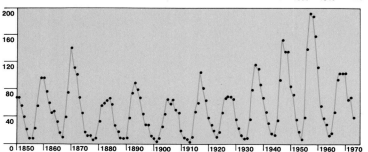

The Sunspot Cycle
The historical record of sunspot numbers shows the prominent 11-year period which was first identified in 1848, and also shows that the sunspot cycle virtually disappeared between 1650 and 1715. Early records, prior to 1840, are not very complete but are good enough that the existence of the Maunder Minimum is well documented. Sunspots are regions of intense magnetic activity and so are evidence of an 11-year period in the changing magnetic field of the Sun. Other phenomena which are associated with the solar magnetic field, such as flare activity, also correlate with the 11-year period. Terrestrial phenomena linked with solar activity, like the "northern lights" or Aurora Borealis and their Southern hemisphere counterparts, the Aurora Australis, are best seen at times of sunspot maximum. Observation of sunspots has given important clues to the nature of the magnetic field in the Sun and solar-type stars but it is still far from well understood. The undoubted importance of magnetic effects on the structure and energy transport of stars means that this is a very important area of research in modern astrophysics.

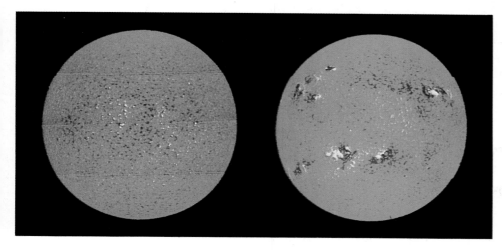

Above: *Comparison of full disc magnetograms of the quiet Sun of 26 January 1976 and the active Sun of 3 January 1978. Yellow indicates positive (north) polarity and blue, negative (south) polarity.*

studied this "Maunder Minimum" (named after a nineteenth century solar astronomer who first pointed it out) and has also discovered several previous episodes of greatly reduced solar activity. He has shown that these periods were all coincident to some degree with decades of colder-than-average climate over many parts of the Earth. Typical cold episodes lasted 50 years, with gaps of a few centuries between them.

On a time scale of individual solar cycles, many studies have claimed to show 11-year periodicity in weather records of various kinds. However, these results must always be treated with scepticism since they are selected from thousands of possible weather histories. In several cases very strong correlations have disappeared in the cycle immediately after an "effect" was discovered. Nevertheless, some periodic weather phenomena may exist. The best known of these is the 22-year recurrence of droughts in the high plains of the western United States, coincident with sunspot minimum following even-numbered solar cycles. Twenty-two years is of course the period of the solar magnetic cycle rather than of sunspot numbers, so this effect could almost certainly be attributed to the magnetic fields in the solar wind which connect the Sun and Earth.

Another type of very short-term weather interaction which has been studied is the effect of solar wind magnetic field orientation on daily weather patterns. John Wilcox and his co-workers at Stanford University have shown that, over a period of many years, the strength of the cyclonic and anticyclonic wind flows in the Earth's middle atmosphere fell quite noticeably during the two days following the passage of an "interplanetary sector boundary". An interplanetary sector boundary is the boundary between a region of space where the solar wind magnetic field points away from the Sun and a region where it points toward the Sun. There are typically about four such boundaries intersecting the Earth's orbit in space, so the Earth crosses one about every seven days. Since high and low pressure systems are the sources of most of our weather, this discovery would seem to show

that the Sun can affect the birth and death of individual storm fronts and fair-weather highs. However, it is still too early for such studies to be used for routine forecasting.

One basic problem with all of the solar-weather interactions proposed so far, unfortunately, is that the actual physical mechanism whereby solar activity modifies our weather has not been determined. Rather, these effects have been simply correlations between observed solar phenomena and observed weather patterns. Finding ways in which the Sun's activity can affect our weather is, in fact, very difficult, since the amount of energy reaching the Earth's lower atmosphere from the solar

Below: *A group of active regions seen near the Sun's limb on 11 September 1973. This ultraviolet image is taken in the light of twice ionized carbon, and shows plasma at a temperature of about 60,000°K.*

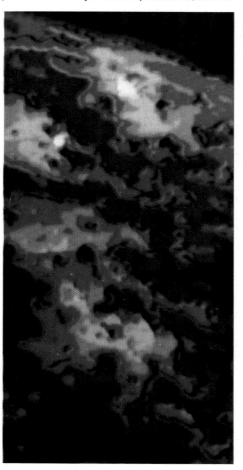

wind and from solar flares is miniscule compared with the energy content of the atmosphere itself. Therefore, some sort of "amplification factor" or "feedback mechanism" must be postulated in order to explain how solar changes can affect the weather.

Another sort of change which would clearly affect the Earth very directly would be variations in the total energy output—i.e. all light and heat—from the Sun. The intensity of the sunlight striking the Earth has been labelled the "solar constant", and the most accurate measurements give its value as 1,373 watts per square metre falling on a surface squarely facing the Sun at the Earth's distance, with a possible error of as much as $20W/m^2$. In fact, however, the solar constant is not constant, but fluctuates slightly. Because these variations are less than 1 per cent and cannot be measured accurately through the Earth's murky atmosphere, it is only within the past few years that observations from spacecraft, such as Solar Max, have reliably shown us how the Sun does vary. Day-to-day variations of 0·2 per cent have been seen, corresponding to a variability of about $3W/m^2$, and there are tentative indications that the Sun's output is about 0·5 per cent lower at sunspot minimum than at sunspot maximum. These levels of variability are too small directly to cause major weather effects, although the correspondence with the solar cycle does agree qualitatively with Eddy's Maunder Minimum hypothesis. Many more years of observation and studies of possible amplification factors are clearly needed.

In comparison with the other stars we see in the sky at night the Sun is average in size and luminosity. In the violence of its flaring and variability it is impressive to us, but nevertheless it is probably well below average, a fact for which we should be grateful, since life would have great difficulty in evolving on planets near very active stars. The Sun and its family of planets form the only true solar system that we know, although we believe that the "averageness" of the Sun would be paralleled by many of its companions in space, and that other stars may have similar arrays of planets. In the following chapters we will take a close look at our Sun's planets and how they have been explored; throughout this journey it is well to keep in mind the many powerful effects that solar radiation can have on planetary atmospheres and surfaces.

RECOMMENDED READING

Fire of Life: The Smithsonian Book of the Sun, Smithsonian Exposition Books, Washington D.C., 1981.

Eddy, John A., *A New Sun: The Solar Results from Skylab,* NASA SP-402, US Government Printing Office, Washington D.C., 1979.

Eddy, John A. (Ed.), *The New Solar Physics,* Westview Press, Boulder, Colorado, 1978.

Frazier, Kendrick, *Our Turbulent Sun,* Prentice-Hall Inc., Engelwood Cliffs, New Jersey, 1982.

Gibson, Edward G., *The Quiet Sun,* NASA SP-303, US Government Printing Office, Washington D.C., 1973.

Harvey, J., Pomerantz, M. and Duvall Jr., T., "Astronomy on Ice", *Sky & Telescope,* Cambridge, Massachusetts, December 1982.

Zirin, Harold, *The Solar Atmosphere,* Blaisdell Publishing Co., Waltham, MA, 1966.

With the invention of space travel, our perception of our environment has been extended beyond the Earth. This is a transition of evolutionary scale, analogous to the emergence of life from the sea.

Since Apollo 11 landed on the Moon in 1969, it has become increasingly evident that the scope of human activity would not be confined much longer to the diminishing resources of a single planet. Rapid development of space transportation technology promises access to the resources of the Solar System. Applied science and technology make it possible to tap the matter and energy of this vast commonwealth as the expanding human population depletes them on Earth.

The prospect has materialized from an era of discovery unrivalled in its impact on the human outlook since the voyages of Columbus and Magellan. Starting with the Mariner 2 fly-by of Venus in 1962, the Solar Commonwealth has been reconnoitred from Mercury to Saturn. Voyager 2 is outbound for encounters with Uranus and Neptune. After 11 years of flight, Pioneer 10 has crossed the known frontier of the Solar System and has entered interstellar space.

Within two decades, United States and Soviet spacecraft have accomplished the preliminary exploration of six of the commonwealth's nine planets and of 37 of its 45 known moons. Evolutionary processes common in varying degree to the inner, terrestrial-type planets were revealed on the Moon by six United States manned expeditions and by the robotic landers and orbiters of the United States and the Soviet Union.

The first men on the Moon and the machines that analyzed its surface and sounded its depths discovered a partially evolved planet. It exhibited the processes of accretion, melting, recrystallization and differentiation which produced the typical "shells" of terrestrial-type planets: the crust, the mantle and the core. The identification of lunar resources by analysis of the rocks and fines and by remote sensing from orbit has shown a potential for industrial development on the Moon.

With it massive carbon dioxide atmosphere and blast-furnace heat, Venus presents an horrendous vision of what Earth might have become as the result of a runaway "greenhouse" effect. Yet, Venus bears resemblance to Earth, not only in size and density, but in topography. Piercing the dense cloud cover, radar surveys have revealed continental-size massifs, oceanic-type basins and volcanic mountains. Like Earth also, Venus has thunderstorms.

Mercury, as expected, presents a densely cratered surface, like that of the Moon, dominated by the great Caloris basin, a feature that appears to confirm the catastrophic bombardment of the inner Solar System 3·9 thousand million years ago. That event was first identified on the Moon.

Further evidence of a catastrophic era of accretion, a great "sweeping up" of smaller bodies of meteoroid or asteroid size by the planets, was found on Mars. The discovery of ancient, fluvial valleys on the Red Planet renewed hope of finding evidence of life on Mars, an expectation nearly abandoned by the results of earlier reconnaissance. Martian topography proved to be spectacular, with massive volcanic mountains dwarfing those of Earth and a rift valley system of continental extent. The attempt to find evidence of life on Mars with automated biological laboratories in two Viking landers has remained enigmatically inconclusive.

Somewhere on the scale of cosmic evolution between a planet and a star, Jupiter was found to be composed mainly of hydrogen in gaseous, liquid and metallic states, with a core of heavy elements estimated at several Earth masses. Its rapid rotation and internal structure generated a powerful magnetic field. Jupiter was found to be emitting more heat than it receives from the Sun. With its four large (Galilean) satellites and 12 smaller ones, it presents the aspect of a secondary Solar System. In common with Saturn and Uranus, Jupiter exhibited rings. Its large moon, Io, was linked to Jupiter by a 10 million ampere electrical current generated by the moon's passage within the Jovian magnetic field. Equally surprising was the discovery of erupting volcanoes on Io, the only body beyond Earth where active volcanism has been found.

Like Jupiter, Saturn was found to be a liquid planet with a core of heavy elements and an inner shell of metallic hydrogen. Long-lived white ovals in its atmosphere are similar to those in the Jovian atmosphere, apparently storm systems, although Jupiter's Great Red Spot, a semi-permanent hurricane in the planet's southern hemisphere, was not duplicated on Saturn.

The magnifence of Saturn's seven great ring systems was beautifully recorded by Pioneer and Voyager spacecraft. Details of the rings' structure revealed their intricate composition of ringlets, spokes, tiny "shepherding" moons and icy and rocky particles. By 1983, examination of Voyager photographs revealed 18 satellites. The largest, Titan, of planetary size, exhibited a nitrogen atmosphere 60 per cent denser than that of Earth (78 per cent nitrogen). Titan has so fascinated planetologists that a committee of them has proposed sending a probe there.

Reconnaissance of the planets and their moons has not only enlarged our perception of the Commonwealth of Sol but has provided new insights into the processes which shaped the Earth, which change it and affect its atmosphere and climate. Interplanetary exploration has enhanced our understanding of our planet — of its uniqueness as an abode of life within the Solar System.

The Origin of the Solar System

Evidence derived from astrophysics, meteorite studies and the composition of planets, moons and asteroids indicates that the Solar System evolved from a supernova explosion 4,500 million years ago in a star-forming cloud of interstellar gas and dust. Shock waves from the explosion compressed fragments of the cloud. Each of them collapsed into a flattened disc in which large scale turbulence pumped angular momentum outwards and mass inwards. These motions were driven by internal heating of the nebula generated by the energy of gravitational collapse.

Within the nebula, dust grains collided and accreted to form larger grains. Accretions grew to asteroid size in thousands of years. After the Sun ignited and dispelled the nebular gas, many of the asteroid-size bodies grew to lunar size within millions of years. As this process continued, the planets formed. Their evolution was circumscribed by three initial conditions: chemical composition, mass, and distance from the Sun.

First Theories

The problem of the origin of our Solar System has been of great interest to scientists since the times of Immanuel Kant (1724–1804) and Pierre-Simon Laplace (1749–1827). An immense range of theories has been proposed, many with little or no detailed correspondence with observations. The advent of the age of space exploration in the 1960s has increased the flow of data by about a factor of a thousand, and has made possible the study of a wide range of

Above: *The German philosopher/scientist Immanuel Kant. The "nebular" hypothesis of the origin of the Solar System proposed by Kant and Laplace is still thought to be substantially correct.*

Right: *The spiral galaxy NGC 2997 is inclined at about 45° to our line of sight, revealing its internal structure. The two spiral arms are peppered with bright red areas of ionized hydrogen which are similar to regions of star formation in our own Milky Way.*

Below: *United States Naval Observatory photograph of the Milky Way running through the constellation Sagittarius. We are here looking towards the Galactic centre.*

phenomena which were previously wholly inaccessible to Earth-based observations. It is scarcely surprising, then, that the range of allowable speculation about the origin of the Solar System has been considerably narrowed. For this reason, our present attention can be focussed upon a relatively narrow range of surviving theories, and we will not attempt to review in detail the history of earlier ideas.

The present view of the origin of the Solar System is a direct descendant of the nebular hypothesis originally proposed by Immanuel Kant, and later developed in detail by Laplace: both envisioned the collapse of a dense cloud of gas and dust into a flattened disc. The Sun then formed in the centre of the disc, while the planets grew from dust aggregations further from the centre. This

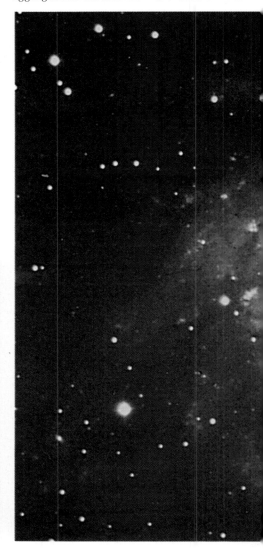

"In the centre of everything is the Sun. Nor could anyone have placed this luminary at any other, better point in this beautiful temple, than that from which it can illuminate everything uniformly."

Nicolaus Copernicus, *On the Revolutions of the Celestial Spheres*

theory has gained support in the intervening centuries, and is now favoured by the large majority of all scientists who work on this problem. However, the passage of time has brought its surprises: there is now strong evidence that the process postulated by Kant and Laplace was triggered by a nearby supernova explosion, which left evidence in the form of odd isotopic abundance patterns in some of the most ancient meteorites.

Three independent lines of evidence relate to the origin of stellar systems: firstly, astrophysical evidence bearing on the conditions in star-forming regions; secondly, a vast literature on the laboratory study of meteorite samples regarding the conditions at their places of formation, at the very beginning of Solar System history; finally, evidence for systematic composition, tem-perature and pressure trends in the early Solar System as reflected in the density, bulk composition, oxidation state, and volatile-element content of a wide range of large Solar System bodies.

A substantial proportion of the astrophysical and planetary data have become available as a result of spacecraft investigations. Further, many of the most exciting and revealing results of meteorite research owe their existence to highly specialized instrumental analysis techniques developed to study the Apollo lunar surface samples.

Astrophysical Evidence

Most stars, for most of their lifetimes, derive their energy from the fusion of hydrogen nuclei to make helium (see page 64). Such stars are the most commonly seen in space, and lie along a narrow band on a diagram of luminosity vs. temperature: the faintest of these Main Sequence (MS) stars have luminosities less than one ten thousandth of that of the Sun, masses of a few per cent of the Sun's, and surface temperatures under 2,500°K. These are commonly called red dwarfs. The brightest of the MS stars have masses which may range up to more than 200 solar masses, with luminosities of several million times that of the Sun and temperatures of tens of thousands of degrees. Some of these stars may be more massive than the upper limit for static hydrogen stars calculated from theory. The massive stars radiate most of their energy as ultraviolet light.

Since the amount of energy liberated by hydrogen fusion is well known, it is easy to

calculate how long it would take for any MS star to "burn" all its nuclear fuel. Detailed calculations on the evolutionary histories of stars further permit an estimate of what fraction of the mass of hydrogen fuel in each star may actually be consumed by fusion reactions.

It has been found that red dwarfs may have MS (hydrogen-burning) lifetimes of up to 10^{12} years, while spendthrift highmass MS stars may burn all their fuel in less than 100,000 years. The fate of a massive star which has evolved beyond the hydrogen-burning phase is well understood: such a star will rush through a series of nuclear fusion processes involving helium, carbon, oxygen, silicon, etc, terminating in a cataclysmic explosion which will disperse the fresh products from these fusion reactions into space at a few per cent of the speed of light. Obviously, if highly luminous MS stars are seen in some region of space, then they must have been formed in the last 100,000 years. The age of our Galaxy is close to 10 thousand million years, and thus star formation must still be going on today.

A similar conclusion applies to the highly-evolved, non-MS stars, the giants and supergiants, which derive most of their energy from fusion of elements heavier than hydrogen. Studies of stellar evolution consider such manifestations as the latest evolutionary phases of the most massive MS stars. Thus we may also conclude that giant and supergiant stars should be found only in and near regions of active star formation.

Yet another relatively rare class of stars can be found in the spiral arms of our galaxy. They are distinguished by modest excesses of luminosity over MS stars of the same colour, and are named T-Tauri stars after the first star of this type to be identified. In addition to their slightly higher luminosity, T-Tauri stars emit an extremely dense stellar wind which carries a total energy flux comparable to their luminosity. Very recently it has been found that a number of the nearest T-Tauri stars have ultraviolet emissions several thousand times that of the Sun. Both the UV and solar wind emissions apparently arise from a very dense corona excited by turbulence or sound waves generated in the lower atmosphere of the star. These T-Tauri stars also have a strong tendency to occur in clusters, and, like the giant, supergiant, and upper MS star populations, they are found in spiral arms but not in gas- and dust-free globular clusters.

The most striking feature of the spatial distributions of these unusual stars is that they are all correlated with each other; they are all found in or around galactic ("open") star clusters which are observed to be expanding and dispersing at a great rate.

The T-Tauri stars tend to be found near the centres of these clusters, the highly luminous MS stars form an expanding shell about the clusters, and the brightest giant and supergiant stars form a rapidly expanding halo about the others. Even more intriguing is the observation that these clusters are centred on dense, chaotic clouds of interstellar gas and dust.

These associations suggest strongly that the dense interstellar clouds spawn young T-Tauri stars which have not yet settled down as well-behaved MS stars. Stars are formed with a wide range of masses; small protostars progress to the red end of the Main Sequence and stay there for a trillion years, while very massive protostars form upper MS stars, evolve through their MS lifetimes, enter the giant and supergiant phases, and destroy themselves by supernova explosions within 100 thousand to a million years.

Since the rates of expansion and dispersal of young galactic clusters will dissipate them completely within 10 to 100 million years, we must conclude that the most violent supernova explosions will tend to occur in the immediate vicinity of star-forming regions, where nearest-neighbour interstellar distances are very small.

Right: *NGC 6589/90, a region of dust and gas in Sagittarius. Our view of the centre of the Galaxy is obscured by huge clouds of such interstellar dust in the direction of the constellation Sagittarius. Light from hot stars within the dust produces the two bright reflection nebulae, known as NGC 6589 and NGC 6590.*

Interstellar Molecules
Fifty-three different molecules have now been identified in interstellar space. Question marks beside four others represent tentative indentifications. They vary in complexity from the host of diatomic molecules seen at left to cyanopentaacetylene at right, which comprises 13 component atoms. With the exception of molecular hydrogen, each accounts for less than 0·1 per cent of the mass of a typical giant molecular cloud complex. Some of these are molecules common on the Earth; others, such as the long cyanoacetylene chains, have never been detected in terrestrial laboratories. Each molecule is identified by its characteristic spectral signature in the radio region.

The space between stars is neither empty nor homogeneous. In fact, a wide range of temperature and density conditions are found in the interstellar medium (ISM). Most of the volume of interstellar space is filled by extremely hot, tenuous gas clouds dominated by ionized hydrogen and helium. These are called H II regions by astronomers, but would better be described as ionized regions. Most of the remaining volume (and most of the mass) of the ISM is found in cooler, denser clouds (H I regions), dominated by atomic H, at temperatures of the order of 1,000°K. There are also extremely dense, cold (< 100K; < −170C) gas and dust clouds dominated by molecular H2 and other molecular species. The spatial distri-

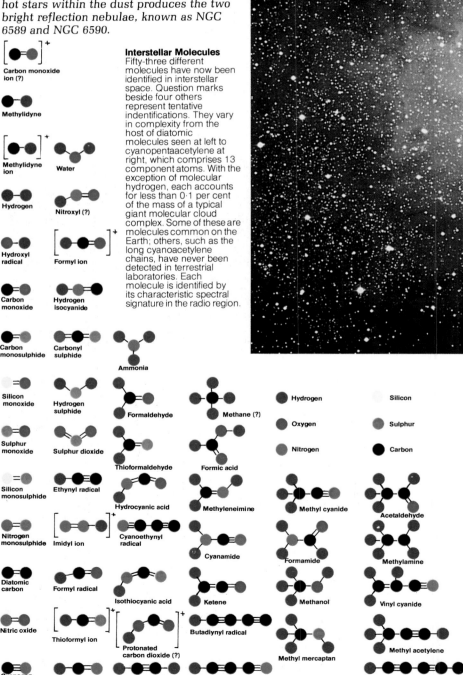

bution of these regions is provocative: the ionized gases form immense spheroidal "bubbles" in the cooler neutral gas, and the dense molecular clouds form clumps, strings, and irregular clusters within the cool gas.

With the development of highly sensitive radio telescopes it became possible to detect a large number of sharp lines in the microwave region, due to rotational transitions by diatomic molecules (containing two atoms) and polyatomic molecules (containing multiple atoms) in dense interstellar clouds. Although limited by the unavailability of laboratory data on many species of interest, this technique has nonetheless documented the presence of several dozen molecular species in dense, cold clouds. Among these

species is a wide range of organic molecules, including hydrocarbons, nitriles, alcohols, carboxylic acids, and aldehydes.

The cooler and denser regions of the ISM also are populated by a variety of structures which are poorly understood and difficult to observe, such as Bok globules and Herbig-Haro objects, which are interstellar clouds of gas and dust. In Herbig-Haro objects young stars emitting infra-red radiation appear to be embedded. Some of these objects appear to be compact, dense clouds about the same size as the Solar System, cold (< 100°K) on the outside and warm (> 1,000°K) in their interiors.

By far the most easily observed region of present-day star formation is the Orion

Nebula, with its rich complex of dense clouds and young stars. Perhaps the most pervasive impression is the extreme complexity of the distribution and motions of its component matter. Uniformly contracting, non-rotating spherical gas clouds are certainly not in evidence.

Meteorite Evidence

A great gap exists between astronomical observations of faint, distant interstellar clouds and the earliest surviving evidence from meteorites. This gap can at present only be bridged by hypotheses which are difficult to test except by reference to these two bodies of evidence. It is likely that a variety of mutually contradictory hypotheses could be proposed to bridge that gap.

The principal role of meteorite study is to unravel information on the composition, temperature, and pressure in the pre-solar nebula at the time of formation of the Sun, planets, and small bodies. This information is largely derived from studies of the composition of meteorites; since the vapour pressures of possible minerals span a vast range, a list of the abundances of the elements in a meteorite contains a wealth of data on the temperature at which the meteorite formed. Materials formed in the pre-solar nebula at high temperatures (near 1,400°K) are refractory minerals, rich in oxides of calcium, aluminium, titanium, etc. At ~1,200°K, metallic iron-nickel alloy and magnesium silicates dominate the assemblage of stable minerals. Below ~ 1,000°K sodium and potassium feldspar are stable, and below 680°K the mineral troilite, FeS, also forms. Metallic iron disappears by oxidation to FeO below ~ 500°K. Hydroxyl silicates such as serpentine are possible below ~350°K. A number of moderately volatile elements with condensation temperatures below 900°K help fill in the temperature scale.

The first and most general lesson to be learned from the study of meteorites is that iron sulphide is ubiquitous and FeO nearly ubiquitous in primitive (non-igneous) meteorites. Hydroxyl silicates occur in the rare class of carbonaceous chondrites, a type of

Structure of the Interstellar Medium (ISM)
About half of the mass of a galaxy like the Milky Way is contained not in stars but in interstellar material. Most of interstellar space is filled by hot, tenuous gas clouds dominated by ionized hydrogen and helium (H II regions, pink areas in diagram). Most of the mass of the ISM is in the form of relatively cool (1,000°K), denser

regions of neutral hydrogen (H I regions, blue areas in diagram) concentrated in the spiral arms. Within the H I clouds are yet denser clouds of molecular gas and dust (black), the dust shielding the molecular gas, mainly H₂, from destruction by interstellar radiation. These cool molecular clouds are closely linked with the process of star formation.

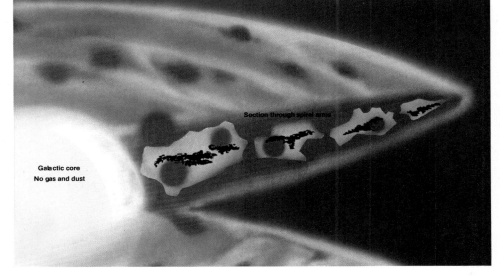

Galactic core
No gas and dust

Section through spiral arms

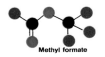

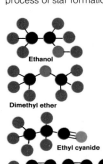

Methyl formate

Ethanol

Dimethyl ether

Ethyl cyanide

Cyanotriacetylene

Cyanotetraacetylene

Cyanopentaacetylene

Above: *A 17·5lb (7·95kg) meteorite found in the Elephant Moraine area of East Antarctica. It has been classified as a Shergottite, a type of stony meteorite of probably planetary rather than asteroidal origin. Isotopic analysis suggests that the meteorite originated in a Martian volcanic region.*

Right: *This meteorite fragment with a mass of 1·09oz (31g) was found by a research team in the Allen Hills area of East Antarctica in 1981-82. Identified as an anorthositic breccia, in mineral structure it closely resembles rocks found in the Descartes highlands on the Moon by the Apollo 16 expedition in 1972.*

stony meteorite composed largely of silicate grains or chondrules. However, these may be of secondary, not nebular, origin. Formation temperatures ranging from 650° down to ~ 350°K are found. However, all the known meteorites with formation temperatures below about 450°K belong to the carbonaceous chondrite family; they are rich in organic matter, magnetite, water-soluble salts, and claylike minerals strongly suggestive of formation in the presence of liquid water within an asteroidal parent body. All the other meteorites which have primitive, unmelted textures and tiny bead-like inclusions of glass (called chondrules) contain at least a trace of native metallic iron-nickel alloy. These primitive chondrule-bearing meteorites are called chondrites.

Once formation conditions of various chondrite classes are deduced in this manner, it would be very useful to know where and when these conditions obtained. The answer to the "when" question can be answered by a variety of radiochemical dating techniques. It is found that the primitive meteorites all formed about 4,500 million years ago, within a time interval no longer than 100 million years.

This date represents the time of the last chemical interaction between meteoritic solids and nebular gas, presumably immediately prior to the dissipation of the gaseous nebula and the accretion of the terrestrial planets. However, we see a clear breakdown of the primitive chondritic meteorites into several classes with distinctly different formation temperatures.

It is reasonable to suppose that these classes formed at different heliocentric distances. But where did they form? It seems very likely that the orbits pursued by these meteorites immediately prior to their landings on Earth were closely similar to the orbits of Earth-crossing asteroids. It therefore is important to examine the compositions of Earth-crossing and Belt asteroids in order to compare them to the various classes of chondritic meteorites.

The second main kind of evidence provided by meteorites concerns the availability of heat sources to drive the internal evolution of planets. The most familiar of these sources are the long-lived (~ 1 billion-year half-life, i.e. the time it takes half the radioactivity to decay) radioactive isotopes of potassium (K), uranium (U), and thorium (Th); ^{40}K, ^{235}U, ^{238}U, and ^{232}Th. In addition, a few of the carbonaceous chondrites contain highly refractory calcium- and aluminium-rich inclusions (CAI's) which bear the signature of the decay of an extinct short-lived (~ 1 million-year half-life) radioisotope of aluminium, ^{26}Al.

The presence of ^{26}Al in the early Solar System is significant. Since the half-life for ^{26}Al decay is only 0·7 million years, its presence in meteoritic solids requires that those solids were formed within about two million years of the time of synthesis of ^{26}Al. That synthesis, of course, took place in a supernova explosion. Therefore, the origin of the Solar System and that supernova explosion must have occurred within a time interval of less than about 2 million years at about 4,500 million years in the past. It would be most unreasonable to suppose that such a coincidence was accidental. It seems more likely that either the supernova explosion triggered the formation of the Solar System, or that the explosion and the formation of the Solar System were both caused by the collapse and evolution of a dense, massive interstellar cloud.

Such a collapse would result in the formation of 100 to 100,000 stars with a wide range of masses, most of them forming over a time interval of about 1 million years. The most massive of these stars will evolve to the supernova stage while stellar formation is still going on nearby.

Nebulae present in this environment would experience very intense ultraviolet irradiation from nearby newly-formed T-Tauri stars and highly luminous, hot stars on the high-mass end of the Main Sequence, in addition to severe shock-wave processing by nearby supernovae.

Planetary Evidence

The first suggestion that conditions in the early Solar System might have caused systematic compositional trends in the planets was that of Harrison Brown 30 years ago. He pointed out that the small, dense, rocky planets close to the Sun gave way to even smaller ice + rock bodies further from the Sun, with the Jovian planets (Jupiter, Saturn, Uranus and Neptune) attaining compositions almost as rich in volatile elements as the Sun itself. The simplest interpretation of these composition classes is that small bodies close to the Sun were too warm for the condensation of ices.

This idea can be tested somewhat more rigorously by considering the densities of Solar System bodies in detail. It is known, for example, that Mercury has the highest intrinsic (uncompressed) density of any planet. Venus and Earth have the next

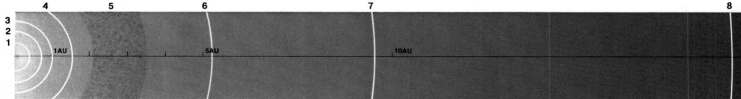

highest intrinsic densities (4·4 gm/cm³), and Mars is yet lower (3·7gm/cm³). Only three asteroids have even approximately known densities, and they appear to be in the range 2·4 to 3·5gm/cm³. The four large Galilean satellites of Jupiter follow a clear density trend, dropping from ~ 3·4gm/cm³ to ~ 1·4gm/cm³ (uncompressed) with increasing distance from Jupiter. The satellites of Saturn appear to cluster near 1·2gm/cm³ (and Pluto has a density close to 1·0.)

A considerably larger body of compositional data derives from photometric and spectroscopic studies of over 250 asteroids. It has been found that the most common types of meteoritic material falling on Earth, the metal-bearing "ordinary" chondrites, are rare or absent in the asteroid belt. Instead, the belt contains several broad and overlapping compositional bands of asteroids, generally dominated by carbonaceous chondrites. Igneous meteorite types, such as stony irons, irons, and achondrites (i.e. without chondrites), are found to be fairly common near the innermost edge of the belt,

while very volatile-rich materials analogous to but more extreme than the carbonaceous chondrites are found near the outer edge of the belt.

The achondrites, characterized by tightly crystallized igneous minerals and almost complete loss of liquid metal-sulphide melt, are apparently complementary to the iron and stony iron meteorites, with all three classes produced by melting of asteroid-sized parent bodies. The presence of these density-separated classes near the inner edge of the asteroid belt shows that the early stages of planetary evolution, with melting, density-dependent differentiation, and outgassing of volatile elements occurred there, but not farther from the Sun.

These observations serve to demonstrate the strong dependence of the composition of undifferentiated solid material on distance from the Sun. The place of origin of the carbonaceous chondrites seems well established; almost anywhere in the asteroid belt. The "ordinary" chondrites, however, are found to be vanishingly rare; apparently the

belt was too cold for metallic iron to be there. If they are in fact derived from Earth-crossing asteroids, as seems very likely from dynamical arguments, the problem is not solved, merely deferred; the Earth-crossers encounter the terrestrial planets so frequently that they have very short life expectancies.

An average Earth-crosser cannot expect to survive longer than a few tens of millions of years, or about 1 per cent of the age of the Solar System. Why then do we have any Earth-crossers today? Studies of the orbital evolution of small bodies show that asteroids from particular parts of the belt, and comets with particular types of orbits, may be perturbed by gravitational interactions with the planets so as to place them in Earth-crossing orbits. It appears that the present orbits of these asteroids cannot be traced back unambiguously to their ultimate place of origin. This prevents a clear comparison being made between their formation conditions and those of other meteorites, the planets, and their satellites.

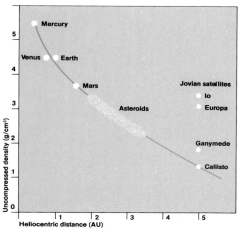

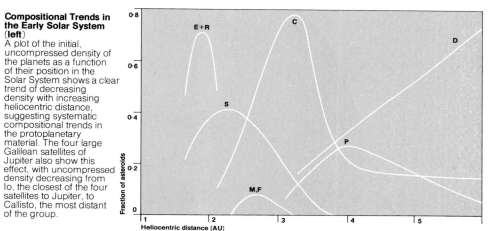

Compositional Trends in the Early Solar System (left)
A plot of the initial, uncompressed density of the planets as a function of their position in the Solar System shows a clear trend of decreasing density with increasing heliocentric distance, suggesting systematic compositional trends in the protoplanetary material. The four large Galilean satellites of Jupiter also show this effect, with uncompressed density decreasing from Io, the closest of the four satellites to Jupiter, to Callisto, the most distant of the group.

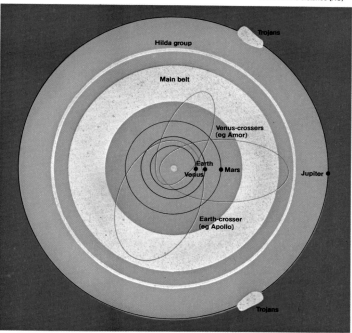

Heliocentric Planetary Distances (below)
1 Mercury.
2 Venus.
3 Earth.
4 Mars.
5 Asteroid belt.
6 Jupiter.
7 Saturn.
8 Uranus.
9 Neptune.
10 Pluto.

The scale drawing at bottom illustrates the relative semi-major axes of the orbits of the planets. Nearer the Sun we find the so-called "terrestrial" planets Mercury, Venus, the Earth and Mars, which are small, dense, rocky bodies. Outside the asteroid belt is the realm of the Jovian planets, which have substantial ice mantles and are rich in volatile elements. The different compositions of the planets give important clues towards the determination of conditions in the early Solar System at the time of formation of the planets.

Asteroid Orbits (left)
The majority of asteroids travel in orbits of relatively low eccentricity between about 2·2 and 3·5 astronomical units from the Sun, forming the "asteroid belt" shown left as a wide orange band. The belt lies between the orbits of Mars and Jupiter. A much smaller group (the Hilda group) orbit at about 4 AU, in a position of dynamical resonance with the orbit of Jupiter. For similar dynamical reasons asteroids are also found at the so-called Lagrangian points, in the same orbit as Jupiter but either preceding or following the planet by some 60°. These are known as the Trojan asteroids. A small number of minor planets have highly eccentric orbits which at perihelion bring them inside the orbits of the Earth or Venus. Three examples are shown in the diagram. Of these, one is an Earth-crosser, like the asteroid Apollo; the other two are, like Amor, Venus-crossers.

Composition of Asteroids (above)
Information on the composition of asteroid material can be derived from measurement of their albedos (reflectivities) and spectral characteristics. These show that the asteroid belt is highly structured in composition. The distribution of the various compositional types is found to vary systematically with heliocentric distance. Distinct peaks in the compositional types E,R,S,M,F,C,P and D are found at distances ranging from 1·8 to 5·2 astronomical units. The inferred composition of the asteroids in each radial region is consistent with the theory that they accreted from the solar nebula at or near their present locations. Of the more important types C asteroids resemble carbonaceous chondrites, S asteroids are "stony" and the D type are probably "super-carbonaceous" material.

9

10

The prediction that the asteroid belt would be found to be dominated by carbonaceous chondrites was made in 1970, by the author and others, at a time when only a single asteroid reflection spectrum—a means of determining chemical structure by reflected light—was available. Curiously, that asteroid, Vesta, was found to have a spectrum of chemical elements indistinguishable from that of laboratory samples of basaltic achondrites, a class of igneous (differentiated) meteorites. Today, with spectral data on over 250 asteroids available, Vesta is still unique! The significance of the presence of small differentiated asteroids in the belt is unclear because they may be fragments of larger bodies which were disrupted by collisions.

Vesta, however, is a large asteroid, and no apparent Vesta-like debris of smaller asteroids can be found near its orbit. It is clear that Vesta somehow managed to differen-

tiate despite its mass, which is entirely negligible on the scale of true planetary bodies. The heat released by the decay of long-lived radionuclides (radioactive elements) cannot melt Vesta because it is so small that, over billions of years, heat leaks out and is lost to space rather than accumulating to cause melting.

There are close chemical similarities (and some distinctive differences) between the basaltic achondrites and the basin basalts on the Moon. After the Apollo 11 lunar landing in 1969 it was at first thought that early melting of the Moon was caused by rapid accretion of the Moon from small bodies, perhaps in a time as short as 30 to 100 years. This seemed implausible to many scientists, and the discovery that Vesta had a similar basaltic surface confirmed their scepticism. Vesta is so small that even

instant accretion would liberate only enough heat to raise its temperature 40 degrees. Thus a heat source other than long-lived radionuclides or accretion heating must have melted Vesta; possibly also the Moon.

T-Tauri Phase Heating

Two other possible heat sources were available in the early Solar System. One, was the decay of the short-lived radionuclide ^{26}Al. The other was heating by the T-Tauri phase superluminous Sun. We not only expect such a stage in the early evolution of the Sun from theory and from observations of other young stars, but we also see direct evidence for it in the abundance patterns of rare gases implanted in very high concentrations in some meteorites.

Relative Sizes of the Planets
1 Mercury.
2 Venus.
3 Earth and Moon.
4 Mars.
5 Jupiter.
6 Saturn.
7 Uranus.
8 Neptune.
9 Pluto.

A Io.
B Europa.
C Ganymede.
D Callisto.
E Titan.
F Triton.

The relative sizes of the planets and their major satellites are here compared with a segment of the solar disc, drawn to the same scale. A sunspot group and a giant solar prominence seen above the solar surface are also shown to scale. The planetary satellites (A-F) together with the Earth's Moon are all those satellites in the Solar System which are larger

The dense T-Tauri solar wind carried enough energy to induce strong electric currents in the interiors of weakly conducting bodies. Ohmic heating then would rapidly warm them to the melting point. Observations of numerous T-Tauri stars suggest that they settle down to the Main Sequence in about 10 million years, and this heat source must accordingly die out within the same time period. The ability of an asteroid to extract energy from the solar wind depends sensitively on the electrical and thermal conductivity of the asteroid, its distance from the Sun, and its size.

The abundances of the volatile elements in planetary atmospheres are yet another potential indicator of the conditions of origin of planets. There are, however, several severe complications. Among the chemically active volatile elements, hydrogen, carbon, nitrogen, oxygen, sulphur, chlorine, fluorine (H, C, N, O, S, Cl, F), the first five are soluble in core-forming metal melts. Since Mercury, Venus, Earth, and possibly Mars have metallic cores which may have acquired soluble volatiles, it is likely that the atmospheric inventories of these elements does not account for their total planetary abundance.

In the case of Mars, substantial loss of all atmospheric constituents is possible by thermal, nonthermal, and explosive (impact) escape mechanisms. The crustal inventories of water and carbon dioxide on Mars are poorly known, but possibly very large.

Planetary Atmospheres

Mercury, which was studied during three separate fly-bys by the Mariner 10 space-craft, shows no evidence of the presence of even a trace of an endogenous atmosphere (i.e. one originating within the body). Venus, studied in detail by a long series of Mariner, Pioneer and Soviet Venera craft, has 92 atmospheres pressure of carbon dioxide plus an unknown amount of crustal carbonate minerals, somewhat larger in sum than the terrestrial crustal carbon inventory, which is almost entirely in the form of calcium and magnesium carbonates. The atmospheric nitrogen content on Venus is about twice as high as on Earth. A variety of sulphur gases and the halide acids HCl and HF are all present in the atmosphere of Venus as a result of the high surface temperature, averaging near 740°K.

The atmosphere of Mars consists of about 6 millibars of carbon dioxide containing about 2 per cent nitrogen. Both Venus and Mars have only traces of atmospheric water vapour. The Martian polar caps and regolith

than the smallest planet, Pluto: the other tiny moons of Mars and of the outer planets are not shown. The different compositions and structures of the planets are reflected in their appearances here, based on close-up photographs from space missions. The inner planets are rocky and, except for Venus, have relatively thin atmospheres, whereas the visible surface of the outer planets, like that of Venus, is the top of a swirling mist of clouds. Although the Earth's Moon is far from being the largest of the planetary satellites it is (with the probable exception of Pluto's moon Charon) the most massive in comparison to its primary planet. In many ways the Earth-Moon system should be regarded as a double planet. The exact size of Pluto is still not well determined; it is too small to show an appreciable disc when viewed from Earth and measurement of its size is based on modern techniques of speckle interferometry which can help to eliminate the effects of scintillation caused by instabilities in the Earth's atmosphere. The bright rings of Saturn are easily seen as they comprise icy particles which are highly reflective: the dark, rocky rings of Uranus, however, were only detected by their obscuring effect on the light of stars which are occulted by the passage of Uranus and its ring system between them and Earth.

and xenon (Ne, Kr and Xe) are close to the solar ratios (declining in abundance with increasing atomic number) or the "planetary" ratios seen in chondritic meteorites and in the atmospheres of Earth and Mars. Unfortunately, the Soviet and American mass spectrometer data on these gases are flatly contradictory, and no satisfactory theoretical explanation of either set of data is presently available.

A further complicating factor is the marginal detection of deuterium on Venus in amounts which would give Venus a D:H ratio 100 times as high as on Earth. This might imply that the original hydrogen (water) content of Venus was at least 100 times the present amount (but still only 0·1 per cent of the amount of water on Earth). Alternatively, it might imply that the main hydrogen carrier during the formation of Venus was polymeric organic matter, not bound water in silicate minerals. Both complex molecules in interstellar clouds and the polymers in carbonaceous meteorites have D:H ratios of about 0·01, similar to the D:H ratio of Venus.

A Genetic Scenario

The foregoing brief survey of observational constraints on the origin of the Solar System now suggests the sequence of events which gave rise to our Solar System. There is no unanimity of agreement on any aspect of this history, but at least we can convey the present majority view. Like all views in science, it is subject to revision on the basis of new observational discoveries or new theoretical insights.

contain abundant condensed and absorbed water and carbon dioxide. The Venus atmosphere appears to have a deuterium to hydrogen (D:H) ratio about 100 times as high as that on Earth.

The compositions of the atmospheres of Venus and Mars were studied in detail by the Pioneer-Venus and Soviet Venera probes and by the two Viking Mars landers. In addition to chemically active gases such as carbon dioxide, water vapour, and nitrogen, both missions studied the rare gas contents of these planets.

The abundances and isotopic composition of the rare gases tell a complex and obscure story; the primordial rare gases are most abundant on Venus, some 100 times less abundant on Earth, and nearly 100,000 times less abundant on Mars. The abundance of ^{40}Ar, radiogenic argon from potassium 40 (^{40}K) decay, is nearly the same on Venus as on Earth, but is nearly 100

times lower on Mars. The ratio of the abundance of ^{40}Ar to primordial Ar (^{36}Ar plus ^{38}Ar) is about 300 on Earth and 3,000 on Mars, but is close to 1 on Venus.

The comparison between Earth and Mars can be taken to suggest early loss of volatiles on Mars. Volatile elements originally may have been about equally abundant on the two planets. Only a minor fraction of the Martian volatiles, those released late (after substantial decay of the billion-year radionuclide ^{40}K) are present today.

While this "Earth-like analogue" view of Mars limps in a number of particulars, it is not the Earth-Mars comparison which shows the inadequacy of assuming that all planets started out the same. Rather, it is the enormous abundance of the primordial rare gases on Venus.

The interpretation of the Venus data depends critically on whether the relative abundances of primordial neon, krypton

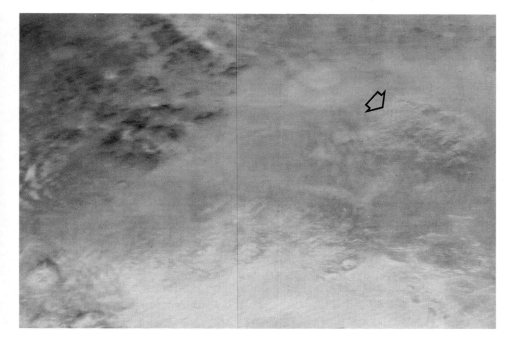

Above: *In this Viking Orbiter 2 photograph of a Martian dust storm, a turbulent, bright dust cloud (arrowed) is being blown eastward across the great Argyre basin on the surface of Mars.*

The origin of our Solar System, like the origins of stellar systems in general, occurred in a region of dense, cool, interstellar gas and dust clouds. The mass of the cloud complex was probably in the range of 1,000 to 100,000 times the mass of our Sun. Most of this mass was collected into new stars with a wide distribution of masses, probably within a time period of about 10 million years. At least one supernova explosion occurred in that cloud, and a number of T-Tauri and upper MS stars with enormous ultraviolet emissions must have been present. The supernova shockwave(s) compressed and triggered the collapse of a number of small cloud fragments, and highly radioactive debris from these explosions was embedded in these pre-stellar nebulae.

Each pre-solar cloud fragment collapsed into a flattened disc, pumping angular momentum outwards and mass inwards by means of large-scale turbulent motions.

These motions were driven and maintained by the internal heating of the nebula caused by the conversion of the gravitational energy of collapse into heat.

The heat was generated throughout the interior of the nebula, and lost from the outer surfaces of the disc by radiation. The inner regions of the disc, within the present orbit of Mercury, reached temperatures high enough to vaporize all the inherited interstellar dust, which of course completely erased all isotopic anomalies caused by the nonuniform injection of supernova debris.

Within the realm of the terrestrial (rocky) planets (Mercury, Venus, Earth, Moon and Mars), out to the inner edge of the asteroid belt, temperatures were high enough to permit a good degree of equilibration between the solar-composition nebular gas and the dust grains, but not high enough to vaporize the major rock-forming elements. Toward the centre of the asteroid belt the maximum temperatures were not high enough to permit a close approach to equilibrium; reaction rates are extremely dependent on temperature. One consequence of the low temperatures in the asteroid belt is that pre-solar materials,

such as interstellar organic matter and supernova ejecta, may survive as distinct and virtually unaltered entities. From the outer portions of the asteroid belt to the orbit of Pluto, ices as well as more conventional mineral grains were condensed, again with the most volatile materials being condensed only at the greatest distances from the Sun.

If the mass of the solar nebula were near one solar mass, then the outer portions would fall victim to dynamical instabilities which would cause the shedding of rings from the outer edge. If, however, the mass of the nebula were near the lower limit of the permissible range (about 0·01 solar mass), it would have been stable against such disruptions.

The dust component of the nebula engages in a variety of roles. *First,* the dust provides infra-red opacity, which hinders radiative cooling of the interior and helps maintain steep temperature gradients, and hence also convection. *Second,* small dust grains are readily transported by that turbulence, which tends to homogenize the dust within the gas. *Third,* dust grains always experience a gravitational acceleration directed toward the symmetry plane of the disc, and therefore would tend to sediment out unless prevented from doing so by these turbulent motions. *Fourth,* dust grains *collide* and *accrete* to form larger grains. *Fifth,* dust grains, unlike gas, tend to follow Keplerian (elliptical) orbits; the pressure-gradient force, which lowers the effective gravitational acceleration of gas parcels, is negligible for grains. They therefore feel a larger effective gravity, and tend to orbit the Sun at a larger speed than the local gas. The resultant aerodynamic drag makes the dust grains spiral in toward the Sun.

As a result of grain growth and sedimentation, a dense dust layer forms at the equatorial plane of the nebula. The very high local concentration of grains causes accretion to run away, and asteroid-sized bodies are formed within thousands of years. The nebular gas will dissipate as soon as the Sun ignites. In several nebular evolution calculations, the nebula survives only about 100,000 years.

Once the nebula has been dispersed, accretion of asteroid-size bodies will slowly

Physical Conditions in the Proto-solar Nebula
The temperature and pressure structure within the solar nebula at the time of the formation of the planets will have had a strong effect on the composition of the planets as a function of their distance from the Sun. Within the present orbit of Mercury, the disc became sufficiently hot to vaporize all solid material. Between Mercury and the asteroid belt interstellar dust was virtually destroyed but in this region the temperature was not sufficiently high to vaporize rock-forming elements. The rocky terrestrial planets are hence found here. Within the asteroid belt, where the initial temperatures were lower, pre-solar grains of interstellar organic matter could continue to exist, while from the belt out to the edge of the proto-planetary nebula both interstellar grains and ices were condensed. Within this region one would expect to find the most volatile (easily destroyed) materials only at the largest heliocentric distances, where the temperature was lowest. The type of material available for the formation of planets would thus depend on the temperature in the proto-planetary nebula at the orbit of each planet, and is reflected in the present day composition of the planets. The figure at right shows the temperature (above) and pressure (below) distribution in the nebula at the time of formation of the planetary system we see today. The scale of the diagram extends to the present-day orbit of Saturn.

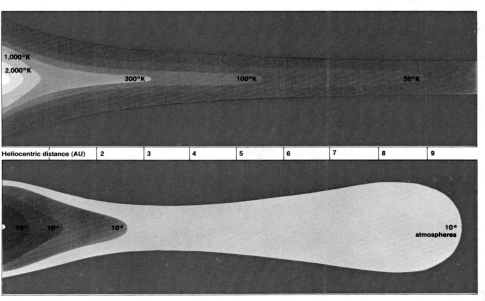

f stars. Recombination radiation of hydrogen (red) and starlight reflected from dust (blue) are both seen in this photograph.

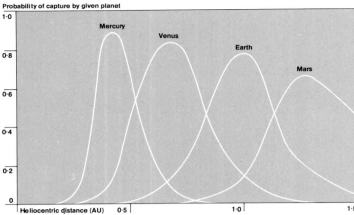

Probability of capture by given planet

Mercury   Venus   Earth   Mars

Heliocentric distance (AU)

Sampling of Preplanetary Solids during Accretion
As each planet formed, it accreted material from a wide range of orbital radii. The figure at left shows the probability that a small mass at any heliocentric distance should be accreted by each of the terrestrial planets. We can see from this how perhaps 25% of the Earth's mass was originally in a solar orbit closer to either that of Mars or of Venus. The composition of each planet can be significantly affected by the accretion of material from regions that are well away from its final orbit.

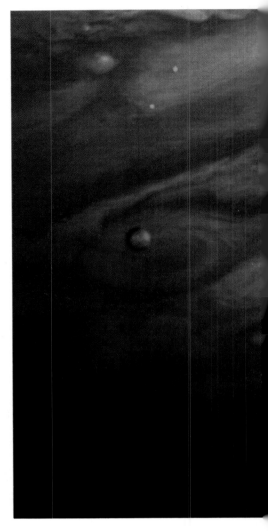

progress up to the lunar size range. After some 10 million years, about 200 lunar-sized bodies and a lesser mass of small bodies would survive. These bodies encounter each other infrequently, and high-speed encounters may result in disruption rather than accretion. The time required for these bodies to collect into a small number of planets in stable orbits is about 100 million years. This process goes most quickly close to the Sun, where orbital periods are short and the spatial density of solid material is found to be highest.

Each growing planet accretes solids over a wide range of orbital radii. Perhaps 25 per cent of the mass of Earth originally formed nearer to Venus or Mars, and similar breadth of sampling is expected for the other terrestrial planets.

The tiny proportion of the mass of each planet which originated far outside that planet's orbit may dominate the supply of volatile elements to the planet. Indeed, even post-accretion bombardment by very small masses of extremely volatile-rich bodies (carbonaceous asteroids and ice-bearing comets) may be a major source of planetary volatiles.

The Jovian Planets

The formation of the Jovian planets (Jupiter, Saturn, Uranus and Neptune) may occur through large-scale nebular instabilities or through the gravitational capture of cold nebular gas by solid planetesimals with masses at least ten times that of Earth. In either case, the volatile-element abundances on the Jovian planets should be the sum of two components, one due to captured solar gas and the other to the locally condensed materials. Clearly the Jovian planets must have originated as gravitationally bound entities while the nebular gas was still present.

Accreting planets store some unknown proportion of their accretion energy as heat, and radiate the rest into space. The accretion of small bodies deposits energy in planetary atmospheres and on their surfaces, whence the heat is readily lost. However, an accreting terrestrial planet will be struck by bodies with masses of at least 1 per cent, and possibly up to 10 per cent of the planetary mass. Such impacts deposit heat efficiently in the interior and may force early melting, differentiation, and outgassing of the planet.

If, for example, Mars began to develop an atmosphere when it had 50 per cent of its present mass, then half of its accretionary

history would have involved extremely violent impacts in a tenuous atmosphere. Explosive blow-off of the earliest atmospheric gases would be unavoidable.

It is customary to speak of differences between planets as due to either different initial conditions or different evolutionary paths. This view should be modified by the realization that the evolutionary courses available to a planet may be very closely circumscribed by the initial conditions. The *three fundamental initial conditions, composition, mass,* and *heliocentric distance,* are to some degree already interconnected because of the relationships between planetary composition and distance. Evolutionary processes such as solar heating, *radiogenic* heating, solar wind heating, sweeping, accretion, melting behaviour, etc., are intimately related to these initial conditions.

The ability of a planet to generate an atmosphere and hydrosphere is obviously in the same category. It would not be surprising if advances in the understanding of planetary evolutionary paths give as their largest payoff a better insight into initial conditions.

Research Frontiers

We may expect continuing progress in the study of dense molecular clouds and nearby star-forming regions. Radio interferometry—a technique of high resolution observation using two or more radio telescopes—has begun to explore the complex internal structure and motions of dense clouds, and these studies will be important contributors to our understanding of the earliest history of our solar nebula. There is some possibility that the dynamics of supernova shock wave impacts on interstellar clouds will also become better understood. Theoretical studies of the physics and chemistry of evolving accretion discs are being actively pursued.

One crucial problem in the interpretation of asteroid data is the establishment of relationships between meteorite types and asteroid locations, including the difficult question of the composition, origin and fate of Earth-crossing asteroids. Spectroscopic study of asteroids is continuing, and the Spacewatch asteroid-search program at the University of Arizona will soon begin discovering large numbers of Earth-crossers. At least a ten-fold increase in our data base on these bodies should be achieved within a few years.

The trends which relate the compositions of planets to their heliocentric distance and size have been incompletely explored. Geo-

Above: *This Voyager 1 image of Jupiter also shows two of its satellites. Io, left, is Europa. Jupiter's retinue of satellites resembles a little solar system; further study of it should advance our understanding of the origin of the Solar System.*

Below: *Engineers working on the Galileo Jupiter atmosphere probe which is due to be launched via the Space Shuttle in 1986 and to arrive at Jupiter in August 1988.*

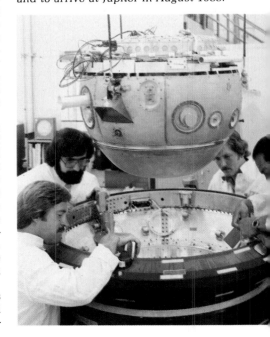

Pluto and beyond. Comet and asteroid missions are therefore an integral part of the study of the planets, and such missions will surely provide much insight into the initial compositions of planetary bodies. However, most nearby (Earth-crossing) asteroids are of uncertain provenance, and their places of formation are very poorly known. Likewise, most of the comets that have well-determined orbits have passed through the blast furnace of perihelion passage many times, and may have been seriously altered in composition and structure. Thus a properly planned programme of asteroid and comet exploration would require the comparative study of a variety of bodies in a wide selection of orbits, without unduly favouring the most accessible. The main *long-range* attraction of the Earth-crossing asteroids may be their content of precious metals; the main attraction of old comets such as Halley's may be geological (or aesthetic!). But both of these classes are of *immediate* exploratory interest because of their propensity to collide with the planets. Not only have they had important chemical and climatological effects since the time of planetary formation, but they lurk in our future as well. An impact of one such body ended the Cretaceous era and gave mammals the run of the Earth. Finding and characterizing such bodies is clearly important, and can be done very well in just a few years of effort.

All told, it should be clear that modest progress will be made in the next few years, but that we should not expect to obtain a fully satisfactory understanding of the origin of the Solar System in the near future.

One bright hope is the impending emergence of a new source of relevant information; it should be possible within the next few years for astronomers to detect planets in orbit about many of the nearest stars by use of the Space Telescope to be launched in 1986 (see Chapter 1). It is our frank expectation from all that we have discussed above that the conditions required to form stars should by themselves suffice to form planetary systems as well. If this generalization is true, then planets should be numerous throughout the Galaxy.

The detection of extrasolar planetary systems, combined with the continuing study of the satellite systems of Jupiter, Saturn and Uranus (which resemble little solar systems) will surely lend considerable breadth and depth to our present perspective on Solar System origins. A fundamental statistical obstacle has faced students of this subject, who have traditionally studied a handful of planets in a single stellar system; they are unable to decide which of the features they observe are universal properties of planetary systems everywhere, and which are mere local idiosyncracies. This obstacle may soon be removed.

chemical data on the crustal composition of Mercury, Venus, Mars and the Galilean satellites of Jupiter are urgently needed, but the prospects of gathering them are not at present likely.

Soviet Venus spacecraft may provide useful information on the abundances of a few of the most abundant rock-forming elements at a few points on the surface, and the Galileo Jupiter orbiter will return global compositional maps showing the distribution of some of the major surface minerals on the Galilean satellites. There are no plans for any future Mars or Mercury missions by any nation. Indeed, the only future planetary exploration missions now planned are Galileo and the next round of Soviet Venera spacecraft. Cometary missions to Halley's comet are planned by the USSR, the European Space Agency (ESA), and by Japan, with the United States watching from the sidelines.

An extremely valuable perspective on the modern state of the planets would be provided by comparing the planets to the primitive, unmelted, undifferentiated matter out of which they formed. Fortunately for us, we have evidence, provided by our studies of meteorite samples, that many small, ancient, and undifferentiated bodies still survive in the Solar System. Many asteroids and most fresh comets would fall into this category. Studies of primitive asteroidal and cometary bodies at a wide range of distances from the Sun may tell us directly how the composition of pre-planetary solids varied, from the orbit of Mercury to

Below: *US and Dutch technicians prepare the Infra-red Astronomical Satellite (IRAS) for launch. The satellite, launched on 25 January 1983, has, among many astronomical successes, discovered a shell or ring of particles surrounding Vega, the third brightest star in the sky. The material has been interpreted as a possible planetary system at a different (earlier) stage of development from our own familiar Solar System.*

RECOMMENDED READING

Beatty, J.K., O'Leary, B. and Chaikin, A., *The New Solar System*, Sky Publishing Co. Cambridge, Mass., 1982.

Hartmann, William K., *Moon and Planets*, 2nd edition, Wadsworth Publishing Co. Belmont, California, 1983.

Wood, J. *The Solar System*, Prentice-Hall, New York, 1979.

The Earth

From the Moon, we have seen the Earth as a blue planet, mottled white with clouds. Its blue sky is the result of the diffraction of sunlight by oxygen in the atmosphere. It was the view of the Blue Planet from Apollo 8 on Christmas Day 1968 that showed mankind the singularity and fragility of the only known abode of life in the Universe.

Earth is the third planet from the Sun, orbiting it at an average distance of 92,953,000 miles (149,589,000km) in a (tropical) year of 365 days, 5 hours, 48 minutes and 46 seconds. Slightly flattened at the poles, the Earth's equatorial diameter is 7,926·6 miles (12,756·3km), 26·6 miles (42·7km) more than its polar diameter, 7,900 miles (12,713·6km). Its equatorial bulge appears to be typical of rapidly rotating planets.

Largest of the terrestrial (rocky) planets, Earth's density is 5·52 times that of water (5·52g/cm³). Its atmosphere consists principally of nitrogen (78·09 per cent) and oxygen (20·95 per cent), with smaller percentages of argon, carbon dioxide, neon, helium, krypton, xenon, methane and hydrogen. Water vapour constitutes about 0·2 to 0·4 per cent by volume and is considered part of the hydrosphere which consists of the oceans, ice caps, lakes, rivers and streams.

The Earth rotates with a period of 23 hours 56 minutes 04 seconds on its axis which is inclined 23·5 degrees to the plane of its orbit (the ecliptic). A number of measurements have shown that Earth's period of rotation, that is, the length of the day, is growing longer as the result of the slowing of its rotational velocity (1,034·8mph, 1,665·3km/hr at the equator) by tidal friction with the Moon, Earth's single satellite.

The inclination of the axis varies from 22 to 23·5 degrees over a period of 41,000 years in response to the gravitational effects of the Sun, Moon and planets. It is the axial tilt or obliquity that produces the seasons, with their temperature variations, as the angle at which sunlight strikes parts of the surface changes with the revolution of the Earth around the Sun. The 41,000 year tilt cycle has been linked to long-term climate variations as obliquity changes result in changes in the intensity of sunlight reaching various parts of the surface.

The Earth's orbit is an ellipse with a variation of about 3 million miles (4·8 million kilometres) between the planet's distance from the Sun at perihelion, when it is closest, and aphelion, when it is farthest away. In the present epoch, Earth reaches

EARTH: BASIC DATA	
Equatorial Diameter*	1E; 7,926·6 miles (12,756·3km)
Mass*	1E; 13·2 x 10²⁴lb (5·98 x 10²⁴kg)
Density	3·19oz/in³ (5·52g/cm³)
Volume*	1E
Surface Gravity*	1E; 32·17ft/sec² (9·78m/sec²)
Escape Velocity	6·96 miles/sec (11·2km/sec)
Period of Rotation	23hr 56min 04sec
Inclination of Equator (to Orbit)	23° 27'
Distance from Sun (Semi-major axis)	1AU; 92·95 x10⁶miles (149·59 x 10⁶km)
Siderial Period	365·26 days
Orbital Speed	18·5 miles/sec (29·8km/sec)
Orbital Eccentricity	0·017
Inclination of Orbit (to ecliptic plane)	0·00
Number of Satellites	1

*Earth = 1

Precession (right)
The gravitational pull of the Sun and Moon on the Earth's equatorial bulge makes the Earth's axis circle slowly around, completing one cycle of precession in 25,800 years. During this period, different stars lie above the North Pole and act as "pole star". At present, the pole star is Polaris; in 3,000 BC it was Alpha Draconis, and in AD 14,000 it will be Vega. The Moon's inclined orbit causes a slight waviness in the precessional motion. This nutation, or nodding movement, has a period of 18·6 years.

The Earth's Inclination
The Earth's axis is tilted away from the vertical of its orbital plane by some 23·5°. In June, the Sun thus shines more directly on the northern hemisphere, giving more concentrated heat and causing summer conditions. The glancing sunlight on the southern hemisphere gives less intense heat. Six months later, the position is reversed. The Earth is closest to the Sun, and moves fastest, in January.

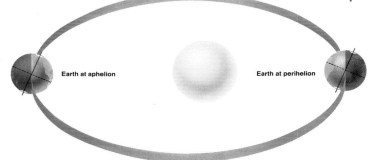

Earth at aphelion   Earth at perihelion

perihelion during midwinter in the northern hemisphere and aphelion at midsummer.

The Earth's orbital velocity increases by 0·59 miles/sec (0·96km/sec) at perihelion. Northern hemisphere winters are shorter and tend to be warmer as a result, than those in the southern hemisphere. Conversely, at aphelion northern hemisphere summers are longer and tend to be cooler than those of the southern hemisphere.

This Earth-Sun geometry is reversed every 12,900 years with the precession of the equinoxes. Gravitational effects of the Sun, Moon and planets on Earth's equatorial bulge cause the axis to sway clockwise in a slow circle, like the motion of a spinning top, with a period of 25,800 years.

The summer solstice is thus being shifted toward perihelion with the result that in the future, as in the past, northern hemisphere summers will be shorter and hotter and winters, longer and cooler. Because of the

present elevations of the continents, some climatologists believe that this arrangement is conducive to another ice age.

One astronomical effect of precession is a change in the pole star. At present, the north star is Alpha in Ursa Minor (Polaris). When the Pyramids of Egypt were being built, it was Alpha Draconis. About 12,000 years hence, it will be the bright star, Vega. Because the Sun and the Moon are not in the same plane, their combined gravitational influence on the Earth varies causing a slight wave in the precessional movement called nutation, or nodding. The period of one nutation is 18·6 years.

All of these variables—the eccentricity of the Earth's orbit, the obliquity of the axis, precession and even nutation—together with the Earth's distance from the Sun and the density and composition of its atmosphere contribute to the uniqueness of the Earth as the abode of life.

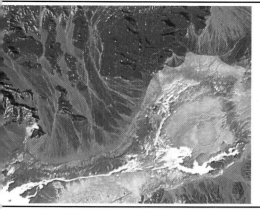

"... the vast loneliness up here at the Moon is awe-inspiring and it makes you realize what you have back there on Earth. The Earth from here is a grand oasis in the big vastness of space."

James A. Lovell, *Transmission from Apollo 8 in lunar orbit, Christmas Day,1968*

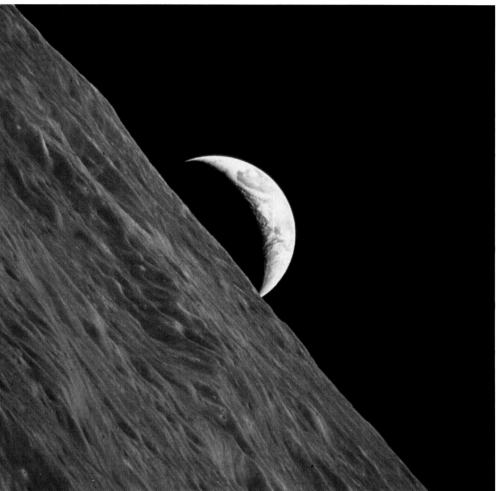

Above: *From their elevated orbits, satellites provide unique information on the Earth's surface, oceans and atmosphere. This Apollo 9 picture reveals the complexity of thunderclouds over the Amazon Basin.*

Left: *Earth rises above the horizon of its natural satellite, the Moon, in a picture taken by Apollo 17 astronauts. The barren Moon is a typical rocky planet: the "Blue Planet" Earth is the exception, with its water, oxygen atmosphere, and teeming life.*

The Physical Earth

The total surface area of the Earth is approximately 197 million sq miles (510·2 million km²). About 70·8 per cent is covered by water and 29·2 per cent is land. Most of the continental land lies in the northern hemisphere in the present period of geologic time (the Quaternary). The polar regions reflect this arrangement. The geographical north pole is in an ocean surrounded by continents while the south pole is in a continent surrounded by ocean. The south polar continent, Antarctica, is nearly covered by an ice sheet (exceptions are high mountain ridges and dry valleys) with an extent of 5·48 million sq miles (14·2 million km²). The Antarctic ice cap forms the planet's main heat sink.

Earth is the most active and highly differentiated of the terrestrial planets. Its crust is constantly being renewed and reprocessed by the convection of the under-lying mantle. The driving force is heat from the interior, believed to be generated by the decay of radioactive elements.

The crust ranges in thickness from 20 to 34·8 miles (32 to 56km) under continents and 3 to 4 miles (4·8 to 6·4km) under oceans. Below, the mantle extends about 1,800 miles (2,900km) to an outer core of liquid metal, principally iron, with a radius of about 1,120 miles (1,800km). At the centre lies a solid inner core, believed to be nickel, iron and sulphur, with a diameter of about 2,000 miles (3,200km).

The rotating Earth generates electrical currents within its metallic core. The dynamo effect is believed to be the source of the Earth's magnetic field which forms the actual geophysical frontier with the interplanetary medium. The magnetic field shields the surface from much of the particle radiation emitted by the Sun and other stars. The extent to which it protects living organisms from lethal doses is not fully understood, but evidence in seabottom cores has shown that many species of sea animals have become extinct when the magnetic field reversed its polarity. Evidence in rocks has shown that the Earth's magnetic polarity reverses in epochs of about 750,000 to 1,700,000 years. The present polarity has been estimated to have existed for 730,000 years. Before that, the orientation of magnetized particles in the rocks shows a compass needle would have pointed south.

The mass of the Earth has been calculated at 5·98 x 10²⁷ grams. The principal elements in portions of the crust that have been analyzed are oxygen, 46 per cent; silicon, 28 per cent; aluminium, 8 per cent; calcium, sodium, potassium and magnesium, 11 per cent. Principal concentrations of industrial metal in the upper crust are aluminium, iron and magnesium in terms of abundance per cubic kilometre.

Exploration

The exploration of the Earth as a planet from space was an outgrowth of the International Geophysical Year (IGY) of 1957-58. Reconnaissance of the surface, atmosphere and near space environment has been carried out since 1957 principally by American, Russian and Western European satellites in three programmes: geographical, geodetic and environmental surveys of the surface and sub-surface of the planet ball; analysis of the density, composition and motions of the atmosphere; observations of magnetic fields, sub-atomic particles in regions beyond the atmosphere and studies of Earth-Sun relationships.

The first major discovery in circumterrestrial space by satellites was the existence of zones of trapped electrons in the Earth's magnetic field. This led to a second major discovery, the size and shape of the geomagnetic field, the vast force field generated in the planet core.

Investigation of the metes and bounds of the field, the magnetosphere, led to a third major discovery, the existence of a stream of particles emanating from the corona of the Sun—the solar wind. These discoveries were made almost as soon as rocket technology enabled the space-faring powers to put Geiger counters, magnetometers and electron traps into orbit. They revolutionized the conception of the Earth in space, of the Earth-Sun connection and of space itself.

Earlier conceptions of a continuum of nothingness of "ether" changed to one of an interplanetary medium alive with magnetic fields and streams of particles blowing outward from the Sun among the worlds of the Solar System. The wind was an effect of the expanding atmosphere of the Sun, the heliosphere.

The solid ball of the planet was thus immersed in shells or spheres of matter and energy: the atmosphere, its upper level of electrified particles, the ionosphere, the magnetosphere and the heliosphere.

How far did the heliosphere extend? A partial answer came 25 years after Sputnik 1 opened the space age. In 1982, Pioneer 10 reported that the solar wind was blowing between Uranus and Neptune. It thus appeared to extend to the outermost region of the Solar System, beyond Pluto and the comets. Beyond lay the interstellar medium where high energy atomic nuclei, protons and electrons, the cosmic rays thrown out by exploding suns, raced across the Universe.

The Belts

The zones of trapped radiation above the atmosphere were deduced by James A. Van Allen and his colleagues at the State University of Iowa from data returned by three United States Explorer satellites during 1958. These were Explorer 1, launched 31 January 1958; Explorer 3, launched 26 March 1958, and Explorer 4, launched 26 July 1958. They were elements in the first successful American satellite programme, Project 416 (four satellites for $16 million). Explorer 2 failed.

The discovery of the radiation zones, or "Van Allen belts", was deduced at first from negative evidence. Explorers 1 and 3 carried Geiger counters which reported radiation for part of their orbits and then mysteriously

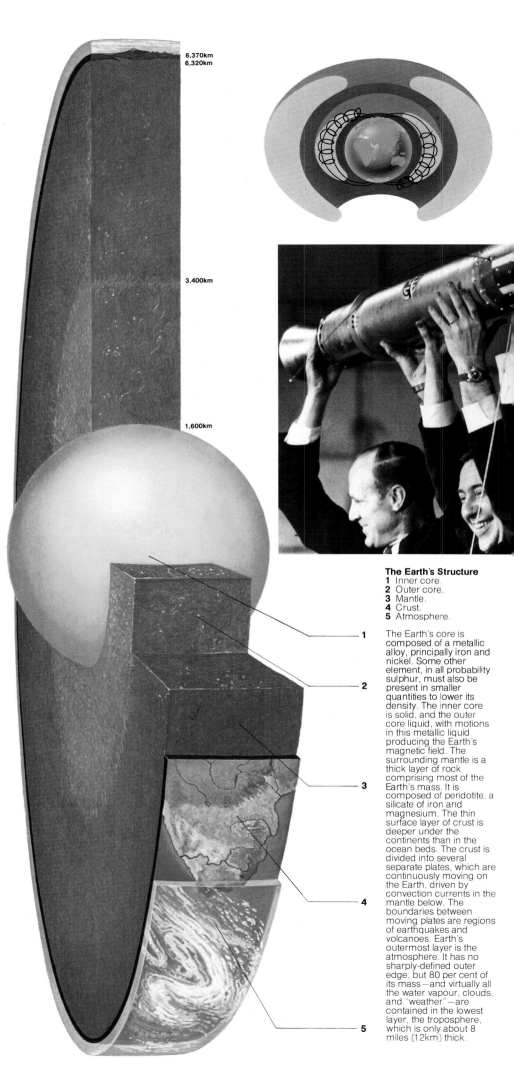

6,370km
6,320km

3,400km

1,600km

The Earth's Structure
1 Inner core.
2 Outer core.
3 Mantle.
4 Crust.
5 Atmosphere.

The Earth's core is composed of a metallic alloy, principally iron and nickel. Some other element, in all probability sulphur, must also be present in smaller quantities to lower its density. The inner core is solid, and the outer core liquid, with motions in this metallic liquid producing the Earth's magnetic field. The surrounding mantle is a thick layer of rock comprising most of the Earth's mass. It is composed of peridotite, a silicate of iron and magnesium. The thin surface layer of crust is deeper under the continents than in the ocean beds. The crust is divided into several separate plates, which are continuously moving on the Earth, driven by convection currents in the mantle below. The boundaries between moving plates are regions of earthquakes and volcanoes. Earth's outermost layer is the atmosphere. It has no sharply-defined outer edge, but 80 per cent of its mass—and virtually all the water vapour, clouds, and "weather"—are contained in the lowest layer, the troposphere, which is only about 8 miles (12km) thick.

The Van Allen Belts
These are two zones of electrically-charged particles, roughly doughnut shaped and lying around the Earth's equator at distances of 1·6 and 3·5 Earth-radii from the centre of the Earth. The particles come from the Sun, and are trapped by the Earth's magnetic field. The outer Van Allen belt consists of high-speed electrons. The inner belt contains some electrons, but its main constituent are protons (hydrogen nuclei).

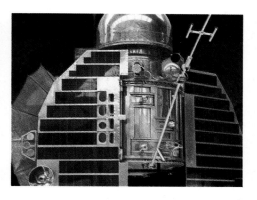

Above: *Only Mars 1 of the three Soviet Mars probes of 1962 successfully reached interplanetary space. It found charged particles well beyond the Van Allen belts, but its radio failed before it reached Mars.*

Above left: *Dr W.H. Pickering, Dr James Van Allen and Dr Wernher von Braun (l to r) hold aloft a full-scale model of Explorer 1. Van Allen provided Geiger counters which discovered the radiation belts now named after him.*

Above: *Explorer 7, launched in October 1959, established a link between the radiation belts and activity on the Sun. Solar flares boost the intensity of particles in the belts, causing aurorae and magnetic storms.*

shut down when they reached apogee, the highest point. The probable explanation was that the counters were being saturated by regions of intense radiation at higher altitudes. Explorer 4, equipped with a counter capable of recording higher radiation densities, confirmed the explanation.

Explorer 4 data enabled the Iowa investigators to plot high radiation intensities to 1,300 miles (2,090km). The radiation zone seemed to consist of electrified particles, principally electrons, trapped in the Earth's magnetic field and spiralling back and forth between the poles along magnetic lines of force.

The extent of the field was sounded by Pioneer 1, launched by the US Air Force on 11 October 1958 to hit the Moon. The probe fell short. It reached an altitude of only 70,700 miles (113,830km). However, it recorded intensities of trapped radiation as far out as 10,000 miles (16,090km).

Two peaks of trapped radiation at 2,000 and 10,000 miles (3,218 and 16,090km) were reported by Pioneer 3, launched 6 December 1958 by the Army Ballistic Missile Agency for the new National Aeronautics & Space Administration (NASA). The radiation then faded to assumed interplanetary levels at 40,000 miles (64,360km). There appeared to

be two principal zones or belts of trapped radiation: the inner and outer belts.

Although the discovery of the radiation belts is credited to the early American space probes, Sputnik 2, launched 3 November 1957, three months before Explorer 1, is claimed by some Russian scientists to have found the inner radiation belt.[1]

Sputnik 2 is the capsule that carried the dog, Laika, which perished after surviving long enough to suggest that man also could endure the low gravity of orbital free fall. The probe was equipped with instruments that could have detected the radiation zone. However, its altitude was too low in the northern hemisphere to encounter the inner zone and although it was high enough in the southern hemisphere to detect the belt, the data were recorded only in Australia. The Russians had failed to give the Australians their code and the Australians declined to forward the record.[2]

---

1 Soviet Space Programs (I), Staff Report, Committee on Aeronautic and Space Sciences, 1966. Report of Mstislav V. Keldysh, President USSR Academy of Sciences, on the fifth anniversary of Sputnik 1.
2 Dungey, J.W., Imperial College of Technology, London. op cit.

Although the full extent and intensities of the zones were not measured until later, their discovery in 1958 is widely considered as the most significant scientific event of the IGY. In 1959, a concept emerged of a vast field of magnetic force, generated deep within the Earth, extending far beyond the planet and interacting with particles radiating from the Sun. It was mapped by the data from the small 99lb (45kg) satellite, Vanguard 3, launched by NASA on 18 September 1959.

New information about the trapped radiation came from Explorer 7, launched on 13 October 1959. Its radiation counter reported changes of radiation intensities in the lower part of the inner zone during a magnetic storm on 28 November 1959.

That storm effectively dramatized the effect on Earth of these high-energy emissions from the Sun. Not only did radiation levels surge in the belts, but brilliant auroras appeared in the polar regions as charged solar particles cascaded into the atmosphere, disrupted the ionosphere and blacked out long distance radio and radio-telephone communication in the higher latitudes of the northern and southern hemispheres.

Data establishing the existence of a third radiation belt were claimed by Soviet scientists from the reports of Mars 1, which the Soviet Union launched on 1 November 1962 toward Mars. Before its radio failed, Mars 1 reported a region of intense radiation far beyond the second, or outer belt. Similar data were returned in August 1961 by Explorer 12, but American investigators located the radiation zone beyond the magnetic field boundary and did not consider it trapped in the Earth's field. Explorer 12, launched on 15 August 1961 into a 181 x 47,990 mile (292 x 77,232km) orbit, traversed the belts every 26½ hours. Its 2-watt radio detected wide variations in electron density in the zones and reported that solar protons were trapped in the outer belt.

The Solar Wind

The existence of a stream of particles (plasma) coming from the Sun had been predicted as early as 1919 by the British physicist, F. A. Lindemann (Lord Cherwell). Ludwig F. Biermann of the Max Planck Institute, Munich suggested that it would explain why comet tails always pointed away from the Sun no matter which way the

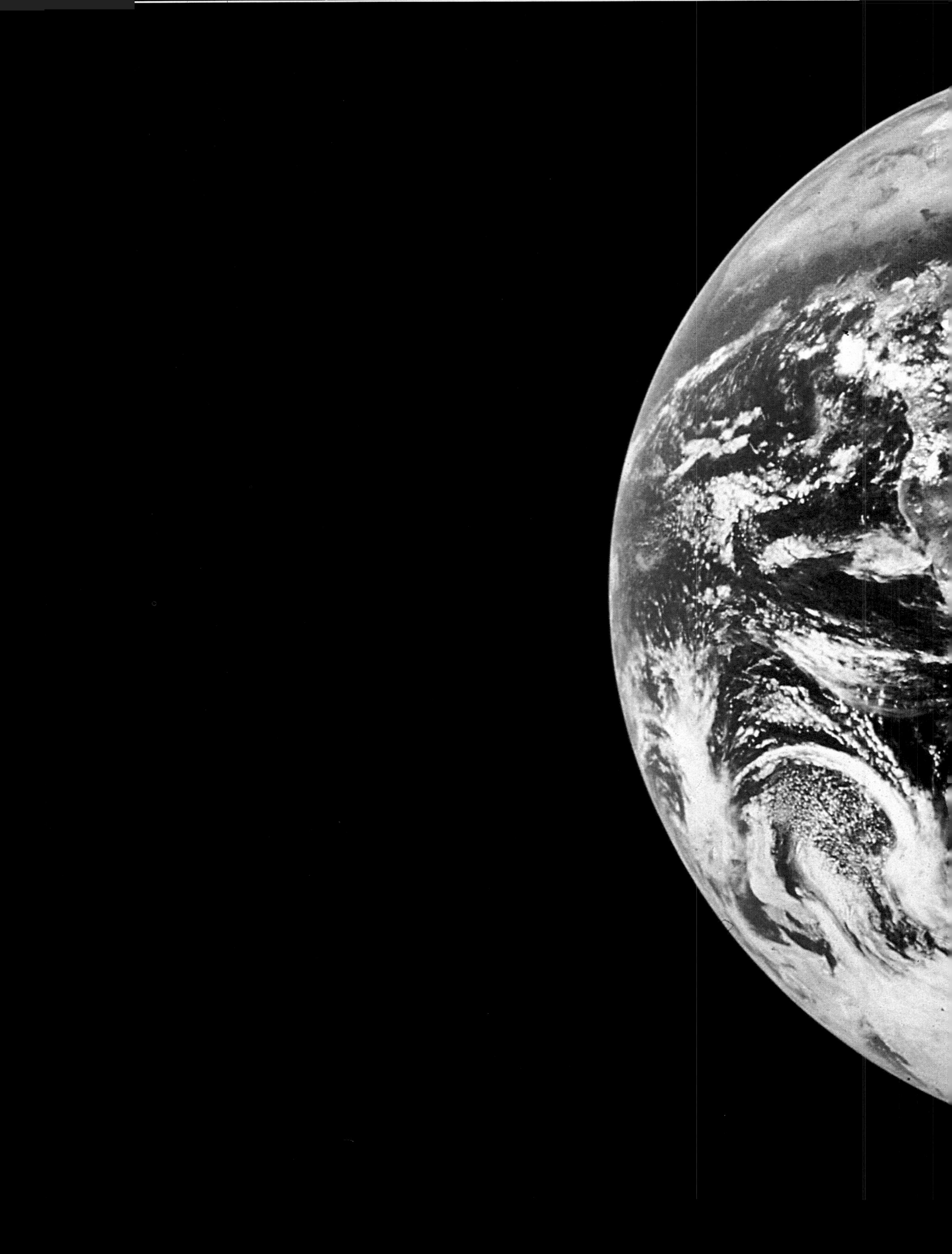

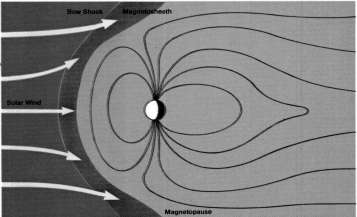

Above: *The first deep space robot explorer, Pioneer 5, was launched on 11 March 1960 into an orbit around the Sun, between Venus and the Earth. It extended the record distance for communication by a factor of 55. Pioneer 5 studied the interplanetary magnetic field and the solar wind.*

comet was moving—like flags on sailing ships flying in the direction of the ship's heading. It remained for space vehicles, however, to prove that the wind from the Sun does indeed blow among the worlds.

Before Luna 2 hit the Moon on 13 September 1959, its particle detectors told a story of greater scientific interest than the first impact on the Moon. En route, the detectors found a stream of positively charged particles at 40 Earth radii (158,450 miles, 255,000km). They were identified as low-energy solar protons moving briskly through the interplanetary medium.

Luna 3, launched around the Earth-Moon system on 4 October 1959, detected the stream beyond 40 Earth radii. Sputnik 8, boosted into low Earth orbit on 12 February 1961, launched a probe to Venus which reported a flux of billions of protons per square centimetre per second a million kilometres from Earth before its radio failed.

Although these early Soviet measurements of a particle stream moving past the Earth beyond the magnetic field were suggestive,

it remained for NASA's Mariner 2, launched to Venus on 27 August 1962, to establish that these particle streams represented a steady flow of plasma from the Sun. Pioneer 1, Pioneer 5, Explorer 10, Explorer 12 and Cosmos 2 contributed data, but the extent of the solar wind remained speculative until the Jupiter probe, Pioneer 10, reported the solar wind blowing far beyond Saturn.

The discovery of the solar wind provided a means of determining the shape of the magnetic field. Its general configuration was defined by Explorer 10, launched on 25 March 1961 into a 100 x 144,975 mile (160 x 233,305km) orbit. The spacecraft's 2·2lb (1kg) plasma detector sent back only 58 hours of data, but they were enough to depict a field boundary at 22 Earth radii (87,192 miles, 140,319km). At that distance, the solar "plasma" alternately appeared and disappeared. When it was present, Explorer's magnetometer reported that the Earth's magnetic field was weak and fluctuating, but when the plasma was absent, the field was strong and steady.

The on-off effect showed that the field was keeping out the plasma except where gaps in it allowed the wind from the Sun to penetrate far enough to reach Explorer 10 detectors. A picture emerged from these data of the solar wind flowing around the magnetic field like a stream around a rock.

On the sunward side of the Earth, the

magnetic field boundary appeared to be closest to the planet, at 10 Earth radii (39,632 miles, 63,780km). This was explained as a result of compression by the solar wind. On the night side, the magnetosphere extended outward like the tail of a comet beyond the orbit of the Moon. Explorer 12 returned data which depicted a boundary region of about 60 miles (96km) separating the magnetosphere from interplanetary space. The region was called the magnetopause. It was defined as a turbulent frontier where the solar wind broke upon the magnetosphere like a sea upon a beach. During the period of 1963-65 when the Sun was relatively quiet, Pioneer 6, launched on 16 December 1965 into solar orbit between Earth and Venus, reported the solar wind blowing steadily at 191 miles/sec (307·5 km/sec).

The Shape of the Earth

Before the space age, it was known that the Earth was somewhat flattened at the poles, with an equatorial bulge nearly five times higher than Mount Everest. The bulge has been explained as a displacement of mass caused by the centrifugal force of the Earth's rotation. Observers have found the same kind of bulge on Mars, Jupiter and Saturn which also rotate rapidly.

It was Vanguard 1, launched on 17 March 1958, that measured the bulge and other

The Magnetosphere (left)
The region of influence of the Earth's magnetic field is enclosed by the solar wind to form the magnetosphere. It is compressed on the Sunward side (left) by the wind's pressure; on the Earth's night-time side, it forms a long magnetotail. The Van Allen belts are now seen as just one feature of the magnetosphere, where particles are concentrated most densely. Beyond the magnetopause, the magnetosheath consists of solar wind particles caught up in turbulent motion around the magnetosphere; there is a bow shock where the solar wind hits it.

The Earth's Atmosphere
1 Thermosphere.
2 Mesosphere (ionosphere extends through **1** and **2**).
3 Stratosphere.
4 Troposphere.

Earth's gravity ensures that the density of the atmosphere falls off uniformly with height, so that its pressure drops by a factor of 100,000 for each rise in height of 50 miles (80km). But otherwise the structure of the atmosphere is not simple. The temperature depends on absorption of solar energy. In the troposphere, temperature decreases with height above the warm Earth, to reach −60°C at 8 miles (12km). In the strato-sphere temperatures rise because ozone here absorbs solar ultraviolet to reach 0°C at 30 miles (50km). Temperatures fall again in the mesosphere to −100°C to rise in the ionosphere and exosphere towards the high temper-ature of the solar wind. The ionosphere consists largely of ionized atoms and free electrons, which reflect long-wavelength radio waves back to Earth, particular layers are called D, E, F1 and F2. The atmosphere is also a shield, protecting us from solar electrons and X- and UV radiation, cosmic rays and meteors.

miles (km)
350 (560)
300 (480)
250 (400)
200 (320)
F2 Layer
150 (240)
100 (160)
F1 Layer
E Layer
50 (80)
D Layer
10 (16)

Above left: *Aurorae—Northern or Southern Lights—occur when the solar wind is active. Its electrons penetrate the Earth's magnetosphere, and are directed to the poles. Here they collide with atoms in the ionosphere, causing green and red glows.*

peculiarities of the Earth's figure with precision. Vanguard's orbit, 404·9 x 2,461·5 miles (651·6 x 3,961·3km), was so stable that it enabled observers to make the first geodetic measurements from space. Minor perturbations in the orbit as it was tracked by radio indicated gravitational anomalies which reflected greater or lesser concen-trations of mass in the planet. Analysis of the anomalies showed that the Earth is shaped more like a pear than like an apple, with the stem toward the north pole. The equatorial bulge was shown to be greater than expected. These shapings were inter-preted as indications that the primordial Earth was considerably more plastic and malleable and more responsive to the forces of rapid rotation and tidal effects of the Moon that it is now.

Data showing that the equatorial bulge is greater than could be accounted by the present rate of rotation confirmed the theory that the Earth was spinning faster in the far past than it is now. Persistence of the primordial bulge despite a slowing of rota-tion has been interpreted as evidence of increasing rigidity of the mantle over time. Vanguard data indicated, however, sufficient plasticity to account for evidence of mantle convection and its effects: sea floor spread-ing and continental drift. Vanguard thus played a significant role in establishing the theory of Plate Tectonics which depicts the crust of the Earth as consisting of separate plates. The plates are afloat on the mantle and are moved by its convection, a process proposed as early as 1912 as the theory of continental drift and sliding.[3]

---

3 The plates encompass oceanic and continental crust. The principal ones are the African, American, Eurasian, Indian, Pacific and Antarctic. Minor plates are the Aegean, Arabian, Caribbean, Nascan, Turkish and Philippine.

Above: *Sputnik 3, was surprisingly large; 140in (355cm) long and weighing 2,962lb (1,327kg). Its elliptical orbit ranged from 135 to 1,158 miles (217 to 1,864km), allowing study of the upper ionosphere and the Van Allen belts.*

Atmosphere

Before the advent of rocket research, the nature of the atmosphere above aircraft and balloon altitudes was highly speculative. A region of electrified particles, the iono-sphere, was known to exist at high altitudes and to reflect radio waves, but its extent, origin and particle density were not fully determined.

Sputnik 3 measured atmospheric density directly for the first time in 1958 and reported ionization data—measurements which were later made by Samos 2, a United States Air Force satellite, in January 1961. Sputnik 3 also observed the topside of the ionosphere with a radio frequency mass spectrometer. On the basis of its reports plus those made by Venus and lunar probes, the Soviet Academician, K. I. Gringauz, con-cluded that the Earth is surrounded by a variable atmosphere of ionized gas—a "geo-corona" in which the flux of electrons rose and fell with solar activity.

Cosmos 2, in April 1962, showed that changes in solar activity resulted in changes in the distribution of charged particles and also in chemical types. Gringauz speculated that the Earth's ionized, gaseous envelope extended 12,430 miles (20,000km).

Although attempts to define an energy linkage between the heliosphere, the atmos-phere of the Sun, and the atmosphere of the Earth appeared to be a principal goal of early geophysical satellites, there were no un-equivocal results that could be applicable to long or short term weather forecasting, a prime objective of the new technology. Meteorological satellites appeared about the same time as the more exotic interplanetary, lunar and deep space probes. A preliminary effort to survey the atmosphere was made by Vanguard 2 which returned rather poor cloud photos in February 1959. A wobble in the spacecraft degraded the data.

The Geophysical Satellites

Following the first probing of the ionosphere by Sputnik 1 and the discovery that the Earth is slightly pear-shaped by Vanguard 1, more than 100 specialized satellites have been placed in orbit by the space-faring powers to look at the Earth as a planet and to analyze its near-space environment.

In the United States, the National Aeronautics and Space Administration carried out these investigations mainly with a class of satellites called Explorer. Explorer 1 set the pace in 1958 by detecting the first clues to the Van Allen radiation belts.

A parallel series of satellites called Cosmos was developed by the Soviet Union. Although the Explorers were identified with environmental research, the functions of the Cosmos series were more diversified.

Both powers developed geodetic satellites which enabled them to refine measurements of the Earth's surface. In the USSR, these machines were alluded to but not specifically identified, presumably for military reasons. In the United States, the satellite geodetic programme has been more openly conducted. NASA began developing a series of Geodynamic Experimental Ocean Satellites (GEOS) with the launch of Explorer 22 on 10 October 1964. A main objective of the programme was to refine the geoid, the shape of the planet ball at sea level.

As a practical matter, the precise determination of the geoid is the basis for measuring elevation (positive and negative relief) on Earth. In the United States, the geoid is the zero point for National Geodetic Vertical Datum (NGVD). Coastal zone construction restrictions and flood insurance rates are based on elevations above (or below) NGVD.

The technique of geodetic mapping required precise tracking of a satellite in order to detect variations in its orbit. As Vanguard 1 demonstrated, these were caused by variations in the gravitational field which indicated variations of mass within the planet. Orbital variations of Vanguard had shown gravitational "lows" in the northern hemisphere. These represented lower mass areas of the mantle, suggesting the pear shape. A reverse effect had been found on the Moon by Lunar Orbiter 5 in 1967. Variations in its orbit had revealed concentrations of mass so high that at first they were considered by some scientists as buried planetoids. Later, it was surmised that these "mascons" were the product of partial melting.

Explorer 22 carried mirrors so that it could be tracked by laser beams from ground stations. This experiment in tracking a satellite was repeated on Explorer 27. Both satellites also sounded electron densities in the ionosphere.

Explorer 29, later designated GEOS 1, carried military tracking devices. It was launched from Cape Canaveral on 6 November 1965 and carried a Doppler radio tracking experiment which measured orbital variations by changes in radio signal frequency.

On 1 July 1966, a passive GEOS satellite, consisting of a large balloon that was automatically inflated in orbit, was launched from NASA's Western Test Range (WTR) at Lompoc, California. PAGEOS as it was called served as an optical ranging target.

Above: *ESA's GEOS-2 magnetospheric research satellite is fitted into its payload fairing before launch on a McDonnell Douglas Delta rocket. The motor below the satellite boosted it to geostationary orbit.*

Below: *A test version of the European ISEE 2 spacecraft (silver cylinder) is mounted atop the large NASA ISEE 1 satellite for vibration tests: the two were launched together to study the solar wind.*

GEOS 2 (Explorer 36), launched from the WTR on 11 January 1968, carried a radar altimeter as well as laser reflectors. The radar altimeter provided a cross check with laser tracking from the ground.

The most sophisticated satellite in this series was GEOS 3, a 750lb (340kg) machine, which was launched from the WTR into a 524 miles (843km) orbit on 9 April 1975. It carried its own radar altimeter and laser reflectors. In addition, it was tracked by ground radar and also by Applications Technology Satellite 6 from geostationary orbit. ATS-6 could observe half of the GEOS 3 orbit and track it by receiving radio ranging signals from GEOS.

GEOS-ESA

Two other types of GEOS (Geosynchronous Orbit Scientific Satellites) were launched by NASA from the Eastern Test Range (ETR-Cape Canaveral) into geostationary orbit on 20 April 1977 and 14 July 1978 for the European Space Agency. They were built by the British Aircraft Corporation as prime contractor for the European STAR Consortium of ten West European countries. GEOS-ESA were designed to measure magnetic and electric fields in space near the Earth as they responded to changes in solar wind intensities.

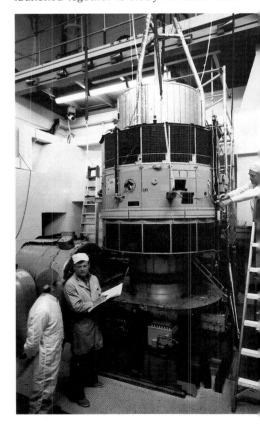

A joint NASA-ESA survey of Earth's magnetosphere and the solar wind was made by three International Sun-Earth Explorer satellites (ISEE). ISEE 1, built by NASA, and ISEE 2, built by ESA, were launched by a single Delta 2914 rocket on 22 October 1977 from the ETR into a looping 174 x 87,000 mile (280 x 140,000km) orbit. ISEE 3, built by NASA, was launched into a "halo" orbit about a gravitationally balanced point on the Earth-Sun line 1 million miles (1·61 million km) from the Earth on 12 August 1978.

The 1 and 2 satellites in Earth orbit several thousand miles apart measured solar wind intensities and the strength of the magnetic fields near the Earth while ISEE 3 monitored the solar wind and fields at greater distance.

Nearer the Earth, NASA launched two International Satellites for Ionospheric Studies (ISIS) built by Canada on 30 January 1969 and 1 April 1971 into near polar orbits from the WTR. Both were instrumented to measure electron densities in the ionosphere. Two earlier ionosphere sounders, Alouette 1 and Alouette 2, built also by Canada, were launched by NASA from the WTR on 29 September 1962 and 29 November 1965. Ionospheric research was particularly important to Canada where much of the country's long distance radio and telephone communications were affected by the impact of energetic emissions from the Sun on the ionosphere.

Of importance to NASA in the Space Shuttle era are the electrical effects of the ionosphere on the vehicle electrical systems and scientific cargoes. Special ionospheric electrical studies were made by the Space Shuttle *Columbia* during its four orbital test flights in 1981-82.

Lower altitude observations of the atmosphere were carried out by three Atmospheric Explorer satellites. They monitored photochemical processes and energy transfer in the upper atmosphere, including the formation of ozone. The three satellites were Explorer 51, launched on 16 December 1973 and Explorer 54, launched on 6 October 1975 into polar orbits from WTR and Explorer 55 launched on 20 November 1975 in equatorial orbit from ETR. Similar investigations had been made in 1963 by Explorer 17 and in 1966 by Explorer 32.

A Spanish ionospheric observatory, Intasat 1, was launched piggyback with NOAA 4 on 15 November 1974 by NASA for the Instituto Nacional de Technica Aeroespacial of Spain. Earlier, a German satellite, Aeros 1, had been launched on 16 December 1972 to explore the atmosphere at altitudes of 135 to 537 miles (218-864km).

Ionospheric and magnetospheric studies were continued in 1981 by two Dynamics Explorer satellites launched together into polar orbit from the WTR on 3 August. A Solar Mesosphere Explorer launched on 6 October of the same year into polar orbit reported chemical pollution in the high atmosphere and measured its effect on ozone density and distribution.

Starting on 4 September 1964, NASA launched a series of six Orbiting Geophysical Observatories (OGO) from both the Eastern and the Western Test Ranges. Their mission was to observe particles and mag-

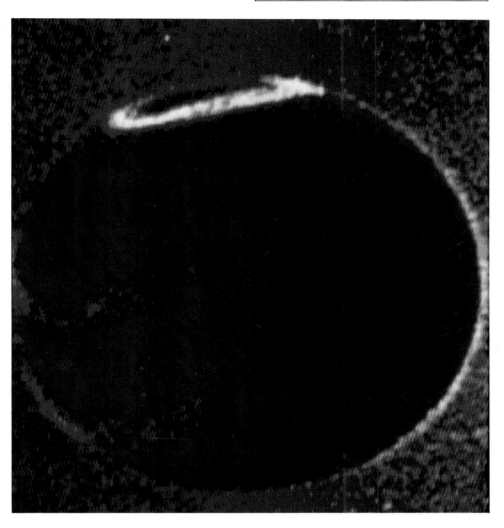

Above: *Dynamics Explorer's ultraviolet view of the Earth's nightside shows a "crown" of aurorae around the magnetic pole. Oxygen causes the two bands at left, and hydrogen the broad glow (right).*

Below: *Technicians check out Dynamics Explorer 2. The two Dynamics Explorers were launched together into polar orbits, to study interactions between the ionosphere, magnetosphere and plasmasphere.*

Above: *OGO 4 in launch configuration for vacuum tests. In orbit, the solar panels (front) are unfolded, and the booms (right) and antennas deployed, making it 49ft (15m) long and 20ft (6m) wide overall.*

Above: *An array of sensors carried by the scientific satellite Intercosmos 20. This Eastern bloc satellite performed ocean and surface sensing, and relayed meteorological data.*

netic fields during a part of the 11-year solar cycle. The OGO satellites returned volumes of data from a wide range of altitudes, reaching as far as 71,920 miles (115,740km). OGO 4, launched on 28 July 1967 and OGO 6, launched on 5 June 1969 monitored the effects of maximum solar activity on fields and particles near the Earth. The OGO satellites, in sum, carried 130 experiments into orbit, performed 1·2 million hours of experiments and transmitted data that were used in 300 reports and scientific papers.

Soviet Satellites

As early as Sputnik 1, which measured electron density from 125 to 375 miles (200–600km) the Soviet Union also made detailed measurements of the upper atmosphere and near Earth space. These investigations were by numbers of Cosmos and Elektron satellites and also by Luna, Mars and Venera probes en route to the Moon, Mars and Venus.

Sputnik 3, in orbit 15 — 25 May 1958, reported a predominance of atomic oxygen at 310 miles (500km) altitude where Soviet scientists concluded the atmosphere becomes "atomic" rather than molecular.

The Cosmos series was announced on 16 March 1962 with the launch of Cosmos 1. Although satellites called Cosmos perform observations not related to geophysical and environmental research, and frequently related to photographic reconnaissance, more than a score of these machines have been identified as upper atmosphere, ionosphere, magnetosphere and solar wind observatories. The Cosmos explorer-type satellites were instrumented to observe the composition of the atmosphere, electron densities in the ionosphere, the energy composition of the radiation belts and the effects of solar particle and electromagnetic radiation on the ionosphere and its radio propagation characteristics.

Among the Cosmos satellites reported as having provided data on these subjects were Cosmos 1, 2, 4, 8 and 11 in 1962; 17 and 19 in 1963; 25, 49 and 54 in 1964; 108 and 137 in 1966; 196 in 1967; 261 in 1968 and 381 and Cosmos 385 in 1970. Since then, many other Soviet satellites and the Salyut space stations have provided similar data in conjunction with experiments.

In 1964, the USSR launched a series of four Elektron satellites. They were designed to survey the ionosphere and the radiation belts. Elektron 1 and 2 were double launched by a single rocket on 30 January 1964 and Elektron 3 and 4 were double launched by a single rocket on 11 July 1964. These machines did more than monitor the belts. They read the composition of the upper atmosphere, reporting the presence of helium at all altitudes and predominance of hydrogen nuclei above 560 miles (900km). They found changes in the geometry of the ionosphere with time of day. In the upper layer, the mean thickness was 125 miles (200km) at noon. It swelled to 185 and 250 miles (300 and 400km) in the morning and evening.

In a series of international Cosmos flights, called Intercosmos, the Russians conducted joint experiments with Soviet bloc countries. Intercosmos 1 carried instruments supplied by the German Democratic Republic and Czechoslovakia to observe the effects of solar ultraviolet and X-rays on the structure of the upper atmosphere in 1969. Also, the German Democratic Republic, Bulgaria, Czechoslovakia, Hungary, Cuba, Poland and Romania participated in upper atmosphere experiments the same year on Intercosmos 2. During 1970, two more Intercosmos satellites studied radiation in space near the Earth and solar X-rays; launches occurred regularly throughout the 1970s, 20 missions having been flown by November 1979.

The failure of the Soviet Union to identify geodetic satellites has led American obser-

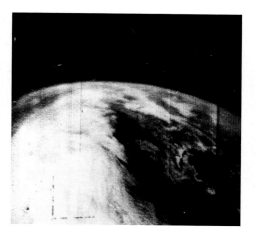

Left: *The first US meteorological satellite, Tiros 1, was covered with solar cells and weighed 263lb (119·5kg). It rolled along in orbit like a wheel, with two Vidicon TV cameras—a wide angle (104°) and a narrow angle (12°)—mounted 180° apart on its rim photographing the Earth beneath.*

Above left, and above: *Since the first Tiros 1 weather picture (left) taken in April 1960, resolution of detail has improved dramatically: the view of the eastern portion of the United States (right) was taken by a polar-orbiting RCA-designed Tiros-N satellite twenty years later.*

Left: *The Gemini 7 crew took this superb picture with a Hasselblad camera. The Red Sea (upper left) branches into the Gulfs of Aqaba and Suez (lower left); at right is the Nile.*

vers to suspect that satellite geodetic data are classified as secret in the USSR. It is supposed that geodetic data may be construed as contributing to the accuracy of missile targeting.

In general, the research satellites of the United States, Western Europe and the Soviet Union have been surveying the same Earth, the same atmosphere and the same near-space region for 25 years. Although the environmental parameters have become well known, a full understanding of their interactions remains beyond the grasp of the international scientific community. The possibility that this question will be illuminated by investigations of other planetary atmospheres has been a strong motive for Solar System reconnaissance and exploration.

Tiros

By 1960, the environmental sciences had progressed to a point where global observation from space had become a practical necessity to improve weather prediction. A new technology of remote sensing by instruments which measured the energy emitted or reflected by the surface was evolving. It could be applied not only to observe physical changes in the atmosphere and clouds but also to monitor temperature, pressure and precipitation and identify chemical elements and minerals on the surface.

Remote sensing technology also became the means by which the planets were to be reconnoitred. Its more immediate application to the Earth, however, was developed to observe the atmosphere and its interaction with electromagnetic and particle radiation from the Sun. Mathematical modelling of the atmosphere and of the oceans had reached a stage where detailed observations of physical processes were required to confirm or enhance the model. Computer analysis leading to the prediction of weather

and sea states seemed to be limited mainly by the availability of world wide data. The response to the problem in the United States, the Soviet Union, Western Europe and Japan was the development of remote sensing meteorological, geophysical and surface observation satellites which could collect and disseminate the data.

Observing the Earth from space was demonstrated in a spectacular way by colour photographs from the manned Mercury and Gemini spacecraft. Although aircraft and sounding rockets had been used routinely to photograph the surface from high altitudes, the pictures astronauts took with hand-held cameras from Gemini illustrated the effectiveness of looking at weather systems, especially storms, from space.

For weather observation, it was necessary to observe in the infra-red as well as the visible light portions of the electromagnetic spectrum in order to obtain images of the clouds and surface at night as well as in daylight. Scanning radiometers using these "windows" could produce two-dimensional images of the energy being radiated from clouds, oceans and land. The energy was sensed by satellite instruments as a voltage or current value. The analogue value which was proportional to the energy being emitted or reflected was put in digital form, either in the satellite or by a ground receiving station, so that it could be analysed by computer. These energy sensing systems were applied to weather observation by a family of Television Infra-red Orbital Satellites (Tiros) which were developed for NASA by the Radio Corporation of America. Tiros 1 began operating on 1 April 1960 in polar orbit.

The Tiros polar orbiting satellites evolved rapidly through three more generations (ESSA, ITOS and NOAA). Each generation was more complex and provided more data than its predecessor, leading to Tiros-N (the NOAA series) which was serving 900 ground stations in 120 countries by 1982.

Tiros 8 with an automatic picture transmission system went into service on 21 December 1963. An advanced Tiros (ESSA 1) was launched on 3 February 1966 for the Environmental Science Services Adminis-

EVOLUTION OF REMOTE SENSING SATELLITES: METEOROLOGICAL

TYPE	LAUNCH DATE	LAUNCH CENTRE	WEIGHT lb (kg)	ORBIT miles (km)	INCLINATION degrees	RESULTS
US Operational						
Tiros 1	1 Apr 60	ETR*	263 (119·5)	427 x 465 (688 x 748)	48·3	First global cloud photographs.
Tiros 8	21 Dec 63	ETR	265 (120·4)	461 x 439 (742 x 706)	58·5	First automatic picture transmission system.
ESSA 1	3 Feb 66	WTR**	305 (138·6)	429 x 518 (691 x 833)	97·9	Advanced Tiros.
ITOS-1	23 Jan 70	WTR	683 (310)	887 x 915 (1,427 x 1,473)	102	Improved Tiros with real time night-day readout.
NOAA-1	11 Dec 70	WTR	676 (306·8)	882 x 910 (1,420 x 1,464)	101·9	24-hr imaging of clouds; monitoring solar protons; temperature profile of atmosphere.
Tiros-N	13 Oct 78	WTR	1,600 (726)	527 x 537 (849 x 864)	98·9	Imaging in visible and infra-red; temperature and moisture profiles of atmosphere; solar monitor.
NOAA-7	23 June 81	WTR	3,097 (1,405)	524 x 536 (844 x 862)	98·9	Global weather temperature and pressure; data from ocean buoys and balloons relayed to ground stations.
NASA Developmental						
Nimbus 1	28 Aug 64	WTR	829 (376)	261 x 575 (420 x 926)	98·6	First high resolution TV and infra-red photos.
Nimbus 6	12 June 75	WTR	1,828 (829)	684 x 693 (1,101 x 1,115)	99·9	Ocean colour sensing; Earth radiation monitor.
Nimbus 7	24 Oct 78	WTR	1,823 (827)	586 x 592 (943 x 953)	99·3	Air pollution monitor added.
GOES 1	16 Oct 75	ETR	1,382 (627)	Geostationary	1·0	Visible and infra-red photos.
GOES 5	22 May 81	ETR	882 (400)	22,029x22,997 (35,451x37,010)	0·52	Photos; atmosphere sounder.
Soviet						
Cosmos 122	25 June 66	Baikonur	4,410? (2,000?)	366 x 400 (589 x 643)	65	First USSR weather satellite.
Meteor 1	26 Mar 69	Plesetsk	4,850? (2,200?)	393 x 427 (633 x 687)	81·2	First operational USSR weather satellite.
ESA						
Meteosat 1	23 Nov 77	ETR	1,543 (700)	Geostationary	0·73	First ESA weather satellite.

*Eastern Test Range   **Western Test Range

tration (ESSA) of the US Department of Commerce. In addition to the atmosphere, its sensors monitored the oceans, solar flares, solar particle density and magnetic storms in space and the ionosphere. The ESSA satellites were launched from NASA's Western Test Range at Lompoc, California southward over the Pacific Ocean into near-polar, Sun-synchronous orbits. They crossed the equator every afternoon and returned daily photographs of the entire planet.

Following the launch of the ninth satellite in this system on 26 February 1969, a third generation Tiros called ITOS (Improved Tiros Operational System) appeared on the launch pad. It could provide night and day radiometer data in real time as well as store data for later transmission. Also, it photographed worldwide cloud cover every 12 hours from polar orbit.

The ITOS satellites replaced the ESSA machines as the National Oceanic and Atmospheric Administration (NOAA) took the place of ESSA. NOAA 1 was boosted into a 910 x 882 mile (1,464 x 1,420km) polar orbit on 11 December 1970. It provided day and night imaging with high and medium resolution television and infra-red scanners and vertical temperature profiles of the atmosphere by scanning radiometers. It monitored also solar proton and electron intensities. Five of these satellites were launched successfully, the last one, NOAA-5, on 29 July 1976. It produced a thermal map of the Gulf Stream and adjacent Atlantic Ocean waters off the coast of Georgia.

Tiros-N, the fourth generation of Tiros satellites, was launched into polar orbit on 13 October 1978. A fleet of eight of these machines was planned by NOAA for service through until 1984. Tiros-N was equipped to provide images and data in the visible, near infra-red and far infra-red portions of the spectrum. It produced vertical temperature

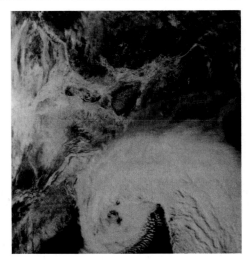

and moisture profiles of the atmosphere and the stratosphere. It monitored the flux of solar particles. Also, it carried electronic devices designed to locate missing aircraft and ships from their radio signals and to relay the data to ground stations. The first operational Tiros-N was NOAA-6, launched on 27 June 1979. It demonstrated the feasibility of charting ocean currents by tracing the development of the Somali Current off East Africa during the summer monsoon.

A third Tiros-N, NOAA-7, was launched on 23 June 1981. With NOAA-6, it observed global weather and transmitted temperature, pressure, radiation and picture data to worldwide ground stations. The two satellites were equipped to collect local weather data from balloons and ocean buoys and transmit them to command and data acquisition stations at Wallops Station, Virginia; Fairbanks, Alaska and a data receiving station at Lannion, France. The data were then processed by NOAA's central computer at Suitland, Maryland and distributed to

Above: *The Tiros-N weather satellite records the great blizzard of 1979 over the eastern United States. The storm on 19 February (left) brought snow and ice which halted commerce the next day (right).*

users all over the world. Both satellites contributed data to the international Global Atmospheric Research Program (GARP). NOAA-7 was the 28th weather satellite in the Tiros family since 1960.

Nimbus and GOES

Beyond the applications satellites, NASA launched seven operating meteorological research satellites called Nimbus into 560 to 685 miles (900–1,100km) polar orbits between 1964 and 1978. Manufactured by the General Electric Company, these machines tested advanced sensing systems. They performed much the same observations as the Tiros series, but they functioned also as experimental machines.

Nimbus 1, launched on 28 August 1964,

Above: *Seen here in Hughes Aircraft Company's anechoic chamber, is the second Japanese weather satellite, Himawari 2. Below the communications antennas is the VISSR scan mirror.*

Top: *The two-ton Nimbus 7, launched in October 1978, was the last of its series. The Earth-sensing instruments conducted the first global monitor of man-made and natural pollutants in the Earth's atmosphere.*

Above: *The vertical structure of a storm cloud is here deduced from a stereo pair of images taken by two Synchronous Meteorological Satellites. The structure is also reflected in the ocean below.*

provided the first, high resolution television and infra-red cloud and surface photographs from a satellite. So precise was its photography that mapmakers were able to correct the location of Mount Siple in Antarctica which had been mapped by aircraft reconnaissance with an error of 45 miles (72km). Rising 9,850ft (3,000m), the mountain was used by pilots as a navigation aid.

The Nimbus satellites tested instrumentation later put into operational use by the Tiros system. A scanning microwave radiometer developed for Nimbus was demonstrated by Nimbus 5 as an aid to polar navigation by determining sea ice boundaries.

Nimbus 6, launched on 12 June 1975, carried a colour scanner which mapped meanders of the Gulf Stream by registering their high chlorophyll content (in plankton). This machine was equipped to measure the Earth's radiation budget (i.e., the amount of heat the Earth receives from the Sun and the amount radiated away into space). It carried out initial tests of the feasibility of a tracking and data relay satellite system which would provide continuous communication between a control centre and orbiting spacecraft, including the Space Shuttle, in lieu of a network of stations along the ground track. The final satellite in this research series, Nimbus 7, was launched on 24 October 1978. It was the first satellite that monitored air pollution. It also measured changes in sunshine intensity at the atmosphere top.

From the polar-orbiting Tiros and Nimbus satellites, NASA took another long step in developing a remote sensing machine that would hover over one spot on the surface in geostationary orbit, 22,300 miles (35,880km) over the equator. At that altitude in an equatorial orbit, a satellite is moving around the Earth at the same rate as the Earth is rotating, so that the satellite appears to be stationary. Five Geostationary Operational Environmental Satellites (GOES) built by Hughes Aircraft Company, were launched from Cape Canaveral from 16 October 1975 to 22 May 1981. They were preceded by two successful experimental geostationary observatories called Synchronous Meteorological Satellites (SMS) in 1974 and early 1975. Two international geostationary meteorological satellites also were launched from the Cape by Deltas, Himawari 1 on 14 July 1977 for Japan and Meteosat 1 for the ESA on 23 November 1977.

Each GOES carried visible light and infrared sensors that provided continuous imaging of the clouds and surface day and night. A NOAA data centre at Wallops Station received data from the satellite and converted them to a format the field stations could use. The reformatted data were sent back to the satellite and retransmitted to field stations across the United States including Miami, San Francisco, Anchorage and Honolulu.

GOES 1 was moved to 60° east longitude over the Indian Ocean to support the GARP (Global Atmospheric Research Program) effort and its data were processed by a European Space Agency ground station in Spain. Other GOES spacecraft were positioned to overlook the western hemisphere at 75°, 105° and 135° west longitude. These

Full-disc image of the Earth taken by Meteosat-1 from geostationary orbit in the infra-red (11 micron) channel. From the IR and visible band images acquired every 30 minute

machines provided images of large areas of North and South America and the surrounding oceans every 30 minutes.

GOES satellites collected data from thousands of remote observing stations on land, sea and in the air and relayed the data to the NOAA centre. The spacecraft carried in addition to their imaging systems a magnetometer, solar X-ray telescope and particle detector to observe the Sun, magnetic field fluctuations and the energies and trajectories of solar particles.

International Systems

Japan's synchronous meteorological satellite was positioned over the western Pacific Ocean to cover the planet from Hawaii to Pakistan with visible light and infra-red scanners. The satellite also carried a solar particle detector.

ESA's Meteosat 1 was stationed over the eastern Atlantic Ocean where it monitored the weather of Europe, Africa and some parts of eastern South America for two years. A second Meteosat was launched for ESA on the third test flight of the ESA launcher, Ariane, on 19 June 1981. Riding piggyback with it was an experimental Indian communications satellite called Apple. This machine was followed by a NASA-launched Indian satellite called Insat-1, a combined weather and communications satellite capable of broadcasting television directly to community television centres throughout India as well as providing weather information. This satellite failed on 4 September 1982, running out of fuel after manoeuvres designed to free a jammed antenna, but a modified vehicle—Insat-1B —was launched by STS-8 in August 1983.

The Soviet Union unveiled its meteorological satellite system in 1966, based on the Cosmos series of experimental satellites. The system, Meteor, provided continuous coverage by two or three satellites orbiting at the same time at about 560 miles (900km) altitude at an inclination of 81·3°. The Meteor satellites furnished the same services as the NOAA machines, sending day and night images, atmospheric temperature and pressure profiles, data on the Earth's thermal balance and the flux of charged particles to 60 ground stations across the Eurasian land mass which processed the data.

China announced it was developing a low orbit meteorological satellite called Metsat, following the Tiros design, and planned a geostationary machine in 1985.

Applications Satellites

The link between the US meteorological and public service satellites was a series of Applications Technology Satellites (ATS) which were designed mainly for experimental communications. Starting in 1966, the ATS programme culminated in ATS-6, a 3,086lb (1,400kg) machine, which served as a special experimental and broadcasting station in geostationary orbit. ATS-6 was launched on 30 May 1974 and at first was positioned over the equator at 94° west longitude where it broadcast educational and health television programmes to the Rocky Mountain region and Alaska. It was used in a Veterans Administration experiment testing the exchange of medical information; a satellite instructional television

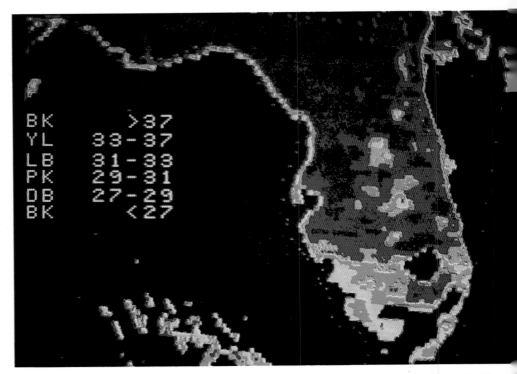

Above: *GOES-1 infra-red monitor reveals Florida's temperature in winter 1977. Colour coding is keyed at left, in °F; of the land regions, only yellow and light blue are above freezing. Other patches are clouds.*

experiment; a tracking and data relay experiment with Nimbus and GOES satellites; two wave propagation experiments; a test of a cesium ion engine; a spacecraft attitude pointing experiment; a radio beacon experiment; environmental measurements experiment; low energy proton and electron detection; solar cosmic ray monitoring; auroral particles experiment and a solar cell radiation damage test.

In 1975, this massive satellite, the largest and most thoroughly instrumented communications test machine at that time, was moved to 35° east longitude over Kenya where it provided satellite communications for the historic Apollo-Soyuz manned space flight in which American astronauts and Russian cosmonauts linked up in orbit and visited each other's spacecraft. ATS-6 was built by Fairchild Industries for the Goddard Space Flight Center.

Solar Max

The meteorological satellites were equipped primarily to measure solar radiation in the visible and infra-red band of the spectrum wherein most of the Sun's radiant energy is emitted. These emissions control the weather in the lower atmosphere. The intensity at which this energy reaches the top of the atmosphere is called the solar constant. One of the main questions pertaining to climatic fluctuation on Earth is whether the solar constant actually is constant or whether it varies and, if so, how much.

Although the solar constant has been determined as 1·37 kilowatts per square metre (plus or minus 0·02kw), ground and satellite observations have indicated some fluctuation in the range of a few tenths of 1 per cent. Is this enough to affect weather and climate? The answer might settle the

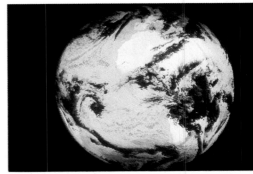

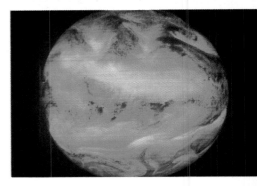

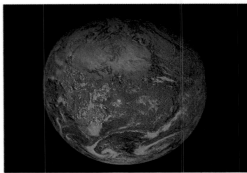

Above: *Multi-wavelength Meteosat images. Infra-red (top) shows temperatures of clouds and of surface between them; cloud structure is enhanced in the false colour view (bottom). Six-micron image (middle) shows water vapour in upper troposphere.*

EVOLUTION OF MAJOR EARTH-OBSERVING SPACE PLATFORMS						
TYPE	LAUNCH DATE	LAUNCH CENTRE	WEIGHT lb (kg)	ORBIT miles (km)	INCLINATION degrees	RESULTS
US Unmanned Satellites						
GEOS 1	6 Nov 65	ETR	386 (175)	688 x 1,405 (1,108 x 2,262) (as of 6 Nov 65)	59·4	Made geodetic measurements.
Landsat 1	23 July 72	WTR	1,800 (816)	562 x570 (905 x 918)	95·1	First satellite to image Earth resources.
ATS-6	30 May 74	ETR	2,050 (930)	Geostationary	1·6	Applications Technology multipurpose satellite.
GEOS 3	10 Apr 75	WTR	531 (241)	515 x 533 (828 x858)	114·9	Ocean and island mapping.
Seasat 1	27 June 78	WTR	5,070 (2,300)	482 x 500 (776 x 800)	108	First satellite equipped with radar camera.
Solar Max	14 Feb 80	ETR	5,104 (2,315)	352 x 353 (566 x 569)	28·5	Solar constant monitor; first satellite to be retrieved by Shuttle.
Landsat 4	16 July 82	WTR	4,280 (1,941)	438 x438 (705 x 705)	98·3	First satellite to photograph surface in natural colour with thematic mapper.
Manned orbital platforms						
Salyut 1	19 Apr 71	Baikonur	40,785 (18,500)	123 x 129 (198 x208)	51·5	Prototype Soviet manned space station.
Skylab 1	14 May 73	ETR	164,865 (74,783) includes OWS, AM, MDA & ATM.	273 (440) variable	50	Manned space station. Earth, Sun and comet observations through 8 Feb 74. Carried solar observatory and Earth experiments package.
Salyut 6	29 Sep 77	Baikonur	41,674 (18,900) excludes ferries	133 x 159 (214 x256) variable	51·6	Most extensively occupied Soviet space station; made Earth, Sun and astronomical observations
Salyut 7	19 Apr 82	Baikonur	41,890 (19,000)	211 x211 (340 x 340)	51·6	Most recent Soviet space laboratory; docking units may allow addition of modular units in orbit.
STS-2	12 Nov 81	ETR	212,000 (96,163)	139 x 139 (224 x 224)	38	First manned spacecraft equipped with radar camera. SIR-A photos revealed ancient river beds under Sahara Desert.

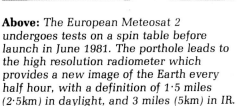

Above: *The European Meteosat 2 undergoes tests on a spin table before launch in June 1981. The porthole leads to the high resolution radiometer which provides a new image of the Earth every half hour, with a definition of 1·5 miles (2·5km) in daylight, and 3 miles (5km) in IR.*

Above: *Exhibition model of the Soviet Meteor-2 weather satellite. Infra-red and visible cameras at the lower end point continuously at the Earth, while the solar panels swivel to follow the Sun. The spacecraft is three-axis stabilized by momentum wheels.*

long standing question of whether solar variation was the primary cause of Pleistocene ice ages, the last of which ended barely 12,000 years ago.

Data from two satellites have a bearing on this question. One was Nimbus 7 in polar orbit which reported short-term decreases in the solar constant. The second machine was the Solar Maximum Satellite launched due east from Cape Canaveral on 14 February 1980 in a 353 mile (569km) orbit.

Solar Max, managed by the Goddard Space Flight Center, had the primary mission of observing solar flares during the maximum period of the Sun's 11-year cycle of violent surface eruptions in 1980–81. Of more immediate interest to climatologists, the satellite carried a solar constant monitoring package which reported two decreases of 0·1 per cent lasting about one week each.

Nimbus 7 had measured the same events as exceeding 0·3 per cent.[4] A continuing correlation of fluctuations in solar radiation with global temperature might indicate whether the variations have any short or long term climatic effect. But many other factors had to be taken into account, such as the heat-trapping effect of increasing concentration of carbon dioxide in the atmosphere and the heat loss effect of dust and aerosols from volcanoes.

The Landsat Series
The weather satellites had demonstrated the utility of remote sensing for meteorology, but the new technology had wider applica-

4 Evans, J.V. "The Sun's Influence on the Earth's Atmosphere and Interplanetary Space." *Science.* Vol 216, No 4545.

tion. It might also be profitably used to monitor conditions on the ground.

In response to demands from the United States Departments of the Interior and Agriculture, NASA developed a satellite equipped with cameras and scanners to monitor vegetation, bare soil and rock, snow and ice, bodies of water and urban areas. It was called the Earth Resources Technology Satellite (ERTS).

The first machine in the series, ERTS 1 (later Landsat 1), was launched into a 570 mile (918km) polar orbit on 23 July 1972. It weighed 1,800lb (816kg) at launch and was shaped like an oversized ocean buoy with wings (solar panels). Its remote sensing instruments were a return beam vidicon camera system and an advanced radiometer called the Multi-Spectral Scanner. ERTS-1 circled the Earth 14 times a day, returning to its initial orbital path every 18 days. It thus could show changes in surface conditions, ground cover, croplands, ice and snow. The television cameras, designed to photograph the surface in colour, failed, but the Multi-Spectral Scanner (MSS) produced such remarkably detailed surface images that the cameras were not missed.

The MSS sensed reflected solar energy from the ground in green, red and near infra-red portions of the spectrum, using four spectral bands (0·5 to 0·6; 0·6 to 0·7; 0·7 to 0·8 and 0·8 to 1·1 micrometres). These wavelengths were the spectral reflections of various kinds of surface features from forests to strip coal mines. The scanner took four readings for each 1·1 acre on the ground—one for the intensity of reflected green light, one for the intensity of reflected red light and two for the intensity of reflected infra-red radiation. These intensity levels were converted into digital form and transmitted to ground stations in the United States and 10 other nations. The receiving stations relayed the data to a central processing facility at NASA's Goddard Space Flight Center, Greenbelt, Maryland.

When processed, the data were presented as a photograph, in black and white (with shadings) or false colour to distinguish the various features of a scene. False colour was used in order to depict images in the invisible infra-red band. The MSS produced a scene covering 13,214 sq miles (34,225 sq km) with a resolution of less than a football field (or 262ft, 80m). In false colour, the scenes looked like surrealistic paintings. Forests appeared in scarlet, croplands in red and pink plaid, urban areas in deep or dark blue, mountains in brown and surface mines in streaks of bright red.

Colour representations were not consistent from one type of scene to another. In Oregon, cleared land was shown in yellow and in Idaho, as brown. Second growth conifer and old conifer forests could be distinguished by shades of green. Farmland sometimes showed up in violet and sometimes in magenta. These were beautiful pictures but for practical purposes each required a legend to identify features.

A second Earth resources satellite, Landsat 2, was launched on 22 January 1975. Its orbit was synchronized with that of Landsat 1 so that the two could provide nearly complete global coverage (except for polar areas) every nine days. With the two satellites operating, NASA, NOAA and the Department of Agriculture experimented with the joint use of the Landsats and the meteorological satellites to forecast wheat production in the United States and the Soviet Union.

Landsat 1 was operated continuously for six years until stabilization problems persuaded NASA to shut it down on 16 January 1978. Landsat 3 which was launched on 5 March 1978 replaced it to resume nine day global coverage. The MSS of this spacecraft operated in a fifth waveband; thermal infra-red, 10·4 to 12·6 micrometres.

Ten years after the first Landsat went into orbit, a new and more powerful resources satellite, Landsat 4, was launched into polar orbit at 438 miles (705km) altitude on 9 July 1982. It weighed 4,280lb (1,941kg) at launch. The prime contractor was the General Electric Company. In addition to an improved MSS, Landsat 4 carried a new instrument: the Thematic Mapper, a super radiometer with seven spectral bands and a resolution of 98ft (30m) (compared with the four/five bands and 262ft [80m] MSS resolution).

With the Thematic Mapper's extra bands, it became possible to depict surface scenes in natural colour, so that grass would appear green instead of MSS red. The addition of a blue-green band on the Mapper made it possible to see considerable depth in clear water. This capability enabled scientists to make bathymetric measurements, map reefs and survey uncharted islands and atolls. Additional infra-red bands enabled geologists to identify a wider variety of rock and soil types, especially those bearing clay

Above: *A Hughes technician adjusts the thermal blanket on Landsat 4's Thematic Mapper. The louvres and radiative cooler help maintain temperature control.*

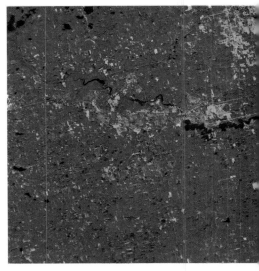

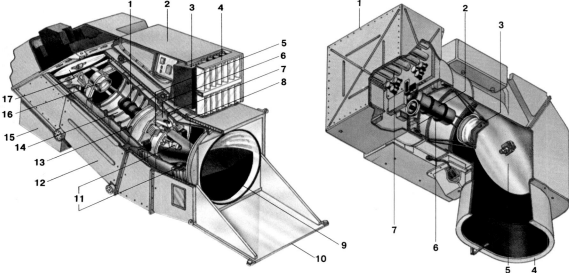

Thematic Mapper
1 Central baffle.
2 Electronics module.
3 Multiplexer.
4 Thermal control. louvres.
5 Hybrid preamplifier.
6 Calibration shutter.
7 Onboard calibration black body.
8 Relay optics assembly.
9 Radiative cooler.
10 Earth shield.
11 Alignment and focus mechanisms.
12 Mainframe.
13 Primary mirror.

14 Optical metering structure.
15 Aperture sunshade.
16 Secondary mirror.
17 Scan mirror.

The Thematic Mapper is a "super" MSS which is sensitive to seven spectral bands, five visible and one near-infra-red with a maximum resolution of an area square of 98·4ft (30m); and one band in the thermal infra-red with a resolution of an area square of 393·6ft (120m).

Developed by Hughes (as is the MSS), the TM is a brand-new instrument which can scan in both directions. Two focal plane detector arrays (Bands 1-4 on one, 5-7 on the other) receive the projected ground scene, sixteen individual detectors handling the high resolution bands and four concentrating on the thermal infra-red band (Band 6). Data rate is 32kbps. Information is digitized for transmission to Earth.

Multi-Spectral Scanner
1 MSS detector assembly (responds in four spectral bands).
2 Light baffle.
3 Ritchey-Chrétien type telescope optics.
4 Earth shield.
5 13in (33cm) oscillating scan mirror.
6 Relay mirror.
7 Detectors—six per spectral band; 6 x 4 total matrix in focused area. (Bands 1-3: photomultiplier tubes; band 4: silicon photo diodes).

The MSS, a mechanically scanning radiometer generally similar to the device fitted aboard earlier Landsats though with a modified optics and scan mechanism to take into account a lower orbit, scans four bands in the visible and near-infra-red portions of the spectrum, producing a continuous, 115-mile (185km) swath of ground image data in a stream with an output of 15·06 megabits per second. Ephemeris and

attitude information is handled at 8 kilobits per second by the telemetry system link, flight time information being coded in the stream. Fibre optics within the MSS send ground-reflected light received by an oscillating mirror to the equipment's sensors, which are sensitive to 0·5 to 1·1 micrometre wavelengths. The mirror scans in the forward direction only; spacecraft motion results in a continuous image strip.

minerals. The clay minerals often accompany deposits of copper, lead, zinc and uranium. Landsat 4 imagery became potentially useful for metals prospecting.

The new machine was designed to deliver 800 scenes a day from its Multi-Spectral Scanner and Thematic Mapper, each scene covering 13,214 sq miles (34,224 sq km). With its 98ft (30m) resolution, the Mapper could make an inventory of fields as small as five to 10 acres. Its seven spectral bands enabled observers to distinguish among crops such as corn, soybeans and wheat as well as diagnose the condition of all types of vegetation in terms of moisture and blight.

NOAA which manages the Landsat operational programme estimated the market for

Below: *The Thematic Mapper's first image from space, on 20 July 1982, revealed Detroit (top right), Wayne County airport (middle) and Lake Erie (lower right).*

services in 1981, prior to Landsat 4, at about $6 million a year. In that year, 36 per cent of all Landsat data was sold to the private sector in the United States; 33 per cent to foreign users; 12 per cent to educational and research institutions and state and local governments in the United States and the balance to federal agencies. By the end of 1981, 100 countries were using Landsat data for natural resource inventory.[5]

Seasat

Another type of Earth observation satellite more advanced than the early Landsats was launched by NASA into a 497 mile (800km)

---

5 Landsat D Report, NASA, 21 June, 1982.

polar orbit on 24 June 1978. It was called Seasat and was designed principally to test the use of microwave instruments, including radar, to scan the oceans of the world.

Seasat used the venerable and reliable Agena rocket frame as its main bus. In addition to four microwave sensors, it carried a visible light and infra-red radiometer. Of particular importance on this machine was a synthetic aperture radar which emitted microwave energy to take pictures of the surface. The radar camera produced images with a resolution of 82ft (25m) over a swath 62 miles (100km) wide. The instrument directed microwaves at an angle (side-looking radar) so that the reflected beam would show relief—hills,

Landsat 4
1 RF compartment.
2 TDRS high-gain antenna.
3 Powered hinges.
4 Solar array jettison mechanism.
5 Solar array.
6 Sun sensors.
7 Multi-spectral scanner.
8 Wideband module and antennas.
9 X-band antenna.
10 S-band antenna.
11 Communications and data-handling module.
12 Thematic mapper.
13 Signal conditioning and control unit.
14 Earth sensor.
15 Propulsion system thruster.
16 Propulsion module (hydrazine).
17 Power module.
18 Multi-mission modular spacecraft (MMS) support structure.
19 Attitude control module.
20 Adapter.
21 S-band omni antenna (2).
22 Instrument module primary structure.

23 Global Positioning System (GPS) antenna.
24 2 axis gimbal.

Landsat 4, launched on 9 July 1982, is the most advanced of NASA's Earth resources satellites. It comprises a Multi-mission Modular Spacecraft (MMS), which provides power, attitude control, communications and data handling, and propulsion; and an Instrument Module (IM). The satellite improves considerably the technology of remote sensing of the Earth, thereby aiding resource management. In some senses, it is a test vehicle: for example, it is assessing the capabilities of the new Thematic Mapper (TM) and also demonstrating the feasibility of the system in respect of user participation. However, it also ensures the continued availability of MSS data—previously available from similar equipment aboard Landsat 1, 2 and 3—and offers users a transition from MSS to the high-resolution TM. A transition adapter provided the mating structure for the IM and MMS. It also provides 3 mounting points to a cradle which in turn mounts in the Shuttle cargo bay for retrieval. Power is generated from a solar array, for conditioning and regulation by the MMS; output is 2200 watts, with storage in 50 amp/hr batteries for night use. Data transmission is performed in a variety of bands, both directly to ground stations and also using TDRS. Attitude control is very precise and achieved by an inertial reference unit, updated from two star trackers. Torquer magnets unload the momentum wheels. 5lb hydrazine thrusters enable orbital altitude to be varied for Shuttle rendezvous and to repeat ground swath coverage. For the first time in a NASA satellite a Global Positioning System (GPS) is incorporated: using data supplied by navigation satellites, Landsat 4's computer can calculate the craft's position and velocity, signals being received by means of a GPS antenna. In August 1983, loss of electrical power and TM direct ground link failure forced NOAA to authorize the launch of the backup Landsat D-prime craft in early 1984. Landsat 4 may be revived by a Shuttle repair mission in 1985/6.

Technical Data
Launch weight: 4280lb (1,941kg).
MMS bus units: 48 x 48 x 12in (1·2 x 1·2 x 0·3m) each.
Solar array: 4 panels, each 90 x 59in (2·3 x 1·5m)
Power output: 2,200W.

valleys, mountains and ocean waves in considerable detail. The image was assembled from the echoes.

This radar camera had a "lens" consisting of an antenna 30·7ft (9·35m) long and 6·9ft (2·1m) wide. It collected microwave energy reflected from a target as an optical lens collects light. By mounting the antenna on a platform which was moving around the Earth at 4·85 miles/sec (7·8km/sec), the aperture of the antenna-lens was synthesized or extended from 30·7ft (9·35m) to 7·95 miles (12·8km).

Seasat failed after only four months in orbit, but its radar camera returned surface pictures which were remarkable for their high resolution and detail. Because radar creates its own illumination and clouds are transparent to it, the camera could photograph the surface at night as well as day, through clouds or clear skies.

Shuttle Imaging Radar

A similar radar camera was tested aboard the second orbital flight of the Space Shuttle *Columbia* (12-14 November 1981). The instrument was assembled by NASA's Jet Propulsion Laboratory from spare parts of the Seasat instrument.

As the Space Shuttle *Columbia* passed over North Africa on its 27th orbit on 14 November 1981, an experimental radar imaging system in the cargo bay acquired images of the Eastern Sahara, the driest region on Earth.

When the images were analyzed at the US Geological Survey, Flagstaff, Arizona, geologists were astounded to see networks of broad river valleys and tributary channels instead of the flat sand surface depicted by Landsat pictures. They were looking at a fluvial landscape underlying the sand, one sculpted millions of years ago by flowing water during less arid climatic times when the Sahara was a grassy savannah. Some of these bygone rivers disclosed by radar had

flood plains as wide or wider than that of present Nile Valley, hundreds of kilometres to the east.

The Shuttle Imaging Radar "camera" (SIR-A) had functioned like a time machine. Its signals (23cm wavelength at a frequency of 1·3 Gigahertz) penetrated the loose, dry sand like sunlight through glass to reveal the ancient topography of the Sahara buried 1 to 5 metres below the present surface of the desert. The regional geology suggested that the largest valley systems had formed about 40 million years ago, during the Tertiary Period of geologic time.

Superimposed on these large valleys are networks of smaller channels formed in the last 2 to 3 million years during the Quaternary, the present period of geologic time. The channels were carved by running water during brief intervals of wetter climate which coincided with known episodes of human occupation of the region.

The ability of SIR-A to see through several metres of dry sand was unexpected. Although penetration of totally dry sand by 23cm signals was considered theoretically possible, the magnitude of the discovery as a breakthrough in remote sensing technology was not realized until the post-flight film was analyzed by the geologists at Flagstaff.

A detailed report of the experiment, its results and its implications for future research in geology, archaeology and planetology was prepared by scientists who analyzed the data. The report was published in *Science*, the journal of the American Association for the Advancement of Science on 3 December 1982.[6]

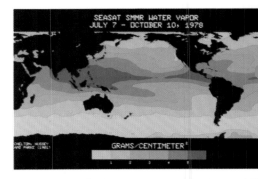
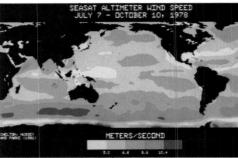
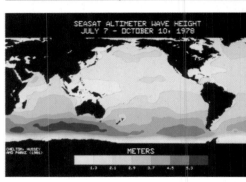

Above: *Seasat's microwave radiometers, radar altimeter and SAR registered the concentration of water vapour (top); the height of waves (bottom); and, from the sea roughness, the wind speed (centre).*

---

6 "Subsurface Valleys and Geoarchaeology of the Eastern Sahara Revealed by Shuttle Radar". J.F. McCauley, G.G. Schaber, C.S. Breed and M.J. Grolier, US Geological Survey; C.V. Haynes, University of Arizona; B. Issawi, Egyptian Geological Survey; C. Elachi and R. Blom, Jet Propulsion Laboratory.

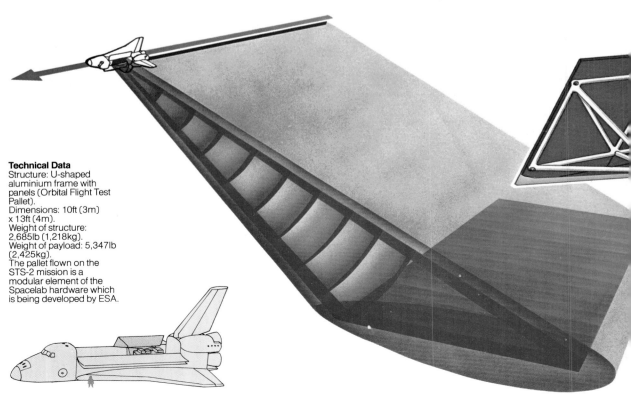

Synthetic Aperture Radar
Adapted from Seasat's imaging radar (1978), SIR-A is a synthetic aperture radar imaging system consisting of a 30·7ft (9·35m) antenna, a radar sensor, an optical recorder and an optical processor. The signal is radiated through the side-looking planar antenna, returned echoes being received by the antenna and amplified by the receiver; the many thousands of echoes gathered by the equipment enable a high-resolution image to be generated and recorded on film. This image represents the scattering of radar energy by characteristics such as ground roughness, slope and moisture content, and is made up according to time delay, Doppler shift and echo strength. The "synthetic aperture" appellation stems from the effective elongation of the radar "lens" (i.e. the antenna) caused by the motion of the Shuttle. A radar image 31 miles (50km) wide was built up along the Shuttle's ground track, covering a total area around the world of 3,861 sq miles (10,000km²). Resolution was about 131ft (40m.

Technical Data
Structure: U-shaped aluminium frame with panels (Orbital Flight Test Pallet).
Dimensions: 10ft (3m) x 13ft (4m).
Weight of structure: 2,685lb (1,218kg).
Weight of payload: 5,347lb (2,425kg).
The pallet flown on the STS-2 mission is a modular element of the Spacelab hardware which is being developed by ESA.

Adapted from the Seasat satellite's synthetic aperture radar system (SAR) flown in 1978, SIR-A acquired eight hours of data on the two day mission which was reduced from five days because of a partial failure of *Columbia*'s fuel cell power supply.

The radar imagery was obtained in strips representing 31 miles (50km) wide swaths on the surface. It covered about 6·2 million miles (10 million km) of *Columbia*'s ground track in North America (to 40·83° north latitude) Central America, South America (to 35·59° south latitude); north and south Atlantic Ocean; southern Europe and the Mediterranean Sea; north, central and south Africa; Iran and the Arabian peninsula; the Indian Ocean, India, Indonesia, the southern Soviet Union, China,

Australia and areas of the Pacific Ocean.

The SIR-A antenna, 30·7ft (9·35m) long and 6·56ft (2m) wide, was designed to collect imagery at a velocity of 4·35 miles/sec (7km/sec) with a resolution of 131ft (40m). The antenna has 896 transmitting elements which transmitted 1,624 signals a second.

The two dimensional image was formed by the reflected signal time delay, the Doppler shift in frequency and the signal strength which determined the brightness of each scene component. The radar sensor generated an FM signal which was radiated by the antenna to the surface. Echoes were collected by the antenna, amplified by the receiver and recorded on optical film. The image is a representation of the surface contour, slope and roughness.

Below: *This radar image of the swampy coast of New Guinea, acquired by the imaging radar system (SIR-A), is colour-coded to show ocean and rivers blue, and vegetation in green and orange.*

Below right: *The SIR-A's discovery of dried-up river valleys beneath the Selima Sand Sheet of the Sahara is seen in the 31 miles (50km) wide strip superimposed on a Landsat 2 MSS view of the desert.*

Serendipity

After the film was processed at NASA's Jet Propulsion Laboratory, it was sent to the US Geological Survey's Branch of Astrogeologic Studies at Flagstaff for interpretation. The SIR-A images of Egypt and Sudan were first examined by SIR-A guest investigator Carol S. Breed, a geologist who was familiar with the region from previous field studies.

She and her colleagues had recently described networks of ancient stream valleys emanating from a high plateau near the Libyan border. On Landsat images, these valleys disappear beneath the sands in the region imaged by SIR-A.

At once, she realized that she was looking at a strange landscape from which the modern, featureless expanse of windblown sand had vanished. In its place, was an integrated, fluvial topography portrayed in light and dark tones on the radar image.

So startling and geologically significant was this discovery that USGS and JPL experts organized an expedition to the Egyptian

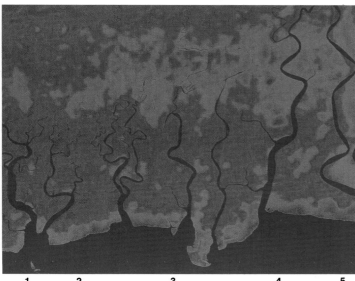

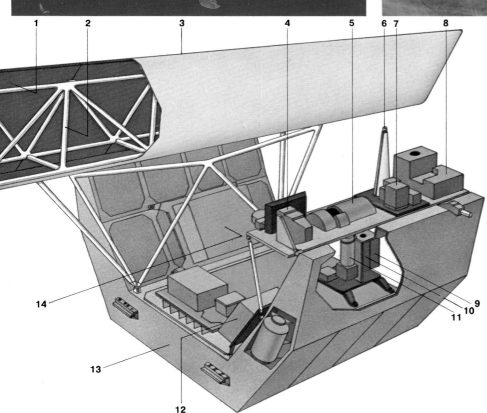

OSTA-1 Pallet
1 Epoxy-fibreglass honeycomb panel (7).
2 Aluminium tubular truss.
3 SIR-A synthetic aperture imaging radar antenna.
4 SIR-A optical recorder (film capacity: 3,600ft/ 8hrs).
5 Ocean color experiment (OCE).
6 FILE conical sunrise sensor.
7 Feature identification and location experiment (FILE).
8 Measurement of air pollution from satellites experiment (MAPS).
9 SMIRR film camera (2).
10 Shuttle multi-spectral infra-red radiometer (SMIRR).
11 7in (17·8cm) SMIRR telescope.
12 OCE module.
13 Spacelab pallet for mounting OSTA experiments.
14 SIR-A electronics module.

The OSTA-1 Shuttle pallet carried five remote-sensing experiments. The Shuttle Imaging Radar-A (SIR-A) was a system designed to map geologic features of the Earth, with a view to locating mineral, petroleum and oceanic resources. However, the most startling revelation

proved to be a hitherto unknown sand-buried drainage system in the Eastern Sahara. The Ocean Color Experiment (OCE) aided mapping of algae concentrations by distinguishing high-chlorophyll regions of the sea. The Measurement of Air Pollution from Satellites (MAPS) investigated the carbon monoxide content of the troposphere, while the Feature Identification and Location Experiment (FILE) was carried out to help develop an automated system to select promising regions and reject others in land surface surveillance. Finally, the Shuttle Multi-spectral Infra-red Radiometer (SMIRR) complemented SIR-A by identifying spectral signatures of rock types from IR data collected. Within the Orbiter, two further experiments relating to lightning observation and the response of plants to moisture levels in micro-gravity were conducted. Developed by NASA's Office of Space and Terrestrial Applications, OSTA-1 provided an early demonstration of the Space Shuttle's scientific and research roles in Earth exploration.

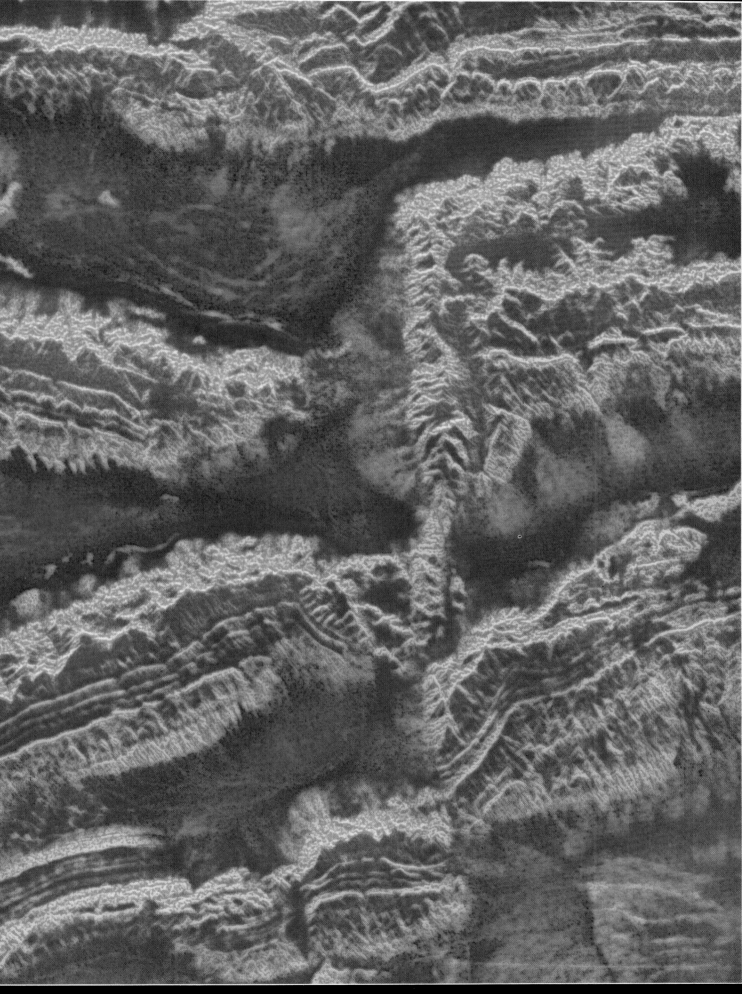

desert in September 1982 to confirm it *in situ*. The Americans, including archaeologist William McHugh, were joined by scientists of the Egyptian Geological Survey. The Egyptians brought a labour force to dig pits and search for river sediments for verification of the SIR-A penetration results. The workmen had dug barely a metre deep when they found river gravels. In the gravels, they turned up stone tools made by prehistoric people who intermittently occupied the region before it became hyperarid. The scientific team cited archaeological evidence of human occupation of the region dating back 200,000 years or more. Intermittent periods of rainfall alternated with arid periods. In one age, the Sahara was a grassy plain crossed by streams and dotted by lakes and ponds; in another, a dry, flat expanse of sand and barren rock.

In their report in *Science*, the authors suggested that the buried dry valleys of the Arbain Desert are relics of Tertiary systems (2 to 40 million years ago) that drained the Eastern Sahara before the rise of general aridity in the early Quaternary, about 2 million years ago. These systems pre-dated the appearance of early man and the integration of the Egyptian Nile with its Central African headwaters.

From the SIR-A images, investigators have concluded that the Arbain Desert peneplain was carved by large streams during the Tertiary Period and by smaller streams or "wadis" during the Quaternary Period. These rivers flowed in directions different not only from the present flow of Nile but also of the water table in Egypt which slopes northward from high ground in the southwest toward the Qattara Depression and the Nile delta. Prior to the onset of hyperadity, the region was inhabited by early man in the Lower Paleolithic, by Neanderthal man in the mid-Paleolithic and by successive Neolithic cultures of modern man.

The joint report is notable not only for its detailed descriptions but for its unqualified statement of the discovery: a rarity in scientific literature. It said:

"The SIR-A radar saw below the sand sheet a dramatically different and predominantly fluvial subsurface terrain known previously only to stone age people."

Other Deserts

Although the X-ray capability of SIR-A to peer below the surface looks promising as a research tool, it is limited to arid regions. Surface moisture attentuates the signal. Other deserts from which SIR-A images were acquired on the mission were the Taklamakan, Badain, Jaran, Ulan Buh and Mu Us in China; the Kara Kum in the Soviet Union; the Rajasthan in India; the Thar in Pakistan; several desert areas in central Australia and An Nafud in Saudi Arabia.

The implications of the SIR-A imagery for extra-terrestrial exploration were cited in the report. It noted that the ancient fluvial landscape under the Arbain

"resembles features of probable fluvial origin in the northern plains and equatorial regions of Mars that also lack running water at present."

It added:

"We can only speculate on the potential

of imaging radar to reveal subjacent topography through the dry or frozen eolian veneer that mantles many areas of Mars."

Planetary scientists quickly proposed an orbiting radar camera for Mars where arid, desert conditions might also reveal ancient, subsurface conditions of the past. The use of the radar camera to photograph the surface of Venus through its dense clouds has been proposed in a new Venus orbiter called Venus Radar Mapper (VRM), (see Chapter 8). Thus, in eight hours on the second orbital test flight of *Columbia*, terrestrial and astrogeologists discovered that space science had delivered to them a powerful, new research tool.

The SIR-A experiment was conducted by Charles Elachi of JPL, principal investigator, and co-investigators Walter E. Brown, JPL; Louis Dellwig, University of Kansas; Anthony W. England, NASA/Johnson Space Center; Max Guy, Centre National d'Études Spatiales, France; Harold MacDonald, University of Arkansas; R. Stephen Saunders, JPL and Gerald Schaber, U.S. Geological Survey.

SMIRR

In addition to SIR-A, *Columbia* carried four other remote sensing experiments on the second mission (12-14 November 1981). They were the Shuttle Multi-spectral Infrared Radiometer (SMIRR), a non-imaging sensor designed to identify chemical clues to mineral deposits in rocks and soil; a Feature Identification and Location Experi-

Above: *The American space station Skylab; at upper left, with four solar panels deployed, is the Apollo Telescope Mount. Skylab itself has only one solar panel; its second was damaged on launch.*

ment (FILE), a scanner developed to automate the selection of ground targets; an ocean colour analyzer and an air pollution monitor.

These experiments were placed on an engineering model of the Spacelab pallet in the cargo bay. They acquired sufficient data to test their effectiveness despite curtailment of the mission.

The SMIRR experiment looked at 50,000 miles (80,000km) of *Columbia*'s ground track in swaths 328ft (100m) wide. The instrument identified limestone, clay (kaolinite), iron oxide minerals and apparently a potassium aluminium sulphate mineral, alumite by their reflections of infra-red radiation.

The Jet Propulsion Laboratory reported that a remote area of Baja California exhibited mineral clues of gold, silver, copper, lead and zinc deposits in the data collected by SMIRR. Identification of clay minerals was obtained for the first time from orbit with this instrument. The space agency noted that clays in sedimentary rocks are important clues to the existence of deposits of petroleum, copper, gold and silver.

Skylab and Salyut

The most ambitious and costly Earth observation platform sent into orbit by the United States was the Skylab space station

Above: *Skylab's Earth Terrain camera, with an 18 inch (46cm) lens, recorded this true colour view of San Francisco Bay, stretching from San Francisco (bottom left) to Stockton (top right) in 1974.*

which was manned for 171 days between 25 May 1973 and 8 February 1974 by three successive crews.

Developed from the third stage of the Saturn V rocket, Skylab was a demonstration project which NASA hoped would lead to the development of a permanent space station. However, it was heavily damaged during its launch on 14 May 1973 and only the strenuous efforts of its crews and ingenious repairs kept the station operating. The station was abandoned when the third crew departed in 1974 and re-entered the atmosphere four years sooner than expected on 11 July 1979. It broke apart over the Indian Ocean and pieces of it rained down on Western Australia despite efforts to control entry and impact.

The station, consisting of a solar observatory, airlock, a multiple docking adapter for Apollo spacecraft, Apollo CSM, and a workshop, was 118·5ft (36·1m) long and weighed 98·4 tons (100 tonnes). It was launched into a 270 mile (435km) orbit by two stages of the Saturn V launch vehicle and was occupied by three crews of three astronauts each for 28, 59 and 84 days.

During manned occupation, about 10 per cent of the time was taken up with repair details, sometimes in space suits outside

Above: *Soyuz T-4 cosmonauts Vladimir Kovalenok and Victor Savinykh (lower left) aboard the Soviet space station Salyut 6, which fulfilled important Earth-observation functions. Kovalenok is atop the BST-1M far-infra-red telescope used for studying the Galactic centre.*

the station. Scientific experiments covered the fields of solar physics, stellar astronomy, space physics, Earth observations, life sciences (how to live in orbit) and materials processing.

The Earth Resources Experiments Package (EREP) consisted of a multi-spectral camera capable of photographing the Earth in the visible and infra-red portions of the spectrum; a terrain camera using high resolution colour film to photograph the ground; an infra-red spectrometer; a multi-spectral scanner; a combination microwave radiometer and radar altimeter and an L-band (heat sensing) radiometer.

These remote sensing systems acquired images of forests, prairies, croplands, mountains, lakes, rivers, the oceans and urban areas. They recorded sea states, ice cover on the Great Lakes (during the winter of 1973-74), sea ice, snow extent and ground temperatures. Some of the spectacular photographs showed a quiescent volcano in New Zealand, smoking Mount Etna in Sicily, Crater Lake in Canada which from space was obviously an impact feature and a dendritic pattern of furrows radiating from the Grand Canyon of Arizona — a pattern resembling the river valleys and their branching tributaries photographed by Mariner 9 on Mars.

Skylab's solar observatory made 200,000 images of the Sun and photographed the full cycle of a solar flare. The comet Kohoutek was observed as it passed through the Solar System while Skylab was operating.

The Soviet Union launched a series of smaller space stations called Salyut starting in 1971. Like Skylab, these vehicles were equipped for Earth, solar and astronomical observations and materials processing experiments. They were visited regularly by crews flown up to them in Soyuz spacecraft.

The most successful and busiest of the Salyut stations was Salyut 6, launched on 29 September 1977 and finally closed out after 44 months of nearly continuous use in 1981. Its successor, Salyut 7, was launched on 19 April 1982.

By mid-1982, the main function of a manned space station from the NASA viewpoint had evolved from Earth observation to that of a materials processing laboratory, construction base and deep space launch platform.

A manned presence was no longer necessary to conduct Earth reconnaissance. That task had been taken over by machines.

RECOMMENDED READING

Asimov, I., *The New Intelligent Man's Guide to Science,* Basic Books, New York, 1965.

Brooks, C. E. P., *Climate Through the Ages,* Dover Publications, Inc., New York, 1970.

Gamow, George, *A Planet Called Earth,* Viking Press, Inc., New York, 1963.

Hynek, J. A. and Anderson, N. D., *Challenge of the Universe,* McGraw Hill, New York, 1963.

Lewis, R. S., *Appointment on the Moon,* Viking Press, Inc., New York, 1969.

Lewis, R. S., *From Vinland to Mars,* Quadrangle New York Times Book Co., New York, 1976.

Whipple, F. C., *Earth, Moon and Planets,* Harvard University Press, Cambridge, Mass., 1968.

Wukeling, G. E., *Handbook of Soviet Space Science Research,* Gordon & Breach, New York, 1968.

The Moon

If a date can be assigned for the beginning of extraterrestrial exploration, it may well be 20 July 1969 when the first men set foot on the Moon. Neil Armstrong and Edwin E. Aldrin commenced the investigation of the surface after landing the Lunar Module *Eagle* in the Mare Tranquillitatis while Michael Collins remained in lunar orbit in the Apollo 11 Command Module, *Columbia*.

Although smaller than three of the Galilean moons of Jupiter (Io, Ganymede and Callisto) and Saturn's Titan, our Moon is the second largest satellite in relation to its primary in the Solar System. The Earth-Moon system is often regarded as a double planet system, with its centre of gravity in the Earth.

The Moon's rotation about its axis and its revolution around the Earth are synchronous, with a (sidereal) period of 27·32 days. As a result, the same side of the Moon (the near side) always faces Earth. The physiographic effect of this orbital-rotational resonance has produced marked differences in the sides. About one-third of lunar near side consists of dark-hued basins (the so-called "maria" or "seas", as the ancients thought of them). Lunar far side, the side turned away from Earth, is largely free of the basin structure.

With an equatorial diameter of 2,160 miles (3,476km), the Moon is 27·25 per cent of the size of Earth, with 0·02 per cent of Earth's volume and 0·01 per cent of Earth's mass. The Moon's density of about 3·3g/cm³ (compared with Earth's 5·5g/cm³) suggests

THE MOON: BASIC DATA	
Equatorial Diameter*	0·273E; 2,160 miles (3,476km)
Mass*	0·0123E
Density	1·91oz/in³ (3·3g/cm³)
Volume*	0·0203E
Surface Gravity*	0·165E
Escape Velocity	1·48 miles/sec (2·38km/sec)
Period of Rotation	27·322 days
Inclination of Equator (to Orbit)	6° 41'
Distance from Earth	252,667 miles (406,610km) max 221,423 miles (356,330km) min
Siderial Period	27·322 days
Synodic Period	29·53 days
Orbital Speed	0·63 miles/sec (1·02km/sec)
Orbital Eccentricity	0·0549
Inclination of Orbit (to ecliptic plane)	5° 09'
*Earth = 1	

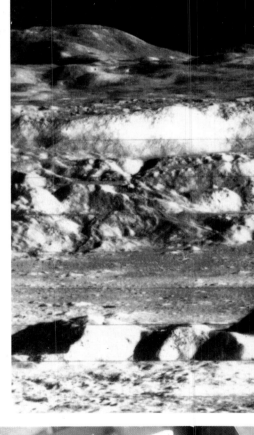

to some investigators that it was formed in another part of the Solar System, but others disagree and believe it accreted near the Earth.

The Moon's semi-major axis of revolution around the Earth—i.e., its average distance from Earth's centre—is 238,855 miles (384,390km). Its orbit is an ellipse ranging from 221,423 miles (356,330km) at perigee, the point nearest Earth, to 252,667 miles (406,610km) at apogee, the point farthest away from the Earth.

Except for light gases deposited by the solar wind, the Moon does not have an atmosphere, and surface temperatures change rapidly and drastically in sunshine and shadow. At the equator, temperatures

Synchronous Rotation
The tidal pull of Earth's gravity has gradually slowed the Moon's rotation. Its "day" now lasts as long as its period of revolution about the Earth. As a result, one side permanently faces us. From outside the Earth-Moon system however, the Moon can be seen to make one complete revolution per orbit, as shown in this diagram by the arrows indicating the fractions of a complete revolution achieved during orbit. Because this orbit is elliptical, the Moon travels at different speeds depending on its distance from the Earth. As a result, the rotation is not always "in step" with the position in the orbit, and it is then possible to glimpse normally-hidden regions of the Moon. "Libration" enables us to see up to 59 per cent of the whole lunar surface.

"Appearing unannounced, the moon
Avoids a mountain's jagged prongs
And sweeps into the open sky
Like one who knows where she belongs."

W. H. Auden, *Nocturne*

Moon would certainly turn out to be an example of the primordial material from which the terrestrial planets evolved.

This view was challenged by a group of planetary scientists who were convinced that the Moon was, or had been, volcanically hot enough to have melted its primordial condensate into chemical fractions of varying densities to form a crust, mantle and possibly, a core. If this was the case, and the Moon was structurally analogous to the Earth, planetologists could assume that all terrestrial bodies tended to evolve by similar processes.

The cosmological implications of the origin and composition of the Moon thus made it a fascinating challenge to science. Was the Moon cold and dead like a meteorite or hot and differentiated, as the result of radiogenic heating, like the Earth? And where had it come from? Its origin and evolution were listed by the Space Science Board of the United States National Academy of Sciences as one of the most important scientific questions of the 20th century.

The debate between "hot" Moon and "cold" Moon schools became polarized around conflicting interpretations of evidence. The hot Moon school asserted that many of the craters on the Moon appeared to be volcanic. Its advocates insisted that the magma (melted rock) which appeared to have paved the maria must have had a volcanic origin. (The term maria, the plural of the Latin mare, or sea, refers to the dark,

Above: *Hailed as "the picture of the decade" in 1966, Lunar Orbiter 2's dramatic oblique view of the prominent crater Copernicus was taken from an altitude of 28·4 miles (45·7km). The ancient, collapsed mountains rimming the crater rise to more than 1,000ft (1,600m). The distant mountain is the Gay-Lussac Promontory.*

Left: *Edwin Aldrin, second man on the Moon, poses inside the Lunar Module for Neil Armstrong after both had completed an EVA on 20 July 1969. The era of extraterrestrial exploration had truly arrived.*

ranging from 101°C at noon to −152·7°C at midnight have been recorded at the Mt. Wilson, California observatory. Temperature measurements before and during an eclipse showed a drop from 71°C to −78·8°C in a period of only one hour.

The new world Armstrong and Aldrin reached has approximately the area of the new world Columbus discovered nearly five centuries earlier. Tranquility Base, however,

was the gateway to a wider frontier — the Solar System.

Before the exploration of the Moon, our understanding of the Solar Commonwealth was gained from studies of electromagnetic and particle radiation, telescopic observations, measurements of the Solar Wind by early satellites and analyses of meteorites which fell to Earth.

The 46·3lb (21kg) of rocks and soil which the crew of Apollo 11 returned to Earth on 24 July 1969 provided the material for the first, systematic study of the origin and evolution of another body in space. As the study progressed through five more lunar expeditions, it resulted in a new consensus of the structure and evolution not only of the Moon but also of all the terrestrial (ie Earth-like or rocky) planets in the Solar System.

In the pre-Apollo era, a respected segment of scientific opinion held that the Moon had the composition of chondritic meteorites; that it had never differentiated, as the Earth had, to form a crust, mantle and core. As such a primitive and inactive body, the

Below: *". . . one giant leap for mankind" as a spacecraft from Earth hangs over the silent plains of a new world. Here, the Apollo 12 Lunar Module Intrepid heads for touch down in the Oceanus Procellarum. Herschel, the large crater at far right, lies almost dead centre of the Moon's visible hemisphere.*

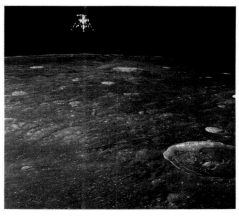

low-lying areas of the Moon which observers in antiquity believed were seas.)

But another explanation of the dark maria had been advanced by Grove Karl Gilbert (1843–1918) of the US Geological Survey in 1893 and had become a tenet of the cold Moon school. Gilbert had observed the Moon for 18 nights through the 26½-inch refractor telescope of the US Naval Observatory. He concluded that only impacts of falling bodies could have produced the craters he saw. The smooth, grey areas were the product of collisions of great objects with the surface, Gilbert surmised.

A number of distinguished scientists entered the controversy. In 1961, the Nobel laureate chemist, Harold Clayton Urey (1893–1981) explained the difference he noted between Earth and Moon.[1]

"Terrestrial rocks have undergone
a long fractionation in the crust of
the Earth, apparently due to partial
melting processes which have
caused the flow of material from
the deep interior to the surface. This
sort of differentiation seems not to
have been present on the Moon."

On the other side, Fred L. Whipple, Director of the Smithsonian Astrophysical Observatory, asserted that there was abundant evidence of volcanic activity on the Moon. The larger craters, however, obviously were the result of impacts by asteroids, planetoids or meteorites.[2]

In the view of Ralph B. Baldwin, an astrophysicist-industrialist, most of the lunar surface had been formed by large impacts early in the Moon's history, but there was evidence of igneous action—rock formation by heat and pressure—as a secondary process.[3]

Patrick Moore, a British astronomer, suggested in 1963 that

". . .we begin with a Moon which
has a solidifying crust lying over
a hot viscous magma."[4]

Jack Green, a geophysicist with the Douglas Aircraft Company, proposed in 1966 that the maria were basalt, an igneous rock produced by volcanism on Earth.[5]

Gerard Kuiper (1905–1973) concluded in 1954 when he was Director of the Yerkes and McDonald Observatories that the Moon must have melted as a result of radioactive heating. He maintained that this was a uniform process in planetary evolution and analysis of the lunar rocks would prove it.[6]

In parallel with this debate was a three-sided controversy about the origin of the Moon. Kuiper maintained that it had formed near the Earth as a two-planet system and Urey proposed that it had formed elsewhere in the solar nebula and had been captured, an event which critics insisted was dynamically unlikely. A third scenario had been advanced at the end of the nineteenth century by Sir George Darwin (1854–1912), second son of Charles Darwin. It described a fission process whereby the Moon was spun off a rapidly rotating, molten Earth, as a great blob of matter which went into orbit close to the Earth and gradually receded as the result of tidal forces. This idea was supported by an American astronomer, William H. Pickering (1858–1938), who suggested that the Pacific Ocean Basin was the fission scar. Some fission theorists pointed to the Moon's density, $3·3g/cm^3$, as evidence that it was composed of Earth's crustal and upper mantle material which were less dense than the whole Earth average of $5·5g/cm^3$.

The Moon's Structure
1 Core (possibly molten).
2 Lower mantle.
3 Middle mantle.
4 Upper mantle.
5 Crust.

One of the purposes of the Apollo missions was to establish a network of seismic stations which would monitor "moonquakes" and meteor impacts, and eventually enable a picture of the Moon's structure to be drawn up. The moonquakes, however, are many times weaker than their counterparts on Earth and they occur a lot deeper inside: between 375 and 500 miles down (600-800km). Although only a few thousand occur annually, they have given scientists a basic understanding of the lunar interior. There is, almost certainly, a small molten iron core which has led to weak magnetization of the lunar rocks. Its presence is inferred from a meteorite impact on the Moon's farside whose shock-waves did not pass through the (presumably) liquid centre. The overlying lower mantle is also partly molten, while the olivine-rich upper and middle mantles are solid and dense. The Moon's basaltic crust is extremely thick and rigid. It consists mainly of plagioclase rich materials.

1,738km
1,680km
1,430km
750km
c300km

Origin of the Moon: A Russian View

"Our physical-mechanical scheme of the development of the Moon is based on the theory that during the time the Earth was accreting, a satellite cluster of small bodies and particles formed around it. The particles and small bodies had been in heliocentric orbit in the same zone as the protoplanetary cloud in which the nucleus of the Earth was growing. As a result of inelastic collisions near the Earth, a certain fraction of the particles changed to geocentric orbits.

"In this scheme, the Moon represents the final product of the assembly of the particles and bodies of the satellite cluster. Its depletion of volatile elements (e.g. water, lead) and enrichment with refractory material (e.g. silicates) relative to the Earth can be explained in the following way.

"Because the circumterrestrial cluster was a later formation than the Earth, lunar material existed longer in a scattered state, both in the protoplanetary cloud and in circumterrestrial orbits. The lag in accretion was at least 50 to 100 million years. During this time, small bodies and particles were colliding at velocities of three to five and five to seven kilometres a second depending on their location with respect to the growing nucleus of the Earth.

"A time period of 100 million years is characteristic for the dissipation of light gases from the region of the terrestrial planets by the solar wind. The wind is capable of ionizing and blowing atoms of any elements right out of the Solar System, if the space is free for radiation.

"Collision of solid particles with velocities of several kilometres a second causes evaporation of

Above: *Cosmonauts study pictures of the Moon sent back by Luna 9 in 1966. Yuri Gagarin is in the foreground at left.*

Two Approaches To Exploration

With the onset of the space age, both the American and Russian programmes of lunar exploration evolved through several stages of increasing technological complexity in concert with the development of more powerful launch vehicles that could lift heavier payloads.

A significant difference, however, became apparent in the final stage of each programme. The Ranger, Surveyor and Lunar Orbiter stages of the United States programme were oriented toward the support of manned exploration, Antarctic style, in the climactic Apollo stage. This orientation was not evident in the Soviet Luna programme which relied on automated and remotely controlled vehicles to perform scientific studies in lunar orbit and on the surface, and to return soil samples to Earth.

To a limited extent, the American system of manned exploration and the Russian system of exploring with automata were complementary. The scientific findings of both programmes were similar and reinforcing. From the American point of view, the deployment of 12 astronauts at six landing sites across the near face of the Moon to set up experiments and collect samples provided a more extensive field of operation and a much higher yield and closer control of samples than the Soviet effort. Soviet scientists asserted that the Luna series provided a more practical model for exploring the terrestrial planets.

Both powers experienced early failures, but the USSR achieved a number of "firsts" which had political significance in a climate of technological competition.

Luna 2 achieved the first man-launched impact on the Moon and Luna 3 made the first photographs of lunar far side in 1959; Luna 9 scored the first soft landing on the Moon and Luna 10 was first to enter lunar orbit in 1966; Zond 5, a spacecraft of the manned Soyuz type, was first to fly around the Moon and return safely to Earth in 1968; Luna 16 accomplished the first automated soil sample return to Earth from the Moon and Luna 17 deployed the first wheeled, self-propelled vehicle on the lunar surface in 1970.

The fact that the Soviets did not crown these accomplishments with a manned presence on the Moon or in orbit around it has intrigued Western observers. An American view suggests that although the Soviets demonstrated a capability of a manned circumlunar flight with the unmanned Zond missions in 1968, they lacked a launch vehicle as powerful as the Saturn V to lift 110,000lb (50,000kg) payloads to lunar orbital manoeuvres and landing.[7]

1 Urey, H.C., "The Moon and Planets" in (Eds.) Berkner, L.V. and Odisha, H., *Science in Space*, McGraw Hill, New York, 1961.
2 Whipple, F.L., *Earth, Moon and Planets*, 3d ed., Harvard University Press, Cambridge, Mass, 1968.
3 Baldwin, R.B., *Measure of the Moon*, University of Chicago Press, Chicago, 1963.
4 Moore, P., *Survey of the Moon*, Norton, New York, 1963.
5 Green, J.S., "Lunar Exploration and Survival", a paper published by Advanced Research Laboratories, Douglas Aircraft Co., 1966.
6 Kuiper, G.P., "Origins of the Moon," a paper, Proceedings, National Academy of Sciences, Vol. 4, 1954.
7 *Soviet Space Programs, 1966-70*, Staff Report, Committee on Aeronautical & Space Sciences, US Senate, 1971.

A Russian map of the Moon's visible side as seen through a moderately large telescope, compiled by Ivan Katiayev, an engineer-cartographer. The dark, solidified lava plains are evidence that the process of accretion and bombardment contributed to heating the surface rocks in the past

material, particularly of volatile elements and those with a low melting point. A certain fraction of evaporating elements recondenses into particles within the cluster; the remainder is expelled from the cluster by the solar wind.

"Particles absorbed by a growing Earth fall into it with high velocities. They, too, are evaporated but the powerful gravitational field of the Earth prevents the evaporating material from slipping away. Also, the inner, denser, more opaque part of the cluster keeps volatiles from being blown away.

"In summary, the Earth received relatively more volatiles and the Moon relatively a higher proportion of refractory materials because (1) the Earth accumulated earlier than the Moon from material passing through a shorter sequence of collisions and (2) the Earth's stronger gravitational field prevented volatile elements from being blown away by the solar wind."

(The author cited the work of Professor Edward Anders and his colleagues at the University of Chicago on basalt samples returned from the Mare Tranquillitatis by Apollo 11 which established the depletion of volatiles on the Moon and its enrichment in refractory elements).

"Once the cluster of particles and small bodies formed in Earth orbit, several conditions for the accretion of the Moon must be satisfied. It had to be completed at a distance known to be less than 30 Earth radii (191,136·9km) and close to 20 Earth radii (127,424·6km) based on the limitations of tidal evolution of the lunar orbit and the geocentric momentum of the cluster. The temperatures resulting from accretion must have been high enough to create the lunar crust and produce the basaltic lavas that flooded the maria. A third condition of accretion must account for structural asymmetry of the Moon, including concentrations of mass (as detected by both Soviet and American orbiting vehicles).

"Having these conditions, we will select one of three versions of accretion of the Moon: (1) Formation of an Earth-Moon system from a binary nucleus by absorption of particles from heliocentric orbits; (2) gradual growth of the Moon from a small nucleus in a cluster; (3) accretion of the Moon from several large satellites grown in the circumterrestrial cluster.

"We note that the first and second versions lead to a low initial temperature of the Moon and do not cause the observed, large irregularities in its structure. We dwell on the third version—the possibility of formation of several large satellites of the Earth having autonomous supply zones.

"Within 20 to 25 Earth radii, a system of two or three large satellites could have formed, with masses of one-half to one-third the present Moon. In the presence of tidal friction, such a system could exist only as long as required for approach of the orbits and collision. A probable collision within 10 Earth radii is numbered in days and, within 20 radii, in years.

"The fusion of two orbits into one body is a very rapid process, lasting about an hour. The energy given off is sufficient to heat the entire mass to several hundred degrees above its equilibrium temperature.

"Participation of large bodies, comparable to each other in mass, in the formation of the Moon gives the most acceptable initial temperature from the point of view of subsequent evolution of the Moon. Moreover, the possibility is developed for the creation of large irregularities in structure and composition as a consequence of the irregular differentiation of the interior of the Moon."

Excerpted from *The Origin of the Moon* by Ye. L. Ruskol, O. Yu. Schmidt Institute of the Physics of the Earth, Moscow; Proceedings of the Soviet-US Conference on the Cosmochemistry of the Moon and Planets, Moscow, 1974.

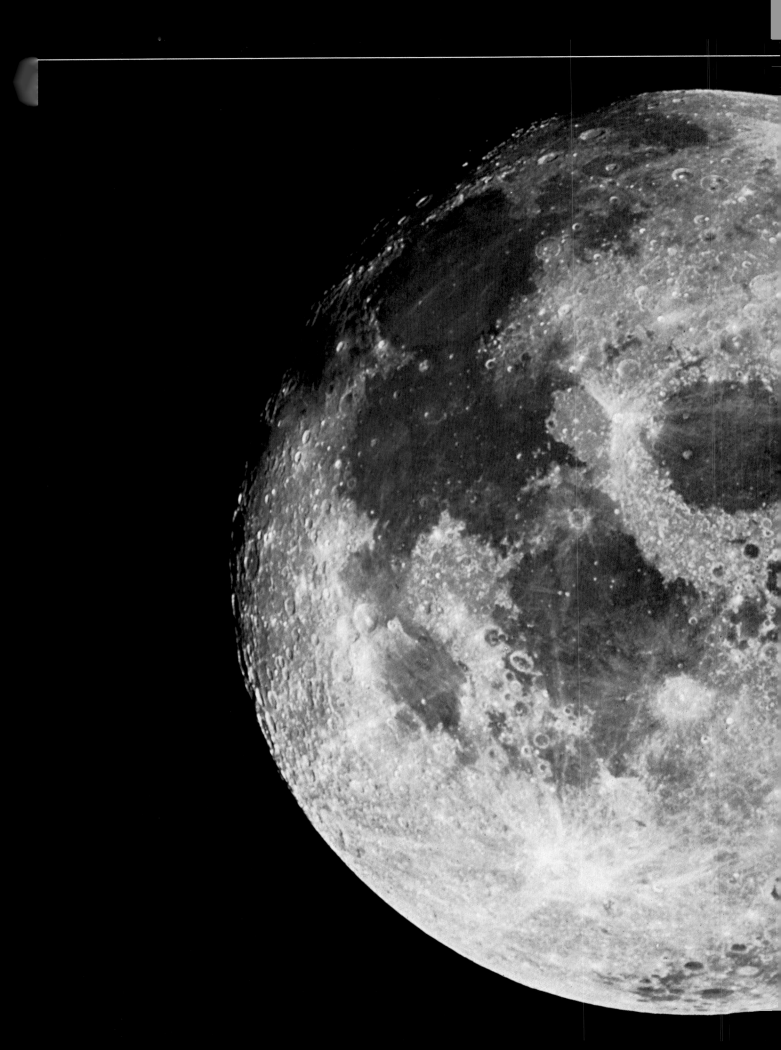

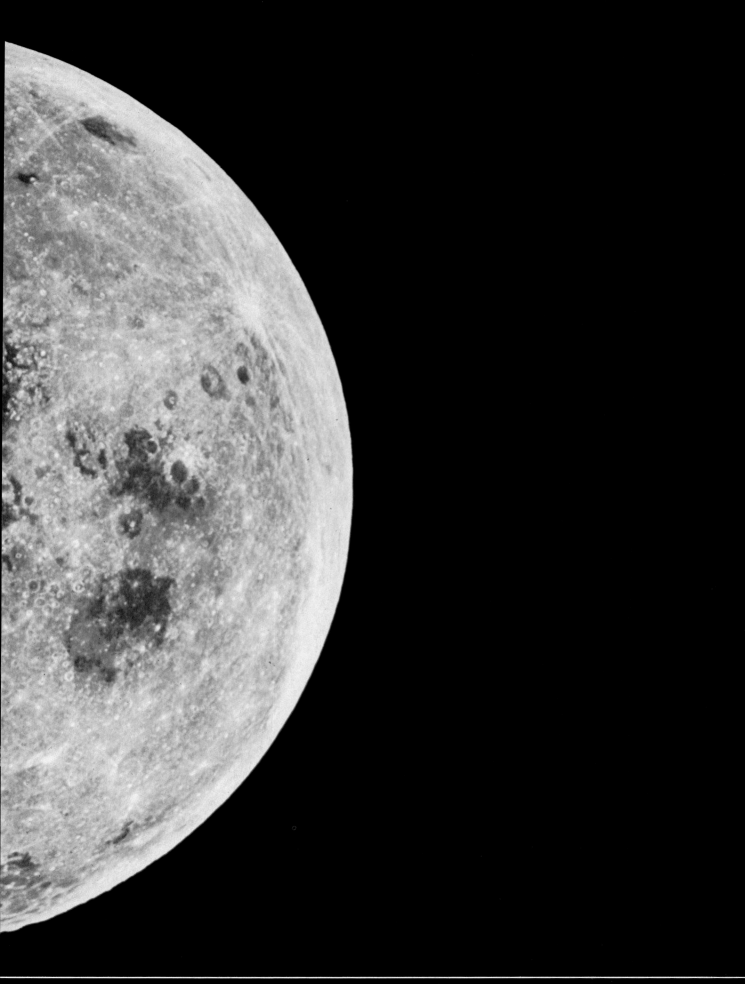

Early Luna Vehicles

Launched on 12 September 1959, Luna 2 hit the Moon about 268 miles (432km) from the visible centre. Luna 3, launched on 4 October 1959, second anniversary of Sputnik 1, flew by lunar far side and took pictures which were developed aboard the spacecraft. The pictures were transmitted to Earth by radio facsimile as the vehicle went into barycentric (Earth-Moon) orbit. Early transmission was poor and later attempts failed to re-transmit the picture data. After 198 days of a continually changing flight path, Luna 3 entered the atmosphere and broke up during re-entry.

Although indistinct, the far side photos were improved sufficiently by computer enhancement to enable Soviet cartographers to produce the first far side atlas.

Higher quality far side photographs were radioed to Earth by Zond 3, a Soviet interplanetary experimental vehicle which was launched on 18 July 1965. It took 25 photographic frames from an altitude of 5,682 miles (9,145km) as it raced by the Moon toward the orbit of Mars and on to heliocentric orbit. These photos confirmed Luna 3 picture details—which were again confirmed by US Lunar Orbiter far side surveys in 1966.

Early US Probes

Starting with Able 1, 17 August 1958, the United States launched nine probes toward the Moon before the tenth, the Ranger 4 camera probe, achieved lunar impact, crashing on far side on 27 April 1962 without returning picture data.

Ranger 4 was an element of a three-pronged reconnaissance programme of the US National Aeronautics & Space Administration. It was designed to photograph, map and gather preliminary chemical data about the lunar surface in support of Project

Spacecraft Landings
Lunar landing sites, both Russian and American, tend to cluster about the Moon's equator. This reflects the fact that near equatorial sites are well illuminated, whereas polar regions are in shadow. The Russian Luna 9 was the first probe to soft-land on the Moon, in the west of the Oceanus Procellarum, in 1966. The US programme for lunar exploration evolved through a series of crash-landing Ranger craft, the exploratory Surveyor landers and the Lunar Orbiter series, which mapped the Moon in unprecedented detail in preparation for the Apollo missions. Two Orbiters were put into polar orbits to map possible highland landing sites. The manned Apollo series began with two landings in maria regions, for reasons of safety; but later landings took place in the geologically distinct uplands. At the same time as Apollo, the Russians resumed their unmanned Luna landings with such craft as Lunas 16, 17, 20, 21, 23 and 24.

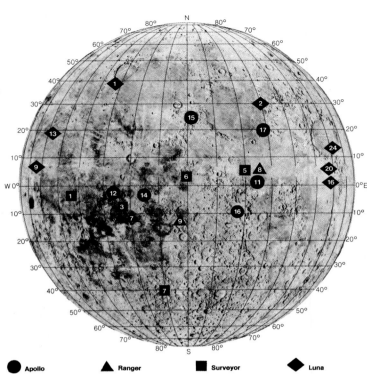

● Apollo ▲ Ranger ■ Surveyor ◆ Luna

Apollo and its objective of landing a man on the Moon. Although these programmes were motivated by international competition, their lasting contributions to human knowledge far outweighed their political purpose which lost its importance as soon as it was achieved.

The first project, Ranger, was a series of photographic impact probes designed to transmit close-up pictures of the surface as they hurtled toward it. The first effective one was Ranger 7. It crashed in the crater Tycho on 31 August 1964, transmitting 4,306 photographs until impact. Ranger photo resolution exceeded by an order of magnitude the resolving power of the most powerful

telescopes. The photos revealed craters nested within craters, down to 10in (25·4cm) diameter. Ranger 7 revolutionized mankind's image of the lunar surface which now could be seen to be much more densely cratered than observers had imagined.

Instead of knife-edge rims and scarps as depicted by artists' renditions in popular science features, the Ranger photos showed a dense population of craters and potholes with rims gently rounded, like dimples made by raindrops in sand. The edges seemed to be eroded, although the Earthly agents of erosion, wind and water, were absent.

SUCCESSFUL LUNAR MISSIONS					
SPACECRAFT		**DATE**	**LAUNCH VEHICLE**	**WEIGHT lb (kg)**	**RESULTS**
Luna 2	(USSR)	12 Sep 59	A-1	860 (390)	First vehicle to hit Moon. Impact near visible centre.
Luna 3	(USSR)	4 Oct 59	A-1	614 (278)	First lunar photos covering 70 per cent of far side.
Ranger 7	(US)	28 July 64	Atlas-Agena	806 (366)	Returned 4,306 close-up photos of soil before impact in Mare Nubium.
Ranger 8	(US)	17 Feb 65	Atlas-Agena	808 (368)	Returned 7,137 close-up photos before impact in Mare Tranquillitatis.
Ranger 9	(US)	21 Mar 65	Atlas-Agena	808 (368)	Returned 5,814 close-up photos before impact in Crater Alphonsus.
Zond 3	(USSR)	18 July 65	A-2-e	2,095 (870)	Returned 25 photos of lunar far side before taking up solar orbit.
Luna 9	(USSR)	31 Jan 66	A-2-e	221 net (100)	Achieved first soft landing on the Moon and returned photos from Oceanus Procellarum.
Luna 10	(USSR)	31 Mar 66	A-2-e	540 net (245)	First spacecraft to achieve lunar orbit. Returned surface gamma, infra-red radiation and fluorescent data for two months.
Surveyor 1	(US)	30 May 66	Atlas-Centaur	2,194 (995)	Soft landing near Flamsteed crater; returned 11,237 photos of surface and soil consistency data.
Lunar Orbiter 1	(US)	10 Aug 66	Atlas-Agena	850 (385)	Returned first sequence of photos for lunar photomap of near side.
Luna 11	(USSR)	24 Aug 66	A-2-e	540 net (245)	Returned data similar to those of Luna 10 from lunar orbit.
Luna 12	(USSR)	22 Oct 66	A-2-e	3,607 (1,636)	Returned photos and scientific data from lunar orbit.
Lunar Orbiter 2	(US)	6 Nov 66	Atlas-Agena	860 (390)	Returned 205 photos of Apollo landing sites and far side features from lunar orbit.
Luna 13	(USSR)	21 Dec 66	A-2-e	3,506 (1,590)	Returned photos and soil strength data from Oceanus Procellarum after soft landing.
Lunar Orbiter 3	(US)	5 Feb 67	Atlas-Agena	849 (385)	Continued photomapping of near side for Apollo landing sites.
Surveyor 3	(US)	17 Apr 67	Atlas-Centaur	2,283 (1,035)	Returned close-up surface photos, excavated soil with shovel after soft-landing in Oceanus Procellarum.
Lunar Orbiter 4	(US)	4 May 67	Atlas-Agena	860 (390)	Returned 163 photo frames of near side from lunar orbit.
Explorer 35	(US)	19 July 67	Thrust-Aug. Delta	229 (104)	Returned surface radiation data from lunar orbit and detected Earth's magnetic field deflecting solar wind as Moon passed through the field's "tail".
Lunar Orbiter 5	(US)	1 Aug 67	Atlas-Agena	860 (390)	Concluded photomap of lunar near side from lunar orbit.
Surveyor 5	(US)	8 Sep 67	Atlas-Centaur	2,216 (1,005)	Made first chemical analysis of lunar soil in Mare Tranquillitatis and returned 19,119 surface photos. Established existence of basaltic lava as mare surface material.
Surveyor 6	(US)	7 Nov 67	Atlas-Centaur	2,223 (1,008)	Made chemical and mechanical tests of lunar soil in Sinus Medii and returned 30,065 photos of surface.
Surveyor 7	(US)	7 Jan 68	Atlas-Centaur	2,293 (1,040)	Dug trench and made chemical analysis and mechanical tests of sub-surface soil; returned 21,274 photos after soft-landing near north rim of Tycho crater.
Luna 14	(USSR)	7 Apr 68	A-2-e	540 net (245)	Returned data on Earth-Moon interactions, lunar mass distribution and charged solar particles from lunar orbit.
Zond 5	(USSR)	14 Sep 68	D-1-e	12,300 (5,600)	First circumlunar biological mission; capsule containing fly larvae, wheat seeds, bacteria and turtles; recovered in Indian Ocean..
Zond 6	(USSR)	10 Nov 68	D-1-e	12,300 (5,600)	Second circumlunar flight with biological specimens recovered after return to Soviet Union using lifting re-entry to reduce velocity. First lunar spacecraft to return to country of origin.
Apollo 8	(US)	21-27 Dec 68	Saturn V	66,986 (30,385)	First manned flight to lunar orbit; Borman, Lovell and Anders recovered in Pacific Ocean splashdown after 10 orbits of the Moon.
Apollo 10	(US)	18-26 May 69	Saturn V	94,693 (42,953)	Second manned flight to lunar orbit; Stafford, Young and Cernan flew 31 orbits of the Moon; Stafford and Cernan descended to 9 miles (14.5km) of the surface in the LM *Snoopy*.

Left: *An Atlas-Agena rocket carrying the survey probe Ranger 7 lifts off for the Moon on 28 July 1964. Ranger 7 returned 4,306 photographs to Earth before a deliberate crash-landing in Mare Nubium.*

Below: *Model of Luna 9, the first soft-landing moonprobe, on display at the Exhibition of National Economic Achievements, Moscow. The landing capsule is shown open beneath the descent craft.*

The crash landing photo reconnaissance continued with Ranger 8 which sent back 7,137 photos of the western Mare Tranquillitatis on 20 February 1965 and Ranger 9, which transmitted 5,814 photos of the crater Alphonsus in the lunar terrae or highlands on 24 March 1965.

Some of the photos taken from higher altitudes revealed sinuous fault structures and dimpled craters which were interpreted as signs of volcanism. But the album of

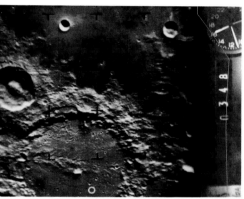

Left: *24 March 1965: Ranger 9 close-up of the large lunar crater Alphonsus which is over 80 miles (129km) in diameter.*

17,259 photos from Ranger made it evident that impacts of bodies of all shapes and sizes from space had been the force that cratered and pulverized the surface. The Moon had undergone an intense bombardment for millions of years.

By the mid-1960s, the United States and the Soviet Union were racing neck to achieve the first soft landing of an automatic vehicle on the Moon.

With the development of more energetic upper stage rockets, the USSR embarked on a programme of soft landings, starting in 1963. They experienced the customary early failures. Launched on 2 April 1963, Luna 4 missed the Moon by 5,000 miles (8,000km); Cosmos 60, launched on 12 March 1965 failed to leave Earth orbit; Luna 5, launched on 9 May 1965, crashed in Mare Nubium; Luna 6, launched on 8 June 1965, missed the Moon by 100,000 miles (160,000km); Luna 7, launched on 4 October 1965, crashed in Oceanus Procellarum as did Luna 8, launched on 3 December 1965.

The first successful soft landing was achieved on 3 February 1966 by Luna 9, which descended into Oceanus Procellarum and began photographing the scene. The descent vehicle weighed 3,490lb (1,583kg) but the operating "station" which separated from the landing bus had a mass of only about 220lb (100kg).

The automatic station deployed a 3·3lb (1·5kg) camera which photographed the landing site to a distance of 1 mile (1·6km). The station transmitted photofacsimiles and radiation measurements for about 72 hours. The landscape depicted by Luna 9 gave the impression of ancient lava flows pulverized by meteoritic bombardment.

Because the vehicle stood only about two feet high, the panorama was limited. There was enough detail in the pictures, however, to show that the maria surface was suffici-

SUCCESSFUL LUNAR MISSIONS					
SPACECRAFT		**DATE**	**LAUNCH VEHICLE**	**WEIGHT lb (kg)**	**RESULTS**
Apollo 11	(US)	16-24 July 69	Saturn V	96,900 (43,953)	First manned landing on the Moon. Armstrong and Aldrin brought the LM *Eagle* down in Mare Tranquillitatis; set up experiments; photographed area; collected 46·3lb (21kg) of rocks and soil; spent 151min 40sec in extravehicular activity (EVA) while Collins orbited the Moon a total of 30 times in CSM *Columbia*.
Zond 7	(USSR)	7 Aug 69	D-1-e	13,225 (6,000)	Unmanned circumlunar flight test returned to Earth.
Apollo 12	(US)	12-24 Nov 69	Saturn V	96,995 (43,997)	Second manned lunar landing. Conrad and Bean brought LM *Intrepid* down in Oceanus Procellarum. Set up experiments, took pictures, collected 75-6lb (34·3kg) samples while Gordon orbited Moon in CSM *Yankee Clipper*. Two EVAs of 7hr 45min total.
Luna 16	(USSR)	12 Sep 70	D-1-e	4,145 (1,880)	Made soft landing in Mare Faecunditatis, collected 3·56oz (101g) of soil and returned it to USSR.
Zond 8	(USSR)	20 Oct 70	D-1-e	13,225 (6,000)	Unmanned circumlunar flight with biological specimens. Returned to Earth.
Luna 17	(USSR)	10 Nov 70	D-1-e	4,084 (1,836)	Landed Lunokhod 1, automated roving vehicle weighing 1,667lb (756kg) in Mare Imbrium. Vehicle tested soil returned scientific data for 10½ months.
Apollo 14	(US)	31 Jan-9 Feb 71	Saturn V	111,435 (50,547)	Shepard and Mitchell landed LM *Antares* on Fra Mauro Formations while Roosa orbited in CSM *Kitty Hawk*. Lunar explorers used rickshaw-type cart to haul equipment. Emplaced experiments, took photos, collected 94·4lb (42·8kg) soil samples. Shepard drove golf ball in televised stunt. Two EVAs totalling 9hr 23min.
Apollo 15	(US)	26 Jul-7 Aug 71	Saturn V	107,407 (48,720)	Scott and Irwin landed at Apennine Mountain front near Hadley Rille in LM *Falcon* while Worden circled in CSM *Endeavour*. Deployed LRV surface vehicle, battery powered. Three EVAs totalled 19hr 07min. Emplaced heat flow experiment; collected 169·1lb (76·7kg) samples. Crew deployed 79·3lb (36kg) sub-satellite in lunar orbit.
Luna 19	(USSR)	28 Sep 71	D-1-e	9,435? (4,280?)	Lunar orbiter sending photos and scientific data to Earth. Measured lunar gravitational fields, gamma radiation, magnetic field and solar wind.
Luna 20	(USSR)	14 Feb 72	D-1-e	4,145 (1,880)	Second sample return mission. Landed Mare Crisium, collected 3·5oz (100g) of sub-surface soil in hollow drill and returned sample to Soviet Union in same manner as Luna 16.
Apollo 16	(US)	16-27 Apr 72	Saturn V	116,605 (52,892)	Young and Duke landed in Descartes highlands in LM *Orion* with second lunar roving vehicle while Mattingly orbited in CSM *Casper*. Three periods of EVA totalled 20hr 14min. Returned 207·8lb (94·3kg) samples. Second sub-satellite of 79·3lb (36kg) deployed in lunar orbit on return trip. CSM *Casper* carried instrumentation for extensive radiometric surveys of lunar surface in its Scientific Instruments Module bay while in lunar orbit.
Apollo 17	(US)	7-19 Dec 72	Saturn V	116,510 (52,849)	Cernan and Schmitt landed in Taurus Mountains region near Littrow crater in search for evidence of recent volcanism. Third Rover deployed from LM *Challenger* while Evans orbited in CSM *America* and made radiometric surveys of surface. Lunar surface explorers set EVA record of 22hr 4min and a long distance record of 21 miles (33·8km) in Rover. This last and longest Apollo mission (301hr 51min) returned 243·4lb (110·4kg) samples. No evidence recent volcanism found.
Luna 21	(USSR)	8 Jan 73	D-1-e	12,345 (5,600)	Landed Lunokhod 2, second automated roving vehicle, in Le Monnier crater where it made soil strength and composition measurements and functioned as rolling lunar observatory.
Explorer 49	(US)	10 June 73	Thrust-Aug. Delta	723 (328)	Entered lunar orbit and made radioastronomy observations from far side.
Luna 22	(USSR)	29 May 74	D-1-e	12,345 (5,600)	In lunar orbit, took surface photographs and collected radiation data.
Luna 23	(USSR)	28 Oct 74	D-1-e	12,345 (5,600)	Landed in Mare Crisium but failed to collect soil sample when drill was damaged.
Luna 24	(USSR)	9 Aug 76	D-1-e	12,345 (5,600)	Succeeded in collecting soil sample and returning it to USSR from Mare Crisium in same manner as the Luna 16 and 20 missions.

ently firm to support the mass of a landing vehicle of greater size and not composed of deep dust as some theorists had predicted. Officials of the US National Aeronautics & Space Administration interpreted the Luna 9 data as signifying that maria regions generally would be safe for a manned landing.

The Little Gold Box

US Surveyor 1, with a net weight of 620lb (281kg), landed on 2 June 1966 in southwest Procellarum. It returned 11,237 photos which depicted a relatively smooth surface of dark material encircled by hills. Close up, the surface looked like a freshly ploughed field.

Following the failure of Surveyor 2, Surveyor 3 came down in eastern Procellarum on 20 April 1967 and transmitted 6,315 photographs of a heavily cratered Moonscape. The two landings left no doubt that the maria surface was firm enough to support a vehicle with the mass of the Lunar Module (3,086lb, 1,400kg) then in production. Fears that a landing craft might be drowned in dust or crash through a brittle crust into a crevasse were set to rest. However, the dense population of craters within craters, gouges and potholes made it clear that a manned landing in such a region would take piloting skill—and luck.

Then, on 10 September 1967, Surveyor 5 landed in southwest Mare Tranquillitatis. It carried a chemical analyzer housed in a six-inch box, plated with gold. The box emitted a stream of alpha particles (protons) from radioactive curium 242 and sensed the energies of those scattered back to it from impact with the soil. Energy levels of the reflected particles identified chemical elements in the soil in the periodic table between hydrogen and silicon.

After 900 minutes of operation, data transmitted to Earth revealed that the soil had the chemical composition of basalt, an igneous rock formed by volcanic processes on Earth. Basalt forms the Palisades of the Hudson River, the Columbia River Plateau, much of the Hawaiian Islands and of Iceland. The message from Surveyor's Little Gold Box told of great basaltic lava flows that had filled the basins in the far past.

Although the hot Moon school regarded the message as proof of volcanism, cold Moon advocates argued that large areas of the surface could have undergone melting by the energy released in the impacts of planetoids or asteroids, especially those large enough to have created the major basins.

Surveyor's identification of basalt in Tranquillitatis did not alone confirm volcanism, but it lent credence to the hot Moon thesis that the Moon had been partially melted in the past. The experimenters who designed and interpreted the results of the chemical analyzer seemed to think so. They reported:

"The overall analysis indicated
that the lunar surface at the
Surveyor 5 landing site is a silicate
rock similar in composition to
materials available on Earth. The
results are more comparable to the
chemical composition of the
continental crust of the Earth than to
that in the outer regions of the Sun." [8]

Meteorites are believed to have the bulk chemical composition of the outer regions of the Sun.

Surveyor 6 landed in the Sinus Medii, a level plain near the centre of lunar near side. It, too, carried a little gold box which also reported basalt. Surveyor 7 alighted on 10 January 1968 in the light-coloured lunar highlands on the ejected material north of Tycho, a hilly region in the southern hemisphere. Compared with the dark, basaltic basins, the highland soils were not only lighter in colour but contained a lower abundance of iron group elements including titanium and copper. The alpha particle scattering instrument showed that the highland soils also were less dense than the maria basalt.

A consensus developed among lunar science investigators in the Ranger and Surveyor programmes that the upper part of the Moon had been cooked by volcanic or plutonic (deep, radiogenic) heating. Perhaps the whole Moon had been melted at one time, some suggested.

Surveyor data supported a scenario of a primordial molten Moon where heavier elements had settled toward the centre while the lighter ones had floated to the surface. While this cooking was going on for millions of years, no cosmic chef spooned off the scum, which had collected at the surface of the cauldron and formed the silicate crust—a crust smashed to smithereens by the bombardment of planetoids, asteroids and meteors. As the surface cooled and the crust hardened, new episodes of heating were generated by the radioactive heat engine within the Moon. Fiery magma erupted through the crust, especially through fissures and cracks made by the great impacts that produced the basins, and into the basins poured the red hot lava from the interior to pave the bottoms with basalt.

Orbital Reconnaissance

Luna 10, launched on 31 March 1966, was the first spacecraft to achieve an orbit around the Moon. The 540lb (245kg) automatic station entered an elliptical orbit inclined 71·8 degrees to the lunar equator on 4 April. It bore instruments designed to count meteoroid impacts, observe the Moon's thermal characteristics, magnetic field and surface radiation and return data on the Moon's gravitational field. The orbiter carried no camera, but it did score another first—the first broadcast of a tape recording of the Soviet Union anthem, the "Internationale",

Above: The footprint made by Surveyor 3 on the Moon when it bounced on landing due to the failure of the verniers to shut off. The furrows just above the leg were made by the scoop-and-claw soil test device.

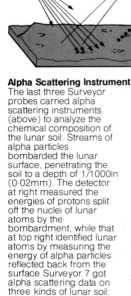

Alpha Scattering Instrument
The last three Surveyor probes carried alpha scattering instruments (above) to analyze the chemical composition of the lunar soil. Streams of alpha particles bombarded the lunar surface, penetrating the soil to a depth of 1/1000in (0·02mm). The detector at right measured the energies of protons split off the nuclei of lunar atoms by the bombardment, while that at top right identified lunar atoms by measuring the energy of alpha particles reflected back from the surface Surveyor 7 got alpha scattering data on three kinds of lunar soil: fine soil, rock and subsurface material.

Technical Data
Height: 10ft (3·05m).
Width across extended legs: 14ft (4·27m).

Weight after jettison of retro-rocket: 620lb (281kg)
Prime contractor: Hughes.

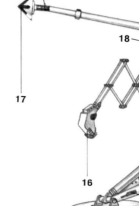

18—

17

16

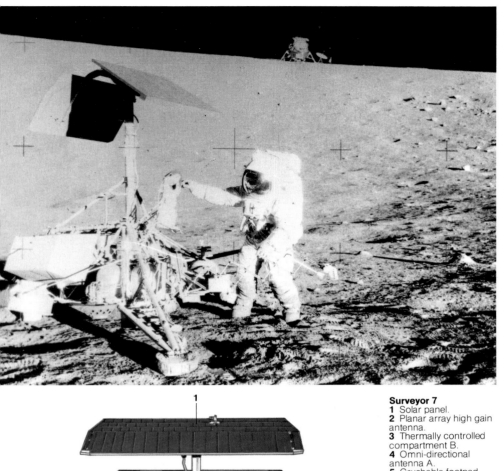

Left: *Thirty-one months after it landed in the Oceanus Procellarum, Surveyor 3 is examined by Apollo 12 astronaut Alan Bean. The TV camera and soil scoop were returned to Earth for study.*

from the Moon. This was done for the edification of the 23rd Congress of the Communist Party of the Soviet Union which was in session at the time. It was said that the event brought the delegates to their feet.

The second Soviet lunar orbiter, Luna 11, was launched on 24 August 1966. It carried gamma and X-ray spectrometers and made the first general survey of the chemical provinces of the lunar surface. Luna 12, launched on 22 October 1966, photographed the surface from orbit. Luna 13, launched on 21 December 1966 landed in Oceanus Procellarum on 24 December to make soil tests and take close-up Moonscape photos. In addition, this vehicle deployed telescoping rods which

8 Developers and investigators of the alpha particle scattering experiment were Anthony Turkevich, Professor of Chemistry, University of Chicago; James H. Patterson, Argonne National Laboratory, Argonne Illinois and Ernest Franzrote, Jet Propulsion Laboratory, Pasadena, California.

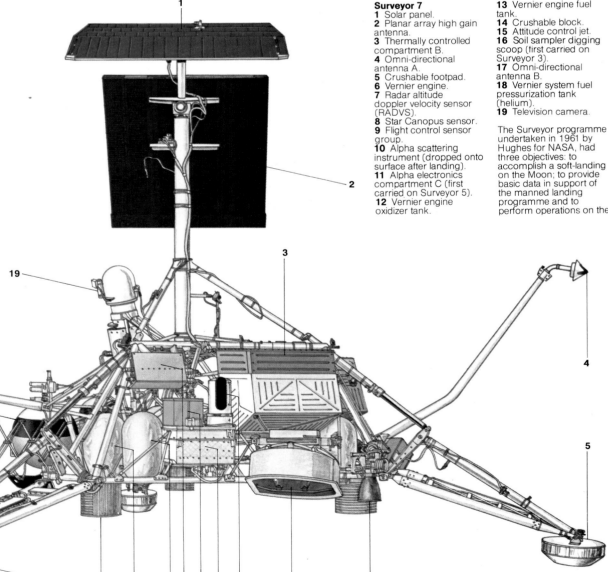

Surveyor 7
1 Solar panel.
2 Planar array high gain antenna.
3 Thermally controlled compartment B.
4 Omni-directional antenna A.
5 Crushable footpad.
6 Vernier engine.
7 Radar altitude doppler velocity sensor (RADVS).
8 Star Canopus sensor.
9 Flight control sensor group.
10 Alpha scattering instrument (dropped onto surface after landing).
11 Alpha electronics compartment C (first carried on Surveyor 5).
12 Vernier engine oxidizer tank.
13 Vernier engine fuel tank.
14 Crushable block.
15 Attitude control jet.
16 Soil sampler digging scoop (first carried on Surveyor 3).
17 Omni-directional antenna B.
18 Vernier system fuel pressurization tank (helium).
19 Television camera.

The Surveyor programme undertaken in 1961 by Hughes for NASA, had three objectives: to accomplish a soft-landing on the Moon; to provide basic data in support of the manned landing programme and to perform operations on the Moon that would reveal new scientific data. The successful missions of Surveyors 1, 3, 5 and 6 confirmed the potential landing sites for the Apollo flights, releasing Surveyor 7 to carry out a purely scientific mission in the lunar highlands, and so allow comparison between highland and mare regions. The probes achieved considerable success despite the loss of two craft; these achievements may be summarised as follows:

Surveyor 1: first fully-controlled lunar landing; established lunar surface could support spacecraft; first pictures of solar corona from Moon; first on-surface colour pictures of lunar surface. Landed: near Flamsteed Crater.

Surveyor 3: First extra-terrestrial excavation; first colour pictures of Earth from Moon; first controlled bearing tests of lunar surface. Landed: Ocean of Storms.

Surveyor 5: First on-site chemical analysis of lunar surface; found that lunar rock has basaltic composition similar to Earth; first detection of magnetic particles in lunar soil; first restart of rocket motor on Moon. Landed: Sea of Tranquillity.

Surveyor 6: First launch from lunar surface; first controlled movement on Moon; established chemical uniformity of luna maria. Landed: Sinus Medii.

Surveyor 7: First soft-landing in lunar highlands; discovered larger rocks and fewer craters; established that rocks have higher albedo than on maria; revealed highland material has lower iron content than mare material; detected and photographed laser beams from Earth. Landed: NW of Tycho Crater in the Moon's south-central highlands.

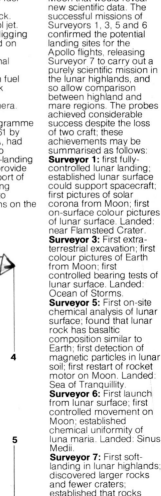

thumped the surface by means of gunpowder explosions to test density and cohesion. The results showed that the soil in this region was less dense than the average density of terrestrial soils; these findings, however, were not confirmed by Surveyor tests and Apollo expeditions.

A probability that some planetoids were buried below the basins was indicated by the third phase of US pre-Apollo reconnaissance of the Moon—a project called Lunar Orbiter. Between 1966 and 1968, five spacecraft carrying high resolution cameras were launched into low orbits around the Moon.

The fifth in the series, Lunar Orbiter 5, was launched into a polar orbit of the Moon on 1 August 1967. Variations in its orbital path disclosed the existence of large concentrations of mass (mascons) in Mare Orientale, Mare Smythii, Mare Humboldtianum and Crater Grimaldi. These masses exerted increased gravitational pull on orbiting spacecraft.

Designed primarily to make high resolution photographs of the surface from an orbital altitude of 30 nautical miles (55·56km), the Lunar Orbiters not only scouted potential landing sites for the Apollo Lunar Module but paid scientific dividends as well. Their instruments reported that radiation levels at the surface were low and would not endanger the astronauts. The discovery of the mascons added a surprising new element to lunar evolution. It also provided a warning that Apollo pilots orbiting the Moon in preparation for a landing of the Lunar Module would have to take these gravitational anomalies into account in calculating descent trajectories. Before considering the achievements of the Apollo missions, it is appropriate to look at the latter stages of Soviet lunar exploration.

Luna Third Phase

Lunar flight logs do not include any successful Soviet missions in 1967 when American Surveyors and Lunar Orbiters monopolized the lunar scene in preparation for Apollo. After a 16 month hiatus, the USSR launched Luna 14 towards lunar orbit on 7 April 1968. In the absence of authoritative data, the orbiter is estimated to have had a mass of 3,560lb (1,615kg), the same as Luna 10, its predecessor. It carried an experiment array similar to that of Luna 10 and performed radio communications tests with Earth stations.

The third series of Luna missions, from Zond 4 and Luna 15 onwards, was lofted by the new and more powerful D-l-e launcher which had been developed by 1965. It could lift heavier payloads than the A-1 and A-2-e launch vehicles used in the earlier phases of the programme, but it did not appear in Soviet reports until 1968.

The Soviet step-up in launch thrust paralleled that of the United States progression from Thor-Able, Atlas-Agena to Atlas-Centaur. The third phase Lunas were the first automated machines designed to land on the Moon after manoeuvring in orbit to reach a selected landing site, instead of hitting a surface target by direct ascent.

The initial mission in phase 3 was Luna 15, launched on 13 July 1969, three days before Apollo 11. Inasmuch as both the

Soviet unmanned and the American manned vehicles would be on a lunar flight trajectory and in lunar orbit at the same time, NASA queried the Soviet Space directorate about Luna 15's flight path to be certain it would not interfere with the first Apollo lunar landing mission. Soviet space officials assured NASA that there would be no interference.

However, the nature of the Luna 15 mission was not divulged. It entered lunar orbit as Apollo 11 approached the Moon. The new tactic of manoeuvring vehicles in orbit before a landing raised the question of whether Luna 15 was to be an orbiter or a lander. Doubt was settled on 21 July when Luna 15 crashed in Mare Crisium. It was to have been a lander and many observers believe its mission was to pick up a sample of lunar soil and fly it back to the Soviet Union, thus giving another first to Soviet space enterprise—the first return of a lunar soil sample. For if that had been the Luna 15 mission, it certainly could have returned such a sample to Earth before the crew of Apollo 11 could have brought their 46·3lb (21kg) of rocks and soil to the Lunar Receiving Laboratory at Houston, Texas. Whatever was intended, the probe succumbed to a 300mph (480km/hr) impact. The Soviets flew five more missions programmed to return lunar soil samples to Earth. These were Luna 16, 18, 20, 23 and 24, but only Luna 16, 20 and 24 succeeded. Each returned a sample the weight of which was of the order of 3·52oz (100gr).

Launched on 12 September 1970, Luna 16, with a mass of 4,145lb (1,880kg), landed in Mare Faecunditatis after making several orbits of the Moon to locate the landing site. Once on the ground, the vehicle's television camera showed the control team on Earth what the site looked like. Following this inspection, Earth control instructed the robot to sink a hollow drill as far as it would go into the lunar regolith and extract a core.

The drill penetrated about 10·33in (26·25cm) before hitting a hard place, presumably a rock. A core sample of 3·63oz (103gr) was lifted out of the drill hole and dumped into a

Below: *A technician at the USSR Academy of Sciences holds the ampule of lunar rock returned by Luna 24's re-entry module. The rock-carrier contains only 6oz (170g)— the highest sample weight of the series.*

canister atop the vehicle. The canister was then sealed.

The Luna samplers consisted of two stages, a descent stage which lowered the entire craft to the surface from orbit and which also served as a launch platform for the ascent stage. This was designed to lift off the descent stage when the sample was safely aboard and fly back to Russia. The landing area was in Kazakhstan.

Luna 16 performed the lift-off and fly-back manoeuvre and the return capsule parachuted down to Kazakhstan on 24 September 1970.

Luna 18, launched on 2 September 1971, crashed in Mare Faecunditatis, but Luna 20,

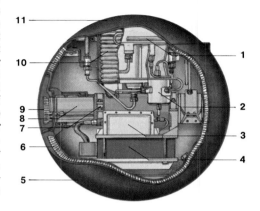

Luna 16 Return Capsule
1 Antenna.
2 Antenna switch.
3 Radio transmitter.
4 Storage battery.
5 Protective heat shield.
6 Capsule shell.
7 Sample container retaining spring.
8 Container for lunar sample.
9 Container cover and locking mechanism.
10 Parachute compartment (containing braking and main parachutes).
11 Parachute compartment cover.

Luna 16's return capsule parachuted down to Earth on 24 September 1970; having separated from the ascent stage, the capsule deployed parachute, whip antennas and metallic "needles" for radar location on re-entry, and a homing beacon was

activated to enable helicopters to pin-point the craft. The sample itself was revealed to be a single core weighing just over 3·6oz (100gr) taken from the north-eastern region of the Sea of Fertility; subjected to dosimetric, biological and toxicological tests, it resembled granular dark grey powder and under the microscope was shown to comprise materials of two major aggregates—angular, basalt-like magmatic rock particles and more complex, caked particles, many vitrified from the lunar surface. Over 70 chemical elements were detected, as were short-lived radio-nucleides formed under the influence of the solar wind, and a high content of space-originated inert gases.

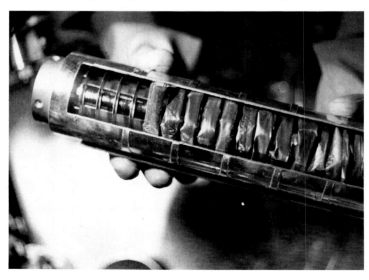

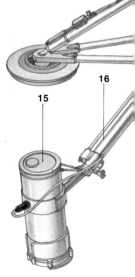

15

16

launched on 14 February 1972, returned a sample slightly in excess of 3·5oz (100gr) from Mare Crisium. The next attempt, Luna 23, was launched on 28 October 1974. It landed successfully in Mare Crisium but was abandoned after its drill broke. The last of these samplers, Luna 24, was launched on 9 August 1976, again to Mare Crisium. It succeeded in collecting a soil sample and returned it to the USSR.

The similarity of the two-stage samplers with the US Lunar Module with its descent and ascent stages is striking. The Soviet machines were smaller, about 12·8ft (3·9m) tall compared with the 22·96ft (7m) high LM, and were crudely constructed inasmuch as

they were not required to maintain life support. But both operated in much the same way.

A second automatic system of exploring an extra-terrestrial body was demonstrated by Luna 17. Launched on 10 November 1970, it entered an orbit around the Moon on 15 November and two days later landed in Mare Imbrium. There it discharged the first, self-propelled, wheeled surface vehicle, Lunokhod 1.

This vehicle had eight wheels, each powered independently by an electric motor, and was shaped rather like a circular bathtub with a lid on it. Inside the lid were solar arrays which provided electric power when

the lid opened out. At nightfall, the lid was closed to protect scientific instruments inside. Chemical batteries provided what power was needed and the interior of the craft was warmed by a radioactive isotope heater (see picture on page 140).

Upon landing, Luna 17 automatically let down a ramp and out rolled Lunokhod onto the basaltic plains of Imbrium. The vehicle had a mass of 1,667lb (756kg), somewhat heavier than the 1,545lb (700kg) loaded weight of the Lunar Roving Vehicle, the manned, 4-wheeled vehicle, brought to the Moon by the last three Apollo missions.

Lunokhod 1 was operated by radio control from Earth by a four man crew consisting of

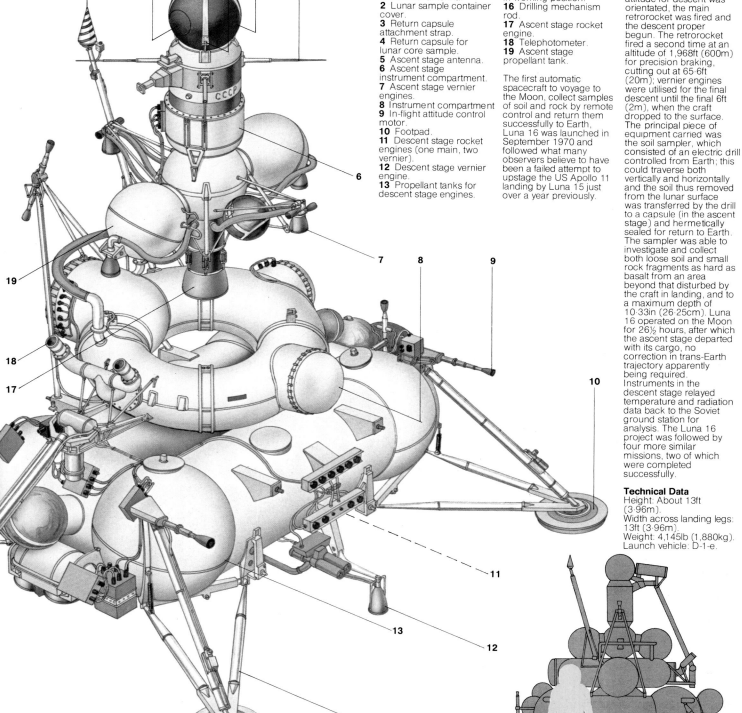

Luna 16
1 Descent stage omni directional antenna.
2 Lunar sample container cover.
3 Return capsule attachment strap.
4 Return capsule for lunar core sample.
5 Ascent stage antenna.
6 Ascent stage instrument compartment.
7 Ascent stage vernier engines.
8 Instrument compartment
9 In-flight attitude control motor.
10 Footpad.
11 Descent stage rocket engines (one main, two vernier).
12 Descent stage vernier engine.
13 Propellant tanks for descent stage engines.

14 Landing leg.
15 Drilling device, shown in working position.
16 Drilling mechanism rod.
17 Ascent stage rocket engine.
18 Telephotometer.
19 Ascent stage propellant tank.

The first automatic spacecraft to voyage to the Moon, collect samples of soil and rock by remote control and return them successfully to Earth, Luna 16 was launched in September 1970 and followed what many observers believe to have been a failed attempt to upstage the US Apollo 11 landing by Luna 15 just over a year previously.

From a corrected lunar orbit, the Luna 16 lander's attitude for descent was orientated, the main retrorocket was fired and the descent proper begun. The retrorocket fired a second time at an altitude of 1,968ft (600m) for precision braking, cutting out at 65·6ft (20m); vernier engines were utilised for the final descent until the final 6ft (2m), when the craft dropped to the surface. The principal piece of equipment carried was the soil sampler, which consisted of an electric drill controlled from Earth; this could traverse both vertically and horizontally and the soil thus removed from the lunar surface was transferred by the drill to a capsule (in the ascent stage) and hermetically sealed for return to Earth. The sampler was able to investigate and collect both loose soil and small rock fragments as hard as basalt from an area beyond that disturbed by the craft in landing, and to a maximum depth of 10·33in (26·25cm). Luna 16 operated on the Moon for 26½ hours, after which the ascent stage departed with its cargo, no correction in trans-Earth trajectory apparently being required. Instruments in the descent stage relayed temperature and radiation data back to the Soviet ground station for analysis. The Luna 16 project was followed by four more similar missions, two of which were completed successfully.

Technical Data
Height: About 13ft (3·96m).
Width across landing legs: 13ft (3·96m).
Weight: 4,145lb (1,880kg).
Launch vehicle: D-1-e.

a commander, driver, radio man and navigator. Four television cameras mounted on the vehicle showed them where it was going. Automatic sensors on the tub shut off power if it inadvertently approached a hole or crevasse the cameras failed to see. The vehicle could go backward as fast as it could go forward and make hairpin turns.

In contrast to the US Apollo-LRV, essentially a battery-powered, lunar jeep, Lunokhod was a well-equipped scientific observatory in its own right. It deployed rods that thumped the soil to measure its density and bearing strength; an X-ray spectrometer which reported soil chemical data and which also doubled as an X-ray telescope to observe celestial X-ray sources; a cosmic ray detector and a laser mirror which reflected laser beams directed to it from observatories in the Crimea and France.

Designed to operate for three lunar days (of 14 days each), Lunokhod continued collecting and reporting scientific data for over 10 months, including nine lunar days and part of the tenth. It covered about 6·5 miles (10·5km) of ground (compared with 17·4 miles (27·9km) by the Apollo 15 Rover) and telecast more than 20,000 pictures to receiving stations on Earth.

The second automated roving vehicle, Lunokhod 2, was carried to the Moon by Luna 21 which was launched on 8 January 1973. Lunokhod 2 carried the same instrumentation as its predecessor but covered more ground—23 miles (37km)—during the three lunar days it was operating. It telecast 80,000 pictures to Earth. The crew nearly 233,000 miles (375,000km) away consisted of a commander, driver, radio man, navigator and engineer. Lunokhod 2 explored a region 112 miles (180km) north of the Apollo 17

Above: *A copy of the Russian lunar rover, Lunokhod 2, which was delivered to the Mare Serenitatis in January 1973 by Luna 21. Stereo TV cameras are clearly visible (left); communications antennae are above; hinged lid contains solar cells.*

landing site between the Taurus Mountains and Mare Serenitatis.

Soviet scientists cited the Lunokhods, as well as the sample-return Lunas, as prototypes of the machines and systems that would be deployed to explore the terrestrial planets in lieu of manned expeditions. In the United States, critics of the expense of Project Apollo argued that the Soviet-style automata could perform the same job at a fraction of the cost. The argument remained speculative, however; while Apollo costs were a matter of public record, Luna costs were not. Estimates of comparative programme costs could not be substantiated.

A third type of Luna sent to the Moon in the third phase of Soviet exploration was Luna 19, launched on 28 September 1971, and Luna 22, launched on 29 May 1974. They were advanced, orbital reconnaissance vehicles capable of making high resolution and wide area photographic surveys. Each was equipped also with instruments that indicated chemical and mineral assemblages of regions of the surface; that analyzed the particles and fields of space near the Moon; reported the intensity of the solar wind and high energy emissions from solar flares and even monitored radio emissions from Jupiter. As though this were not enough, both vehicles returned data on concentrations of mass within the Moon as the "mascons" affected their orbits. Each of the vehicles operated for about a year.

Zond

A separate class of vehicles called Zond appeared in the Soviet lunar flight programme in 1968 and continued for part of 1969. Western observers regarded the class as a precursor to manned lunar missions.

The Zond spacecraft exhibited the configuration of a Soyuz manned spacecraft, but lacked the forward work module. The vehicle was 17·38ft (5·3m) long, 7·54ft (2·3m) in diameter, and had a mass of about 12,345lb (5,600kg), according to British and American estimates.

The first of the series, Zond 4, was launched on 2 March 1968 to the vicinity of the Moon's orbit, but not directly to the Moon. Judging from later flights in the Zond series, the trajectory was designed to bring it back to Earth, but no return was reported and it was assumed by observers that the test flight failed.

Zond 5 was launched on 14 September 1968 on a successful circumlunar flight which brought it back to Earth in seven days. It re-entered over the South Pole and splashed down in the Indian Ocean, where it was recovered.

Zond 5 was a Soyuz-type spacecraft with a recoverable cabin module, heavily shielded to withstand re-entry at lunar return velocity. It carried parachute packs, scientific instruments, radios, temperature regulating devices for the cabin and a power supply in the forward module. Attached was a Service Module with extendable solar panels, a radio telemetry system, flight control instruments, stabilization systems, attitude control thrusters, course correction rockets and chemical storage. It appeared to be an unmanned manned space ship.

Instead of a human crew, however, Zond 5 carried biological experiments including turtles, flies, worms, a spiderwort plant, seeds of wheat, pine and barley and bacteria cultures. The experiments were designed to test the effect of cosmic rays and high energy solar radiation on life forms flying beyond the protective envelope of the Earth's magnetic field. Earth orbital manned flights remained within the magnetic shield, but flights to the Moon went far beyond it, into the unshielded realm of the interplanetary medium.

It was following the return of Zond 5 that NASA confirmed its intention of sending Apollo 8, the second manned Apollo mission,

Above: *A view inside the Soviet sample-receiving laboratory, where rocks returned by Luna and Lunokhod missions were received and processed in sterile conditons.*

Above: *Edwin Aldrin, pilot of the Apollo 11 Lunar Module (right) stands before the first Apollo experimental package. At centre is the Passive Seismic Experiment Package; beyond, the Laser-Ranging Retro-Reflector. Other instruments are cameras.*

to orbit the Moon in December 1968. It seemed evident that the Soviets had the capability of making a manned, circumlunar flight in the fourth quarter of the year.

On 10 November the Soviets launched Zond 6 around the Moon. It returned 17 November in a remarkable fashion. Re-entering the atmosphere over the South Pole, it was manoeuvred so that it skipped out like a flat stone skipping across water and then it entered again, this time on a descent path that enabled it to land in the Eastern Soviet Union instead of the Indian Ocean.

Early in December, it was formally announced that Zond 4, 5 and 6 were dedicated to perfecting a manned spacecraft to go around the Moon. Although Zond 6 had performed well, Academician Anatoliy A. Blagonravov, a principal spokesman for Soviet space programmes, was quoted by Moscow Radio as saying that further unmanned tests would be required before men could be sent around the Moon. Shortly thereafter, Apollo 8, with Frank Borman, James Lovell and William Anders aboard, was launched to the Moon on 21 December, flew 10 orbits of the Moon on Christmas Eve and returned on 27 December.

The Soviets continued testing with Zond 7 which was launched on 7 August 1969. It circled the Moon in a 1,250 miles (2,000km) orbit on 11 August and returned on 14 August using the double skip manoeuvre of

Zond 6. The final shot in the series, Zond 8, was launched on 20 October 1970. It transmitted television photos of Earth from 40,400 miles (65,000km) and passed within 685 miles (1,100km) of the Moon. This time, the spacecraft with a full complement of specimens re-entered over the North Pole and splashed down in the Indian Ocean.

Tranquility Base

Analysis of the rocks and fines which Apollo 11 brought back from the Mare Tranquillitatis showed that in addition to basaltic igneous rocks, the astronauts had picked up another type of rock called "breccia". This is an aggregate of small rock fragments and soil compacted into coherent mass. The soil scooped up by Armstrong and Aldrin turned out to be a mixture of crystallized fragments and pieces of glass. Mixed in with it were residues of iron meteorites and some pieces that looked as though they had been derived from bedrock. The rubbly, rough soil appeared to be the product of myriad impacts. The lunar science team referred to it as the "regolith".

The rounded crater rims and rolling hills indicated that some process of erosion was working on the airless and waterless Moon. It was the continuous bombardment of space dust falling on a surface unshielded by an atmosphere, the Lunar Sample Analysis Planning Team suggested.[9]

The little gold boxes on Surveyors 5, 6 and 7 had shown that the most common elements on the Moon were oxygen and silicon, as on the surface of the Earth. However, there appeared to be a lower abundance of sodium on the Moon than on Earth and the Moon seemed to be richer in elements heavier than silicon.

The minerals which turned up in Apollo 11 samples included pyroxene, a silicate found in igneous rocks containing calcium, sodium, magnesium, iron or aluminium; plagioclase, a feldspar high in calcium and sodium and ilmenite, a mineral composed of iron, titanium and oxygen. Three new minerals were found. The Sample Analysis Planning Team referred to them as pyrox-manganite, ferropseudobrookite and chromium-titanium spinel, a hard, crystalline mineral. Free metallic iron and troilite, a ferrous sulphide found in meteorites, showed up in the samples as common accessory minerals. They are rare on Earth.

All the rocks exhibited high concentrations of titanium, scandium, zirconium, hafnium, yttrium and rare earth elements, but low concentrations of sodium. The volatile elements such as bismuth, mercury, zinc, cadmium, thallium, lead, chlorine and bromine were significantly depleted compared to their supposed abundance in the primitive Solar System. There was no evidence of water.

From the depletion of volatile elements—those that boil off early as temperature rises—the Sample Analysis Planning Team inferred that the Moon had accreted in a part of the solar nebula where temperatures were higher than the region where Earth is thought to have formed.

If so, the Moon must have been captured. But although the hypothesis of capture is easy to reach on this basis, it remains incredibly difficult to explain in terms of planetary-satellite dynamics.

9 *Science*: Report of the Lunar Sample Analysis Planning Team, Vol. 167, No. 3918, 3 Jan 1970.

143

Potassium-argon and other radiometric methods of dating the rocks showed they were formed 3·7 billion (ie $3·7 \times 10^9$) years ago. If the Moon's age is reckoned at 4·6 billion years, like the age of the Earth, the igneous rocks in Mare Tranquillitatis crystallized 900 million years after the formation of the Moon, presumably from a melt of primordial rocks. In this way, a period of lunar volcanism could be inferred beginning several hundred million years after the Moon accreted from grains, gases and planestimals in the solar nebula. A single exotic rock fragment showed up in the Apollo 11 collection. It yielded an age of 4·4 billion years.

The depletion of volatile elements which suggested that the Moon formed in a hotter part of the nebula than did the Earth tended to support opponents of the fission theory. If the Moon had spun off the Earth, the separation must have occurred before 4·3 billion years ago, the Sample Analysis Planning Team concluded. Furthermore,
"such a hypothesis must now take account of certain definite differences in chemical composition."

Apollo 12

For an expedition whose investigators spent less than two hours actually doing field work, Apollo 11 yielded remarkable results. The sample analysis showed that at some time between 4·4 billion years, the age of the oldest rock, and 3·7 billion years, the age of most of the basalts, an episode of melting had occurred on the Moon. Surveyor had indicated it; Apollo 11 proved it.

The first manned lunar mission dedicated to exploration was Apollo 12. Although Apollo 11 carried scientific instruments, including a seismometer and a laser reflector, its primary purpose was to fulfil President John F. Kennedy's 1961 commitment to land a man on the Moon and bring him safely back before the decade was out. Apollo 11 did this; its scientific fall-out was a bonus.

On 19 November 1969, the Apollo 12 astronauts, Charles "Pete" Conrad, Jr and Alan L. Bean landed in Oceanus Procellarum 1,300 miles (2,106km) west of Tranquility

10 *Science*: Report of the Lunar Sample Analysis Planning Team, Vol. 167, No. 3918, 3 Jan 1970.

Base in the Lunar Module *Intrepid*. Overhead, Richard F. Gordon orbited the Moon in the CSM, *Yankee Clipper*.

Intrepid was targeted to a pock-marked field where Surveyor 3 had landed 31 months before. The region was strewn with debris splashed out of the crater Copernicus eons ago and was interesting because of variety of rocks that might be lying there. Conrad brough the LM down to within 790ft (240m) of Surveyor. A mission objective called for Conrad and Bean to hike across the cratered field to Surveyor, photograph it, inspect it carefully and bring back some camera lenses for analysis at Houston. When they reached the spacecraft, they found it covered by a layer of tan dust, but otherwise in nearly mint condition. It seemed to them that Surveyor 3 could stand for a

Above: *Apollo 12 astronaut Alan Bean starts to deploy the ALSEP experiment package from the stowage bay at the rear of the LM. Instruments included a magneto-meter, and a passive seismic experiment.*

thousand years in that benign environment. Nothing rusts on the Moon, but micro-meteoroids could score the paint and the glass on the spacecraft.

Intrepid carried the Apollo Lunar Surface Experiments Package (ALSEP) which included two devices essential to an understanding of the Moon—a cluster of four seismometers to record moonquakes and meteorite impacts and a magnetometer to detect a magnetic field, if any.

A magnetic field, such as Earth's, was not expected on the Moon because of its slow

LUNAR SURFACE OPERATIONS										
MISSION CREWMEN	LANDING DATA					EXTRAVEHICULAR ACTIVITY			SAMPLES COLLECTED lb (kg)	SURFACE STAYTIME hr. min. sec.
	AREA	LATITUDE	LONGITUDE	DATE	TIME GMT hr. min. sec.	TRAVERSE VEHICLE	DIST. TRAVELLED miles (km)	DURATION hr. min. sec.		
Apollo 11 Armstrong Aldrin	Sea of Tranquillity	0·7°N	23·4°E	20 July 69	20:17:40	None	~0·62 (~1)	02:31:40	46·3 (21·0)	21:36:21
Apollo 12 Conrad Bean	Ocean of Storms	3·2°S	23·4°W	19 Nov 69	06:54:36	None	First: ~0·62 (~1) Second: 0·8 (1·3) Total: ~ 1·42 (~2·3)	First: 03:56:03 Second: 03:49:15 Total: 07:45:18	First: 36·8 (16·7) Second: 38·8 (17·6) Total: 75·6 (34·3)	31:31:12
Apollo 14 Shepard Mitchell	Fra Mauro	3·6°S	17·5°W	5 Feb 71	09:18:11	Modular equipment transporter	First: ~0·62 (~1) Second: 1·86 (3·0) Total: ~ 2·48 (~4)	First: 04:47:50 Second: 04:34:41 Total: 09:22:31	First: 45·2 (20·5) Second: 49·2 (22·3) Total: 94·4 (42·8)	33:30:31
Apollo 15 Scott Irwin	Hadley-Apennines	26·1°N	3·7°E	30 July 71	22:16:29	LRV-1	First: 6·4 (10·3) Second: 7·8 (12·5) Third: 3·2 (5·1) Total: 17·4 (27·9)	Standup: 00:33:07 First: 06:32:42 Second: 07:12:14 Third: 04:49:50 Total: 19:07:53	First: 32·0 (14·5) Second: 76·9 (34·9) Third: 60·2 (27·3) Total: 169·1 (76·7)	66:54:53
Apollo 16 Young Duke	Descartes	9·0°S	15·5°E	21 Apr 72	02:23:35	LRV-2	First: 2·6 (4·2) Second: 6·9 (11·1) Third: 7·1 (11·4) Total: 16·6 (26·7)	First: 07:11:02 Second: 07:23:11 Third: 05:40:03 Total: 20:14:16	First: 65·9 (29·9) Second: 63·9 (29·0) Third: 78·0 (35·4) Total: 207·8 (94·3)	71:02:13
Apollo 17 Cernan Schmitt	Taurus-Littrow	20·2°N	30·8°E	11 Dec 72	19:54:57	LRV-3	First: 2·1 (3·3) Second: 11·7 (18·9) Third: 7·2 (11·6) Total: 21·0 (33·8)	First: 07:11:53 Second: 07:36:56 Third: 07:15:08 Total: 22:03:57	First: 31·5 (14·3) Second: 75·2 (34·1) Third: 136·7 (62·0) Total: 243·4 (110·4)	74:59:40

Note: The total times given for EVA duration are based upon the times at which cabin pressure reached 3·0psi during depressurization and repressurization, except for Apollo 11 which is based on the times of hatch opening and closing; and Apollo 12 which is based on times of egress and ingress.

Above: *Alan Shepard, Apollo 14 commander, shields his eyes from the brilliant Sun on his first moonwalk. The picture was taken by Edgar Mitchell through the window of LM Antares.*

rotation and assumed lack of a metallic core. It was considered probable that the dynamo effect which is believed to generate a magnetic field had never occurred there.

It was with considerable surprise, therefore, that investigators saw the first transmissions from the Apollo 12 magnetometer indicating the existence of a remanent

Below: *Apollo 12's Charles Conrad — with photographer Alan Bean reflected in his visor — holds a sample of moonrock in his Special Environmental Sample Container.*

magnetic field in the rocks of 36 gammas. Although this is a minute fraction of the Earth's field, it showed that a strong, background field had existed at the time the rocks in Procellarum crystallized and were magnetized by it. In light of the dynamo theory, the data meant that the Moon not only rotated rapidly in the far past, but had some semblance of a metallic, possibly liquid core.

At Procellarum, the basaltic rocks and fines were of another generation than those at Tranquility Base; Procellarum rocks were 500 million years younger. Their ages of crystallization hovered around 3·2 billion years ago. Two new pieces of information were apparent. The Moon had a magnetic field then. The episodes of melting had continued for 1·4 or 1·5 billion years. A new scientific scenario was taking shape.

Until 3·2 billion years ago, the Moon had been volcanically active. Then the lunar heat engine had shut down. Whether it was completely dead was uncertain, for there were persistent reports of gas emissions and strange fogs from the rim of Aristarchus and the interior of Alphonsus.

The search for a piece of the original crust was rewarded when Conrad and Bean picked up a "genesis" rock the size of a small lemon. It subsequently was dated at 4·6 billion years old. It contained 20 times more uranium, thorium and potassium than any other sample.

Fra Mauro

In April 1970, the National Aeronautics & Space Administration turned its attention to the highlands. Apollo 13 was launched toward a highland region called the Fra Mauro Formation, but never got there. En route to the Moon, an oxygen tank in the Service Module overheated and exploded, severely damaging the life support system. By using the Lunar Module oxygen reserve, the crew was able to survive and return directly to Earth after flying around the Moon.

Apollo 14 reached the Fra Mauro Formation on 5 February 1971. Alan B. Shepard and Edgar Dean Mitchell landed the Lunar Module *Antares* in a hilly region, 110 miles (178km) east of the Apollo 12 site.

The Command Module pilot, Stuart A. Roosa, remained in orbit in the mother ship,

Kitty Hawk, photographing the surface while waiting for his colleagues to finish their work on the ground and blast off in *Antares'* upper stage to rejoin the Command and Service Module for the trip home.

A major mission objective was to send seismic shock waves into the ground to measure the depth of bedrock. The waves which Shepard and Mitchell generated by firing small explosive charges with a device called a "thumper" would be reflected on reaching bedrock to an array of three geophones (sound detectors) laid out at intervals on the surface.

This was the first attempt to perform an active seismic experiment on the Moon. It had been done many times on the Antarctic and Greenland ice caps to measure the depth of the ice, but the seismic energy did not penetrate the rubbly regolith with the ease it penetrated ice. The experiment revealed a layered structure in the topsoil to a depth of about 100ft (30m), the maximum range of the seismic waves in this medium. Seismic reflections indicated a layer of powdery material at 27·8ft (8·5m). Density increased below that level, but bedrock was not reached.

The most effective seismic experiment was performed while the Apollo 14 CSM was still in orbit. Early on 4 February 1971, the third stage of the Saturn V launcher hit the Moon 130 miles (210km) southwest of the Apollo 12 site with the energy of 11 tons of TNT. Seismic waves generated by the impact were picked up by the Apollo 12 seismometers and caused the whole region to ring like a bell for three hours. The surprising amount of reverberation was interpreted as indicating a considerable depth of unconsolidated material in the Procellarum region. A similar effect had been observed when the third stage of the Apollo 13 Saturn V launcher hit the Moon in April 1970. Signals from both third stage impacts did not reveal any change in unconsolidated regolith material to a depth of 21 to 24 miles (34-39km). Crustal rocks had been smashed to at least that depth.

The Apollo 14 magnetometer detected a high magnetic field in the Fra Mauro region, three times stronger than that at the Apollo 12 site. It gave additional evidence that the Moon had generated a strong field in earlier eons. It also lent credence to the existence

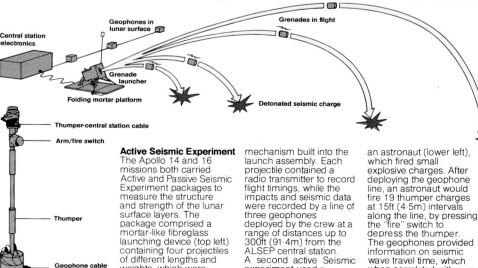

Active Seismic Experiment
The Apollo 14 and 16 missions both carried Active and Passive Seismic Experiment packages to measure the structure and strength of the lunar surface layers. The package comprised a mortar-like fibreglass launching device (top left) containing four projectiles of different lengths and weights, which were launched by a firing mechanism built into the launch assembly. Each projectile contained a radio transmitter to record flight timings, while the impacts and seismic data were recorded by a line of three geophones deployed by the crew at a range of distances up to 300ft (91·4m) from the ALSEP central station. A second active Seismic experiment used a "thumper" device held by an astronaut (lower left), which fired small explosive charges. After deploying the geophone line, an astronaut would fire 19 thumper charges at 15ft (4·5m) intervals along the line, by pressing the "fire" switch to depress the thumper. The geophones provided information on seismic wave travel time, which when correlated with range, indicated wave velocity.

Central station electronics

Geophones in lunar surface

Grenades in flight

Grenade launcher

Folding mortar platform

Detonated seismic charge

Thumper-central station cable

Arm/fire switch

Thumper

Geophone cable and reel

ORBITAL EXPERIMENTS

SURFACE EXPERIMENTS

Experiment	Number	Apollo 11	Apollo 12	Apollo 13	Apollo 14	Apollo 15	Apollo 16	Apollo 17
Multi-Spectral Photography	S-158		●					
Cm Window Meteoroid	S-176					●	●	●
UV Photography – Earth and Moon	S-177			●	●	●	●	●
Gegenschein* from Lunar Orbit	S-178			●	●	●	●	●
Gamma-Ray Spectrometer	S-180					●	●	●
X-Ray Fluorescence	S-161			●		●	●	
Alpha Particle Spectrometer	S-162			●		●	●	
S-Band Transponder (CSM/LM)	S-164					●	●	●
S-Band Transponder (Subsatellite)	S-164					●	●	
Mass Spectrometer	S-165					●		●
Far UV Spectrometer	S-169							●
Particle Shadows/Boundary Layer	S-170					●	●	
IR Scanning Radiometer	S-171							●
Bistatic Radar	S-173			●	●	●	●	●
Magnetometer (Subsatellite)	S-174					●	●	
Lunar Surface Magnetometer	S-209		●			●	●	
Solar Wind Spectrometer	S-031		●			●		
Suprathermal Ion Detector	S-033		●		●	●		
Passive Seismic	S-034	●	●		●	●	●	
Active Seismic	S-035				●		●	
Lunar Sounder	S-036							●
Charged Particle Lunar Environment	S-037				●	●		
Cold Cathode Ion Gauge	S-038		●		●	●		
Heat Flow	S-058					●		●
Lunar Field Geology	S-059	●	●		●	●	●	●
Laser Ranging Retro-Reflector	S-078	●			●	●		●
Solar Wind Composition	S-080	●	●		●	●	●	
Cosmic-Ray Detection (Helmets)	S-151						●	●
Cosmic-Ray Detector	S-152					●	●	
Lunar Surface Closeup Photography	S-184	●	●		●			
Portable Magnetometer	S-198				●		●	
Far UV Camera/Spectroscope	S-199						●	
Lunar Gravity Traverse	S-200						●	
Soil Mechanics	S-201		●		●	●	●	●
Lunar Ejecta and Meteorites	S-202							●
Lunar Seismic Profiling	S-203							●
Surface Electrical Properties	S-204							●
Lunar Atmospheric Composition	S-205							●
Lunar Surface Gravimeter	S-207							●
Lunar Neutron Probe	M-515							●
Lunar Dust Detector	S-229		●	●				●

*Celestial counterglow: a faint glow in the sky believed to be sunlight reflected by interplanetary dust.

of a metal core. The expedition had been supplied with a modularized equipment transporter (MET), a 2-wheeled, rickshaw-like cart, complete with rubber tyres, to haul equipment and samples. It tested the utility of a wheeled vehicle on lunar soil.

The final Apollo 14 experiment involved the crew. Shepard, Mitchell and Roosa underwent the 21-day quarantine required by Public Health Service before being released to their homes. Like the crews of Apollo 11 and 12, they were free of any lunar biogenic contamination. It was final proof that Moon was sterile. Life had not appeared there until the *Eagle* landed.

With the completion of the Fra Mauro mission, there were two working seismic stations on the Moon—at Fra Mauro and Procellarum. The first station set up at Tranquility Base had failed after several months. From the two stations, Houston received intermittent seismic signals of impacts of small meteorites, most of them on Far Side.

In addition, signals which seemed to be generated by weak Moonquakes were received at monthly intervals, three to five days before lunar perigee, when the Moon was nearest Earth. It was speculated that the heightened gravitational attraction of the Earth pumped magma into cracks between the rocks and created shock waves.

Two laser beam reflectors had been set up on the Moon, one at Tranquility Base, the other at Fra Mauro. They consisted of 100 silica corner reflectors in an aluminium frame 17·9in (46cm) square. Each was designed to reflect a ruby laser beam fired at it through a telescope on Earth back to the telescope. Two observatories took part in the laser experiments—the Lick Observatory at Mt Hamilton, California and the McDonald Observatory, Mt Locke, Texas. Travelling at the speed of light, the beam's round trip time would define the average distance between Earth and Moon. It was expected that laser measurements would eventually narrow

distance uncertainty to within 245ft (75m), from the existing uncertainty of 1,640ft (500m). Such a refinement would improve the accuracy of calculations of the rate at which the Moon is receding from the Earth as it is accelerated by tidal effects. Beam measurements would also indicate fluctuations in the Earth's rotation and the length of the day and provide a measurement of continental drift.

A gas detector (cold cathode gauge) set up by Shepard and Mitchell at the landing site reported gases which seemed to have a volcanic origin. A similar gauge had been left at the Apollo 12 site, but had failed.

Was the Moon still hot enough to emit tenuous wisps of gas from its interior? A Russian astronomer, N. Kozyrev, had reported gas emissions from the central peak of the crater Alphonsus in 1958. Luminous hazes had been seen by others in the craters Aristarchus, Eratosthenes and Plato. It was speculated that if Moonquakes indicated subsurface pools of hot magma, the pools probably were the source of the gas emission.

Hadley-Apennines

The Apennine Mountain region was the target of Apollo 15. Astronauts David R. Scott and James B. Irwin landed the Lunar Module *Falcon* on 30 July 1971 in a mare plain called Palus Putredinus (Marsh of Decay) at the eastern edge of the Imbrium Basin, 644 miles (1,036km) northeast of Fra Mauro. The landing site lay between the front of the Lunar Apennine Mountains which form the southeastern rim of Imbrium and a canyon called the Hadley Rille. The term, "Marsh of Decay", suggested that gases might have been seen there, but no emissions were detected by the expedition.

While the Command Module pilot, Alfred M. Worden, remained in orbit aboard the CSM *Endeavour* and photographed the surface, Scott and Irwin unloaded the Lunar Roving Vehicle: a four-wheeled, battery powered "jeep" from the Lunar Module and

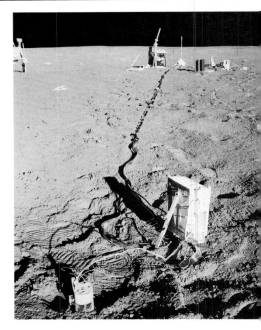

Above: *The Apollo 14 Suprathermal Ion Detector and its accompanying Cold Cathode Gauge were set up to detect the flow of ions in the solar wind.*

drove it along the mountain front. They stopped to collect rocks, admire the scenery and take photographs.

A major objective of this expedition was to determine if heat was flowing out of the lunar interior. Scott and Irwin struggled to sink a pair of thermal probes into the regolith to a depth of 10ft (3m), but soil resistance was so high they were able to reach a depth of only 5·3ft (1·62m) with one probe and 5·25ft (1·6m) with the other. These insertions were sufficient, however, to enable the probes to sense a 1·75 degrees Centigrade rise in temperature per metre of depth.

The experimenters reported:
"The conclusion is that if the observed lunar heat flow originates

from radioactivity, then the Moon must be more radioactive than the classes of meteorites that have formed the basis of Earth and Moon models in the past."[11]

Scott and Irwin extended the lunar instrument network by setting up a magnetometer, seismometers and a third laser mirror. From orbit, X-ray and gamma ray spectrometers aboard the *Endeavour* drew a broad scale chemical map of a swath of the surface over which the spacecraft orbited.

The orbital survey confirmed the chemical differences between maria and highland rocks that had appeared in the samples. As suspected from their light colour, the highlands had a high concentration of aluminium and silicon compared with the basins. The gamma ray spectrometer showed a concentration of radioactive elements—uranium, thorium, potassium—and of iron in the western maria on Near Side. Their abundance was an order of magnitude lower in the eastern highlands on Far Side. There were distinctive chemical lunar provinces.

As Apollo 15 thrust out of lunar orbit to return home, the crew deployed a hexagonal box 30·7in (78cm) long and 14·2in (36cm) across into lunar orbit. The subsatellite

was instrumented to detect energetic particles and plasma near the Moon. The data showed that the Moon creates a cavity in the Solar Wind (as does the Earth).

Apollo 15 was the first of the three later (J-type) expedition spacecraft to carry a Scientific Instrument Module (SIM) in a bay of the Service Module (SM). The instruments were gamma ray, alpha particle and mass spectrometers, an X-ray fluorescence instrument, a magnetometer and automatic cameras. The spectrometers and the X-ray instrument collected galactic background data as Apollo 15 approached the Moon and as it returned to Earth, and lunar surface data as the Command and Service Modules (CSM) of the spacecraft orbited the Moon while commander and lunar module pilot were exploring the surface. The magnetometer monitored space and lunar magnetic fields and the cameras photographed the CSM ground track. The SIM conferred upon the Apollo spacecraft some of the functions of an independent satellite. The actual subsatellite released from the SIM-bay as the crew prepared to leave lunar orbit mapped the remanent lunar magnetic field and measured high and low energy solar particles in lunar orbit. The spectrometers surveyed the gross chemical composition of the surface along the ground track. Gamma ray intensity indicated that radioisotopes of potassium, uranium and thorium were higher in the western maria (lowland basins) than in the eastern and highland regions of the Moon.

Viewing Far Side from low orbit, Worden described the landscape of the side never seen from Earth as "very hummocky" with subdued craters and few distinctive lava flows. Maria basins did not appear until *Endeavour* passed over the crater Tsiol-

Left: *The first Lunar Rover—folded in preparation for its flight to the Moon on Apollo 15—is inspected for fit in the LM at the Kennedy Space Center.*

Below: *Apollo 15's CSM Endeavour was the first in the series to carry a Scientific Instrument Module on board. Its instruments carried out large-scale remote sensing of the lunar surface. This enabled cross-correlation of much surface data and helped with planning the Apollo 17 mission.*

kovsky. The ship's laser altimeter showed that the surface of Far Side was 3 to 6 miles (5 to 10km) higher than that of Near Side.

The seismic stations at Procellarum, Fra Mauro and Hadley-Apennines confirmed a thick crust. It was 40 miles (65km) thick at Fra Mauro. Continental crust on Earth averages 25 miles (40km) in thickness.

Reviewing the four expeditions, NASA scientists concurred that the Moon was a planet. It was more like the Earth than like meteorites, However, chemical differences appeared to deny any parental connection.

On the Moon, the ratio of potassium to uranium was lower than on the Earth. The Moon was greatly depleted in volatile elements. It seemed to be devoid of any water. Its abundance of oxygen (in the rocks) was lower than that of Earth. It had no atmosphere, and may never have had one, although gases were detectable by sensitive instruments near the surface.

By 1972, lunar science conferences had produced a scenario of evolution in which the Moon had undergone several episodes of heating, chiefly from radioactive isotope decay. In the first 300 to 400 million years, a low density scum of anorthosite floated to the surface of the Moon-planet to form the crust which was then cratered and pulverized by infalling planetoids, asteroids, meteorites and comets.

Three crustal provinces formed: two types of basins and the highlands.

The basins were sculpted out of the crust by infalling bodies of considerable size. Imbrium was thought to have been created 3·9 billion years ago by a planetoid as big as the Island of Cyprus.

Once the large basins were formed, lava erupted from the interior and flowed into them. It was speculated that Earth's ocean basins may have been formed by similar processes and later filled with water.

Tranquillitatis represented one type of basin crust. Its basaltic floor was found to be rich in iron and titanium. Another province seemed to be represented by Procellarum. Its basalt contained a lot of potassium (K), rare earth elements (REE) and phosphorus (P). To this assemblage, the geology team

11 Apollo 15 Preliminary Science Report, NASA SP-289, 1972.

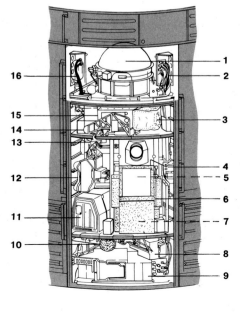

Apollo SIM-bay (SIM door shown removed)
1 Cryogenic oxygen tank.
2 SM-SIM interface cabling.
3 Mapping camera film cassette (transferred to Command Module by astronaut EVA during trans-Earth flight).
4 GN_2 controls.
5 GN_2 bottle.
6 Panoramic camera.
7 Panoramic camera film cassette (transferred to CM by EVA).
8 Mass spectrometer.
9 Alpha and X-ray spectrometer.
10 Gamma ray spectrometer (shown without protective cover).
11 Particles and field subsatellite.
12 EVA foot restraint.
13 Multiple operations module.
14 Laser altimeter.
15 Mapping camera.
16 SM-SIM interface cabling.

ut, Dr Harrison Scl

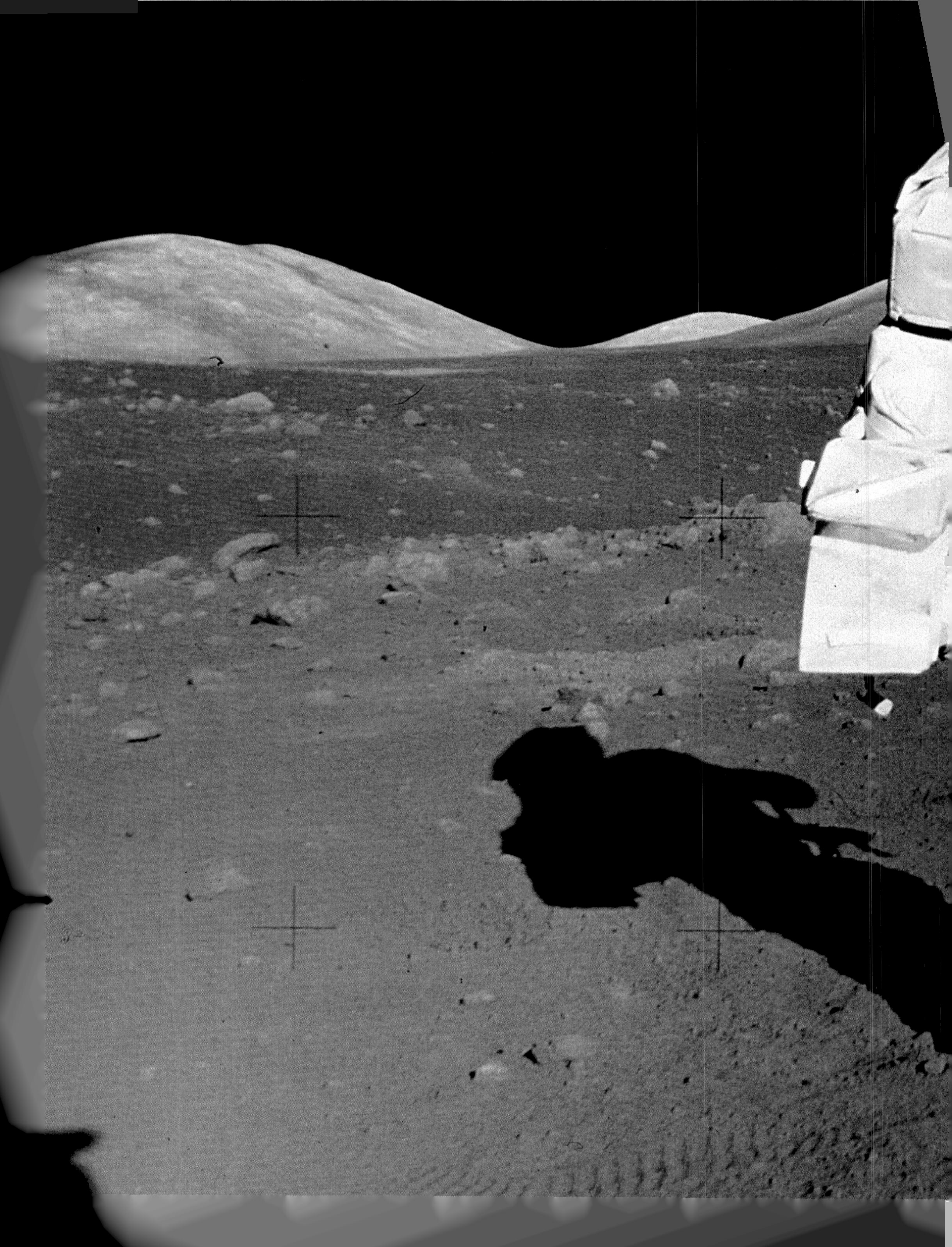

assigned the acronym KREEP. The highlands which the astronomers of the Renaissance thought of as continents (Terrae) consisted principally of the calcium-aluminium silicate rock called anorthosite.

The failure to find rocks younger than 3·1 billion years and only a few "genesis" rocks which seemed to be older than 4·2 billion years indicated that episodes of melting had continued about 1·1 billion years. Volcanism had ended 3·1 billion years ago, but the Moon was still hot at depth. After 45 days of operation, the Apollo 15 heat flow experiment reported a flow of 3·3 millionths of a watt per square centimetre, or about one-half the average flow on Earth.[12]

Apollo 16

A repetition of the heat flow experiment was attempted on the Apollo 16 expedition to the region in the highlands called Descartes. John Young and Charles M. Duke landed the LM *Orion* on a landscape called the Cayley Formation on 20 April 1972. Thomas K. Mattingly remained aloft in the CSM *Casper*.

The two probes were set in the ground in good order, but before any data could be collected, Young caught his boot in the cable and broke if off one of the probes. Repair was not possible and the experiment was abandoned.

A surprisingly high magnetic field of 313 gammas was registered by the expedition's magnetometer. It was three times as strong as the 103 gamma field detected at Fra Mauro and 30 times the highest reading at Hadley-Apennines. These data implied the existence of a Moon-wide magnetic field of 1,000 gammas, about one-thirtieth of the Earth's field at the equator.

Another "genesis" rock was found in the Cayley Formation, a breccia (composite) No. 67483 which exhibited an age of 4·25 billion years. Original pieces of the crust — or what was thought to be the crust — were being found as erratics all over the Moon. Vainly were such ancient rocks sought on Earth, but none have been reported up to this writing. The oldest Earth rocks found in Greenland were about the median age of the lunar rocks.

Meanwhile, a phenomenon of considerable importance as a probable stage in the evolution of the planets were perceived by a group of investigators who were working on dating the rocks.

Data from Apollo 14 and 16 samples and from another sample picked up in the highlands in February 1972 by the Soviet's Luna 20 lander and returned to Russia showed that a 150 million year period that involved intensive melting and recrystallization of rocks had taken place from 3·95 to 3·8 billion years ago. This was interpreted by Gerald Wasserburg and his colleagues at the California Institute of Technology as evidence of a cataclysmic bombardment of the Moon. The basins may have been created in this period.[13]

The bombardment appeared to be a late stage in the accretion of the Moon, which was sweeping up left over debris from the condensation of the planets. But a question of great importance remained to be answered. Where had the projectiles come from? Why had they appeared more than 500 million years after lunar formation? Where had they been stored all this time?

Similar evidence of catastrophic bombardment was to be found later on Mercury. Portions of Mars were heavily cratered. Craters were found on Venus. Earth had probably not escaped such a bombardment, but the scars had been healed by tectonic and erosion processes which were continually altering the surface.

A number of scenarios were generated at NASA's Lunar Science Conferences to explain the phenomenon. A credible one suggested that a vast number of planetesimals, asteroids, planetoids and meteors had remained in the region between Mars and Jupiter — the asteroid belt. They were perturbed out of their orbits by the big planet, Jupiter, and came hurtling into the inner Solar System to crash into the terrestrial planets. How and

Below: *Apollo 16 commander John Young walks away from the site in the Descartes highlands where he has deployed the Apollo Lunar Surface Experiments Package. Power comes from the Radioisotope Thermoelectric Generator (background right). Just below is the heat flow experiment. The Lunar Surface Magnetometer is upper left.*

The Moon of Apollo 17 Astronaut, Harrison Schmitt

"The probability is very great that the synthesis of the geology of Apollo and Luna will become one of the fundamental turning points in the history of all science. For the first time men have been presented with the opportunity to interpret their own Earth through an understanding of a second planet. This second planet which we call the Moon is now a pitted and dusty window into the Earth's own origins and evolution.

"Sunset on the Far Side of the Moon was not always so starkly tranquil as it is now. About 4·6 billion years ago, when the Moon was approximately its present size, the Sun probably set on a glowing, splashing sea of molten rock. Storms of debris still swept this sea, mixing, quenching, outgassing and remelting a primitive, melted shell.

"This outer shell and possibly the entire Moon appears to have been melted by the great thermal energy released by the last violent stages of the formation of the terrestrial planets. The actual processes by which this energy was released and, in fact, the processes by which the materials of the Moon and Earth came together in space remain subjects of heated debate.

"Inside the melted shell, the crust and upper mantle of the Moon were gradually taking form through processes associated with the

Geologist Harrison Schmitt working with the Lunar Roving Vehicle on the Apollo 17 mission, at Station 4, on the rim of Shorty crater, where he discovered orange soil. Distant peak in the centre background is Family Mountain.

fractional separation of phases on a planetary scale. At the base of the melted shell or possibly in the center of the completely melted Moon, an immiscible, dense liquid of iron and sulfur probably accumulated as the melting took place. The initial separation of silicate minerals in the outer melted shell then produced a combined crust and upper mantle a few hundred kilometers thick; the crust rich in calcium and aluminium (anorthitic plagioclase) and the upper mantle rich in magnesium and iron (pyroxene and olivine).

"Most of the major chemical differentiation we have observed on the Moon may have been established with the formation and cooling of the outer melted shell. This differentiation included the fractionation of siderophile and chalcophile elements into the immiscible iron-sulfur liquid; the fractionation of many major, minor and trace elements between the crust and upper mantle during the fractional crystallization of silicate minerals; and the loss of volatile elements from the crust and upper mantle as the continued rain of primordial debris mixed and splashed the outer melted shell in the vacuum of space."

Excerpted from *Evolution of the Moon: The 1974 Model*, by Harrison H. Schmitt, proceedings of the Soviet-American Conference on the Cosmochemistry of the Moon and Planets, Moscow, 4-8 June 1974.

ray detector, Ronald E. Evans circled the Moon in the CSM *America* which was equipped with infra-red, ultraviolet and gamma ray sensors.

The gravity meters were a new experiment on the Moon. They were brought to detect gravitational waves propagating through the Universe. The Moon was regarded as an ideal platform for this kind of research. It was seismically quiet, compared with Earth.

No evidence of recent volcanism was found, but Cernan and Schmitt found something else: glassy orange soil. It turned out to have interesting implications. A number of volatile elements, rare on the Moon, had condensed on the orange soil grains, including bromine, silver, zinc, cadmium and thallium. Volatiles also had been associated with the green glassy fines found at Hadley-Apennines. The glasses indicated that there may be more volatiles on or in the Moon than supposed. Water might still exist as ice in the permanently shadowed craters of the polar regions.

Lunar programme scientists have asked NASA to attempt to verify this possibility by launching an instrumented satellite to lunar polar orbit, as a follow up to Apollo. Beyond this proposal, no further exploration of the Moon has been planned by either the USSR or the United States.

Work continues, however, on the 836·6lb (379·5kg) of lunar rocks and soil brought back by Apollo. Only a small fraction has been thoroughly analyzed, but it was enough to enable a leading lunar physicist, the late Paul W. Gast, to remark:

"I think we have now come to the point where we all recognize that we have a planet before us, the Moon. . . . That has changed the whole concept of the composition of the planets. A chemically heterogenous Solar System such as we are beginning to see from the Moon is certainly a fundamentally different Solar System from one where you basically make everything out of chondrites."[15]

when they came was speculative, but the evidence they had come was unmistakable. There is little doubt that the Moon intercepted some that were coming at Earth.

A Lunar Core

During 1972, the final year of the Apollo expeditions to the Moon, the interior of the Moon remained to be delineated. The thick crust appeared to merge with a denser mantle. Was there a core?

Seismic evidence said there was. On 13 May 1972, the stations at Procellarum, Fra Mauro and Descartes recorded the impact of a sizable meteorite on Far Side. Shear waves from the impact failed to pass through the centre of the Moon — an indication that it was in a molten state. Shear waves do not

pass through a liquid. A molten core was implied, but its composition remained speculative. A small iron or iron sulphide core with a radius of 310 to 435 miles (500 to 700km) was calculated by investigators of the University of California at Los Angeles on the basis of the Moon's moment of inertia ratio.[14]

Orange Glass

A final attempt to locate evidence of volcanism more recent than 3·1 billion years ago was made on the last expedition, Apollo 17. Astronauts Eugene Cernan and Harrison H. (Jack) Schmitt landed the LM *Challenger* in a valley between the Taurus Mountains and the Littrow crater on 11 December 1972.

Schmitt, a geologist and the only scientist to go to the Moon, believed that evidence of relatively recent volcanism would turn up there. Worden had reported cinder cones in the region as he cruised in lunar orbit the previous year in *Endeavour*. While Cernan and Schmitt drove their Lunar Roving Vehicle around the landing site in search of recent rocks, and erected seismometers, gravity meters, a mass spectrometer and a cosmic

Left: *John Young drives the Lunar Roving Vehicle at its maximum speed of 8·7mph (14km/h) in this scene from the Apollo 16 mission. The Rover was electrically powered, and could negotiate slopes of 20°.*

12 Apollo 15 Preliminary Science Report, NASA SP-289, 1972.
13 Tera, F., Papanastassiou, C.S., Wasserburg, G.J. "Lunar Time Scale and Summary of Isotopic Evidence for a Terminal Lunar Cataclysm", Fifth Lunar Science Conference, Houston, 1974.
14 Kaula, W.M. et al, "Apollo Laser Altimetry and Inference as to Lunar Structure", Fifth Lunar Science Conference.
15 News conference, NASA, Washington, DC, 27 Oct 1972, in Lewis, R.S., *Voyages of Apollo*, Quadrangle-New York Times Book Co., New York, 1974.

RECOMMENDED READING

Alfven, A. and Arrhenius, G., *Evolution of the Solar System*, NASA, Washington, D.C., 1976.
Cortright, E.M., *Apollo Expeditions to the Moon*, NASA, Washington, D.C., 1975.
Hallion, R.P. and Crouch, T.D., *Apollo: Ten years Since Tranquility Base*, Smithsonian Institution Press, Washington, D.C., 1979.
Lewis, R.S., *Appointment on the Moon*, Viking Press, New York, 1969.
Lewis, R.S., *The Voyages of Apollo*, Quadrangle-New York Times Book Co., New York, 1974.
Lewis, R.S., *From Vinland to Mars: A Thousand Years of Exploration*, Quadrangle-New York Times Book Co., New York, 1976.
Moore, Patrick, *A Survey of the Moon*, Norton, New York, 1963.
Schmitt, Harrison H., "Evolution of the Moon: the 1974 Model", Proceedings of the Soviet-American Conference on the Cosmochemistry of the Moon and Planets, Lunar Science Institute, Houston.
Whipple, Fred L., *Earth, Moon and Planets*, 3d ed., Harvard University Press, Cambridge, Mass, 1968.
Wilford, John N., *We Reach the Moon*, Norton, New York, 1969.
Baldwin, R.B., *Measure of the Moon*, University of Chicago Press, Chicago, Ill, 1963.

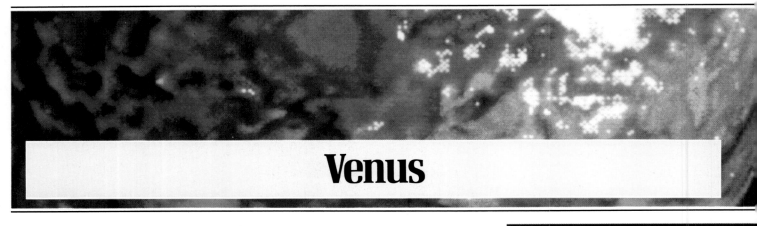

Venus

In the ancient world, Venus was perceived as two stars. The Greeks called it "Phosphoros" in the morning and "Hesperos" in the evening. Babylonians, Egyptians and Chinese also regarded it as two stars. It was the Greek mathematician, Pythagoras (582–507 BC), who unified the perception of Venus by proving that it was a planet, the Greek term for wanderer, among the fixed stars.

The brightest object in the heavens at evening after the Moon, Venus had a special significance for ancient peoples. The Mayans based a remarkably accurate calendar on its apparitions. Greeks and Romans invested the silvery body with qualities of love and beauty. It was the antithesis of Mars.

In the Rennaissance, Venus had a critical role in establishing the doctrine that the Earth revolved around the Sun. Galileo Galilei (1564–1642), observing Venus with his small telescope, discovered that it exhibited phases like the Moon. The discovery proved that Venus changed its position in the heavens relative to the Earth and Sun and therefore, like Earth, circled the Sun. Under investigation by the Italian Inquisition for advocating the "heresy" of heliocentrism, Galileo reported his discovery cryptically. *"The mother of loves"*, he wrote, *"imitates the forms of Cynthia (the Moon)."*

Venus was also the key to determining the distance from the Earth to the Sun. In the eighteenth century, Edmond Halley (1656–1742), British Astronomer Royal, proposed that observations of the transit of Venus across the face of the Sun from two different points on Earth would provide a means of determining the parallax of the Sun.[1] Once this was known, the distance from Earth to the Sun could be calculated by trigonometry.

The transit of Venus across the Sun occurs only twice every 130 years. On the basis of transits in 1761 and 1769, solar parallax was determined as 9 seconds of arc. This value was refined by later observations to 8·7942 to yield an average Sun–Earth distance of 92,600,000 miles (149,600,000km) —the astronomical unit (AU). During the transit of 1761, a Russian astronomer, Mikhail V. Lomonosov (1711–1765) observed a haze around the Venerian disc. He concluded that it was an atmosphere.

Although Venus is Earth's closest neighbour, the "mother of loves" remained an entrancing mystery for centuries. Its surface was perpetually hidden by dense clouds so that not even its period of rotation could be determined with any degree of exactness.

In 1890, the Italian astronomer, Giovanni Virginio Schiaparelli (1835–1910), concluded

VENUS: BASIC DATA	
Equatorial Diameter*	0·95E;7,519 miles (12,100km)
Mass*	0·815E
Density	3·04oz/in³ (5·26g/cm³)
Volume*	0·857E
Surface Gravity*	0·91E
Escape Velocity	6·4 miles/sec (10·3km/sec)
Period of Rotation	243 days
Inclination of Equator (to Orbit)	~0°
Distance from Sun (Semi-major axis)	0·72AU; 67·19 x 10⁶ miles (108·1 10⁶km)
Siderial Period	224·7 days
Synodic Period	583·9 days
Orbital Speed	21·7 miles/sec (35km/sec)
Orbital Eccentricity	0·007
Inclination of Orbit (to ecliptic plane)	3·394°
Number of Satellites	0
*Earth = 1	

Above: *Galileo Galilei who, in 1610, discovered the phases of Venus with his telescope. From these, he inferred that Venus circled the Sun.*

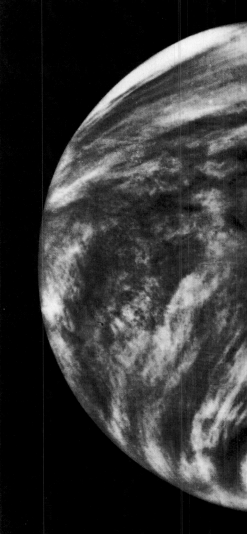

Above: *Mariner 10 image of Venus from 447,400 miles (720,000km). The streaky cloud markings are a sign of the rapid circulation of Venus' atmosphere.*

that the period of the rotation of Venus was the same as the period of its revolution around the Sun, 225 days. This estimate stood until 1962 when radar scans from the big antennas at Goldstone, California indicated that the rotation of Venus was 250 days plus or minus 50 days. This value was later corrected to 243·1 days and the rotation was found to be retrograde.[2]

With an equatorial diameter of 7,519 miles (12,100km), Venus is nearly Earth's twin in size. Compared to the value 1·0 for Earth, Venus exhibits a density of 0·956

$(5·26g/cm^3)$, a mass of 0·815 and volume of 0·857. Its orbit around the Sun is nearly circular, with a mean distance from the Sun of 67,194,700 miles (108,136,365km). Venus comes nearest Earth at inferior conjunction (when both are on the same side of the Sun) at a distance of 25,974,000 miles (41,800,000km). This arrangement recurs every 19 months and has set the timetable for launching probes to Venus.

Because of its relative proximity to Earth and similarity in size, Venus has been considered as a probable abode of life,

" . . . now glowed the Firmament
With living Saphirs: Hesperus that led
The starrie Host, rode brightest. . . "

John Milton, *Paradise Lost*

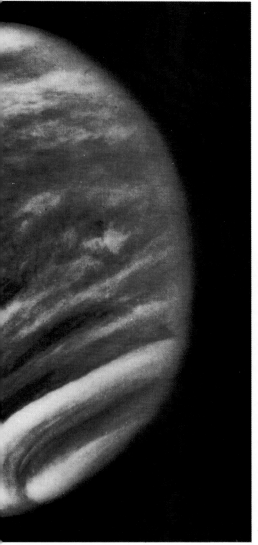

especially since it has long been known to have an atmosphere. It was visualised in fiction as a planet of warm oceans and steaming jungles, the habitat of giant reptiles like those roaming the Earth in the Mesozoic Era. This view seemed reasonable in the absence of any specific knowledge about the environment of Venus. Inasmuch as it is 30 per cent closer to the Sun than Earth, the Venerian surface temperature might be expected to be about 38°C assuming an atmosphere similar to Earth's.

Below: *The first deep space probe, Pioneer 5, in preparation for its launch by Thor-Able booster on 11 March 1960. The technician is testing one of the arms that deployed the craft's four solar panels.*

The reconnaissance of Venus with space-craft began in 1960 as soon as the space-faring powers, the United States and the Soviet Union, had developed rockets powerful enough to hurl interplanetary payloads.

The United States National Aeronautics & Space Administration launched Pioneer 5 towards Venus on 11 March 1960. The 95lb (43kg) probe was instrumented primarily to make soundings of fields and particles in the interplanetary medium. Its Thor-Able launcher did not impart enough energy to send the probe as far as the orbit of Venus and it remained in solar orbit between the Earth and Venus where it returned a great deal of historic data, especially on the Sunward boundary of the Earth's magnetic field.

The following year, the Soviet Union fired the 1,419lb (644kg) Venera 1 at Venus from a Sputnik carrier vehicle in parking orbit around the Earth. Launched on 12 February 1961 on an A-2-e booster, Venera 1 flew past Venus within 62,000 miles (100,000km) on 19 May 1961, but its communications failed en route and nothing was heard from it. Radar showed, however, that a trail to Venus had been blazed.

Mariner 2

NASA's interplanetary investigation pro-gramme in the early 1960s centred on Mars and Venus. The agency's Jet Propulsion Laboratory at Pasadena, California created the basic design of a 1,000lb (454kg) probe for the reconnaissance of both planets during launch opportunities in the period 1962–1964. The basic probe was called "Mariner". Mariner A was targeted for Venus and Mariner B, for Mars.

The booster for Mariners A and B was to be Atlas-Centaur, consisting of the reliable Atlas missile and a not-so-reliable, newly developed upper stage called Centaur. It was the first rocket to use hydrogen as fuel. Centaur's twin hydrogen-oxygen engines put out 30,000lb (13,605kg) of thrust, nearly double that of the predecessor upper stage, the Agena B. The hydrogen-oxygen engines were designed to be restarted after delivering the probe to Earth parking orbit to propel it either outward to Mars or inward to Venus and Mercury.

By mid-1961, however, Centaur's reliability remained too uncertain for a Venus mission in 1962 when Venus approached inferior

The Orbit of Venus
The visibility of Venus, and the phases it shows, depend on its position with respect to the Earth as it circles the Sun. When it is at superior conjunction, it is furthest from Earth and hidden behind the Sun. As it moves to the east of the Sun, it becomes steadily more visible as an "evening star". During the early part of this cycle it is almost full, but too distant and too close to the Sun to be seen well. As it nears inferior conjunction, Venus' apparent size increases, but its phase diminishes. The best time to observe Venus is at quadrature, when it is at greatest elongation. (Cycle repeats on W.)

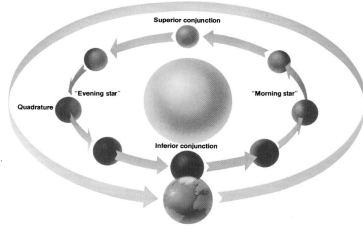

1 Parallax is the apparent change in the position of a distant object resulting from a change in the position of the observer.
2 In a direction opposite to that of its motion around the Sun.

conjunction.[3] In order to realize the 1962 launch opportunity, NASA had to rely on the Agena B upper stage, with 15,000lb (6,800kg) of thrust.

Mariner was redesigned to reduce its launch weight to 447lb (203kg), with 40lb (18kg) of scientific instruments. The redesign was accomplished in 11 months. Four reduced Mariner spacecraft known as Mariner R were manufactured, two for Venus and two for Mars.

First up was the Mariner R that became Mariner 1. It was launched from Cape Canaveral on 22 July 1962, but a guidance failure in the Atlas caused it to go astray and the Atlantic Missile Range safety officer reluctantly blew it up lest it crash into Atlantic ship lanes.

The back-up spacecraft, Mariner 2, was launched early in the morning of 27 August 1962. It narrowly escaped the fate of Mariner 1 when the Atlas guidance allowed the launch vehicle to roll to within 3 degrees of the Agena's limit of sensing the horizon. Had the limit been exceeded, the flight would have been aborted.

With Mariner attached, the Agena separated from the Atlas and pitched down 15 degrees to a flight attitude parallel with the horizon. Then its engine fired for 3 minutes and 15 seconds and it entered an orbit of 115 miles (185km).

Agena-Mariner coasted for 16·3 minutes. At a point in the orbit northeast of the Island of St Helena, the Agena engine was fired by the onboard sequencer for 2 minutes and 19 seconds. Mariner was injected into a trajectory that would take it Sunward so that it would fly past Venus and then enter an orbit around the Sun between Venus and Earth for the rest of cosmic time.

Mariner was a technological descendant of the Ranger lunar photo probes, with an adaptation for interplanetary navigation. It had the general shape of a pyramidal ocean buoy with wings. The base was a hexagonal frame of magnesium and aluminium. Two solar panels extended from either side, each 59in (150cm) long and 29·5in (75cm) wide. The pair carried a total of 9,800 silicon photovoltaic cells which converted sunlight into 148 to 222 watts of direct electrical current. During manoeuvres in space, when the panels were not facing the Sun, energy was supplied by a silver-zinc celled battery with 1,000 watt hours capacity. The battery could be recharged by the solar panels.

Atop the frame rose the pyramidal superstructure of aluminium tubing which gave the vehicle an overall height of 12ft (3·65m). This structure supported the solar panels and scientific instruments. An omni antenna was mounted at the top.

Attached directly to the hexagonal "bus" was a liquid fuel rocket engine for trajectory correction, a high-gain dish antenna, Sun sensors, Earth sensors and an array of boxes housing electronic components, the attitude control system, a data processing system, the flight computer and a timer-sequencer.

The Sun sensors and the Earth sensor were linked to the computer which fired nitrogen gas jets to control Mariner's flight attitude. It was designed to fly with the high-gain dish antenna facing Earth and the solar panels facing the Sun. If it drifted out of this orientation, the sensors informed the

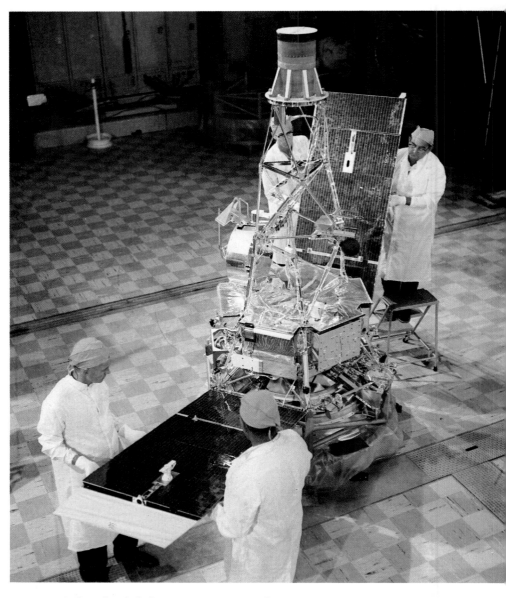

computer. When this failed to correct drift, as it did occasionally, the flight team at JPL sent corrective radio signals.

A Wind Between The Worlds

Mariner 2 was instrumented not only to observe Venus on a fly-by but also to collect data on magnetic fields and particles during the cruise to Venus. It carried a magnetometer to measure the strength of the interplanetary magnetic field as well as the magnetic field of Venus. A Geiger tube registered the flux of high-energy cosmic rays encountered on route. A solar plasma detector picked up low energy particles, mainly protons, from the Sun. There was also a cosmic dust detector.

In order to reach the orbit of Venus, Mariner 2 was launched in a direction opposite to the direction Earth moves around the Sun. It thus lost some of Earth's orbital velocity. In doing so, its flight path followed a long, parabolic curve Sunward.

Mariner's injection velocity of 7·03 miles/sec (11·31km/sec) would have caused it to cross the orbit of Venus 231,100 miles (372,000km) from the planet if not corrected. The miss distance was too great to allow the scientific instruments to acquire good data.

On 4 September 1962, a mid-course correction was made. The computer fired the

Above: *Engineers attach solar panels containing 9,800 solar cells to provide electrical power for the first Venus fly-by probe, Mariner 2. Its similarity to the early Ranger design is apparent.*

manoeuvering engine for 27·8 seconds to increase Mariner's velocity in the direction opposite to the way Earth was moving around the Sun. The effect of this was to decrease Mariner's Earth-relative velocity by 58·6mph (94·4km/h) and to increase its velocity relative to the Sun by 44·7mph (72km/h).[4]

In early September, Mariner's trajectory was 69,600 miles (112,000km) nearer the Sun than Earth's orbit. The spacecraft trailed the Earth by 1,483,900 miles (2,388,000km). But as it moved ever nearer the Sun, Mariner began to overtake the Earth like a racehorse on the inside track and by 31 October, it had caught up and was passing Earth.

By 7 December, the Venerian gravitational field was pulling the spacecraft toward the planet. On 12 December, as Mariner approached within a million kilometres of Venus, one of the two solar panels failed, presumably because of a short circuit. In order to conserve power, the flight team sent a radio signal turning off the engineering telemetry. The planetary experiments were then turned on.

Mariner encountered Venus on the night side on 14 December 1962 and flew behind it to view the day side. Its closest approach was 21,522 miles (34,636km) from the surface. The flight team calculated that it was moving at a Sun-relative velocity of 87,890mph (141,440km/h). On 27 December, the spacecraft reached perihelion, its closest approach to the Sun, after a journey of 65,127,000 miles (104,809,000km). On 3 January 1963, a radio signal was sent from NASA's Deep Space Instrumentation Facility at Johannesburg, South Africa to shut down the spacecraft power and communication systems.

The Structure of Venus
1 Rocky core.
2 Mantle.
3 Crust.
4 Thick atmosphere.

As compared to the other terrestrial planets, very little is known about the interior structure of Venus. Only recently have spaceprobes (such as the US Pioneer-Venus mission) been able to make gravity measurements of the planet, and map broad surface features. Basalt was identified on the surface by Venera landers. Because of the similarity in size and density, Venus is believed to have a structure like that of the Earth. Its slightly smaller core reflects its lower density, but its

Mariner 2 was not heard from again, despite later attempts to reactivate communication.

At Venus, Mariner's magnetometer failed to detect any magnetic field, confirming a supposition that the planet's slow rotation did not generate one. The microwave radiometer, sensing radio energy reflected from the surface, indicated a surface temperature of 422°C on both night and day sides. It was supposed that atmospheric circulation carried day side heat around to the night side.

Cloud temperatures sensed by the infrared radiometer ranged from 92·4°C at the bottom of the cloud decks to −92·4°C at the top. It was calculated from these results that the clouds began 45 miles (72km) above

composition is uncertain. Venus does not reveal the presence of a magnetic field, as a result of its slow rotation, despite possibly possessing an iron/silicate core similar to that we have identified in the Earth. Above the core lies a mantle. Above this, Venus' rocky crust shows no sign of recent large-scale tectonic activity. A distinct highland-lowland surface topography was mapped by the Pioneer-Venus Orbiter. A highland region, Ishtar Terra, larger than the continental United States, was revealed standing several miles above the mean planetary radius. It is overlain by a dense atmosphere of carbon dioxide.

the surface and extended to an altitude of 59·6 miles (96km). These estimates were to be modified in later years.

Atmospheric density and composition were calculated indirectly. The density at the surface was estimated at 20 Earth atmospheres, a gross underestimate.

The high surface temperature was a strong indication that carbon dioxide was the main constituent of the atmosphere. Its heat-trapping or "greenhouse" effect would account for the furnace heat at the surface.[5]

The effect of the planet on Mariner's flight path enabled the science team to calculate the mass of Venus at 0·81485 of 1 Earth mass.

During the cruise from Earth, Mariner 2 surveyed the interplanetary medium. The dust monitor showed that concentrations of cosmic dust were 10,000 times less than the concentration near Earth. The plasma detector confirmed the hypothesis of the solar wind. It had been postulated years earlier as an explanation of the motion of comet tails which always streamed away from the Sun. Pioneer 5, the first attempt at Venus, had detected evidence of such a wind blowing from the Sun.

Mariner 2's detector showed a tenuous wind blowing between the worlds and filling the interplanetary medium with dissociated protons and electrons to form a neutral gas or "plasma". The data indicated that the wind was blowing outward at velocities of 185 to 500 miles/sec (300—800 km/sec). The discovery of the solar wind suggested that the inner planets lay within the outer atmosphere of the Sun. How far it extended beyond the Earth would not be known for another 20 years.

During the mission of Mariner 2, new efforts were made at the Goldstone Deep Space Instrument Facility to refine the period of Venus' rotation. One of Goldstone's 26 metre antennas transmitted signals to Venus and a second dish picked up their reflections. The results showed a retrograde rotation with a period of 230 days plus or minus 40 to 50 days.

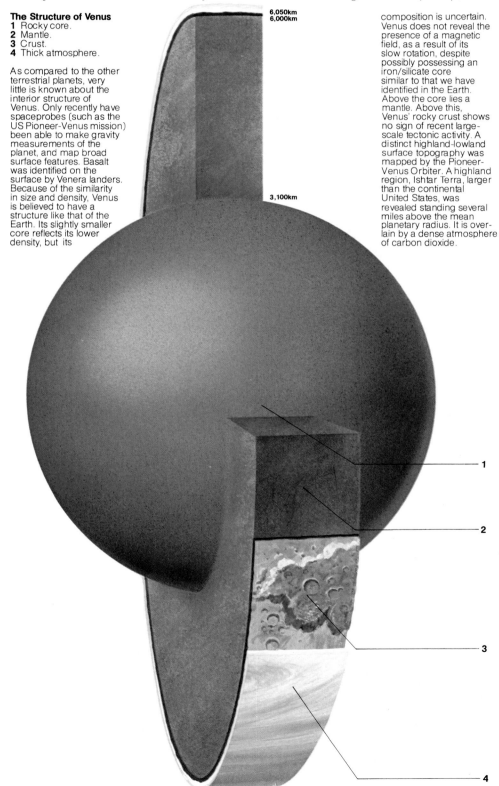

6,050km
6,000km
3,100km

1
2
3
4

3 Launching at inferior conjunction when Venus was closest to Earth allowed a minimum energy trajectory and a shorter cruising time.
4 The paradox is explained by the laws of planetary motion propounded in the 17th century by Johannes Kepler (1571–1630). The orbit of a planet is an ellipse. The radius vector of each planet (the line joining its centre with the centre of the Sun) moves over equal areas of the ellipse in equal times. Thus, a planet nearer the Sun moves around it faster than a planet farther away. At launch, Mariner was orbiting the Sun at Earth's velocity, 66,600mph (107,179km/h). In order to reach Venus which orbits the Sun at 78,407mph (126,180km/h) an hour, Mariner had to gain additional velocity relative to the Sun of at least 12,229mph (19,680km/h). Actually, it gained more as it was accelerated by the gravitational fields of Venus and the Sun.
5 Carbon dioxide in the atmosphere absorbs heat radiated from the surface of a planet and re-radiates some of the heat back to the surface, raising surface temperature. Since glass traps heat similarly in a botanical greenhouse, the heat trapping process of a carbon dioxide atmosphere is called the greenhouse effect. A dense carbon dioxide atmosphere on Venus is believed to have caused a runaway greenhouse effect.

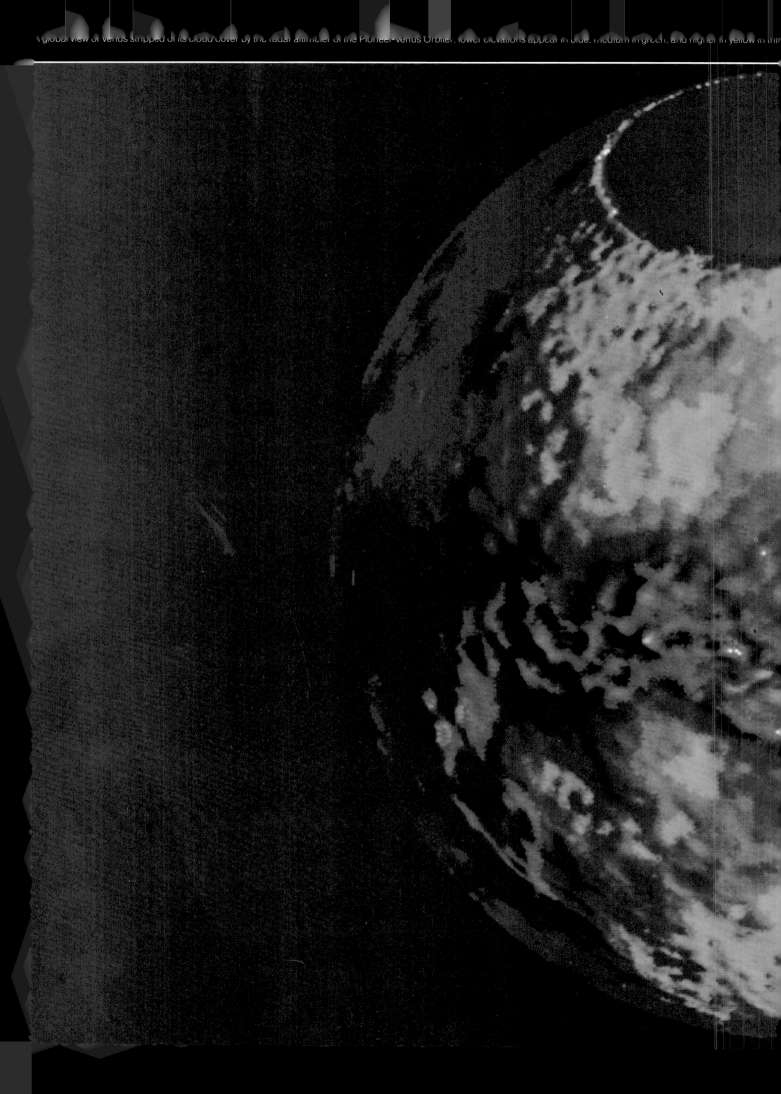

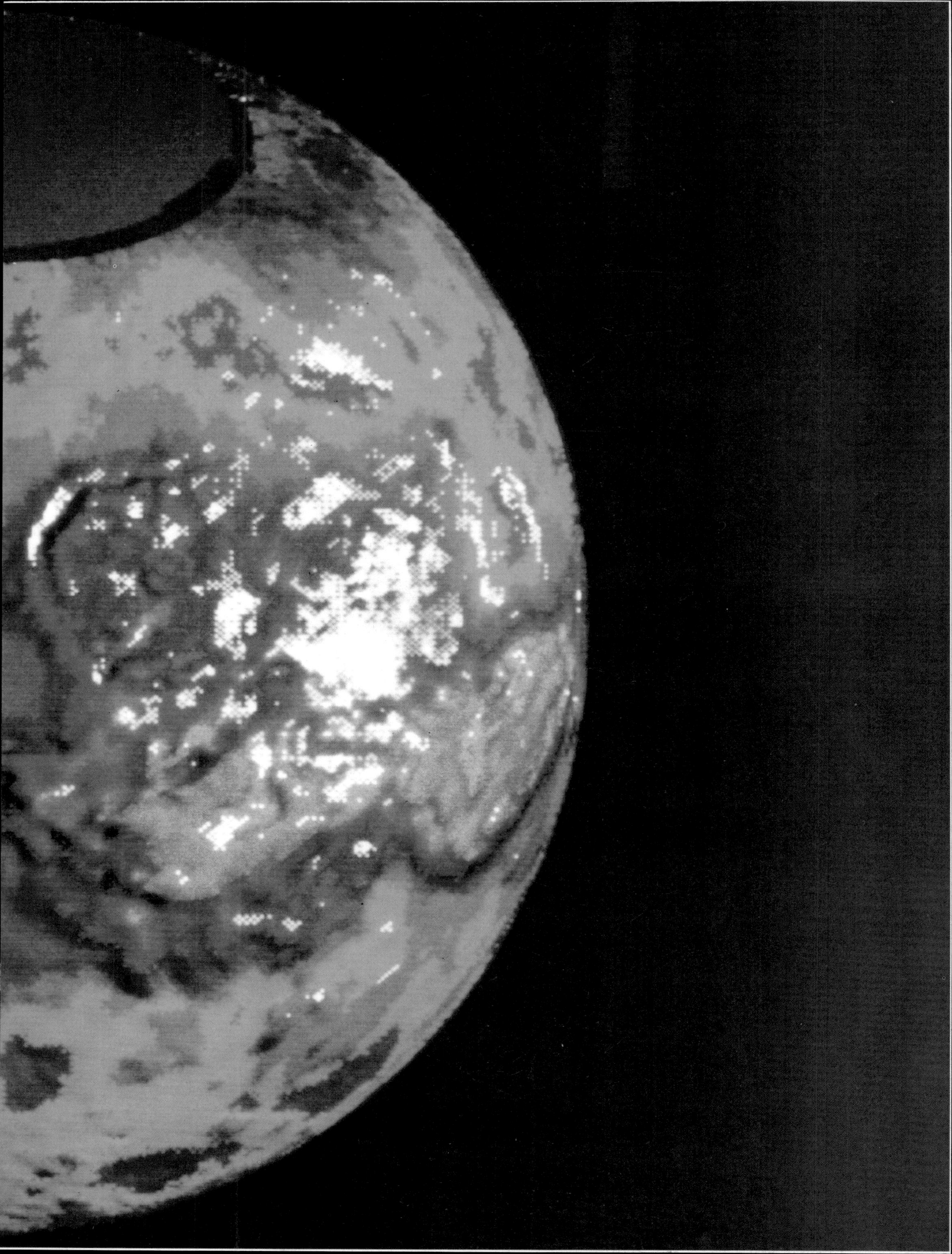

The Russian Probes

After Mariner 2, NASA turned its attention to Mars and fitted its Mariner R vehicles for a reconnaissance of the red planet. In addition to Venera 1, the Soviet space programme meanwhile had launched four probes to Venus during the 1961–62 opportunity, but none succeeded in getting out of Earth orbit.

At the next Venus launch opportunity, the Russians launched Zond class vehicles on 27 March and 2 April 1964 from the space centre at Tyuratam. The March launch failed in Earth orbit. The probe launched in April passed Venus on 19 July 1964, but communications failed en route.

Two more Zonds were fired at Venus at the next inferior conjunction. The first, launched on 12 November 1965 passed Venus at an altitude of 14,800 miles (23,800km) on 27 February 1966 and was designated Venera 2. The second, launched on 16 November 1965, struck the surface on 1 March 1966. It was the first vehicle to land on another planet. Communications failed in both probes which were tracked by radar.

A third Venus probe was launched on 23 November 1965, but it failed to leave Earth orbit.

The first Soviet spacecraft to return atmospheric data directly from Venus was Venera 4, a 2,439lb (1,106kg) vehicle launched on 12 June 1967. As it encountered the veiled planet, it dropped a 846lb (384kg), egg-shaped capsule into the clouds on 18 October to survey the atmosphere. Descending by parachute, the capsule radioed data to the Venera 4 bus on density, temperature and composition. The bus relayed the data to Earth, where signals were received in the USSR and also at Jodrell Bank, England for 94 minutes. The last signal disclosed atmospheric pressure of 22 atmospheres. The pressure later was interpreted as indicating an altitude of 15 miles (24km).

During descent, the capsule reported temperatures of 38·5°C rising to 274°C when signals ceased. Gas analyzers showed that the atmosphere was 90 to 95 per cent carbon dioxide, 0·4 to 0·8 per cent oxygen and up to 1·6 per cent water vapour.

The main bus carried a magnetometer, cosmic ray counters, charged particle sensors and gas detectors. It found a weak corona of hydrogen on the night side at an altitude of 6,164 miles (9,920km). The hydrogen was interpreted as signifying loss of water, presumably as the result of greenhouse effect heating, at some time in the past.

Mariner 5

One day after Venera 4 encountered Venus, on 19 October 1967 NASA's Mariner 5 flew past the planet at an altitude of 2,440 miles (3,928km). Mariner 5 had been launched on 14 June, two days after Venera 4.

Mariner 5 had been the back-up for NASA's Mars fly-by, Mariner 4. Modified for Venus, Mariner 5 in most respects was similar to its predecessor Venerian probe, Mariner 2. However, it carried more sophisticated radio receiving as well as transmitting equipment and its solar panels had been shortened and placed away from the bus to reduce the effects of overheating which may have caused one of Mariner 2's panels to fail.

Mariner 5 carried a magnetometer, plasma detector, trapped radiation detector and an ultraviolet photometer. Unlike its Mars counterpart, it had no camera. The dense clouds effectively prevented imaging the surface in the visible spectrum. Like Venera 4, Mariner 5 found that carbon dioxide was the main component of the atmosphere. The abundance was estimated at 70 to 90 per cent from Mariner 5 data.[5]

The ultraviolet photometer found a cloud of atomic hydrogen at 11,800 miles (19,000km) altitude, but no high altitude atomic oxygen. Mariner 5 beamed radio signals through the atmosphere as it flew around the planet. In addition to providing some information on the molecular structure of the atmosphere, this method, called radio occultation, had been first tried successfully by Mariner 4 at Mars. It effectively defined the low density of the Martian atmosphere. But the result at Venus was entirely different. At lower levels, the dense atmosphere of Venus extinguished the radio beam.

The regions where the Venera 4 capsule descended and where Mariner 5 began radio occultation were on the night side near the equator. Data from both vehicles showed it was as hot there as on the day side, confirming the Mariner 2 finding that temperature distribution was fairly even over the planet.

A technical memorandum from the Jet Propulsion Laboratory noted a contrast between Venus and the Moon where the temperature falls hundreds of degrees during the long night. On Venus, the dense atmosphere not only prevents cooling at night but it may distribute the heat with warm winds from the day side, the memorandum said. It added:

"Light rays are bent around the planet in the lens-like atmosphere, just as Mariner's radio signals were bent. The bending varies with wavelength, so that the beam is spread as well as bent; thus, the Sun at night appears as a horizontal rainbow smear."

The memorandum concluded:

"Venus appears to offer roasting heat, a choking atmosphere, crushing pressure and murky skies, to which forbidding weather and hostile terrain may perhaps be added."

At the Jet Propulsion Laboratory, the experimenters said that below 6 miles (10km), the refractivity of the atmosphere was so high that radio or light waves entering at a tangent would be distorted into a spiral and could not escape. The effect led to a whimsical speculation that the Venus "light trap" would distort light to such an extent that an explorer on the surface might see the back of his head when looking in front of him.

Below: Venus fly-by probe Mariner 5. The most obvious features are the four solar panels, the high-gain antenna dish, with magnetometer and low-gain antenna below, and the heat-control louvres.

Right: Engineering replica of the Soviet Venera 4 craft, which entered Venus' atmosphere in 1967. The lower capsule parachuted through the clouds relaying data to the bus (above).

Veneras at Venus
Eleven Soviet spaceprobes have penetrated the atmosphere, and landed on Venus. Venera 4, the first atmospheric probe, was crushed by pressure as it descended through deeper layers—a fate shared also by Veneras 5 and 6. Veneras 7 and 8 both landed successfully, measuring pressures of 90 atmospheres at the surface. Veneras 9 and 10 transmitted the first TV pictures of the surface, while 11 and 12 detected the incidence of thunderstorms. Veneras 13 and 14 landed at a site agreed jointly with the US—Phoebe Regio—and drilled soil samples.

The problem of the precise period of Venus' rotation continued to be investigated by radar. Tracking from Goldstone and the radio telescope at Arecibo, Puerto Rico during 1966–67 determined the rotation period as 243 days plus or minus 0.6 days and confirmed that Venus was slowly turning on its axis in a direction opposite to that of the Earth and Mars. Could the retrograde rotation be accounted for by the impact of a large planetoid? The Mariner science team offered no other speculation.

Because its retrograde rotation is slower than its period of revolution around the Sun, the day-night cycle on Venus is only 117 Earth days long. Daylight is 58.5 days and night 58.5 days.

Veneras 5, 6, and 7

One problem of exploring the Venerian surface was analogous to that of exploring the ocean bottoms of Earth—the crushing effect of pressure. After five years of probing by the United States and the Soviet Union, the full extent of Venerian surface pressure remained undetermined.

The Soviets again tackled the problem in 1969, launching Venera 5 on 5 January and Venera 6 on 10 January. Both vehicles had a launch weight of 2,490lb (1,130Kg). Venera 5 dropped a landing capsule in the Venerian atmosphere on 16 May and Venera 6 released its lander the next day. Both capsules transmitted during parachute descent, Venera 5 for 53 minutes and Venera 6 for 51 minutes. Surface atmospheric pressure was calculated from the data as 100 atmospheres and temperatures about 500°C.

These returns, however, were modified by more precise data from Venera 7 which indicated that neither Venera 5 nor Venera 6 survived long enough to transmit from the surface. Venera 7 appears to be the first probe to have succeeded in doing so.

A cylindrical vehicle sprouting solar panels like its predecessors, Venera 7 weighed 2,600lb (1,180Kg) at launch on 17 August 1970. As it approached Venus on 12 December 1970, a cooling system was turned on to reduce the temperature inside its 1,091lb (495Kg) landing capsule to −8°C.

Russian space engineers employed a new method of separating the lander from the Venera 7 bus. As the bus entered the atmosphere on 15 December at a velocity of 7.2 miles/sec (11.6km/sec), it began to wobble and lost its sensor lock on Earth. The effect generated a signal that caused the lander to separate from the bus. The capsule plummeted down until it was slowed by rising pressure to 820ft/sec (250m/sec). A parachute was then deployed and a radio antenna thrust out. Radio signals were received for 35 minutes. Then they faded out.

American observers assumed that the Venera 7 lander had been crushed like its predecessors, but on 26 January 1971, the Russians announced that they had been able to extract another 26 minutes of data from tape recordings. The additional information was buried in interplanetary radio noise and had to be separated by computer. The data had a signal strength of only 1 per cent of the earlier transmissions, an indication of a misalignment of the lander antenna on landing. It may have toppled or been blown over.

The faint signals reported surface temperature at 475°C, plus or minus 20 degrees, and the pressure, 90 atmospheres, plus or minus 15. These values have been confirmed by later probes.

The full horror of Venus as a planetary hell with a lid of clouds was now being revealed. It made desiccated Mars appear tolerable by comparison.

In 1972, the Soviets shot another capsule into the Venerian atmosphere. Venera 8 was launched on 27 March from the Baikonur Cosmodrome. Its pre-cooled lander separated from the carrier bus at Venus on 22 July and reached the surface on the day side where it transmitted for 50 minutes.

Surprisingly, illumination studies showed that sunlight penetrated the clouds and reached the surface, making lander photography feasible without floodlighting. In fact, the illumination was described as comparable to a cloudy afternoon in Moscow. Radiometer and spectrometer scans of the surface showed the signatures of uranium, thorium and potassium, in abundances similar to those on Earth. The surface rocks yielded a chemical composition that suggested granite, indicating that chemical differentiation had occurred to form the crust of Venus, presumably during a primordial molten era. Venus, despite its retrograde rotation, heavy atmosphere and blast furnace climate, was beginning to appear structurally more like the Earth.

Again, day side and night side temperatures were similar, ranging from 462° to 476°C. Atmospheric pressure was reported at 1,300lb/in² (compared with Earth's sea level pressure of 14.7lb/in²).

6 Mariner 5 did not make direct measurements of atmospheric composition. This was deduced by radio signal refraction and attenuation in the upper atmosphere from which the molecular weight of the principal gas, carbon dioxide, was computed.

Mariner 10

Emboldened by the success of the Mariner programme, NASA launched the 1,109lb (503kg) Mariner 10 on 3 November 1973 on a two planet reconnaissance of Venus and Mercury. The flight trajectory was calculated so that as Mariner 10 passed Venus, the planet's gravitational field would sling the spacecraft around toward Mercury. The programme by then had access to the high-energy upper stage Centaur which replaced the Agena atop the Atlas booster.

The "gravity assist" technique was successful. Mariner 10 flew past Venus at an altitude of 3,595 miles (5,784km) on 5 February 1974. Its flight path was deflected as planned causing the spacecraft to fly-by Mercury at an altitude of 450 miles (724km) on 29 March 1974 and take up a solar orbit which brought it back to encounter Mercury again on 21 September 1974 and a third time on 16 March 1975.

Mariner 10 carried a pair of telescopic cameras to photograph the surface of Mercury. En route, it returned a stunning array of pictures of the clouds of Venus. Spacecraft instruments included two magnetometers, an ultraviolet spectrometer and a charged particle detector. As Mariner 10 passed Venus, the ultraviolet spectrometer detected not only hydrogen and helium in the high clouds but also atomic oxygen. The abundance of atomic oxygen was 10 times that

seen at Mars, suggesting dissociation of a considerable volume of water vapour.

If surface water had existed on Venus in the past and had boiled off as a runaway greenhouse effect heated the planet, there might be a clue, a residue of some ancient ocean in the form of deuterium, the heavy isotope of hydrogen. With a higher atomic weight, deuterium might have remained as hydrogen escaped into the high atmosphere and to space. The ultraviolet spectrometer searched for deuterium, but failed to detect any. Deuterium was to turn up as an unexpected result of atmospheric probing on a later mission.

Photographs in ultraviolet light of the Venerian clouds showed a pattern of banding like the clouds of Jupiter. The whole atmosphere appeared to be rotating symmetrically with the planet. Evidence of convection was seen in the region of peak solar heating.

Mariner 10 went on to Mercury, leaving Venus to Soviet probes for the next 4 years.

Veneras 9, 10, 11, and 12

The photographic breakthrough on the surface of Venus was achieved by two Soviet missions, Venera 9, launched on 8 June 1975, and Venera 10, 14 June 1975. They were new and heavier planet explorers, combining orbiters and landers, with a launch weight of 11,023lb (5,000kg). They required the more powerful D-1-e

launchers instead of the A-2 series which had boosted the earlier Veneras. The Soviet transition in launch vehicles was parallel to that made by NASA in replacing the upper stage Agena with Centaur. Discovery went hand in hand with advancing technology. The Veneras arrived at Venus in October and took up orbits around the planet. The Venera 9 lander separated from the orbiter bus on 22 October and the Venera 10 lander from its bus on 25 October.

Each lander, with a launch weight of 3,440lb (1,560kg) including entry sphere,

Below: The first-ever picture of Venus' surface, from Venera 9, shows angular rocks up to 2ft (0.6m) across. The stripes are transmissions from its other instruments.

that country's Pioneer-Venus 1 and 2 probes using the same 1978 launch window and entering the Venerian atmosphere the same month as the Soviet Venera 11 and 12 soft-landed on the planet. In-flight exchanges of information, for example, enabled trajectory patterns to be established, and both the Soviet and US spacecraft made simultaneous measurements of the solar winds (or atomic particles streaming from the Sun) for later comparison and evaluation.

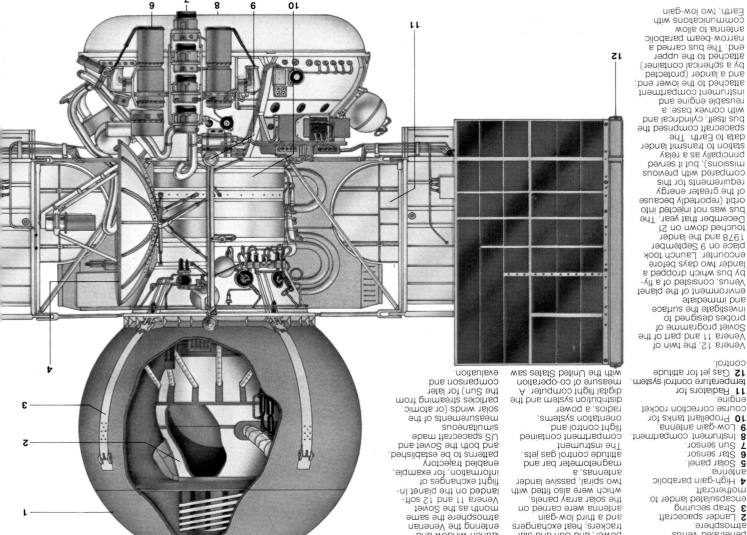

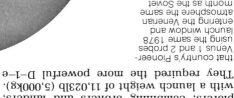

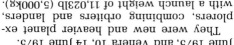

Venera 12

1 Protective shell, jettisoned after lander penetrated Venus' atmosphere.
2 Lander spacecraft.
3 Strap securing encapsulated lander to mothercraft.
4 High-gain parabolic antenna.
5 Solar panel.
6 Star sensor.
7 Sun sensor.
8 Instrument compartment.
9 Low-gain antenna.
10 Propellant tanks for course correction rocket engine.
11 Radiators for temperature control system.
12 Gas jet for attitude control.

Venera 12, the twin of Venera 11 and part of the Soviet programme of probes designed to investigate the surface and immediate environment of the planet Venus, consisted of a fly-by bus which dropped a lander two days before encounter. Launch took place on 9 September 1978 and the lander touched down on 21 December that year. The bus was not injected into orbit (reportedly because of the greater energy requirements for this compared with previous missions), but it served principally as a relay station to transmit lander data to Earth. The spacecraft comprised the bus itself, cylindrical and with convex base: a reusable engine and instrument compartment attached to the lower end; and a lander (protected by a spherical container) attached to the upper end. The bus carried a narrow-beam parabolic antenna to allow communications with Earth, two low-gain

antennas to communicate with the lander, two solar cell arrays for electric power, and Sun and star trackers; heat exchangers and a third low-gain antenna were carried on the solar array panels, which were also fitted with two spiral, passive lander antennas, a magnetometer bar and attitude control gas jets.

The instrument compartment contained flight control and orientation systems, radios, a power distribution system and the digital flight computer. A measure of co-operation with the United States saw was encased in an insulated, spherical shell 7·87ft (2·4m) in diameter for entry into the atmosphere. Each entered pre-cooled to −8°C. Descent through the atmosphere, for a time retarded by parachutes, was accelerated by allowing the landers to free fall, protected by an aerodynamic shield. Near the surface, where atmospheric pressure was high, the rate of descent was 23ft/sec (7m/sec). The shock of impact was taken up by a crushable doughnut shaped shell.

The landers began to photograph their day side landing sites two minutes after touchdown. Venera 9 landed at 33 degrees north latitude and 293 degrees longitude in or near a region later identified as Beta Regio, a plateau. The capsule seemed to have come down on the slope of a stony hill.

The cameras may have been looking up hill for the horizon was only several dozen feet away. The photographs had high resolution and showed heaps of stones, many with sharp edges. Their appearance appeared to be the result of volcanic or tectonic processes.

Lander 9 transmitted photographs and data for 53 minutes and then fell silent. During transmission, the temperature inside the capsule did not exceed 60°C. Lander 10 settled on an undulating, stony plain about 18 degrees of latitude south of lander 9. Its photographs showed a horizon several hundred feet distant. The surface appeared older than the surface in the lander 9 site. Gamma ray spectrometer readings indicated a predominantly basaltic crust, with uranium, thorium and potassium in Earthlike abun-

dance at both landing sites. The Soviet Academician, M. V. Keldysh of the Institute of Applied Mathematics, stated that:

"Comparison of the evidence for the Moon, the Earth, Venus and Mars testifies that the same geochemical process occurs in all terrestrial planets, subdividing them into shells; the outer one, the crust, being constituted for the most part by basalt." [7]

Both Venera orbiters performed radio occultation experiments with their transmitters as they went behind the planet. Signals passing through less dense regions of the upper atmosphere confirmed previous findings of the multilayer structure of the clouds and showed the existence of an ionosphere, a region of charged nuclear particles above the atmosphere.

The Veneras found that the Venus ionosphere was closer to the planet ball and thinner than Earth's ionosphere. Orbiter radar surveys showed flat and mountainous relief, with a maximum altitude variation of 1·8 to 3 miles (3 to 5km).

The Soviets sent two more Venera spacecraft in the 11,000lb (5,000kg) class to Venus in 1978. Both dropped landers equipped with cameras, but surface photos, if any, were not released.

Venera 11 was launched on 9 September and Venera 12 on 14 September 1978. Lander 12 reached the surface first on 21 December and operated for 110 minutes. Lander 11 came down about 500 miles (800km) away on 25 December and operated for 95 minutes. Their data were relayed to Earth by their buses, which flew on into solar orbit.

Both capsules took samples of the atmosphere during their descent, which was slowed at first by parachutes and later by an aerodynamic braking disc that fitted around the cylindrical waist of each lander like a wide collar. This appears to have been successful, for the descent of Lander 12 lasted an hour, the longest of any Soviet lander.

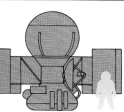

Venera 12 Lander
1 Parachute compartment.
2 Scientific instruments for atmospheric cloud cover analysis.
3 Aerodynamic braking disc.
4 Pipes to carry coolant from mothercraft to lander.
5 Internal electronics.
6 Crushable shock absorber.
7 Main support ring (mounts research instruments and experiments).
8 Support struts.
9 Telephotometer windows, protected by ejectable cover.

10 Scientific instruments.
11 Helical antenna (for communications with mothercraft).

The Venera lander was carried in a spherical shell fitted with inner and outer heat insulation to protect the machine from high temperatures during atmosphere entry; it was also cooled before separation from the bus. The lander itself carried scientific and equipment compartments, the aerodynamic shield, the landing device (a crushable torus), and

antennas. The instruments comprised a telephotometer imaging system for returning surface pictures; a gamma ray spectrometer for soil survey; a densitometer; and sensors to evaluate atmospheric temperature and pressure during the slow descent, plus an accelerometer and a mass spectrometer to measure atmospheric density, and a nephelometer and a photometer to relay data about cloud structure during the descent.

Technical Data
Gross launch weight: 11,023lb (5,000kg).
Weight of lander: 3,440lb (1,560kg).
Shell diameter: 7·9ft (2·4m).

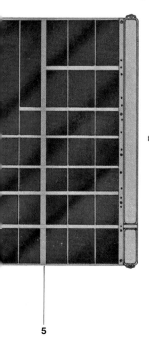

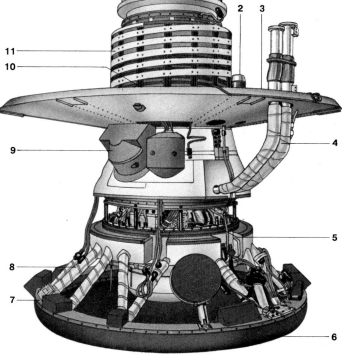

Above: *The Venera 12 bus is readied for launch in 1978. The convex white torus houses instruments, and encircles the reusable propulsion unit. Note low-gain antennas are in stowed position.*

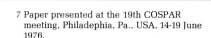

7 Paper presented at the 19th COSPAR meeting, Philadephia, Pa., USA, 14-19 June 1976.

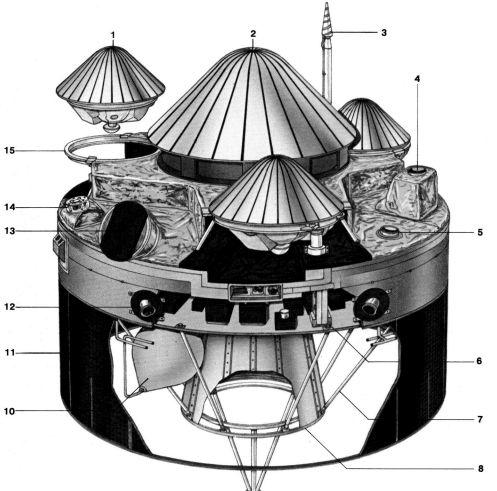

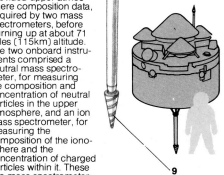

Temperatures reported by the landers at the surface were 446° to 460°C. Pressure was a uniform 88 atmospheres. Of considerable interest to students of planetary evolution was the finding that the ratio of Argon 36 to Argon 40 was 200 to 300 times greater than on Earth. The relative depletion of Argon 40, a decay product of radioactive Potassium 40, was interpreted as an indication that chemical evolution had been retarded on Venus, compared with Earth.

Both vehicles detected frequent lightning strokes during descent. After landing, Lander 11 acoustic sensors reported a loud noise like thunder.

The Pioneers

NASA, too, returned to Venus in 1978, this time with new exploration vehicles in the Pioneer class. In contrast to Mariner, largely an in-house development of the Jet Propulsion Laboratory, two Pioneer spacecraft for Venus were built by industry with Hughes as prime contractor. The project was managed by NASA's Ames Research Laboratory at Mountain View, California.

The Pioneer-Venus programme consisted of two spacecraft, an orbiter (Pioneer-Venus 1) and five atmosphere probes (Pioneer-Venus 2). The Orbiter and Multi-probe were launched separately by Atlas-Centaurs. Both

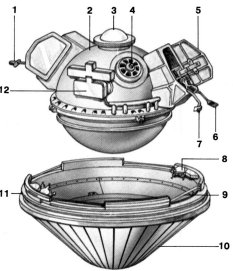

Pioneer-Venus Multi-probe
1 Small probe.
2 Large probe (centred on bus spin axis).
3 Forward omni antenna.
4 Ion mass spectrometer.
5 Axial thruster.
6 Equipment shelf.
7 Equipment shelf support strut.
8 Central thrust tube.
9 Widebeam omni antenna.
10 Propellant tank.
11 Solar panel cylinder.
12 Radial thruster.
13 Star sensor.
14 Neutral mass spectrometer.
15 Probe support structure.

Carrying similar heat control systems, experiment compartments, solar panels, batteries, power distribution systems, omni antennas and communications systems, data processing systems, Sun and star sensors and attitude control systems to those of the Orbiter, though not the high-gain dish antenna of that craft, the Pioneer-Venus Multi-probe was launched on 8 August 1978, almost three months later than its companion but on a more direct trajectory, enabling it to arrive within five days of the first mission. The Multi-probe vehicle was a modified Orbiter bus, but it was designed to drop four probes (one large and three identical smaller probes) into the Venerian atmosphere and itself enter as a fifth probe. The bus provided a stable spinning platform for the probes, which separated from it when about 20 days away from Venus encounter. Following ejection of the

individual probes, the bus provided upper atmosphere composition data, acquired by two mass spectrometers, before burning up at about 71 miles (115km) altitude. The two onboard instruments comprised a neutral mass spectrometer, for measuring the composition and concentration of neutral particles in the upper atmosphere, and an ion mass spectrometer, for measuring the composition of the ionosphere and the concentration of charged particles within it. These two mass spectrometer instruments were attached to the equipment shelf with their inlets projecting above the flat top of the bus cylinder. These experiments were the mission's only atmospheric composition measurements between 93 and 71 miles (150-115km). The bus, carrying a more powerful transmitter than any of its probes, returned data to Earth for a period of two minutes at 1,024bps before its destruction. Data from the bus, and from the smaller probes as well, were returned during a critical 1hr 38min period. These almost simultaneous signals were received and handled by the two Deep Space Network antennas at Canberra, Australia, and at Goldstone, California; triangulation measurements involving these two stations and those at Guam and at Santiago enabled craft trajectory changes to be monitored and atmospheric wind characteristics around Venus to be assessed as a result.

Technical Data
Diameter of bus: 8·2ft (2·5m)
Length of bus (from bottom to top of main probe): 9·5ft (2·9m).
Total weight of bus: 1,993lb (904kg).
Total weight of instruments: 112lb (51kg).
Diameter of Large Probe: 5ft (1·5m).
Weight of Large Probe: 696lb (316kg).
Diameter of Small Probes: 2·6ft (0·8m) each.
Weight of Small Probes: 198lb (90kg) each.

Pioneer-Venus Large Probe Descent Profile
The Large Probe was the first to reach Venus, 5 minutes before the leading Small Probe (North) and 1½ hours ahead of the bus. As it hit the edge of Venus' atmosphere, at a speed of 7 miles/sec (11km/sec), its heat shield slowed it, causing very intense deceleration forces until it reached a height of some 50 miles (80km), the altitude of the haze layers (top of diagram). Once into the main clouds (yellow) at 42 miles (68km) altitude, the probe deployed its parachute and jettisoned the aeroshell. At the clouds' lower edge, 28·5 miles (46km) up, the probe released the parachute and fell freely, slowed only by the dense lower atmosphere to hit the surface in a "hard landing" 56 minutes after it first entered the atmosphere.

Pioneer-Venus Small Probe
1 Net flux radiometer.
2 Titanium pressure vessel.
3 Antenna housing.
4 Ground coolant access cover.
5 Atmosphere structure door (shown open).
6 Atmosphere structure temperature sensor.
7 Atmosphere structure pressure inlet and spin control vane.
8 Yo-yo cable cutter.
9 Yo-yo despin cable (to slow spin rate on descent).
10 Carbon phenolic heat shield.
11 Probe/bus interface ring for separation clamp.
12 Nephelometer door (shown closed).

The three Small Probes deployed by the Pioneer-Venus Multi-probe, each carrying three instruments, were, like the Large Probe, fitted with heat shields to protect the pressure vessel, which was attached

to an aeroshell and aft cover; however, the pressure vessels did not separate from aeroshell or afterbody during deployment. Retarded only by atmospheric density during descent, each probe was fitted with three doors to provide the instruments access to the Venerian atmosphere. The instruments themselves measured atmospheric pressure, density and temperature: a nephelometer looked through two sapphire windows, and a heat deposition (net flux) radiometer extended sensors outside on booms (each external radiometer sensor on each small probe had two diamond windows). A "yo-yo" system — two weights swung out a distance of 8ft (2·4m) from each craft — was employed to slow the craft's rotation rate. One Small Probe was targetted on Venus's day side (as was the Large Probe); the other two on the night side.

Orbiter and Multi-probe spacecraft were based on a common bus design—a flat cylinder 8·2ft (2·5m) in diameter and 3·94ft (1·2m) high. Each bus provided a spin-stablized platform, the Orbiter for scientific instruments and the Multi-probe for the probes. Hydrazine fuelled thrusters maintained spin and attitude.

The Orbiter which carried 12 scientific instruments and a million bit data memory was equipped with a powerful, solid fuel rocket which was fired to insert it into orbit around Venus at encounter. With its antenna mast, the Orbiter stood 14·76ft (4·5m) high and weighed 1,283lb (582kg) at launch, including 100lb (45kg) of instruments.

Three of the instruments observed electrons in the ionosphere. Three more, plus the radio, analyzed the atmosphere. The Orbiter also carried a detector to pick up bursts of gamma rays from the Galaxy; a magnetometer; a cloud photopolarimeter which returned photographs of the clouds and a radar mapper to continue the surface mapping started by Veneras 9 and 10. Two instruments, a plasma analyzer and electric field detector, observed the interaction of the solar wind and the ionosphere.

The Orbiter was launched on 20 May 1978 and was inserted into a near polar orbit around Venus on 4 December after travelling a "type 2" trajectory which is one that takes a spacecraft more than 180 degrees around the Sun, so allowing the co-ordination of the two vehicles. The Multi-probe was launched on 8 August 1978 on a shorter, "type 1" trajectory so that it reached the vicinity of Venus on 9 December, only five days after the Orbiter began circling the planet.

The Multi-probe weighed 1,993lb (904kg), including 112lb (51kg) of instruments. The basic Pioneer bus was modified to carry four mushroom-shaped probes—a large one mounted at the centre of the bus and three small ones around it. The bus itself entered the atmosphere as a fifth probe.

At a distance of 8·1 million miles (13 million km) from Venus, the four probes were released from the bus. The larger one descended over the day side equator, one of the small probes came down in the mid-northern latitudes of day side and two small probes fell into the northern and southern latitudes of night side. The bus was instrumented to sample the uppermost atmosphere, but was not shielded against entry heating. It burned up 64 seconds after entry at an altitude of 68 miles (110km).

Weighing 696lb (316kg) at launch, the larger probe or "sounder" descended on parachutes to within 29 miles (47km) of the surface, where the parachutes were jettisoned. Then it sank the rest of the way, slowed by aerodynamic braking.

Two of its instruments, a gas chromatograph and a mass spectrometer, measured atmospheric composition directly. Others were protected from heat and pressure inside the pressure vessel and took their readings through diamond and sapphire windows. The infra-red radiometer received its data through a diamond window the size of a US quarter dollar. The window weighed 13·5 carats and was cut in Holland from an industrial grade rough diamond.[8] A nephelometer, which measured the density and structure of clouds, used two sapphire windows and a large cloud-particle-size spectrometer measured particles with a laser beam projected through a sapphire window and reflected by an outside mirror to a sensor.

The three small probes, called "north", "day" and "night" to distinguish them by their destinations weighed 198lb (90kg) each and carried three instruments apiece. Each was contained in a titanium aeroshell with a phenolic carbon heat shield. They descended without parachutes, their plunge slowed by

---

8 United States Customs later remitted to NASA the duty paid on the diamond imported from the Netherlands.

Pioneer-Venus Large Probe
1 Radio transparent window.
2 Aft cover.
3 Antenna.
4 Cloud particle spectrometer window.
5 Command/data unit.
6 Pyrotechnic connector.
7 Transponder.
8 Pyrotechnic control units and battery.
9 Deceleration module.
10 Pilot chute and mortar.
11 Carbon phenolic ablative heat shield.
12 Probe/bus in-flight disconnect.
13 Cut out for atmosphere structure temperature sensor.
14 Aero fairing.
15 Neutral mass spectrometer inlet.
16 Pressure vessel/ deceleration module umbilical cable cutter.
17 Spin vanes.
18 Parachute tower.
19 Titanium descent module.

The main components of both the Large Probe and the three Small Probes carried by the Pioneer-Venus Multi-probe were a forward aeroshell with heat shielding; a spherical titanium pressure vessel housing the instruments and the communications, command and power system; and the aft cover. The Large Probe carried seven instruments. The gas chromatograph (atmosphere structure experiment) and the mass spectrometer measured atmosphere composition directly through ports, while the others observed through windows of sapphire and diamond. The solar flux radiometer used five sapphire windows, the nephelometer (cloud sensor) two sapphire windows, the cloud particle analyzer one sapphire window and the infra-red radiometer one diamond window. This last, 0·75in (18·75mm) in diameter and 0·125in (3·125mm) thick, was the only material that would admit IR rays and yet withstand the temperature and pressure of the Venerian atmosphere. The Large Probe established a radio link with Earth 20 minutes before entry, and at about 42 miles (68km) altitude a mortar fired to open the aft cover, a pilot parachute extracted the main chute, which in turn extracted the pressure vessel containing the instruments for deployment in the atmosphere. Drag plates slowed descent and vanes modulated spin.

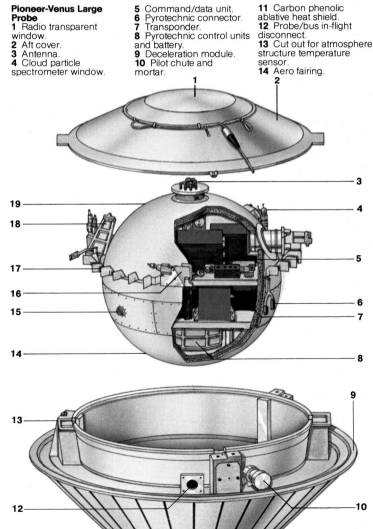

Above: *The Pioneer-Venus Orbiter is launched from Cape Canaveral on an Atlas-Centaur rocket. This preceded the Multi-probe's launch by three months, but the two craft arrived at Venus only 5 days apart.*

Pioneer-Venus Orbiter

1 Log conical spiral omni antenna.
2 Backup high-gain antenna.
3 Despin bearing.
4 Electric field detectors.
5 Electron temperature probe.
6 Plasma analyzer.
7 Forward axial thruster.
8 As 5.
9 Equipment shelf (also houses gamma burst detector).
10 Aft omni antenna.
11 Central thrust tube.
12 Orbit insertion solid propellant motor.
13 Propellant tanks.
14 Solar array.
15 Radial thruster.
16 Radar mapper.
17 Star sensor.
18 Sun sensor.
19 Cloud photopolarimeter.
20 Ultraviolet spectrometer.
21 Neutral mass spectrometer.
22 Ion mass spectrometer.
23 Infra-red radiometer.
24 Retarding potential analyzer.
25 Magnetometer.
26 3-section, deployable magnetometer boom.
27 Sleeve dipole antenna.
28 Despun high-gain antenna.

The Pioneer-Venus mission was carried out in late 1978 by two separate vehicles which shared a "basic bus" design, the Orbiter and the Multi-probe craft. The former was to survey the Venerian atmosphere and near-space environment, produce a rough radar map of the planet, and perform one astronomical experiment, and the latter to direct a number of individual probes towards the planet's surface. The Orbiter was launched on 20 May 1978 and reached its destination early in December that year. It comprised a cylindrical bus fitted with a despun high-gain dish antenna to return scientific data at high rates; a second omni antenna was positioned aft. Protruding radially from the upper ring was a 15·5ft (4·7m) boom extended after launch which carried magnetometer sensors. The instrument array

comprised a cloud photopolarimeter, for measuring the vertical distribution of cloud and haze particles and observing cloud circulation and ultraviolet markings; an infra-red radiometer, to measure heat emission from the planet's atmosphere and to seek water vapour above the clouds; an airglow ultraviolet spectrometer, to observe atmospheric markings visible only through UV filters and to track UV-absorbing cloud and haze masses; a neutral mass spectrometer, for measuring the densities of neutral atoms and molecules in the upper atmosphere and also for identifying noble (ie non-reactive) gases; an ion mass spectrometer, to study the distribution and concentration of positively charged ions from an altitude of 93 miles (150km) to the ionosphere; a solar wind plasma analyzer, measuring the strength, direction, temperature and other properties of the solar wind in the Venerian upper atmosphere; a magnetometer, for determining both spatial and planetary magnetic fields while taking into account the Orbiter's own magnetic energy; an electric field detector, for measuring the electric components of plasma waves in the solar wind and the ionosphere and radio emissions from 100 to 100,000Hz; electron temperature probes, to obtain data relating to the thermal characteristics of Venus' atmosphere; a charged particle retarding potential analyzer, which measured carbon dioxide and oxygen atoms and their surrounding electrons; and a gamma ray burst detector (the only astronomical device on board). In addition, a radar mapper was carried to produce radar maps of the planet's surface features from echoes along the orbital path. Orbiter radio science experiments employed two-way Doppler tracking to detect orbital changes of the craft

caused by variations in the gravitational field, and using X-band signals, gathered data about the characteristics of the Venerian atmosphere. From its highly elliptical orbit, the spacecraft was able to produce ultraviolet images of Venus.

Technical Data
Height: 14·76ft (4·5m) including antenna mast.
Height of bus 3·94ft (1·2m)
Launch weight: 1,283lb (582kg).
Total weight of instruments: 100lb (45kg).
Diameter: 8·2ft (2·5m).
Diameter of dish antenna: 43in (109cm).
Solar array: 77·5sq ft (7·2m²) of 0·8in x 0·8in (2cm x 2cm) cells.
Output of solar array: 226W (near Earth) or 312W (near Venus).
Prime contractor: Hughes Aircraft Co.

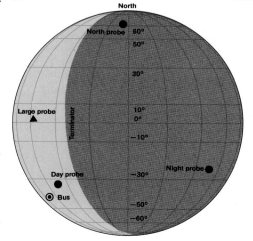

aerodynamic pressure. Only the day probe continued to send data after it reached the surface, where it survived for 67 minutes.

Aphrodite and Ishtar

Spin stabilized at 4·9 revolutions a minute, the Pioneer Orbiter took up an initial orbit of 233 x 41,570 miles (375 x 66,900km). The low point in the orbit (periapsis) was eventually reduced to 93 miles (150km), which as a result gave the vehicle an orbital period of 24·03 hours.

The radar mapper revealed the first, broad scale topography of Venus, covering 83 per cent of the surface from 75 degrees north to 63 degrees south latitude. Two thirds of the planet were covered by rolling plains. About 16 per cent of the surface appeared to be low lying basins, like lunar maria. Two elevated regions of continental size were defined by the radar reflections. One appeared to have active volcanoes. Near the equator appeared a rift valley,

Multi-Probe Entry Locations The four Pioneer-Venus probes and their accompanying bus came down in a variety of locations on both the day and night sides of the planet. The bus burned up on the day side, while the large probe also entered here under parachute descent, sampling the structure of the atmosphere. Three smaller probes made descents as shown.

analogous to one on Mars and the mid-ocean rift system on Earth.

These were preliminary findings. The features became more complex and detailed as the Orbiter continued to survey the planet.

The larger of the two continental features was centred at 5 degrees below the equator and was called "Aphrodite". It was about as large as the northern half of Africa. It consisted of two mountainous regions separated by a plain and extended about 5,965 miles (9,600km).

In the west, mountains rose 26,250ft (8,000m) above the plateau, or about 29,500ft (9,000m) above the mean planetary surface which was defined by the radius of 3,759 miles (6,050km) from the centre. Mountains in the eastern part were more subdued, rising 10,825ft (3,300m) above the plateau and 14,100ft (4,300m) above the mean surface.

The smaller of the two continents was centred at 65 degrees north latitude and

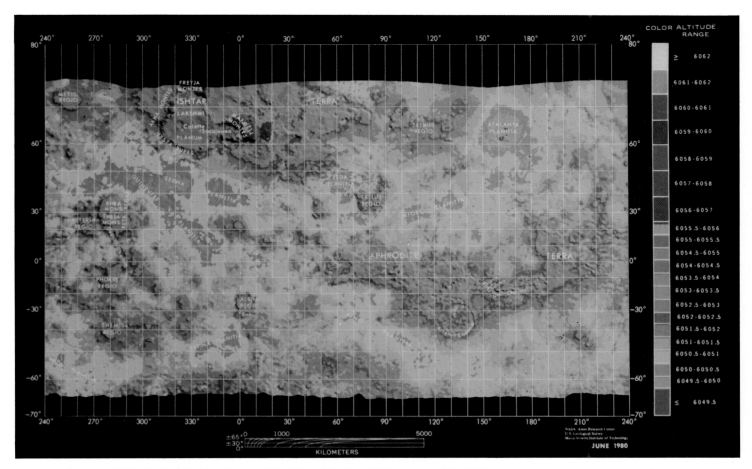

COLOR ALTITUDE RANGE

Range
≥ 6062
6061-6062
6060-6061
6059-6060
6058-6059
6057-6058
6056-6057
6055.5-6056
6055-6055.5
6054.5-6055
6054-6054.5
6053.5-6054
6053-6053.5
6052.5-6053
6052-6052.5
6051.5-6052
6051-6051.5
6050.5-6051
6050-6050.5
6049.5-6050
≤ 6049.5

KILOMETERS

NASA Ames Research Center
U.S. Geological Survey
Mass. Institute of Technology

JUNE 1980

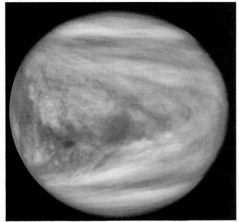

Above: *Colour contour map of about 83 per cent of Venus' surface, prepared from Pioneer Orbiter radar measurements. Sixty per cent of Venus is covered by a flat, rolling plain (blue). There are two main "continents": Ishtar Terra in the north, and the larger Aphrodite Terra at the equator. Maxwell Montes, on the east side of Ishtar, is at 36,100ft (11,000m) the highest point.*

Left: *Venus' upper atmosphere: part of a time-sequence photographed in ultraviolet by the Pioneer Orbiter. The pictures were taken 14 hours apart, and they reveal the permanent Y-shaped cloud feature and the rapid circulation pattern.*

covered an area as large as the United States. It was named "Ishtar", after the Babylonian Earth mother and goddess of love and procreation. Ishtar exhibited several mountain ranges rising 7,550ft to 10,825ft (2,300–3,300m) above a central plain called "Lakshmi". Its most conspicuous feature was a massif called Maxwell Montes which rises 36,100ft (11,000m) above the plain.

Two smaller highland regions were observed. One, Beta Regio, was a volanic pile consisting of two, adjoining shield volcanoes, so-called because they appeared to have been built up by shield-shaped masses of successive lava flows. The volcanoes were judged to extend 1,305 miles (2,100km) north to south. A second minor highland area, Alpha Regio, exhibited an ancient, fissured, rough surface.

The crust of Venus was regarded from the radar data as a single plate, in contrast to the multiple plates comprising the crust of Earth. The lowest point on the planet was

found in the rift valley to the east of Aphrodite. It was 1·8 miles (2·9km) below the mean surface.

Continued radar scans disclosed the existence of a second volcanic region in a section of Aphrodite Terra called the "Scorpion's Tail".

On the great plains of Venus, large craters were detected some with diameters of 250 to 375 miles (400 to 600km) and depths of 656 to 2,300ft (200 to 700m). West of Ishtar appeared a basin centred at 70 degrees north latitude. Its lowest point was 1·67 miles (2·7km) below the plains and its bottom revealed no craters—an indication that it had been floored with lava in relatively recent times.

Atmospheric data from Soviet Veneras and the Pioneer Multi-probe were generally in agreement. The relatively low proportion of Argon 40 found in data from both was estimated by the Pioneer scientific team as about 30 per cent of that on Earth. Inasmuch

as Argon 40 is formed by the decay of radio-active Potassium 40, the apparent depletion of Argon 40 could be accounted for in several ways. It could indicate a lower initial abundance of Potassium 40, a slower rate of decay or a lesser degree of tectonic (crustal shaping) actvity compared with Earth.[9] The third possibility seemed to be consistent with the Soviet interpretation of retarded evolution on Venus. The Argon problem seemed to be a clue in search of mystery.

A profile of the atmosphere derived from Venera and Pioneer probing showed a smog layer about 9·3 miles (15km) thick at the top of the clouds. The main cloud layers drifted below and below them were hazes of varying density. The approximate altitudes of the cloud layers varied. Pioneer Orbiter photos

9 Phillips, R.J. et al., "Tectonics and the Evolution of Venus", *Science*, Vol. 212, No. 4497.

perature map of V

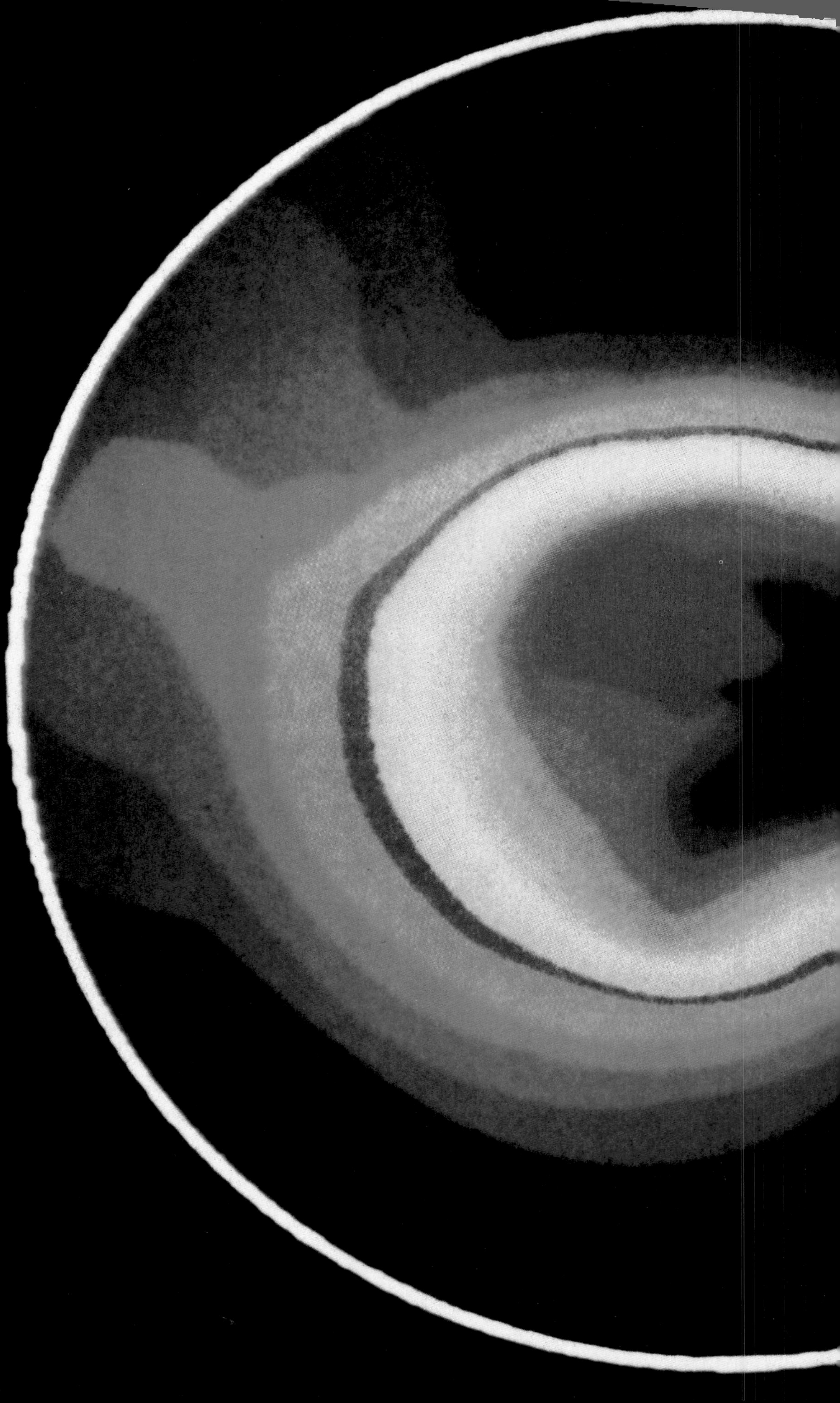

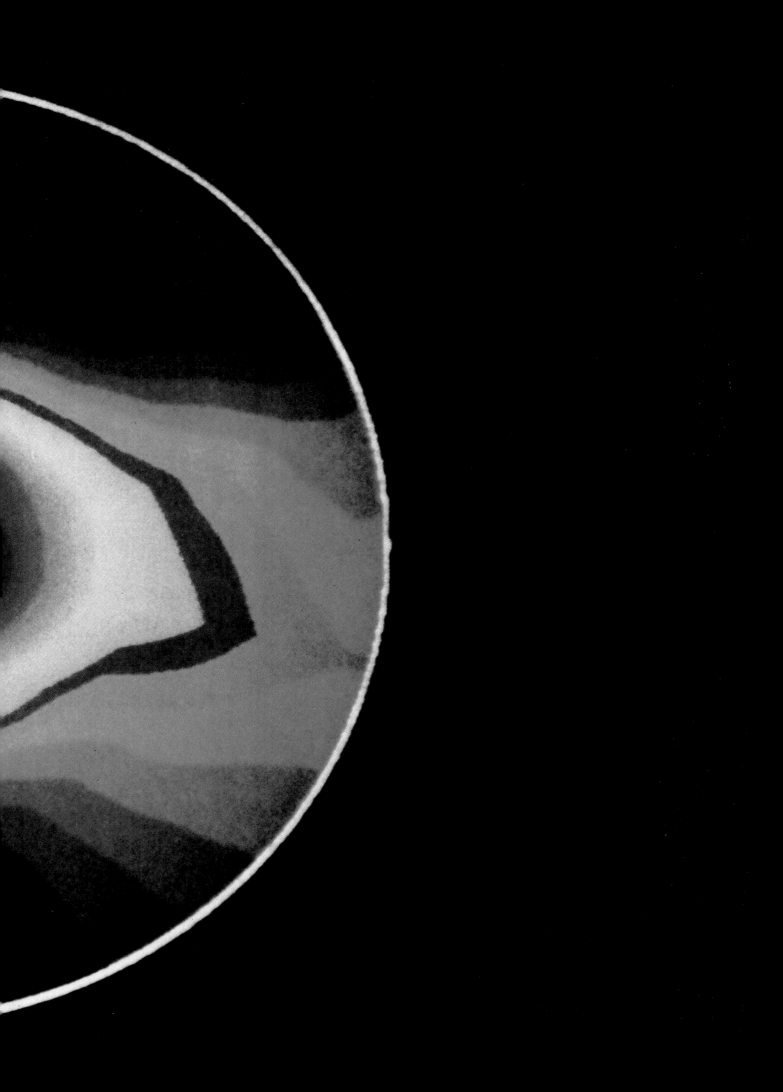

showed a main cloud deck at 37·3 to 40·4 miles (60-65km) above the surface, but soundings by Pioneer and Venera probes showed the bulk of condensation clouds between 35·4 and 30 miles (57 and 48km), with a thin haze below.

The composition of the clouds, however, was consistently reported as a condensate of sulphuric acid, with minor amounts of sulphur dioxide and water vapour. Condensation clouds appeared patchy. They varied in density but in general appeared to be hardly 10 per cent as dense as cumulus clouds on Earth.

A shell of high speed winds blowing from east to west (opposite to the prevailing winds on Earth) encompassed the planet at high altitudes. At the upper cloud level, above 31 miles (50km), the winds were blowing at 224mph (360km/h) in equatorial regions and appeared to be moving around the equatorial circumference of Venus in four days. Wind velocities dropped at lower altitudes. At 31 miles (50km), the speeds were 119mph (192km/h) and at 12·4 miles (20km), 50mph (80km/h). By contrast, more than half of the atmosphere which lies below 12·4 miles (20km) was virtually stagnant. Speeds of 1·86 to 11·2mph (3 to 18km/h) were registered by the probes at altitudes lower than 6 miles (10km).

At the lower altitudes, cross winds blow between the equator and the poles at 15·5mph (25km/h) and exhibit convective circulation. The atmosphere as a whole, however, moves around the planet from east to west as a unit in the direction of the planet's "backward" rotation. Its motion is like that of a solid body, indicating that wind velocities in the polar regions must be much lower than those over the equator.

The lower altitude winds blowing between the equator and the poles are superimposed on the main east-west circulation. Some of the more than 1,000 photos returned by the Pioneer Orbiter show a spiral of wind-driven clouds and haze moving poleward.

Investigators suspected that a polar vortex exists into which cooler layers of air descend and flow back to the equator where they are reheated to rise and move poleward. A cap of haze which extends over the poles may trap any heat rising through the polar vortex.

The energy source of the high speed winds of the upper atmosphere has puzzled observers for years. One suggestion is that as the super-dense, super-hot air near the surface rises, the momentum imparted to it by the planet's slow rotation is increased as air density decreases with altitude.

In more than three years of observation, Pioneer Orbiter photos have shown changes in cloud layers and wind patterns with time. The high altitude smog layer has disappeared and reappeared. The global pattern of the wind circulation has changed. The rotation of the atmosphere as a unit which Pioneer Orbiter observed was not seen by Mariner 10 in 1974. Mid-latitude jet streams detected by Mariner 10 have not been observed by Pioneer.

Deuterium

Unexpectedly, deuterium turned up in an analysis of data from the sounder probe's neutral mass spectrometer. Only traces had

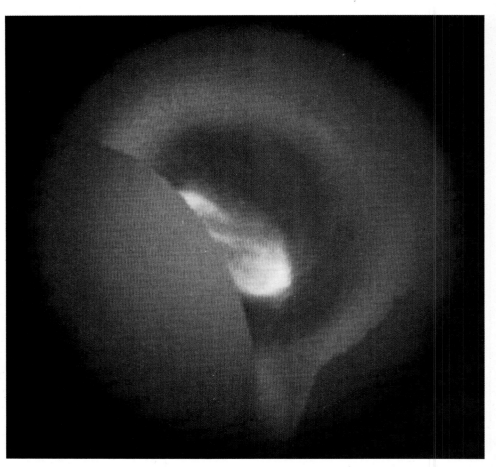

Above: Orbiter infra-red picture of the cloud patterns around Venus' north pole. A crescent of cold, dense cloud surrounds two "eyes" at the pole where warmer, lower clouds are visible.

Right: Contrast-enhanced image of Venus' north pole region, showing the different temperature regimes in the cloud layers. Warmer regions near the equator are part of the twice-daily "thermal tide".

been seen before of the heavy hydrogen isotope, but this time, a remarkable abundance appeared.

As the probe dropped through the clouds at 31 miles (50km) altitude, the spectrometer inlets became clogged with sulphuric acid. The acid contained sufficient traces of water, however, to enable the instrument to measure the ratio of deuterium to hydrogen in Venus' water. Investigators found that the ratio of deuterium to hydrogen in the water drops was 100 times greater than the ratio on Earth. The deuterium enrichment suggested that an enormous volume of hydrogen had escaped from Venus while the heavier atoms of deuterium remained. This effect indicated that at some time in the past history of Venus, an ocean had evaporated as the result of a catastrophic rise in temperature.

The hypothesis of massive destabilization and outgassing of water from Venus implies that solar temperature was lower in the past. This idea is supported by a belief that the luminosity of the Sun has increased 30 per cent since the formation of the planets. An increase in solar temperature high enough to raise surface temperature catastrophically could have occurred late in the history of

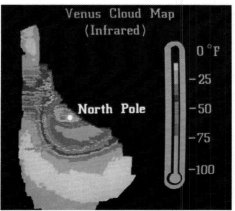

Venus Cloud Map (Infrared)

North Pole

0 °F
-25
-50
-75
-100

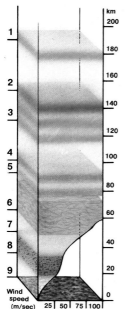

Venus' Atmosphere
1 Weakly ionized layer.
2 Main ionization layer.
3 Weakly ionized layer.
4 Upper hazes.
5 Lower hazes.
6 Tropopause clouds (sulphuric acid).
7 Wind shear.
8 Low hazes, aerosols, dust.
9 Clear atmosphere to surface.

Venus' layered atmosphere, composed mainly of carbon dioxide gas, stretches much further into space than Earth's. The topmost ionized layers result from direct interaction with the solar wind. The main cloud base (**6**) lies below two thin haze layers. The yellowish clouds are composed of sulphuric acid droplets, and although they look opaque, they are more like haze than Earth clouds. Wind speeds at the base of the cloud layer drop dramatically to near-zero at the surface.

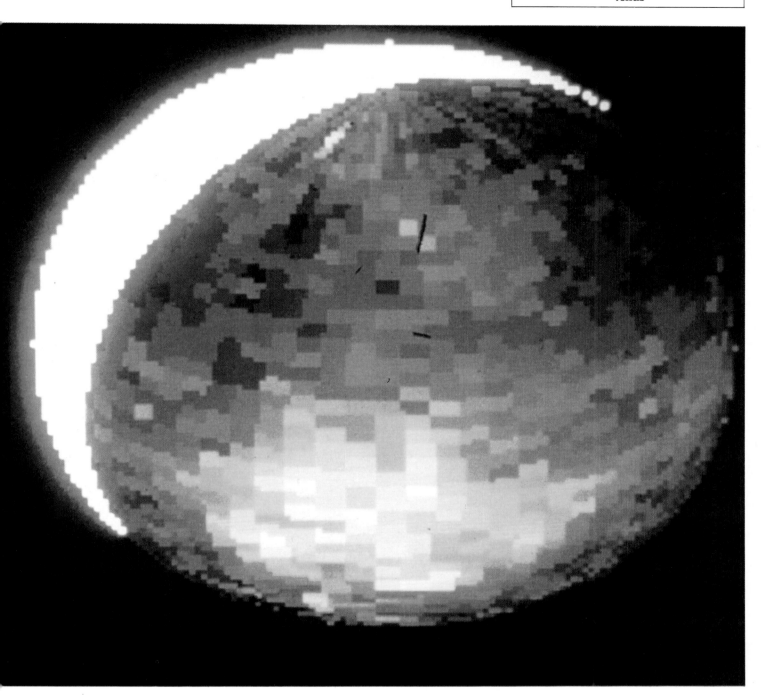

Above: *The ultraviolet sensors on the Pioneer Orbiter reveal not only the sunlit crescent, but also a glow from the nighttime hemisphere caused by fluorescent chemical reactions in Venus' atmosphere.*

Venus.[10] An initial rate of evaporation might then have been accelerated by the onset of the greenhouse effect, allowing hydrogen to escape to the top of the atmosphere and into space while oxygen was absorbed by the rocks on the planet.

The principal contribution to the greenhouse effect on Venus is made by carbon dioxide. Data from Mariner, Venera and Pioneer show that it accounts for 55 per cent of heat trapping. Water vapour, with an abundance of 50 parts per million, accounts for 25 per cent; sulphur dioxide, at 200 parts per million, 5 per cent and clouds and haze, 15 per cent.

The head of the Pioneer-Venus science steering group, Dr Thomas M. Donahue of the University of Michigan, estimated that

the volume of escaped hydrogen could have been equivalent to that in a terrestrial ocean and could have been exhausted in 280 million years. Dr Donahue and his colleagues suggested that after a large volume of water had outgassed from Venus, the runaway greenhouse ensued,

   " and a copious amount of hydrogen
   produced from this water appeared
   in the atmosphere."

Escape of hydrogen would have been powered by solar extreme-ultraviolet heating, they said.[11]

If an ocean had existed on Venus, orbital photography of the order of that achieved by Mariner 9 at Mars (see Mars chapter) would probably show signs of an oceanic basin, along with river valleys and stream beds. While the clouds are opaque to photography in the visible portion of the electromagnetic spectrum, they are transparent to radar imaging. Recent development of synthetic aperture radar which has demonstrated effectiveness in making high resolution sur-

face photographs of Earth through overcast (see pages 122-123) may solve the problem of photomapping Venus from orbit.

Synthetic Aperture Radar (SAR) has been considered since 1978 as a means of mapping the surface of Venus through the dense clouds which are opaque to light photography but transparent to radar. A Venus Orbiting Imaging Radar (VOIR) spacecraft was proposed but dropped from consideration because of cost: about $300 million.

A less expensive Venus Radar Mapper (VRM) mission was developed by JPL scientists in 1982 for submission for funding in the fiscal 1984 NASA budget. It would cut the projected VOIR costs by omitting atmospheric experiments and reducing the high resolution objective of VOIR.

10 Phillips, R.J. et. al., "Tectonics and the Evolution of Venus", *Science*, Vol. 212, No. 4497.

11 Donahue, T.M. et al., "Venus Was Wet: A Measurement of the Ratio of Deuterium to Hydrogen", *Science*, Vol. 216, No. 4546.

SUCCESSFUL MISSIONS TO VENUS

SPACECRAFT		DATE	LAUNCH VEHICLE	WEIGHT lb (kg)	RESULTS
Mariner 2	(US)	27 Aug 62	Atlas-Agena	447 (4,447)	First scientific data from Venus fly-by 14 Dec 62.
Venera 3	(USSR)	16 Nov 65	A-2-e	2,439 (1,106)	Landed 1 March 66. First impact on another planet.
Venera 4	(USSR)	12 June 67	A-2-e	2,439 (1,106)	Landed 18 Oct 67. Returned first data on atmosphere.
Mariner 5	(US)	14 June 67	Atlas-Agena	540 (245)	Venus fly-by Oct 67. Returned atmosphere data.
Venera 5	(USSR)	5 Jan 69	A-2-e	2,490 (1,130)	Descent capsule sounded atmosphere, 16 May 69.
Venera 6	(USSR)	10 Jan 69	A-2-e	2,490 (1,130)	Descent capsule sounded atmosphere, 17 May 69.
Venera 7	(USSR)	17 Aug 70	A-2-e	2,600 (1,180)	Descent capsule and lander data, 15 Dec 70.
Venera 8	(USSR)	27 Mar 72	A-2-e	2,600 (1,180)	Descent capsule and lander data, 22 July 72.
Mariner 10	(US)	3 Nov 73	Atlas-Centaur	1,109 (503)	First fly-by of Venus and Mercury; Venus encounter 5 Feb 74.
Venera 9	(USSR)	8 June 75	D-1-e	10,884 (4,936)	First Venus orbiter, 22 Oct 75; first lander photos, 23 Oct 75
Venera 10	(USSR)	14 June 75	D-1-e	11,098 (5,033)	Venus orbiter and lander, 25 Oct 75; photos same day.
Pioneer-Venus 1	(US)	20 May 78	Atlas-Centaur	1,283 (582)	Venus orbiter with radar mapper, 4 Dec 79.
Pioneer-Venus 2	(US)	8 Aug 78	Atlas-Centaur	1,993 (904)	Ejected multiple descent probes to analyze clouds and atmosphere, 9 Dec 78.
Venera 11	(USSR)	9 Sep 78	D-1-e	11,023 (5,000)*	Lander returned atmosphere and surface data, 25 Dec 78; no photos.
Venera 12	(USSR)	14 Sep 78	D-1-e	11,023 (5,000)*	Lander returned atmosphere and surface data, 21 Dec 78; no photos.
Venera 13	(USSR)	30 Oct 81	D-1-e	11,023 (5,000)*	Lander returned colour surface photos and atmosphere data, 1 March 82.
Venera 14	(USSR)	4 Nov 81	D-1-e	11,023 (5,000)*	Lander returned colour surface photos and atmosphere data, 5 March 82.

*Estimated weight.
Note: The Soviet Union launched two further craft to Venus—Venera 15 and 16—on 2 June 1983 and 7 June 1983 respectively. If successful, these probes will carry out radar mapping of the surface from October 1983 onwards.

In addition, the cost of establishing the spacecraft in a circular orbit could be reduced by allowing it to take up an elliptical orbit around Venus. SAR engineering advances have made it feasible to design a system that would photomap the surface satisfactorily from elliptical orbit. Further economies could be realized by using spare hardware from the Voyager programme and possibly from the Galileo Jupiter mission planned for 1986.

Objectives of the Venus Radar Mapper were cited by the JPL group as mapping at least 70 per cent of the surface of Venus at 0·62 miles (1km) resolution and obtaining surface relief from radar altimeter data with 328ft (100m) resolution. The VRM spacecraft would also make gravity field measurements over areas not covered by the Pioneer-Venus Orbiter. It will use a dual purpose antenna to collect data and relay them to Earth.

In a newsletter circulated among interested scientists, the JPL group commented that while understanding of the Venerian atmosphere is relatively complete, the geology and solid body geophysics of the planet "remains sketchy and incomplete". The communication noted that the Soviet Venera landers (see below) had obtained physical measurements and pictures of a few small areas on the surface, but the observations were localized and could not readily be placed in global perspective.

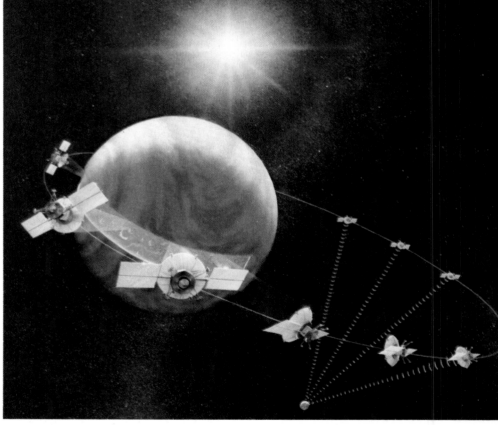

Also, the newsletter commented, the locations of Venera landing sites were dictated largely by celestial mechanics constraints. The Venera landers were dropped off their carrier vehicles while approaching Venus on interplanetary trajectories. Consequently, a lander touchdown site was largely dictated by the characteristics of the trajectory.

Earth-based radar mapping, the letter said, is limited to equatorial and mid-latitude regions of one hemisphere of Venus because the orbital periods of Earth and Venus and the slow rotation of Venus causes the same hemisphere of Venus to be visible at every close approach.

The Pioneer-Venus Orbiter's radar altimeter made a topographic map of essentially the entire planet at 62 miles (100km) resolution, the letter continued. Although the map enables observers to

Above: *The instruments aboard the Venera 13 Lander are prepared for flight. The saw-tooth lip to the landing ring is evident (compare with Venera 12 on page 161).*

Left: *The Venus Radar Mapper, due for launch in 1988, is designed to map Venus from orbit with a resolution of 0·6 miles (1km).*

Below: *Panorama of Venus' surface from Venera 13. The orange colouration is the result of absorption of blue light by the clouds. At the bottom is the saw-toothed landing ring (for stabilization), with a discarded lens cover just above. To the right is a colour calibration standard.*

identify the planet's major physiographic features, it does not have the resolution to indicate geologic processes that formed the features. The letter summed up:

"Venus is a unique laboratory for comparative planetology. Its similarity to the Earth in size, composition and proximity to the Sun implies that any differences between Earth and Venus will be due to small but significant factors."

The 1982 Veneras

The USSR resumed surface photography of the day side of Venus with two 11,023lb (5,000kg) Veneras carrying landers at the 1981–82 opportunity. Venera 13 was launched on 30 October 1981 and landed on 1 March 1982. Its twin, Venera 14, was launched on 4 November 1981 and landed on 5 March. Both landers separated from their buses which continued in solar orbit and relayed lander radio signals to Earth.

During their descent, both landers analyzed the composition of the atmosphere with results confirming previous findings. In addition, the landers measured the intensity and frequency of lightning strokes, which some scientists associated with volcanic activity on Venus.

On the basis of surface radar profiles made by Pioneer-Venus Orbiter, American scientists recommended to the Venera scientific team landing sites of particular interest to the exploration programmes of both countries. The landers came down on an upland region called Phoebe Regio, southeast of the volcanic Beta Regio. Each machine carried a hollow core drill of the type devised for advanced Luna landers on the Moon. The cores were deposited in a test chamber and analyzed by X-ray fluorescence. The surface rock and fines were identified as basalt. The mechanical strength of the ground was measured by a rod which was pressed into the soil by springs. The rod also was used to measure electrical conductivity of the soil.

Venera 13 operated on the surface for 127 minutes and returned eight panoramic views. The pictures were taken through red, blue and green filters successively, radioed to Earth and recombined to form colour images. Venera 14 also sent back colour pictures in this manner. Photo and

scientific data were relayed to Earth by the Venera buses.

Temperature and pressure data were within the ranges found by earlier probes, 465°C and 94 atmospheres at the surface. Early photo transmissions showed large, thick, surface boulders of dark grey rock, with eroded faces. Between the outcrops of rock, the surface was covered by a brownish black, fine grained dirt. Academician Valeriy Barsukov, head of the Soviet Institute of Geochemistry and Analytic Chemistry, was quoted by the Soviet news agency, Tass, as remarking that basalt covered 60 to 70 per cent of Venus.

At the end of 1982, after 20 years of investigation, the history of Venus was barely understood. The principal mystery is why its environment differs so drastically from that of Earth, in view of the fact that both planets formed near each other in the same part of the solar nebula and their early evolution seems to have been similar.

As Professor Keldysh (see also page 161) remarked, Venus has undergone a process of chemical differentiation that is now seen as typical of terrestrial planets. But the evolution of its crushing, suffocating atmosphere, the onset of the greenhouse phenomenon and the disappearance of its water remain in the realm of speculation.

It has been considered axiomatic that planets of similar size and density follow a similar evolutionary path. However, this premise has been challenged by the presently returned data from Venus, in the opinion of a group of Pioneer scientists.[12]

---

12 Phillips, R.J. et al., op. cit.

RECOMMENDED READING

Donahue, T.M. et al., "Venus Was Wet: A Measurement of the Ratio of Deuterium to Hydrogen", *Science*, Vol. 216, No. 4546.
Jet Propulsion Laboratory staff, *Mariner Mission to Venus*, NASA-McGraw Hill, New York, 1963.
Lewis, R.S., *From Vinland to Mars*, Quadrangle-New York Times Book Co., New York, 1976.
Philips, R.J. et al, "Tectonics and the Evolution of Venus", *Science*, Vol. 212, No. 4497.
Venus, Special Report, Science Year, World Book Encyclopedia, Chicago, Ill., 1977.
Young, A. & L., "Venus", *Scientific American*, Vol. 233, No. 3, Sept 1975.

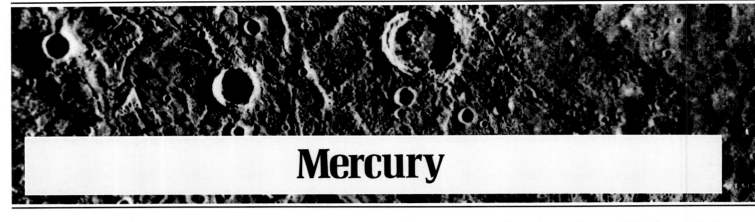

Mercury

Mariner 10 was one of five multi-planet, fly-by missions on which NASA embarked in the 1970s. Four were aimed at the outer planets in the late 1970s.[1] The targets of Mariner 10 were Venus and Mercury.

The concept of multi-planet reconnaissance by a single spacecraft arose quite early in the space age. A "grand tour" of the outer planets—Jupiter, Saturn, Uranus and, possibly, Neptune—was proposed by a team of young engineers and mathematicians at National Aeronautics & Space Administration centres in 1961-62. It would be quite feasible when the outer planets were in alignment circa 1977, the group suggested. Once the spacecraft encountered Jupiter, the big planet's gravitational field would hurl the vehicle on to Saturn whose gravitational field would accelerate the tour bus to Uranus and from there to Neptune and then out of the Solar System.

The concept was interesting from the viewpoints of science and economy. Using a single spacecraft on a multi-planet survey saved launch costs as well as vehicle costs.

In mid-1968, the Space Science Board of the United States National Academy of Sciences endorsed a two-planet mission that would fly past Venus and Mercury during the 1973 launch opportunity for Venus. The Board suggested that the mission be accomplished with a single launch in order to conserve funds available for planetary exploration.[2] The project was implemented by NASA in 1969 as a single launch, dual-planet, gravity-assist mission.

Because Mariner 10 was required to operate closer to the Sun than any previous spacecraft, the basic design was modified to provide protection from solar radiation. Mercury's average distance from the Sun is 36 million miles (57·9 million km), or 0·387 astronomical units (AU), nearly one-half that of Venus.

The spacecraft's instruments had to be protected from intense heat and the solar input to the vehicle's photovoltaic cells had to be reduced. The panels (two rather than four of previous Mariners) were redesigned so that they could be rotated away from the Sun as Mariner 10 approached Mercury. A sunshade was installed to protect the main

---

1 The missions were Pioneer 10 to Jupiter and its satellite system; Pioneer 11 to Jupiter and Saturn; Voyagers 1 and 2 to Jupiter, Saturn and Uranus.
2 Giberson, W.E. and Cunningham, N.W., "Mariner 10 Mission to Venus and Mercury", Acta Astronautica, Vol. 2, Pergamon Press, 1975.

MERCURY:BASIC DATA	
Equatorial Diameter*	0·38E, 3,031 miles (4,878km)
Mass*	0·055E
Density	3·18oz/in³ (5·5g/cm³)
Volume*	0·056E
Surface Gravity*	0·38E
Escape Velocity	2·67 miles/sec (4·3km/sec)
Period of Rotation	58·6 days
Inclination of Equator (to Orbit)	~0°
Distance from Sun (Semi-major axis)	0·3871AU; 36 x 10⁶miles (57·9 x 10⁶km)
Siderial Period	87·97 days
Synodic Period	115·88 days
Orbital Speed	29·7 miles/sec (47·8km/sec)
Orbital Eccentricity	0·206
Inclination of Orbit (to ecliptic plane)	7·004°
Number of Satellites	0
*Earth = 1	

bus, along with special blankets and reflective and painted surfaces.

Mariner 10 was manufactured for the Jet Propulsion Laboratory by the Boeing Aerospace Co. in Kent, Washington. It was the sixth in the Mariner series and JPL management emphasized the use of existing designs and hardware.

As Mariner 10 left the Earth on 3 November 1973, its two television cameras with 4·92ft (1·5m) telescopes, its ultraviolet experiment consisting of airglow and occultation spectrometers and its charged particle telescope were turned on. This was done in order to calibrate the instruments in the well known regions of the Earth-Moon system.

The airglow ultraviolet spectrometer observed the emissions of hydrogen, helium and atomic oxygen from Earth as baseline data with which to compare emissions expected at Venus and Mercury. During the first week of the cruise, the cameras made five mosaics of the Earth and six of the Moon at the resolutions expected when Mariner flew by Venus. Earth images enabled the imaging team to compare the clouds of Earth with the clouds of Venus.

Trajectory corrections on the Venus leg of the journey were made on 13 November 1973 and 21 January 1974. Guidance engineers estimated that an error of 1 kilometre at Venus would result in missing the aiming point at Mercury by 620 miles (1,000km).

The mission seemed to come perilously close to failing in January when the spacecraft automatically switched from its main power system to the backup power system. If the failure causing the switchover was common to both systems, the mission was lost.

Controllers at the JPL Mission Control and Computing Center in Pasadena were prepared for the worst. From then on, the mission relied on the backup power system.

The Venus Flywheel

In late January 1974, Mariner 10 observed the Comet Kohoutek with the ultraviolet spectrometer. The instrument detected emissions of neutral hydrogen over a range of 17 degrees from the comet's nucleus. The observation was much more extensive than was possible from Skylab (which was orbiting the Earth at the time) because the proximity of the Earth limited Skylab observations.

Left: *Lift-off of the Venus and Mercury probe Mariner 10 from Launch Complex 36B at Cape Canaveral on 3 November 1973. The launch vehicle is an Atlas rocket topped with a powerful Centaur upper stage.*

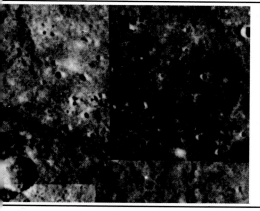

"Through the electronic sight and other "senses" of our automated probes, colour and complexion have been given to worlds that existed for centuries as fuzzy discs or indistinct points of light."

NASA Facts, *Our Planets At A Glance*

Above: *Mariner 10 undergoes a pre-launch check at the Boeing Space Center, Kent, Washington, where it was manufactured for NASA. Technicians working with space-probes must always wear surgical garments so as to prevent contamination of the many sensitive electrical components. The two tiltable solar panels are deployed, and extensive thermal shielding is evident.*

Right: *The 210ft (64m) antenna at Goldstone, California is part of the Deep Space Network. A microwave tower relays data from the dish to the Network Operations Control Center at JPL in Pasadena.*

Mariner 10 raced by Venus at a nearest altitude of 3,595 miles (5,784km) on 5 February 1974, returning spectacular photographs of banded clouds in ultraviolet light and identifying hydrogen, helium and atomic oxygen in the high atmosphere (see Venus chapter).

The gravitational field and orbital energy of Venus accelerated the 1,110lb (503kg) spacecraft to Mercury. Controllers at Pasadena made a trajectory correction on 16 March 1974 by changing velocity 58·4ft/sec (17·8m/sec).

The change shifted encounter from 6,200 miles (10,000km) above the sunlit side to within 437 miles (703km) of the dark side of Mercury on 29 March 1974, based on a planetary radius of 1,515·6 miles (2,439km). Mariner's twin television cameras began photographing the planet on 23 March at a distance of 3·3 million miles (5·3 million km).

One half of the sunlit side of the planet was visible on the approaching leg and the other sunlit half was visible on the departing leg. During these segments of the fly-by, the cameras took pictures at 42-second intervals. A total of 2,482 exposures were transmitted to the Deep Space Network antennas at Goldstone, California, Madrid, Spain and Tidbinbilla (Canberra), Australia and relayed to the Jet Propulsion Laboratory for processing.

Mercurian gravitation deflected Mariner 10 into a solar orbit with twice the period of

Mercury's revolution around the Sun. The Mercurian year is approximately 88 days. After passing Mercury on 29 March, Mariner 10 was due to fly-by the planet again approximately 176 days later.

In preparation for the second pass, JPL made two course changes on 9 and 10 May in order to bring the spacecraft to within 21,100 miles (34,000km) of the sunlit side of the planet. However, another course correction on 2 July shifted closest approach to 29,665 miles (47,740km) above 40 degres south latitude for a view of the southern hemisphere. The second encounter came on 21 September 1974, two Mercurian years after the first. Mariner transmitted 1,954 more exposures on that sweep.

On its third passage on 16 March 1975, two Mercurian years later, Mariner 10 flew over the dark side northern hemisphere at an altitude of 193 miles (310km) and transmitted 1,091 exposures of the sunlit areas it could "see" during approach and departure.

Of the total exposures listed, JPL reported that photo data fully processed (i.e., full images) totalled 983 for the first encounter, 506 for the second and 349 for the third. The differences are accounted for by excluding optical navigation, Moon searches and photometric testing data.

With a diameter of 3,031 miles (4,878km), Mercury is smaller than Mars but its higher density, 5·5g/cm³, gives it a gravitational field only 1 per cent less than that of Mars and 2·2 times that of the Moon. These characteristics were determined by telescopic observation which also noted some surface features resembling the maria on the Moon.

Thus, even before the mission of Mariner 10, it appeared that internally Mercury was more like the Earth than like the Moon, but externally, its surface was probably lunar. Gravitationally, it was comparable to Mars.

Because, for an Earth-based observer, Mercury is never more than 28 degrees from the Sun, it has been difficult to study. It can be seen only for a short time in the morning and evening.

In ancient times, Mercury, like Venus, was believed to be two stars. Classical Greek astronomers called the morning apparition Apollo and the evening one Hermes, the Greek name of a god identified by the Romans as Mercury. Heraclitus of Ephesus (c.535—475 BC) concluded that the morning and evening stars were the same.

Next to Pluto at the other "end" of the Solar System, Mercury's orbit has the highest eccentricity of Sol's family (0·206). At perihelion, it is 28·6 million miles (46 million km)

from the Sun; at aphelion, about 43·5 million miles (70 million km). Its average orbital speed is 29·7 miles/sec (47·8km/sec) (compared with 18·5 [29·8] for Earth).

In 1880, Giovanni Virginio Schiaparelli (1835–1910), whose observations of Mars and Venus are described elsewhere in this section, concluded that Mercury's day was the same length as its year, 88 days. Thus, like the Moon, one face was always turned toward its primary. This view was shared by other observers including Percival Lowell (1855–1916) in the United States and E.M. Antoniadi (1870-1944) in France.

Synchronous rotation around its axis and revolution around the Sun meant that one side of Mercury was bathed in perpetual daylight and the other side immersed in darkness and cold. Fiction writers seized upon the opportunity to suppose a twilight zone where Mercury's vast wealth of metal could be mined.

The synchronism of Mercury's periods of rotation and revolution around the Sun became suspect in 1962 when radio astronomers at the University of Michigan detected thermal emissions from the dark side. The emissions would not have been detectable if the dark side always faced away from the Sun.

In 1965, Cornell University scientists sent radar pulses to Mercury from the radio telescope at Arecibo, Puerto Rico. The Doppler shift in the radar reflections (caused by the rotation of the planet) showed that Mercury was turning on its axis once in approximately 59 days. The period was later refined to 58·6 days.

A new relation was apparent between Mercury's 88 day year and its 58·6 day rotation. Instead of 1 to 1, the ratio was 3 to 2. During one rotation, Mercury moved two thirds of the way around the Sun. It was then calculated that since the period of rotation was two-thirds of a Mercurian year, Mercury had a very long solar day.[3] It was approximately 175·9 (Earth) days or two Mercurian years long. That happened to coincide precisely with the period of Mariner 10's orbit around the Sun after the spacecraft passed Mercury on 29 March 1974.

Relativity

In the modern history of science, Mercury is an important link in the proof of the general theory of relativity which Albert Einstein (1879–1955) presented in 1915. In that year, Einstein was able to show that the general theory provided the only satisfactory explanation of a long standing Mercurian mystery. The mystery concerned the precession of the perihelion of Mercury's orbit.

Perihelion, the point in the orbit nearest the Sun, had been observed to advance about 600 seconds of arc per century as the line of apsides (long axis) of Mercury's elliptical orbit slowly moved around the Sun. Newtonian physics explained that most of the precession was influenced by the gravitational attraction of other planets, but it failed to account for about 43 seconds of arc. Several possibilities were considered including the existence of an unseen planet between Mercury and the Sun, a planet called "Vulcan". Despite such hypotheses, no such planet could be found.

Einstein applied the mathematics of his general theory to the problem. In place of the Newtonian concept of gravitation as an attracting force that acts at a distance, Einstein substituted a field concept. It held that material bodies like the Sun produce a curvature in space and time which forms a gravitational field. The path of a body in the field is defined by the space-time curvature. Einstein was able to show that the missing 43 seconds could be accounted for by the field equations of general relativity theory. Most theoretical physicists accepted his proof, but not all.

In 1967, Mercury was the target of additional proof. The Lincoln Laboratory of the Massachusetts Institute of Technology sent radar waves to Mercury when it was at superior conjunction on the other side of the Sun from Earth. As the waves reached Mercury and were reflected back to Earth, they passed close to the Sun. A time delay was observed, showing that the path of the waves had been deflected by the mass of Sun as predicted by the general theory.

Caloris

With a solar orbit of 175·9 days, Mariner 10 not only matched the period of Mercury's solar day but was also in resonance with the 87·9 day orbit of the planet and its 58·6 day rotation. It was as a result of this remarkable feat of gravity-assist navigation, that Mariner 10 encountered Mercury every two Mercurian years. It could photograph the planet and make other scientific observations again and again, provided its power, attitude control and communications systems continued to operate.

There was one drawback. Because Mercury spins three times in two of its years, the same hemisphere was illuminated by the Sun each time Mariner 10 flew by. The other hemisphere was always dark. On

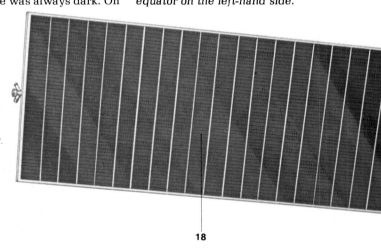

Above: *The crater-scarred surface of Mercury, photographed from a distance of 130,000 miles (210,000km) by Mariner 10. Although superficially similar to the Moon, Mercury's terrain has fewer smooth plains and many more "wrinkle ridges". The mountains ringing the 839 mile (1,350km)-wide Caloris Basin are visible near the equator on the left-hand side.*

Mariner 10
1 Low-gain antenna.
2 Airglow ultraviolet spectrometer.
3 Television camera (2).
4 Scan platform.
5 Charged particle telescope.
6 Occultation ultraviolet spectrometer.
7 Cruise Sun sensor.
8 Magnetometer.
9 Sunshade.
10 Acquisition Sun sensor.
11 Reaction control jets (roll and yaw).
12 Plasma science experiment.
13 Infra-red radiometer.
14 Thermal control blanket.
15 Heat shield.
16 High-gain antenna (motor-driven).
17 Canopus tracker.
18 Tiltable solar array.
19 X-band radio transmitter (hidden behind Canopus tracker).

Mariner 10, launched on 3 November 1973, was an extremely successful space probe designed to investigate and report on the physical characteristics of the two innermost planets, Mercury and Venus. For the first time in a major space venture, the gravity-assist technique was used, the pull of Venus being harnessed to provide enough energy for the craft to continue on to its smaller neighbour. The planets' relative alignment

was crucial to the outcome of the mission, and hence the programme had to be rigidly scheduled in order to take advantage of the launch "window" that would be available during the last few months of 1973. The vehicle was essentially a standard Mariner spacecraft, but modified for the special demands of the project: for example, two rather than four solar panels were employed, movable in order to protect them from intense solar heat; and a passive thermal protection system was incorporated

in order to take account of Mercury's high surface temperatures. Equipment comprised two TV cameras, an X-band radio transmitter, a scanning electron spectrometer, a scanning electrostatic analyzer, an infra-red radiometer, a charged particle telescope, two UV spectrometers and two magnetometers. Mariner 10 had six principal experiments on board: the Extreme Ultraviolet Experiment analyzed planetary atmospheres; the Infra-red Radiometer measured the temperature of the two

planets; the Plasma Experiment investigated solar wind within the Venerian orbit; the Charged Particle Experiment measured such particles near Mercury and observed solar flares; the two magnetometers, boom-mounted, correlated magnetic effects within the immediate vicinity of the probe itself; and the television cameras recorded both narrow- and wide-angle pictures, each camera taking a 700-scan-line, 832-pixel/line frame every 42 seconds for relay to Earth.

its three operating passes, Mariner 10 was thus able to photograph parts of only one hemisphere.

Inasmuch as differences exist between hemispheres of the Earth, the Moon and Mars, it is probable that Mercury's unseen hemisphere may hold surprises.[4] Mariner 10 was able to scan approximately one-third of the surface of Mercury during the 17 months it functioned. It transmitted a total of 5,514 photographs to the 210ft (64m) antennas of the Deep Space Network.

As the picture data were processed at the Jet Propulsion Laboratory, Mercury emerged as another, rougher version of the Moon. The principal land forms were craters and basins. There were long, sinuous cracks, analogous to lunar rilles; and ridges that ran hundreds of miles. Cliff-like scarps which do not appear on the Moon crossed the cratered landscape.

Compared to the Moon, which was merely desolate, Mercury was harsh, forbidding, and without an atmosphere except for a trace of helium from decay of radioactive elements and the solar wind. There was no water.

Like the Moon, Mercury bears the scars of the full accretionary period of planetary evolution. On the Moon, this period was reckoned as 600 million years, terminating with a catastrophic bombardment of planetoids, asteroids, meteors and comets 3·9 billion years ago. The sequence appeared to much the same on Mercury.

The most spectacular feature photographed by Mariner 10 was a circular basin 839 miles (1,350km) in diameter which dominated the northwest quadrant of the sunlit hemisphere. The basin was centred at 30 degrees north and 195 degrees west.[5] It was named "Caloris" because of its location in a region which receives maximum heating from the Sun at perihelion.

The Caloris Basin was seen to be rimmed by mountains rising 1·25 miles (2km) above the floor. About 93 miles (150km) beyond the rim appeared a secondary range of mountains. Members of the photo analysis team have commented on the similarity in the structure of this Mercurian basin to that of Mare Imbrium on the Moon. The youngest of the circular maria on the Moon, Imbrium is about 80 per cent of the diameter of its Mercurian counterpart and is believed to have been formed during the terminal phase of accretion 3·9 billion years ago. Caloris may also have been created then. The difference in size may be the result of the higher acceleration of Mercurian gravity.

3 The solar day is the time between successive sunrises at a given point on the planet.
4 On Earth, one hemisphere is mostly ocean, the other mostly land. The north pole is an ocean surrounded by land and the south pole is a continent surrounded by ocean. Most of the large basins on the Moon are clustered on near side. On Mars, the southern hemisphere is more heavily cratered than the northern. On both Earth and Mars, the south polar ice cap is more extensive than the north polar cap.
5 The volume of photographs sent back by Mariner 10 required the construction of a grid system for Mercury.

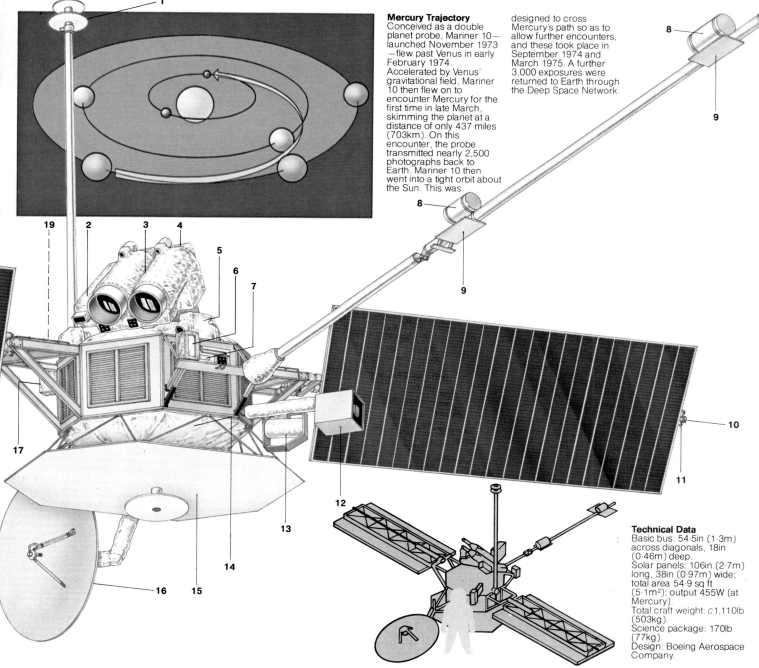

Mercury Trajectory
Conceived as a double planet probe, Mariner 10—launched November 1973—flew past Venus in early February 1974. Accelerated by Venus' gravitational field, Mariner 10 then flew on to encounter Mercury for the first time in late March, skimming the planet at a distance of only 437 miles (703km). On this encounter, the probe transmitted nearly 2,500 photographs back to Earth. Mariner 10 then went into a tight orbit about the Sun. This was designed to cross Mercury's path so as to allow further encounters, and these took place in September 1974 and March 1975. A further 3,000 exposures were returned to Earth through the Deep Space Network.

Technical Data
Basic bus: 54·5in (1·3m) across diagonals, 18in (0·46m) deep.
Solar panels: 106in (2·7m) long, 38in (0·97m) wide; total area 54·9 sq ft (5·1m²); output 455W (at Mercury).
Total craft weight: c 1,110lb (503kg).
Science package: 170lb (77kg).
Design: Boeing Aerospace Company.

Like Imbrium also, Caloris apparently was gouged out of the surface by the impact of a body tens of miles in diameter. Depending on velocity, the diameter of the planetoid that created Imbrium was calculated at 40 to 117 miles (64 to 188km) by the American astrophysicist, Ralph B. Baldwin.[6]

Other features of the Caloris region were reminiscent of the Moon. Between the primary and secondary mountain rings appeared a relatively flat surface, with scattered hills or domes. In one area, the hilly landscape resembled the Rook Mountains of Mare Orientale on the Moon, the team noted. The floor of Caloris was fairly level and seemed to be filled with "plains material" which showed a concentric pattern of ridges and cracks. Plains material was believed to have been derived from magma or lava, either extruded from the interior of the planet by volcanism or the product of extensive melting of the surface by the heat of impact.

The ridges were 1 to 8 miles (1·5 to 13km) wide and rose about 1,000ft (300m). Some of them extended for 186 miles (300km). They were transected by cracks which seemed to represent a late deformation of the crust. The cracks ranged from a width of 3,000ft (700m) (the best resolution of Mariner's telescopic lenses) to more than 5·6 miles (9km). They appeared to be several hundred metres deep. Their floors were flat. In this respect and in contour, they resembled lunar rilles.

Beyond the secondary mountain ring rolled the plains, partially cratered and scored by radial valleys. Several valleys were 75 miles (120km) long and 10 miles (16km) wide. Like the valleys radiating from the lunar Mare Imbrium they may have been scoured by missiles from the impact zone. The Caloris region valleys cut through ancient craters which had the appearance of having been flooded with lava. The valleys had been formed after episodes of cratering and volcanism.

The cracks, the ridges and valleys, all secondary effects of the Caloris impact, extended about 620 miles (1,000km) from the primary mountain rim and then faded into cratered plains.

A tertiary effect of the impact was seen on the opposite side of the planet, 180 degrees around Mercury from Caloris. It was a jumbled landscape of uneven hills, some 3 to 6 miles (5 to 10km) wide and up to 5,000ft (1·5km) high. Shock waves from the Caloris impact seemed to have travelled through the planet with enough force to rumple the antipodal surface.

The craters were structurally similar to those on the Moon and had undergone a similar kind of degradation. The photo analysis team concluded that similar erosive processes had been at work on Mercury as on the Moon, especially the impacts of micrometeoroids.[7] They had smoothed the juts and crater rims on the Moon like cosmic sandpaper. Some differences were noted also between lunar and Mercurian craters. Material ejected by impact did not travel as far from the craters on Mercury as it did from lunar counterparts. Secondary craters made by the ballistic impact of ejected rocks were closer to the main craters on Mercury than on the Moon. These differences were

attributed to Mercury's greater gravitational field which reduced the range of splash.

Further comparison of the Moon and Mercury showed that on the basis of the areas covered by Mariner 10, there are fewer large basins on Mercury than on the Moon, the photo analysis team observed. The photographic coverage revealed eight basins larger than 186 miles (300km) in diameter, including a 217 mile (350km) basin at the north pole and one of similar size at 45 degrees south latitude.

Since only a third of the planet's surface was seen, it was possible that it had at least 24 basins 186 miles (300km) in diameter or larger, the analysis group suggested. For comparison, the group noted that 24 basins in the same size range have been charted on the Moon which has only one-half of Mercury's surface area.[8] Moreover, no basins between 310 and 800 miles (500 and 1,300km) in diameter showed up in the Mercury photos, but there are five in that range on the Moon, the team noted.

There was a suggestion in these comparisons that the projectile bombardment during the accretionary period of inner

The Structure of Mercury
1 Iron core
2 Silica-rich mantle with heavily-cratered surface.

Although Mercury appears to be remarkably Moon-like in both appearance and composition — its mantle is probably composed of light, silica-rich rocks — any resemblance is superficial. Mariner 10 confirmed that Mercury has a very high average density, which can only mean that the planet's interior is made up of much denser material, such as iron. In this way, Mercury is far more similar to the Earth. Under a relatively thin 400 mile (640km) mantle of light rocks, 80 per cent of the planet's mass resides in a huge iron core 2,237 miles (3,600km) in diameter. Although it is hidden, this vast mass of cooling iron has had visible effects on Mercury. The wrinkle-ridges which cross the planet's surface were probably created by the core's slow contraction. Mercury's weak magnetic field may also be generated in the spinning iron core.

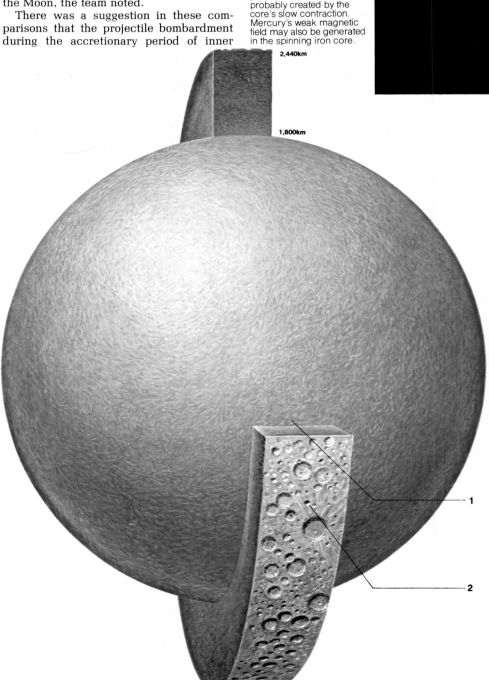

2,440km

1,800km

Above: *Mercury's heavily-cratered south pole, photographed by Mariner 10 from 53,200 miles (85,100km) on its second encounter in September 1974.*

planet evolution was more intense in the vicinity of the Earth-Moon system than at Mercury where Mariner did not see any other impact feature comparable to Caloris.

However, there were some similarities in crater distribution. The cratering on the Mercurian plains appeared to have the same distribution as that at the Apollo 14 landing site, Fra Mauro, on the Moon. But the density of cratering on the plains appeared lower than on the light coloured lunar highlands.

Volcanism

Although no direct evidence of volcanism, such as cones, domes or flow fronts, was seen, it was considered by members of the analysis team that the plains material had a volcanic origin. In this case, it followed that Mercury was probably differentiated into a crust, mantle and core like the other terrestrial planets and the Moon.

Some team members considered it unlikely that plains material filling the Caloris, north polar and southern mid-latitude basins could have been derived from impact melting because the fill appeared equal to the volume of material thrown out of the basin. The visible evidence supported volcanism.

However, an alternative possibility was suggested by Bruce C. Murray, head of the Mariner 10 television group. It was possible, he said, that the plains material consisted of ejecta from huge impacts

"conceivably located on the hemisphere of Mercury that was in shadow during the three Mariner 10 encounters."[9]

The possibility could explain the paucity of large basins seen on Mercury by Mariner 10, compared with the number on the Moon. The great lunar basins are concentrated on the near side of the Moon. Perhaps they were concentrated on one side of Mercury as well—the side Mariner 10 could not see.

If the origin of the plains material had been molten magma erupting from the interior, it could be assumed that iron rich silicates formed the upper crust, like those of the lunar regolith. The television group noted that similarities in structure and albedo (reflectivity) of the plains and cratered terrains to the lunar surface supported an assumption of silicate composition.

With that composition, the Mercurian crust would be expected to have a density of 3 to $3 \cdot 3 \text{g}/\text{cm}^3$. If so, the interior of Mercury must consist of a large iron core to give the planet its overall density of $5 \cdot 5 \text{g}/\text{cm}^3$.

The television group cited estimates of a crust 310 to 375 miles (500 to 600km) thick and an iron core, part of which may be liquid, occupying 75 to 80 per cent of the interior. The scarps running hundreds of miles in length were surmised to be the result of contraction of the crust by slow cooling of the iron core.[10]

During each of the three operating encounters, Mariner 10's infra-red spectrometer made temperature measurements. The noon temperature was calculated at 427° to 510°C at the equator. On the dark side, the temperature fell to −210°C. Day side temperature was in the range of the surface

temperatures on Venus; dark side temperatures in the range of those of lunar night.

At first encounter, the spacecraft's magnetometers found a magnetic field which was strong enough to deflect the solar wind around the planet, as Earth's field does. Surface magnetic field intensities ranged from 350 gammas at the equator to 700 gammas at the poles (compared with an average of 30,000 gammas on Earth). Although relatively weak, the magnetic field was surprising. Because of Mercury's slow rotation, none was expected. Planetary magnetic fields are supposed to be generated by the dynamo effect of a rapidly rotating body with an iron core. Mercury had the iron core, but lacked the rapid rotation.

A sequence of episodes in the evolution of Mercury has been proposed by Murray.[11] The earliest after formation is the fractionation and reassemblage of its elements into the large iron core and the silicate mantle and crust. This process was completed before cratering began as the planet swept up debris in the inner Solar System.

The next episode consisted of the obliteration of many early craters during a period of volcanism when magma erupted from the interior and spread out over the surface, covering the shallower craters and partially filling the deeper ones.

During the terminal bombardment, the Caloris impact occurred, the counterpart, it appears, of the Imbrium lunar impact.

The next episode was the formation of the plains from widespread volcanism. The final episode consisted of a "light peppering" of impacts after heavy bombardment ceased.

For the last 4 billion years, Mercury appears to have been quiescent. To the extent that its evolution can be equated with that of Moon, it is only partially understood.

Further investigation of Mercury is not planned in this decade. Although it is doubtful that a photomap of the unseen hemisphere will change the perception of Mercury significantly from that created by Mariner 10 observations, there is interest among planetary scientists in taking another look. Unfortunately, Mariner 10 did not carry enough fuel to change its solar orbit so that it could see the hidden hemisphere.

6 Baldwin, Ralph B., *The Measure of the Moon*, University of Chicago Press, Chicago, Ill., 1963.

7 Murray, Bruce C., "Television Observations of Mercury by Mariner 10", Conference on Cosmochemistry of the Moon and Planets, Moscow, 1974.

8 Ibid.

9 Ibid.

10 Ibid.

11 Murray, Bruce C., "Mercury" *Scientific American*, Vol. 233, No. 3, September 1975.

RECOMMENDED READING

Cross, C.A., "The Planet Mercury", *Spaceflight*, London, Nov 1978.

Dunne, J.A., *The Voyage of Mariner 10*, NASA, US Govt. Printing Office, Washington, D.C., 1977.

Guest, J., "Solar System, a Special Review", *New Scientist*, London, 1975.

Lewis, R.S., *From Vinland to Mars*, Quadrangle, New York, 1976.

Moore, P., *The Planet Venus*, Faber & Faber, London, 1959.

Murray, B.C., "Mercury-Mariner 10 Results", *Scientific American*, New York, Sept. 1975.

Murray, B.C. & Burgess, E., *Flight to Mercury*, Columbia University Press, New York, 1977.

Newland, I., *First to Venus, the Story of Mariner 2*, McGraw Hill Book Co., New York, 1963.

NASA-JPL authors, *Mariner R, Mission to Venus*, McGraw Hill Book Co., New York, 1963.

Various authors, "The Planet Mercury", *Journal of Geophysical Research, Special Issue*, Vol. 80, American Geophysical Union, Washington, D.C., June 1975.

Mars

For thousands of years, Mars, the red planet, has played a role in the mythology, literature and science of human cultures. In antiquity, it was Nergal, the Chaldean incarnation of vengeance; Ares, the Greek god of war, and Mars, the Roman war god. Its "martial" aspect was derived from its minatory red-brown colour, a celestial symbol of blood and destruction hanging over the world of men.

Apart from myth, Mars has a fictional history which for several centuries has been intertwined with the results of scientific observation. A junction of the scientific and fictional histories of Mars occurred in 1877 when the "seeing" of the planet was exceptionally clear.[1] Mars was at opposition then, on the same side of the Sun as Earth and nearly at its miniumum distance from Earth.

In Washington, D.C., the American astronomer, Asaph Hall (1829–1907), studied Mars night after night through the 26-inch refracting telescope of the United States Naval Observatory. The outcome of his effort was the discovery that Mars has two small moons. Hall said that he named them Phobos and Deimos (fear and flight) after the mythological horses that drew the chariot of Mars, the war god, across the heavens, although in Greek mythology they are the sons of the god of war, Ares.

Although new in science, Hall's discovery was not new in literature. In *Gulliver's Travels* (1726), Jonathan Swift related that the astronomers of Laputa had discovered two "lesser stars or satellites that revolve around Mars". As a man of letters, Swift (1667–1745) may have known that Johannes Kepler, the German mathematician, had predicted the existence of two moons circling Mars. Kepler (1571–1630) whose laws of planetary motion are the genesis of modern astrogration based this assumption on a progression: if Jupiter had four moons, as reported by Galileo in 1610, and the Earth, only one, then Mars orbiting between them must have two—especially since Venus had none. The notion of two Martian moons was picked up by other writers. Voltaire (1694–1778) referred to it in the novel *Micromégas* (1750).

Like the moons, the surface of Mars was "known" to literature before its details could be seen. Earth-based photographs of the Martian disc cannot resolve detail less than

Right: *The first really detailed map of Mars, prepared by Giovanni Schiaparelli in Milan during close oppositions between 1877 and 1888. The inconspicuous (and non-existent) canals are sketched in.*

MARS: BASIC DATA	
Equatorial Diameter*	0·53E; 4,213 miles (6,780km)
Mass*	0·107E
Density	2·25oz/in³ (3·9g/cm³)
Volume*	0·15E
Surface Gravity*	0·38E
Escape Velocity	3·17 miles/sec (5·1km/sec)
Period of Rotation	24hr 37min 23 sec
Inclination of Equator (to Orbit)	24°
Distance from Sun (Semi-major axis)	1·52AU; 141·2 x 10⁶miles (227·3 x10⁶km)
Siderial Period	686·98 days
Synodic Period	779·94 days
Orbital Speed	15·04 miles/sec (24·2km/sec)
Orbital Eccentricity	0·093
Inclination of Orbit (to ecliptic plane)	1·85°
Number of Satellites	2
*Earth=1	

200 miles (320km) across. The most powerful Earth telescopes could not identify mountain ranges on Mars as large as those on Earth or the Moon.

Schiaparelli's Canali

However, another rare conjunction of science and speculation occurred in 1877. The Italian astronomer, Giovanni Virginio Schiaparelli (1835–1910), also was studying Mars that year through the Brera Observatory telescope in Milan. He painstakingly recorded the areographic location of 62 large surface features, to which he gave such classical names as Elysium, Amazonis, Utopia. Moreover, Schiaparelli made drawings of a network of linear features which he called "canali" or channels. It is evident from Schiaparelli's reports that he regarded the lineaments as large, natural waterways transecting the planet. Even under the most favourable

"seeing" conditions, the "canali" would have to be vast indeed to be resolved by telescopes of the nineteenth century.

Although lineaments on Mars had been seen by others, including the papal astronomer, Fra Pietro Angelo Secchi (1818–1878) in 1858 and Johann Schroeter (1745–1816), a German astronomer, in 1785, it was Schiaparelli's detailed description of them as waterways that resulted in one of the most exciting and controversial scenarios in the history of astronomy: the Martian canals.

Over the next nine years, Schiaparelli developed a "canali" network with observations at five apparitions of Mars. The lineaments acquired the names of large terrestrial rivers, such as the Indus, Ganges, Hiddekel (Tigris) which seemed to establish their fluvial nature. The "canali" were not always visible. They appeared and disappeared as astronomers looked for them over decades. The only persistent features of Mars were the polar ice caps. Although they varied in extent, apparently with the seasons, they did not vanish as the "canali" seemed to do.

Nevertheless, the canal scenario evolved into a scientific romance as other astronomers adopted it, notably the Americans, William H. Pickering and Percival Lowell. Studying Mars with the Harvard Observatory telescope in Peru, Pickering (1858–1938) identified 200 dark areas where the canals seemed to intersect. He called them "oases". Lowell (1855–1916), a wealthy amateur astronomer, mapped the canals from the observatory he founded at Flagstaff, Arizona. He became convinced that they were the work of intelligent beings struggling to survive in a dehydrating environment.

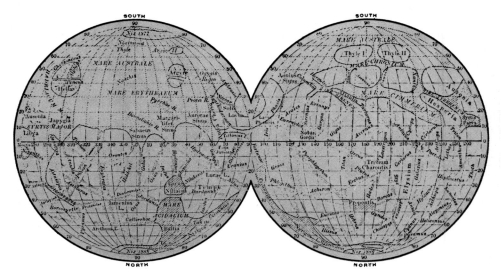

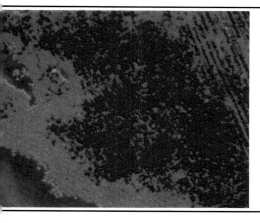

"Red on the south horizon, brighter than
For fifteen years, the little planet glows,
And brightest yet its kindled themes impose
On the imaginings of man."

"Red on the south horizon, brighter than
For fifteen years, the little planet glows,
And brightest yet its kindled themes impose
On the imaginings of man."

Robert Conquest, *For the 1956 Opposition of Mars*

Lowell's Hypothesis

Lowell published these views in books: *Mars and its Canals* (1906) and *Mars as the Abode of Life* (1908). The canal network had been constructed to irrigate deserts by drawing water from the ice caps as they partially melted in spring. This hypothesis seemed to be supported by waves of darkening which could be seen in the middle latitudes in the Martian spring—vegetation?

The dying planet concept had a strong influence in fiction. It set the scene for H.G. Wells' *War of the Worlds* (1898) and its radio adaptation in 1938 by Orson Welles and the Mercury Theater which simulated news reports of a Martian invasion of New Jersey, and created a minor panic in the United States. From Edgar Rice Burroughs to Ray Bradbury and Robert Heinlein, Mars has served as a strange and romantic locale of fantasy and science fiction.

For nearly a century, the fictional history of Mars popularized the idea that life might exist there. That possibility enhanced the exploration of Mars as a prime objective of both the United States and the Soviet Union early in the space age. In 1969, the United States Space Task Group Report to President Nixon called for a manned landing on Mars in the 1980s as an appropriate sequel to Project Apollo.

The Character of the Planet

Except for the Moon, Mars is the only planet on which some surface markings can be seen from Earth and except for Venus, Mars come closest to Earth. When opposition occurs at a point in the orbit of Mars where it is nearest the Sun (perihelion), the distance between Earth and Mars is 34·4 million

Below: *These four photographs of Mars taken with the 61in (1·5m) Catalina telescope in 1967 show the best resolution available before spaceprobes arrived.*

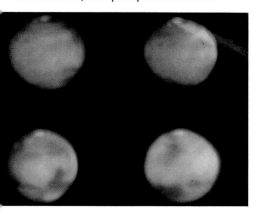

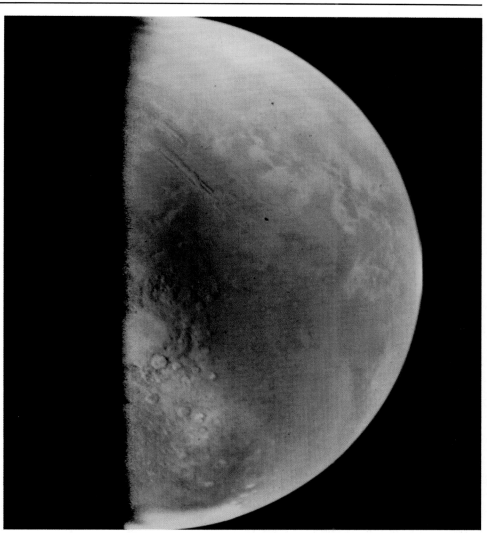

Above: *A Viking Orbiter photograph, taken in 1976, shows the dramatic improvement in image quality. The enormous Argyre impact basin dominates the picture (bottom).*

miles (55·39 million km). This closest approach comes every 15 to 17 years. Mars' average distance from the Sun is 141·2 million miles (227·3 million km) or 1·52 astronomical units (AU).[2]

The equatorial diameter of Mars, 4,213 miles (6,780km),[3] is about 53 per cent that of Earth's (7,927 miles, 12,756km); the mass of the red planet is only 10·7 per cent that of Earth; the density of Mars is $3·9g/cm^3$ compared with Earth's density of 5·52 and surface gravity on Mars is 38 per cent that of Earth. Still, the two planets have strong similarities and these, like the fictional history, also suggested that Mars is the most

likely abode of life beyond the Earth.

Like Earth, Mars is tilted on its axis of rotation. The inclination of the equator to the plane of the orbit is 24 degrees, only one-half degree greater than Earth's tilt. As a result, Mars has seasons—summer, autumn, winter, spring—as Earth has. Because Mars is half again as distant from the Sun as Earth is, the Martian (sidereal) year is longer: 686·9 (Earth) days long, and its seasons are correspondingly longer. Spring in the nor-

1 The "seeing" was enhanced by the unusual clarity of the Martian atmosphere which can, at times, obscure the surface when laden with dust.
2 An astronomical unit is the distance from the Earth to the Sun, averaging 92,953,000 miles (149,598,000km).
3 Like Earth, Mars is slightly flattened at the poles.

thern hemisphere of Mars and autumn in the southern last 199 days; summer in the northern and winter in the southern hemisphere last 182 days; autumn in the northern and spring in the southern last 146 days and winter in the northern and summer in the southern last 160 days. The seasons on Mars are uneven in length because of the eccentricity or oval shape of its orbit around the Sun. Its eccentricity is 0·093, compared with the Earth's 0·017.

The eccentricity of the Mars orbit accounts for the fact that its south polar ice cap is larger than the north polar cap. During the south polar winter, Mars is farther from the Sun than during summer and as it reaches maximum distance (aphelion), it is moving more slowly around the Sun. As a result, the autumn-winter half year in the southern hemisphere is 381 days, 75 days longer than the spring-summer half year of 306 days.

Like Earth, Mars has a nearly 24 hour day. The Martian period of rotation is 24 hours 37·4 minutes, or 41·4 minutes longer than the Earth day of 23 hours 56 minutes. The similarities of the length of the day and procession of the seasons contributed to the illusion of a habitable Mars.

The Early Probes

The Soviet Union was first to try spacecraft reconnaissance of Mars. It launched two probes on 10 and 14 October 1960. Both failed to reach Mars orbit. Two years later, the Soviets tried again. Mars 1, a 1,970lb (894kg) probe, was launched toward Mars on 1 November 1962. It was instrumented to measure plasma, radiation, magnetic fields and dust as it sped toward Mars. By 4 December, the probe had reached a point 6·8 million miles (11 million km) from Earth and the Soviet new agency, Tass, reported that Mars 1 was expected to fly-by Mars at a distance of 120,000 miles (193,000km) in June 1963. Whether it did so was not established, for on 21 March 1963 radio communication with the probe failed, ostensibly because of misalignment of the spacecraft's antenna which could not be corrected. During the Mars 1 flight, data radioed to Earth confirmed the existence of a third "outermost" radiation belt at 50,000 miles (80,000km) from Earth which had been predicted by Soviet scientists on the basis of earlier satellite data.

In the United States, the National Aeronautics & Space Administration developed a Mars probe akin to Mariner 2, an interplanetary reconnaissance vehicle which had made a successful fly-by of Venus in 1962 (see Venus chapter).

The NASA Mars probe, Mariner 3, was launched on 5 November 1964. A fibreglass shroud protecting the spacecraft during ascent through the atmosphere failed to be jettisoned when the launch vehicle exited the atmosphere. Electricity generating solar panels and radio antenna folded beneath the shroud could not be deployed, and so the craft went silently on its way to become lost in space.

Mariner 4

On the morning of 28 November 1964, the 575lb (261kg) probe called Mariner 4 was launched from Cape Canaveral aboard an Atlas-Agena rocket. This time, the shroud did come off when the vehicle entered a parking orbit around the Earth at 100 miles (160km) and the Atlas main booster fell away. As the probe passed over the Indian Ocean, the Agena engine was ignited a second time. It boosted velocity to 25,600mph (41,200km/h), well above Earth escape velocity.

Mariner 4 was launched into a solar orbit in the same direction as the Earth was travelling around the Sun. While on Earth, Mariner 4 was moving around the Sun at Earth's orbital velocity of 66,662mph (107,280km/h). Its launch added 25,600mph (41,200km/h) to this, giving the quarter ton spacecraft a total velocity of 92,262mph (148,480km/h) relative to the Sun.

Once the Agena engine had done its work and dropped away, Mariner 4 was moving faster than Earth around the Sun. Its extra velocity sent it into a higher orbit than Earth's—an orbital path that took it out to the orbit of Mars. Inevitably, the gravitational pull of the Earth and the Sun reduced the spacecraft's velocity, until by the first week of December it was 7,085mph (11,400km/h) relative to Earth and 73,680mph (118,572 km/h) relative to the Sun.

Like its twin, Mariner 3, Mariner 4 was an octagonal box with four panels containing photovoltaic (solar) cells which extended

Below: *Mariner 4, showing low-and high-gain antennas (top), four solar panels with stabilization vanes, and the TV camera (below main body). It passed Mars at a distance of 6,083 miles (9,789km) in 1965.*

from the top like blades of a fan. Each of the panels was 6ft (180cm) long and 3ft (90cm) wide. The four carried a total of 28,000 cells which supplied up to 195 watts of power to the craft.[4] Atop the aluminium alloy box was a dish-shaped, high-gain antenna and rod-shaped low-gain antenna, to which was attached a magnetometer for detecting a Mars magnetic field, if any. Overall, Mariner was 9·02ft (2·75m) high and 22ft (6·7m) across with solar panels extended.

The box carried a television camera with a small reflecting telescope. The camera was programmed to take 22 photographs through orange-red and blue-green filters in a period of 26 minutes as Mariner 4 made its closest encounter with Mars. The pictures were stored on tape for transmission to Earth after Mariner had passed the planet. The box also carried a plasma detector, cosmic ray telescope, dust detector and a trapped radiation counter. All data including the pictures were transmitted by an 8-watt radio.

A Sun sensor kept the solar panels facing the Sun by signalling the central computer to correct the spacecraft's attitude when the solar panels drifted away from the Sun. Attitude control was maintained by firing nitrogen gas jets. A second sensor kept the high-gain antenna pointed Earthward by sighting on the yellow star, Canopus. Thus flew Mariner 4 to Mars: its solar panels facing Sunward and its high-gain antenna looking Earthward.

The probe crossed the interplanetary sea of particles and fields between Earth and Mars in 228 days. A single mid-course change was all that was required to maintain the planned trajectory. It increased the velocity of the spacecraft by 30mph (45km/h) on 4 December 1964.

Left: *Mariner 4's single TV camera took 22 pictures of Mars' surface, although the last three—taken on the night side—were blank. The photographs were transmitted to Earth after the encounter, because the radio transmission rate of 8·33 bits per second was very slow when compared to the recording rate of 10,700 bits per second.*

Right: *The Mariner 4 frames revealed Mars to be a disappointingly barren, inert planet, covered in craters—more like the Moon than the Earth. Instead of volcanoes, vegetation and evidence of water, the camera showed ancient crater-scarred plains which had remained unchanged for millions of years.*

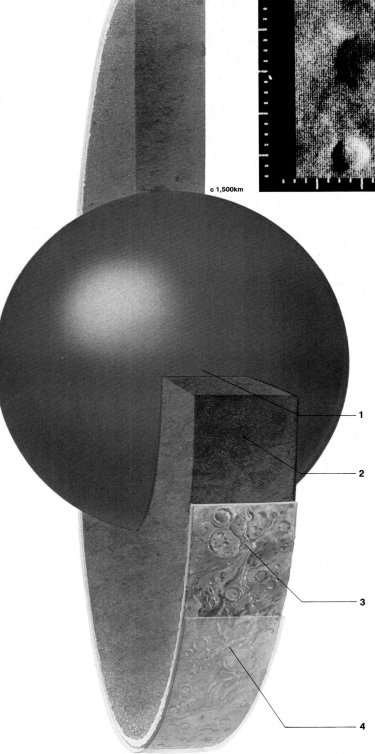

3,390km
c 3,350km

c 1,500km

The Structure of Mars
1 Rocky core.
2 Mantle.
3 Crust.
4 Atmosphere (mainly CO_2).

Little is known about the detailed structure of Mars, despite sophisticated mapping and sampling of its surface layers. From studies of its moment of inertia, its weak magnetic field (several thousand times weaker than the Earth's) and its density, it seems likely that Mars has a core largely made of rock—with perhaps a little iron mixed in— estimated to have a radius between 800 and 1,250 miles (1,300 to 2,000km). Surrounding this is a mantle with a thickness of c.1,150 miles (1,850km). Convective currents of molten rock, responsible in the past for the Martian volcanoes, may still flow within this region. Mars' crust is composed of low-density rock, and has an estimated range in thickness from 30 to 125 miles (50 to 200km), reaching its greatest depth under volcanic regions. It is likely that much of the Martian water is frozen into the soil as permafrost. As well as the non-uniformity in depth, the crust exhibits a non-uniform surface. It ranges from ancient, crater-scarred plains, through regions of deep canyons, to huge volcanic mountains. The thin Martian atmosphere exerts only one-hundredth the surface pressure of the Earth's. Over 96 per cent is carbon dioxide, and clouds of CO_2 ice are formed at high altitudes. Extensive dust storms occur near the surface.

Mars Encounter

On the evening of 14 July 1965, Mariner 4 flew across the Martian equator and passed over the southern hemisphere, where it was winter—as it was in the southern hemisphere of Earth. At that time, Mars was 134 million miles (216 million km) from Earth and Mariner's 8 watt radio signal took 12 minutes to reach NASA's Deep Space Network receiving stations in Australia, California and South Africa.

Mariner's camera began taking pictures as soon as the illuminated disc of Mars came into view of the camera's telescope. The first photograph was taken at an altitude of 10,500 miles (16,900km). It showed a 200 mile (320km) stretch of a bright region called Elysium. The photograph was of poor quality. Even after computer enhancement, it remained dim, its definition vague. Picture number 2 was slightly better. It showed a region 185 miles (297km) wide from east to west and 500 miles (800km) long from north to south between Elysium and Amazonis, another bright area thought to be desert.

Picture quality and definition improved as Mariner came closer to the surface and the camera lens was able to view it directly. Picture 3 showed a region 174 by 308 miles (280 by 496km) at the western edge of Amazonis. A ridge appeared. A winding valley could be discerned. It looked like a lunar rille, a crack in the surface.

At closest approach Mariner 4 raced by the planet at an altitude of 6,082·6 miles (9,788·8km). In picture 5, circular features appeared—craters. They became clearer in

---

4 At the end of each panel was a wedge-shaped vane. It was designed to use light pressure from the Sun to stabilize the probe, but its effectiveness was dubious.

pictures 6, 7 and 8 as the spacecraft passed over the southern hemisphere. In size the craters ranged from 1·74 to 109 miles (2·8 to 175km) across. The cratered landscape continued to unfold through pictures 9 through 14. The southern hemisphere of Mars was definitely lunar in appearance. Crater walls 12,800ft (3,900m) high appeared, some rimmed with white frost. At picture 20, Mariner 4 crossed the terminator and entered the night side so that the last three pictures, 20, 21 and 22 were blank.

Photographic reception took 10 days. Transmission was slow because the radio was limited. Each picture was composed of 40,000 bits. It took 8·5 hours for an entire frame to be received. The first pictures of the surface of Mars from a space probe were a shock to many in the scientific community who expected to see a more Earthlike and less lunar landscape. No mountains, wide valleys, river courses nor ocean basins appeared. There were no clouds, no volcanoes, no continental platforms. Mars seemed to be an inert planet. The magnetometer failed to detect a magnetic field. In terms of magnetic field theory, the lack of such a field suggested the absence of a metallic core that would generate it in a planet rotating as rapidly as Earth.

As Mariner 4 passed behind Mars, relative to Earth, its radio continued beaming telemetry signals through the red planet's atmosphere until the body of the planet blocked the signals altogether. As the spacecraft cleared the planet, the signals once more penetrated the atmosphere. This occultation procedure was one of the most important experiments of the flight. As the radio signals passed through the atmosphere, they were distorted, and the degree of distortion indicated the density of the atmosphere. The first spacecraft measurement of

Below: *Mariner 7 lifts off for Mars from Launch Pad-36A at Cape Canaveral on 27 March 1969 atop an Atlas-Centaur launch vehicle. A month earlier, Mariner 6 had also been launched.*

the Martian atmosphere showed that instead of the expected range of 10 to 80 millibars, atmospheric pressure ranged only from 10 to 20 millibars or from 1 to 2 per cent of Earth's sea level atmospheric pressure.

For those hoping to find some hint of conditions that might support life on Mars, the results of the occultation experiment were disappointing. The pressure was too low to allow liquid water to exist on the surface. Without water, life could not exist; at least life as known on Earth. In 26 minutes of photography and 45 minutes of occultation, Mariner 4 destroyed a scenario that had been sustaining illusions about Mars for nearly a century. The Mars it depicted seemed to be as barren and lifeless as the Moon.

On 29 July 1965, the Mariner photos were projected on a screen at the White House in Washington, D.C. for President Lyndon B. Johnson and members of congressional space committees. The President's reaction expressed the general view. He said that, speaking as a member of the generation

"that Orson Welles scared out of its wits, . . . it may be, it just may be, that life as we know it, with its humanity, is more unique than many have thought and we must remember this."

The 1969 Mariners
Advancing rocket technology made it possible for NASA to launch a pair of improved fly-by probes to Mars during its 1969 opposition. They were designated Mariners 6 and 7.

The upper stage Agena rocket was replaced by the more powerful Centaur atop the Atlas. Centaur's twin RL-10 engines were the first to burn hydrogen and oxygen as propellant. The product of combustion was, of course, steam and these new steam engines yielded the highest specific impulse (ratio of thrust to weight) of any chemical propulsion system.

Weighing 910lb (413kg) at launch, Mariner 6 and Mariner 7 were similar in design to Mariner 4, but carried two television cameras instead of one, a larger high-gain antenna and more electric power than their predecessor. With solar panels deployed, the 1969 Mariners measured 19·03ft (5·8m) across and were 10·83ft (3·3m) high from the base of the octagonal bus to the top of the low-gain antenna mast. The sunlight pressure vanes were eliminated at the tips of the solar panels so that attitude control was dependent on the nitrogen thrusters. The new Mariners relied on the sun and Canopus sensors for orientation in the flight. The mid-course correction motor was carried in the bus along with the electronics. The wide and narrow angle television cameras were mounted on a scan platform with a larger turning arc than that of Mariner 4. The spacecraft designers and the Jet Propulsion Laboratory hoped to achieve better pictures and faster transmission.

In addition to the cameras, each of the new Mariners carried an infra-red spectrometer, infra-red radiometer and an ultraviolet spectrometer. These instruments would survey the planet's physical characteristics. The radio would be used once more to measure the density of the atmosphere as

Above: *Heavily-cratered region photographed by Mariner 7's narrow-angle TV camera. Despite its proximity to the asteroid belt, the source of meteoroids, Mars is far less heavily-cratered than the Moon.*

each spacecraft was occulted by the planet. The infra-red radiometer measured infra-red emissions from the ground or from clouds in two wavelength ranges. Temperature could be calculated from the energy emitted in each. Infra-red thermal emissions from the polar ice caps might indicate whether they were water ice or frozen carbon dioxide, or both. From the ultraviolet spectrometer, scientists monitoring the vehicles at JPL expected to get some indication of the chemical composition of the atmosphere and of the surface rocks.

Mariner 6 was launched on 24 February 1969 aboard Atlas-Centaur. Thrust into the 100 mile (160km) high parking orbit, it was boosted to escape velocity by a second burn of the powerful Centaur engines. Mariner 7 was then launched on 27 March. It was NASA's first successful double planetary launch.

The flights of both vehicles were uneventful. Mariner 6 encountered the red planet on 31 July 1969 and passed within 2,106 miles (3,390km) of the equator. Mariner 7 arrived on 5 August 1969, flying 2,177 miles (3,504km) over the south pole. The two probes sent back a total of 201 photographs, Mariner 6, 75 and Mariner 7, 126. Improved picture quality and photography covering a larger area of the planet modified the initial impression of Mars as a lunar desert.

Polar Regions

Passing over the south polar region where it was winter, Mariner 7 showed that the northern edge of the ice was fairly sharp and regular. In winter, the south polar ice cap of Mars covers about the same proportion of the red planet's surface as the Antarctic ice sheet covers on Earth. The Martian north polar cap in winter is smaller and analogous to the spread of winter sea ice in Earth's Arctic Ocean.

Beyond the south polar cap appeared large, circular craters, one estimated at 80 miles (130km) across. A hood of clouds or haze hung over the polar region. It was interpreted as vapour moving halfway around Mars from the north polar ice sheet which was evaporating in the northern summer.

It now appeared that ice was transferred as vapour from the summer pole to the winter pole through the Martian atmosphere, a phenomenon unknown on Earth. Whether the south polar ice was water or dry ice still was not clear from spectrometer data. Nor could the thickness be determined, although the ice sheet seemed to be considerably thicker than the thin rime of frost that some observers had supposed.

The infra-red and ultraviolet spectrometers diagnosed the atmosphere as consisting mainly of carbon dioxide, not nitrogen as formerly believed. Small amounts of nitrogen, oxygen and water vapour were detected. New and discouraging data came from radio signals passing through the atmosphere as both spacecraft rounded the planet. Density was reported at 7 to 8 millibars, or less than 1 per cent of Earth's sea level atmospheric pressure. The prospects for liquid water on the surface vanished. With them faded the prospects for life, inasmuch as biologists insisted that life could not exist or even evolve without free water.

With improved definition and resolution, the 1969 Mariner photos revealed differences between Martian and lunar craters. Mars was considerably less cratered than the Moon, despite the proximity of Mars to the asteroid belt, the source of cratering projectiles. The floors of the Martian craters appeared to be flatter, the rims less sharp than those of lunar craters. Some erosion process evidently was working on Mars. It had erased craters in the smooth mid-latitude region called Hellas.

Near the equator, Mariner 6 photos showed a badlands region of jumbled, chaotic ground extending across equatorial Mars for hundreds of miles. The source of this jumbled landscape was puzzling. Equatorial temperatures ranged from $3.6°$ to $9.84°C$ during the day and from $-52.5°$ to $-101.75°C$ at night.

Silicates were identified in the surface rocks by the ultraviolet spectrometer. Apparently the Martian crust had undergone chemical differentiation as had the crusts of the Earth and the Moon. It confirmed a theory that the process of evolution is consistent for terrestrial planets, at least in the Solar System.

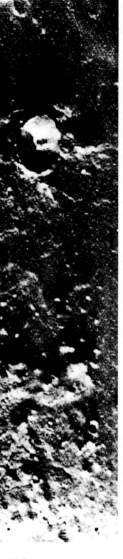

Below: *Mariners 6 and 7 were almost identical in design to Mariner 4, but carried two TV cameras for high- and low-resolution pictures. They were designed to search for possible landing-sites.*

Above: *Mariner 7 colour image of Mars, reconstructed from three colour-filter photographs. Dark central feature is the Meridiani Sinus, and hazes are visible at the terminator and near the north pole.*

Beyond the enigmatic badlands appeared another curious feature of Mars. Mariner 6 photographed the rim of a huge crater, some 500 miles (800km) across. The rim was whitened, as though coated with frost. It was located at the areographic coordinates of a feature called "Nix Olympica" (the snows of Olympus) which was depicted as a white dot on the International Astronomical Union map of Mars, made from years of telescopic observations. What was Nix Olympica? Was it indeed a mountain as some astronomers who charted it had supposed? The Mariner 6 photo of the great crater suggested that here was an enormous caldera[5] of a volcano, greater than any known on Earth. Mars now began to look more Earthlike than lunar.

The 1971 Launches

At the 1971 Mars opposition, NASA launched two spacecraft and the Soviet Union, three at the red planet, First up was Mariner 8. The Centaur engines failed to ignite after it was launched by the Atlas on 8 May 1971 and the vehicle fell into the Atlantic Ocean.

On 10, May, a Soviet vehicle, identified only as Cosmos 419, was fired into Earth parking orbit, but it failed to leave it and plunged back to Earth.

Mars 2, a Soviet probe weighing 10,250lb (4,650kg) at launch, went up on 19 May. It reached the vicinity of Mars on 27 November, entered an elliptical orbit around the planet and released a metric ton lander to the surface. The lander presumably crashed for nothing further was heard from it.

Right: *Soviet technicians prepare Mars 3 for launch in May 1971. The lander transmitted TV pictures for 20 seconds after touchdown, and then abruptly stopped.*

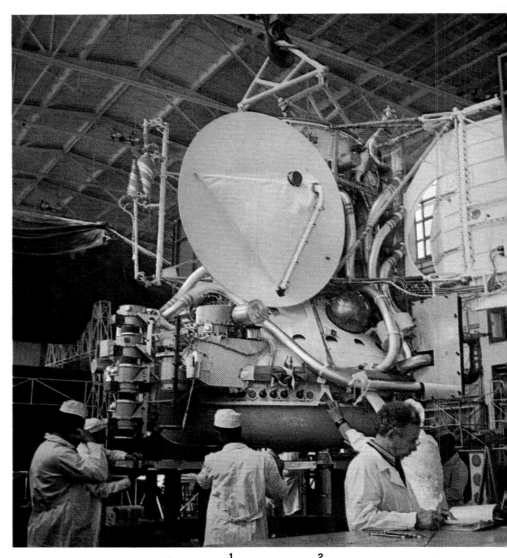

Mars 3
1 Aerodynamic braking cone.
2 Automatic research station.
3 Radar altimeter aerial.
4 Main parachute (stowed in container).
5 Instruments for automatic control system.
6 Descent capsule separation engine.
7 Radiators for thermal control.
8 Solar panel.
9 Propellant tanks.
10 Sensors for automatic navigation system.
11 Instrument compartment.
12 Course correction and braking engine.
13 Optical sensors for astro-orientation system.
14 Low-gain antenna.
15 High-gain parabolic antenna.
16 Antenna for French-supplied "Stereo" experiment.

Mars 3, the second of two identical probes launched by the Soviet Union in May 1971, was a two-component spacecraft consisting of an orbiter and a lander. The latter, launched before Martian orbit was achieved, was soft-landed using a complex system of aerodynamic braking, parachute deployment and retro-rockets. It contained a TV system, instruments for measuring wind speed,

temperature and pressure, a mass spectrometer to examine the composition of the atmosphere, and soil analysis instruments. The orbiter contained an IR radiometer for measuring temperature changes on the planet's surface, an IR photometer for mapping surface relief, a visible light photometer for studying atmospheric dust particles, an ultraviolet photometer for upper atmosphere study, and TV camera systems. In addition, a French-designed "Stereo" experiment for studying solar radio emissions was carried.

Technical Data
Height: About 13·5ft (4·1m) with lander.
Diameter: About 6.56ft (2m) across base.
Array span: About 19·4ft (5·9m).
Launch weight: 10,250lb (4,650kg).

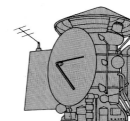

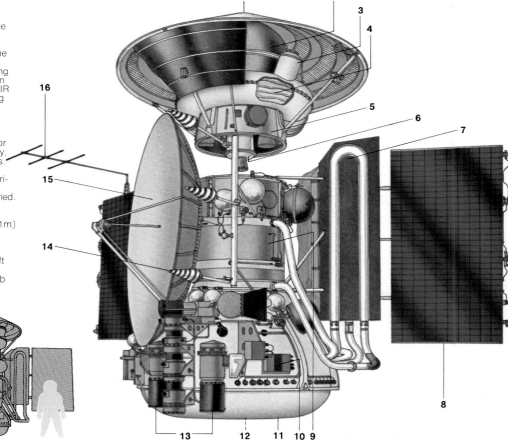

186

The Mars 2 orbiter carried two television cameras, an infra-red radiometer, a water vapour detector, an infra-red photometer which was designed to measure surface elevations by changes in atmospheric density with surface altitude and an ultraviolet photometer to determine the composition of the upper atmosphere.

Mars 3, a twin of Mars 2, was launched on 28 May 1971. The second Soviet probe went into orbit around Mars on 2 December 1971 and released its lander. Using parachutes and braking rockets, the Mars 3 lander reached the surface at 45 degrees south latitude and 158 degrees west longitude near a supposed basin called Sirenum Fossae. Twenty seconds after the lander began television transmission, all signals from it ceased. Russian sources suggested an antenna failure, possibly caused by a violent dust storm which was raging all over Mars in December 1971. The storm interfered with surface photography by both Soviet orbiters, but in January, as the storm abated and the dust cleared somewhat, photos reached Moscow showing a dark, lunar maria-like surface and some bright clouds. Moscow Radio reported on 26 January 1972 that conditions ascertained on Mars by the Mars 2 and Mars 3 orbiters were compatible with the existence of life in the form of micro-organisms and primitive plants.

In March 1972, Tass reported that the orbiters were continuing to explore the surface by taking pictures and measuring temperature, pressure, density and atmosphere composition. Shortly thereafter, Tass stated that the work of Mars 2 and 3 was nearing completion.

Mariner 9

Meanwhile, Mariner 9, NASA's second attempt to put a camera spacecraft in orbit around Mars, was launched successfully on 30 May 1971. Only one mid-course correction was required to put the vehicle into position for orbital insertion by its 300lb (136kg) thrust braking-engine on 13 November 1971. A 15-minute firing established Mariner 9 in an oval orbit of 862 × 10,634 miles (1,387 × 17,113km) inclined at 65° to the equator. The periapsis or low point was raised to 1,027 miles (1,653km) to improve radio communication with Earth as the Earth-Mars geometry changed in 1972.

Less massive than the Soviet orbiters, Mariner 9, weighing 2,270lb (1,030kg) at launch, had nearly twice the mass of the earlier Martian Mariners. In addition to its orbital manoeuvring engine and load of fuel, it had larger cameras, a larger high-gain antenna and a full set of diagnostic instruments to analyze the chemistry of the surface and the atmosphere.

Its shape was similar to that of the earlier Mariners, featuring the same octagonal bus. It had the same attitude control and Sun-Canopus sensor systems. Essentially, its mission was to make a photographic map of Mars, in the manner of the Lunar Orbiters, but the surface features disclosed by its orbital photography were so spectacular that the photomapping achievement seemed secondary.

In three months, Mariner 9 answered scientific questions that had been debated for years: the cause of the wave of darkening

Above: *View of the underside of Mariner 9, showing the scan platform with its wide- and narrow-angle TV cameras, and the UV and IR spectrometers.*

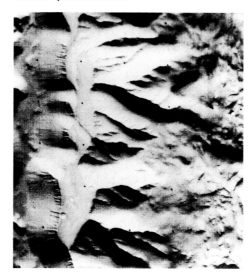

Above: *Mariner 9 image of the central section of Mars' vast canyon system, the Valles Marineris. The photograph covers an area of 36x27 miles (58x43km).*

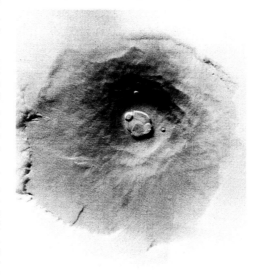

Above: *Mariner 9 mosaic of Mars' biggest volcano, Olympus Mons. The 16·4 mile-high (26·4km) mountain measures approximately 300 miles (500km) across.*

in spring, the origin of the badlands, the nature of Nix Olympica, the existence of canals.

The planetwide dust storm which had blinded the Soviet orbiters also shrouded the surface from Mariner as it led the two Russian vehicles in an international dance around Mars in the last quarter of 1971. With an orbital period 11·9 hours, Mariner 9 made two revolutions of Mars a day. On its 95th orbit late in December, vague land forms began to appear in its photographs. Dark spots showed up in the blurred atmosphere like islands. As the dust settled in January, the spots resolved into a massive chain of mountains stretching across the equator.

Olympus Mons

In the northern hemisphere, about 18 degrees above the equator and 135 degrees west longitude, the crater called Nix Olympica emerged as the caldera[5] of a gigantic volcano, surrounded by smaller vents. It was a shield volcano, built up by successive lava flows forming terraces of shield-shaped structures. The volcano was calculated as 373 miles (600km) across and 18 miles (29km) above the base. It rose like a monument between another volcanic pile, the Tharsis Ridge, and the plains of Amazonis. Once its structure was visible, Nix Olympica became identified as Olympus Mons—Mount Olympus on Mars. The terrestrial Mount Olympus in Thessaly, mythological home of the gods of ancient Greece, could have fitted comfortably in the crater of its Martian namesake.

Six hundred and eighty-five miles (1,100km) to the southeast appeared a row of three more giant, shield volcanoes forming the Tharsis Ridge. They were named Arsia Mons, Avonis Mons and Ascraeus Mons from south to north. Three smaller volcanoes flanked the ridge to the north and east. Another group of volcanoes appeared in photographs of the region called Elysium. The largest, Elysium Mons, stretched 155 miles (250km) across and was 9·3 miles (15km) high. Northward reared another mighty mountain, Alba Patera, with an apparent diameter nearly as large as that of Olympus. Lava flows radiating 500 miles (800km) from the crater could clearly be seen in the Mariner 9 photographs.

It was evident now that volcanism had been a persistent activity on Mars for hundreds of millions of years. There was more: east and south of the Tharsis Ridge stretched a plateau which appeared to be scored by crustal faults. The faults merged south of the equator to form a series of steep walled canyons extending more than 2,500 miles (4,000km) east and west and covering a region 435 miles (700km) wide. In some places, canyon depths were estimated at four miles (6·5km).

These Martian canyonlands were designated collectively as Valles Marineris (Mariner Valley). They revealed a long history of tectonic (crustal deformation) activity in addition to the evidence of ages of volcanism.

North of this great rift system, the Mariner 9 cameras picked up another feature—a

---

5 A caldera is a large, bowl-shaped volcanic depression, usually caused by the collapse of the top of a volcanic cone.

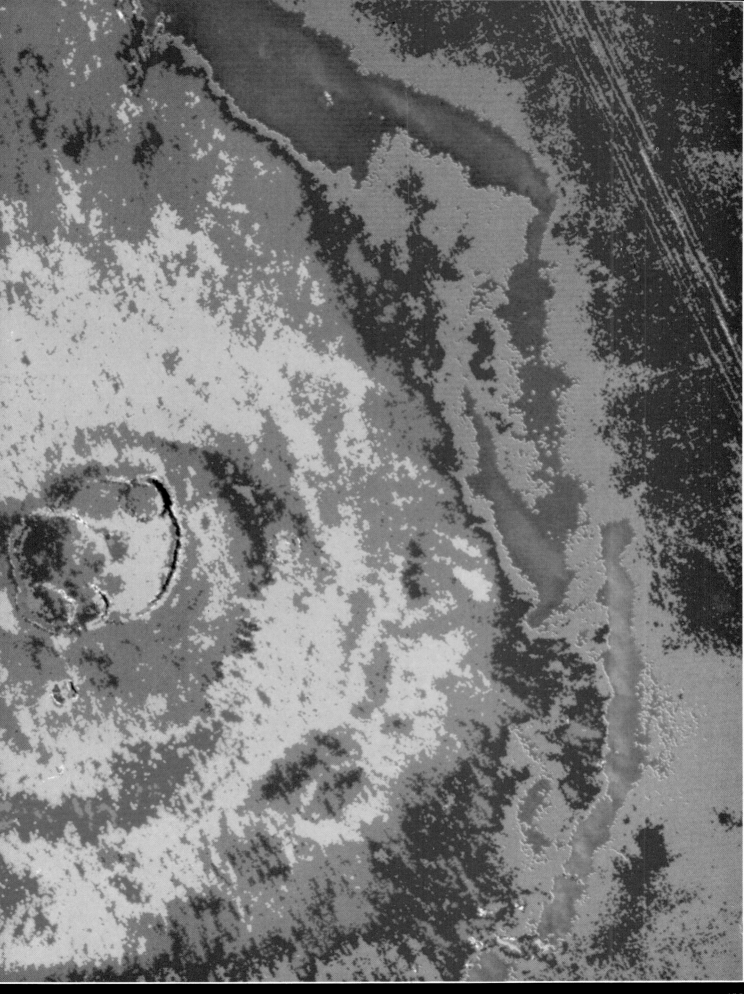

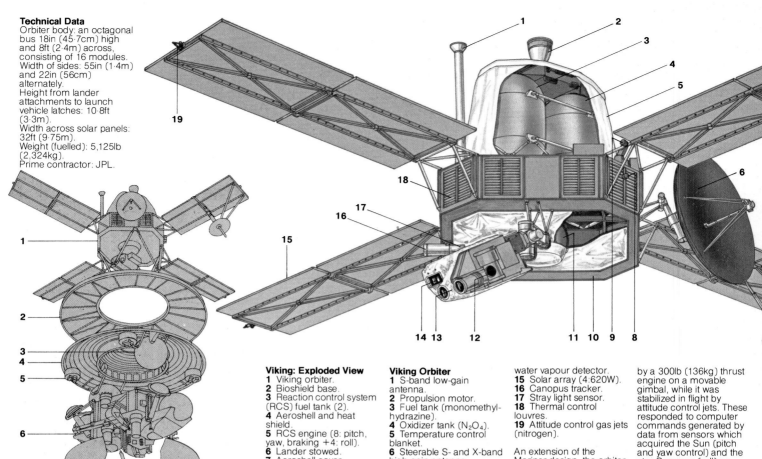

Technical Data
Orbiter body: an octagonal
bus 18in (45·7cm) high
and 8ft (2·4m) across,
consisting of 16 modules.
Width of sides: 55in (1·4m)
and 22in (56cm)
alternately.
Height from lander
attachments to launch
vehicle latches: 10·8ft
(3·3m).
Width across solar panels:
32ft (9·75m).
Weight (fuelled): 5,125lb
(2,324kg).
Prime contractor: JPL.

Viking: Exploded View
1 Viking orbiter.
2 Bioshield base.
3 Reaction control system
(RCS) fuel tank (2).
4 Aeroshell and heat
shield.
5 RCS engine (8: pitch,
yaw, braking +4: roll).
6 Lander stowed.
7 Aeroshell cover.
8 Bioshield cap.

A two-stage vehicle, Viking
consisted of the orbiter, the
navigable carrier, and the
lander, encapsulated at
launch in a bioshield, and
in an instrumented
aeroshell which protected
and aligned it during the
preliminary descent.

Viking Orbiter
1 S-band low-gain
antenna.
2 Propulsion motor.
3 Fuel tank (monomethyl-
hydrazine).
4 Oxidizer tank (N_2O_4).
5 Temperature control
blanket.
6 Steerable S- and X-band
high-gain antenna.
7 Relay antenna.
8 Cruise Sun sensor.
9 Sun gate sensor.
10 Orbiter bus.
11 Pressurant tank
(helium).
12 Infra-red thermal
mapper.
13 Visual imaging
cameras.
14 Mars atmospheric

water vapour detector.
15 Solar array (4:620W).
16 Canopus tracker.
17 Stray light sensor.
18 Thermal control
louvres.
19 Attitude control gas jets
(nitrogen).

An extension of the
Mariner design, the orbiter
was constructed to fulfil
five basic functions: to
guide the spacecraft to
Mars orbit; to survey the
landing sites; to support
the lander during descent;
to carry out scientific
studies of Mars; and to act
as a communications relay
station for the lander. Main
propulsion was provided

by a 300lb (136kg) thrust
engine on a movable
gimbal, while it was
stabilized in flight by
attitude control jets. These
responded to computer
commands generated by
data from sensors which
acquired the Sun (pitch
and yaw control) and the
star Canopus (roll) as
navigation references.
Communication was by
two-way S-band radio links
which relayed data, and
received Earth commands.
An X-band link was used
for radio science
experiments. The main
science instruments (see
right) were mounted on a
movable scan platform.

network of subsidiary valleys, with dendritic
branches. They looked remarkably like dried
river beds and stream beds, with tributary
streams flowing into them. After months of
analysis, the Mariner imaging team concluded that the strange, sinuous valleys had
a fluvial origin. There were obvious markings
of headwaters, tributaries and channel
mouths. There were braided sediments,
islands, sand bars in the channels. Some of
the channels were crisp, as though recent;
others were eroded, as though ancient. The
contrast suggested more than one era when
water flowed on Mars.

With the data from Mariner 9, the
fictional and natural histories of Mars
merged. Schiaparelli's "canali" did indeed
exist on Mars, but they were not those he
believed he saw. The productive life of
Mariner 9 ended on 27 October 1972 when
its supply of nitrogen stabilization gas ran
out. It had operated 516 days since launch
and 349 days in orbit around Mars. The
spacecraft had sent more than 7,300 television photos to Earth, not only covering
the entire surface of Mars but also close-up
scenes of the moons, Phobos and Deimos.

Right: *KSC engineers mate the first Viking
Orbiter craft to its lander, encapsulated in
its aeroshell. Two Viking probes were
launched towards Mars in August and
September 1975.*

Mars Atmospheric Water Vapour Detector
1 Head electronics.
2 Neon reference source.
3 Detector slit assembly.
4 Radiator.
5 Diffraction grating.
6 Collimator mirror.
7 Wavelength servo motor.
8 Telescope mirror.
9 Order isolation filter.
10 Raster assembly.
11 Calibration assembly.

This infra-red spectrometer detected the distribution of water vapour over Mars in an absorption band at 1·38 micrometres wavelength, and provided pressure data when water was found to be present. Infrared radiation from the surface was reflected by a mirror onto a fine grating which spread the spectrum onto five lead sulphide detectors. The intensity of the IR radiation detected was related to the amount of water vapour through which it had passed. The MAWD measured water vapour over a 1·9 x 15 mile (3 x 24km) area every 4·5 seconds, to an accuracy of 1 precipitable micron. (This is a measure of the depth of water that would form at the surface if all the vapour in the measured atmospheric column were precipitated.) During the Martian summer a maximum abundance of c 100 precipitable microns occurred over dark material in the north polar region. The summer residual polar cap was found to consist of dirty water ice. Water vapour was rising here and moving towards the equator. Total Mars vapour content remained constant at the precipitable equivalent ·f 1·3km³ of ice.

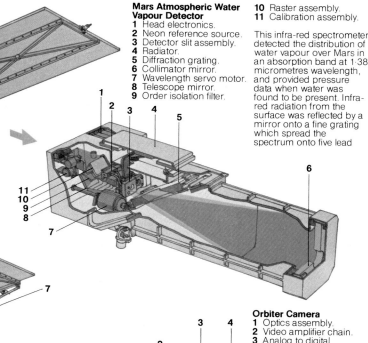

Orbiter Camera
1 Optics assembly.
2 Video amplifier chain.
3 Analog to digital converter.
4 Vidicon power supply.
5 Focus and deflection coils.
6 Digital sequencing logic.
7 Image sensor.
8 Shutter assembly.
9 Filter wheel.

The orbiter's imaging system consisted of two identical telescopic TV-type cameras which could resolve features of 328ft (100m) on Mars from an altitude of 932 miles (1,500km). Each used a TV-style vidicon tube for picture acquisition. A six-colour filter wheel, controlled by the flight data subsystem, allowed images to be built up in colour. The cameras' focal length was 475mm, and a picture could be taken every 4·48sec. The image formed on the 1·5in vidicon tube and was then scanned by an electron beam which converted it into electrical signals. These were read out on a 7-track tape recorder, and data radioed to Earth one track at a time. An image was composed of 1,056 lines, each made up of 1,182 pixels. Each pixel was transmitted as a 7-bit word, so a complete image consisted of over 8·7 million bits. The cameras, which had independent power and control systems, operated alternately, one taking a picture while the other erased its last image from the vidicon tube.

Infra-red Thermal Mapper
1 Planet port.
2 Scan mirror.
3 Telescope (one of four).
4 Electronics.
5 Detectors.
6 Space port.
7 Power supply and motor drive.
8 Reference.
9 Inlet.

This mapper was designed to read Mars' surface and atmospheric temperatures from orbit. It was also required to determine the temperature of any frost or clouds, and to investigate the nature of any moisture or condensation detected. Its four channels, each served by a telescope focussed on 7 antimony-bismuth detectors, measured IR radiation from 0·2 to 24 micrometres in five different spectral bands. The forward motion of the orbiter would bring a ground point successively into view of the four staggered detector arrays, one at a time. Three channels could determine surface temperature to an accuracy of 1°C, the fourth to 0·36°C. Each detector viewed Mars through a 0·3° field of view equivalent to a 5 mile (8km) circle on the surface. The instrument's optics included a 45° mirror, which could be moved to three positions to view the planet, deep space or a reference surface at a known temperature, three 2·3in (5·75cm) and one 1·5in (3·75cm) diameter reflector telescopes.

Soviet Efforts

The first half of the 1970s witnessed the most intensive international effort in planetary investigation since the exploration of the Moon. In 1973, the Soviets launched four more vehicles to Mars, two orbiters and two landers. Because of weight and distance, each vehicle was launched separately.

The two orbiters, Mars 4 and 5, weighed 10,250lb (4,650kg) each at launch. Mars 4, launched on 21 July 1973, arrived in the vicinity of Mars on 10 February 1974, but continued on into solar orbit when its retrorocket engine failed 1,300 miles (2,100km) from the surface. Mars 5, launched on 25 July 1973, was injected into an orbit of 1,094 × 22,059 miles (1,760 × 35,300km) around Mars on 12 February 1974. It transmitted photographs of the surface to Earth, confirming the volcanic structures seen by Mariner 9.

Mars 6 and 7 contained landing capsules with a launch weight of 1,400lb (635kg) each; total payload weight was 10,250lb (4,650kg). Mars 6 was launched on 5 August 1973 and reached the surface of Mars in the southern hemisphere on 12 March 1974.

Left: *Viking 2 Orbiter image of the dawn side of Mars in August 1976. At top, swathed in clouds of ice crystals, is the huge volcano Ascreaus Mons. Below are the canyons of the Valles Marineris.*

However, its radio transmission ceased 148 seconds after its parachutes opened. Before transmission cut off, Mars 6 radioed the first direct readings of the chemical composition of the atmosphere. They showed that carbon dioxide was the major constituent and indicated an unexpectedly high concentration of argon. Mars 7 was launched on 9 August 1973 and encountered Mars on 9 March 1974 but continued on into solar orbit, missing Mars by 808 miles (1,300km).

The Russian argon data excited Mars scientists in the United States who were preparing the Viking mission to seek evidence of life in the Martian soil. A high concentration of the inert gas was interpreted by specialists in planetary atmospheres as indicating a denser atmosphere on Mars in the past. This interpretation supported the assumption that the channels shown by Mariner 9 were fluvial.

On the basis of the data returned by the 1973 Mars probes, R.M. Sagdayev, Director of the Institute of Space Research, Moscow said that Mars was more Earth-like than previously supposed. It was geologically active, at least in the past, and possibly had surface water at some time in its history, he said.[6]

6 *Soviet Space Programs, 1971–75 Staff Report,* U.S. Senate Committee on Aeronautical and Space Sciences, Vo. 1.

Viking

The Viking Project, a reduced version of a Mars exploration programme called Voyager in the 1960s, was prepared for launch in 1975.[7] Although developed under tight economic constraints, Viking was still the most expensive reconnaissance effort by NASA since Apollo.

The project comprised two Viking spacecraft, each consisting of an orbiter and a lander. Each had a combined launch weight of 7,758lb (3,519kg). The orbiter, based on Mariner technology, weighed 5,125lb (2,325 kg) and the lander, 2,633lb (1,194kg). The lander was developed from lunar Surveyor technology.

The capability of American space engineering for miniaturization, required in the early years of missile development to achieve lighter payloads, found its highest expression in the Viking lander. The lander bus, weighing only 1,270lb (567kg) without shielding, engines and fuel, carried two automated chemical laboratories, a complete weather station, a seismology station, the equivalent of a photographic studio, two computers, an automated backhoe and shovel which dug a trench, scooped up a handful of soil and deposited it in apertures atop the vehicle and a conveyor which distributed soil samples to the laboratory system. The organic chemical laboratories and incubators and the inorganic chemical laboratories were the miniaturized equivalent of facilities that might be expected to occupy a research centre.

Viking 1 was launched on 20 August 1975 aboard a Titan III E-Centaur, the most powerful booster system in the American inventory next to Saturn. Navigation was controlled at the Jet Propulsion Laboratory and the spacecraft's orientation in flight was directed by Sun and Canopus sensors.

The orbiter was an uprated version of Mariner 9 with approximately the same dimensions and similar instrumentation. Dual television cameras were built to a higher resolution and were designed to resolve 328ft (100m) surface details from an altitude of 930 miles (1,500km). Mounted with them on the scan platform were the radiometers and spectrometers that would read cloud and surface temperatures and measure atmospheric water vapour.

In launch position, the lander was tucked against the base of the orbiter. Its three landing legs and two extendable 8·2ft (2·5m) booms were retracted on the hexagonal titanium bus. The lander measured 9·84ft (3m) across and stood 6·56ft (2m) tall on its 4·26ft (1·3m) legs and 12in (30·5cm) footpads.

Thoroughly sterilized to prevent contamination of Mars with Earth microbes, the lander was encased in an egg-shaped bioshield of woven fibreglass on an aluminium frame during ascent through Earth's atmosphere. When each Viking spacecraft exited Earth's atmosphere, the bioshield cap was thrown off by explosives. The bioshield base remained on the vehicle to Mars and was dropped after the lander was separated from the orbiter. During interplanetary flight

Right: *Lift-off of Viking 2 from Cape Canaveral on 9 September 1975. The launch vehicle is a Titan III E-Centaur, then the most powerful US booster after Saturn V.*

Right: *Viking 2 panorama of the Martian surface. The horizon is about 1·8 miles (3km) away. The "rusty-red" colour of most of the rocks is caused by a thin layer of hydrated iron oxide, or limonite.*

and entry into the Martian atmosphere, the lander was enclosed in an aeroshell which was dropped when the lander descended to 21,000ft (6,400m).

Viking 1 was inserted into orbit around Mars on 19 June 1976 by a firing of its 300lb (136kg) thrust hydrazine engine. The orbit was elliptical, with a periapsis (low point) of 940 miles (1,513km) over the prospective landing site. However, the landing site which had been selected from Mariner 9 photos and radar scans from Earth turned out to be too rough for a safe landing when viewed by the orbiter. Additional photo surveys by the orbiter and radar scans from the big antenna at Goldstone, California and the radio telescope at Arecibo, Puerto Rico located a smoother site to the northwest.

The Viking 1 lander separated from the orbiter and began its descent by firing its braking engine on 20 July 1976. It was encased in an aluminium alloy aeroshell that was designed to shield it from temperatures up to 1,500°C during entry through the Martian atmosphere.

In the shell, the lander essentially functioned as an independent spacecraft. The

---

7 The designation, "Voyager", was shifted to a later project for the reconnaissance of Jupiter, Saturn and Uranus.

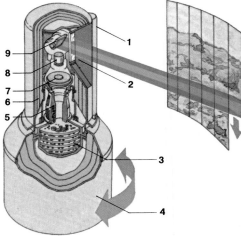

Surface Sampler Collector Head
1 0·08in (2mm) primary sieve.
2 In-flight retaining tab.
3 Solenoid actuator/vibrator.
4 Surface contact switch/rotation position switch (internal).
5 Backhoe retainer.
6 180° rotation motor (internal).
7 Lid open indicator switch.
8 Backhoe.
9 Magnetic array.
10 Brush.
11 Temperature sensor (external).

12 Secondary sample retention area.
13 Lid.
14 Disaggregation teeth.

This automated shovel was used to dig soil samples and deliver them to the lander for analysis. Its lid was raised when the scoop was pushed into the soil, and closed when it was filled. The head was then retracted on its boom assembly, positioned over an inlet on the lander, rotated, and vibrated, so causing soil to sprinkle through the sieve. The backhoe was for trenching.

Lander Camera
1 Dust cover.
2 Entrance window.
3 Processing electronics.
4 Mounting mast.
5 Azimuth drive motor.
6 Thermal insulation.
7 Photosensor array.
8 Optics.
9 Scanning mirror and elevation drive.

The lander's two identical facsimile cameras could view the entire circumference of the landing site from the footpads to a point 40° above the horizontal. Images were built up by sequential line scans—each line made up of 512 pixels—acquired by a nodding mirror which reflected light to a diode sensor. Each "nod" scanned one vertical line of the scene; then the camera moved 0·04° in azimuth to scan the adjacent line. Twelve diodes were employed: one acquired a survey black-and-white image; three recorded colour through red, blue and green filters; three operated in the near-infra-red bands; four (at different focal positions) produced high-resolution pictures (2mm at 3m); one with a protective filter imaged the Sun. The signals were digitized and stored for transmission to Earth; a black-and-white panorama took 10 minutes to receive, colour about 30 minutes.

Viking Lander
1 S-band low-gain antenna.
2 Facsimile camera No 2.
3 Lens cover/duster.
4 UHF antenna (relay).
5 X-ray fluorescence funnel and spoiler.
6 Magnet and camera test target (3).
7 Biology processor.
8 Seismometer.
9 10 x 10in (254mm x 254mm) grid pattern.
10 Radar altimeter electronics.
11 Magnifying mirror.
12 S-band high-gain antenna (direct).
13 Radioisotope Thermo-electronic Generator power source (inside cover) (2).
14 Wind sensors.
15 Ambient temperature sensor.
16 Low level electronics.
17 Terminal descent hydrazine propellant tank (2).
18 Roll engine (4).
19 Hinge dust cover.
20 Landing shock absorber.
21 Temperature sensor.
22 Boom magnet cleaning brush.
23 GCMS processor.
24 18-nozzle terminal descent engine (3).
25 View mirror.
26 Terminal descent landing radar (on underside of lander).
27 Furlable boom.
28 Magnet and backhoe.
29 Collector head.
30 Thermocouple.

The Viking lander had two basic missions: to land safely; and to enable its instruments to conduct seven different types of investigation on the surface. These were:
Biology: which sought to detect evidence of micro-organisms in the soil.
Molecular analysis: which searched for organic and some inorganic compounds in the soil and analyzed atmospheric composition.
Inorganic chemistry: by use of the X-ray Fluorescence Spectrometer.
Meteorology: using wind speed/direction, temperature and atmospheric pressure sensors on an extended boom.
Seismology: by using seismometers to detect Marsquakes.
Physical properties: using mirrors on the surface sampler boom, leg-mounted stroke gauges and current-measuring circuits to determine soil properties.
Magnetic properties: using magnets on the collector head to detect magnetic particles in the soil. In addition, radio science investigations of the site were conducted during lander-orbiter communications.
The hexagonal lander was made of an aluminium-titanium alloy and insulated with fibreglass and dacron cloth. Its six subsystems comprised three terminal descent engines; two communications systems; a radar altimeter and terminal descent landing radar; a guidance control and sequencing computer; two 35W RTGs (**13**) and four nickel-cadmium re-chargeable batteries; and the data acquisition and processing unit.

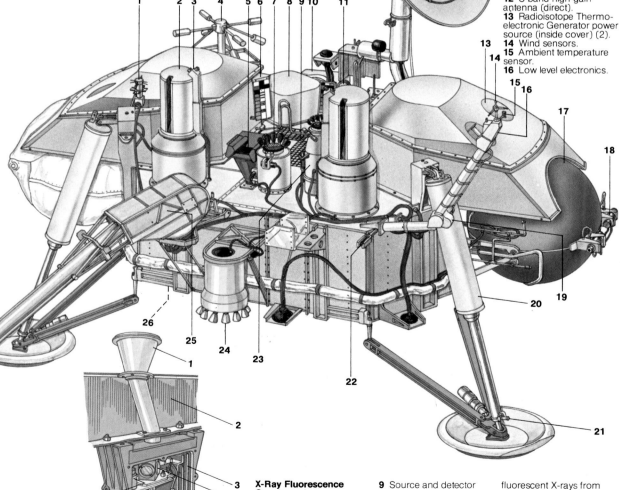

X-Ray Fluorescence Spectrometer
1 Funnel.
2 Lander insulation.
3 High voltage power supply.
4 Window to sample area.
5 Low voltage power supply.
6 Dump cavity.
7 Electronics.
8 Dump mechanism.
9 Source and detector array.

This inorganic chemistry analysis instrument identified elements in soil samples which were deposited in an analysis chamber. Iron and cadmium X-ray sources produced radiation energetic enough to excite fluorescent X-rays from elements in the soil between magnesium and uranium in the periodic table. Gas-filled proportional counter detectors reacted by emitting electrical pulses proportional to the energy of the X-ray photons from the excited element, which could thus be identified.

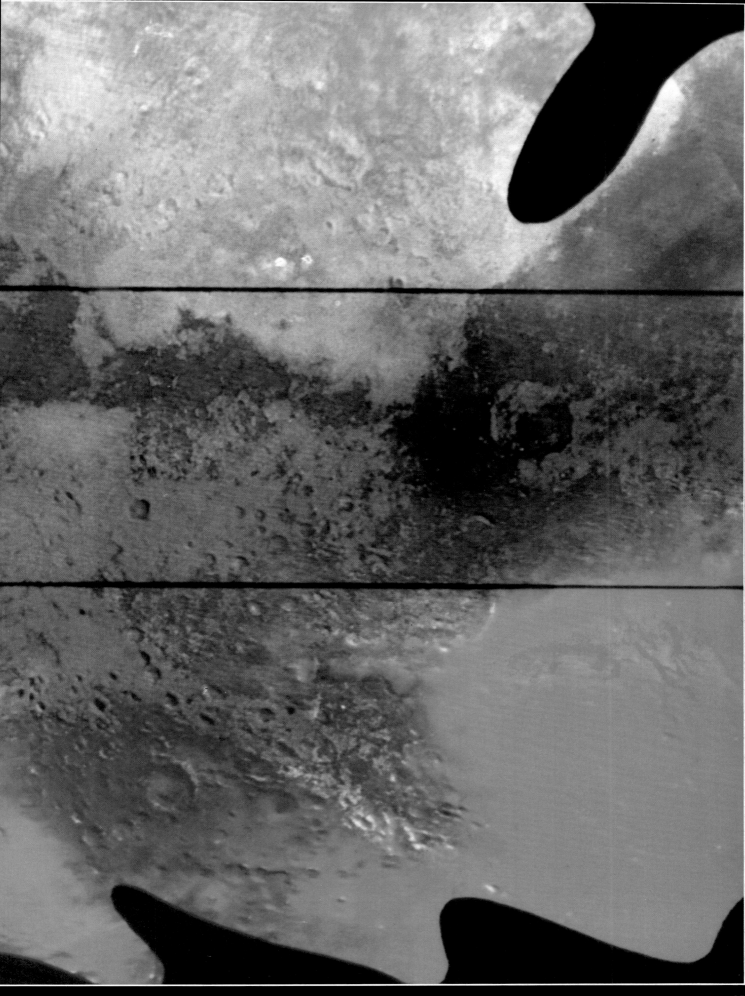

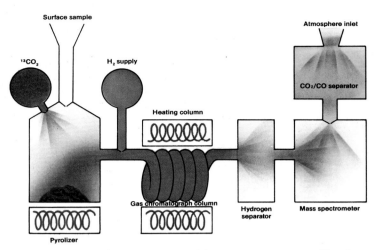

Gas Chromatograph Mass Spectrometer (GCMS)

This instrument was used on the landers to perform chemical analyses of the Martian soil. About 100mg of soil was transferred into the GCMS hopper and the sample was pulverized and then heated to 500°C, to vaporize any organic material present. The vapour was then swept into a gas chromatographic column to separate out the constituents, which were then heated progressively from 50° to 500°C in order to release different organic molecules for delivery to the spectrometer. Here the vapour was ionized and focused by magnetic and electronic units on to an electron multiplier tube, the impulses so produced creating profiles of the component parts. However, the GCMS failed to detect any organic compounds.

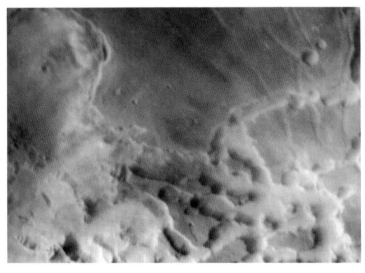

Above: *The Viking Orbiters frequently recorded mists on Mars. Here, clouds of water-ice fill the labyrinthine canyons of the Noctis Labyrinthus, at the western end of the Valles Marineris complex.*

shell carried 12 reaction control engines fuelled by 408lb (185kg) of hydrazine. The lander's guidance computer fired these to align the vehicle for descent and also as braking thrusters during the early stage of the descent.

The aeroshell carried a mass spectometer which identified gases in the upper atmosphere and pressure and temperature sensors which enabled the science team to construct a density-temperature profile as the vehicle descended. The data were radioed to the orbiter which relayed them to Earth. It was during this phase of the mission that nitrogen was identified in the atmosphere. It was another positive indication of the prospect of life.

Because round-trip radio communication took 38 minutes during this period, landing manoeuvres had to be controlled by the lander's computer. The initial descent was slowed by the aeroshell and the attitude control jets to 3·7 miles (6km) altitude. A pressure sensor then fired a mortar which deployed a 53ft (16·2m) parachute. Seven seconds later, the aeroshell was jettisoned. At approx. 4,900ft (1·5km) altitude, the parachute was jettisoned. Three throttleable retro-rockets attached to the lander frame commenced firing for the final stage of the descent under computer control. At touchdown, they were shut off by a landing pad switch.

The Viking 1 lander came down in a lowland desert called Chryse Planitia (the Golden Plains) at 22·4 degrees north latitude and 48 degrees west longitude at 1153·06 Universal Time (Greenwich Mean Time) or 4·13pm Mars local time on 20 July 1976. Travelling at the speed of light, the landing radio signal from Viking 1 did not reach Earth until 19 minutes, 1 second later, at 1212·07 Universal Time (GMT) or 0512·07 Pacific Daylight Time. The first black and white photo of the landing site showed an Earthlike field strewn with broken rocks and a near horizon. The lander's twin facsimile cameras stood 5·25ft (1·6m) above the ground, about eye level for a person of average height. The scene was desolate but not strange. Science was learning that planetary surfaces look somewhat alike.

Above: *Viking 1 Orbiter mosaic of part of Mars' northern hemisphere. The view is dominated by the 2,500 miles (4,000km)-long Valles Marineris canyon system. Three Tharsis volcanoes are on the left.*

Left: *Viking 2 view of the Red Planet and its red sky in November 1976. Colour-matching is made possible with the craft's colour calibration charts (foreground). The high-gain antenna (top) relays the data.*

The first colour photo from Lander 1 revealed a reddish brown landscape, strikingly similar to a plot of Arizona desert, with a light blue sky beyond the horizon. The sky colour astonished observers until colour values were rectified (by comparing them with colours painted on the lander). The revised photo showed a pink sky. It was tinted by the red dust in the atmosphere.

Viking 2 was launched on 9 September 1975 and inserted into orbit around Mars on 7 August 1976. Lander 2 touched down at 2237·50 Universal Time on 3 September in a slightly rolling, stony region called Utopia Planitia (Plains of Utopia) at 47·6 degrees north latitude and 225·7 degrees west longitude about 4,040 miles (6,500km) from Lander 1. Viking 2's landing signal reached the Jet Propulsion Laboratory 20 minutes, 30 seconds later at 1558·20 PDT. It was 9·49am local time on Mars.

Lander Operations

Except for the Lander 1 seismometer, which could not be uncaged, all of the instruments on both landers returned data. A small servo-motor extended the meteorology boom which returned the first weather report from Mars on 21 July: light winds from the east in late afternoon changing to light winds from the southeast after midnight. Maximum wind speed was 15mph (24km/h). Temperatures ranged from −84·7°C just after dawn to −29·7°C in late afternoon. Pressure was steady at 7·7 millibars.

Under computer control, the shovel and backhoe were extended on their boom. The backhoe scraped a trench and the shovel scooped up a handful of soil. The soil was dumped into inlets to the three biology experiments, the gas chromatograph mass

spectrometer test cell and the X-ray fluorescence spectrometer test cell.

Each of the three biology experiments was designed to register an organic chemical process unique to living organisms. The first to yield data was the gas exchange experiment. It was designed to show evidence of living organisms by exchange of gases resulting from metabolic activity. The experiment was based on an assumption that micro-organisms existing in the Martian soil were dormant because of lack of water. If this was the case, moisture added to a soil sample under controlled conditions might bring them to life and start metabolic activity.

A cubic centimetre of soil was conveyed automatically to 0·53in³ (8·7cm³) container. To the normal Martian atmosphere were added helium and krypton, mainly to increase pressure in the test cell, and a nutrient of organic compounds and inorganic salts. Then the soil was humidified, providing moisture that might revive any dormant microbes, and incubated for seven days, The initial result was startling. Oxygen was detected immediately by the gas chromatograph mass spectrometer. However, the amount tapered off after two hours. There was no change when nutrients were added.

Next, the soil was made wet with more moisture. Additional oxygen did not appear, but carbon dioxide was emitted. Although exciting, the results did not fit the expected pattern of gas exchange. Before the test was repeated, the sample was heated to 145°C to kill any organisms present. But sterilization did not stop the production of oxygen when the sample was moistened again. The experimenters concluded that the gas exchange was the result of some inorganic chemical reaction peculiar to the Martian soil. It did not have a biological origin, they said.

A second experiment tested for the assimilation of carbon by micro-organisms from the atmosphere. A quarter of a cubic centimetre of soil was deposited in a 0·24in³ (4cm³) test cell with an atmosphere of radio-

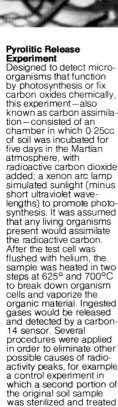

Pyrolitic Release Experiment
Designed to detect micro-organisms that function by photosynthesis or fix carbon oxides chemically, this experiment—also known as carbon assimilation—consisted of an chamber in which 0·25cc of soil was incubated for five days in the Martian atmosphere, with radioactive carbon dioxide added; a xenon arc lamp simulated sunlight (minus short ultraviolet wavelengths) to promote photosynthesis. It was assumed that any living organisms present would assimilate the radioactive carbon. After the test cell was flushed with helium, the sample was heated in two steps at 625° and 700°C to break down organism cells and vaporize the organic material. Ingested gases would be released and detected by a carbon-14 sensor. Several procedures were applied in order to eliminate other possible causes of radio-activity peaks, for example a control experiment in which a second portion of the original soil sample was sterilized and treated in the same way.

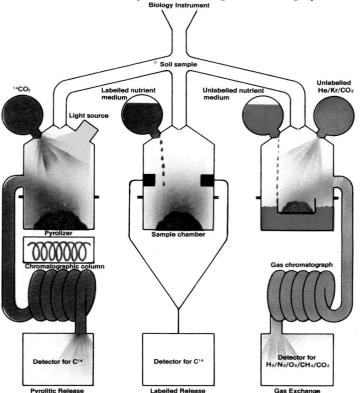

Biology Instrument

Soil sample

¹⁴CO₂ · Labelled nutrient medium · Unlabelled nutrient medium · Unlabelled He/Kr/CO₂

Light source

Pyrolizer

Chromatographic column

Sample chamber

Gas chromatograph

Detector for C¹⁴

Detector for C¹⁴

Detector for H₂/N₂/O₂/CH₄/CO₂

Pyrolitic Release · Labelled Release · Gas Exchange

Labelled Release Experiment
The labelled release experiment was designed to detect evidence of metabolism in the Martian soil. The soil was put in an incubation cell with an enclosed Martian atmosphere and moistened with small quantities of organic components (labelled with carbon-14) in a nutrient "soup". The atmosphere was continuously monitored during the 11-day incubation period by radio-activity detectors to sense any excretion of carbon gas such as might result from the assimilation of the nutrients by organisms present; a curve of cumulative radio-activity might indicate the metabolic growth rate of the organism. At the end of the incubation period the test cell was purged with helium and a fresh sample prepared and analyzed. Labelled gas was in fact released during this experiment. Control cycle tests with sterilized soil were run and resulted in reduced evolution of radioactive gas.

Gas Exchange Experiment
This device measured the uptake of carbon dioxide, nitrogen, methane, hydrogen and oxygen during up to twelve days of incubation of a 1cc soil sample. The sample was suspended in a porous cup and moistened with water vapour, with or without added nutrient, and the incubation was arranged to take place in an atmosphere of carbon dioxide, krypton (introduced as a calibration standard) and helium. Gases within the single test cell were analyzed every few days by a gas chromatograph. Any detection of hydrogen, oxygen, nitrogen or methane indicated, it was considered, organic metabolism. A control experiment with sterilized soil was again available. Early results showed a significant release of oxygen, but as with the labelled release experiment this may have been caused by oxidation rather than by organic processes. In each of the biology experiments, data were gathered electronically for transmission to Earth by the lander.

MISSIONS TO MARS					
SPACECRAFT		DATE	LAUNCH VEHICLE	WEIGHT lb (kg)	RESULTS
Mariner 4	(US)	28 Nov 64	Atlas-Agena	575 (261)	Mars fly-by on 14 July 65; 22 photos.
Mariner 6	(US)	24 Feb 69	Atlas-Centaur	910 (413)	Mars fly-by on 31 July 69; 75 photos.
Mariner 7	(US)	27 Mar 69	Atlas-Centaur	910 (413)	Mars fly-by on 5 Aug 69; 126 photos.
Mars 2	(USSR)	19 May 71	D-1-e	10,250 (4,650)	Entered Mars orbit on 27 Nov 61; lander failed.
Mars 3	(USSR)	28 May 71	D-1-e	10,250 (4,650)	Entered Mars orbit on 2 Dec 71; lander failed after reaching surface.
Mariner 9	(US)	30 May 71	Atlas-Centaur	2,270 (1,030)	Entered Mars orbit on 13 Nov 71; photomapped Mars surface.
Mars 4	(USSR)	21 July 73	D-1-e	10,250 (4,650)	Mars fly-by on 10 Feb 74; apparently failed to enter orbit.
Mars 5	(USSR)	25 July 73	D-1-e	10,250 (4,650)	Entered Mars orbit on 12 Feb 74; returned photos.
Mars 6	(USSR)	5 Aug 73	D-1-e	10,250 (4,650)	Landed 12 March 74; transmission failed during descent.
Mars 7	(USSR)	9 Aug 73	D-1-e	10,250 (4,650)	Mars fly-by on 9 March 74; lander attempt failed.
Viking 1	(US)	20 Aug 75	Titan III-Centaur	7,758 (3,519)	Entered Mars orbit on 19 June 76; lander set down on 20 July 76; long-term orbital and ground scientific observations and biology tests.
Viking 2	(US)	9 Sep 75	Titan III-Centaur	7,758 (3,519)	Entered Mars orbit on 7 Aug 76; lander set-down on 3 Sep 76; long-term orbital and ground scientific observations and biology tests.

active carbon oxides. The soil was incubated in the glow of a 6 watt xenon lamp, simulating sunshine on Mars, for 120 hours at temperatures of 8° to 26°C. Then the lamp was turned off, the test cell was heated to 120°C and the radioactive atmosphere was vented.

In two steps, the cell temperature was raised to 700°C to break down any organic compounds that had been synthesized. The residue was oxidized to form carbon dioxide which was then passed to a radiation counter. If the counter found radioactive carbon in the gas, it meant that something in the soil had synthesized organic compounds from the atmosphere. The result would be evidence of life.

Test Results

This test was run six times in Lander 1 and four times in Lander 2. The results showed that some atmospheric carbon had been fixed in the sample, but they showed also that assimilation took place in a pre-sterilized sample. Again, the experimenters were unable to say whether the results could be interpreted as evidence of life or as some unexpected inorganic chemical reaction peculiar to the soil of Mars.

The results of these two experiments were construed as either negative or ambiguous, but the third experiment gave a clearer signal. It showed that whatever was in the soil was able to metabolize a nutrient labelled with radioactive carbon and release it in a waste product.

The labelled release experiment was done several times in Landers 1 and 2 over a six month period. About one-half cubic centimetre of soil was placed in the test cell and moistened with a nutrient solution contain-

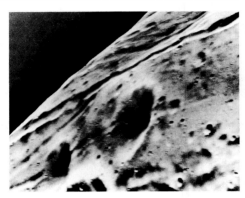

Above: *Viking Orbiter 1 view of the Martian moon Phobos from only 75 miles (120km). The smallest features visible are 32ft (10m) across. This northern region is heavily cratered and crossed with deep grooves.*

Summary of Non-Biological Findings: The Viking Project

Photographic: The northern hemisphere of Mars is characterized by extensive volcanism, including the largest volcanoes found in the Solar System. The southern hemisphere is more densely cratered. The great rift sytem, Valles Marineris, may be analogous to rift systems on Earth and Venus and the product of similar tectonic processes. In equatorial regions there is extensive evidence of catastrophic flooding, but the source of water is undetermined.

Erosion appears to have been extensive in the northern highlands. Terraced deposits in the polar regions show rapid erosion and also rapid deposition. Judging from crater counts, major surface features are a billion years old or older.

Hydrosphere: The hydrosphere of Mars exists as water vapour in the atmosphere, as water ice at the poles and, conjecturally, as permafrost under the surface. Water vapour in the atmosphere ranges from near zero in the winter hemisphere to 85 parts per million around polar ice in summer. By mid-summer, the atmosphere above the north polar cap is saturated, indicating a permanent cap of water ice over which carbon dioxide (dry) ice is precipitated out of the atmosphere in winter.

Atmospheric moisture moves from one hemisphere to the other as the seasons change. Planetary abundance of water in the vapour state is 1·3 cubic kilometres.[8] The volume of water frozen at the poles is estimated as orders of magnitude greater. An even larger volume may be contained underground as permafrost.

Polar Observations: Viking's infra-red thermal mapper indicated that super-cooling occurs at the winter pole. This effect may cause atmospheric carbon dioxide to precipitate out as dry ice, especially at the south pole. The effect may account for lander weather data showing a drop in atmospheric pressure during the southern winter.

The equipment on the Viking landers was designed to be able to withstand long periods of extreme operating conditions. This image was taken at the end of a Martian winter and shows frost-covered rocks. The view is to the rear end over the top of Lander 2 looking south-east.

Observations at the north pole in the summer showed that the residual cap was dirty water ice at a temperature -73° to -63°C.

Entry Observations: The upper atmosphere consists mainly of carbon dioxide with small amounts of nitrogen, argon, carbon monoxide and nitrogen oxide. The ratio of the isotopes nitrogen 15 to nitrogen 14 is enriched, indicating a denser atmosphere in the past. This supports the hypothesis that the apparent river and stream beds were cut by flowing water. The present thin atmosphere would not permit liquid water to accumulate on the surface.

Landing Sites: Both landing sites revealed the same orange-brown colour, contributed possibly by the mineral maghemite (Fe_2O_3) which was noticed clinging to the permanent magnets on the lander digging tools. The rocks, ranging in size from a few centimetres to two metres, are basaltic igneous, a type found on Earth, the Moon and Venus.

At Chryse Planitia, the topography is undulating. The landscape appears to be the product of the mechanical and chemical breakdown of the upper layers of a volcanic flow of basalt. Utopia Planitia is a flat plain, strewn with boulders that appear to have been ejected from a crater in the vicinity.

Marsquakes: A local event with the Richter scale energy of 2·8 was detected 68 miles (110km) from lander 2. Shear wave reflections indicated that the crust is 9·3 miles (15km) thick. The signal was damped out in a few minutes, suggesting the presence of water or frost in the crust. By contrast, the Moon rings for a long time after a seismic event.

Meteorology: Because of the condensation of carbon dioxide at the poles, atmospheric pressure varies from summer to winter by 30 per cent. Winds generally were mild at the landing sites, less than 66ft/sec (20m/sec). Daily temperatures varied between -123°C and -43°C at night and mid-afternoon in summer at the sites.

ing carbon-14, the labelling isotope. if metabolism occurred, radioactive carbon would be released in the waste gas and detected by the radiation counter. The result would indicate that some form of Martian life had made a hearty meal of the labelled nutrient.

When the nutrient was injected into the incubation chamber, radioactivity began to appear immediately. It rose from a background level of 500 counts per minute to 7,500 counts per minute in 24 hours. It then levelled off at about 10,500 counts per minute after seven days. When more nutrient was added, additional labelled gas was released briefly. The amount in the test cell decreased and then began to rise slowly again.

It was evident that some agency in the soil was performing or imitating metabolism, but it was not growing. The increase in the release of the labelled gas was not exponential as might be expected with the growth of a microbial colony.

For the third time, the spokesman for the biology team expressed doubt that the results constituted a clear signal of life on Mars. It was suggested that a non-biological agency in the soil could have produced the results. It might be a strong oxidizing agent created by ultraviolet light reaching the surface of Mars which is not shielded from it by ozone as is the surface of the Earth. If soil particles were coated with such an agent it might not only release oxygen but it might also oxidize labelled nutrients to emit labelled carbon dioxide. When a soil sample was scooped up from beneath a rock, where it had been protected for eons from ultraviolet radiation, the test results were the same.

The labelled release experiment group believed there is a real possibility that their experiment detected evidence of life on Mars, but the biology team as a whole has not been able to accept that conclusion.

Below: *Close-up view of Mars' north polar cap in summer from Viking Orbiter 2. The 37x18·5 mile (60x30km) region shows a 1,640ft-high (500m) scarp (top) covered in water-ice. Ice has sublimed away on the slopes, showing layered deposits.*

A major aspect of doubt was the result of soil tests by the gas chromatograph mass spectrometer which failed to yield any trace of organic compounds in the soil at both landing sites. This result alone seemed to negate any acceptance of a biological explanation of any of the experiment results, for the team had to deal with the question of how life could have developed in the absence of organic compounds.

Summarizing the biology results, the Viking Project Scientist, Gerald A. Soffen, observed that the biology results were by far the most complex of all the investigations;

"While inorganic chemical reactions may be sufficient to explain the data seen, . . . biological processes cannot be ruled out at this time." [8]

The question of life on Mars has been narrowed by these investigations, but not resolved. The question remains: is there some form of life in the red soil or something else that imitates it?

If there is a chemical imposter, its nature remains a mystery. Such is the legacy of Viking.

8 Soffen, G.A., "Scientific Results of the Viking Project", *Journal of Geophysical Research*, Vol. 82, No. 28, 20 September 1977.

RECOMMENDED READING

"Scientific Results of the Viking Project", *Journal of Geophysical Research*, American Geophysical Union, Washington D.C., 1977.
Glasstone, S., *The Book of Mars*, NASA, Govt. Printing Office, Washington D.C., 1968.
Lewis, R.S., *Appointment on the Moon*, Viking, New York, 1969.
Lewis, R.S., *From Vinland to Mars*, Quadrangle, New York, 1976.
Pollack, J.B., "Mars", *Scientific American*, New York, Sept 1975.
Various authors, *The Martian Landscape*, photos of the Viking Mission. NASA, Govt. Printing Office, Washington, D.C.
Various authors, *Atlas of Mars*, Viking Orbiter photos, NASA, Govt. Printing Office, Washington, D.C.
Various authors, *Viking Mars Expedition 1976*, Martin Marietta Corporation, Denver, Colorado, 1978.

Above: *A dusty day at the Viking 1 landing site, showing a series of trenches (right) dug for soil samples to a depth of 12in (30cm). The vertical "arm" is the boom for the meteorological experiments.*

Soils: At both landing sites, the fines consisted of iron rich clay, iron oxides and oxides of silica. These were interpreted as a common weathering product of a basaltic lava flow.

Soil samples were analyzed for the presence of organic molecules, but none was found. The science team did not believe that life could have evolved on Mars in the absence of organic material. It was speculated that organic molecules were destroyed by ultraviolet radiation which reaches the surface of Mars in the absence of ozone.

The Moons: The two, irregularly shaped moons of Mars are probably captured asteroids. Mariner 9 and Viking Orbiter photographs showed that both were heavily cratered and very dark.

Phobos, the inner moon, is the larger. It is 10 by 14 miles (16 by 23km) and revolves around Mars in 7·7 hours from west to east at 3,790 miles (6,100km) from the surface. Deimos, 5·6 by 8 miles (9 by 13km), has an orbital period of 30·3 hours at 12,428 miles (20,000km) from the surface. It also moves from west to east.

The Extended Mission: The Viking orbiters and landers were scheduled to perform a basic mission from the summer of 1976 to the beginning of conjunction in November when Mars moved behind the Sun.

After conjunction the scientific team extended the mission from year to year and Orbiter 2 was shut down on 24 July 1978 when it used up its nitrogen attitude control gas.

Orbiter 1 continued to photograph Mars and collect scientific data until 8 August 1980. Engineers at the Jet Propulsion Laboratory switched off its transmitter as its gas ran out.

Lander 2 was shut down in mid-March 1980 because of a power failure. Lander 1, however, was still operating in the summer of 1982 six years after it landed. It was programmed to return photographs, weather reports and engineering data every eight days until 1994—but was eventually reported to be out of commission on 8 March 1983.

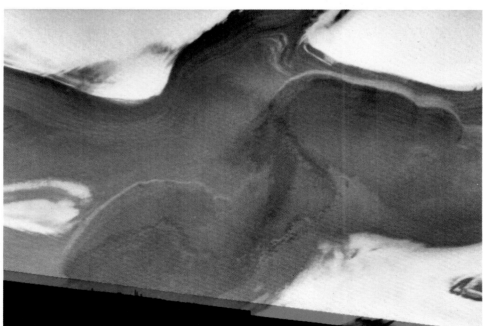

The Giant Planets: Jupiter and Saturn

THE principal mass of the Solar System lies beyond the asteroid belt which forms a transition zone between the rocky planets of the inner Solar System and the gaseous-liquid giants beyond. This arrangement has been accounted for to some extent by the tendency of the refractory elements, with high melting points, to condense into planets nearer the Sun and the tendency of volatile elements, with low boiling points, to form planets farther away.

From Mercury to Saturn, planet density generally decreases with distance from the Sun. It drops from 5·5 times that of water at Mercury to 0·7 times water at Saturn. Beyond Saturn, the symmetry of this profile is broken. Uranus and Neptune appear to be denser than Jupiter and Saturn. Pluto's bulk density was calculated in 1980 at $1.14g/cm^3$ — slightly higher than water.

Nevertheless, the predominant density gradient in the Solar System is repeated by satellites of Jupiter, which is often viewed as a star that did not succeed.

Jupiter, consisting mainly of hydrogen and helium, occupies 1,317 times the volume of Earth, but only 318 times Earth's mass. Its density ($1.3g/cm^3$) is 23 per cent of Earth's and barely higher than that of water. Yet Jupiter alone contains more mass than all the other bodies of the Solar System combined beyond the Sun. Jupiter's period of rotation, 9 hours 55·5 minutes at the equator, is the most rapid of all the planets.

With its retinue of 16 moons, two larger than Mercury and two about the size of Earth's Moon, Jupiter and its satellites form a system of their own, an analogue of the Solar System. Although Jupiter apparently

JUPITER: BASIC DATA	
Equatorial Diameter*	11·23E; 89,015 miles (143,252km)
Mass*	318E
Density	0·75oz/in³ (1·3g/cm³)
Volume*	1,317E
Surface Gravity*	2·64E
Escape Velocity	37·3 miles/sec (60km/sec)
Period of Rotation	9hr 55min 30sec
Inclination of Equator (to Orbit)	3°
Distance from Sun (Semi-major axis)	5·2AU; 483·4 x 10⁶miles (778 x 10⁶km)
Siderial Period	11·86 tropical years
Synodic Period	398·8 days
Orbital Speed	8·14 miles/sec (13·1km/sec)
Orbital Eccentricity	0·048
Inclination of Orbit (to ecliptic plane)	1·305°
Number of Satellites	16
*Earth = 1	

began its career as a proto-star, it did not gain enough mass from the nebula to start thermonuclear reactions in its interior. Still, the heat produced by its accretion of mass was sufficient to create a density profile among its larger satellites analogous to that of the Solar System. Volatile elements were driven outward to condense into the big, icy satellites, Ganymede and Callisto. The more refractory materials of the "Jovian System" accreted nearer Jupiter to become Io and Europa with higher densities.

The Grand Tour

Ever since Galileo Galilei turned his 8-power telescope on Jupiter in 1610, astronomers astrophysicists and cosmologists have been fascinated by the Big Planet. As the centuries passed, observers realized that out there was a solar system within a

Above: *A composite image of Jupiter at three infra-red wavelengths shows detail not visible optically. The planet appears unchanged at 1·6 microns (blue); but the 2·2 micron emission (green) reveals methane-poor poles, and the (red) 4·8 micron bands arise in Jupiter's hot core.*

Solar System, a planet that might be considered as a star that had never caught fire.

Three years after the space age opened as an outgrowth of the International Geophysical Year (1957–58), NASA scientists and engineers began plotting methods of sending an instrumented probe on a grand tour of the outer planets.

Circa 1977–78, the planets, Jupiter, Saturn, Uranus and Neptune would be aligned on the same side of the Sun. With precise navigation, a spacecraft could planet hop from one to the other and then continue out of the Solar System. The energy requirement for such a voyage, covering 40 times the distance between the Earth and Sun, exceeded by far the capacity of man-made propulsion systems. In order to make the grand tour, the spacecraft would have to borrow gravitational and orbital energy from one planet to boost it on to the next.

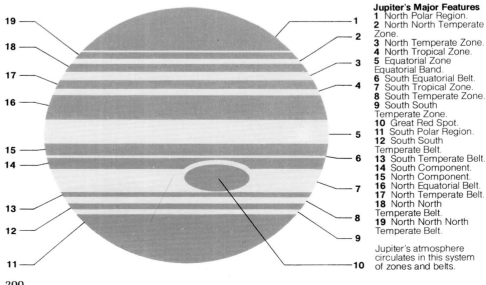

Jupiter's Major Features
1 North Polar Region.
2 North North Temperate Zone.
3 North Temperate Zone.
4 North Tropical Zone.
5 Equatorial Zone Equatorial Band.
6 South Equatorial Belt.
7 South Tropical Zone.
8 South Temperate Zone.
9 South South Temperate Zone.
10 Great Red Spot.
11 South Polar Region.
12 South South Temperate Belt.
13 South Temperate Belt.
14 South Component.
15 North Component.
16 North Equatorial Belt.
17 North Temperate Belt.
18 North North Temperate Belt.
19 North North North Temperate Belt.

Jupiter's atmosphere circulates in this system of zones and belts.

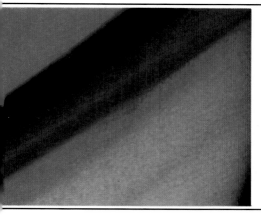

> "... when I was viewing the heavenly bodies with a spyglass, Jupiter presented itself to me; and because I had prepared a very excellent instrument for myself, I perceived ... that beside the planet there were three little stars, small indeed, but very bright."
>
> Galileo Galilei, *Observational Notes for 7 January 1610*

If the vehicle could reach Jupiter under its own power, it could be navigated to pass close enough to the big planet to be seized by its gravity field and thus acquire enough of its orbital velocity to accelerate towards Saturn. The "gravity assist" process could be repeated at Saturn to accelerate the vehicle to Uranus and at Uranus to Neptune and, possibly, to Pluto.

A grand tour mission was plotted by the engineering faculty and students at the Illinois Institute of Technology and by the staff of the Jet Propulsion Laboratory and other NASA centres. Harnessing the gravitational and orbital energy of the planets appealed to NASA not only as a challenge in physics, but as an economical means of exploring the outer planets at a time when the funding of Project Apollo took the lion's share of the American space budget.

Several elaborate reconnaissance vehicle systems were considered. The Space Science Board of the US National Academy of Sciences endorsed a project called TOPS, an acronym for Thermoelectric Outer Planet Spacecraft. The vehicle had a launch weight of 1,540lb (700kg). It would be accelerated to the outer planets by a propulsion system called the ion drive. Ion engines had been

developed at NASA's Lewis Research Center, Cleveland in the early 1960s. They produced thrust by magnetically accelerating and expelling positively charged mercury ions.

The ion engine required a long-term source of electrical energy, either solar cells or a nuclear reactor. Because the electrical output of solar cells would decrease with distance from the Sun, a nuclear power source would be more efficient, especially for a spacecraft going to Jupiter where solar energy dwindled to 4 per cent of its intensity at Earth.

The Space Science Board estimated that with reactor power, a fairly heavy payload could be flown as far as Pluto in less than four years. The TOPS concept did not materialize. It was too costly in a period when NASA was being required to cut expenditures. Although a small reactor for spacecraft had been developed, NASA would not risk launching it because of the radiation hazard if the launch failed.

If any outer planet exploration was to be done, spacecraft using chemical propulsion and gravity assist would have to do it. Nuclear generation of electric power would be restricted to compact radioisotope thermoelectric generators producing less than 0·5kW from the decay of plutonium.

Above: *Nerve-centre of NASA's planetary exploration programme, the Space Flight Operations Facility at the Jet Propulsion Laboratory in Pasadena, California. Graphics displays relate to Viking operations on Mars. The same Facility later controlled the Voyager missions.*

Pioneer

The economical, near-term solution was the modification of the utilitarian Pioneer spacecraft for a flight to Jupiter. The Pioneers had proved reliable as solar orbiting monitors of fields and particles near the Earth. Three "Jupiter class" Pioneers were built by TRW Systems, Redondo Beach, California, two for Jupiter and one spare. Each had a launch weight of 570lb (258kg), within the capacity of the Atlas-Centaur to boost it out to Jupiter. The modest cost programme, designed to "test the water" beyond Mars, was managed by NASA's Ames Research Laboratory near San Francisco.

It was the destiny of Pioneers F and G (Pioneers 10 and 11 after launch) to reconnoitre first the asteroid belt, which was feared to be a serious hazard to navigation. If one or both vehicles survived a trip through the belt, the next hazard would be

Above: *Jupiter's north polar regions, as seen by Pioneer 10's sister-craft Pioneer 11, from 372,800 miles (600,000km). The picture shows in detail the transition regions between Jupiter's belts and zones.*

Left: *Technicians work on the magnetometer boom on Pioneer 10, the first probe to fly past Jupiter on 3 December 1973. The probe has now left the Solar System.*

the fierce radiation zones of Jupiter. High-energy radiation in the massive Jovian magnetic field might wreck communication systems.

The only feature of the TOPS programme which survived in the Pioneers was the thermoelectric auxiliary power system. Four small radioisotope generators were installed in each spacecraft to produce 140 watts of electricity for the radio, navigation system and 11 scientific instruments. Each Pioneer carried 55lb (25kg) of scientific equipment.

A critical instrument was the imaging photopolarimeter (IPP) which looked at the reflective properties of the Jovian atmosphere to indicate the shape and size of cloud particles, the abundance of gas above the clouds and gather data that could be processed by computer into pictures of the planet. Because the Pioneers were spin-stabilized, the IPP telescope swept across the surfaces of Jupiter and its satellites 7·8 times a minute to build an image line by line. It was not capable of being pointed precisely at a target. Its colour images, developed in the computer at Ames from the red and blue components of reflected light, were quite detailed, however.

Mariner Jupiter-Saturn

Although one of the spacecraft, Pioneer 11, would be targeted for Saturn if all went well at Jupiter, the Pioneer missions did not fulfill the expectations of the grand tour plan. Congressional budget cutting had forced the space agency to abbreviate the tour in 1972, and rely on Pioneer for a look at Jupiter and, hopefully, another at Saturn. But the resourceful Jet Propulsion Laboratory

came up with a low cost addition that would restore most of the grand tour—a pair of Mariner spacecraft adapted for outer planet reconnaissance. They would supplement and enlarge on the Pioneer effort.

The Mariners were not spin-stabilized. Computer-directed attitude control by gas jets enabled them to provide precise instrument pointing from a movable scan platform. Moreover, computer flight control gave the Mariners a degree of freedom from ground command that the closely monitored and ground-directed Pioneers lacked. At Saturn, 85 light minutes from Earth, this was an advantage.

Two Mariner missions to Jupiter and Saturn were planned. The first was to fly-by Jupiter in March 1979 and Saturn in November 1980. The second would reach Jupiter in July 1979 and Saturn in August 1981, with the option of proceeding to Uranus. A significant cost reduction was sought by having the programme manager, the Jet Propulsion Laboratory, assemble the Mariner components rather than awarding the integration task to a private contractor.[1] In 1977, NASA changed the title of the project from Mariner Jupiter-Saturn to Voyager, a title once applied to a proposed Mars landing mission in the 1960s.

---

1 The National Aeronautics and Space Administration divided the construction of unmanned spacecraft between industrial contractors and its own facility, the Jet Propulsion Laboratory. Thus, while the Pioneers were built by an industrial contractor, TRW Systems, the Voyagers were put together in-house by JPL from parts supplied by sub-contractors.

So far as Jupiter and its moons were concerned, the Pioneer and Voyager missions exhibited a redundancy in outer planet exploration which might have been avoided if the TOPS programme had been adopted in the first place. Instead of one or two vehicles headed for Jupiter, there were four. The Pioneers would break the trail; the Voyagers would follow and continue to Saturn. These were the most ambitious fly-by programmes of the space age and if they were successful, mankind would have completed a preliminary survey of the solar commonwealth.

Although Jupiter's volume, mass, rotation and revolution had been determined before the space age, features of its atmosphere, such as the Great Red Spot, and of its satellites eluded precise definition from Earth. Details of atmospheric composition, the existence of a magnetic field, the source of Jupiter's radio and particle emissions, even the exact number of its satellites (12 known in 1970) were undetermined or speculative.

Peering at Jupiter on the night of 7 January 1610, Galileo had described the larger moons as "three little stars, small but very bright". At first, he believed they were fixed stars. After discovering a fourth "star", Galileo was able to discern their motion as satellites of Jupiter. About a month before Galileo's sightings, a German astronomer, Simon Mayer, also known as Simon Marius (1573–1624), saw the satellites, or so he later reported. Mayer named them Io, Europa, Ganymede and Callisto after the Greek mythological lovers of Zeus (or Roman Jupiter), but the moons, although retaining Mayer's nomenclature, have since been known as the "Galilean" satellites.

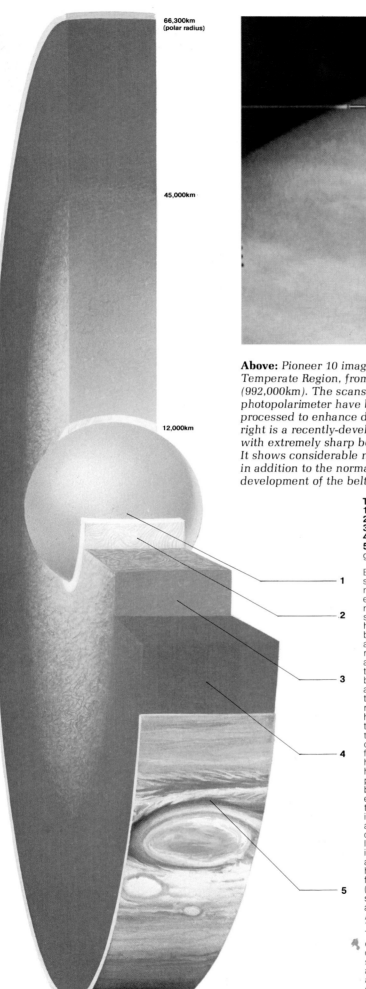

66,300km
(polar radius)

45,000km

12,000km

Above: *Pioneer 10 image of Jupiter's North Temperate Region, from 616,400 miles (992,000km). The scans of the imaging photopolarimeter have been computer-processed to enhance detail. On the right is a recently-developed cloud feature with extremely sharp boundaries. It shows considerable north-south motion in addition to the normal east-west development of the belts and zones.*

The Structure of Jupiter
1 Possible core.
2 Possible "sea" of helium.
3 Liquid metallic hydrogen.
4 Liquid hydrogen.
5 Cloud tops—hydrogen gas.

Because Jupiter captured so much of the early solar nebula, it is made almost entirely of hydrogen—the material of the Sun and stars. Most of this hydrogen is in liquid form, but at its centre Jupiter almost certainly has a rocky core amounting to about 9 per cent of its total mass. The core must be at a temperature of about 30,000°K to explain the fact that Jupiter radiates twice as much heat as it receives from the Sun. Above a possible thin "sea" of helium, most of Jupiter's mass is in the form of liquid metallic hydrogen at extremely high pressures. Below pressures of 3 million bars, liquid hydrogen extends in a deep layer up to the atmosphere, where it becomes gaseous. The atmosphere itself is composed of several layers: water droplets, ice crystal clouds, ammonium hydrosulphide clouds and frozen ammonia crystals (see diagram of vertical structure of the atmosphere on page 207). At the very top is a thin "smog" of hydrocarbons. The brownish coloration of Jupiter's belts probably comes from traces of sulphur and carbon in the atmosphere, although the agent responsible for the colour of the Great Red Spot may be phosphorus.

Their discovery had a profound effect on the world view of seventeenth century Europe. The spectacle of satellites circling a distant planet contributed to the displacement of the Earth from its accepted cosmological position as the centre of the Universe. In addition, they contributed to the discovery of a great universal constant—the speed of light. In 1675, Olaus Romer (1644–1710), a Danish astronomer, observed that the satellites were eclipsed by Jupiter 16 minutes and 40 seconds earlier when Jupiter was on the same side of the Sun as Earth than when Jupiter was on the opposite side. It thus appeared that it took light 16 minutes and 40 seconds to travel twice the radius of Earth's orbit. Dividing twice the Earth's orbital radius, approximately 185,920,394 miles (299,201,690km), by 1,000 seconds yields 185,920 miles/sec (299,202km/sec). That is close to the speed of light which has been determined as 186,247·25 miles/sec (299,727·7km/sec).

Pioneers 10 and 11

The Jupiter Pioneers were built to operate for at least 700 days to make the billion kilometre flight on a minimum energy trajectory. With their 9ft (2·7m) diameter high-gain dish antennas, the Jupiter Pioneers looked like metal parasols shading hexagonal boxes of equipment and scientific instruments. They were 9·5ft (2·9m) tall from the adapter ring at the interface with the Centaur rocket to the tip of the medium-gain antenna which was elevated on struts above the big dish. A low-gain "omni" antenna was extended 2·5ft (0·76m) behind the equipment bay. The four radioisotope electrical generators, were attached to two booms well away from the instruments. A third boom held the magnetometers away from the generators.

Attitude control and velocity propulsion was provided by three pairs of hydrazine-fuelled thrusters attached to the rim of the dish antenna. They were pointed so that one pair could be fired to propel the spacecraft forwards; the second pair could propel it backwards and the third pair could spin the vehicle to stabilize it.

In addition to the imaging photopolarimeter (IPP), the scientific instruments were a Geiger tube telescope to detect radiation; an asteroid-meteoroid sensor; two magnetometers to sense the magnetic fields in space and at Jupiter; a cosmic ray telescope; an infra-red radiometer, an ultraviolet photometer, a charged particle counter and a plasma analyzer. The plasma analyzer monitored the solar wind. Each Pioneer carried two radio receivers and two 8-watt transmitters. Flight control was monitored by Canopus and Sun sensors. The Pioneers were actually controlled directly from Ames, so that constant communication was required. These vehicles were not equipped with computers that controlled their successors, the Voyagers.

Pioneer F was launched on 2 March 1972 (3 March, GMT) from Cape Canaveral, Florida and became Pioneer 10 as it was injected into the Jupiter trajectory at 8·9 miles/sec (14·3km/sec). Pioneer G was launched on 5 April 1973 (6 April, GMT) after its predecessor had negotiated the asteroid belt without a scratch, and became Pioneer 11.

Both vehicles sped outward from the Sun, passing the orbit of the Moon in only 11 hours (compared with 72 hours on Apollo flights) and the orbit of Mars in 84 and 97 days respectively, compared with 229 days for Mariner 4.

The launch of Pioneer 10 was so accurate that only one principal velocity correction of 30·8mph (49·6km/h) on 7 March was required to bring the spacecraft to within 85,500 miles (137,600km) of Jupiter's cloud tops. The distance was reduced to 80,500 miles (129,600km) by two minor velocity changes accomplished on 23 and 24 March so that Pioneer 10 would fly behind the near moon, Io, to sound for an atmosphere suspected of

Jupiter's Magnetosphere
Jupiter has the largest and most complex magnetosphere of all the planets, extending to about 90 Jupiter radii around the planet in the plane of its equator, where the magnetic field is weakest. As well as serving to shield Jupiter from the solar wind, this magnetic bubble also acts as a powerful particle accelerator. Plasma, much of it generated by the volcanic moon, Io, moves along the field lines to the turbulent outer magnetosphere, where the particles are thrown back towards the planet via the plasma sheet. They then return to the polar field lines, and the process is repeated, with the particles gaining added energy each time.

Pioneer 10 and 11
1 RTG deployment damping cable.
2 Spin/despin thruster.
3 Imaging photopolarimeter.
4 Geiger tube telescope.
5 High-gain antenna.
6 Magnetometer.
7 Trapped radiation detector.
8 Plasma analyzer.
9 Meteoroid detector sensor panel.
10 Medium-gain antenna.
11 Cosmic ray telescope.
12 Infra-red radiometer.
13 Charged particle instrument.
14 Thrusters.
15 Sun sensor.
16 Stellar reference assembly light shield.
17 Radioisotope thermoelectric generator (RTG) (2).
18 RTG power cable.
19 Asteroid-meteoroid detector sensor.
20 Separation ring.
21 Low-gain antenna.
22 Thermal control louvres.
23 Ultraviolet photometer.

Pioneers 10 and 11, launched on 2 March 1972 and 5 April 1973 respectively, were the first probes tasked with the exploration of the outer planets: Pioneer 10 was targetted at Jupiter, thence it flew on until it passed the orbit of Neptune and so left the Solar System (June 1983); Pioneer 11 also encountered Jupiter, but then, using gravity assist, it intercepted Saturn. It is due to depart the Solar System in a direction approximately opposite to Pioneer 10 in 1986. Designed to fit within the 10ft (3m) diameter shroud of the Atlas-Centaur launch vehicle, each probe had hydrazine attitude control and propulsion systems, electrical power produced by boom-mounted nuclear generators, and temperature control effected by aluminized plastic blankets and radioisotope and electric heaters. Two identical receivers (one back-up) were fitted for communications; a 9ft (2·74m) diameter high-gain antenna pointed continuously at Earth. Eleven scientific instruments were carried. The helium vector magnetometer measured the fine structure of the interplanetary magnetic field and the fluxgate magnetometer the strength of intense planetary magnetic fields. The trapped radiation detector measured the particles in the Jovian and Saturnian fields. The other instruments comprised an asteroid-meteoroid detector, an ultraviolet photometer, an infra-red radiometer, an imaging photopolarimeter and a charged particle composition instrument, while a plasma analyzer measured the solar wind. A cosmic ray telescope, for measuring proton flux and chemical element identification, and a Geiger tube telescope, for use in the Jovian and Saturnian radiation zones, completed the scientific package.

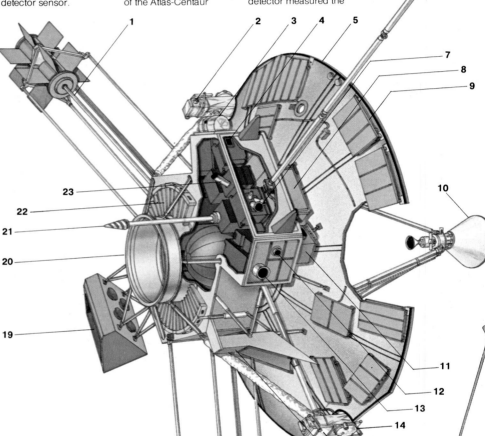

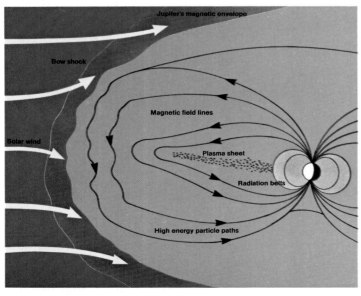

Jupiter's magnetic envelope
Bow shock
Solar wind
Magnetic field lines
Plasma sheet
Radiation belts
High energy particle paths

Technical Data
Length: 9·5ft (2·9m) from conical medium-gain antenna to launch vehicle adapter rim.
Equipment compartment: hexagonal box 14in (36cm) deep with 28in (71cm) long sides.
Total weight: c 568lb (258kg).

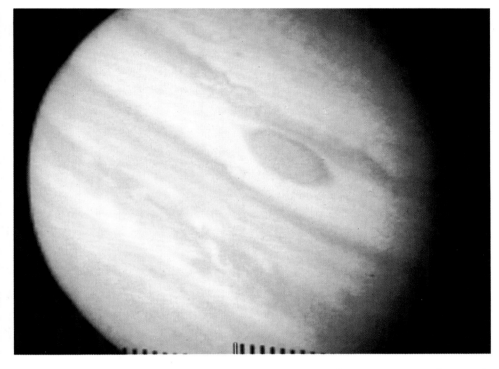

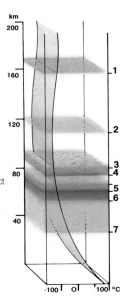

Mission Profiles

Pioneer 10: The voyage to Jupiter took some 21 months and covered a distance of about 600 million miles (1,000 million km). The asteroid belt was successfully navigated after about six months flight.

The Jupiter encounter lasted about two months, the closest approach being made on 3 December 1973, 80,500 miles (129,600km) from the cloud tops. Jupiter's gravitational field then swung the spacecraft on a

trajectory that took it past the orbits of the outer planets and out of the Solar System in 1983. Pioneer 11: Passing Jupiter (nearest distance 67,800 miles, 109,100km from the centre) in December 1974, Pioneer

11 then used that planet's gravity to send it back across the Solar System to intercept Saturn, closest encounter being on 1 September 1979. The pass was within 13,300 miles (21,400km) of Saturn's cloud tops.

Above: *Pioneer 10 image of Jupiter. The Great Red Spot is very prominent and the red moon (right of Spot) is Io. "Teeth marks" at the bottom are an artefact of the TV camera's scanning system.*

Jupiter's Atmosphere
1 Stratosphere.
2 Troposphere.
3 Hydrogen gas.
4 Ammonia ice clouds.
5 Ammonium hydrosulphide clouds.
6 Water ice clouds.
7 Water droplets.

Vertical structure of Jupiter's atmosphere, from light-scattering and infra-red measurements aboard the Pioneer craft. The uppermost layers of the atmosphere are composed of transparent gas — hydrogen/helium — and below are several distinct layers of cloud at steadily increasing temperatures. The highest ammonia ice clouds, at pressures of 0·7 Earth atmospheres, form Jupiter's pale zones. The lower belts are made up of ammonium hydrosulphide, while clouds of ice crystals and, finally, liquid water drops, lie at the lowest levels.

being present by transmitting radio signals through it.[2]

As Pioneer 10 broke trail to Jupiter, no navigation hazard threatened the mission as menacing as the obstacle course of the asteroid belt. It was believed to be swarming with planetoids and rocks. Or so it appeared to observers on Earth. Pioneer 10 entered the belt on 15 July on the 135th flight day. Ames controllers were relieved and surprised to find that the detectors showed no appreciable increase in dust or debris. On 2 August, the trajectory analysis showed that Pioneer 10 flew within 5·47 million miles (8·8 million km) of a 1,100yd (1km) rock called Palomar-Leyden. On 2 December, the vehicle passed within 5 million miles (8 million km) of a 15 mile (24km) planetoid, Nike. These were its nearest misses. Although the belt did not appear to be the hazard to navigation that pre-flight analysts had feared, an increase

2 The radio occultation experiment sent a radio beam grazing the satellite to Earth. Distortion of the signal indicated the existence of an atmosphere and its approximate density. The experiment had first been performed at Mars by Mariner 4 in 1965.

in dust was recorded as Pioneer 10 penetrated deeper into the region between Mars and Jupiter.

Pioneer 10 observed massive solar storms on 2 and 7 August. They were recorded also by Pioneers 6, 7, 8 and 9 in solar orbits nearer Earth, providing observations over an enormous radial distance from the Sun. By the end of February 1973, Pioneer 10 emerged from the belt. The density of space dust dropped off to pre-belt, interplanetary levels. As Pioneer 10 flew on during the spring of 1973 toward its rendezvous with Jupiter, Pioneer 11 was launched by Atlas-Centaur and Ames control charted a course that would use Jovian gravity to bend the flight path and boost it toward Saturn.

In November 1973, Pioneer 10 passed the orbit of the asteroidal moon, Sinope, and entered the Jovian system at a distance of 14,336,000 miles (23,071,000km) from Jupiter's centre. In rapid succession, it crossed the orbits of the outer moons, Pasiphae, Carme and Ananke. On 26 November, it encountered the bow shock wave where the solar wind breaks upon the Jovian magnetosphere like the sea upon the shore. It was then 4·66 million miles (7·5 million km) from the planet's centre.

The Jovian magnetosphere, a great bubble in the solar wind shaped by Jupiter's magnetic field, appeared to be spongy. It contracted and expanded with the varying intensity of the solar wind. Consequently, Pioneer 10 instruments showed it crossing the bow shock repeatedly. At one time, it was within the bubble, and at another it was outside, in the solar wind.

Pioneer 10 passed the outer Galilean satellite, Callisto, on 3 December. It entered a zone of high radiation at 5 Jupiter radii (222,542 miles, 358,130km). Scientific instruments began to react to false commands generated by the radiation. It was as though Jupiter was seizing control of the vehicle. As Pioneer 10 passed the near moon, Io, a false command shut down the imaging photo-polarimeter and Pioneer 10 failed to get pictures of the moon.

Late on 3 December 1973, Pioneer 10 made its closest approach, 80,500 miles (129,600km) from the clouds and then passed behind Jupiter. The spacecraft continued to radio pictures and scientific data as it sped away. By late winter, it was headed towards the bright star, Aldebaran, in the constellation of Taurus.

Scientific Returns

An early major finding of Pioneer 10 was the unexpectedly low density of dust and debris in the asteroid belt.

It measured the extent of the Jovian magnetic field as it contracted and swelled with the solar wind. The field extended over a region of 420 Jupiter radii (18,686,400 miles, 30,072,000km), a distance, a NASA report noted, equal to 72 per cent of the distance between Earth and Venus.

Pioneer 10 made its first finding that the strength of the solar wind does not wane with distance from the Sun on the cruise to Jupiter. There was no increase in interstellar cosmic radiation from which the solar wind shields the Solar System.

Magnetometer data showed that the magnetic field of Jupiter is reversed relative to

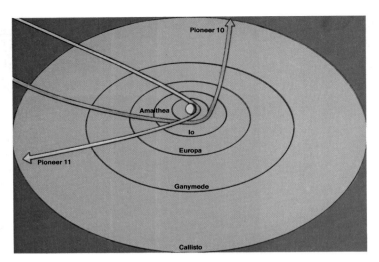

Pioneer-Jupiter Encounters
Pioneer 10 and Pioneer 11 were sent into the Jovian system on different trajectories to explore specific aspects. Pioneer 10 passed the planet at a distance of 80,500 miles (129,600km) on 3 December 1973, having already probed the extent of the Jovian magnetosphere. It swung around the planet in a counter-clockwise direction as viewed from the celestial North pole. As Pioneer 11's approach was even closer (25,850 miles, 41,600km), there was more radiation risk. However, the steep approach minimised this, and allowed images of the polar regions to be obtained.

Earth's field. On Jupiter, the compass needle would point south. Field strength ranged 4 to 30 times the strength of Earth's field (2 to 15 gauss compared with Earth's 0·5 gauss). The Jovian field appeared to be the source of the so-called galactic electrons which had been detected by an Interplanetary Monitoring Platform in 1964. Jupiter turned out to be a strong emitter of energetic particles, like the Sun.

As a result of its rapid spin, 9 hours, 55·5 minutes at the equator, Jupiter is flattened at the poles 10 times more than is Earth. The equatorial diameter, 89,015 miles (143,252km), is 4,807 miles (7,736km) greater than the polar diameter, 84,208 miles (135,516km).

Pioneer 10's imaging photopolarimeter returned pictures of Ganymede with a resolution of 236 miles (380km), showing surface features like lunar maria. At Io, a cloud of gas, thought to be atomic hydrogen, was detected by the ultraviolet spectrometer. The IPP returned a sequence of ever larger and sequentially more detailed pictures of the clouds of Jupiter as Pioneer sped towards it. The whole atmosphere appeared to be in turbulent motion. In the north tropical zone, the clouds were elevated above those in surrounding regions. Part of the equatorial cloud region seemed to be higher than clouds of the temperate zone. In the southern hemisphere, the Great Red Spot was photographed again and again by the IPP.

This feature has been measured as being 24,000 miles (38,500km) across, a gigantic eye in the face of Jupiter. A smaller Red Spot about one-tenth the diameter of the great one was seen in the northern hemisphere. Curiously, it hovered at about the same latitude above the equator as the great one hovered below. There was no question from these sightings about the nature of the red spots. They were semi-permanent hurricanes, rotating counter-clockwise. Ascending gases were flowing outward at the top of these features, several miles above the surrounding cloud deck.

The ultraviolet spectrometer peered 150 miles (240km) into the clouds. It identified the make-up of the atmosphere as 82 per cent hydrogen, 17 per cent helium and 1 per cent other gases. The gaseous atmosphere was deep. At its lower boundary, 596 miles (960km) below the clouds, gaseous hydrogen became a liquid under pressure. At a depth of 14,900 miles (24,000km) below the clouds (the visible surface of Jupiter) the liquid

became metallic hydrogen. In this state, the hydrogen conducted electricity. The vast Jovian magnetic field is thought to be generated in this region by the planet's rapid rotation. At the base of the hydrogen mass, heat, it was speculated, would change the metallic state to a liquid state.

At the centre of the planet, the overall density of Jupiter indicated the existence of a rocky core, perhaps equal to the combined masses of Venus, Earth and Mars, but compressed to a volume about equal to that of Earth. The Jovian density, 1·3 times that of water, did not support a consensus of an iron core.

Moving rapidly through the intense Jovian radiation belts, Pioneer 10 received a radiation dose of 500,000 rads.[3] If that did not silence the spacecraft, the crew at Ames was sure nothing else at Jupiter would.

In the spring of 1982, Pioneer 10 was moving serenely on its journey between the orbits of Uranus and Neptune at circa 25 astronomical units (2,237 million miles, 3,600 million km from Earth). The instruments were on and the 8-watt radio sent back data showing that the solar wind was still blowing out there as strongly as ever. A year later, Pioneer 10 passed Pluto (then inside Neptune's orbit) on 25 April 1983, and then the orbit of Neptune on 13 June 1983, so leaving the known Solar System.

Pioneer 11

Aimed to skim the high latitudes of Jupiter where radiation exposure was lower, Pioneer 11 passed through the asteroid belt as smoothly as its predecessor. It encountered Jupiter on 3 December 1974, a year after Pioneer 10. Its closest approach was 25,850 miles (41,600km) above the clouds or 67,800 miles (109,100km) from the centre of the planet.

Like Pioneer 10, Pioneer 11 carried a plaque which identified it as an artefact of a civilization of the third planet of the star, Sol. Depicted on the 6 × 9in (15 × 23cm) plate of anodized aluminium were the figures of the human male and female, a schematic diagram of the Solar System, giving its location in relation to 14 pulsars and the centre of the galaxy. The message reflected

---

3 Rad is an acronym for radiation absorbed dose. The radiation at Jupiter was a hundred thousand times the lethal dose for a human being (5 rads).

Above: *"Like a Cyclopean eye", said NASA of this Pioneer 11 photograph of Jupiter's Great Red Spot, taken from a distance of 683,500 miles (1,100,000km).*

a belief that somewhere in the Universe, the spacecraft would be found by a species intelligent and curious enough to make sense out of it.

Pioneer 11 data supplementing the findings of Pioneer 10 contributed to a new perception of the Jovian system. The number of satellites rose to 13, later to 15, finally to 16. Analyses of the clouds showed that they are composed largely of condensed ammonia compounds and water. The uppermost clouds consist entirely of ammonia crystals. Cloud colours of red, yellow and rust orange were thought

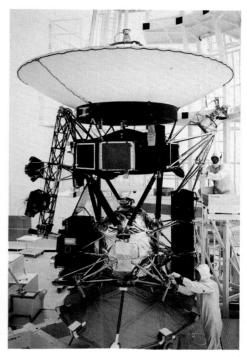

Above: *A model of the Voyagers that was used for electrical and countdown tests is checked out at the Kennedy Space Center a few months before the launches of Voyagers 1 and 2 for Jupiter and Saturn.*

The Voyagers

With the larger, computer-controlled Voyager spacecraft, the opportunity arrived in 1977 to attempt the grand tour, omitting Pluto. Project Voyager, as programmed by the Jet Propulsion Laboratory, was a 10-year, multi-planet investigation which extended Mariner technology to its limit.

Each of the two Voyager spacecraft was eight times heavier than the Pioneer vehicle at launch and required the Titan IIIE plus Centaur upper stage, the most powerful launcher in the American inventory (next to the Saturn V Moon rocket) to send it off to Jupiter.

Voyager launch weight was 4,555lb (2,066kg), including a 2,758lb (1,251kg) propulsion module which gave the spacecraft a final boost after separation from the upper stage Centaur. The Mariner-type spacecraft had a mass of 1,797lb (815kg). Shaped like a mushroom, Voyager was 9·84ft (3m) tall, dominated by the 12ft (3·66m) dish antenna. It was attached to a 10-sided aluminium frame 18·5in (47cm) high and 5·8ft (1·78m) across with 10 compartments containing electronic assemblies. Inside the decagonal frame was a spherical hydrazine tank which supplied propellant to four manoeuvring engines and 12 attitude control thrusters attached to the frame.

The solid rocket propulsion module was suspended below the frame by a truss. The rocket was ignited after Voyager separated from Centaur and burned for 43 seconds, adding 4,475mph (7,200km/h) to injection velocity. At burnout, the propulsion unit was jettisoned.

Attitude control was maintained by a Sun sensor and two trackers of the yellow star, Canopus. Three radioisotope thermoelectric generators provided 423 watts of power during the early part of the flight from the

to be the product of these ammonia compounds reacting to ultraviolet sunlight.

A massive ionosphere was sounded, a region of electrified particles above the neutral atmosphere, rising 2,500 miles (4,000km) above the clouds. It was many times thicker and much hotter than expected.

Atmospheric data collected by Pioneer 11 showed that temperatures in the clouds were not excessively high, a finding that supported a long debated NASA programme to drop an entry probe into the atmosphere.

The data from both Pioneers confirmed that Jupiter has an internal heat source. It radiates 1·9 times as much heat as it receives from the Sun. The internal energy (heat) was calculated at 10^{17} watts. The poles were as warm as the equator.

Next to the Sun, Jupiter is the strongest emitter of radio noise in the commonwealth. Radio signals in the 3 centimetre wavelength appeared to emanate from temperature-induced motion of molecules in the atmosphere. Decimetric signals (1·18 to 27·5in, 3 to 70cm) were attributed to electrons spiralling around magnetic field force lines. Decametric signals (tens of metres) were produced by other electron motion.

Overall, the ratio of helium to hydrogen in the Jovian atmosphere approximated the ratio in the atmosphere of the Sun. Planetary scientists could speculate that if Jupiter had acquired sufficient additional mass, the Solar System would have been double star system. In that case, it is doubtful that a planet like Earth might have evolved.

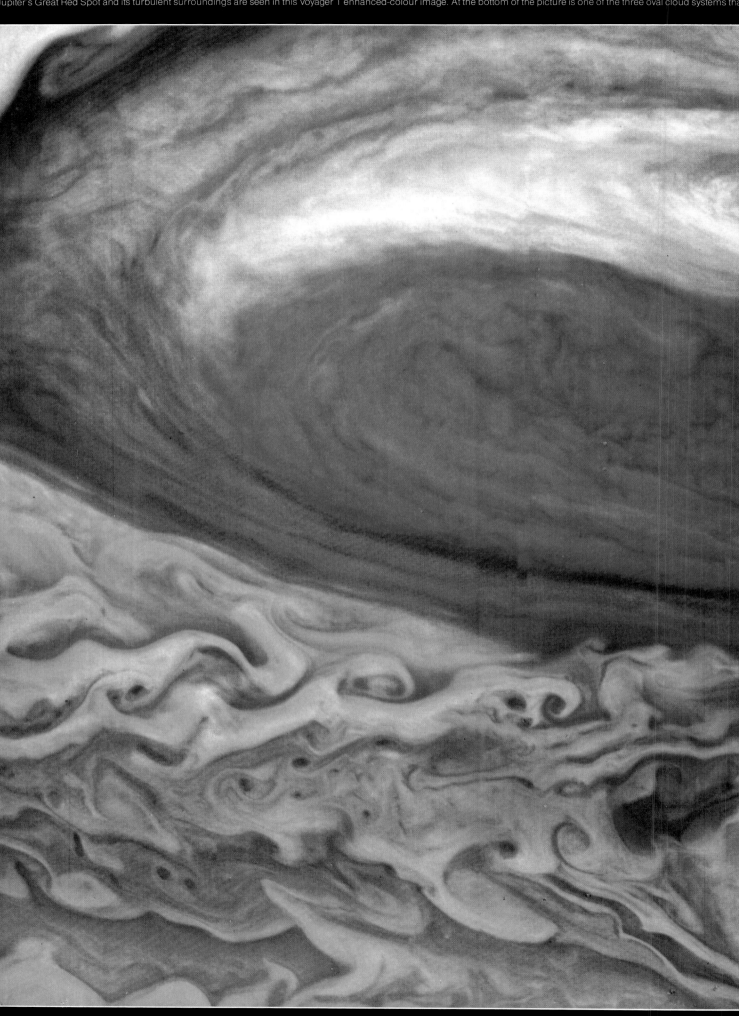

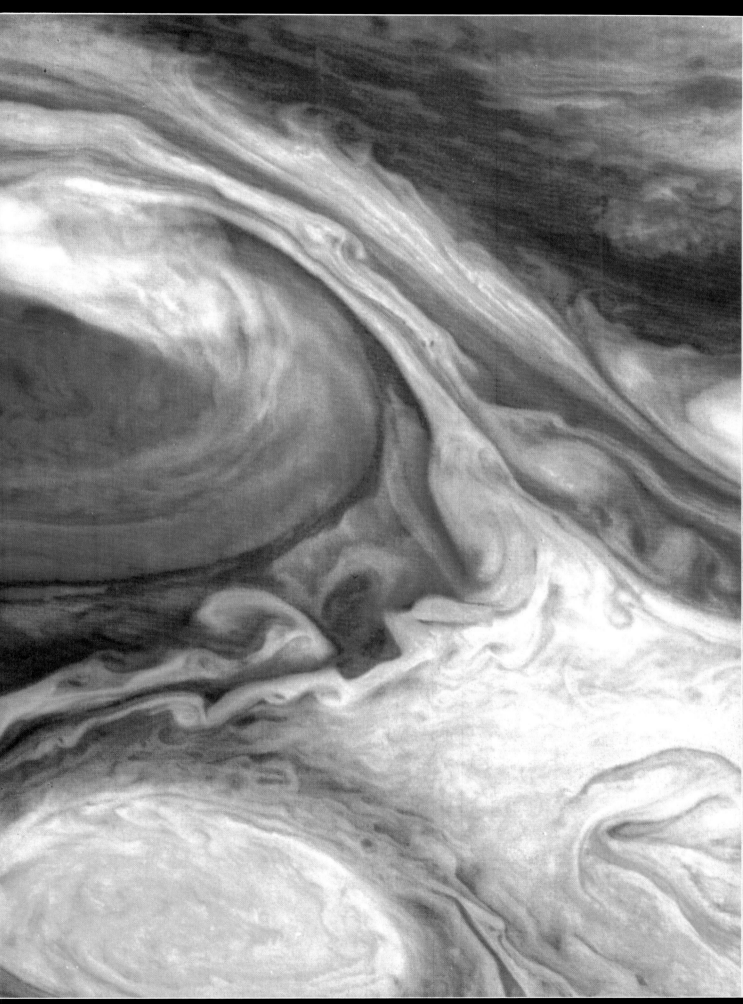

decay of plutonium 238. As decay progressed, the power level faded to 384 watts at Saturn. The generators were mounted on a boom which was extended after the spacecraft separated from its launcher.

In flight, the spacecraft was controlled by command, flight and attitude control computers. Only trajectory corrections were commanded from the ground. Voyager carried two radio receivers. One was a stand-by and automatically came on line if the other failed. S-band and X-band transmitters with a power range of 9·4 to 28 watts flashed data over a range of a billion kilometres at 115,200 data bits a second. When the spacecraft was behind a planet, data were stored on tape for later transmission.

Made to operate farther from the Sun than any other machine, the Voyagers were insulated from heat loss by thermal blankets of aluminized mylar and heated by small radioisotope heaters. At Saturn, solar heating was expected to be 1 per cent of that at Earth.

The Voyagers were programmed to look at 15 bodies (or more) in the Solar System, including Jupiter, Saturn, Uranus and Neptune and some of their satellites. They carried three classes of instruments which were designed to collect information about the physical and chemical nature of these bodies and their radiation environment.

One group consisted of optical scanners which were mounted on the Voyager scan platform. While the spacecraft was flying in a stable attitude, the platform could be rotated to point the instruments at a target. The instruments were two television cameras, one wide, the other narrow angle; an infra-red spectrometer and radiometer which registered atmospheric and cloud composition as well as energy balance of a planet or satellite; an ultraviolet spectrometer which also assessed atmospheric composition and gases; and a photopolarimeter which measured methane gas, molecular hydrogen and ammonia above the clouds of Jupiter and Saturn.

Another set of instruments measured the strength of magnetic fields and the energies of charged particles, from low-energy particles in the solar wind to high-energy galactic cosmic rays. These were the plasma detector, low-energy particle detectors, two solid state cosmic ray telescopes and four magnetometers. Planetary radio astronomy experiments were carried out by a special radio receiver. It listened for emission of radio signals from the planet which were picked up with 32·8ft (10m) whip antennas. The radio communications system was used to sound planetary and satellite atmospheres and ionospheres by transmitting radio signals through them to Earth. The signals also enabled analysts to measure the spacecraft's trajectory change as it passed near a planet or moon. The measurements indicated the body's mass, density and probable shape.

Like the Pioneers, the Voyagers carried a greeting to the Universe. It was imprinted on a 12in (30cm) gold plated, copper phonograph record containing sounds and images of life on Earth. A NASA committee selected 115 images which were encoded in analog form on the record and sounds of life on Earth including thunder, bird songs, whales communicating, volcanoes, human laughter

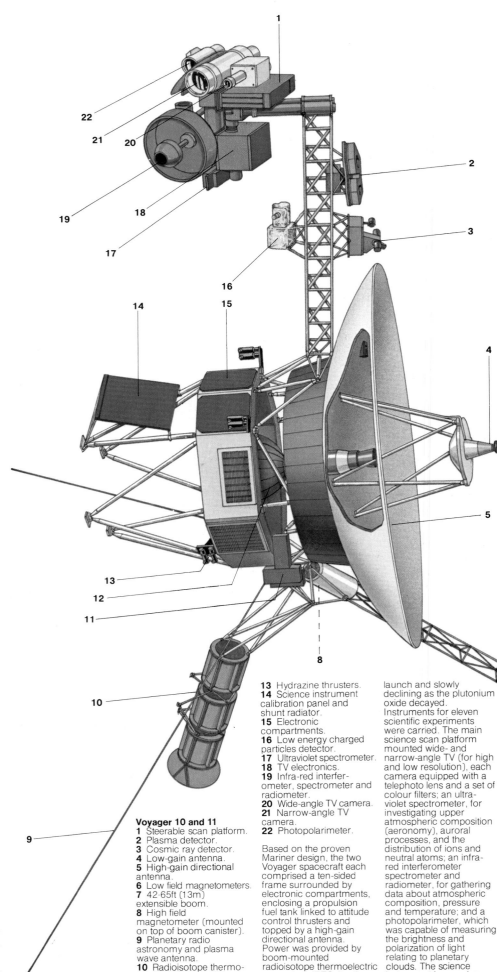

Voyager 10 and 11
1 Steerable scan platform.
2 Plasma detector.
3 Cosmic ray detector.
4 Low-gain antenna.
5 High-gain directional antenna.
6 Low field magnetometers.
7 42·65ft (13m) extensible boom.
8 High field magnetometer (mounted on top of boom canister).
9 Planetary radio astronomy and plasma wave antenna.
10 Radioisotope thermo-electric generator (3).
11 Star trackers.
12 Propulsion fuel tank.

13 Hydrazine thrusters.
14 Science instrument calibration panel and shunt radiator.
15 Electronic compartments.
16 Low energy charged particles detector.
17 Ultraviolet spectrometer.
18 TV electronics.
19 Infra-red interferometer, spectrometer and radiometer.
20 Wide-angle TV camera.
21 Narrow-angle TV camera.
22 Photopolarimeter.

Based on the proven Mariner design, the two Voyager spacecraft each comprised a ten-sided frame surrounded by electronic compartments, enclosing a propulsion fuel tank linked to attitude control thrusters and topped by a high-gain directional antenna. Power was provided by boom-mounted radioisotope thermoelectric generators (RTGs) rather than by solar arrays, producing 450W at

launch and slowly declining as the plutonium oxide decayed. Instruments for eleven scientific experiments were carried. The main science scan platform mounted wide- and narrow-angle TV (for high and low resolution), each camera equipped with a telephoto lens and a set of colour filters; an ultra-violet spectrometer, for investigating upper atmospheric composition (aeronomy), auroral processes, and the distribution of ions and neutral atoms; an infra-red interferometer spectrometer and radiometer, for gathering data about atmospheric composition, pressure and temperature; and a photopolarimeter, which was capable of measuring the brightness and polarization of light relating to planetary clouds. The science instrument boom also carried plasma, cosmic ray and low energy

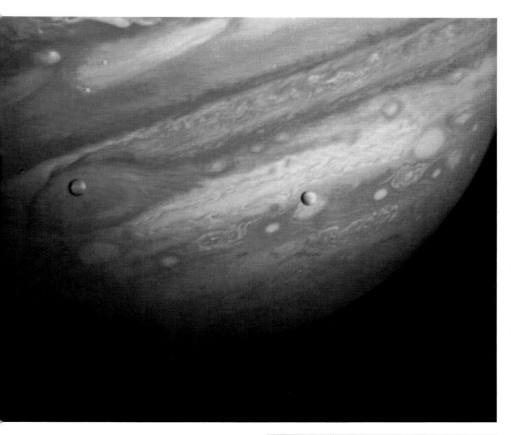

Above: *From 12·4 million miles (20 million km) the Great Red Spot dominates this view of Jupiter from Voyager 1. Io (left) and Europa (right) float above. The resolution is about 250 miles (400km).*

Right: *Although Voyager 1 did not fly over Jupiter's poles, computer reconstruction produced this view of the north pole. The regular spacing of cloud features is evident.*

Technical Data
Weight, spacecraft: 1,797lb (815kg).
Weight, scientific instruments: 254lb (115kg).
Height: 9·84ft (3m).
Diameter, high-gain antenna: 12ft (3·66m).
Basic frame: 10-sided aluminium bus, 18·5in (47cm) high; 5·8ft (1·78m) across.

6

7

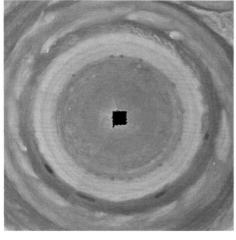

charged particle detectors. Two antennas were fitted for planetary radio astronomy and plasma wave investigation in planetary magnetospheres, and a further, extendable 42·5ft (13m) boom mounted low- and high-field magnetometers, direct sensing instruments designed to mesure the magnetic fields surrounding the planets and the spacecraft. Communications to Earth are effected via the high-gain antenna, with a smaller, low-gain antenna as back-up. The transmitter power, at 23W, was ostensibly low,

although data were relayed at 115,200bps from Jupiter; data storage facilities were also provided, by means of a tape recorder with a capacity of 500 million bits. Special "hardening" techniques protected components, especially the electronic microcircuits, against the high levels of radiation encountered as the space-craft passed through the planetary magnetospheres.

and the launch of the Saturn V rocket. Messages in 56 languages including 6,000-year-old Akkadian and musical selections ranging from the Bach Brandenburg Concerto Number Two to a Navajo Indian chant and Chuck Berry's "Johnny B. Goode" were included in the audio portion of the record which was to be played with the accompanying needle and cartridge at 16²/₃ revolutions a second. A list of instructions assumed that any space-faring species that found the record would be able to play it.

Voyager 2 was launched on 20 August 1977, 16 days before Voyager 1, but encountered Jupiter on 9 July 1979, four months later. Voyager 1, launched on 5 September 1977, encountered Jupiter on 5 March 1979, after passing Voyager 2 on 15 December 1978 about 105 million miles (170 million km) from Earth. The later launch of Voyager 1 put it on a shorter path.

Voyager 1's instruments were turned on several days after launch to observe interplanetary magnetic fields, solar high- and low-energy particles and the solar wind

during the cruise to Jupiter. On 18 September 1977, Voyager 1's television system acquired an historic picture of the crescent Moon and the crescent Earth. The passage through the asteroid belt was uneventful. Voyager 1 began transmitting photographs of Jupiter from a range of 165 million miles (265 million km). Detailed pictures began coming into the Deep Space Network (DSN) stations in mid-January 1979 at a range of 29·2 million miles (47 million km).

The Deep Space Network
The DSN, which has evolved from the global tracking system built for Vanguard in 1957—58, consists of three major transmitting, receiving and tracking stations at Goldstone, California in the Mojave Desert; Robledo de Chavela, near Madrid, Spain and Tidbinbilla near Canberra, Australia.

Each station is equipped with a giant, steerable dish antenna, 210ft (64m) in diameter, with the signal-collecting area of a football field, and two 85·3ft (26m) steerable antennas. With three stations located nearly equidistant around the Earth, NASA can track and communicate with spacecraft anywhere in the Solar System.

Most commands from the Jet Propulsion Laboratory, which operates the Deep Space Network, are transmitted from Goldstone's 400 kilowatt transmitter. The transmitters in Spain and Australia are limited to 100 watts radiated power.

The three stations receive and record continuous streams of data from interplanetary spacecraft. The Voyagers transmitted at only 23 watts of power at rates up to 115,200 bits per second. In addition to scientific and photo data, the Voyagers transmitted engineering telemetry and range rate information from which controllers at JPL could determine the "health" of the spacecraft and their course. The DSN provided tracking information on flight direction, velocity and distance from Earth. Course change commands were sent from the Mission Control and Computing Center to one of the DSN stations, processed by computer for accuracy and transmitted to the spacecraft at 16 bits per second.

Plasma waves were detected near Jupiter with a special receiver linked to the 10 metre whip antennas. Some wave frequencies were in the audio range so that vibrations generated by the spacecraft could be heard in the receiver as sounds. Controllers at JPL reported hearing transmissions that sounded like a 5-gallon can being struck with a leather-covered mallet when the attitude control jets fired. There were other sounds whose origin was not so obvious. One piercing whine was described as sounding like a whale singing. The television transmissions had acquired a sound track.

On 10 February 1979, Voyager 1 crossed the orbit of Sinope, the outermost Jovian satellite at 14·3 million miles (23 million km) from the cloud tops which form the visible surface of Jupiter. The closest approach was 216,865 miles (349,000km) from the centre, 172,750 miles (278,000km) from the cloud tops (5 March). Voyager cameras at this stage were taking pictures every 48 seconds. Radio tracking indicated that Voyager 1 had been accelerated by Jupiter to a velocity of 62,140mph (100,000km/h).

The spacecraft's ultraviolet spectrometer registered an energetic auroral display over the poles. As solar wind pressure rose and fell, Voyager 1 repeated the Pioneer experience of crossing and re-crossing the magnetosphere boundary as it contracted and expanded.

The Voyager scientists had a special interest in Io as a result of the Pioneer discovery of a powerful electric current linking the near moon with the Jovian ionosphere. Trained on Io, the ultraviolet spectrometer detected a ring of ionized sulphur circling Jupiter in Io's orbit. As Voyager 1 approached Io, the television cameras picked up large, shallow depressions on the moon's surface, suggesting lunar-like basins. The spacecraft passed close enough to photograph a portion of Io's surface with a resolution of 10 miles (16km).

On 5 March, huge, crater-like holes were revealed in the surface and after some consultation at JPL were identified as volcanic calderas. Two conspicuous ones were quickly named Pele and Prometheus, in the mythological tradition of nomenclature. Pele was a shallow caldera, about 620 miles (1,000km) in diameter. Prometheus appeared to be an active volcano as the photographs came in. The discovery of a satellite about the size of Earth's Moon with currently active volcanoes was hailed as a stunning breakthrough by NASA. It was the only body in the Solar System exhibiting active volcanism besides the Earth. There were volcanic mountains on Mars and Venus, but they seemed to be long dead. Io was exhibiting erupting volcanoes even as Voyager passed.

The spacecraft flew within 71,500 miles (115,000km) of Ganymede and the cameras saw an icy surface, pocked with impact craters. On 6 March, the cameras were turned on the surface of Callisto at the closest approach range of 78,300 miles (126,000km). The pictures showed an icy surface littered with craters up to 125 miles (200km) across. One huge depression which looked like a bull's eye seemed to be an impact basin. The photo interpretation team named it Valhalla, straying from Greek to Norse mythology for the source of the name.

On 7 March, the cameras yielded another major discovery. Bradford A. Smith, the imaging science team leader, announced that a thin, flat ring of particles had been photographed around Jupiter—a Saturnian-style ring. The Jovian ring measured less than 18·6 miles (30km) in thickness and was orbiting the planet at an altitude of 35,420 miles (57,000km) from the clouds. Jupiter became the third planet to be shown to have one or more rings, after Saturn and Uranus.

On 8 March, Voyager 1 took more pictures of Io. This time, a volcano in the process of erupting was visible at a range of 2·5 million miles (4·1 million km). The plume, identified as sulphur dioxide, was seen as a bluish puff on the limb of the moon. Eight more volcanic eruptions were discerned later in the Io photographs.

On its dark side, Jupiter exhibited a massive aurora, 18,000 miles (29,000km) long. It first appeared as a long, white streak. Brighter streaks showed up near it. Stupendous bolts of lightning were observed as they flashed in and above the clouds where the aurora pulsated.

Voyager 2

As Voyager 1 flew on to Saturn, Voyager 2 came on the Jovian scene. It made its closest approach on 9 July, at 404,000 miles (650,000 km) from the cloud tops, speeding at 45,360 mph (73,000km/h).

The new cloud photos showed that Jupiter's weather was changing. A turbulent region west of the Great Red Spot had begun to break up and pull away from the feature. To the South of the Red Spot, white ovals were drifting east. They appeared to be smaller, semi-permanent storms. The Red Spot had drifted to the west since Voyager 1 saw it.

Voyager 2 was directed to a more distant approach than its predecessor in order to observe more accurately the newly discovered ring. Once located, it could be seen by telescopes from Earth.

Voyager 2 observations showed that the ring was 4,040 miles (6,500km) wide. Matter between it and the cloud tops seemed to extend all the way to merge with the clouds. Near the cloud tops appeared a second ring, very faint.

On Io, a volcano called Loki was erupting. Voyager 2's ultraviolet spectrometer showed that it was emitting a plume 110 miles (175km) long.

Voyager 2 photos of Ganymede lent it a strong resemblance to Mercury, although its density is less than one-half that of Mercury. A pattern of surface grooves which had showed up in Voyager 1 pictures was resolved into mountain ranges by the Voyager

Above: *Io, viewed by Voyager 1 from 535,600 miles (862,000km). The circular features are live volcanoes, most prominent of which is Prometheus (centre).*

Below: *An eruption takes place on Io's limb. Inset shows the greenish-white plume extending to a height of 100 miles (160km).*

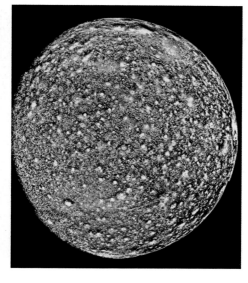

Above: *Voyager 1 image of Ganymede, at 3,275 miles (5,270km) diameter, Jupiter's largest moon. It is heavily impact-scarred, and the white spots and linear filaments may be the result of more recent impacts.*

2 cameras. Voyager 2 saw a side of Ganymede which had been hidden from Voyager 1. It was heavily cratered like Callisto and was dominated by a circular feature resembling an ancient impact basin. This feature had been sighted by Pioneer 10 and named Regio Galileo.

Europa, second of the Galilean satellites from Jupiter, displayed the topography of a billiard ball. It seemed generally flat and featureless, except for a network of lines suggesting crustal deformation. It is a

Above: *Callisto is the most heavily-cratered body yet observed in the Solar System. In this Voyager 2 photomosaic, craters 60 miles (100km) across uniformly cover the entire surface.*

transition satellite between the terrestrial Io and the huge ice balls of Ganymede and Callisto.

Although both Voyagers functioned with precision at Jupiter, they were not free of malfunctions. Voyager 1's photopolarimeter ceased operating and only the Voyager 2 instrument was available at Saturn. Voyager 2 lost one of its two radio receivers on the outbound flight. The back-up receiver failed partially, making it difficult for JPL programmers to instill flight commands in the

spacecraft computer.[4] However, both vehicles were operational as they departed the Jovian system with great velocity toward their next target, Saturn.

The Jovian Planets

The Pioneer and Voyager missions confirmed the view that the Galilean satellites decreased in density with distance from the primary body. They were more like small planets orbiting a surrogate star than like planetary moons.

The inner satellites, Io and Europa, exhibited lunar masses of 1·2 and 0·67 respectively. The outer "planets", Ganymede and Callisto, had 2·03 and 1·45 lunar masses respectively. The density profile dropped from 3·52g/cm^3 at Io to 3·00 at Europa, 1·95 at Ganymede and 1·8 at Callisto. The density profile not only imitated the Solar System, but planet size was also roughly analogous to the system's arrangement. The

4 Voyager 2's primary radio receiver failed on 5 April 1978. The computer switched to the back-up receiver. The back-up developed a faulty tracking loop capacitor which prevented it from locking on a signal from Earth as the frequency varied. The variation occurs as a result of the Doppler shift caused by the spacecraft's velocity and the Earth's rotation. Engineers worked around the malfunction by programming ground computers to control transmission frequency so that the signals would reach Voyager 2 at a frequency the receiver could accept. An automated command sequence for the Saturn encounter was stored in Voyager 2's computer so that it could continue performing experiments and transmitting data if the back-up receiver failed. This precaution has also been taken for the Uranus encounter.

Above: *Jupiter's faint ring system shows in this Voyager 2 colour composite image as two light orange lines. Because the spacecraft moved between exposures, Jupiter's limb is colourfully double-exposed.*

Right: *Voyager 2 image of Jupiter's equatorial regions, colour-enhanced to reveal more detail. The bluish edges of the wispy plumes (centre) may lie in deeper, warmer regions of the atmosphere.*

outer "planets" of Jupiter were larger than the inner ones, with an apparently larger abundance of volatile elements and a smaller abundance of refractories.

Io, with a diameter of 2,262 miles (3,640km), exhibited a slightly variable orbit about 261,950 miles (421,600km) from the centre of Jupiter. The Voyager cameras recorded its multi-coloured surface of bright reds, oranges, yellows and whites, the product of extensive volcanism. The surface of this remarkable "planet" was singularly free of impact craters. Probably, they had been filled in by volcanic fallout. Dark-hued volcanic calderas appeared, surrounded by rings of deposits, mainly sulphur and sulphur dioxide.

Six of the eight eruptions which Voyager 1 had photographed as it departed Jupiter were still going on when Voyager 2 arrived. Plumes of dust and gas rose up to 175 miles (280km) above the dark openings which were shaped like open pits in the surface rather than the volcanic mountains of Earth or Mars. In addition to Pele, Prometheus and Loki, the calderas were named Volund, Amirani, Maui, Marduk and Masubi for ready reference. Each of the calderas and the immediate flows around them averaged about 62 miles (100km) in diameter.

A whitish, doughnut shaped area of fallout surrounded Prometheus on the equator. Pele had a fallout region 620 miles (1,000km) long and 435 miles (700km) wide. South of Loki, a U-shaped feature appeared in some of the Voyager 1 photos. The infra-red inter-ferometer spectrometer (IRIS) on Voyager 1 detected a temperature of 17°C there, very hot compared with the surrounding surface temperature of −146°C. Other volcanic "hot spots" were detected, associated with cal-deras along the equator. The plumes emitted from these volcanic wells were much greater than any known on Earth. The JPL staff calculated that each plume carried 10,000 tons of material a second above the surface, more than 100 billion tons a year. The fallout from the great volcanic plumes was believed to account for the uncratered appearance of Io's surface. The debris had filled the craters.

Although a cynosure for the imaging team, the volcanic features covered only a fraction of the surface. Several rugged mountain chains appeared in the Io photos, together with long, curved cliffs, or scarps,

KNOWN SATELLITES OF JUPITER (1982)			
NAME	DIAMETER miles (km)	DISTANCE FROM PLANET miles (km)	PERIOD (days)
1979J3	25 (40)	79,550 (128,020)	0·29
Adrastea (1971J1)	25 (40)	79,860 (128,520)	0·29
Amalthea	150 (240)	112,650 (181,300)	0·489
1979J2	50 (80)	137,780 (221,725)	0·67
Io	2,262 (3,640)	261,950 (421,600)	1·769
Europa	1,945 (3,130)	416,900 (670,900)	3·551
Ganymede	3,275 (5,270)	664,900 (1,070,000)	7·155
Callisto	3,007 (4,840)	1,168,000 (1,880,000)	16·689
Leda	1·3-8·5 (2-14)	6,903,500 (11,110,000)	240
Himalia	110 (170)	7,127,000 (11,470,000)	250·6
Lysithea	3·7-20 (6-32)	7,276,000 (11,710,000)	260
Elara	50 (80)	7,295,000 (11,740,000)	260·1
Ananke	3·7-17 (6-28)	12,863,000 (20,700,000)	617
Carme	5-25 (8-40)	13,888,000 (22,350,000)	692
Pasiphae	5-28·5 (8-46)	14,478,000 (23,300,000)	735
Sinope	3·7-22 (6-36)	14,727,000 (23,700,000)	758
Note: The orbital periods are expressed in Earth days.			

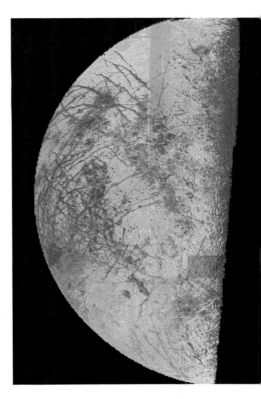

Below: The Valhalla impact basin on Callisto measures 1,615 miles (2,600km) across. The ring-shaped fracture lines indicate that the impacting body may have come close to penetrating Callisto's crust.

Above: A computer-generated, false colour, Voyager 2 image of Europa. Red, vein-like features are thought to be cracks in the 6·2-mile (10km) deep water ice crust that may have become filled with frozen mud.

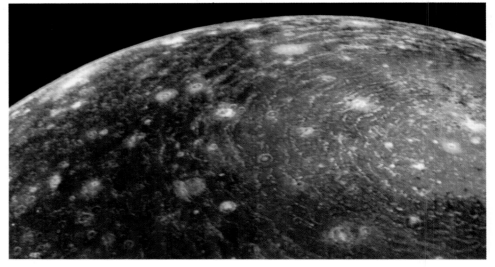

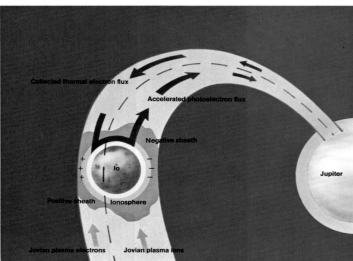

Jupiter's Radio Emissions
After the Sun, Jupiter is the strongest radio source in the sky. It emits bursts of radiowaves, which arise during interactions with its volcanically-active moon Io. By moving through Jupiter's strong magnetic field, Io's ionosphere becomes positively charged on one side, negatively on the other, which produces a potential of 400 kilovolts across the moon. When Io reaches the right position in its orbit, it can "close the switch" to produce strong electric currents in Jupiter's field lines. Current flows along the "circuit" to Jupiter's electrically-conducting ionosphere and back to Io, giving rise to enormous radio bursts. The power of the current generated is $10^{12}W$.

like those seen on Mercury. They indicated crustal motion. Near the poles, mountains rose several miles. With its volcanoes, its mountains and its sinuous scarps, Io seemed more terrestrial than Jovian.

The volcanic heat source was attributed to crustal flexing by the tides which Jupiter's massive gravity raised on Io. The ring of charged particles circling Jupiter in the orbit of Io was shown in Voyager 2 data to consist of sulphur and sodium ions, presumably thrown off the surface of Io by volcanic eruptions. The ring measured 42,900 miles (69,000km) in thickness. In ultraviolet light, its brightness corresponded to a radiated power of a million-million watts.

The Io flux tube, first detected by Pioneer 10, was defined by Voyager data as an electrical current of 10 million amperes flowing from Io to Jupiter with a power of

10^{12} watts. It was dynamo-generated by the motion of Io as it orbited.

Some of Jupiter's radio emissions were attributed to the complex interaction of Io with Jupiter. The impact of charged particles spilling out of a circum-Jovian ring into the Jovian atmosphere was suspected as the cause of Jupiter's auroras.

Jupiter's second moon, Europa, with a diameter of 1,945 miles (3,130km) and density of 3g/cm³, appeared dull by comparison with Io. Europa's smooth, bright surface suggested that the planet was covered by an ocean of ice, perhaps 62 miles (100km) thick. From a distance, Europa looked like a dirty snowball. Closer inspection by Voyager 2 revealed that the smooth surface had a web of dark streaks, some running a distance of 1,865 (3,000km). The streaks resolved into lines which were interpreted as chasms, ridges or valleys up to 45 miles (70km) wide. Tectonic processes altering the surface had been at work on Europa. A few impact craters were seen.

Further examination brought forth smaller, light coloured streaks, like threads. They appeared to be about 6 miles (10km) wide and several hundred metres high. Instead of running in straight lines, the lighter streaks form a scalloped pattern with smooth curves, 100 to several hundred kilometres in extent. The surface turned out to be well covered with a network of these symmetrically curving white lines as well as by the darker, straighter streaks.

It was speculated that Europa's frozen ocean covered a rocky mantle. What tectonic processes were active in the Jovian sub-planet could only be speculated from the strange mesh of streaks and curvilinear white lines.

Ganymede with a diameter of 3,275 miles (5,270km) was the largest sub-planet in the Jovian system, larger than Mercury. It appeared to be half ice and half rock. From a distance, parts of the surface appeared grooved. The grooves on closer inspection turned out to be mountains and valleys. The ridges were 6 to 9 miles (10 to 15km) across and 3,300ft (1,000m) high—similar in scale, a staff report noted, to sections of the Appalachian Mountains of the Eastern USA.

It was surmised by geologists on the Voyager science team than Ganymede has undergone several eras of mountain building. Evidence was seen of faulting, crustal spreading and a sideways drifting of the crust, suggesting its division into plates. The analogy with plate tectonics on Earth suggested convection in the planet's interior. A tenuous atmosphere of water vapour and oxygen was suspected at the surface.

The least fascinating of the Galilean satellites was Callisto, on which there was no sign of volcanism or much else beyond craters. With a diameter of 3,007 miles (4,840km), Callisto was about the size of Mercury. The craters on this outermost sub-planet did not exceed 95 miles (150km) in diameter, and none seen by the Voyagers was deep. Callisto's density of 1·8g/cm³ indicated that much of the surface was ice which did not retain impact scars long.

In addition to the shallow basin dubbed "Valhalla", a second basin was later detected and named Asgard. No mountains were seen. Tectonically, Callisto seemed dead.

Above: *A model of the Galileo Jupiter probe undergoes vibration testing. In the late 1980s, it will penetrate Jupiter's atmosphere. The complete orbiter and probe craft is shown below.*

At the beginning of the Voyager mission, 13 satellites were known in the Jovian system, the 13th having been discovered in the Pioneer photos. The Voyagers found three more, bringing the total to 16. Three small satellites, Adrastea, Amalthea and one known only as 1979 J2 orbit Jupiter between the cloud tops and Io. Beyond Callisto are Leda, Himalia, Lysithea, Elara, Ananke, Carme, Pasiphae and Sinope. A 16th satellite was discovered in the photographs in 1980.

Project Galileo

The successor to the Pioneer-Voyager missions to Jupiter is Project Galileo, targetted to reach the Jovian system in 1988. The dual spacecraft, with a launch weight of 5,147lb (2,355kg), consists of an orbiter and an atmosphere probe.

As of late 1983, Galileo was scheduled to be lifted to low Earth orbit in late May or early June 1986 by the Space Shuttle *Challenger* and boosted to Jupiter by a Centaur second stage rocket. Centaur was substituted for the less powerful Inertial Upper State booster late in 1982 and is expected to reduce flight time from four years to two. (Use of the IUS would require gravity assist from Earth. IUS would put Galileo into a highly elliptical orbit that would bring it back in two years to within 124 miles (200km) of Earth, on a course enabling the spacecraft to gain enough energy from the Earth's gravitational field to reach the Jovian system in 1990.)

About 150 days before Jupiter encounter, the 738lb (335kg) probe will separate from the orbiter and fall into the Jovian atmosphere. After entry, the spherical descent module will jettison its aeroshell and heat shell and deploy a parachute system to slow descent.

Descent module instruments will measure the structure and composition of the Jovian atmosphere and clouds, the vertical distribution of solar energy, the abundance of helium, planetary heat and radio frequency emissions, the flux of energetic particles and lightning strokes. The probe is expected to endure descent for an hour before it is crushed by increasing pressure. During that time, instrument data will be radioed to the orbiter for transmission to Earth.

The orbiter will fire its retrorocket engine to fall into orbit around Jupiter. The orbit, a huge ellipse ranging from 124,280 to 9·3 million miles (200,000 to 15 million km), is intended to allow the orbiter to make 11 orbits in 20 months on trajectories passing close to major satellites. The orbiter will carry a solid state camera system, infra-red and ultraviolet spectrometers, a photopolarimeter, a magnetometer and detectors for plasma, energetic particles and dust.

Galileo is the only United States mission to the outer Solar System planned for the remainder of the 1980s.

storms welling up from deep within the atmosphere. The colour spots in the rings (right) are an artifact of the image processing.

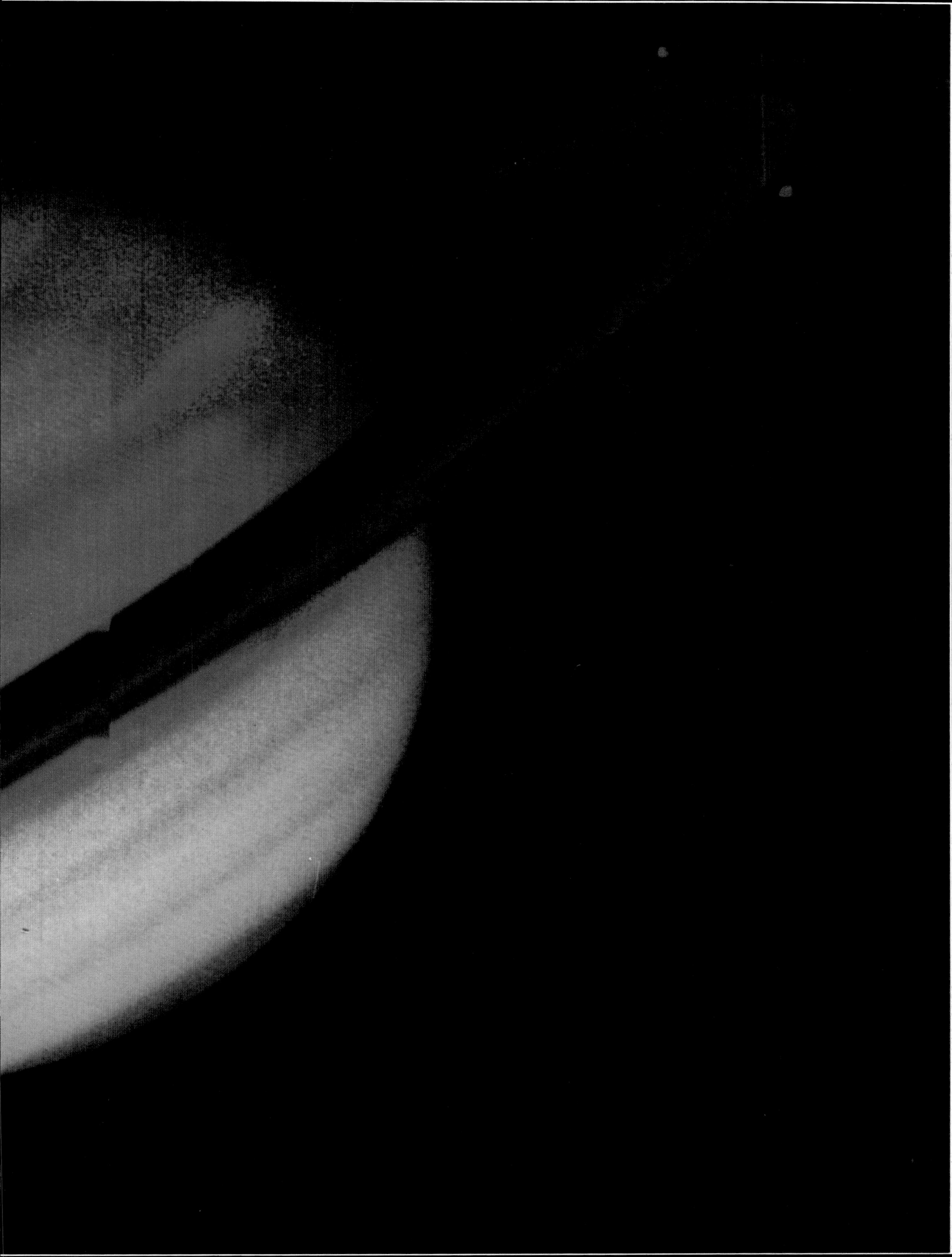

Saturn

Like Jupiter, Saturn with its retinue of 18 moons (as of 1982) emits more heat from its interior than it receives from the Sun.

The first six of its 9 major moons[5] which have been observed by Earth-based telescopes increase in size with distance from the planet. The increase is gradual except for the Mercury-sized moon, Titan, which is more than three times the diameter of the next largest moon, Rhea. Since the beginning of 1980, nine additional moons, all minor ones, have been identified in the Saturn system from both ground-based and spacecraft observations, bringing the total in the system to 18.

In Roman mythology, Saturnus was the god of agriculture. Saturn has not been imbued with the minatory, amorous or mischievous attributes of other celestial bodies. Until its spectacular rings were resolved as separate structures by a Dutch astronomer, Christiaan Huygens (1629–1695) in 1659, it seemed to be a distant companion of Jupiter. Looking at Saturn through his 8-power telescope in 1610, Galileo believed he was seeing three close stars.

The rings were considered solid discs until 1895 when astronomers concluded that they must consist of small, unconsolidated pieces. Solid rings could not exist so close to a great mass without breaking up. Until recently, Saturn was supposed to be the only ringed planet in the Solar System, a phenomenon that fascinated students of planetary evolution. However, in 1977, five rings were discovered around Uranus[6] and in 1979 Voyager 1 identified two rings around Jupiter. Instead of being unique, rings turned out to be a characteristic of the outer planets, representing, it was surmised, partially consolidated matter left over from their accretion.

Saturn is unique, however, as the only planet in the commonwealth lighter than water. Its density was calculated at 0·7g/cm³. Like Jupiter, a large part of Saturn's mass is liquid hydrogen.

The second largest planet in the Solar System, Saturn has a volume 815 times that of Earth, but its mass is only 95·2 times Earth's mass. Its rapid rotation, 10 hours 14 minutes at the equator, has resulted in considerable polar flattening, so that its polar radius, 33,555 miles (54,000km), is 3,933 miles (6,330km) less than its equatorial radius, 37,488 miles (60,330km). Saturn wheels around the Sun every 29·46 Earth years. During its revolution, Saturn's orbit is perturbed by Jupiter so that the orbit varies from 9 to 10·9 AU. Twice as far from the Sun as is Jupiter, Saturn is much colder. It receives (as previously noted) about 1 per cent of the heat that Earth gets.

---

5 The nine moons in order of distance from Saturn are Mimas, Enceladus, Tethys, Dione, Rhea, Titan, Hyperion, Iapetus and Phoebe.
6 The discovery was made by Cornell University researchers flying 40,350ft (12,300m) over the Indian Ocean in a NASA observation aircraft. The researchers, James Elliot, Edward Dunham and Douglas Mink, sighted the rings of Uranus on 10 March 1977 as they were observing the temporary disappearance of a faint star behind Uranus. Independent observations in Australia and South Africa confirmed them.

SATURN: BASIC DATA	
Equatorial Diameter*	9·46E; 74,977 miles (120,660km)
Mass*	95·2E
Density	0·40oz/in³ (0·7g/cm³)
Volume*	815E
Surface Gravity*	1·13E
Escape Velocity	21·75 miles/sec (35km/sec)
Period of Rotation	10hr 14min
Inclination of Equator (to Orbit)	27°
Distance from Sun (Semi-major axis)	9·5388AU; 886·7 x 10⁶miles (1,427 x 10⁶km)
Siderial Period	29·46 tropical years
Synodic Period	378·09 days
Orbital Speed	6·03 miles/sec (9·7km/sec)
Orbital Eccentricity	0·056
Inclination of Orbit (to ecliptic plane)	2·49°
Number of Satellites	18
*Earth=1	

Right: *Saturn with two of its moons, Tethys (above) and Dione, photographed by Voyager 1 from 8 million miles (13 million km). The shadows of Saturn's rings can be seen on the planet.*

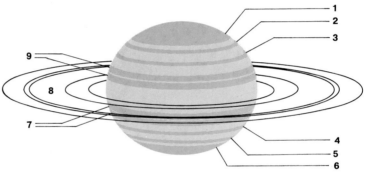

Major Features of Saturn
1 North Polar Region.
2 North North Temperate Belt.
3 North Temperate Belt.
4 South Temperate Belt.
5 South South Temperate Belt.
6 South Polar Region.
7 South Equatorial Belt.
8 Ring system.
9 North Equatorial Belt.

Saturn's highly-flattened disc shares the same banded structure as Jupiter. However, the bands are not as obvious, as they form lower in Saturn's colder atmosphere.

Like Jupiter, the surface of Saturn appears to be the top deck of clouds. It is a multi-layered ball of hydrogen and helium, again like Jupiter and the Sun. It is supposed to have a compressed, rocky core about twice the size of the Earth but 15 to 20 times Earth's mass. The rocky cores of the two giant planets are considered the kernels about which lighter elements accreted as they were blown outward in the nebula by winds and radiant energy from the Sun.

The Rings

Saturn's rings have been identified alphabetically in several sequences of discovery. Those discovered by Earth-based telescopes are designated in order of greatest distance from the planet.

The outer ring, as seen from Earth, was called the "A" ring. Between it and a middle "B" ring was a gap, the "Cassini Division", so named after its discoverer, Giovanni Domenico Cassini (1625–1712), director of the Paris Observatory. A third ring, the "Crepe" or "C" ring, orbited nearer Saturn. These were fairly bright rings, visible to observers using small telescopes. More powerful instruments located a "D" ring between the "C" ring and the clouds. The "A" ring was found to be divided by a gap, called "Encke's Division". It was noticed in 1837 by Johann Franz Encke (1791–1865) at the Berlin Observatory. Later, an "E" ring was sighted farther out than the "A" ring.

Two more rings, "F" and "G", were discovered by Pioneer 11 between the "A" and "E" rings. The seven rings of Saturn are detailed in the accompanying table.

Pioneer at Saturn

Hurled across the Solar System by Jupiter's gravity assist, Pioneer 11 reached the Saturn system in late August 1979, passing through the outermost E ring. Ames controllers made two course corrections in 1975 and 1976 to put the spacecraft on the desired trajectory. Final targeting was completed in 1978.

Pioneer's closest approach was 13,300 miles (21,400km) above the clouds on 1 September 1979. As it moved at a velocity of

Saturn's Atmosphere
1 Clear upper atmosphere (primarily hydrogen/helium).
2 Very thin dust particles.
3 Very thin ammonia haze.
4 Ammonia ice clouds.
5 Clear atmosphere (primarily hydrogen/helium).
6 Ammonium hydrosulphide ice clouds.
7 Water ice clouds.
8 Water-ammonia solution clouds.
9 Clear atmosphere (primarily hydrogen/helium).

Because of Saturn's weaker gravity, its atmosphere is more extensive than that of Jupiter. The clouds condense only deep down, where it is sufficiently warm, and they are overlaid by layers of haze which mask its features.

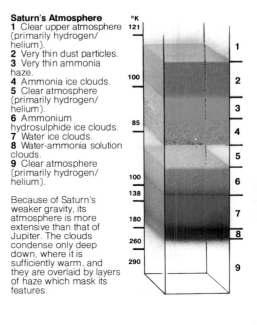

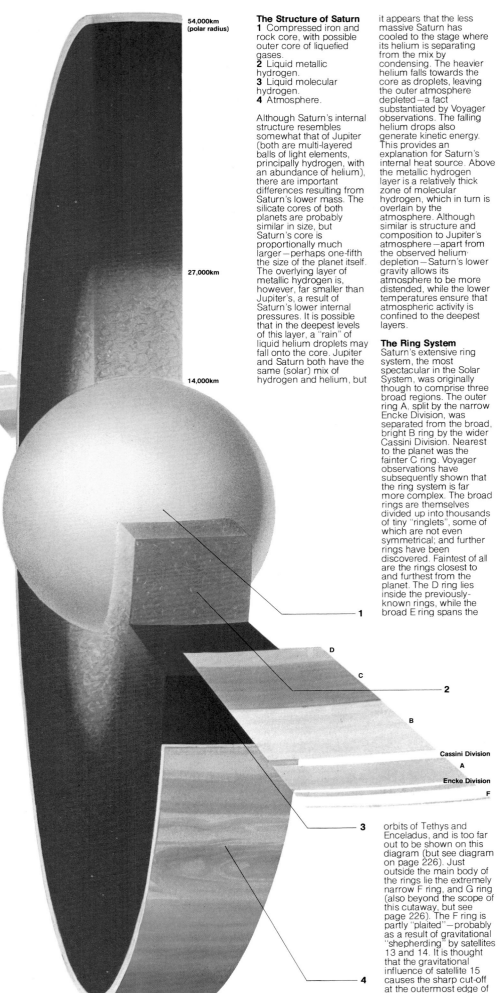

The Structure of Saturn
1 Compressed iron and rock core, with possible outer core of liquefied gases.
2 Liquid metallic hydrogen.
3 Liquid molecular hydrogen.
4 Atmosphere.

Although Saturn's internal structure resembles somewhat that of Jupiter (both are multi-layered balls of light elements, principally hydrogen, with an abundance of helium), there are important differences resulting from Saturn's lower mass. The silicate cores of both planets are probably similar in size, but Saturn's core is proportionally much larger—perhaps one-fifth the size of the planet itself. The overlying layer of metallic hydrogen is, however, far smaller than Jupiter's, a result of Saturn's lower internal pressures. It is possible that in the deepest levels of this layer, a "rain" of liquid helium droplets may fall onto the core. Jupiter and Saturn both have the same (solar) mix of hydrogen and helium, but

it appears that the less massive Saturn has cooled to the stage where its helium is separating from the mix by condensing. The heavier helium falls towards the core as droplets, leaving the outer atmosphere depleted—a fact substantiated by Voyager observations. The falling helium drops also generate kinetic energy. This provides an explanation for Saturn's internal heat source. Above the metallic hydrogen layer is a relatively thick zone of molecular hydrogen, which in turn is overlain by the atmosphere. Although similar is structure and composition to Jupiter's atmosphere—apart from the observed helium depletion—Saturn's lower gravity allows its atmosphere to be more distended, while the lower temperatures ensure that atmospheric activity is confined to the deepest layers.

The Ring System
Saturn's extensive ring system, the most spectacular in the Solar System, was originally though to comprise three broad regions. The outer ring A, split by the narrow Encke Division, was separated from the broad, bright B ring by the wider Cassini Division. Nearest to the planet was the fainter C ring. Voyager observations have subsequently shown that the ring system is far more complex. The broad rings are themselves divided up into thousands of tiny "ringlets", some of which are not even symmetrical; and further rings have been discovered. Faintest of all are the rings closest to and furthest from the planet. The D ring lies inside the previously-known rings, while the broad E ring spans the

orbits of Tethys and Enceladus, and is too far out to be shown on this diagram (but see diagram on page 226). Just outside the main body of the rings lie the extremely narrow F ring, and G ring (also beyond the scope of this cutaway, but see page 226). The F ring is partly "plaited"—probably as a result of gravitational "shepherding" by satellites 13 and 14. It is thought that the gravitational influence of satellite 15 causes the sharp cut-off at the outermost edge of the A ring.

SATURN RING DATA		
FEATURE	**DISTANCE FROM CENTRE** miles (km)	**NOTES**
Equatorial radius	37,488 (60,330)	Near 100 millibar level
D-ring inner edge	41,630 (67,000)	Seen only in forward-scattering light
C-ring inner edge	45,500 (73,200)	
B-ring inner edge	57,300 (92,200)	
B-ring outer edge	73,000 (117,500)	Inner edge of Cassini Division
A-ring inner edge	75,200 (121,000)	Outer edge of Cassini Division
Encke Division	83,000 (133,500)	About 124 miles (200km) wide
A-ring outer edge	84,600 (136,200)	
F-ring	87,400 (140,600)	About 62 miles (100km) wide; three components; eccentric
G-ring	105,600 (170,000)	Seen only in forward-scattering light
E-ring inner edge	130,500 (210,000)	
E-ring outer edge	186,400 (300,000)	

Note: The exact level of Saturn's cloud tops is not known, but is believed to be deeper than the 100 millibar level, the planet's equatorial radius. The top layers of Saturn's clouds are assumed to be 39,350 miles (63,330km) from the centre of the planet.

70,900mph (114,100km/h), the imaging photo-polarimeter scanned the surface with the spacecraft's spin at the rate of 7·8 times a minute. The first detailed images of Saturn, its rings and its big moon, Titan, were radioed to Earth 85 light minutes distant.

Pioneer's instruments found a magnetic field and consequent zones of trapped radiation. Like the radiation belts of Jupiter, the Saturn belts emitted radio energy. The infra-red sensor found that Saturn was radiating 2·5 times more heat than it was receiving from far off Sol. Photometer readings of the moons Iapetus, Rhea, Dione and Tethys indicated their composition of ice and rock.

The "F" and "G" rings were discovered as the spacecraft passed below the ring plane. Pioneer trajectory data during its passage of Saturn indicated a new mass determination for the planet. It suggested a central core of heavy elements, probably a predominance of iron; an outer core of compressed, lique-fied gases, including methane, ammonia and water, and the bulk of the planet, hydrogen and helium. Deep within this mass, the hydrogen was believed to be in a liquid metallic state under pressure. Nearer the surface, it assumed a liquid molecular state and above that, it became atmosphere.

These suppositions, based on the mass determinations, led to a hypothesis that electrical currents were generated in the shell of metallic hydrogen by the dynamo effect of Saturn's fast rotation, producing an extensive magnetic field. Magnetometer measurements of the field showed that it was not as powerful as Jupiter's. At the cloud tops, it seemed to be weaker than Earth's field at the surface. Nevertheless, it was strong enough to produce a magneto-sphere which, like that of Jupiter and Earth, created a huge "bubble" in the solar wind, or heliosphere. Saturn's bubble was like Jupiter's, expanding and contracting with changes in solar wind intensity.

Pioneer data showed that the "G" ring consisted of diffuse particles. Orbiting near it was a new satellite, one of 9 that were to be found in the complex Saturnian system as the Voyagers followed.

Pioneer's infra-red instrument logged an average surface temperature on Saturn of −173°C. The rings were colder, about −200°C, indicating they were mostly ice.

Flying behind the planet, Pioneer transmitted radio signals through the upper atmosphere. They revealed the presence of an extensive ionosphere. The ultraviolet spectrometer detected a cloud of hydrogen around the rings, presumably emanating from them. On its departure path, the spacecraft's imaging photopolarimeter obtained a fuzzy image of Saturn's large moon, Titan. This was recorded at the limit of the IPP's resolution; more detailed investigation was left to the Voyagers. Pioneer 11 retreated from the ringed planet at the end of September to become a wanderer in the interstellar continuum like Pioneer 10. Behind it, the Voyagers were coming up fast.

Voyager 1

Voyager 1 arrived a year later. It began photographing Saturn on 22 August 1980 at a range of 66·7 million miles (109 million km), making its closest approach 78,300 miles (126,000km) from the cloud tops on 12 November 1980. By the time the encounter sequence ended on 15 December 1980, Voyager 1 had transmitted 17,500 pictures back to JPL and millions of bits of data.

The narrow- and wide-angle cameras saw an atmosphere similar to Jupiter's. There were alternating light and dark belts, circulating storm regions which appeared as whitish ovals, remarkably like the white ovals of Jupiter. Saturn's marking was dimmed by a layer of thick haze over the cloud tops. A haze had been observed at Jupiter also, but there it was considerably thinner.

By measuring the motion of cloud patterns and markings, the imaging team could estimate wind speeds. They were high. East winds blew at 1,100mph (1,770km/h) at the equator, but wind velocity dropped off with increasing latitude to nearly zero at 40 degrees north and south. Saturn's equatorial winds were four times stronger than those at Jupiter.

The helium content of the predominantly hydrogen atmosphere was calculated at 11 per cent, lower than the percentage of helium at Jupiter. Auroras were seen at the limbs of the planet. In ultraviolet light, an auroral ring circling the entire planet appeared at 80 degrees south latitude.

Radio noise betrayed the presence of lightning, but flashes were not seen. In addition to Earth, lightning had been detected at Jupiter and Venus. It seemed to be a characteristic effect of planetary atmospheres. On Venus, thunder had been heard by a Russian probe.

The classical "A", "B" and "C" rings were found to consist of hundreds of ringlets, some circular, others elliptical in shape. Even the gaps between the rings showed ringlets. Five were seen in the Cassini Division. Pioneer's "F" ring actually consisted of three separate ringlets, intertwined in the high resolution Voyager's pictures. The inner and outer edges of the rings were accompanied by two small satellites, one on each side. One was 125 miles (200km) and the other 137 miles (220km) in diameter. The JPL

PRINCIPAL SATELLITES OF SATURN (1982)			
NAME	DIAMETER miles (km)	DISTANCE FROM PLANET miles (km)	PERIOD (days)
Mimas	244 (392)	115,300 (185,600)	0·942
Enceladus	310 (500)	147,900 (238,040)	1·370
Tethys	659 (1,060)	183,100 (294,670)	1·888
Dione	696 (1,120)	234,500 (377,420)	2·737
Rhea	951 (1,530)	327,500 (527,100)	4·518
Titan	3,194 (5,140)	759,250 (1,221,860)	15·945
Hyperion	255 x 162 x 137 (410 x 260 x 220)	920,300 (1,481,000)	21·276
Iapetus	907 (1,460)	2,212,600 (3,560,800)	79·33
Phoebe*	137 (220)	8,049,000 (12,954,000)	550·45
*Phoebe's motion is retrograde			
Note: The orbital periods are expressed in Earth days.			

staff characterized them as "shepherd satellites" as though the small moons were tending the ring.

A third satellite, 18·6 miles (30km) in diameter, was discovered near the outer edge of the "A" ring; a fourth and fifth, 56 by 25 miles (90 by 40km) and 62 by 56 miles (100 by 90km) respectively, were found sharing an orbit 56,620 miles (91,120km) from the cloud tops; a sixth with a diameter of 100 miles (160km) was seen in the orbit of the moon, Dione, moving about 60 degrees ahead of it.

Radio waves beamed through the "E" and "F" rings showed that they consist of myriads of tiny particles, but the "C" ring was made up of larger ones, in the range of 6·6ft (2m), while "A" ring particles were 26·2ft to 32·8ft (8 to 10m) in size.

Six of Saturn's minor moons were photographed by Voyager 1 as it approached the ringed planet. Two of them, designated as 1980 S1 and 1980 S3, had been detected by ground-based observation earlier in 1980. The Voyager 1 cameras picked them up about 75 days before the spacecraft encountered Saturn. The two moons appeared to share the same orbit around the planet.

On the basis of Voyager 1 data and ground-based observations, Jet Propulsion Laboratory scientists concluded that these two co-orbiting satellites initially had been identified as a single satellite called Janus in 1966. In its 1981 listing of the satellites of Saturn, JPL eliminated Janus from the table.

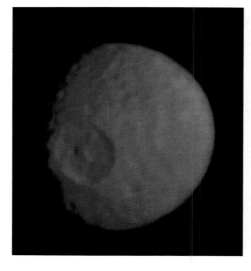

Above: *The appearance of Saturn's icy moon Mimas is dominated by a 60-mile (100km) diameter crater, one-quarter the size of Mimas itself. The impact which caused it almost shattered the moon, as cracks on the far side indicate.*

Above: *Voyager 1 view of Enceladus, Saturn's brightest and palest-coloured moon. Voyager 2 flew much closer, within 56,000 miles (90,000km), revealing that the 310-mile (500km) diameter satellite showed signs of an active interior. The surface is crossed by grooves and faults.*

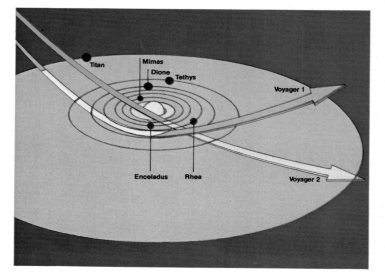

Saturn Encounters
Illustrated here are the different trajectories flown by Voyagers 1 and 2 past Saturn (closest encounters were 12 November 1980 and 25 August 1981 respectively). The angle of Voyager 2's approach and better illumination resulted in improved imaging of the dynamic ring system. A massive computer reprogramming effort after Voyager 1 altered the trajectory of the second to probe to allow for this closer examination. The trajectories were chosen to complement one another, so that satellites seen poorly by Voyager 1 would be photographed in more detail by Voyager 2, which was then diverted towards Uranus.

Above: *Tethys, photographed here by Voyager 1 from 354,000 miles (570,000km), is a little smaller than Dione, but shares the same icy composition. The surface is heavily cratered. Cracks and valleys cover other parts of the surface.*

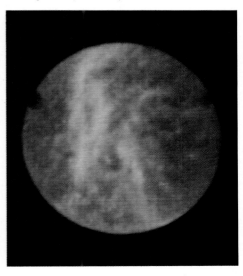

Above: *Like Dione, the trailing hemisphere of Saturn's 951-mile (1,530km) diameter moon Rhea has wispy markings superimposed on a heavily-cratered terrain. This Voyager 1 view has been colour-enhanced to bring out the contrast. The resolution is about 20 miles (32km).*

Above: *This Voyager 1 photomosaic of the 696-mile (1,120km) diameter moon Dione shows an icy surface pitted heavily with craters, some 60 miles (100km) across. Cracks are caused by faults in the ice.*

However, the name, Janus, the Roman god of beginnings, of gates and of the Universe, may be restored by the International Astronomical Union to the larger of the co-orbiting moons, 1980 S1, although it is only two-thirds the supposed size of the "original" Janus and is not the innermost satellite of Saturn as the original was thought to be.

On the arrival leg of the encounter, Voyager 1 photographed spoke-like features radiating outward across the B-ring. They appeared as a portion of the ring emerged from Saturn's shadow and dissipated in a few hours in sunlight. The spokes seemed to consist of small particles, judging from their scattered light.

Voyager 1 observed all of Saturn's larger satellites except Phoebe which, judging from its retrograde orbital motion, is probably a captured asteroid. Mimas, Enceladus, Tethys, Dione and Rhea were spherical bodies composed mostly of water ice. Tethys appeared to be pure ice. The density of Dione indicated 40 per cent rock.

The satellite diameters were measured as follows: Mimas, 244 miles (392km); Enceladus, 310 (500); Tethys, 659 (1,060); Dione, 696 (1,120); Rhea, 951 (1,530) and Titan, 3,194 (5,140). The Voyager 1 measurement of Titan reduced its supposed diameter about 10 per cent and it thus had to yield pride of place as the Solar System's largest moon to Jupiter's Ganymede, it now being second largest.

Mimas, Tethys, Dione and Rhea were heavily cratered, but Enceladus appeared smooth. One huge crater on Mimas covered one third of its diameter. Across Tethys stretched a valley 465 miles (750km) long and 37 miles (60km) wide, apparently a fracture of the crust. Sinuous, branching valleys were observed on Dione amid expanses of smooth plains.

Titan's atmosphere was mainly nitrogen — the gas that makes up 78 per cent of Earth's atmosphere — and, surprisingly, it was 60 per cent denser than Earth's, a phenomenon that made the planet-sized moon unique. Although larger than Mercury, Titan's density of 1·92g/cm³ was less than one-half that of Mercury and only two-thirds that of the Earth's Moon. Surface temperature was calculated at −180°C. This value intrigued planetary scientists because it is near the triple point of an

abundant gas on Titan, methane, just as Earth's average temperature is near the triple point of water. At the triple point, slight variation in temperature could change the state of methane on Titan from a gas to a liquid and from a liquid to a solid.

This circumstance suggested that methane on Titan is the counterpart of water on Earth. Rivers of liquid methane might be imagined flowing into a methane sea, under methane clouds in a nitrogen sky. In this far, cold world, methane snow might be falling at the higher latitudes on methane glaciers, while in slightly warmer regions, methane rain might fall. It was tempting to build an analogue of Earth on this dim, small world, illuminated by the great disc of Saturn and its icy rings as well as by the faraway Sun.

Voyager 1 detected a hydrogen cloud around Saturn and atoms of hydrogen and oxygen were detected in the region from Tethys to Titan.

In mid-December 1980, Voyager 1 departed the Saturnian system and on 19 December, its scan platform instruments—the cameras and spectrometers—were turned off. Voyager 1 was then committed with the Pioneers to interstellar space.

Throughout the historic journey, Voyager 1 had functioned with only one potentially crippling problem. The scan platform on which the remote-sensing instruments were mounted became jammed in February 1978 during a calibration test. Designed to move in both azimuth and elevation, the platform became stuck in azimuth. This prevented accurate pointing of the wide and narrow angle television cameras, the infra-red interferometer-spectrometer and radiometer, the ultraviolet spectrometer and the photopolarimeter. Voyager engineers believed that the azimuth gears were being blocked by bits of debris, probably left over from pre-launch processing. After three months of attempting to slew the platform back and forth, the engineers succeeded in crushing the debris and freeing the gears so that the platform worked properly.

Voyager 2

Functioning adequately despite one wholly disabled radio receiver and a partly disabled back-up, Voyager 2 arrived at Saturn in the summer of 1981. It made its closest approach on 26 August at a distance of 62,760 miles (101,000km) from the cloud tops. It, too, developed a scan problem.

The scan platform jamming on Voyager 1 was repeated on Voyager 2 110 minutes after its closest approach to Saturn. As Voyager 2 emerged from Saturn's shadow, controllers at JPL discovered to their dismay that the platform was stuck at 260 degrees in azimuth and 20 degrees in elevation. The problem had developed during a period when Voyager 2 was out of communication with Earth.

Controllers managed to work around the malfunction by slewing the entire spacecraft so that crucial photographs could be taken, but this emergency procedure used precious fuel which was needed for the continuing mission to Uranus. After more than 67 hours of testing, the scan platform began to respond to ground commands and shortly thereafter it was returned to the control of the onboard computer.

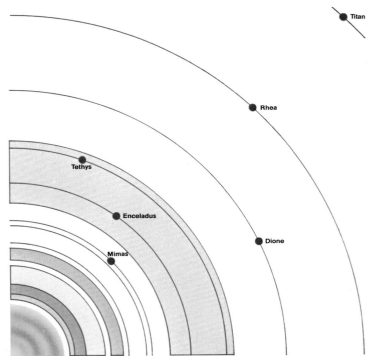

Satellite Orbit Locations
The Voyagers discovered that Saturn has many more rings and satellites than expected. Here, the locations of the major moons are compared to the extent of the ring system. The sharp edge of the A ring is thought to be gravitationally confined by a tiny moon 1980S28 (S15). The extremely narrow F ring is shepherded on each side by the moonlets 1980S27 and 1980S26 (S14 and S13). Between F and G rings are two satellites which share the same orbit, the co-orbital moons 1980S1 and 1980S3. These are probably two parts of the same body split up by an impact. Further out lie the narrow G ring and the first of Saturn's major moons, Mimas. The next two major moons Enceladus and Tethys actually orbit within the broad, faint E ring. Tethys shares its orbit with two small moonlets, and Dione with one (Dione B), which lies in a gravitationally stable position. Rhea and Titan lie beyond.

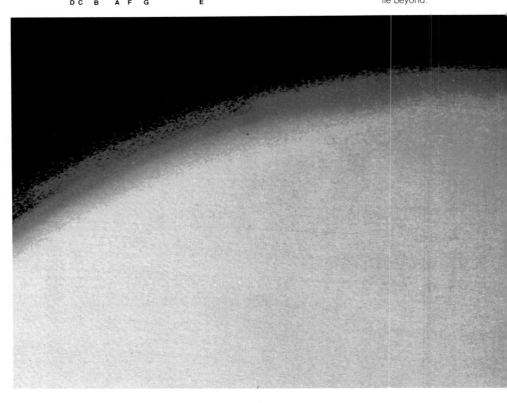

Although most of the observation programme at Saturn had been accomplished before the platform jammed, some of it was lost. Observations of Enceladus were not completed. Close-up images of Tethys and observations of the dark side of the rings were missed. In addition, infra-red measurements of ring material as Voyager 2 entered Saturn's shadow and some ultraviolet spectroscopy data were lost.

Despite the platform problem, however, the imaging and remote-sensing instruments completed most of the observatory phase of the mission. After it was returned to working order, the platform continued to operate properly and controllers expressed confidence that it would continue to do so for the Uranus encounter. Voyager 2 transmitted

Above: *Thick haze layers on Saturn's largest moon, Titan—colour enhanced in this Voyager 1 image—reach to 310 miles (500km) above its surface. They may contain organic molecules.*

more than 18,500 pictures of Saturn and its moons. The photographic return of both Voyagers at Jupiter and Saturn is estimated at more than 70,000 pictures.

Scientific Returns

Voyager 2 made a detailed study of Saturn's atmosphere which disclosed remarkable similarities with the atmosphere of Jupiter. Long-lived oval features resembled the white ovals on Jupiter. On both planets, these features represented anticyclone systems.

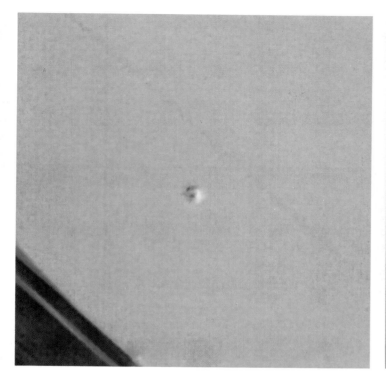

One of the Saturnian ovals measured 4,000 by 3,000 miles (6,440 by 4,830km). Wind velocity in it appeared to be 223mph (100 metres/sec).

As on Jupiter, high speed jet streams were detected on Saturn. Their direction of flow alternated from east to west in the higher latitudes. The jet streams appeared to be energized by small-scale eddies in the Saturnian atmosphere, as on Jupiter. A dominant easterly jet stream indicated that the winds on Saturn are not confined to the clouds but extend deep into the atmosphere. Like Jupiter also, Saturn displayed intermittent plumes of convective clouds.

Passing behind Saturn, the Voyager 2 radio beam probed regions of the atmosphere near 36·5 degrees north latitude and 31 degrees south latitude, supplementing polar and equatorial scans by Voyager 1. Atmospheric temperatures were calculated as ranging from −191°C at a high altitude (70 millibars) to −130°C at a lower level (1·2 bars or 1·2 Earth atmospheres). At the 100 millibar level (0·1 Earth atmospheres), infrared measurements showed that temperatures in the north polar region were 10°C colder than mid-latitude temperatures at the same pressure level. The Voyager science team suggested that this was a seasonal effect.

At high latitudes, above 65 degrees, ultraviolet radiation absorbing gases were detected in the upper atmosphere on Saturn, as they had been detected on Jupiter. The science team surmised that the absorbing material consisted of hydrocarbon molecules formed by auroral activity in the polar regions and convected by the wind systems toward toward the equator. ultraviolet radition emitted by the aurora indicated that it occurs within 12 degrees of the pole. The science team speculated that the aurora was the product of the precipitation of energetic particles into the high atmosphere.[7]

---

7 Stone, E.C. and Miner, E.D., "Voyager 2 Encounter with the Saturnian System", *Science*, Vol. 215, No. 4532, 29 Jan 1982.

Above: *Voyager 2 colour image of the F ring and its inner shepherding satellite, 1980S27 (S 14), seen against Saturn's disc. The A ring, with the Encke Division, is in the lower left-hand corner.*

Above: *Voyager 2's photopolarimeter observations of the occultation of a star by the rings, with subsequent computer processing, produced this image of the Encke division with its central ringlet.*

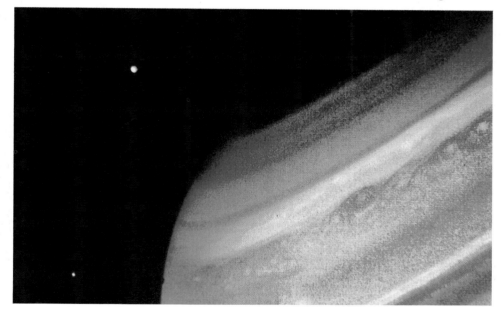

Above: *A short-wavelength composite image of Saturn's northern hemisphere reveals complex weather patterns normally hidden by haze. The large spot is 1,864 miles (3,000km) across.*

Voyager 2's photopolarimeter was able to measure ring thickness to some extent by observing light from the star Delta Scorpii shining through the rings. A few gaps were seen in the rings and where the gaps appeared, the ring thickness appeared to be 660ft (200m) at the edge.

The B-ring exhibited an elliptical shape, with a difference of about 86·7 miles (140km) in its semi-major and semi-minor axes. The F-ring was seen in Voyager 2 photos to consist of one bright strand and four fainter ones, each 43·4 to 62·1 miles (70 to 100km) across. The strands did not appear to be braided nor intertwined (as earlier reported from Voyager 1 data) and the strands were no longer characterized as separate "ringlets" after their structure was examined in the Voyager 2 images.

From observation of Delta Scorpii starlight shining through the F ring, the photopolarimeter revealed that the brightest strand was subdivided into a number of narrower strands, each about 1·8 miles (3km) wide. Clumps of matter could be seen in the F ring at fairly uniform intervals of 5,595 miles (9,000km).

Voyager 2 provided new data on the mysterious "spokes" which had been seen between the outer edge of the B ring and

1·72 Saturn radii (64,448 miles, 103,716km) from the planet's centre. The spokes were identified as clouds of micrometre-sized particles. Some were narrow and radiated outward like spokes in a wheel. These were judged to have been more recently formed than wide, less radially oriented spokes which appeared to be remnants of earlier "epochs" of spoke formation, the science team report. The recent spokes were seen to be co-rotating with Saturn's magnetic field.

From the observations of Pioneer 11 to Voyager 1, and thence to Voyager 2, the ring configurations and structures appeared progressively more elaborate. The rings of Saturn were more than a spectacle; understanding how they formed and how they changed has been considered of fundamental importance to theories of the origin and evolution of planets and of planetary systems.

Voyager 2 returned data on all of Saturn's known satellites, which at the beginning of 1983 number 18, including a rather dim companion of Mimas. There are indications in the photographic and charged particle data that additional satellites may be found.

New information on the masses of two of Saturn's major moons, Iapetus and Tethys, was derived from tracking Voyager as it passed through the system. The science team reported that revised mass data for these moons and also for Mimas showed a tendency among the major ones toward decreasing density with increasing radial distance from Saturn, except for Titan. A similar density scale is exhibited by the Galilean satellites of Jupiter and by the planets of the Solar System, except for Uranus and Neptune.

Generalizing further, the science team noted that the brighter satellites appear to be more highly evolved than the darker ones which seem to be primitive and often irregularly shaped. The brighter surfaces of the more evolved moons, such as Tethys and Enceladus, may be the result of internal activity which produced areas of high reflectivity on the surface.

Phoebe, the outermost Saturnian satellite, has retrograde orbital motion, like the four outer Jovian satellites (Sinope, Pasiphae, Carme and Ananke) and, like them, may be a captured asteroid. If it is, it would be the first asteroid beyond Mars to be photographed by spacecraft. (The moons of Mars, Phobos and Deimos, photographed by Viking orbiters in 1976, are suspected asteroids also.) Voyager 2 images showed that Phoebe is generally spherical, about 137 miles (220km) in diameter, spinning on its axis every 9 hours.

In Voyager 2 photographs, Iapetus exhibited the greatest range of reflectivity (albedo) of any other body in the Solar System, according to the science report. Its bright areas reflected 50 per cent of the sunlight. Dark material was concentrated on the leading hemisphere of Iapetus as it moved around the planet and was probably swept up by the moon. The trailing hemisphere was cratered. Crater floors appeared dark, indicating that the craters had been filled with dark material, possibly lava, like lunar craters.

Hyperion displayed evidence of heavy bombardment by meteorites and asteroids. Its cratering and irregular shape rule out

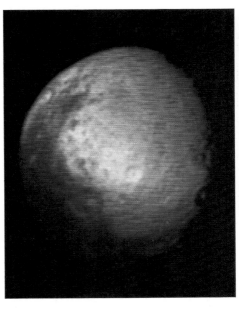

Above: *Saturn's two-tone moon Iapetus, photographed by Voyager 2, showing most of its icy trailing hemisphere, which is over ten times as bright as the dark leading hemisphere. Craters are evident.*

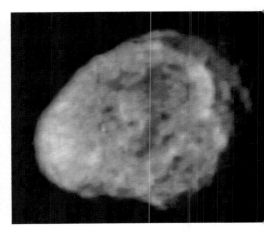

Above: *Voyager 2 close-up of Hyperion from 300,000 miles (500,000km). The moon is heavily cratered and—unexpectedly for a body this large—highly irregular. It seems to be composed of water ice.*

Below: *The surface of Enceladus, seen here in a Voyager 2 close-up, resembles Jupiter's moon Ganymede, but is 10 times smaller. The smoothed over regions show signs of recent geological activity.*

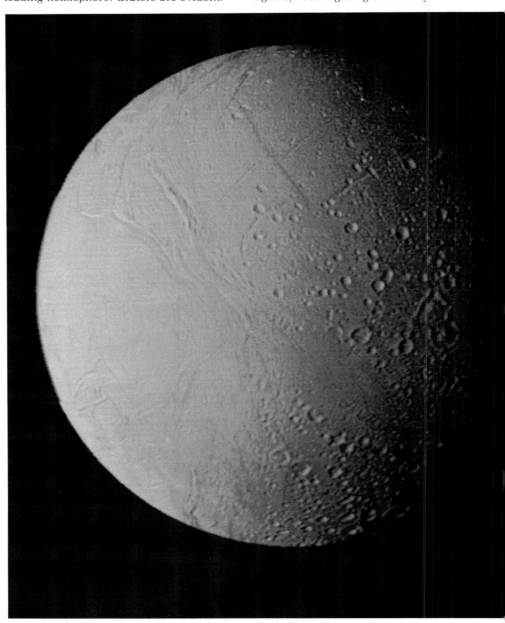

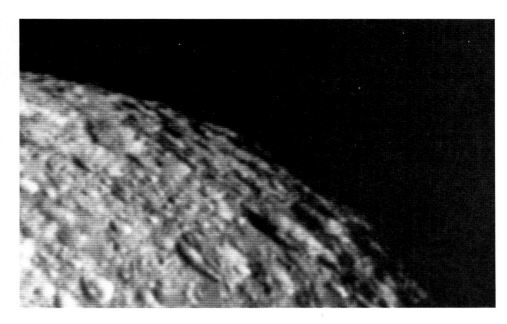

Above: *The trenched and cratered surface of Tethys: regrettably only one high resolution frame of the moon was obtained as a result of Voyager 2's scan platform jamming shortly after closest encounter.*

Below: *A farewell to Saturn from the receding Voyager 2 as it looked back at the dark underside of the rings and their shadow against the brilliant globe. Next target: Uranus, 24 January 1986.*

Saturn's planet-sized moon, Titan, was scanned more remotely by Voyager 2, the report said. There was no measurable change in the haze layer which extended to an altitude of 114 miles (183km) in the north and 145 miles (233km) in the south in Voyager 1 and 2 data. The lack of change was interpreted by some observers as indicating a large, seasonal lag in atmospheric turnover on Titan, a manifestation of a massive atmosphere. A thinner haze lay above the main one at 195 miles (314km).

Titan's atmosphere was found to be the source of a ring of neutral hydrogen atoms around Saturn between 8 and 25 radii or 299,910 miles (482,640km) and 937,210 miles (1,508,250km). At a mean density of 20 hydrogen atoms per cubic centimetre, it was calculated that 10^{27} atoms per second would be required to supply the ring from Titan's atmosphere assuming a neutral hydrogen lifetime (against ionization) of about 10^8 seconds (3·17 years).

Not to be outdone by Jupiter, Saturn, also, was broadcasting radio signals. The emission source was its magnetosphere. The science team noted that recurring radio emissions discovered by Voyager 1 indicated that Saturn's magnetic field possessed large-scale asymmetry resulting in radio emissions with every rotation of the planet. But Voyager 2 found no evidence for any significant asymmetry of the field. The science team reported that it was

*"left with a rather enigmatic situation
to understand the basic source of
Saturnian kilometric radiation
modulation, other than the small,
dipole tilt."* [8]

This question was only one of many that became the legacy of Voyager as Voyager 2 departed the Saturnian system in the autumn of 1981 and was boosted by the planet's gravitational attraction toward an appointment with Uranus. The spacecraft was to begin observing Uranus in late 1985 and make its closest approach on 24 January 1986. From there, it would be accelerated by Uranian gravity to encounter Neptune and the big moon, Triton, on 24 August 1989.

It took 20 years to realize the Grand Tour once it had been proposed. It would take another 20 years to resolve all the data.

8 Ness, N.F. et al, "Magnetic Field Studies by Voyager 2: Preliminary Results at Saturn", op. cit.

any past internal activity that would have modified the surface. The science report surmised that Hyperion may have the oldest surface in the Saturn system.

Looking at Tethys, Voyager 2 cameras recorded an impact basin 248·5 miles (400km) in diameter. The gouge covered nearly one-third of the moon; the satellite Mimas could have fitted into it. The science team believed that the impact occurred when Tethys was in a molten or partially molten state allowing the moon to recover its original spherical shape. Another great scar was seen on the surface, a trench, possibly a crustal fracture, that extended 270 degrees around the moon. It was named Ithaca Chasma and is thought to have been caused by expansion of the moon's interior.

The most geologically evolved of Saturn's moons appears to be Enceladus. Five types of surface units have been identified including three kinds of cratered plains. The youngest of the plains units appeared to be only a few hundred million years old. They are crossed by grooves and faults, indicating crustal folding under compression.

Studies of the Voyager photos have produced hints that the surface of Enceladus may still be tectonically active as a result of internal heating. Linear faults and ridged plains with curvilinear valleys are visible, like those on Jupiter's Ganymede and on Mercury. The science team regarded Enceladus as too small to have produced the heating by radioactive decay. The source of heat, it was speculated, may be tidal interaction with Dione. The surface temperature was measured at −201°C.

RECOMMENDED READING

Cruickshank, D.P.; Morrison, D., "The Galilean Satellites of Jupiter", *Scientific American,* Vol. 234, No. 5, May 1976.

Fimmel, R.O.; Swindell, W.; Burgess, E., *Pioneer Odyssey, Encounter With a Giant,* NASA, Washington, D.C., 1974.

Ingersoll, A.P., "Meteorology of Jupiter", *Scientific American,* Vol. 234, No. 3, March 1976.

Ingersoll, A.P., "Jupiter and Saturn", *Scientific American,* Vol. 245, No. 6, December 1981.

Lewis, R.S., *From Vinland to Mars,* Quadrangle-New York Times Book Co. New York, 1976.

Morrison, D.; Samz, J., *Voyager to Jupiter,* NASA, Washington, D.C., 1980.

Whipple, F.L., *Earth, Moon and Planets,* Harvard University Press, Cambridge, Mass., 1968.

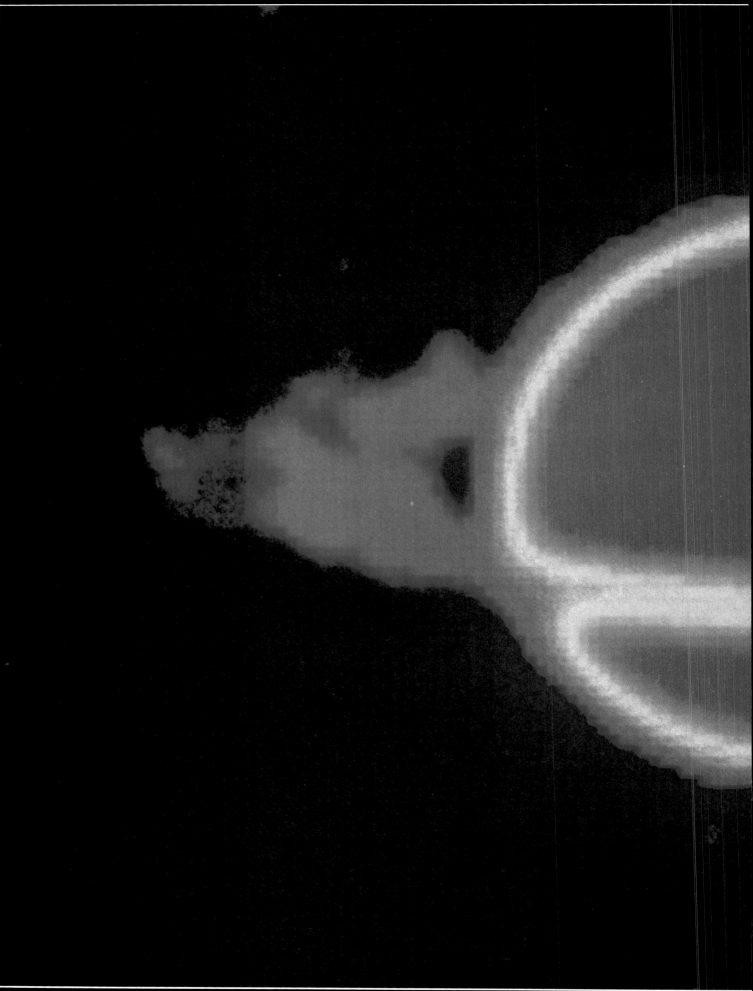

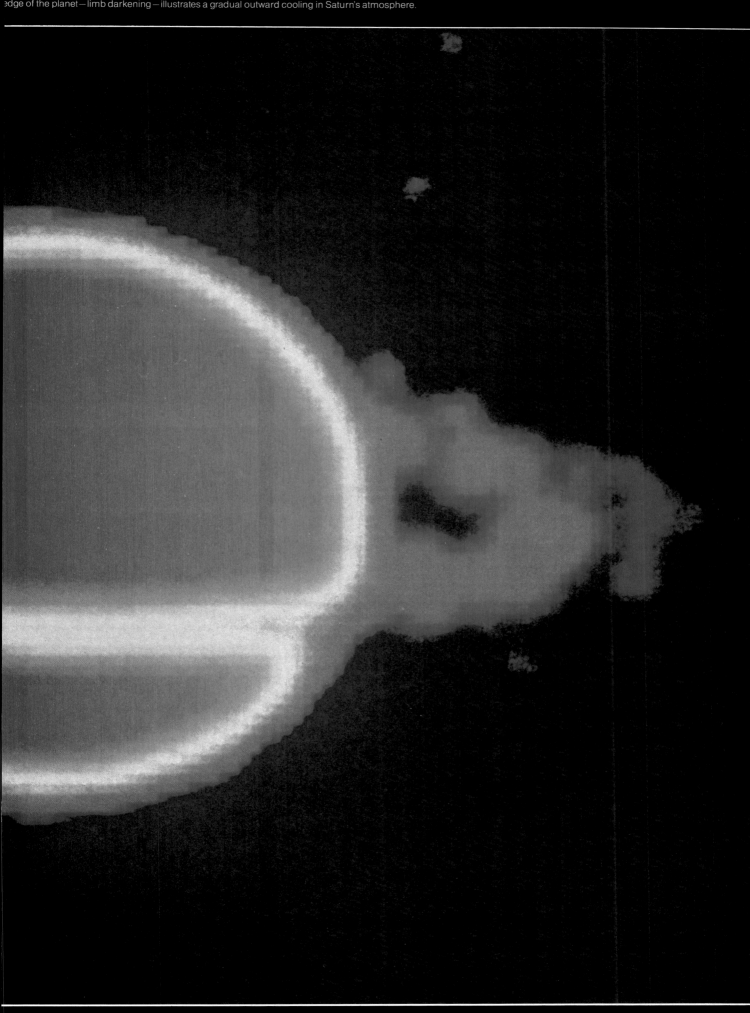

The Outer Planets

At the edge of the Solar System, the outer planets, Uranus, Neptune and Pluto and their satellites form the *terra incognita* of the 1980s. All the other major bodies of the Commonwealth of the Sun have been reconnoitred by spacecraft imaging and remote sensing instruments. These distant worlds and their extraordinary satellite systems seem to defy much of the order that is apparent among the planetary bodies nearer the Sun. It remains for the Space Telescope and Voyager 2 to bring this far frontier into clearer focus and complete the reconnaissance of the Solar System.

Far from the Sun, well beyond the orbit of Saturn, lies the largely unexplored territory of the outermost planets Uranus, Neptune and Pluto. Together with their satellites, these planetary systems comprise eleven unfamiliar and uncharted worlds which the age of space exploration is only now beginning to open up for us.

Thrusting outwards from its encounter with Saturn the Voyager 2 spacecraft is on its way to make the first close-up, scientific, reconnaissance of Uranus (in 1986) and Neptune (1989). The Space Telescope, to be launched in 1986 will help to sweep away many of the scientific mysteries which surround Pluto and its moon, Charon.

Here on the fringe of the Solar System, much of the apparent order that is characteristic of the planets nearer the Sun is missing. We find that Uranus and Pluto have spin axes so inclined to the plane of their orbits that at certain times during their orbital "year" they appear to be almost "rolling" along their orbital paths. Uranus is in fact approaching this condition now and by the end of the decade the Earth-based observer will look almost directly down on the planet's South pole.

Neptune's and Pluto's mean distances from the Sun are both at odds with the enigmatically simple Bode's Law of planetary distances and surely undermine any pretence that it may have a true physical basis.[1]

---

1 Bode's Law (Johann Bode, 1747–1826) purported to perceive a mathematical relationship between planetary distances from the Sun. The relationship is based on the sum of the figure 4 and a series of numbers starting with 0 for Mercury, 3 for Venus, 6 for Earth, 12 for Mars, 24 for the asteroid belt, 48 for Jupiter, 96 for Saturn and 192 for Uranus. When 4 is added to each of these numbers and then divided by 10, the result is the approximate distance in astronomical units from the Sun to the planet to which the number refers. Thus, adding 4 to the number 6, for Earth, yields 10 which divided by 10 gives 1 astronomical unit.

URANUS: BASIC DATA	
Equatorial Diameter*	3·90E; 30,879 miles (49,693km)
Mass*	14·54E
Density	0·92oz/in³ (1·6g/cm³)
Volume*	50E
Surface Gravity*	1·07E
Escape Velocity	13·7 miles/sec (22km/sec)
Period of Rotation	0·75 days (?)
Inclination of Equator (to Orbit)	98°
Distance from Sun (Semi-major axis)	19·18AU; 1,783·4 x 10⁶miles (2,870 x 10⁶km)
Siderial Period	84·01 tropical years
Synodic Period	369·66 days
Orbital Speed	4·2 miles/sec (6·8km/sec)
Orbital Eccentricity	0·047
Inclination of Orbit (to ecliptic plane)	0·8°
Number of Satellites	5
*Earth=1	

Pluto's orbit is the most highly inclined of that of any planet. It has such a pronounced elliptical shape that, even though it spends most of its orbital journey as the most distant planet, it finds itself at the present time closer to the Sun than the next most distant planet, Neptune. Because of their large size and mass Uranus and Neptune are truly giants in the planetary scheme of things, but Pluto on the other hand is a mere pygmy. It would take in excess of four hundred Plutos to equal the mass of one Earth.

The satellite systems which circulate about these planets are no less extraordinary. Uranus has a halo of fine rings, while at Neptune none are seen—or have yet to form. Uranus' almost clockwork family of satellites contrasts starkly with the drastic disorder seen in Neptune's or, for that matter, with the singular nature of Pluto's relatively large moon.

These planets are distinguished from others not only by their physical and orbital properties but also by the fact that they are all relatively recent discoveries. Uranus was the first of these three planets to be discovered. This chance event occurred in 1781, during observations by the then amateur astronomer, William Herschel (1738–1822) in England, and it inexorably led to the prediction and discovery of Neptune by the French mathematician Urbain Leverrier (1811–1877) and the German astronomer Johann Galle (1812–1910) in 1847. The discovery, a triumphant application of Newton's law of gravitation, in turn led to the early prediction by the American astronomer Percival Lowell (1855–1916) of a body beyond Neptune, and the ultimate discovery of Pluto by another American, Clyde Tombaugh in 1930.

NEPTUNE: BASIC DATA	
Equatorial Diameter*	3·81E; 30,199 miles (48,600km)
Mass*	17·2E
Density	1·33oz/in³ (2·3g/cm³)
Volume*	42E
Surface Gravity*	1·41E
Escape Velocity	15·5 miles/sec (25km/sec)
Period of Rotation	0·75 days
Inclination of Equator (to Orbit)	28·8°
Distance from Sun (Semi-major axis)	30·058AU; 2,794 x 10⁶miles (4,497 x 10⁶km)
Siderial Period	164·83 tropical years
Synodic Period	367·49 days
Orbital Speed	3·36 miles/sec (5·4km/sec)
Orbital Eccentricity	0·009
Inclination of Orbit (to ecliptic plane)	1·8°
Number of Satellites	2
*Earth=1	

Above: *Astronauts train underwater with a model of the Space Telescope. When launched in 1986, it should add enormously to our knowledge of the outer Solar System.*

This chain of discoveries may not yet be at an end. Some astronomers argue that evidence (albeit rather weak) exists for the presence of yet another planet beyond Pluto! If so, such a planet must be very small and very faint for the sky has already been searched dilligently and completely for the presence of objects as much as 40 times fainter than Pluto.

"What in its ruddy orbit lifts the blood,
Like a perturbed moon of Uranus,
Reaching to some great world in ungauged darkness hid."

Coventry Patmore, *The Unknown Eros*

Orbits of the Outer Planets
When Uranus was discovered in 1781, it doubled our estimate of the size of the Solar System. The discovery of Neptune in 1847 almost doubled it again. Pluto's orbit, however, presents quite a different aspect. It is inclined at 17° to the plane of the ecliptic, bringing it far above and below the orbits of the other planets. It is also markedly eccentric. At aphelion, Pluto is half as far again from the Sun as Neptune; while at perihelion, it lies within Neptune's orbit (as is currently the case until 1999). The highly-inclined orbit ensures that they will never collide.

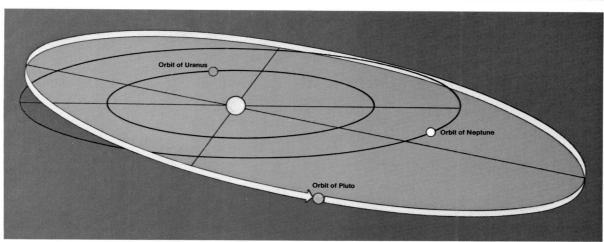

Properties of Uranus and Neptune

Uranus and Neptune have sufficient similarities in their gross properties of mass, size, and telescopic appearance to have been considered in the past as "sister" planets by many astronomers. However, as recent space exploration of Venus and Mars has clearly demonstrated, superficial similarities are likely to be misleading, and, when a detailed appraisal becomes available, the unique character of each object clearly emerges. We already have subtle clues which indicate that significant differences exist between them.

Astronomers consider that detailed knowledge of the chemistry and physical structure of these two planets will be crucial elements in the process of understanding how planets formed, how they evolve, and the nature of the mechanism by which the Solar System came into being. The reason is that they have properties which are almost midway betwen those of the terrestrial type planets on one hand and the large gaseous planets. Jupiter and Saturn, on the other. Their properties therefore are expected to impose unique constraints on theories of how the Solar System was put together and how planets originated.

When seen through a large telescope, Uranus and Neptune have a definite green colour and a fuzzy appearance. Little else is apparent to the eye. The colour is due to the presence of large quantities of methane gas in their atmospheres which strongly absorbs red light; the fuzzy appearance is partly due to the ubiquitous effects of turbulence in

Left: *Artist's impression of Uranus, painted just after the discovery of its rings in 1977. Uranus orbits the Sun pole-on with its rings "vertical" to its path.*

233

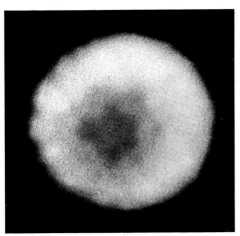

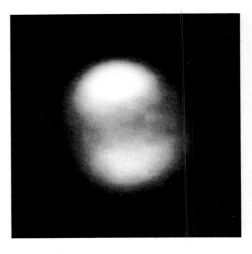

Left: *At infra-red wavelengths of 8900 Å, one of the wavelengths absorbed by methane gas, Uranus shows banks of polar haze surrounding the dark central latitudes. The bright surrounding limb probably results from back-scattering of light in a high layer of ice particles or dust grains.*

Right: *Four exposures of Neptune, in the 8900 Å band (first three) and in the 7550 Å continuum (far right). Neptune differs from Uranus in having a bright southern hemisphere and a dark band of absorption in the north. These images were obtained by Brad Smith and Harold Reitsema with a charge-coupled device fitted to the 60in (154cm) Catalina Observatory telescope.*

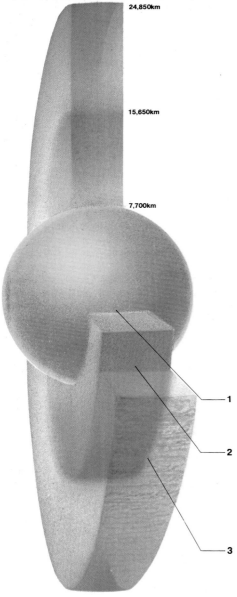

24,850km

15,650km

7,700km

— 1

— 2

— 3

The Structure of Uranus
1 Iron/silicate core.
2 Ice layer.
3 Hydrogen/helium gas.

Models for the interiors of Uranus and Neptune have been calculated on the basis of the planets' properties and on the behaviour of gas at high pressures and low temperatures. Uranus probably has an iron/silicate core in which a magnetic field may be generated. This is overlain by a mantle of water, ammonia and methane (strong methane absorption gives Uranus its greenish tinge), above which is a layer of greatly compressed hydrogen and helium gas. Uranus' atmosphere is very cold and clear, and there are seldom any clouds or hazes. Although Uranus is larger than Neptune, its density is much lower and, unlike Neptune, it does not emit any excess heat from its interior.

the Earth's atmosphere that easily distorts the appearance of such distant objects. But the main reason for the fuzzy appearance is the strong darkening towards the circumference of each planet that is the result of the depth of their relatively clear atmospheres.

"Air" on Uranus and Neptune is primarily made up of a mixture of molecular hydrogen (H_2) and helium (He). In fact, Uranus was the first astronomical object on which molecular hydrogen, one of the most prevalent forms of matter in the Galaxy, was first detected by Gerhard Herzberg, a Canadian spectroscopist. Methane (CH_4) is a minor constituent but has important consequences for it allows us, with modern electronic cameras, to view these planets in a way which shows that their rather bland, featureless, appearance is quite misleading. Electronic pictures taken in the infra-red light that methane absorbs show banks of polar haze on Uranus and bands of mid-latitude clouds and possibly the analogue of terrestrial cyclones on Neptune. The two planets are not only unlike one another but they are clearly different from Jupiter and Saturn.

These differences are more than skin deep. Our knowledge of the mean density and size, together with knowledge of the behaviour of materials at high pressure and density that has been developed in terrestrial laboratories, show that Uranus and Neptune must be constructed mainly from a mixture of rock and ice. Unlike rocky Earth and Mars their atmospheres are very deep, perhaps with base pressures approaching 200,000 times that on the Earth, but the atmospheres are nevertheless a minor part of their bulk. In this they contrast with Jupiter and Saturn where the atmosphere is the dominant component of the planet.

The ice is not pure water but almost certainly includes large quantities of ammonia and methane as well. That we have only indirect evidence for this introduces one of the intriguing scientific research problems of current interest about these planets. Ammonia, a common molecule, is quite clearly seen on Jupiter and Saturn. Since ammonia has a high cosmic abundance it was expected to show up in radio observations of Uranus and Neptune. On the contrary the observations show no obvious trace of the gas; either in the radio spectrum or in the brightness of the emission.

Additionally, and unlike the other three giant planets, Uranus' radio spectrum has

been found to be seasonally variable in brightness. Some astronomers believe that the ammonia is hidden from view by being chemically trapped in an "invisible" form, perhaps in combination with hydrogen sulphide or some other constituent deep in the atmosphere. The "non-explanation" of the radio spectrum of these two planets is a major research problem in planetary astronomy.

Conditions in the deep interior of a planet are difficult to visualize. Perhaps the simplest (but not very accurate) analogy to the structure and composition of Uranus and Neptune would be to visualize them as giant, dirty snowballs enveloped by a deep atmosphere. In the interior the pressures

Below: *The International Ultraviolet Explorer satellite before launch on 26 January, 1978. It has detected strong ultraviolet emission from Uranus, probably caused by aurorae at the poles.*

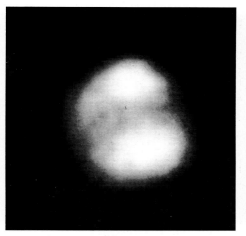

are high and temperatures hot and there is probably no distinct "surface" which differentiates the atmosphere from the interior. Water and ammonia, the primary constituents, ionize at depth and become electrically conducting. Methane disassociates into carbon and hydrogen and one research scientist, Marvin Ross at the University of California Livermore laboratory, has speculated that conditions in the deep interior of Uranus and Neptune are possibly just right for the large scale formation of diamonds!

Magnetic Fields

Both planets are thought to be strongly magnetized since they meet the basic requirements for the induction and growth of a magnetic field by dynamo action: rapid rotation and electrical conductivity within the interior. We have no proof as yet that this is so for Neptune, but there is evidence of it for Uranus. Faint bursts of radio noise of the kind associated with the precipitation of energetic electrons trapped in a magnetosphere have been discovered emanating from the direction of Uranus by Larry Brown of the Goddard Space Flight Center in data obtained by the Interplanetary Monitoring Platform 6 spacecraft during the period from 1971 to 1976.[2] More recently John Clarke at the Space Science Laboratory at the University of California, Berkeley has observed bright ultraviolet emissions from the planet with the Earth-orbiting International Ultraviolet Explorer spectrometer. These emissions are so bright that they are believed to be prominent polar aurorae occurring on the planet caused by beamed electrons colliding with hydrogen in the upper atmosphere—a sure indication that a powerful magnetic field is present.

The magnetospheric properties of Uranus are of great interest to space scientists who specialize in understanding complex interactions of charged particles with large scale magnetic and electric fields in space. Uranus is special because of its peculiar axial orientation. At the moment the south magnetic pole is pointing almost into the direction of the flow of the solar wind and may act as a giant scoop collecting the interplanetary gas and dumping it directly into the planet's upper polar atmosphere. A very unusual situation.

That the two planets rotate reasonably rapidly was discovered quite early after the invention of the astronomical spectrograph. The precise length of the day, or period of

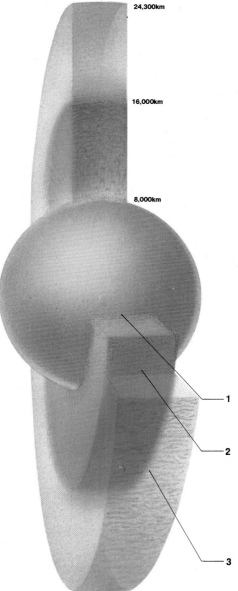

24,300km

16,000km

8,000km

The Structure of Neptune
1 Iron/silicate core.
2 Ice layer.
3 Hydrogen/helium gas.

Like Uranus, Neptune probably has a rocky core at a temperature of 7,000°C and a pressure of 20 million Earth atmospheres. Because Neptune is denser, however, its core may be slightly larger than that of Uranus. Above the core is an icy layer of water, methane and ammonia, and it is possible that convective motions in the ionized water could generate a mantle magnetic field—although none has been detected yet. The overlying atmosphere, although similar to that of Uranus, is surrounded by a thin and variable upper-atmosphere haze. Neptune emits far more excess heat from its interior than does Uranus, probably because the Sun-warmed atmosphere of Uranus acts as a valve to prevent heat loss.

rotation, is however not well known for either planet and the story of attempts to pin these quantities down is one that underscores the fragility of knowledge of faint distant objects.

The rotation periods of both planets were believed to have been determined to within a few minutes in the late 1930s. However, when scientists began working with the US National Aeronautical and Space Administration (NASA) in the mid 1970s to plan space missions to these planets it was decided to check and remeasure these important data. Surely modern instrumentation and the large telescopes of today could lead to improved results!

Six independent astronomical investigations were started using the biggest telescopes and best instrumentation. Soon it became apparent that the results which had been accepted for over a quarter of a century were substantially incorrect; unfortunately, this was the only point of agreement. The new results are in fact discordant and, in the case of both planets, fall into two distinct groupings. All that can be said at present is that the periods of rotation are not far from 18 hours in both cases. A resolution of this problem is not expected until Voyager 2 reaches Uranus in 1986 or the Space Telescope is able to apply its great resolving power to the problem at about the same time.

Seasons

Both planets rotate about polar axes that are strongly inclined to their orbital planes and, as in the case with the Earth, their atmospheres undergo seasonal temperature changes throughout their year. For Neptune with its 28·8 degree tilt the effects should be moderate in range although observations of short term fluctuations in the infra-red emission from the planet indicate rapidly changing weather patterns in its atmosphere. Uranus, however, is tilted at 98 degrees to its orbital plane and for it we may expect a much more dramatic range of seasonal changes.

---

2 The Interplanetary Monitoring Platforms were a series of Explorer-class spacecraft which performed a variety of studies of the interplanetary environment. Allied with this series were two radio astronomy satellites, Explorers 38 and 49, which were designed to measure galactic and solar radio noise by using the Moon for occultation and focussing.

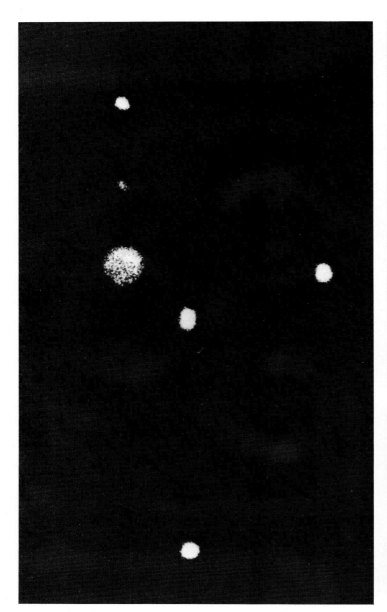

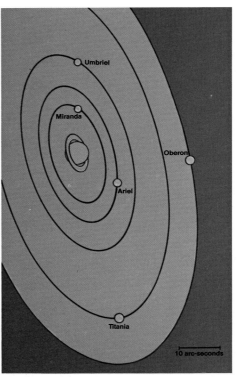

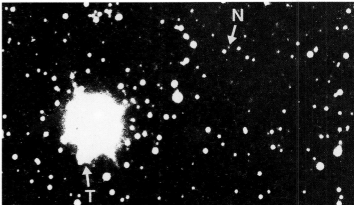

Unlike any of the other planets (except tiny Pluto) the polar regions on Uranus actually receive more heat from the Sun than do the equatorial regions; about 1·5 times as much. What kind of atmospheric circulation exists on the planet as a result of this has yet to be explored in detail but some recent theoretical models suggest that the Uranian atmosphere at some latitudes may become almost "explosively" unstable in the Uranian equivalent of "spring".

Extreme seasonal changes may be the cause behind the time-variable radio emissions which were discovered in 1978 by Michael Klein of the Jet Propulsion Laboratory, and J. A. Turanago of the University of Zaragoza, Spain. The phenomenon has most recently been interpreted by Samuel Gulkis of the Jet Propulsion Laboratory who suggests two explanations. In the first, ammonia could be concentrated by the action of the Uranian meteorology into the equatorial regions of the planet. As a result copious radio emissions from deep, hotter regions of the atmosphere would find it relatively easy to escape from the polar regions. Then, as the view of Uranus from Earth progresses from an equatorial one to a polar one (this takes about 21 years) the radio spectrum will appear to get progressively stronger.

The alternative idea is that ammonia is absent from the atmosphere and that an ocean of water exists at its bottom. In this case meteorological conditions would produce haze at the poles and clear viewing over the equator.

An ocean, or, more correctly, a liquid surface has special physical properties that make it appear to be only half of its actual temperature. As a result, this hypothetical Uranian situation again leads to an excess of radio emissions in the polar region. The alternate scenario then, like the first, will give a reasonable explanation of the radio observations. This latter view of Uranus is presently not considered likely by most astronomers; but the range of the possibilities that are being seriously considered should demonstrate the uncertainties in our knowledge.

A fundamental difference between the two planets is that Neptune apparently has within it a powerful machine for creating energy that is absent on Uranus. Observations of the infra-red radiation flowing out of Neptune's atmosphere show that the planet is emitting just over twice as much heat as it receives from the Sun. In Uranus' case an approximate balance is observed. Since the excess energy flows are truly

Above: *Photograph of Neptune taken by Charles Veillet with the 142in (3·6m) Canada-France-Hawaii Telescope at Mauna Kea. It shows the two faint moons: Nereid (top right, arrowed) and Triton (below Neptune, marked with a "T").*

prodigous this is a substantial matter which involves the entire fabric of the planet. It is thought that the energy produced in Neptune is a result of a slow contraction of the planet which converts gravitational energy into heat. Why such a fundamental process should have stopped on Uranus and not on Neptune is a significant puzzle. The best guess is that Uranus' position nearer the Sun results in a condition in the outer parts of its atmosphere—not duplicated on the more distant Neptune—that "chokes-off" the flow of heat from the interior and prevents further gravitational collapse.

Satellites

If our knowledge of the planets themselves is coarse and controversial, then our insight into the nature of their satellites is less than rudimentary. Only the crudest data are available. Uranus has five known satellites in what astronomers refer to as an extremely regular system. Except for Miranda, the

THE SATELLITES OF THE OUTER PLANETS									
	URANUS						**NEPTUNE**		**PLUTO**
	MIRANDA	ARIEL	UMBRIEL	TITANIA	OBERON	RING SYSTEM	TRITON	NEREID	CHARON
Mass (Em)	0·000014?	0·00022?	0·000087?	0·00073?	0·00042	?	0·057?	0·000003?	0·0002?
Diameter miles (km)	180 (290)	500 (805)	340 (547)	620 (998)	555 (893)	—	1,985 (3,194)	185 (300)	475 (764)
Orbital Period (day)	1·414	2·520	4·144	8·706	13·46	—	5·877	?	6·4
Rotation Period (day)	1·414	2·520	4·144	8·706	13·46	—	5·877	?	6·4
Orbital Eccentricity	0·017	0·0028	0·0035	0·0024	0·0007	Approx 0·0	0·0	0·75	0·?
Orbital Inclination (degrees)	0·8	3·4	0·0	0·0	0·0	0·0	160·0	27·6	105·0
Mean distance from Planet (pr)	5·13	7·54	10·5	17·2	23·0	1·7-2·1	14·6	227	7·7?
Temperature (°C)	-215	-215	-215	-215	-215	-215	-225	-225	231
Note: the following abbreviations have been used in this table—Em: Earth mass; pr: planetary radii. The orbital and rotation periods are expressed in Earth days.									

faintest and most recently discovered, their orbits lie in a single plane, travel on circular paths, and have orbital periods which bear special relationships (Laplacian resonances[3]) to one another that tend to perpetuate the configuration.

We have only snatches of information about their physical and chemical characteristics. Their diameters could range from extremes of 185 to 1,250 miles (300 to 2,000km) depending on how well they reflect light, and they are known to have water-ice on their surfaces. Possibly they are similar to the icy satellites around Saturn such as Enceladus, Tethys and Iapetus. Robert Brown at the University of Hawaii finds their spectra similar to these objects. Other, smaller satellites probably await discovery at Uranus. This seems certain from the special nature of ring systems.

Neptune has two known satellites—Triton, a massive object, and Nereid—a cosmic speck. These two represent a system that is as irregular in its known properties as can be imagined. Measurements of the colour, brightness, and variability of Triton seem to indicate that it is a largely rocky object, with patches of methane ice on its surface and a tenuous methane atmosphere. For many years it was believed that Triton must be the largest satellite in the Solar System but very recent infra-red observations of its emission of thermal radiation indicate that its diameter

Below: *The infra-red view of Uranus overleaf was obtained by David Allen, using the 150in (3·81m) Anglo-Australian Telescope. Here, a night assistant sits at its control console, from which he operates the telescope via a sophisticated computer.*

is near 1,990 miles (3,200km); that is, somewhat smaller than the Earth's Moon.

Perhaps the most surprising fact which we have learned about Triton is that it may be on the verge of extinction—at least in astronomical terms! Its orbit is so inclined to Neptune's equator (160 degrees) that it moves around the planet in the opposite direction to the rotation of the planet. As a result, the large tides that Triton raises in Neptune which tend to dissipate large amounts of the moon's orbital energy ensure that Triton's orbit must be slowly decaying and that eventually the satellite will fall into the planet.

Thomas McCord of the University of Hawaii has made rough estimates of the time it will take this to happen and finds that the show will be over for Triton in 10 to 100 million years—a short time, astronomically speaking. Triton may never enter Neptune's atmosphere as a solid body. As it gets close enough, enormous tidal forces would be expected to break it up. Much of the debris would stay in orbit and perhaps form a system of rings similar to those seen today around Jupiter, or Saturn, or Uranus.

Triton's only known companion is a tiny object called Nereid about which we know very little except that it must be at least 185 miles (300km) in diameter. Its chief distinguishing characteristic is that it has by far the most eccentric orbit of any known satellite.

These remarkable orbital properties of Neptune's satellites have aroused considerable interest. American astronomers R. S. Harrington and T. C. Van Flandern have speculated that in the astronomically recent past a relatively large or massive object

passed through the Neptune system (no physical impact is required) and the object's gravitational force caused what was once a regular satellite system to turn into the chaotic configuration which we see today. Their theory also suggests that a physical impact may have occured with a proto-Pluto satellite assumed to be in orbit around Neptune at that time. The subsequent disruption of this object could have ejected large fragments from Neptune's gravitational pull and formed the Pluto-Charon system. Unfortunately, these are unlikely situations and there is no way of confirming the theory.

The idea that Pluto originated as a satellite of Neptune is in fact an old one. It was first developed by R. A. Lyttleton in England and later by the American-Dutch astronomer Gerard P. Kuiper (1905–1973). The primary factor that led to the idea was the observation that Pluto moves inside Neptune's orbit when it is close to perihelion. As a consequence one might suppose that if Pluto's orbit were traced back to the distant past it might at some point in its history end up near Neptune itself. However, calculations

---

3 Laplacian resonances: A satellite moves around its parent planet in a periodic orbit. If it is also affected by a gravitational force from another satellite in a periodic way, and the periods of the orbit and the impressed force are in the ratio of small integer numbers, then they are said to be in a resonant condition. Such resonances, first successfully analyzed by Pierre Simon de Laplace (1749–1827) are common in the outer Solar System. They represent situations of substantial dynamical stability or very slow dynamical evolution. The latter is probably the case for the satellites of Uranus.

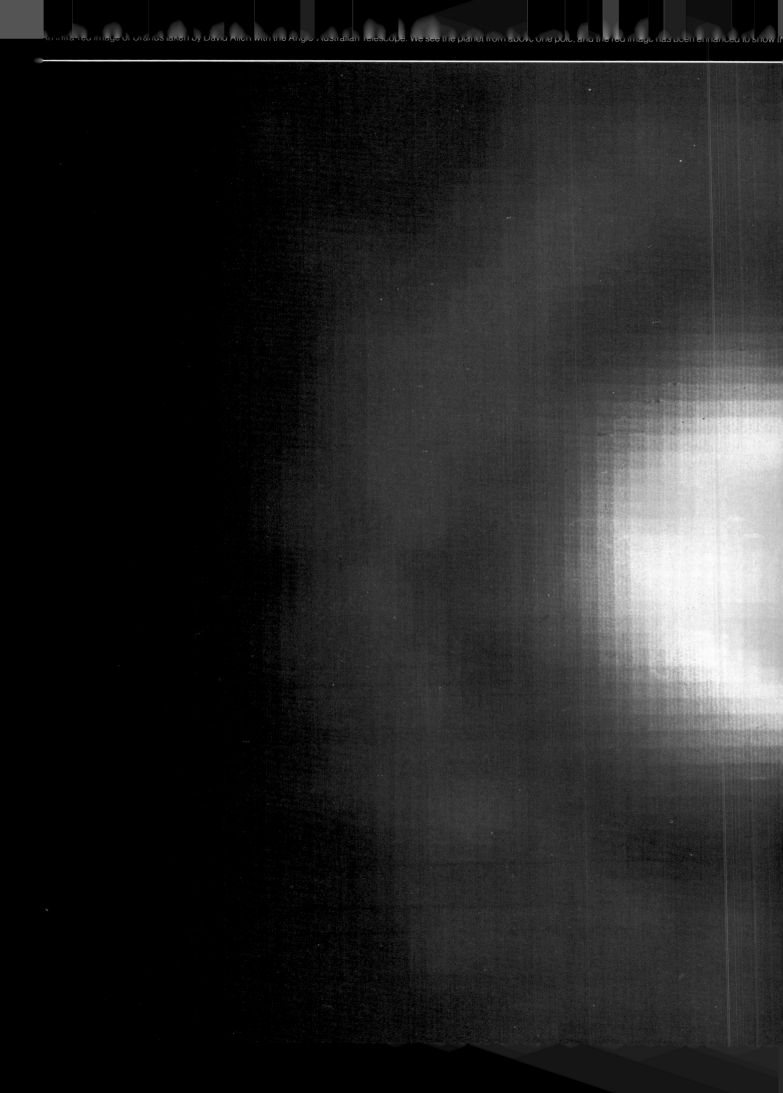

An infra-red image of Uranus taken by David Allen with the Anglo-Australian Telescope. We see the planet from above one pole, and the red image has been enhanced to show t

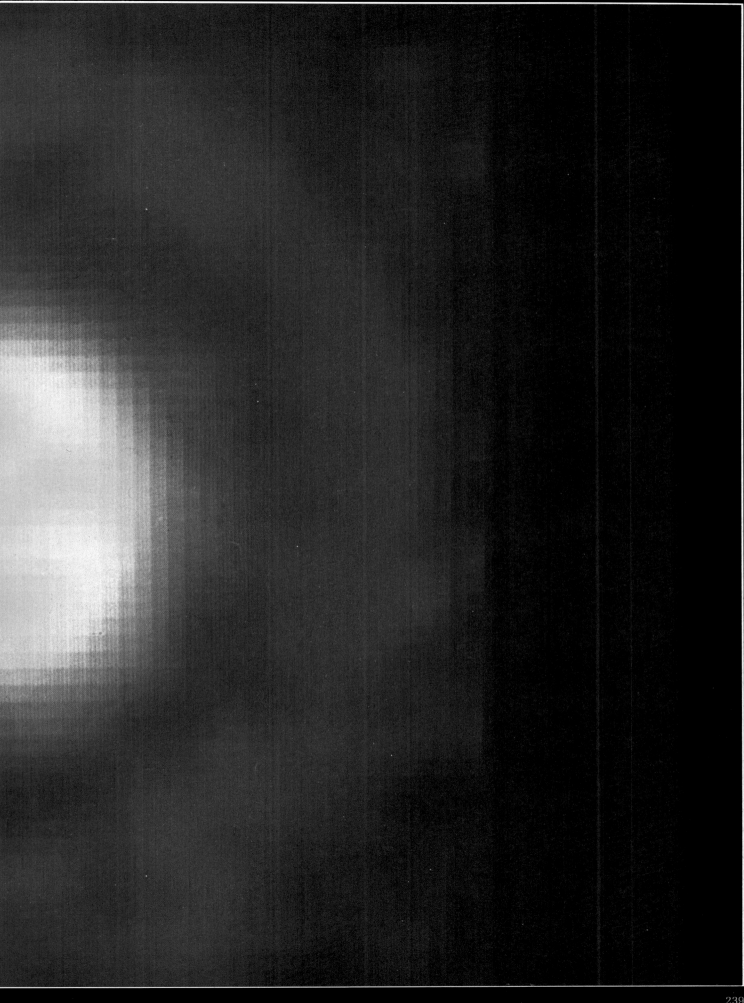

Above: *The Kuiper Airborne Observatory carries a 36in (0·91m) infra-red telescope in a C-141 StarLifter. Researchers using it discovered the rings around Uranus during an occultation experiment in 1977.*

Uranus' Ring System
The nine rings of Uranus were discovered in 1977 when they unexpectedly occulted a star. Seen here projected onto the planet's equatorial plane, they are extremely narrow and very dark; quite unlike the ring systems of Saturn and Jupiter. Only the β ring (7·5 miles or 12km) and the ε ring have significant widths. This outermost ring has a width which varies from 12·5 to 62 miles (20-100km) depending on its distance from Uranus.

show that Pluto has never been anywhere close to Neptune; in fact it comes much closer to Uranus.

The Rings Around Uranus

Most discoveries in the outer Solar System have occurred in modern times and many remarkable tales and controversies abound. Sir William Herschel, when an amateur, was sure that his new discovery was a comet and had to be persuaded by professionals that he had discovered a planet, Uranus! John Adams, an English mathematician (1819–1892) who was the first to predict the position in the sky where a new planet (Neptune) would be found, was sadly neglected by his Astronomer Royal, and when Urbain Leverrier, who could not apparently get his Parisian contemporaries to look, and Johann Galle found the planet, an international incident ensued. These stories, and perhaps many more, are matched by the discovery of rings of material orbiting Uranus.

In an experiment intended to follow a rare occultation of star SAO 158687 behind the planet Uranus on 10 March 1977 as a probe of the planet's upper atmosphere, James Elliot and his associates at the Massachusetts Institute of Technology equipped the NASA Kuiper Airborne Observatory (a C-141 aircraft) with special high speed photometric equipment to resolve light "flashes" known to occur during such events. At almost the last minute an error in the position of the

star to be occulted was found and, at considerable expense (and discussion), the airborne expedition was moved to the southern hemisphere to operate out of Perth, Australia. The equipment had been barely switched on and directed at the planet for twelve minutes when an unexpected "glitch" occurred in the data, which was observed in real time. This was followed by a sequence of four more unexpected and worrisome events before the main occultation event at the planet was observed. In published tape recordings of the conversation between the experimenters it is possible to share the excitement of discovery, as worry about the health of the equipment turned first to speculative ideas and then to almost uncontainable excitement. The "glitches" were quickly recognized to be short occultation events as the star passed behind rings encircling the planet!

The properties of these rings are now reasonably well established. There are at least nine of them, some very narrow and two that are more diffuse. They reside between 25,500 and 32,300 miles (41,000 and 52,000km) from the planet and the

narrowest are probably less than 2.5 miles (4km) wide! Such small sizes are detectable at the great distance of Uranus because the spatial resolution during the occultation is determined by the angular size of the star being occulted. Stars are so distant that they are effectively point sources of light.

The Uranian rings have a completely different character from those at Saturn and Jupiter. They consist of a multitude of narrow elementary strands of material. They are evidently constrained in some way, perhaps by small, and as yet undiscovered, satellites that "shepherd" the ring material, i.e. prevent the natural tendency of colliding material within the rings to disperse by the action of phased gravitational forces. We already know that such a phenomenon is responsible for the maintenance of the Saturn F-ring, as observations from Voyager spacecraft have proved.

Uranus' outer ε-ring is an example of a diffuse ring and has some rather special properties. The ring is elliptical in shape with the region furthest from the planet the most spread out. This configuration is observed to maintain itself as the entire

PLUTO: BASIC DATA	
Equatorial Diameter*	0·20E (?); 1,583 miles (2,548km) (?)
Mass*	0·002E (?)
Density	0·66oz/in³ (1·14g/cm³)
Volume*	(?)
Surface Gravity*	(?)
Escape Velocity	(?)
Period of Rotation	6·3 days
Inclination of Equator (to Orbit)	(?)
Distance from Sun (Semi-major axis)	39·44AU; 3,673·6 x 10⁶miles (5,912 x 10⁶km)
Siderial Period	248·4 tropical years
Synodic Period	366·74 days
Orbital Speed	2·92 miles/sec (4·7km/sec)
Orbital Eccentricity	0·25
Inclination of Orbit (to ecliptic plane)	17·17°
Number of Satellites	1
*Earth = 1	

Above: *Enlarged portions of the discovery plates for the planet Pluto. Pluto (arrowed) has moved significantly between the first plate (taken 23 January 1930) and the second, taken six days later.*

The Structure of Pluto
Little is known about Pluto's structure and composition. Its low density implies that it is almost entirely composed of water ice and frozen gases, and it is not known if it has a rocky core. Its surface is highly reflective and covered in frozen methane.

Pluto's Satellite
Although Charon has not yet been clearly seen — most images of it are highly processed — it has been established that its orbit is very steeply inclined, (see table on page 237).

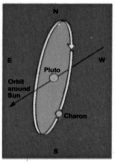

pattern precesses around the planet within a period of about 264 days. The precession is caused by gravitational forces that arise from the equatorial bulge of the planet, due to the planet's rotation. How the ε-ring maintains its form in the face of these precessional forces is as yet an unsolved problem.

No ring sytem has yet been found about Neptune even though recent occultation events have been closely monitored. Some theoreticians believe that none will be found since they speculate that ring systems would be unstable and would break up in such a peculiar satellite system. On the other hand if there has been a major disruption of Neptune satellite system in the recent astronomical past there should be plenty of orbiting debris and perhaps Neptune's rings have yet to form!

Pluto's Properties

Pluto is the smallest planet in the Solar System and recent estimates put its radius at about 800 miles (1,300km). It is therefore substantially smaller than the Earth's Moon. In 1978 J. W. Christy and R. S. Harrington of the US Naval Observatory made the remarkable discovery that Pluto had a moon which has since received the name Charon. This was an important discovery for measurements of the orbital period of Charon (6.3867 days), and its distance from Pluto tells us that Pluto is a very small planet; roughly 5 times less massive than Earth's Moon.

Pluto is so tiny it seems truly remarkable it was ever discovered. Percival Lowell, the founder of Lowell Observatory in Flagstaff, Arizona, expanded on the mathematical techniques of Adams and Leverrier and predicted where Pluto (he called it planet X at the time) would be found in the sky and then executed a search for it in the years before his death in 1916. He was not successful but a new search was instituted by V. M. Slipher (1875–1969), a subsequent director of Lowell Observatory and famous for his discovery of the general recession of galaxies i.e. the redshift, in 1928. In this second search specific predictions were not relied upon but instead the strategy of the

search was a systematic investigation of all objects in the sky around the Zodiac down to a prescribed limiting brightness. The massive amount of work was done by Clyde Tombaugh and in 1930 he found 'planet X' amazingly close to Lowell's predicted position.

Subsequently it was found that the new planet also had orbital properties similar to Lowell's estimates. Even so, it is probable that the coincidence of prediction and observation was a fluke. Now that we know that the actual mass of Pluto is so small, it is certain that this planet could not be responsible for the orbital perturbations of Uranus and Neptune upon which Lowell based his mathematical analysis! Nevertheless Lowell will always be strongly associated with the planet. His observatory found it, and his initials are, as can be plainly seen, the first two letters of the planet's name.

We now know a surprising amount about Pluto and Charon considering their smallness and great distance from us. For example, the orbit of Charon is highly inclined to the orbital plane of the planet and the planet's

rotation axis is tilted in roughly the same direction. We know this because the observed brightness of Pluto is found to vary regularly as the orbital position changes. Not only does the brightness fluctuate periodically telling us the period of rotation, or "Plutonian day", is 6·3867 Earth days but the amplitude of the fluctuations has steadily changed over the past 20 years of observation showing that the planet has a darker equatorial region than the poles (polar ice caps made of methane?). Support for the idea of such polar caps comes from recent spectroscopic observations and also infrared observations which are consistent with a substantial methane atmosphere and also patches of methane frost on the surface.

The true nature of physical conditions on Pluto are still largely beyond our grasp but Lawrence Trafton of the University of Texas has expressed the opinion that the amounts of methane measured to be in the atmosphere would be unstable, that is, would quickly escape from the weak gravitational field of the planet unless something else were there to constrain it. In his terms it would "blowoff"! To accommodate the observations Trafton suggested that substantial amounts of a much heavier gas — perhaps molecular nitrogen or argon — may also be present in the atmosphere which could prevent rapid loss of methane.

Charon

Pluto's satellite Charon is somewhere between 370 to 560 miles (600 to 900km) in radius and roughly ten times less massive than Pluto. In relation to its primary, this makes Charon the largest moon in the Solar System (the next largest is the Earth's Moon which is about 81 times less massive than the Earth). Pluto and Charon are more like a "double" planet than the usual case of a planet with a set of relatively small satellites.

Charon has been observed to move around Pluto with a period equal to the planet's rotation period of 6·3867 days. We therefore probably have the only case of a fully "rotationally locked" system in which the rotation period of both bodies and the orbital period are all equal. An observer on Pluto would see the moon, Charon, locked to the same position relative to the horizon at all times. If the same observer happened to be in the wrong hemisphere he probably would never know that Charon existed.

Future Exploration

The Voyager 2 spacecraft is now on a direct course to Uranus. Programmed to arrive in 1986 the provisional sequence of observations is illustrated (lower right).

Particularly worrisome is the state of the spacecraft's scan-platform on which many of the scientific instruments sit. It moves predictably in one direction but its motion in the orthogonal direction is irregular and possibly quite undependable. This is an exceedingly important matter, for the time available at the Uranus and Neptune encounters is quite brief and it would not be possible to correct an error in pointing of the scientific instruments if the platform became stuck. The two-way communication time at Uranus will be approximately 5 hours and at Neptune 8 hours.

As Voyager approaches Uranus, preliminary plans are to fly the spacecraft as close to Miranda as is reasonable, somewhere between Miranda and Ariel. The spatial resolution which should be achieved by the cameras will depend on the ability of project engineers to carry out manoeuvres that will compensate for the rapid motion of the spacecraft past the target. In principle a ground resolution comparable to that achieved at the Jovian satellites should be possible.

Prime scientific objectives are expected to include measurements of the peculiarly oriented magnetic field and the recently discovered auroral phenomena.

It should be noted that the Voyager 2 instruments were designed for light levels and atmospheric temperatures that are much higher than those at Uranus and Neptune. As a result the scientific return will probably be somewhat less than that which was obtained at Saturn and Jupiter. Nevertheless the magnetospheric experiments and the radio occulation experiment that will probe atmospheric structure are expected to perform without difficulty.

The infra-red interferometer, while lacking sensitivity for measuring stratospheric emissions that might be present and which were abundant at Jupiter and Saturn, should nevertheless, return superb data on the deeper atmospheric structure. The television—or imaging experiment—together with the visible polarimeter instrument can be expected to return spectacular pictures of the satellites as well as probe the fine structure of the rings.

There will also be further exploration of Pluto in the next decade with the Space Telescope, to be launched in 1986. The Planetary/Wide Field camera will easily resolve the moon Charon from its parent planet—and their orbital and global characteristics will become much more precisely known. The Space Telescope will also open up new opportunities in the field of moderately high resolution spectroscopy in the ultraviolet region of the spectrum and it may be that observations with the Faint Object and High Resolution Spectrographs will have much to say about the nature of this peculiar little planet's atmosphere.

We can confidently predict that new discoveries, unanticipated here, will continue to occur. Not the least of them may be several new objects. Some investigators suspect that a "planet X" waits to be found in the far reaches of the Solar System.

Top: On 24 August 1989, Voyager 2 will encounter the final planet on its Grand Tour: the hazy gas-giant Neptune. In this artist's impression, Voyager passes Neptune and its giant satellite Triton, a world thought by some astronomers to resemble the planet Pluto. It is already known that it has an atmosphere and possibly a rock-covered surface.

Above: Voyager 2's next mission target is the ringed planet Uranus, which it will encounter on 24 January 1986. In this artist's impression the nine rings glow dimly, and it is possible to see right through the transparent atmosphere of Uranus to the green depths of its methane layer. Voyager will fly close to Uranus' innermost moon, Miranda.

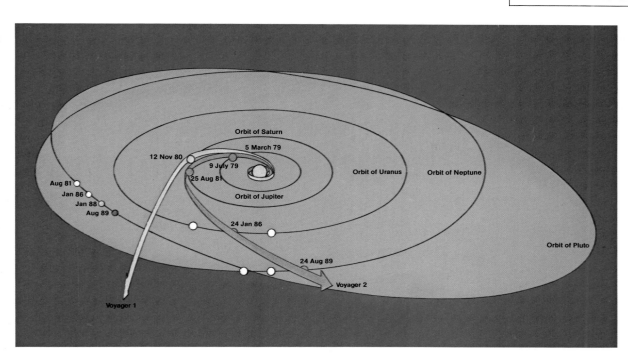

Voyager Flight Paths
The trajectories of the two Voyager spacecraft, as planned by JPL analysts, are charted in this diagram. Close encounters are colour-coded to flight paths. Following its encounter with Saturn on 12 November 1980, Voyager 1 will plass the orbits of Uranus, Pluto (then inside Neptune's orbit) and Neptune between 1984 and 1990, at a steep angle. It will then move steadily out of the Solar System, although it is not directed towards any particular star. Voyager 2 has been accelerated by its encounter with Saturn on 25 August 1981, and will make its closest approach to Uranus on 24 January 1986. Its final destination in the Solar System is Neptune, which it will fly by on 24 August 1989. Although it will be closing in on Pluto's orbit in January 1990, Pluto itself will be too far away for a close encounter. No Pluto probes are planned.

The Uranus Encounter
In early 1986, Voyager 2 will fly through the Uranus system. It will make its closest approach to the planet at 66,500 miles (107,000km) on 24 January 1986 outside the orbit of the satellite Miranda and just inside the orbit of Ariel. The "encounter sequence" depicted here begins 8 hours before closest approach and ends 8 hours after it. During this latter period, there will be a number of occultations when Uranus and its rings will interpose between Voyager and the Earth and Sun. Voyager 2 will start passing behind the rings about 90 minutes after closest approach, and behind the planet some 2 hours after closest approach. The diagram is colour-coded to show the successive phases of ring-Sun and Uranus-Sun occultation, and Uranus-Earth, ring-Earth occultation. During the occultation sequence, the spacecraft will beam radio signals through the rings and the atmosphere of Uranus. Distortion of these waves on reaching the DSN antennas on Earth will provide clues to the detailed ring structure and density of the atmosphere. While Voyager 2 is behind the planet itself, its signals will be blocked, and equally, controllers on Earth will not be able to make contact with the craft. Voyager will also be unable to "see" the Sun, an essential reference for spacecraft attitude control (which keeps its radio antenna pointing directly towards Earth)—and so control will need to be maintained gyroscopically. During this blackout period, the mission controllers hope to photograph the dark side of Uranus to detect lightning strokes, as were observed during the encounter with Jupiter. It is hoped that scan-platform problems will not degrade the encounter.

RECOMMENDED READING
Beatty, J. Kelly, O'Leary, Brian and Chaikin, Andrew, *The New Solar System*, Cambridge University Press and Sky Publishing Corporation, Cambridge, 1981.
Hunt, Garry, *Uranus and the Outer Planets*. Papers from an International Colloquium at Bath, England, Cambridge University Press, 1982.

Minor Planets, Meteorites and Comets

When the first of the outer planet probes, Pioneer 10, was launched to Jupiter on 2 March 1972 (3 March, GMT), mission scientists worried about the survival of the vehicle during its passage through the asteroid belt, the region between Mars and Jupiter.

Astronomers had estimated that this region, a gap 174 million miles (280 million km) wide between the inner and outer planets, is populated by more than 100,000 rocky masses. They range in size from grains of sand to the planetoid Ceres with a diameter 30 per cent of that of the Moon.

Planners of outer planet missions regarded the asteroid belt as an obstacle course, a definite hazard to interplanetary navigation beyond the orbit of Mars. In this sense, Pioneer 10 was a shot in the dark.

By mid-February 1973, Pioneer 10 had cleared the belt without any damage from flying rocks or even a near miss. Data from the spacecraft dust detectors showed that the impact rate of particles no bigger than fine sand had remained approximately the same during passage through the belt as during the flight from Earth to Mars. This finding was confirmed by the subsequent flights of Pioneer 11 and Voyagers 1 and 2 (see Chapter 11). It was one of first discoveries of the outer planet programme. Passage from the terrestrial to the giant planets was open.

The region of the Solar System between Mars and Jupiter had been of special interest to astronomers of the 18th and 19th centuries. Many of them supposed that an undiscovered planet was lurking there. It was predicted by a "law" which expressed a mathematical progression of the distances of the planets from the Sun. The progression had been calculated by Johann D. Titius (1729–1796), a mathematician of Wittenberg, in 1766. It was based on a simple formulation which yielded the approximate position in astronomical units (AU) of each planet then known from the Sun.[1]

Titius's formula was promulgated as a virtual law of nature in 1772 by the director of the Berlin Observatory, Johann E. Bode (1747–1826) and since then it has been

Right: *The Florentine artist Giotto di Bondone (1266-1337) used the 1301 apparition of Halley's Comet as the inspiration for the Star of Bethlehem in his fresco "Adoration of the Magi", which is in the Scrovegni Chapel in Padua. Almost seven centuries later, ESA scientists are calling their 1985/6 Halley's Comet probe "Giotto" in his memory.*

REPRESENTATIVE MINOR PLANETS (in order of discovery)				
NAME	**DIAMETER** miles (km)	**MASS** lb (kg)	**DISTANCE FROM SUN** (AU)	**ORBITAL PERIOD** (years)
Ceres	472 (760)	$2 \cdot 58 \times 10^{21}$ $(1 \cdot 17 \times 10^{21})$	2·766	4·60
Pallas	298 (480)	$5 \cdot 73 \times 10^{20}$ $(2 \cdot 6 \times 10^{20})$	2·768	4·61
Juno	124 (200)	$4 \cdot 4 \times 10^{19}$ (2×10^{19})	2·668	4·36
Vesta	298 (480)	$5 \cdot 29 \times 10^{20}$ $(2 \cdot 4 \times 10^{20})$	2·362	3·63
Hebe	136 (220)	$4 \cdot 4 \times 10^{19}$ (2×10^{19})	2·426	3·78
Iris	124 (200)	$3 \cdot 3 \times 10^{19}$ $(1 \cdot 5 \times 10^{19})$	2·386	3·68
Hygiea	198 (320)	$13 \cdot 22 \times 10^{19}$ (6×10^{19})	3·151	5·59
Eunomia	172 (280)	$8 \cdot 8 \times 10^{19}$ (4×10^{19})	2·643	4·30
Psyche	172 (280)	$8 \cdot 8 \times 10^{19}$ (4×10^{19})	2·923	5·00
Nemausa	48 (80)	$19 \cdot 8 \times 10^{17}$ (9×10^{17})	2·366	3·64
Eros	8·6 (14)	11×10^{15} (5×10^{15})	1·458	1·76
Davida	160 (260)	$6 \cdot 61 \times 10^{19}$ (3×10^{19})	3·190	5·67
Icarus	0·8 (1·40)	11×10^{12} (5×10^{12})	1·078	1·12
Geographos	1·8 (3)	11×10^{13} (5×10^{13})	1·244	1·39

Note: The orbital periods are expressed in Earth years.

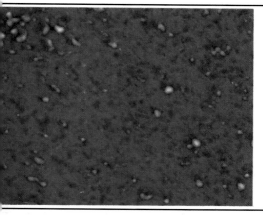

"Mighty talk there is of this comet that is seen a'nights: and the King and Queen did sit up last night to see it, and did, it seems."

Samuel Pepys, *Diaries*, 17 December 1664

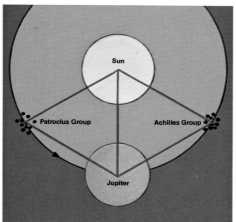

The Trojan Asteroids
Not all asteroids are confined strictly to the asteroid belt. Some have orbits which bring them into the inner Solar System, while others — the Trojan group — occupy stable points in the orbit of Jupiter. These two Lagrangian points, which form equilateral triangles with Jupiter and the Sun, are gravitationally stable positions where small amounts of matter can orbit without disruption. However, Jupiter's elliptical orbit and perturbations from other planets mean that the Trojans stray considerably from their nominal positions. The Trojans form two groups, leading and trailing Jupiter. The leading Achilles group contains the first Trojan to be discovered 588 Achilles, found in 1906. Both the Achilles group and the trailing Patroclus group contain an estimated 700 asteroids. They are large, dark and slightly red in colour, and their elongated shapes suggest that they are split-off fragments from collisions that occurred in the past.

known as "Bode's Law". Some 19th century theorists believed that Bode's Law revealed a remarkable order in the evolution of the Solar System. The validity of Bode's Law seemed to be confirmed in 1781 with the discovery of Uranus at 19·2AU by Sir William Herschel (1738—1822).

Aside from its evolutionary implications, Bode's Law required the existence of a planet at 2·8AU between Mars (1·524AU) and Jupiter (5·203AU).

Nothing of planetary size had been seen there. Astronomers searched the skies for decades, looking for a hidden planet.

In 1801, an Italian astronomer, Guiseppe Piazzi (1746—1826) discovered a small planetoid at about 2·8AU. He named it Ceres after the patron goddess of Sicily, where he had founded the Observatory of Palermo. It turned out to be the largest of the minor planets, with a diameter of about 500 miles (800km). In 1802, Heinrich Wilhelm Olbers of Bremen (1758–1840) sighted another planetoid, Pallas, with a diameter of 298 miles (480km). Juno 124 miles, (200km) was sighted in 1804 and Vesta 298 miles, (480km) in 1807. By 1890, more than 300 asteroids had been charted in the region where Bode's Law said there should be a planet.

Planetoids

Were these planetoids the pieces of a former planet which had somehow broken up? That possibility seemed to be unlikely, for the total mass of more than 500,000 asteroidal bodies estimated by the McDonald and Palomar-Leiden surveys hardly equals 0·004 of the mass of the Earth. This mass included 2,289 asteroids listed as of 1980. Most of the bodies are in orbit around the Sun at 2·3 to 3·3AU; an exception is a small asteroid, Icarus. It passes within the orbit of Mercury at closest approach to the Sun (perihelion) and is one of a number of asteroids which cross Earth's orbit. On 14 June 1968, it passed within 4 million miles (6·4 million km) of the Earth. Another, Hermes, passed Earth at 484,680 miles (780,000km) in 1937. Two other asteroids, Apollo and Adonis, have passed Earth within 3 million miles (5 million km), while another, Geographos, has come within 6 million miles (10 million km).

Astronomically speaking, these passes may be considered near misses and perturbations in the orbits of the Earth-crossing asteroids could bring them nearer. Icarus has been the subject of a study concerned with the propulsion energy that would be required to boost it away from the Earth if it were found to be on a collision course.

At least 14 minor planets called the "Trojans" have been detected in Jupiter's orbit at Lagrangian points, 60 degrees ahead and 60 degrees behind the big planet. A Lagrangian point is found at one corner of an equilateral triangle formed by three astronomical bodies, a small one and two larger ones. Where Jupiter and the Sun occupy two points of such a triangle, a body reaching the third point in Jupiter's orbit will remain there, in equilibrium with the planet and the Sun.

In 1772, the French mathematician, Joseph Louis Comte de Lagrange (1736–1813) predicted that planetoids would be found at these equilibrium points in Jupiter's orbit — and they were, 134 years later. The first of the Trojan asteroids, Achilles, was sighted in 1906 and others were soon found.

Asteroids in orbit ahead of Jupiter were called the Achilles group and those trailing the planet, the Patroclus group, after the Greek heroes of *The Iliad,* Homer's account of the Trojan war. The American astronomer, George O. Abell, estimates that there are 700 or more Trojan minor planets near Jupiter.[2]

A 19th century hypothesis that the asteroids were the residue of a broken-up planet gave way in the 20th century to the theory that these bodies are simply consolidated clumps of matter, or planetesimals, which somehow were prevented from consolidating. Tidal forces of Jupiter have been considered as an inhibitor to consolidation.

No evidence for the break-up of a planet has been found, but there is plenty of evidence for planetary accretion, the process of growth whereby little pieces are amassed by bigger ones. Perhaps the asteroid belt has remained an arena of planetoids and rocks because no planet large enough to sweep them up has ever existed there.

There is evidence, however, that asteroids have been broken up by collision. A probable

Above: *A three-hour exposure with a portrait lens reveals three asteroids as streaks of light on the plate, their tell-tale motion giving them away. Many asteroids have thus been discovered accidentally.*

1 The Titius progression assigned numbers to the position of the planets. Mercury was 0; Venus, 3; Earth, 6; Mars, 12; and so on, the number doubling from Venus on. When 4 was added to the position number and the sum divided by 10, the result gave the approximate distance of the planet from the Sun in astronomical units. In the case of Mercury, the formula yields 0·4AU, somewhat more than Mercury's mean distance of 0·387AU. In the case of Earth, it works out correctly (6 + 4 ÷ 10 = 1AU). The progression gives 1·6AU for Mars (actually 1·524) and 5·2AU for Jupiter (actually 5·203).

2 Abell, George O., *Exploration of the Universe,* 3d ed., Holt, Rinehart & Winston, New York, 1975.

example is the plank-shaped Eros, 12 to 18 miles (20 to 30km) long and 5 miles (8km) thick. It looks like a large fragment of something else.

The collision probability of creating little ones out of big ones—the reverse of accretion—is supported by the identification of 29 "families" of asteroidal objects, with 4 to 62 "members" each. Similarities of family members indicate their origin in a common, parental body.

Meteorites

Like the asteroids, meteorites also derive from parental bodies which, in their case, probably are asteroids. In age, about 4·6 thousand million years, and in general chemical composition, meteorites are similar to the terrestrial planets.

Chemical differences among meteorites can be accounted for by episodes of heating in the parent bodies; and these are analogous to processes which have occurred in the inner planets. The class of meteorites called "chondrites" contains a detailed record of the pre-accretionary stage of the evolution of the Solar System.[3]

Meteorite is a specific term. It denotes an extraterrestrial object that has fallen on the surface of the Earth. A *meteor* or "bolide" is the fireball an incoming extraterrestrial object creates as it ploughs through the atmosphere. Sometimes it explodes or breaks up before impact, strewing fragments over the ground. These are meteorites. In space, the extraterrestrial object is called a meteoroid. If it is small—less than the size of a grain of sand, it is a *micrometeoroid*.

Evidence first seen on the Moon and later on Mars, Venus and Mercury showed that all the terrestrial planets were bombarded heavily by asteroidal or meteoroidal objects 3·9 to 4 thousand million years ago. This process of accretion is evolutionary; it has been seen on the planet-sized moons of Jupiter and Saturn, even on the asteroid-sized moons of Mars. As the aeons passed, the bombardment diminished; the debris left over from the earlier stages of planetary growth was swept up, but not all of it.

Accretion is still going on. On 12 February 1947, a brilliant fireball swept across the skies of Eastern Siberia near Vladivostok. The meteor crashed, gouging 100 craters out of the ground, some 90ft (28m) across. More than 23 tons of iron meteorite fragments were found. The craters covered an area of 2 square miles (5km²).

An earlier Siberian fall occurred in the Tunguska basin on 30 June 1908 when a meteor plunged into a forest. Air waves and ground shock were detected as far away as Western Europe. The projectile apparently exploded before hitting the ground for it did not leave a crater. Some scientists believe the Tunguska event was a comet, not a meteorite. Before entering the atmosphere, the meteoroid mass was an estimated 100,000 tons.

Other meteors have hit the ground and left craters. The largest in the United States is the Barringer Crater near Winslow, Arizona. It is 4,265ft (1,300m) across and 590ft (180m) deep. Its rim rises 148ft (45m) above the ground level. In the area, about 25 tons of iron meteorite fragments have been found as far as 4·3 miles (7km) from the

Above: *Devastation in Siberia: forest trees lie flattened over a region of 1,000sq miles (2,590km²) following the fall of the Tunguska fireball in June 1908. The body may even have been a small comet.*

crater. Impact is believed to have occurred 22,000 years ago.

Other impact craters have turned up in aerial photographs. One in Quebec (the Chubb crater) was discovered in a 1946 Canadian aerial photo. It was 1·9 miles (3km) across and had filled with water to become a lake. Ancient impact craters have been detected all over the world, from northern Illinois to Algeria, but they are hardly noticeable on the ground, having been nearly erased by the tectonic processes of an active planet.

The impact of a large meteorite or asteroid 65 million years ago has been cited as the cause of the great extinction of plants and animals at the end of the Cretaceous Period. Scientists at the University of California, Berkeley theorized that a globe-girdling cloud of dust was ejected into the stratosphere by the impact and prevented sunlight from reaching the surface for several years. As a result, photosynthesis was suppressed, food chains collapsed and animals dependent on them, including marine reptiles, flying reptiles, dinosaurs and others—all perished.[4]

During the Pleistocene Epoch, a huge meteorite with a mass estimated at 315 tons, accompanied by four smaller bodies, struck the Earth near Odessa, Texas. Three craters have been found, the largest 540ft (165m) across. Other meteorite craters have been identified in Kansas, Argentina, Australia, East Pamir, the Island of Oesel in the Baltic Sea, the Empty Quarter of Arabia and the Sahara.

Below: *The Orgeuil meteorite, which fell in Orgeuil, France, in 1864, is one of the rare class of carbonaceous chondrites: stone meteorites containing black, carbon-rich material and some organic matter.*

Large meteorites have survived the fireball phase of entry into the atmosphere and have landed without exploding or breaking into small pieces. The largest is the Hoba West meteorite, found near Grootfontein, Southwest Africa. It has a reported volume of 247ft³ (7m³) and a mass of 45 to 60 tons.

Before reaching the north pole in 1909, Robert E. Peary (1856–1920) discovered four, nickel-iron meteorites in Greenland in 1897. The largest which the Greenlanders called Ahnighito (the tent) weighed 33 tons.

A total of 1,800 meteorites have been listed in the Hey Catalogue of Meteorites, but they are only a fraction of the extraterrestrial debris the Earth sweeps up. Micrometeoroids fall continuously. Their mass has been estimated 10 to 100 tons a day.

Meteorites are classified as irons, stones and stony-irons by their composition. Iron

Below: *The Rowton iron meteorite. One face has been polished and etched with a weak solution of nitric acid in alcohol to bring out the characteristic crystal pattern of the meteorite's structure.*

Below: *The Beddgelert Chondrite, cut to reveal its interior structure. Stony meteorites like this contain round inclusions of minerals such as olivine or pyroxene, called chondrules (Gk chondros, grain).*

Above: *The team of explorers who discovered the Hoba West meteorite in 1920 appear dwarfed by its immense size. This nickel-rich ataxite iron,—the world's largest meteorite—has never been moved.*

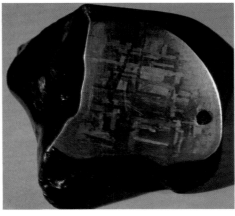

meteorites contain alloys of 85 to 95 per cent iron, the rest, nickel. The stony-irons have 50 per cent iron and 50 per cent silicates. They are relatively rare.

The most common sub-grouping of the stony meteorites are the chondrites, so called because they are an aggregate of millimetre-size, silicate spherules called chondrules. Some investigators say they look like frozen droplets of a melt. Chondrules consist largely of the minerals olivine, pyroxene and plagioclase feldspar embedded in a matrix of similar composition. In the opinion of the University of Chicago scientist Edward Anders, they represent the earliest process of accretion of solid objects from the solar nebula.[5] Stones lacking chondrules form another sub-group, the achondrites.

The chondrites are subdivided chemically according to the proportion of oxidized iron

to reduced iron in their composition. The most highly oxidized are the carbonaceous chondrites, relatively rich in carbon compounds. These, too, have been subdivided into (numerical) types according to mineral structure and volatile content. Type 1 carbonaceous chondrites are regarded by some investigators as the most primitive samples of matter known. Anders characterized them as low temperature condensates from the solar gas.[6]

During the second half of the 19th century, chemists in Europe began accumulating evidence of organic compounds in the carbonaceous chondrites. Inasmuch as organic compounds are associated with living systems, the discovery that the compounds, including hydrocarbons and fatty and aromatic acids, existed in meteorites implied that some form of life had existed on the

extraterrestrial body from which the chondrite came.

Inevitably, the implication aroused a widespread controvery, echoes of which are still heard. In the 19th century, the idea that meteorites were harbingers of life in space was considerably ahead of its time. It was not until well into the 19th century that the extraterrestrial origin of meteorites was accepted by all scientific bodies, including the French Academy. The meteoritic origin of craters like the Barringer Crater in Arizona or the Chubb Crater in Quebec was not established until the present century. The impact theory of craters on the Moon was not fully accepted until spacecraft reconnaissance proved that the craters were not volcanic (see Moon chapter).

3 Anders, E., "Physico-Chemical Processes in the Solar Nebula as Inferred from Meteorites", *Colloquium on the Origin of the Solar System,* Nice, France 3-8 April 1972.

4 Alvarez, L.W.; Alvarez, W., Asaro, F; Michel, H.V., "Extraterrestrial Cause for the Cretaceous-Tertiary Extinction", *Science,* Vol. 208, No. 4448, 6 June 1980.

These authors cite evidence that high concentrations of iridium (a platinum group metal) in Italian, Danish and New Zealand limestone were implanted by splash-out from the impact of an extraterrestrial object at the time of the Cretaceous-Tertiary extinction. The iridium concentrations were 20 to 160 times higher than background levels.

5 Anders, E., "Interrelations of Meteorites, Asteroids and Comets", *Physical Studies of the Minor Planets,* Gehrels, T., ed., NASA, 1972.

6 Ibid.

A well known anecdote in meteorite literature relates that when Thomas Jefferson was president of the United States (1801–1809), he was asked to approve a grant for the study of meteorites by investigators from Harvard College. This enlightened statesman who founded the University of Virginia represented the scientific thinking of his time. He is quoted as having responded that he would rather believe that two Yankee professors would lie than to believe that stones could fall from heaven.

Despite scepticism about the origin of meteorites, the Rosetta stone role of the carbonaceous chondrites became increasingly evident. In 1859, Hungarian scientists found organic compounds in a carbonaceous chondrite that had fallen in Hungary in 1857. In 1868, saturated hydrocarbons were isolated from a carbonaceous chondrite that had fallen near Orgeuil, France in 1864. In 1961, Bartholomew Nagy of Fordham University and associates at Columbia University presented evidence to the New York Academy of Sciences that they had found saturated hydrocarbons in a fragment of the Orgeuil meteorite. In 1969, scientists at NASA's Ames Research Center in California reported the presence of 5 amino acids characteristic of living cells in fragments of a carbonaceous chondrite that had fallen that year in Australia.

Critics of these reports have argued for years that the hydrocarbons represented terrestrial contamination, from the soil in which the chondrites fell or even from the atmosphere. But subsequent investigations turned up organic material embedded under the surface of the stones.

This controversy seems to have yielded to a growing consensus that living systems are not required to account for organic material in meteorites. Such material could have been formed by known chemical processes in the solar nebula and incorporated along with inorganic formations in the accreting solid bodies.[7]

Thus, the meteorites presented the first evidence of the extraterrestrial evolution of pre-biotic compounds and from this evidence it has been reasoned *a priori* that life may arise anywhere in the Universe where conditions allow it.

Conversely, where organic compounds do not exist, it is reasoned that life cannot develop. Indeed, failure to find organic molecules at the Viking lander sites on Mars persuaded the Viking biology team to conclude that evidence of life was not disclosed by the biology experiments—despite tantalizingly positive results from one experiment.

In addition to the organic compounds, the Orgeuil meteorite showed stages of mineral formation which initially was assumed to have taken place at high temperatures in a parent body. There was no doubt that following condensation from the nebula, the chondrites were modified, but it was suggested (1977) that the basic fractionation that produced the pattern of planetary evolution in the chondrites must have occurred during condensation of dust grains from the solar gas.[8] It seemed unlikely that the fractionation process could have occurred in a parent body which could not have been more than a millionth the mass of the Earth.

Most meteorites come from 6 to 11 parent bodies of 62 to 186 miles (100 to 300km) radius, according to Anders, and these bodies relate to 7 asteroid families between 1·9 and 2·8AU whose collision debris crosses the orbit of Mars.[9] Two thirds of the chondrites of low iron content were in major collision 520 million (plus or minus 60 million) years ago and came mainly from one or two bodies. Size of the parent bodies was estimated from cooling rates (as determined from analysis) of the meteorites at 60 to 93 miles (90 to 150km) in radius. The cooling rate of a planetary object is a function of its size. In general, it is lower in larger bodies.

However, type 3 carbonaceous chondrites, with a relatively low amount of volatile material, display cooling rates which indicate they came from bodies of 400km radius, about the size of Ceres. Anders observed,

"Although some people disagree, I think there is more than a slight chance that most meteorites come from the asteroid belt. It would be tremendously embarrassing to our entire profession if it turned out that after a mission to Eros, that pieces of Eros have been reposing in our museums all along."

Below: *A brilliant meteor flashes across the sky during a long photographic exposure of the Cygnus Loop (centre), the remains of an exploded star. The abrupt ending of the meteor trail tells that this body was consumed before it could land.*

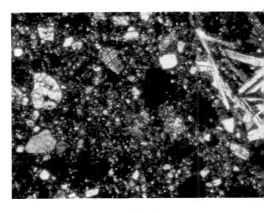

Above: *Etched face of the Stannern Eucrite, a stony meteorite with a structure like terrestrial basalt. The parent body for eucrites may be the asteroid Vesta.*

Meteor Streams

Although meteorite discoveries are infrequent, the occurrence of meteor streams is often regular and predictable. The cascading fireworks displays are seen as the Earth passes through swarms of meteoroids in solar orbit. Some of the meteor swarms are comet debris; others are residues from ancient collisions of asteroidal bodies. Tracks of most spectacular meteor showers radiate from several constellations, and are identified in that way as Earth passes through them at various times of the year.

The most brilliant of the regular showers is the Leonid swarm, seeming to radiate

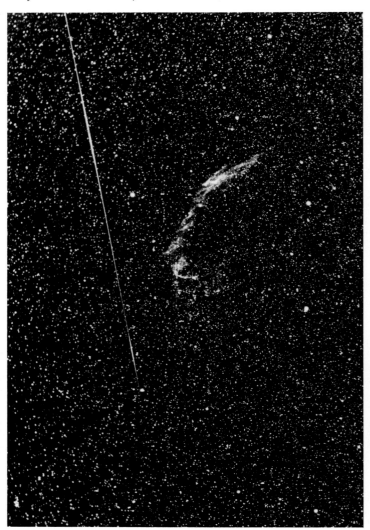

Above: *Tektites—like this 1in (2·5cm) diameter Australite—are glassy, button-shaped objects which bear signs of very rapid heating and cooling.*

from the constellation Leo. The swarm appears in mid-November. Other bright displays are the Perseid meteors in August (from Perseus) and the Aquarids in May (from Aquarius).

A unique class of objects called tektites (small, glassy objects with teardrop or button shape), has been found all over the world.

Below: *"Isti Mirant Stella"—"They marvel at the star". The "star" depicted on the Bayeux Tapestry is in fact Halley's Comet, which appeared just before King Harold's defeat and death at Hastings in 1066. To the French it was a good omen.*

Tektites (from the Greek, tektos, meaning molten) look like solidified globules of melted rock and probably are. Their origin has been in dispute for years.

In the 1960s, tektites became a focus of interest because of a hypothesis that they came from the Moon, hurled out of its gravitational field by violent volcanic eruptions or meteorite impacts. Subsequent analysis of lunar rocks failed to support this idea.

There is divided opinion on whether these golf ball to door knob size black and green glasses are of terrestrial or extra-terrestrial origin. They look as though they have been subject to high aerodynamic heating and this supports claims for extra-terrestrial origin in comets or meteorites. However, they may also have been shaped by flight through the atmosphere after being hurled as molten globules of rock out of exploding volcanoes.

Comets

Although the identification of meteorites as stones from the sky is largely a product of the latter 19th century, comets have been feared as heavenly visitations for thousands of years. In antiquity, they were regarded as portents, usually of some royal event such as the birth or death of a king or of the rise or fall of a kingdom.

The term, comet, comes from the Greek word, kometes, meaning long-haired, a reference to the blurry head of the comet and its tress-like tail. When the Great Comet

(Halley's Comet) was seen in England in the spring of 1066, it was regarded fearfully as a forerunner of the oncoming Norman conquest.[11] Edward the Confessor, last of the Saxon kings, had died early in January of that year. The Anglo-Saxon Chronicle told:

"*then was seen all over England such a sign in the heavens as no man ever before saw.*"

The comet is seen in the Bayeux tapestry.

Such signs had been seen before and would be seen again. Comet apparitions had been supposed to illuminate the deaths of Julius Caesar in 44BC, of Attila in AD453 and of Charlemagne in AD814. In 1456, Halley's comet immobilized with awe a Turkish army beseiging Belgrade and the city's defenders as well.[12]

The appearance of the Great Comet in 1682 inspired the English mathematician-astronomer, Edmond Halley (1656—1742) to attempt to establish its orbit. With the

7 Anders and others have explained that organic molecules can be formed by a cosmochemical version of the Fischer-Tropsch process developed in Germany for the synthesis of fuel. The organics are created by reactions of carbon monoxide, hydrogen and ammonia in the nebula, catalyzed by magnetite (F_3O_4) and silicates.

8 Anders, E. and Owen, T., "Mars and Earth: Origin and Abundance of Volatiles", *Science*, Vol. 198, 4 Nov 1977.

9 Anders, E. "Interrelations, etc.", op. cit.

10 Ibid.

11 Brown, P.L., *Comets, Meteorites and Men*, Taplinger Publishing Co., New York, 1974.

12 Ibid.

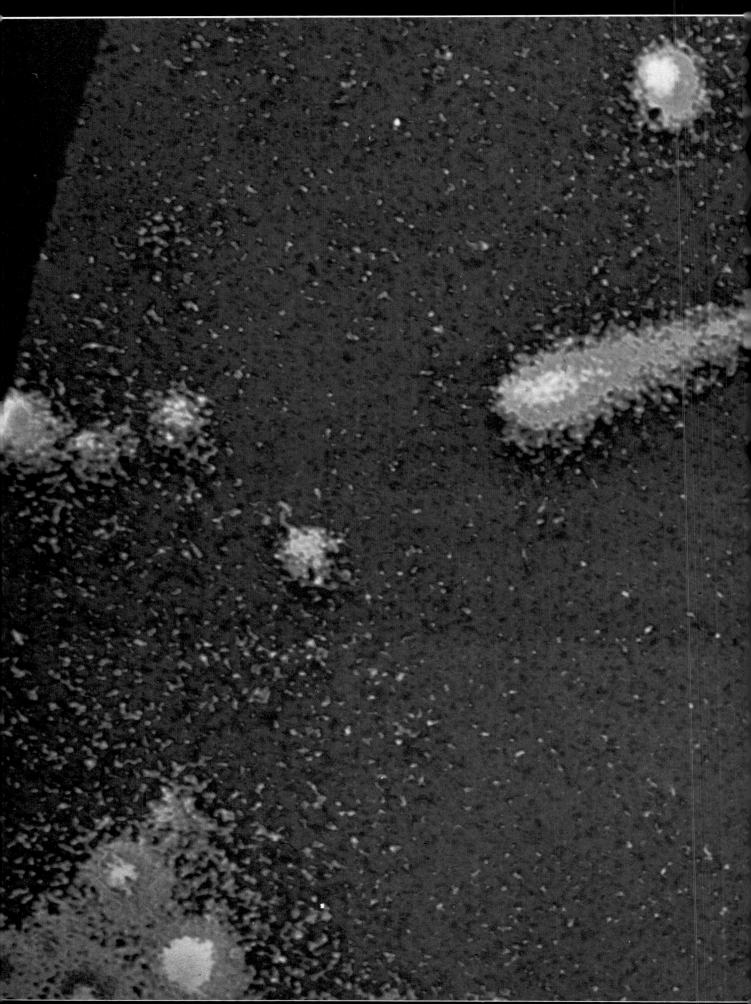

il, consisting of dust and gas, blown out of the comet by the solar wind to a distance of 3 million miles (4·8 million km).

Right: *Comet Arend-Roland, which was easily visible to the naked eye in 1957. The comet's gas tail streams straight out behind. The photograph was taken at the Shternberg Astronomical Institute, Moscow.*

Below: *Comet Ikeya-Seki gleams like a dagger in the twilight sky. Comets are best seen at dusk and dawn as they approach perihelion, and consequently reach their peak of brightness and activity.*

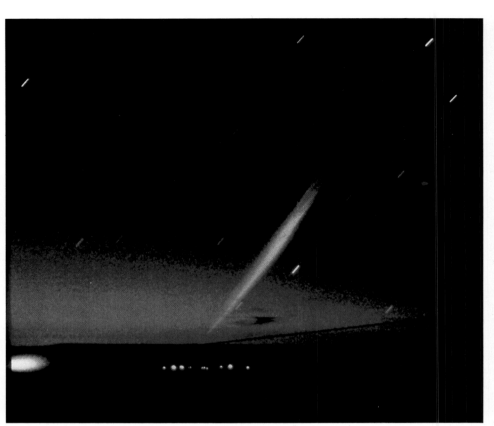

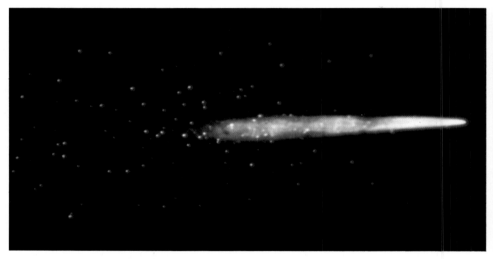

support of Sir Isaac Newton (1643–1727), Halley found that the comet followed an elliptical path which took it more than 3·35 thousand million miles (5·4 thousand million km) from the Sun and brought it back every 75 to 76 years.

When Halley compared the orbit of the 1682 comet with the orbital characteristics of previous comets, he concluded that it was the same comet that had been seen in 1531 and 1607. He was then able to predict that it would reappear in 1758, as it did on Christmas Day of that year.

Halley's Reappearances

Following the apparition of 1758-59, the comet, which had been named for Halley, returned in 1835 and again in 1910. It is due at perihelion (its closest approach to the Sun) on or about 5 February 1986. The predictability of comets suffers from the unpredictable perturbation of their paths by planets and the Sun.

During the apparition of 1910, the head of the comet expanded to a diameter of 342,000 miles (550,000km) and Earth passed through part of the tail at 5 million miles (8 million km) from the head. Experts have played down the effect of Earth passing through the gas-inflated coma, the portion of the head around the nucleus. They predict that the result would simply produce a meteor shower. A collision with the nucleus, however, could be a disaster.

The nucleus is the bright part of the head. It consists of dust, stones and solidified gases or ices made up of water, ammonia, methane, carbon dioxide and dicyanogen.[13] Although tiny compared to the coma around it, the nucleus is denser. Its diameter may range up to 5 miles (8km). It would thus be comparable to the mass of a small asteroid.

In 1927, Comet P/Pons-Winnecke passed Earth at a distance of 3·1 to 3·7 million miles

(5 to 6 million km). Observers at the Meudon Observatory in France reported its nucleus was 0·62 miles (1km) in diameter. A nucleus that size striking the Earth at cometary velocity would have the effect of megatons of high explosives. If the impact came without warning (which seems unlikely), it could hardly be distinguished from a massive nuclear attack.

The American astronomer, Fred Whipple, has described comets as dirty icebergs. About half of the nucleus is stony or metallic. The rest vaporizes as the meteorite approaches the Sun. Whipple estimated that methane would vaporize at a distance of several Astronomical Units. Near Mars, carbon dioxide and ammonia would evaporate and nearer the Sun, the dicyanogen and water would vaporize.

As these gases escape, they cause the coma around the nucleus to expand to the size of Jupiter. Expanding gases fluoresce in solar ultraviolet light and emit visible light brighter than sunlight which is reflected by

Above: *Halley's Comet, photographed on its last close passage through the inner Solar System in 1910. Its tail grew to a length of 20 million miles (32 million km).*

the nucleus. Although visible as a planet-size glowing sphere, the coma is actually hard vacuum. In 1910, observers saw stars shining through the coma of Halley's comet.

The tail is a spectacular feature, consisting of streams of gas which become longer, wider and brighter as the comet approaches the Sun and the volatile materials boil away. Comet tails may extend as far as 93 million miles (150 million km) from the head. They always stream away from the Sun irrespective of the comet's direction. This effect is produced by radiation pressure of sunlight and probably by the solar wind. However, gas emissions from the head exert some braking thrust which may cause the flight path to wobble.

Another widely observed comet in this century is Comet Kohoutek, discovered in

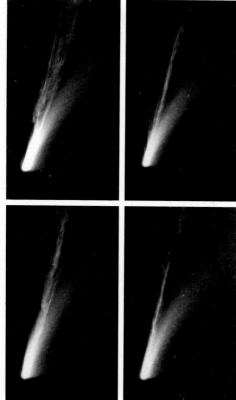

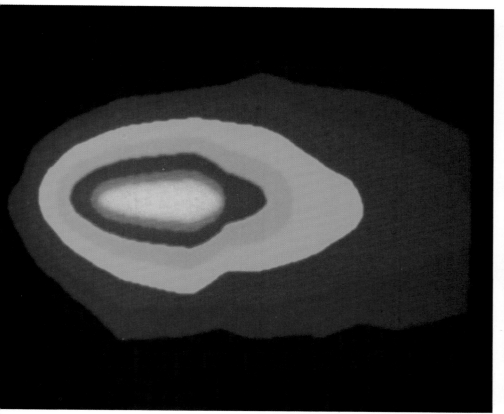

The Structure of a Comet
1 Nucleus or core.
2 Original icy material.
3 Irregular layers of icy material.
4 Porous outer crust.

Until probes intercept Halley's Comet in 1986, the structure of comets will be somewhat conjectural. Currently, Fred Whipple's "dirty snowball" model is thought to be the most accurate. The only solid part of a comet is its stony or metallic nucleus (core), which measures perhaps 6 miles (10km) across at maximum. Icy layers above vaporize as the comet approaches the Sun, but at closest approach, when the ices directly sublime, the head develops a protective dusty crust.

Above: *In May 1983, the Infra-red Astronomical Satellite became the first spacecraft to discover a comet which grew bright enough to be seen with the naked eye. This false-colour IRAS picture of the coma of comet IRAS-Araki-Alcock is at a wavelength of 20 micrometres. It shows a region of escaping gases around the comet's head roughly equal in size to the Earth. The most intense areas (yellow) are the hottest; the blue extension to the right, away from the Sun, indicates dusty material and gas in the comet's tail.*

Above right: *Comet Mrkos, the other bright comet of 1957, showed spectacular activity in its tail. This series of pictures, taken over a five day period in August, reveals jets and flares in the gas tail.*

1973 by the Czech astronomer, Lubos Kohoutek at the Hamburg Observatory, Germany. Kohoutek was the first comet to be observed by men in orbit—by the crew of Skylab 4 aboard the Skylab space station. It was scanned also by instruments aboard Mariner 10 as the spacecraft flew to Venus in 1973. Kohoutek rounded the sun at 0·14AU on 28 December 1973, and shortly thereafter, became fainter and fainter until it disappeared. Contary to expectations, it did not provide a spectacular display and may have broken up. Nevertheless, it provided a scientific feast. Cometeers had theorized that hydrogen should be released from the comet head by photo dissociation of water, but that could not be ascertained from the surface of the Earth because the (Lyman alpha) radiation emitted by hydrogen as its energy state changes does not penetrate the atmosphere.

In 1969-70, NASA observatories, Orbiting Geophysical Observatory 5 and Orbiting Astronomical Observatory 2, detected hydro-

gen around comets Bennett and Tago-Sato-Kosaka. Then, in 1973, Mariner 10 saw hydrogen radiating from Kohoutek to form a 25 million miles (40 million km) corona.

Kohoutek provided an opportunity to scan a comet by microwaves for the first time. The radio scans revealed something new — the spectral lines of molecules of hydrogen cyanide and methyl cyanide. These molecules had been observed in interstellar space, but not in the Solar System until Kohoutek appeared. Their presence in Kohoutek supports a hypothesis that comets were not formed from the solar nebula along with planets and meteorites, but rather from fragments of the interstellar cloud before it contracted to form the solar nebula, according to George Abell.[14] He observed that the distribution of comet orbits is consistent with this theory. Nevertheless, comets are members of the Solar System. If they were interstellar objects, he pointed out, most of them would be approaching the Sun from the Constellation of Hercules toward which the Sun is moving in its Galactic orbit.

The comet catalogue of the British Astronomical Association lists 70 comets with hyperbolic orbits. This suggests to one observer the existence of a population of fast moving comets star-hopping from one periastron (the closest approach to a star) to another.[15] Comets in hyperbolic orbits would not return to the Sun and it is possible they could be pulled by gravitational attraction into another star system.

Approximately 100 comets have been identified as having elliptical orbits which bring them back periodically, like Halley's

13 Whipple, Fred., *Earth, Moon and Planets*, Harvard University Press, Cambridge, Mass., 1968.
14 Abell, G.O., op. cit.
15 Brown, P.L., op. cit.

Giotto

1 Low-gain cardioid antenna.
2 S-band and X-band feed.
3 High-gain dish antenna.
4 Despin mechanism.
5 Travelling-wave-tube amplifier.
6 Optical probe experiment.
7 Hydrazine tank.
8 Mage-1S kick motor.
9 Experiment box.
10 Attitude control thrusters.
11 Rear shield (13·5mm thick Kevlar-49/polyure-thane foam sandwich).
12 GRP strut.
13 Nozzle closure shells.
14 Inner bumper shield.
15 Dust impact detector (DID) system sensor (3+1 on rear shield).
16 Outer bumper shield (1mm thick aluminium alloy sheet).
17 Multicolour camera telescope (modified Ritchey-Chrétien).
18 Camera telescope baffle.
19 Experiment sensors.
20 Solar cell array.
21 Hollow carbon-fibre tripod.
22 Magnetometer sensor (hidden in this view).

By far the most ambitious ESA space project to date, the Giotto probe is due to be launched by Ariane in July 1985 for a rendezvous some eight months later with Halley's Comet, which is reappearing in the inner Solar System at that time on its 30th recorded 76-year periodic return. The spin-stabilized spacecraft will carry ten scientific instruments to study the comet, comprising a camera; neutral mass, ion mass and dust mass spectrometers; a dust impact detector system; two plasma analyzers; a magnetometer; an energetic particles experiment; and an optical probe experiment. An important feature of the spacecraft is its dust protection system, consisting of a 1mm aluminium front sheet and a 13·5mm kevlar/foam rear shield separated by 10in (25cm), to combat the dust cloud produced by the comet as it interacts with the Sun. A solar cell array will provide 190W of power, with four silver-cadmium batteries to boost output while the experiments are in operation and to ensure that electrical power is still available in the event of damage being sustained by the solar array during impact with dust particles. A high-gain dish antenna pointing continuously at Earth during the encounter operates in either S-band (uplink/downlink) or X-band (downlink only) and provides telemetry to the ground station; two low-gain S-band antennas are also fitted, for GTO and near-Earth communications. Halley's Comet has been selected for study not primarily because of its fame: it is the brightest and most predictable of all the intermediate-periodic comets, and a mission to intercept it requires a low launch energy (thus permitting a high-mass payload). Moreover, it will be visible from Earth, for simultaneous ground-based and near-Earth observation.

Mission Trajectory

Giotto's trajectory will take the craft near the comet's post-perihelion crossing of the ecliptic plane on 13 March 1986, about one month after its perihelion passage. Launch by Ariane in tandem with a second spacecraft into GTO will be followed by separation and injection of Giotto into its heliocentric transfer trajectory by means of the latter's solid-fuel kick motor. Halley's orbit is inclined at 162°, and it will cross the ecliptic twice, on 9 November 1985 and again on 11 March 1986. Giotto's closest approach to the Sun will be at a distance of 0·7AU.

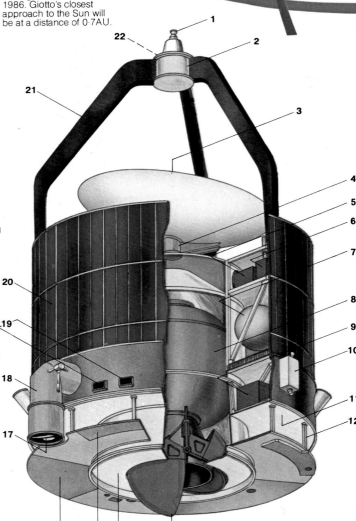

Launch: 10 July 1985

Halley encounter: 13 March 1986

Earth: 13 March 1986

Technical Data
Height overall: 9·72ft (2·964m).
Diameter: 6·1ft (1·86m).
Diameter of high-gain antenna reflector: 4·8ft (1·47m).
Launch weight: 2,094lb (950kg).
Weight at encounter (after kick motor burn-out and hydrazine exhaustion): 1,129lb (512kg).
Fly-by velocity: 42·25 miles/sec (68km/sec.).

Close Fly-By

Giotto will pass directly through comet Halley's coma, targetted at a point 310 miles (500km) sunward from the nucleus. Halley will at that time be 0·89AU away from the Sun and 1AU from Earth. Spacecraft phase angle to the Sun will be 107·2°. The comet's orbit is retrograde (ie opposite to that of Earth—and hence to that of the spacecraft), which makes for an extremely high fly-by velocity, only partly compensated for by a high data rate. Giotto is not expected to survive past the time of closest approach, and thus data will be transmitted in real time, (no spacecraft memory is provided). Battery capacity and ground reception availability will also limit the data-take period.

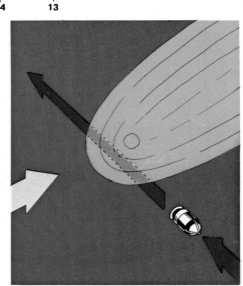

Comet. The periods vary, from Encke's Comet, which comes around every 3·3 years, to Comet Rigolett, with a period of 151 years.

Some comets do not survive their encounter with the Sun. Comet Biela, discovered in 1772 with a period of 7 years, broke in two in 1846. Its major pieces have not been seen since then, but meteor showers were seen at seven year intervals as the Earth passed through Biela's old orbit, until the 20th century.

About 45 comets reach aphelion (the point farthest from the Sun) near Jupiter which has reduced the extent of their orbits. Two comets have nearly circular orbits, one between Jupiter and Saturn, the other between Mars and Jupiter.

The Dutch astronomer, Jan H. Oort has proposed that a great mass of comets exists at 50,000AU, revolving around the Sun far beyond the planetary system. The mass might contain 100 thousand million comets, a relic of the cloud from which the solar nebula formed.

Spacecraft Encounters

Halley's Comet will be the target of probes from the European Space Agency (ESA), the Soviet Union and Japan in 1986. The US National Aeronautics & Space Administration lacked funds for a similar effort, but has diverted International Sun-Earth Explorer-3 (ISEE-3) from a sunward monitoring position to intercept a smaller comet, Giacobini-Zinner, in 1985. ISEE-3 will observe also the behaviour of the solar wind as Halley's Comet approaches, but will not fly close enough to inspect it.

ESA announced plans to send a probe to within several hundred miles of the nucleus of Halley's Comet. The probe, called "Giotto", is to be launched by an Ariane 3 rocket from Kourou, French Guiana on 10 July 1985. It would be expected to encounter Halley's Comet on 13 March 1986 at a distance of 90 million miles (145 million km) from Earth.

Giotto is named in memory of the Florentine painter, Giotto di Bondone (1266-1337). He depicted the 1301 apparition of the comet as a model for the Star of Bethlehem in his fresco, "Adoration of the Magi", for the Scrovegni Chapel in Padua. The Giotto payload includes a camera to take colour images of the coma and nucleus, and spectrometers to analyze the composition and density of gas and dust.

The Soviet Union announced that, in collaboration with France, it would send two "Vega" multiprobes to Halley's Comet; each of them will drop a lander capsule on Venus en route. Vega 1 is to pass through the comet's tail on 6 March 1986 about 6,200 miles (10,000km) from the nucleus and Vega 2 is to pass the nucleus at a distance of 1,862 miles (3,000km) on 9 March 1986.

The Japanese have announced their intention of launching a probe called "Planet A" to Halley's Comet. The probe is to pass c. 62,000 miles (100,000km) from the nucleus.

NASA plans to send ISEE-3 to Comet Giacobini-Zinner in 1985, using the Moon's gravitational field to hurl the 1,056lb (479kg) spacecraft 37 million miles (59·6 million km) from Earth to reach the comet. Comet Giacobini-Zinner was first sighted in 1900 and it passes the Earth and rounds the Sun every 13 years. Its coma has been measured as 31,000 miles (50,000km) in diameter, and its tail as extending 217,500 miles (350,000km).

Part of a three-satellite solar wind and Galactic observatory system, ISEE-3 was launched in 1978 into a "halo" orbit around an Earth-Sun libration point 1 million miles (1·6 million km) from Earth. The libration point (L_1) is the locus in space where the gravitational fields of the Sun and the Earth-Moon system are in equilibrium. A vehicle orbiting such a point remains in the same place relative to the Earth and Sun.

After four years at L_1, the satellite had enough hydrazine fuel left to boost it back to Earth, but not enough for the long journey to the comet. Only by gravitational assist from the Moon could it reach the comet.

On 10 June 1982, NASA's Goddard Space Flight Center fired the satellite engine and broke ISEE-3 out of the halo orbit. The spacecraft took up a looping path around

Below: *US Sun-probe ISEE-3, which was launched in 1978 to monitor the solar wind, undergoing tests at Goddard Space Flight Center. It is being diverted to intercept Comet Giacobini-Zinner in 1985.*

the Earth-Moon system that provided a rare opportunity for a highly instrumented vehicle to investigate the Earth's magnetic tail. This is an elongation of the geomagnetic field which is blown far beyond the Earth by the solar wind. Passing the orbit of the Moon in October 1982, ISEE-3 crossed the tail in November, looped around the Earth and re-entered the tail in December.

On 8 February 1983, ISEE-3 reached the farthest point of its travel "down" the tail (i.e., away from the Earth) and Goddard controllers fired the hydrazine engine to increase velocity. The burn put the satellite into a complex, looping orbit in which it would pass through the geomagnetic tail and swing by the Moon five times. On the final swing-by, it would be accelerated by the Moon out of Earth-Moon system towards its 1985 comet rendezvous.

On 30 March 1983 the spacecraft made its first swing by the Moon at a distance of 13,360 miles (21,500km) from the centre. Successive swing-bys followed, each looping around the Moon's orbit and through the geomagnetic tail.

On the fifth swing-by, scheduled for 23 December 1983, it was calculated that ISEE-3 would graze the surface of the Moon at an altitude of 70 miles (112km) and would be boosted by the lunar gravitational field on the flight path that would allow it to pass within 1,865 miles (3,000km) of Comet Giacobini-Zinner's nucleus in 1985.

The satellite is expected to return data on composition and density of the gases in the head and tail of the comet. It is also expected to show the effect of the solar wind in creating the tail.

On 31 October 1985, ISEE-3 is to make the first of two approaches to the orbit of Halley's Comet at a distance of 86·4 million miles (139·1 million km) from the head sunward or upstream of the incoming comet. Then on 28 March 1986, it is to pass 19·5 million miles (31·4 million km) upstream of the comet. On neither approach will ISEE-3 be in contact with cometary matter, but during each it will monitor the solar wind a day or two before it blows past the comet.

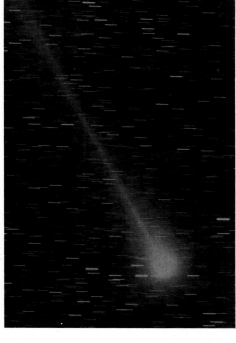

Above: *Comet Giacobini-Zinner on its last close approach in 1972. This small comet, which has a period of 13 years, will be intercepted by the US probe ISEE-3, which will then fly near Halley's Comet in 1986. At its greatest extent, the coma measures 31,000 miles (50,000km) across; the tail extends 217,500 miles (350,000km).*

RECOMMENDED READING

Abell, George O., *Exploration of the Universe* (3rd edition), Holt, Rinehart & Winston, New York, 1975.
Anders, E., "Interrelations of Meteorites, Asteroids and Comets", *Physical Studies of the Minor Planets*, Gehrels, T. (ed.), NASA, Washington, D.C., 1972.
Brown, P.L., *Comets, Meteorites and Men*, Taplinger Publishing Co., New York, 1974.
Whipple, Fred, *Earth, Moon and Planets* (3rd edition), Harvard University Press, Cambridge, Massachusetts, 1968.

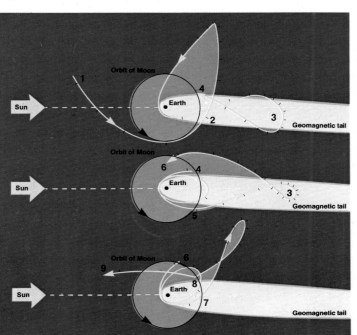

ISEE-3 Flight Path
1 Leave orbit around Sun-Earth libration point, 10 June 1982.
2 First pass through geomagnetic tail, 14-24 October 1982.
3 Further passes through geomagnetic tail.
4 First lunar swing-by, 30 March 1983.
5 Second lunar swing-by, 24 April 1983.
6 Third lunar swing-by, 28 September 1983.
7 Fourth lunar swing-by, 22 October 1983.
8 Fifth lunar swing-by, 23 December 1983.
9 Accelerated out of Earth-Moon system towards comet, January 1984.

This diagram illustrates how ISEE-3 is being manoeuvred through a series of five swings around the Moon, so that it may be accelerated by lunar gravitational force onto a heliocentric course towards an encounter with Comet Giacobini-Zinner (11 September 1985) and then towards the orbit of Comet Halley

If we expand our habitat to include the Solar System, we have the potential resources of 9 planets, 45 moons, thousands of asteroids and a myriad of comets as well as the energy of Sun with which to support an expanding civilization.

The process of utilizing space not only for commercial but for industrial purposes has already begun. As described in the following pages, pharmaceutical, metallurgical and other materials processing experiments have been conducted for more than a decade aboard manned spacecraft and space stations. But this is only the beginning. In the view of modern space theoreticians, an industrial civilization on the Moon and in space is not only possible but probable. Indeed, as a long term prospect, it may be necessary as Earth's resources are depleted.

The nature of extraterrestrial resources has been fairly well defined by observation, reconnaissance and in situ exploration. On the Moon, as Professor James R. Arnold notes, available material resources include aluminum, calcium, iron, magnesium, titanium, potassium, rare Earth elements and phosphorus. Lunar resources are suitable for building a technical civilization in space, in Professor Arnold's view.

However, the sine qua non for such prospective space ventures as factories, colonies, solar power satellites, lunar industry and asteroid mining is a transportation infrastructure. As projected by Kenneth W. Gatland, the transportation system would require a station in near Earth orbit to service and refuel space ships, advanced high capacity shuttles, orbital transfer vehicles and tugs and lunar and planetary landers. More immediately, while the Soviet Union is developing its own Shuttle, the US National Aeronautics and Space Administration is looking at a single-stage-to-orbit, reusable transport in the 21st century and heavy lift vehicles based on present Shuttle solid rocket booster technology.

The Solar Power Satellite pioneer, Peter E. Glaser, states the case for photovoltaic conversion of sunlight into electricity to power microwave generators in space. A transmitting antenna directs a low power, microwave beam to a receiving antenna on the Earth where the microwave energy is reconverted to electricity and distributed through conventional systems. Dr Glaser points out that the construction and maintenance of a Solar Power Satellite system requires a space transportation system capable of placing heavy payloads in low and geostationary orbits. He estimates the capital investment for a solar power system at $1 trillion over a 30-year period.

A leading space pioneer, Krafft A. Ehricke, suggests that because terrestrial resources are limited, it is clear that civilization must enter a "polyglobal phase" in which the resources of other worlds can be tapped. Dr Ehricke suggests that the first stage in the development of a polyglobal civilization is the industrialization of the Moon.

In his projection, lunar development would rely on nuclear rather than solar energy for heat and power to extract oxygen, silicon, iron, aluminum and titanium from the rocks. This would be done at a central processing plant where raw materials, strip mined from the surface, would be melted and their constituent chemical assemblies separated in a centrifuge. Dr Ehricke foresees nuclear fusion technology as the "wellhead" of power on the Moon, with production of hydrogen as a by-product.

In the near term, extra-terrestrial manufacturing prospects are less dramatic. David Dooling reports that, in the view of industrial managers, space manufacturing will be limited to products which can be produced more efficiently and with higher quality in the microgravity environment of low Earth orbit than on the ground. Experimental evidence predicts these products will be crystals, pharmaceuticals, electronic components, optics and superior alloys for specialized uses. However, the economic potential is very high. According to one survey, the market value of materials processing in space is likely to exceed $20 thousand million by the end of the century.

Also in this section, Theo Pirard looks at the programmes of space exploration projected for the 1980s, with especial reference to the smaller space-faring powers, such as India, China, Japan, France, Germany, and Europe in the guise of ESA, who are nevertheless making significant strides forward towards interplanetary space flight.

The exploration of space appears to be following an historic pattern. Like the great explorations of the past, its reconnaissance phase is being followed by economic development. If the past is prologue, the next phase will be settlement.

Extraterrestrial Resources

As on Earth, the rocks and soil of the Moon consist mainly of silicate minerals. The whole periodic table of the chemical elements is there. Is the material of the Moon suitable for building a technical civilization in space? The answer seems to be yes.

The Earth is a very small part of the Universe, and the surface regions that we can mine still smaller. Now that space is accessible to us, it becomes reasonable — for the first time — to look at what we may find there that may be useful to us.

A resource is usually a material object, but it need not be. As we move about the Earth's surface, into low orbit around the planet, we encounter several unfamiliar conditions. The most unusual and promising of these is the reduction of the effective force of gravity to a low or negligible value. Another is the prevalence of high vacuum. A third is the presence of abundant, highly predictable (but interrupted) solar heat and light, in a tight beam easy to direct and concentrate. These conditions, and particularly combinations of them, may permit us to do things we cannot do (or do nearly as well) on Earth. An example under active

study at present is the separation of medically useful substances by electrophoresis (see also Chapter 15). We may expect to see applications also in solid-state materials (semiconductors), alloys, and other systems containing multiple components. Conditions less often considered, but promising, nevertheless, are the gravity gradient force (change of g with altitude), and the rapid movement across the lines of force of the Earth's magnetic field.

At present the charge to users for carrying payloads to low Earth orbit, whether by the Space Shuttle, Ariane, or other booster, is well above $1,000 per kilogram. Thus processing or manufacture in space of materials brought from and returned to Earth must be confined for the present to substances of high intrinsic value.

Looking ahead, this high cost is the greatest barrier to humans moving out to dwell in space permanently, as Professor Gerard K. O'Neill of Princeton University has persuasively urged us to do. The living and working spaces, the material objects we need or want, must now pay this toll to be admitted to orbit. Must this always be true?

There are two ways to overcome this

obstacle. First, we may devise lower cost ways to launch into orbit. This is promising, but progress is slow. A shipping cost below $100/kg is unlikely in this century, or perhaps beyond. Compare the figure, for example, with air fare from the United States to Australia. It is forbidding.

The second approach is to find an alternative source of raw materials. The reason that space is so inaccessible to us is the deep gravitational well of the Earth. In O'Neill's image we are located at the bottom of a 4,000-mile high mountain relative to space. Other planets have the same problem, more or less. But smaller bodies, like the Moon, asteroids, other satellites and comets, hold their surface materials much less strongly.

Of all these celestial bodies, the Moon is nearest and much the best known. The history of lunar exploration is described elsewhere in this volume. Study of the samples returned to Earth, supplemented by geochemical mapping of part of the surface, give us a wealth of information on which to base our plans. We know that the surface is made up almost entirely of finely-dispersed material, roughly of the texture of

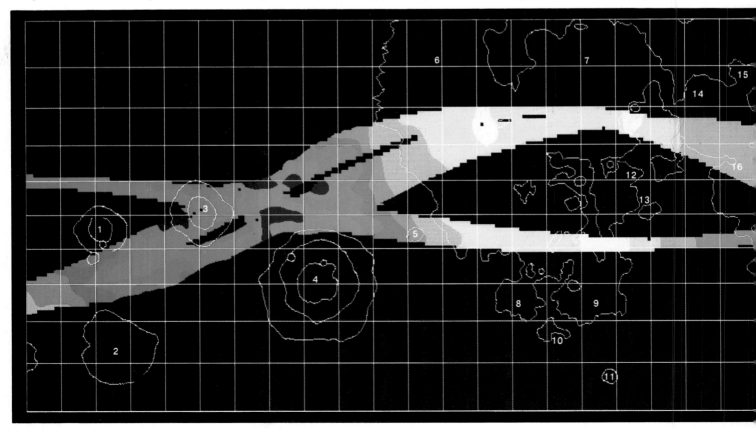

"Sail forth—steer for the deep waters only,
Reckless O soul exploring, I with thee, and thou with me,
For we are bound where mariner has not yet dared to go . . ."

Walt Whitman, *Passage to India*

CHEMICAL COMPOSITION OF BULK SOIL AT THREE APOLLO LANDING SITES[1][2]			
	APOLLO 11 SEA OF TRANQUILLITY	APOLLO 14 FRA MAURO	APOLLO 16 DESCARTES HIGHLANDS
SiO_2	42·04	47·93	44·94
TiO_2	7·48	1·74	0·58
Al_2O_3	13·92	17·60	26·71
FeO	15·74	10·37	5·49
MgO	7·90	9·24	5·96
CaO	12·01	11·19	15·57
Na_2O	0·44	0·68	0·48
K_2O	0·14	0·55	0·13
P_2O_5	0·12	0·53	0·12
MnO	0·21	0·14	0·07
Cr_2O_3	0·30	0·25	0·12
Total[3]	100·30	100·22	100·17

[1] Data given in weight per cent.
[2] Adapted from Criswell, David R. (1978), "Extraterrestrial Materials Processing and Construction", (Final Report), P.IV-32, NSR 09-051-001 (Mod. 24), Lunar and Planetary Inst., Houston, Texas.
[3] Percentage totals appear greater than 100 per cent as the weights of constituents have been rounded up to two places of decimals.

sand, with a few rocks and boulders scattered about, and rare exposures of an underlying rocky basement material. As on Earth, the rocks and soil consist mainly of silicate minerals. The whole periodic table of chemical elements is found there, as it must

be on any solid object in space. There are differences in abundance of elements, and mineral assemblages, from those we find at home, but they are not of crucial importance except in a few problem areas.

What The Moon Can Supply

No "ores" have been found on the Moon, and many Earth scientists doubt that they will be. We must, however, show proper respect for our ignorance; we have hardly begun to explore. The most serious gap in abundance is that of water (or hydrogen). Lunar rocks are very dry. A possible source is to be found at cold traps near the lunar poles which according to our present ideas have not been warmed by sunlight in billions of years. Of course we cannot yet see into these places to verify (or reject) this idea.

The accompanying table shows the chemical composition of bulk soil at three Apollo landing sites. These seem to be representative of the main regions of the moon. Apollo 16 visited the one true highland site, Descartes, which can be taken to represent fairly well the 80 per cent of the lunar surface which is light in colour and high in topography. However, the "typical" highland

soil probably contains somewhat more aluminium (Al) and calcium (Ca) with less iron (Fe) and magnesium (Mg). The Apollo 11 site in the Sea of Tranquillity is filled with dark basaltic mare material, high in Fe and Mg, with a surprisingly high amount of titanium (Ti). The Ti content varies greatly among mare soils; the Apollo 11 site is on the high side but there are richer sites still.

The Apollo 14 site in the Fra Mauro formation represents a special area of the Moon, rich in trace elements including the radioactive elements thorium (Th) and uranium (U). This stuff, called KREEP (the acronym for potassium, rare Earth elements and phosphorus) seems so far to be found only in the western front area of the Moon, near and on the great mare Oceanus Procellarum. Our remote sensing data seem to show that half the radioactivity on the lunar surface is concentrated in this region, a situation without parallel on the Earth.

The material of the Moon certainly seems suitable for building a technical civilization in space. If one examines the material needs of the only technical civilization we know, our own, we find that much of what we require, for structures, roads, and so

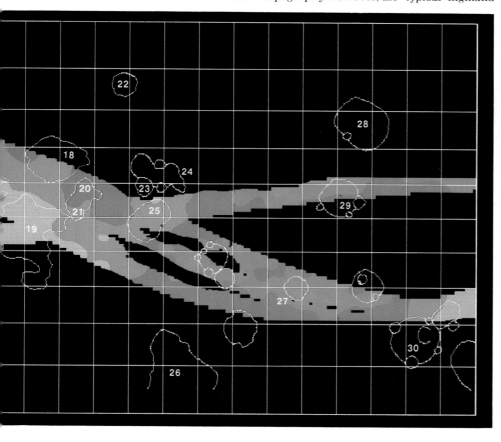

The Distribution of Radioactive Elements on the Moon
1 Korolev.
2 Apollo.
3 Hertzsprung.
4 Mare Orientale.
5 Grimaldi.
6 Oceanus Procellarum.
7 Mare Imbrium.
8 Mare Humorum.
9 Palus Epidemiarum.
10 Mare Nubium.
11 Tycho.
12 Mare Vaporum.
13 Sinus Medii.
14 Mare Serenitatis.
15 Lacus Somniorum.
16 Mare Tranquillitatis.
17 Mare Nectaris.
18 Mare Crisium.
19 Mare Fecunditatis.
20 Mare Undarum.
21 Mare Spumans.
22 Gauss.
23 Mare Marginis.
24 Neper.
25 Mare Smithii.
26 Mare Australe.
27 Tsiolkovsky.
28 Mare Moscoviense.
29 Mendeleev.
30 Mare Ingenii.

This map illustrates the distribution of radioactive elements in a swath covering 20 per cent of the entire surface of the Moon. The concentrations of these elements were measured by Professor James R. Arnold and his colleagues at the University of California, San Diego, from data

collected by the gamma ray spectrometers aboard the Apollo 15 and 16 Command Modules, *Endeavour* and *Casper,* while in lunar orbit during the missions flown in 1971 and 1972. (For an annotated drawing of the SIM-bay and its instruments, see p. 147.) White represents the highest concentration of radioactive elements which appeared in the western maria of the lunar near side. Blue, as seen in the highlands of the lunar far side, depicts the lowest concentrations. The diminution of these concentrations is represented by the colour sequence white to yellow to green to blue. Radioactive elements found on the Moon include thorium, uranium, potassium, aluminium 26 and sodium 22. The Apollo 14 site in the Fra Mauro formation which was found to be rich in KREEP elements (potassium, rare earth elements and phosphorus) is situated between the Mare Imbrium (**7**) and the Mare Nubium (**10**). The coded map was prepared by Dr Philip Davis of the US Geological Survey, Flagstaff, Arizona, and is reproduced by courtesy of Professor Arnold.

Above: *The Apollo 15 CSM orbits the Moon with its Scientific Instruments Module bay (SIM-bay) exposed. The gamma ray spectrometer is situated at the top right corner of the bay in this view.*

Above: *The selenographic north pole (N) lies just outside crater Peary. The Moon's polar regions are in perpetual shadow, a condition that would allow water ice—and hence hydrogen—to exist there.*

Right: *A captured asteroid? This high resolution image of the Martian moon, Phobos, was returned by the spacecraft Viking Orbiter 1 in 1978. The crater Stickney is at the top left.*

on, can be prepared from lunar soil by simple processes already developed here.

For our simplest and largest-scale needs, such as structures, composition is secondary. Materials can be used with little processing; perhaps melting and casting may be the most appropriate. Beyond this we need metals for strength (iron), and electrical conductivity (aluminum), oxygen for life support and propulsion, silicates and silicon for many purposes, and small amounts of the light elements carbon, nitrogen, sulphur and hydrogen (C, N, S, H) for life support. All these except hydrogen are clearly present in sufficient quantity for our needs on the Moon.

We have processes developed on Earth for extracting all these substances in useful form, for more demanding applications. Thus we know it can be done. It is quite another matter, however, to find the processes most suited for application on the Moon or in space. Conditions and costs will be very different. Energy, especially heat, will be cheap and plentiful. Equipment and chemicals brought from Earth will be very expensive. So, for some time at least, will be human labour. This condition will persist until equipment (and people) begin to be produced (or born) in space.

We are now beginning research on space-based processing methods. As in other fields, the best solutions will surely be found only after we have a good deal of experience. The first cars were "horseless carriages", and our first space processes will doubtless show similar lack of finesse;

but they will be a necessary bridge to a space economy.

Getting material off the Moon requires only a few per cent of the energy needed to escape Earth's gravity. The best way to appreciate the difference is to compare the Saturn V rocket used to lift the Apollo astronauts from the Earth with the Lunar Module ascent stage which carried them from the Moon. The former is the size of a large building, while the latter fits into a room. Still, some energy and new technology will be required. O'Neill and his collaborators are developing an electromagnetic launcher, the mass driver, for this purpose, and there are other methods under consideration.

The Asteroids

The Moon has competition as a source of raw materials in space. The asteroids in the belt between Mars and Jupiter are numerous but remote. Some asteroids approach us, however, during their orbits and about fifty are already known which come close to or cross the Earth's orbit. These range typically from one to ten kilometres in diameter. The meteorites which fall from time to time on the Earth (several thousand of these are now recorded) are much smaller bodies which arrive from Earth-intersecting orbits. The relation between Earth-approaching

asteroids and meteorites is not yet well understood, but it is likely that there is at least an overlap in their material properties and composition.

We have not yet visited any asteroid, but we have detailed photographs of the moons of Mars, Phobos and Deimos, which may be captured asteroids. We also have information on the shape and composition of some asteroids from telescopic observation, even though only the largest asteroids show as discs in our telescopes. The smaller objects, including those near the Earth, appear to be irregular, pebble-shaped bodies, rotating with periods of a fraction of a day. Their optical spectra suggest a wide range of compositions, some of which have been tentatively identified with existing meteorite classes. In a number of cases, clear spectral evidence exists for a high concentration of water in some form in the

rocks. We see something similar in a class of meteorites called carbonaceous chondrites (see page 247), and this strengthens the case further.

The adjoining table shows the compositions of a few representative examples of meteorite classes. Perhaps the most interesting factor, beyond the presence of water, is the existence of large amounts of iron-nickel-cobalt alloy and meteoritic iron. Some asteroids have smooth, featureless spectra resembling those of iron meteorites, and may well have the same composition.

Asteroids in the kilometre size range have very low gravitational fields. A human (with his feet well anchored!) could throw material off one. From this point of view asteroids are more attractive for our exploitation than the Moon. For most of the known objects, however, especially those whose orbits around the Sun are inclined by 10 degrees or more to that of the Earth, the energy required to rendezvous and return to near-Earth space more than cancels out this advantage.

One object recently discovered by the California Institute of Technology astronomer Elinor Helin, the asteroid 1982DB, has a low-inclination orbit highly suitable for visit and return. There are probably more like it waiting to be found. The discovery and characterization of such asteroids is an important goal for research.

Research into processes for using asteroidal materials is even less advanced than in the case of the Moon. We can use meteorites as a starting point, but we must be prepared for surprises in composition and structure. However, because we know that water and metallic iron-nickel can confidently be expected on some asteroids, we know that they are potentially useful.

An important question relating to the practical use of asteroidal material is the optimum method of returning it to near-Earth space. One intriguing concept is the use of multiple gravity assist, in which successive close approaches to Venus, the Moon, and ultimately the Earth modify the orbit of the desired material towards the one we want. This procedure was used during the Mariner Venus-Mercury mission, and extensive use of it may be used for the

COMPOSITION[1] OF REPRESENTATIVE METEORITE CLASSES

	CARBONACEOUS[2] CHONDRITE TYPE I ORGEUIL	BRONZITE[3] CHONDRITE	CANYON[4] DIABLO	EUCRITE[5]
Fe	0·00	16·30	~92·38	0·018
Ni	0·00	1·74	7·11	—
Co	0·00	0·09	0·50	—
FeS	15·07	5·48	—	0·33
SiO$_2$	22·56	36·74	—	49·27
TiO$_2$	0·07	0·12	—	0·73
Al$_2$O$_3$	1·65	2·04	—	12·51
MnO	0·19	0·32	—	0·54
FeO	11·39	10·24	—	18·76
MgO	15·81	23·44	—	6·64
CaO	1·22	1·60	—	10·35
Na$_2$O	0·74	0·90	—	0·48
K$_2$O	0·07	0·09	—	0·05
P$_2$O$_5$	0·28	0·27	—	0·10
H$_2$O	19·89	0·15	—	0·16
Cr$_2$O$_3$	0·36	0·55	—	0·31
NiO	1·23	—	—	—
CoO	0·06	—	—	—
C	3·10	0·02	—	—
Total	93·69[6]	100·09	~100·00	100·25

[1] Data given in weight per cent.
[2] Reference: H. B. Wiik, "The Chemical Composition of Some Stony Meteorites", *Geochimica et Cosmochimica Acta*, 9, (1956), 279-289.
[3] Reference: E. Jarosewich and B. Mason, "Chemical Analyses with Notes on One Mesosiderite and Seven Chondrites", *Geochimica et Cosmochimica Acta*, 33, (1969), 411-416.
[4] Reference: E. Goldberg, A. Uchiyama, and H. Brown, "The Distribution of Nickel, Cobalt, Gallium, Palladium, and Gold in Iron Meteorites", *Geochimica et Cosmochimica Acta*, 2 (1951), 1-25.
[5] Reference: M. B. Duke and L. T. Silver, "Petrology of Eucrites, Howardites, and Mesosiderites", *Geochimica et Cosmochimica Acta*, 31, (1967), 1637-1665.
[6] Deficiency in summation is ascribed to ignition loss of organic matter.

Above: *Future NASA satellite communications will be revolutionized by the Tracking and Data Relay Satellite System which will eliminate most of the ground stations in the present network. These are the 60ft (18·3m) antennas at TDRS control centre, White Sands, N.M.*

Galileo mission to explore the satellites of Jupiter. Some propulsive energy would still have to be applied by man-made devices, but it could be much less than for a "brute force" approach. However, the time in transit could be many years.

The use of extraterrestrial materials in space will seem to most people to be an eventuality that may come about only far in the future. This may well be the case. If so, it will probably be more because of political and economic factors, than lack of available means. As David Brin, a University of California physicist, puts it, this particular gold is separated from our present abode by a long stretch of very dry desert.

In the past, people have always found ways to get through, around, or over such difficulties. I believe this will also be true in the future.

RECOMMENDED READING

Arnold, J.R., "The Frontier in Space", *American Scientist*, Vol 68, No 3, May-June 1980.
Bernal, J.D., *The World, the Flesh and the Devil*, Methuen & Co., Ltd., London 1929.
Dyson, F., *Disturbing the Universe*. Harper & Row, New York, 1979.
Johnson, R.D. and Holbrow, C., eds., *Space Settlements, A Design Study*, NASA, Washington, D.C., 1977.
O'Neill, G.K., *The High Frontier: Human Colonies in Space*, Anchor Press, Doubleday, York, 1982.
Taylor, S.R., *Lunar Science, A Post-Apollo View*, Pergamon, London, 1975.

The New Industrial Frontier

Something for nothing is everyone's financial dream, so it seems appropriate that future industries may be based on nothing, or the next best thing. In this case, nothing is the near-absence of the effects of gravity and atmosphere. Proper understanding of how materials behave under these conditions, as opposed to on Earth, is creating the potential for the manufacture in space of products that are better than their terrestrial counterparts.

Of course, the something for nothing aspect is a figurative image. It has taken millions of dollars to arrive at the point where industry can say that the promise of materials processing in space (MPS) is real; millions more will be required to capitalize on this potential.

Estimates vary, but studies place the annual market value of MPS products as high as $20 billion by the end of the century. Another study, however, has argued that the value will be far less than this.

To date a broad range of increasingly complex experiments have been conducted aboard aircraft, sounding rockets, and manned spacecraft. Already, two major US firms are developing what may become the world's first space factory; others are developing facilities that would support it, and other experiments. Much of this potential will be made possible by the management and hardware provided by the US National Aeronautics and Space Administration.

A principal planner in MPS programmes, Donald Waltz of TRW Space and Technology Group, sounded a note of caution:

"Space manufacturing, at least before the year 2000, should not be thought of in terms of space-based factory-type facilities where computers, wristwatches, home appliances, cold remedies, or television sets are produced in assembly lots. Space manufacturing does not envision use of the space environment for jobs better done on Earth; rather, it involves taking advantage of the unique characteristics of space—particularly the aspects of weightlessness —to do useful tasks which cannot be performed as well, or at all, on Earth, and to understand the gravity effects on Earth processes."

He identified five basic areas for materials processing in space: crystal growth, purification/separation, mixing, solidification, fluid processes—and estimated the market value of space product lines at $200-$1,000 million in 1990, to $25,000-$50,000 million in 2000.

Potential products cited by Waltz, fall into four main categories:

1 Pharmaceuticals: Antihaemophilic Factor 8 (AHF-8, a blood clotting agent for haemopheliacs), erythropoietin (for treating anemia); pancreatic T-Beta cells (for natural insulin production); and monodisperse latex spheres, a diagnostic tool.
2 Electronics: semiconductor materials; detector materials; X-ray targets; diodes; solar cells.
3 Optics: lenses; lasers; fibre optics; ceramic waveguides; electronic substrates; unique glasses; narrow-band filters.
4 Advanced alloys; turbine blades; superconductive materials; magnetic materials; corrosion-resistant alloys; nuclear fuel rods; and lubricants.

Waltz predicted that as commercial MPS is developed,

"highly specific facilities will be evolved and dedicated to individual product forms rather than general purpose capabilities which were appropriate to the prior phase."

In common with many new programmes, MPS has gone through an initial phase of unbounded optimism, followed by sharp criticism, and is finally emerging as a mature

science and engineering discipline. The criticism came from the Committee on the Scientific and Technological Aspects of MPS of the National Academy of Science better known as the STAMPS report, in 1978.

It claimed that NASA's programme *"suffered from poorly conceived and designed experiments, often done in crude apparatus, from which weak conclusions were drawn, and, in some cases, over-publicized."*

The report prompted NASA to restructure its programme and place it on a sounder scientific footing. It was countermanded, in effect, by a report from the General Accounting Office, not known as a space supporter, which warned that the US was in danger of losing its lead in this and other areas of space technology. More encouragement came in May 1983 in a National Academy of Public Administration study on "Encouraging Business Ventures in Space Technology". It called for broad efforts to lower barriers and costs to industry attempting to develop commercial activities in space, including the fullest possible use of the Joint Endeavor Agreement and other innovative mechanisms (explained below), and an increase in the emphasis on all aspects of the NASA programme of materials processing in gravity-free conditions.

The Realm of Microgravity

The promise of MPS relies on low gravity and high vacuum. Zero-gravity does not exist. The force of gravity pervades the Universe, never ending though ever varying. The term "weightlessness" is a misnomer. Although weight seems to disappear, it does so on the macroatomic scale. As a satellite orbits a planet, each part is in its own orbit; a particle on the side of a satellite opposite the Earth is in a higher orbit than one closer to the Earth. The vehicle experiences an assortment of little stresses and strains, aggravated by equipment vibration and, where applicable, crew motion. So, materials in space still experience acceleration equal to 1/10,000g, perhaps even as much as 1/100g. A more accurate term for this condition might be free-fall, but microgravity is the currently accepted usage.

The vacuum of space is also relative. The Earth's atmosphere does not end abruptly at

Left: *The realm of microgravity: Skylab 4 astronaut Edward C. Gibson balances fellow crewman Gerald P. Carr on his fingertip, in a demonstration of zero-g in the forward experiment area of Skylab.*

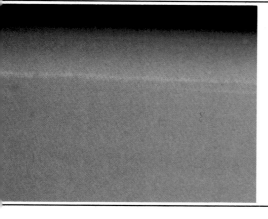

"The escape from gravity which we have all known in our dreams may remind us of life's origin in the oceans; but it may also anticipate a far longer future in space."

Arthur C. Clarke, Foreword, *The Illustrated Encyclopedia of Space Technology*

some arbitrary altitude, but becomes steadily thinner. At 310 miles (500km) it has dropped to 10-8 torr (standard sea-level pressure is 760 torr); an altitude of seven miles (11·26km) is enough to take your breath away. Additionally, spacecraft venting and thruster firings may briefly raise the local pressure; conversely a spacecraft's passage through the exosphere may sweep out a wake that is as hard as 10-15 torr.

The result of minimizing the effects of gravity and atmospheric pressure is that materials may reach "perfection" by being allowed to behave as if they were in a universe of their own. Microgravity should virtually eliminate convection currents caused by temperature gradients, separation of immiscibles, and fractures of solid crystals due to their own weight. Materials can be isolated from container walls, via acoustic or electromagnetic forces, to prevent prevent premature crystallization, internal stresses, or transmission of vibrations from the outside world. Micro-atmospheres may permit greater purity and quality control by reducing unwanted gases present in the best commercial vacuum pumps, and make possible finer control of trace materials used in electronic circuits.

Origins

MPS was born in the early days of the space programme when engineers became concerned about the behaviour of liquid propellants and welding materials in space. Initial tests were conducted with drop towers (2-3 seconds of microgravity) and aircraft flying parabolic trajectories (up to 30 seconds).

The first orbital tests were achieved aboard Soviet Vostok spacecraft and the US Biosatellite 2. Some Saturn rocket stages were equipped with cameras to monitor the behaviour of propellants after engine shutdown.

Apollo 14, 16, and 17 carried several rudimentary experiments, including composite casting, electrophoresis (use of electric fields to segregate fluid mixtures), and fluid transfer equipment. The Skylab manned space station expanded upon these with a total of 160 hours of MPS experiments. The results were striking, with each experiment indicating that microgravity can enhance a product. Even impromptu activities filmed by one crew showed colliding droplets (grape- and orange-flavoured drink) did not mix. During the Apollo-Soyuz Test Project (ASTP) in 1975, another 125 hours of

experimentation was added to America's MPS experience.

To fill the gap between the Skylab-ASTP era and the Space Shuttle-Spacelab era, NASA initiated the space processing applications rocket (SPAR) programme at Marshall Space Flight Center in Huntsville, Alabama, the MPS program manager. SPAR uses Black Brant 5C rockets built in Canada. The experiment apparatus can be up to 16·5in (42cm) wide, 12ft (3·6m) long, and weigh 110-419lb (50-190kg). About six minutes of microgravity is available between rocket burnout and re-entry. Experiments and apparatus are usually basic and often limited to observing model materials (such as ammonium chloride crystallizing in water), or testing new handling techniques, such as an acoustic levitator that uses standing waves to position objects. Nine were flown, of which only one failed (the average for sounding rockets); a tenth was being considered at the time of writing.

Aircraft on which initial tests could be run were also utilised. Aboard a KC-135 (a military version of the Boeing 707) several experimenters can operate experiment gear weighing a few hundred pounds. On a typical mission the KC-135 will fly 40 or so

Above: *This NASA KC-135, a converted USAF cargo aircraft, provides experimenters with about 25 seconds of low-g by flying a prescribed parabolic trajectory between 24,000 and 33,000ft (7·300-10,050m).*

Left: *NASA technicians securing an acoustic levitator assembly during low-g experiments in the converted KC-135 aircraft. The roomy payload bay allows the use of "hands-on" personnel.*

parabolas, each allowing 20-30 seconds of low-g at the top. The penalty is 20-30 seconds of 2-g at the bottom! But it does allow basic techniques to be tested. In like manner, smaller experiments can be handled aboard a NASA F-104B Starfighter with 40-60 seconds of low-g at the top.

To extend the SPAR "bridge", its technology is being adapted to build the materials experiment assembly-A (MEA-A), a box 3·57x3·47x5·54ft (1·09mx1·06mx1·69m) in size and weighing 1,764lb (800kg). It has space for three SPAR-type experiment units plus batteries, radiator, control computer, and data recorders. It will ride in the Shuttle atop the multi-purpose experiment support structure which resembles a trestle bridge. It flew on the seventh Shuttle mission (STS-7) in June 1983. It will be upgraded to the Materials Science Lab by tapping Shuttle resources, and flown nine times by mid-1988.

An MEA-C design is being considered to support more experiments and take advantage of the Shuttle pricing policy which was not established at the time of MEA-A's design. MEA-C would be 14ft (4·26m) wide and 3ft (0·91m) thick, weigh 5,860lb (2,658kg), and hold seven SPAR-type experiments with allowance for growth.

The initial MEA-A experiment units will be a single-axis acoustic levitator to process glass samples; a general-purpose rocket furnace to grow immiscible metal alloys, and a second general-purpose furnace to grow crystals by vaporizing and condensing materials in a closed ampoule.

Another area available for gap-filler experiments is the Space Shuttle middeck cabin. Although experiments placed here must meet stringent safety rules, they also offer the chance for direct crew participation and more frequent flight opportunities. It

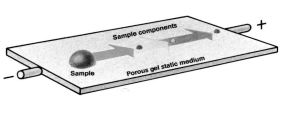

Above: *A beautiful study of* Challenger *taken by the SPAS-01 satellite during the STS-7 flight in June 1983. The MEA box containing materials processing experiments is in the middle of the payload bay.*

Continuous-Flow Electrophoresis System (CFES)
Electrophoresis is the movement of charged particles in solution under the influence of an electrical field. Particles of different charges and sizes move at different rates towards an oppositely-charged electrode; it is thus especially useful for separating the different components of a mixture. Electrophoresis can be performed on a static medium on Earth (**above**), but only a small amount of sample can be treated at one time (c0·01ml). A more productive method is called continuous-flow electrophoresis (**right**). Here a sample is continuously injected into a flowing buffer solution that transports it up a rectangular chamber. An electrical field is applied across the flow, causing the sample to split into separate particle streams that exit through separate collection outlets at the top. CFES is particularly suited to the space environment because there the disturbing effects of gravity experienced on Earth, such as convection currents, bandspreading (the widening of individual streams as they flow), and the collapse of too concentrated a sample around the inlet port, are eliminated. Yields are therefore higher (by a factor of 500 in the first EOS test on STS-4) and the product purity greater. A CFES payload specialist will fly on STS-12.

was first used on STS-3, 23-30 March, 1982, for two experiments, the monodisperse latex reactor, originally proposed for SPAR, and the electrophoresis engineering verification test, an upgrade of an ASTP experiment.

The electrophoresis test used electric fields to segregate materials in a closed column. It was reflown to verify the results of kidney cell separation on ASTP where one cluster of cells showed unusually high urokinase production. Samples of human and animal blood were also segregated as a calibration. Unfortunately, laboratory procedures after the return to Earth allowed the samples to thaw, mix and decay over the weekend following landing. Photographs indicated that the blood tests were successful, however. A reflight is planned.

The latex reactor worked well on its first run, but was a partial failure the second time. Its goal is to produce monodisperse (i.e. all the same size) microspheres of latex that are larger than can be produced on Earth where two microns is the maximum. The spheres are produced by polymerization of latex in solution. In 1g, convection and other effects cause "creaming" and sedimentation. In the STS-3 test, four size groups of spheres were produced, 0·2-0·3, 3·5, 4·5, and 5·5-6·0 microns. A reflight on STS-4 was hampered by an electrical problem, but enough reaction occurred to yield larger spheres. Two more were made on STS-6 and -7.

Latex microspheres have a variety of biomedical uses, including calibration of electron microscopes and of pores in cells, and a classified defence application. A $30 million market already exists for made-on-Earth microspheres. A further possible use for them would be the manufacture of medical "smart bombs" carrying drugs that would become trapped in cancer tumours. This would deliver a lethal dose to the tumour while giving the body as a whole only a small dose.

Other middeck hardware candidates include a three-axis acoustic levitator furnace, hormone purification by isoelectric focussing (a variation on electrophoresis), blood rheology (being studied by an Australian team), automated directional solidification furnace, an acoustic containerless experiments system, and an electromagnetic levitator.

Two Shuttle experiment programmes that may have a major impact on MPS in future years are the Getaway Specials and the Shuttle Student Involvement Program. Many of the former have been purchased by civic and professional groups for use by college students who, in turn, have developed MPS-related experiments. The same is true of the latter which is sponsored by NASA and the aerospace industry. On STS-5, for example, there were two such experiments, one an attempt to grow triglycine sulphate crystals, the other an effort to study the effect of surface tension on convection.

Large Facilities

In parallel with the development of SPAR/MEA, NASA has also developed experiments for Spacelabs 1 (STS-9, Autumn 1983) and 3 (STS-19, Autumn 1984). MPS was one of the major mission areas when Spacelab was being designed.

For Spacelab 1, America has only produced one experiment; it is concerned with fluid distribution in low gravity.

For Spacelab 3, three devices are being built:

1 A fluid experiment system which is a large optical bench that will use holography and Schlieren photography (which shows interfaces between fluids) to study fluid behaviour under microgravity. The key to it is an experiment cell, about six inches per side, inserted inside the optical train. On Spacelab 3, three runs of 18, 34, and 54 hours will be made using the same sample, triglycine sulphate, a

Above: *The McDonnell Douglas CFES rig as installed in the middeck of Challenger in readiness for the STS-7 flight. One of Challenger's fuse panels is to the right of the separation chamber.*

material valuable as an infra-red detector.

2 Drop dynamics module, another optical system, to study the behaviour of free drops.

3 Vapour crystal growth system, to study how crystals grow by vapour deposition (like frost forming on a window) versus saturation in solution.

These facilities will be reused on the Spacelab 8/J mission in 1987. Another facility that was being developed for NASA was cancelled when it ran over budget. It was a solidification experiment system, mounted on a Spacelab pallet, which would have processed large numbers of samples through a furnace.

Because the Shuttle/Spacelab combination is relatively limited in terms of resources and time in orbit, NASA-Marshall has also studied a materials experiment carrier and a materials experiment module that might be attached to a Space Platform for advanced, long-duration work. The carrier would weigh up to 31,084lb (14,100kg), be 19·7ft (6m) long, and hold eight 3,307lb (1,500kg) experiment modules.

Removing Obstacles

Flight hardware is not the only area under active development. In the mid-1970s, NASA recognized legal, managerial and technical obstacles to industry joining it on a commercial basis. The space agency published in the Federal Register (1979). "Guidelines Regarding Joint Endeavors with U.S. Domestic Concerns in Materials Processing in Space". NASA offered to form partnerships with industry where both parties accept some risk and both can expect some profit.

The joint experiments can range from

ground-based research to full-scale demonstrations in space. The requirements are strict, however, with NASA ruling out any "quick-and-dirty" experiments.

Three levels of participation were offered:

1 Technical exchange agreement, where data are shared. The first was signed with John Deere and Co in June 1981 for cast iron and solidification experiments.

2 Industrial guest investigator, where a company details a scientist to work with a counterpart at NASA. The first was signed with TRW for work on solidification experiments; it later fell through.

3 Joint endeavour agreement, where industry develops an experiment for "free" rides aboard the Space Shuttle. The first was signed with McDonnell Douglas Astronautics Co in January 1980.

Details of each endeavour will vary with the company and the work. No money changes hands, thus eliminating contracts that might entitle the US Government to all rights or burden a company with all costs.

McDonnell Douglas and the Ortho Division of Johnson & Johnson have developed a continuous-flow electrophoresis system (CFES). Electrophoresis is a common technique for refining biological materials. The material to be segregated is injected into a

moving buffer solution. An electric field acts on the tiny variations in surface charge that each cell or molecule carries, and gradually pulls the original stream apart.

To test the theory, McDonnell Douglas and Ortho developed an orbital test unit as the start of their electrophoresis operations in space, or EOS.

The CFES rig was given its first flight test on STS-4, 26 June-4 July 1982. Two sets of samples were run, a candidate product (unnamed) and a blend of rat and egg albumins.

The results were encouraging. Output of the single-chamber unit was 500 times greater than is possible to achieve on the ground, McDonnell Douglas said. Albumin calibration samples showed concentrations of 1, 10, and 25 per cent, compared with 0·2 per cent typically obtained on Earth. In addition, the thickness of the flow column was double that which can be maintained on the ground, resulting in four times the flow.

NASA-Marshall director, Dr William Lucas, said that the testing had gone so well that clinical testing of the planned pharmaceutical would begin with material produced on STS-11, scheduled to fly in early 1984. Tests aboard the STS-6 and -7 missions also

Below: *The U-shaped pallet that will fly along with Spacelab on the first mission STS-9. Unlike the experiment module, the pallet will be unpressurized, and directly exposed to the near vacuum of space.*

Bottom: *Payload specialists Dr Robert Parker (left) and Dr Wubbo Ockels inside the flight module of Spacelab at KSC. They are in the main experiment area of the long module.*

were successful, increasing the yield and purity of the CFES output. In June 1983, NASA announced that it would allow McDonnell Douglas to train and fly engineer Charles Walker as a payload specialist to operate CFES. The unit was to be upgraded for an 80-hour pre-production run and required more detailed care than an astronaut could easily be trained to give. A short time later, McDonnell Douglas and the University of Missouri announced their partnership in using CFES to refine T-Beta cells from human pancreases for injection into diabetics as a potential "one shot cure".

Satellite for Lease

McDonnell Douglas plans to fly a prototype production unit on its 7th and 8th joint-endeavour flights in 1985-86. The unit will be 3ft (0·9m) long, 14ft (4·27m) wide, weigh 5,000lb (2,268kg), and contain 24 chambers operating automatically. After that, the company plans to go into commercial production with a free-flying EOS unit launched by the Shuttle. Two options were under study, the Space Platform and an "Orbiting Sixpack" satellite.

The latter moved closer to reality in September 1982 when Fairchild Space & Electronics Co of Germantown, Maryland, confirmed that it was negotiating a joint endeavour with NASA for development of a for-rent satellite called Leasecraft.

Leasecraft will be the "Orbiting Sixpack" version of Fairchild's multi-mission modular spacecraft (MMS) used by the Solar Maximum Mission satellite and Landsat 4. Six power modules would be arranged in a hexagon around a propulsion module. The final configuration is still being devised.

Under the terms of a memorandum of understanding signed 28 September 1982, by Fairchild Industries Chairman, James Uhl, and NASA Administrator, James Beggs, the two organizations

"*will study the potential for a joint endeavor agreement leading to development of a small space platform to be on orbit and available to commercial customers by 1986*"

According to Dr John Naugle, Leasecraft programme manager and former NASA chief scientist, Fairchild would provide customers with everything they need to process materials in space.

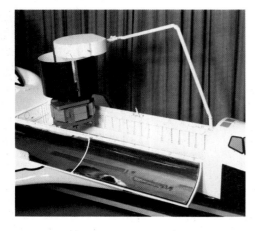

Above: *A model of the Leasecraft in the Shuttle cargo bay, showing the remote manipulator system arm emplacing an electrophoresis module into it.*

The first device to be flown on Leasecraft will be McDonnell Douglas's EOS. On the initial launch, Leasecraft, occupying only five feet or so of the Shuttle payload bay length, and the EOS module, also flat and wide, would be carried and joined together in orbit. The propulsion module would boost Leasecraft to a higher orbit that would decay back to rendezvous altitude within a few months. On return, the Shuttle would use its remote manipulator system to change out products and raw materials, or indeed entire payloads, and replace Leasecraft modules as needed.

Naugle said the cost to develop Leasecraft is estimated at $75-$100 million. He declined to speculate on leasing costs because they will depend on development cost. However, it is planned to be competitive for leasing times from a month (the maximum for a Shuttle sortie) up to about five years. Lease-to-buy contracts might also be available. Production of one or two Leasecraft a year is envisioned.

More Takers

Two more companies have announced MPS plans: Ball Aerospace Systems of Boulder, Colorado, confirmed it was negotiating a joint endeavour on a for-rent materials processing facility, or MPF. Space Industries Inc of Houston, will look at the commercial potential of a manned space station.

Ball Aerospace signed its "memorandum of understanding" with NASA about the same time as Fairchild. Dr Ron Greenwood, Ball's assistant director for commercial space systems, said the MPF would be similar to the MEA-C concept of housing experiments.

Studies indicate that from 1984 onwards "there appears to be a real need for (a) small, affordable spacecraft" in materials processing, he said. The main purpose of the MPF would be to provide experimenters with a laboratory to prove basic materials processes before committing to larger hardware.

Although the design is still being drawn up, Greenwood said the MPF should hold about seven materials experiments, each wider than the 17in (43cm) of the MEA-class and about 40in (102cm) long.

Space Industries Inc and NASA signed a "no-cost" memorandum of understanding "to enter into a no-cost agreement for a limited exchange of non-proprietary data developed during the course of the mission analysis. . ."

Space Industries is a small company set up by Maxime Faget, retired director of engineering at NASA's Johnson Space Center. It is affiliated with Eagle Engineering, the Houston firm that provided integration services for the private Conestoga sounding rocket launch. Eagle is made up largely of ex-NASA engineers and scientists. Among its founders is Hubert Davis, Faget's director of advanced systems at NASA-Johnson.

Davis said Space Industries

"*was formed for the express purpose of exploring the potential of private sector investment and funding in a low-orbit space station.*"

Eagle is providing "front-end capital' to a stock-holder in Space Industries and will be given that firm's systems.

NASA also signed a joint endeavour with GTI Corp of San Diego in January 1982. It was designed to develop a small crystal-growth furnace that other companies would rent, but GTI withdrew later in the year after a survey revealed insufficient market interest to justify the experiment.

A Crystal Growth Furnace

Another joint endeavour with Microgravity Research Associates of Miami was signed in April 1983. The firm was established in 1979 for the purpose of developing a furnace for processing electroepetaxial gallium-arsenide (GaAs) semiconductor materials for use as solar cells and electronic chip substrates. GaAs chips are faster and smaller than comparable silicon chips, and so are expected to be of great value to military, and subsequently civilian computers. The problem with terrestrial production is that they have about a 90 per cent rejection rate, thus making their cost prohibitive. The proposed endeavour will be conducted in three phases in six years—two experimental flights and four prototype flights, both with Shuttle payload bay rigs, then two pilot production runs. Once production starts, the GaAs material is expected to sell for $1,000 a gram if the rejection rate can be reversed.

In joint endeavours, the "free ride" aspect only applies during the development phase. Once the company starts production, it not only pays its own way, NASA also has the right to take over the process if the company refrains from marketing a product that may have powerful benefits for the general public.

European Programmes

The European Space Agency (ESA), Japan, and the Soviet Union also plan to conduct their own MPS flight projects.

Above: MAUS-1; it was designed to take X-ray photographs of gallium and mercury samples as they were heated and allowed to cool, to allow study of the processes that occur before and during solidification.

Left: The German MAUS materials processing experiment being mounted onto a beam atop the Shuttle Pallet Satellite (SPAS-01) which flew on the STS-7 mission. Other MAUS canisters were carried on the OSTA-2 pallet.

ESA is following the US pattern in conducting sub-orbital experiments first, and then flying them on the Shuttle, and planning for operations by deployable carriers.

According to NASA's Office of Technology Assessment (OTA).

"*ESA does not yet consider materials processing to be an applications area per se, but rather an area in which to do basic research that may lead to useful products or processes.*"

ESA's four-year microgravity programme, initiated in January 1982 and budgeted at $52·4 million, also covers life sciences.

The microgravity programme is to have two parts. The first will use Biorack, an Improved Fluid Physics Module, and sounding rockets. Studies of second phase activities include a Microgravity Fluid Science Laboratory and a Multi-User Facility (metal-lurgy/crystal growth/physiology). The decision on Phase 2 activities is to be made in early 1984.

Solaris

France's MPS programme was described by OTA as "modest" with an annual budget of only $1-2 million. France is also participating in West German and Soviet projects, and has experiments booked aboard Space-labs 1 and 3. On Spacelab, France is to provide six of the 33 experiments planned for the materials science double rack (MSDR) and has developed a separate crystal growth unit.

France has bigger plans for Solaris, a miniature, unmanned version of Leasecraft operations. Solaris is being studied by France's National Centre for Space Studies (CNES). A service module, measuring about 6·5x6·5x19·6ft (2x2x6m) and with a mass of 4,850lb (2,200kg), would be launched into a 373 miles (600km) equatorial orbit by an Ariane 4 rocket. It would provide support and 10 kilowatts of electrical power to a 2,205lb (1,000kg) MPS unit designed for seven years of operation. Processing would take 10 hours per sample.

Raw material would be brought up and product and waste removed by a propulsion module carrying a 6·5ft (2m) re-entry vehicle. It would dock with the aid of teleoperator arms and cameras. The re-entry sphere would make a ballistic entry and parachute to a 38·6sq mile (100sq km) area near the launch facility at Kourou, French Guiana.

Although the lack of manned access might limit France's ability to upgrade Solaris to meet market demands, OTA called Solaris "a major potential French initiative" that would generate a lot of business for the Ariane launcher, and "a direct challenge" to ESA, American, and Soviet MPS facilities.

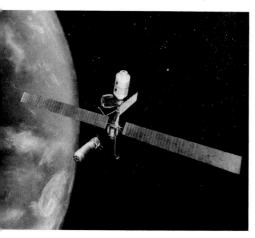

Above: A concept of the Solaris orbital station as envisaged by Matra. The unmanned MPS unit would be serviced by remotely-operated docking modules.

TEXUS

The German MPS programme is intended to meet the as yet undefined needs of the user community, as OTA has noted. The ultimate goal of Government support is substantial involvement of German industry in such areas as chemistry, process technology, metals, composite materials, and crystals.

Initial experiments were made aboard the ASTP (Apollo-Soyuz Test Project) mission. Since then, West Germany's Federal Ministry for Research and Technology (BMFT) has followed a path similar to NASA's MPS programme: sounding rockets experiments are flown then adapted for Space Shuttle, while, in parallel, more complex gear is developed for Spacelab missions.

Germany's equivalent of SPAR is TEXUS (the German acronym for technological experiments under weightlessness). Sweden is a major partner in this programme. The first launch was made in 1977, and two a year are planned during 1981-86. British-built Skylark rockets carry TEXUS experiment modules in launches from ESRANGE at Kiruna, Sweden. A typical TEXUS payload is 14·75ft (4·5m) tall, including support and recovery gear, 15·75in (40cm) wide, and weighs 794lb (360kg). Time in microgravity is about six minutes.

The equivalent of the US MEA is MAUS (autonomous materials processing experiments under weightlessness). This consists of TEXUS-like experiment modules to be flown aboard the Shuttle. A total of 25 Getaway Specials have been purchased and will be combined with US payloads, or with other German payloads. Some MAUS canisters will be attached to the structure holding MEA at no charge; in return, the MEA will be reflown, again with MAUS canisters, on the Spacelab D-1 mission.

The first MAUS was flown aboard STS-5, 11-16 November 1982. It used X-rays to visualize how metals interact when melted and mixed in microgravity. It failed but was reflown, with four more MAUS cans, on STS-7 in June 1983, along with the MEA.

West Germany built the Spacelab 1 Materials Science Double Rack (MSDR) and has 13 of its 33 experiments. MSDR gear includes: high-temperature thermostat, mirror heating facility, isothermal heating facility, capillary measurement equipment, cryostat, fluid physics module, gradient heating facility, and a UHV chamber. The Spacelab D-1 mission, being purchased by West Germany, will carry an improved MSDR. Other gear will include the MEDEA laboratory for metallurgy and crystal growth experiments, and a Process Chamber for fluid physics research.

German industry is participating along lines that appear similar to the US joint endeavour arrangement. MAN Inc is working on "skin technology" involving complex refractory metal alloys for turbine blades that can be melted and resolidified in space with an oxide skin. Volkswagen is interested in immisicible alloys for use in bearings.

Germany is also developing two platforms for conducting MPS research. The first to fly was SPAS-01 (Shuttle Pallet Satellite) on STS-7 in June 1983. It was deployed by the

Shuttle for 12 hours of undisturbed operations while the Shuttle practised rendezvous manoeuvres. Attached were two MAUS containers.

Next will be the Retrievable Carrier, or EURECA. Somewhat akin to Leasecraft, it is an ESA project within the Spacelab follow-on development programme, in which West Germany is taking the lead role. EURECA will operate for two to six months at a time and provide its cargo with as little as 1/100,000g. The overall spacecraft size will be 13·1ft (4m) wide by 4·9ft (1·5m) long. Mass will be 8,600lb (3,900kg), of which 1,764-3,301lb (800-1,500kg) is payload.

Candidate investigations for the Microgravity Retrievable Carrier include:

1 Solidification studies with a materials synthesis facility for low (1,000°C) and high (800-1,600°C) solidification experiments on up to 100 samples, each about 6·2sq in (40cm²) in size.
2 Crystal growth investigations with an ellipsoidal mirror furnace, solution crystal growth, vapour crystal growth, and protein crystal growth facilities.

Below: *Grappled by the RMS arm, the SPAS-01 is parked to permit cooling between flight tests during mission STS-7. The 3,300lb (1,500kg) pallet was constructed by Messerschmitt-Bölkow-Blohm.*

3 A multi-user facility to study how thermal energy moves through fluids, how fluids diffuse into each other, and convective effects.
4 Automatic gradient heating facility from Spacelab 1.
5 Life science experiments.

Japan

Japan's MPS effort, run by the National Space Development Agency (NASDA) is at an earlier stage. Sub-orbital experiments are being conducted with the TT-500-A, a two-stage rocket that provides about seven minutes at 1/10,000g. Because the recovery is in the ocean, NASDA runs a slightly higher risk of hardware loss, and at least one early flight sank before recovery teams could reach it. Two TT-500-A flights a year are planned.

Some Getaway Specials have been reserved by Japan, which is buying half of the Spacelab J mission, now scheduled for 1988. In addition to materials experiments, NASDA also will have a payload specialist aboard to conduct experiments.

Below: *The Materials Science Double Rack that will fly installed in Spacelab 1 in the first Spacelab/Shuttle mission. This unit contains practically all the hardware for the mission's MPS experiments.*

Above: *The payload section of a Japanese TT-500-A sounding rocket, containing MPS experiments developed to test melting and crystal growth in microgravity conditions. It was flown on 14 September 1980.*

Soviet Union

A 1981 Soviet article, released by the Novosti Press Agency, concerning the USSR's MPS programme listed among the many potential products "ideal solid and hollow speres. . . practically 'eternal' ball bearings". Interestingly, this product was held up as a shining promise early in the US programme, then discarded as the physics of MPS became better-known, and when correspondingly the manufacturers of ball bearings improved their production (an indirect though curious benefit of MPS research).

However, the office of Technology Assessment noted that the Soviets are spending three to four times as much on MPS as the United States and have up to 350 scientists engaged in the project. The same Novosti article listed several activites that have been conducted aboard Salyut space stations:

"Sfera (sphere), and Diffuzia (diffusion); the study of the basics of welding and casting; Reaktisa (reaction) and many other experiments in the multipurpose Splav and Krystall furnaces and, finally, the experiment carried out in the Isparitel installation."

The crews that occupied Salyut 5 and 6 operated at least nine different materials processing experiment rigs.

This work was continued aboard the Salyut 7 space station launched in 1982. It carried the computer-controlled Korund furnace that combined qualities of the Splav and Krystall furnaces flown earlier—both heat patterns and sample position could be controlled. Samples could be moved as slowly as 0·04in (1mm) a day or as quickly as 4in (100mm) a minute. It was also much larger than the previous devices, weighing 300lb (136kg) as opposed to the 26·5lb (12kg) of the Magma-F furnace flown on previous missions. Sample size was 1·2in (30mm)—0·4in (10mm) in Krystall and 0·8in (20mm) in Korund,—by 11·8in (30cm) length. A dozen samples can be processed at a time. Materials processed included cadmium selenide and indium antomonide. The article also referred to the processing of a dozen ampules of gallium-arsenide at a time to yield 39·7lb (18kg) of circuit chips.

Vladimir Khryapov, an experiment director, commented,
"There is every reason to believe that we are dealing with an installation of a semi-industrial type.

Below: *The Vietnamese cosmonaut, Pham Tuan, experiencing zero-g aboard Salyut 6 during his flight in July 1980. Valery Ryumin is facing the camera. Note cosmonaut (above) exercising on the veloergometer.*

As for the prospects for industrial production in space, in my view, it is quite real. First of all this will concern semi-conductor materials which do not have enormous weight requirements . . . but which are very expensive to produce on the earth."

As for the future, the article released by Novosti added:
"The primary course of today's Soviet technological experiments in space consists exactly in studying the peculiarities of the course of the processes of heat and mass exchange, crystallization and solidification as well as surface phenomena under zero-g."

More advanced installations were deemed essential. Experiments in the manufacture of improved samples of semi-conductors and other materials were promised. Cosmonaut Konstantin Feoktistov reported in mid-1981 that eventually there will be "whole plants for manufacturing products in zero-g".

As is the case with much of the Soviet space effort, details about these programmes are few. Only the experimental work carried out aboard the Salyut space stations and some precursor work aboard early Soyuz are known abroad. Presumably, the Soviets have conducted sounding rocket experiments akin to SPAR and TEXUS to lay the foundations of the present programme.

RECOMMENDED READING

Dooling, Dave, "The Space Factory", *The Illustrated Encyclopedia of Space Technology,* Salamander Books, London, 1981.

Dooling, Dave, "The First Space Factories", *Space World,* March 1982.

"Freezer Fails, Destroys STS-3 Samples", *Space World,* June-July 1982.

"Latex Reactor on STS-3 Works Well", *Space World,* June-July 1982.

"Industrializing Space—Looking Better", *Space World,* December 1982.

Civilian Space Policy and Applications, Office of Technology Assessment, US Congress, June 1982.

Waltz, Donald M., "The Potential Scope of Space Manufacturing", *Proceedings, 19th Space Congress,* 28-30 April, 1982.

Louviere, Allen J., "Space Manufacturing Systems and the Space Operations Center", *Proceedings, 19th Space Congress,* 28-30 April, 1982.

Randolph, Richard, "NASA-Industry Joint Venture on a Commercial Materials Processing in Space Idea", *Proceedings, 19th Space Congress,* 28-30 April, 1982.

LaFleur, James, "Private Sector Investment in the Space Program: Why, How and When", *Proceedings, 19th Space Congress,* 28-30 April, 1982.

Greger, Gottfried, "The German Material Processing in Space Activities. Spacelab, Space Platforms, and the Future", *Proceedings of the 20th Goddard Memorial Symposium,* 17-19 March 1982.

Seibert, G., "ESA Microgravity Platform Plans and Experiments. Spacelab, Space Platforms, and the Future", *Proceedings of the 20th Goddard Memorial Symposium,* 17-19 March 1982.

"The French Space Effort", *Interavia,* June 1979.

"Solaris: France Proposes Large Unmanned Space-Processing Platform" *Interavia,* May 1981.

ESA Annual Report—1981.

Cacheux, J., Torossian, R., and Do-Mau-Lam, M., "Manufacturing in Space. Space in the 1980s and Beyond", *Proceedings of the 17th European Space Symposium,* 1980.

Chernyshov, Mikhail, "Salyut 7: Over 200 Days in Space", Novosti Press Agency release December 1982.

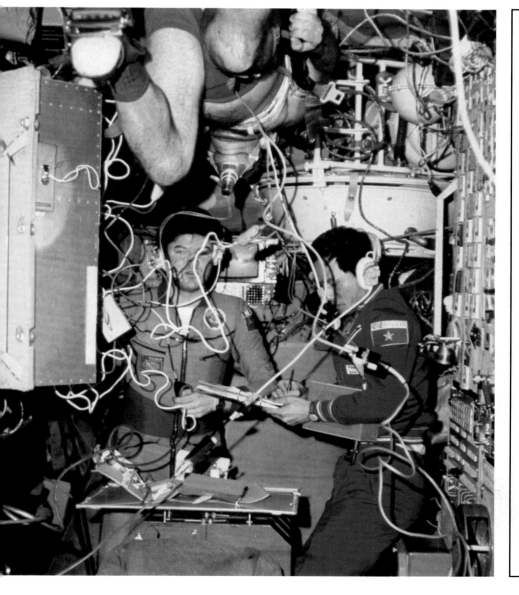

Programmes for the Eighties

The activities of the Scientific Programme Committee of ESA are supported, each year, by a budget amounting to some 100 million dollars. This investment represents a limited resource to realize many important projects in space science. ESA is only able to undertake a new scientific project every two and a half years, and so recognizes the benefit of giving priority to co-operative ventures, and the use of existing spacecraft, suitably modified to mission demands.

With the launch of a 70 million dollars spacecraft called Giotto (see page 254) Europe will undertake its most spectacular mission in space, attempting its first flight beyond Earth orbit into the Solar System to rendezvous with Halley's Comet.

The Giotto probe, weighing 2,094lb (950kg) at launch, is based on the platform of the two successful GEOS spacecraft, which were developed by British Aerospace and the industrial STAR consortium. It will be launched by an Ariane 3 vehicle during the first half of July 1985, together with a communications satellite. Initially placed into a geostationary transfer orbit, it will then fire its own solid rocket motor to inject itself into a heliocentric transfer trajectory to the comet.

Eight months later, precisely at midnight GMT on 13 March 1986, Giotto will undergo a close encounter with the nucleus of Halley's Comet! It will be a fast fly-by (at a velocity of 43miles/sec, 69km/s), some four weeks after the comet's perihelion passage. The likelihood of collision with cometary materials has not been overlooked. Special attention during the design and preparation of the probe has been devoted to the development of the dust protection shield: owing to mass restrictions, this protective system cannot be made of solid material, but is composed of a thin front sheet (0·039in, 1mm aluminium) and a thick rear plate (0·53in, 13·5mm kevlar/foam sandwich) separated by a gap of at least 10in (25cm). When a dust particle penetrates the front sheet, it is vaporized and the resultant gas cloud expands so that the impact momentum is distributed over a large area of the rear shield. Following calculations and tests, it is estimated that Giotto has a good chance of surviving until within a few hundred miles of the cometary nucleus.

The 120lb (54·4kg) Giotto payload, 1/10 of its total mass at encounter, consists of a camera to obtain colour pictures, three spectrometers, plasma sensors and analyzers, a dust impact detector, a magnetometer, detectors for measuring high energy particles,

and an optical probe experiment. The scientific objectives of the Giotto mission are:

1 To provide images of the nucleus; to define details down to a resolution of 164ft (50m); to obtain information on the dimensions, surface structure, rotation of and possible activity in the heart of the comet.

2 To measure the total gas production rate and the total dust flux; to determine the dust-to-gas ratio of a cometary object.

3 To investigate the macroscopic system of plasma interaction between the comet and the solar wind.

4 To characterize the physical processes and chemical reactions that occur in the cometary atmosphere and ionosphere; to identify the volatile components in the cometary coma.

To accomplish these objectives, the Giotto spacecraft carries 10 scientific experiments powered by electricity generated by solar cells and batteries during the delicate fly-by operations. The solar-cell array can provide 190W of power, but this is insufficient when all experiments and one of the two redundant X-band Travelling-Wave-Tube Amplifiers are switched on. Thus four batteries are required both to bridge the gap

Above: *The GEOS 1 spacecraft undergoing trials in the dynamic test chamber at the European Space Research and Technology Centre (ESTEC) in Holland. The Giotto probe is based on a modified GEOS design.*

in power, and to supply full power during the encounter should the solar arrays be damaged as a result of dust-particle impacts. Permanent communications with Giotto will be managed by the European Space Operations Centre (ESOC) in Darmstadt, Germany through two different Earth stations: the 98·4ft (30m) antenna at Weilheim, Germany, will be used during the cruise phase to control the probe; the 210ft (64m) radio-astronomy antenna at Parkes, Australia, is destined to receive Giotto transmissions during the rendezvous with Halley's Comet. Signals from Australia to ESOC will be relayed live via an Intelsat communications satellite.

ISPM

The second ESA mission into the Solar System—ISPM (International Solar Polar Mission)—will be an original enterprise; it will conduct the first scientific exploration of the Sun and its environment outside the ecliptic plane. It was planned initially that this important mission would involve two probes, one European and the other American, both to be launched in 1983 from the Space Shuttle cargo bay. In the spring of 1981, NASA's budget restrictions caused the cancellation of further development of its spacecraft (made by TRW) despite the resulting degradation in the scientific value of the original mission. Another crucial factor was the postponement of the launch date, due to delays in the availability of the Space Shuttle and to vacillation over the choice of upper stage to be used. As a result, the European ISPM probe will be launched alone between 20 and 30 May 1986 into an interplanetary trajectory (first to Jupiter for a fly-by manoeuvre that will swing it out of the ecliptic plane), utilizing the new cryogenic Centaur upper stage. The main parameters of the Solar Polar mission remain essentially similar to those established at the start of the project in 1979. Following a 14-month transit trip to Jupiter, ESA-ISPM will pass over the Jovian cloud tops at an altitude of some 264,000 miles (425,000km). By harnessing the effect of the gravitational field of Jupiter, it will be diverted out of the ecliptic into an orbit that will take it over the solar poles. After this Jupiter encounter with trajectory deviation in July 1987, the European probe will fly for the first time over one polar region of the Sun at a distance of about 2AU. Nearly three years later in June 1990, it will recross the ecliptic plane at a distance of some 1·2AU (perihelion). The mission will end as the solar latitude of the probe drops below 70° at

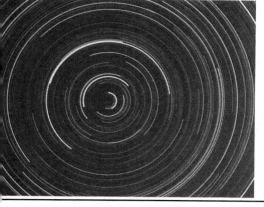

"... listen: there's a hell of a good universe next door; let's go."

e. e. cummings, *pity this busy monster, manunkind*

PROJECT NAME	LAUNCH DATE (launch centre)	TARGET (encounter date)	SPACECRAFT CHARACTERISTICS AND MISSION OBJECTIVES
Venera 15 (USSR)	2 June 83 (Tyuratam)	Venus (October 83)	5-ton spacecraft, 3-axis stabilized, to orbit Venus for radar mapping, to transmit surface pictures with 2-3 miles (3-5km) resolution. Planned to function for one Earth year.
Venera 16 (USSR)	7 June 83 (Tyuratam)	Venus (October 83)	Same as Venera 15 spacecraft and mission. Complementary to Venera 15 for radar mapping.
Venera 17/Vega 1 (USSR-France)	Dec 84 (Tyuratam)	Venus (June 1985) Halley's Comet (March 86)	5-ton spacecraft, 3-axis stabilized, to pass over Venus, to land a scientific capsule and to drop balloons in the Venusian atmosphere; then to encounter the nucleus of Halley's Comet at distance between 62,000 and 6,200 miles (100,000 and 10,000km).
Venera 18/Vega 2 (USSR-France)	Dec 84 (Tyuratam)	Venus (June 85) Halley's Comet (March 86)	Spacecraft and mission identical to Venera 17/Vega 1 (see above). *Note:* Both Russian probes are equipped with many French scientific instruments.
MS-T5/Tansei 5 (Japan)	31 Dec 84 (Kagoshima)	Interplanetary environment	Test probe in solar orbit, spin-stabilized, weighing 320lb (145kg), carrying experiments to analyse solar wind structures, magnetic field, plasma wave.
Giotto (ESA)	July 85 (Kourou)	Halley's Comet (13 Mar 86)	2,094lb (950kg) spin-stabilized cometary probe, to take colour pictures and to make measurements of dust, and plasma close to the nucleus of Halley's Comet (at less than 620 miles 1,000km). First European interplanetary probe.
Planet A (Japan)	14 Aug 85 (Kagoshima)	Halley's Comet (8 Mar 86)	309lb (140kg) spin-stabilized cometary probe, (MS-T5 model in operational configuration), equipped with an ultraviolet TV camera and solar-wind analyzer to observe Halley's Comet at less than 6,200 miles (10,000km).
Galileo (USA-Germany)	May 86 (Kennedy Space Center)	Jupiter atmosphere and Jovian system (Sep 88)	Two-stage spacecraft consisting of a Jupiter atmospheric entry probe (551lb, 250kg) and a Jovian orbiter (1,500lb, 680kg); this dual mission will provide measurements of the atmosphere of Jupiter and will explore the Jovian environment and moons with remote sensing, fields and particle instruments.
ESA-ISPM (Europe)	May 86 (Kennedy Space Center)	Jupiter fly-by (July 87) Perihelion at 1·2AU after solar-polar survey (June 90)	772lb (350kg) spin-stabilized, solar probe, powered by radio-isotope thermoelectric generators, to investigate the properties of the solar corona, the solar wind, the heliosphere, cosmic rays outside the ecliptic plane; to provide a 3-dimensional view of Sun activity.
Venus Radar Mapper (USA)	March-April 88 (Kennedy Space Center)	Venus (July 1988)	1-ton spacecraft, 3-axis stabilized, equipped with a synthetic aperture radar to map the Venusian surface. To be inserted into a near polar elliptical orbit, between 155 and 6,400 miles (250 and 10,300km) to obtain radar photographs of Venusian surface with better than 0·6 miles (1km) resolution.

approximately the end of 1990. The total duration of the mission is scheduled to be 4·5 years.

Compared to Giotto, ESA-ISPM is a very sophisticated spacecraft: while Giotto is a spin-stabilized cylinder powered by solar cells, ESA-ISPM is an irregular body, spin-stabilized, equipped with long booms and provided with Radioisotope Thermoelectric Generators producing 260W of power. It has been developed for ESA by Dornier System (Germany) leading the industrial STAR consortium; British Aerospace is responsible for the precise attitude and orbit control equipment and for the high-gain antenna structure (5·25ft, 1·6m in diameter). When ESA was informed by NASA about its decision to delay the launch of the ISPM probes, the European work was already well-advanced: the spacecraft design was complete, the full industrial team at work, and the hardware fabrication in most sub-systems and experiments under way. ESA decided to adopt a "Build and Store" approach to the completion of the programme. The ISPM Flight Model was completed and delivered to ESA in the latter part of 1983 and it will be left dormant for the next two years. In September 1985 the re-certification process will be started and the probe will be sent to NASA's Kennedy Space Center in January 1986.

Weighing about 772lb (350kg), the ISPM spacecraft carries nearly 115lb (52kg) of scientific payload, consisting of nine principal experiments designed by American and European scientists. Instruments on board the probe will study and analyze the properties of the solar wind and corona, measure energetic particle flows, electro-magnetic radiation from the Sun and from Jupiter, explore their magnetic fields, and improve our understanding of the neutral gas and dust of interplanetary and inter-stellar origin. Most particularly, ISPM will perform solar observations which, combined with terrestrial observations, will permit us a stereoscopic view of various transient phenomena in the Sun's atmosphere. Despite the cancellation of the US-ISPM spacecraft, NASA will contribute to the European ISPM probe; it will provide the Radioisotope Thermoelectric Generators, the launch vehicle in the form of the Space Shuttle, a Centaur upper stage, the control centre

Left: *The European ISPM qualification probe in preparation at Dornier System's plant in West Germany. The parabolic reflector for the high-gain antenna is uppermost in this view.*

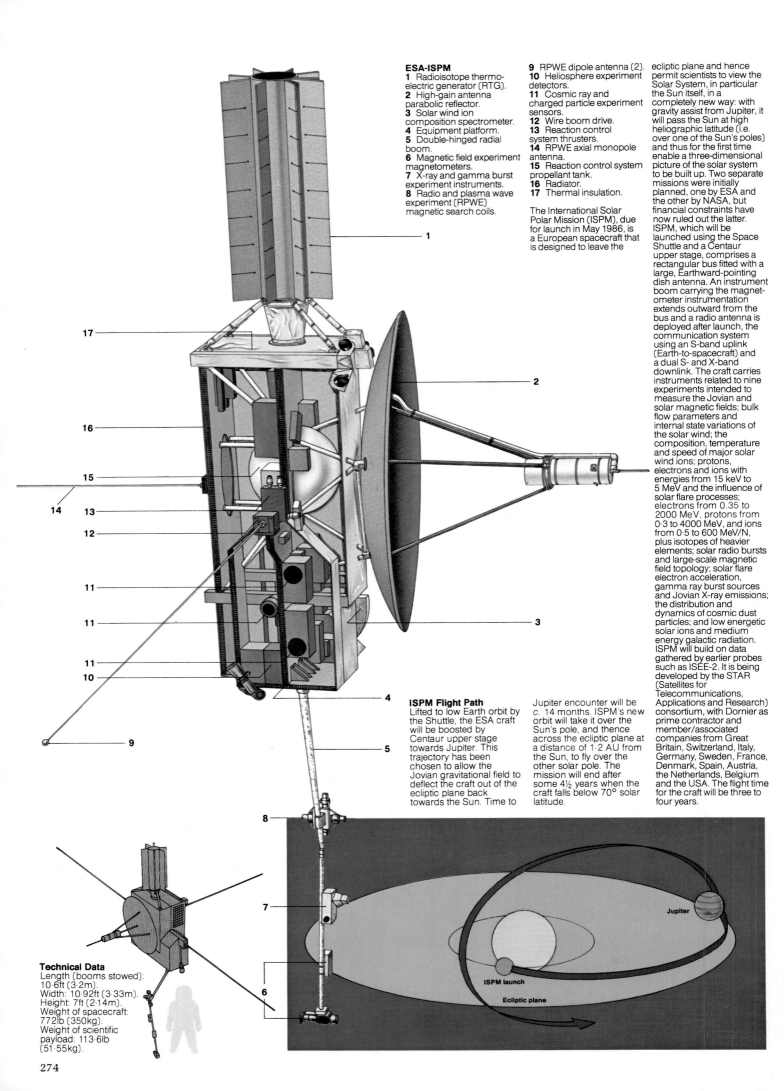

ESA-ISPM
1 Radioisotope thermo-electric generator (RTG).
2 High-gain antenna parabolic reflector.
3 Solar wind ion composition spectrometer.
4 Equipment platform.
5 Double-hinged radial boom.
6 Magnetic field experiment magnetometers.
7 X-ray and gamma burst experiment instruments.
8 Radio and plasma wave experiment (RPWE) magnetic search coils.

9 RPWE dipole antenna (2).
10 Heliosphere experiment detectors.
11 Cosmic ray and charged particle experiment sensors.
12 Wire boom drive.
13 Reaction control system thrusters.
14 RPWE axial monopole antenna.
15 Reaction control system propellant tank.
16 Radiator.
17 Thermal insulation.

The International Solar Polar Mission (ISPM), due for launch in May 1986, is a European spacecraft that is designed to leave the ecliptic plane and hence permit scientists to view the Solar System, in particular the Sun itself, in a completely new way: with gravity assist from Jupiter, it will pass the Sun at high heliographic latitude (i.e. over one of the Sun's poles) and thus for the first time enable a three-dimensional picture of the solar system to be built up. Two separate missions were initially planned, one by ESA and the other by NASA, but financial constraints have now ruled out the latter. ISPM, which will be launched using the Space Shuttle and a Centaur upper stage, comprises a rectangular bus fitted with a large, Earthward-pointing dish antenna. An instrument boom carrying the magnetometer instrumentation extends outward from the bus and a radio antenna is deployed after launch, the communication system using an S-band uplink (Earth-to-spacecraft) and a dual S- and X-band downlink. The craft carries instruments related to nine experiments intended to measure the Jovian and solar magnetic fields; bulk flow parameters and internal state variations of the solar wind; the composition, temperature and speed of major solar wind ions; protons, electrons and ions with energies from 15 keV to 5 MeV and the influence of solar flare processes; electrons from 0.35 to 2000 MeV, protons from 0.3 to 4000 MeV, and ions from 0.5 to 600 MeV/N, plus isotopes of heavier elements; solar radio bursts and large-scale magnetic field topology; solar flare electron acceleration, gamma ray burst sources and Jovian X-ray emissions; the distribution and dynamics of cosmic dust particles; and low energetic solar ions and medium energy galactic radiation. ISPM will build on data gathered by earlier probes such as ISEE-2. It is being developed by the STAR (Satellites for Telecommunications, Applications and Research) consortium, with Dornier as prime contractor and member/associated companies from Great Britain, Switzerland, Italy, Germany, Sweden, France, Denmark, Spain, Austria, the Netherlands, Belgium and the USA. The flight time for the craft will be three to four years.

ISPM Flight Path
Lifted to low Earth orbit by the Shuttle, the ESA craft will be boosted by Centaur upper stage towards Jupiter. This trajectory has been chosen to allow the Jovian gravitational field to deflect the craft out of the ecliptic plane back towards the Sun. Time to Jupiter encounter will be c. 14 months. ISPM's new orbit will take it over the Sun's pole, and thence across the ecliptic plane at a distance of 1.2 AU from the Sun, to fly over the other solar pole. The mission will end after some 4½ years when the craft falls below 70° solar latitude.

Jupiter

ISPM launch

Ecliptic plane

Technical Data
Length (booms stowed): 10.6ft (3.2m).
Width: 10.92ft (3.33m).
Height: 7ft (2.14m).
Weight of spacecraft: 772lb (350kg).
Weight of scientific payload: 113.6lb (51.55kg).

facility at the Jet Propulsion Laboratory, Pasadena, California, and the worldwide services of its Deep Space Network.

Orbital Telescopes

During the 1960s and 1970s Europe acquired a solid reputation in the fields of space astronomy and astrophysics. In that period ESA (and its predecessor ESRO) launched twelve scientific satellites atop NASA vehicles. Four of them were spacecraft devoted exclusively to astronomical research:

1 ESRO-II/Iris (May 1968): to study cosmic rays and solar particles.
2 TD-1A (March 1972): to map the sky in the ultraviolet and to undertake some X-ray studies.
3 COS-B (August 1975): the first official ESA satellite which provided new data about gamma-ray sources in the Universe.
4 IUE (January 1978): an American-European space telescope which performed ultraviolet observations from geosynchronous orbit.

ESA's scientific satellites for the 1980s are the interplanetary probes already described, and astronomy observatories in Earth orbit. They are the Exosat probe (launched on 26 May 1983) and the Hipparcos astrometry[1] satellite (scheduled for launch in early 1987).

Exosat is a half-ton spacecraft built by MBB (Germany) in conjunction with the industrial COSMOS consortium; its mission is to identify cosmic X-ray sources. Exosat, orbiting between 186 miles (300km) and 124,300 miles (200,000km), functions in two operating modes: uninterrupted direct observation of X-ray sources for about 80 hours; and by use of lunar occultation which allows measurements of time, and speed of disappearance and reappearance, of celestial objects behind the Moon. During its two year, 180 orbit lifetime, Exosat will be able to perform roughly 100 Moon occultation manoeuvres and observe over 2,000 targets.

Hipparcos is named after the famous Greek astronomer Hipparchus (c190-120BC) who, by measuring the lunar parallax, determined the distance from the Earth to the Moon. This geosynchronous 1,102lb (500kg) spacecraft, the world's first astrometry satellite, is being developed by Matra, France, leading the industrial MESH consortium. The Hipparcos payload consists of a telescope with two fields of view separated by a wide angle. Operating in the visible light part of the electromagnetic spectrum, this telescope will produce the first accurate catalogue of stellar astrometric parameters for 100,000 selected stars. Another experiment, called Tycho, will provide by photometry (the science of measuring visible light) new stellar data which will result in a catalogue of up to about 400,000 stars.

Turning to the end of this decade and the 1990s, ESA's Scientific Programme Committee has decided to develop the Infra-red Space Observatory (ISO), a 2ft (0·60m) diameter telescope which will supplement observations made by IRAS. Other projects under consideration are the Kepler mission

which calls for the launch by Ariane of a multi-disciplinary orbiter around Mars; the Magellan project for a far- and extreme-ultraviolet spectrographic observatory which would operate in real time; X-80 which is designed to continue the search for cosmic X-ray sources and to study their spectral features; FIRST or a far infra-red and submillimeter space telescope; XMM: a heavy X-ray multi-mirror; SOHO (Solar High-Resolution Observatory); and AGORA (Asteroid Gravity, Optical and Radar Analysis) to study the properties of three main belt asteroids.

German Projects

The Federal Republic of Germany has been actively involved in space activities since 1962. The Helios project, a co-operative venture with NASA flown during the 1970s, witnessed the first close approach to the Sun by two interplanetary probes. Spacelab has marked the first operation, on an international basis, of a reusable space laboratory for manned orbital activities, while the Galileo probe—destined to be the first spacecraft to orbit Jupiter—will use a German retro propulsion module.

Launched from Cape Canaveral by Titan III/Centaurs on 10 December 1974 and 15 January 1976 respectively, two German Helios probes, carrying US experiments, conducted the first detailed close-in measurements of the Sun's surface and solar wind. Each solar spacecraft was developed by German industry led by MBB, with assistance from the French Thomson and Belgian ETCA firms; each was spin-stabilized, and especially protected from over-heating at 0·3AU. Weighing 815kg (370kg), it was powered by solar cells able to withstand maximum temperatures of 165°C at perihelion.

Equipped with two booms and a 105ft (32m) electric dipole, the Helios probes carried magnetometers, a photometer, radiation counters, and analyzers. The long life of their solar mission—Helios 1 was still working satisfactorily eight years after launch—has produced a wealth of new data about the structure and the dynamics of the interplanetary environment close to the Sun, about the manifold effects of solar activity on this environment, and about the plasma of the solar corona. The influence of

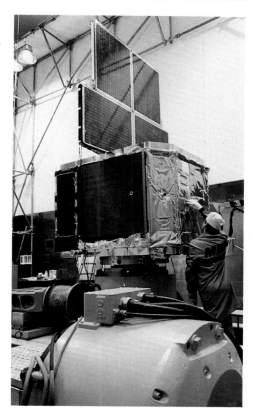

Above: *MBB technicians at work on the flight model of Exosat. This X-ray observatory was launched by Delta 3914 from Vandenberg AFB on 26 May 1983.*

changes in solar phenomena was studied during a large portion of an 11-year solar cycle. Extrapolation of the results obtained in the environment of the Sun, a main-sequence star, when related to other stellar systems in our Galaxy is increasing our knowledge on the entire Universe, far beyond the limits of the heliosphere.

Below: *This diagram illustrates the two modes of Exosat operation: direct observation and lunar occultation. In the latter, Exosat's orbit is adjusted to cause the Moon to interpose temporarily between it and the X-ray source. The resulting data allow the position of the source to be determined with extreme accuracy.*

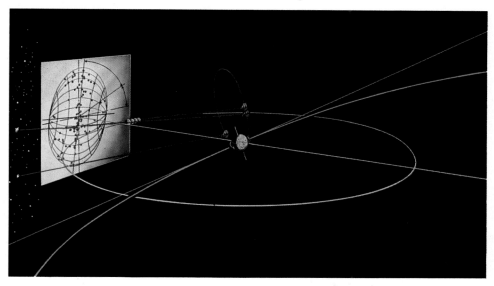

---

1 Astrometry is the branch of astronomy that is concerned with measuring the precise positions and movements of celestial objects.

Galileo

Planned for launch from the Space Shuttle, in May 1986 using a Centaur upper stage, the Galileo probe to Jupiter is a logical follow-on to the successful Voyager missions. Galileo will explore the Jovian atmosphere in 1988-1989 by *in situ* measurements made by a small descent module, and by remote measurements from the main module orbiting Jupiter and "touring" the Jovian system. Under an agreement between NASA and the Federal Ministry of Research and Technology of Germany, DFVLR and MBB-ERNO are supplying the retro-propulsion module to place Galileo in Jovian orbit and to control its trajectory and attitude around Jupiter. A number of German institutes are participating in science investigations to be made by the orbiter and the probe.

The retro-propulsion module is the first important subsystem contracted by NASA from non-US industry for an American interplanetary probe. Using the Earth-storable hypergolic propellant combination MON-1/MMH, and having a usable propellant load capacity of 2,061lb (935kg), it will perform all Galileo's propulsion manoeuvres during its 5-year lifetime. MBB-ERNO is the prime contractor. The deciding factor in selection of the German propulsion system was its outstanding flexibility and its high performance rate (specific impulse: 306 sec); the same engine technology demonstrated its excellent performance on the experimental Symphonie communications satellites.

West Germany is developing two important national projects for basic astronomy research: the first is the German Infra-red Laboratory (GIRL) which is being built by MBB-ERNO, and is designed as a universal, reusable infra-red telescope to be flown on a Spacelab mission (first flight of GIRL is expected in 1986-1987). The other spacecraft, the 2 ton ROSAT space telescope (Dornier System is prime contractor), will be launched in 1987 by the Space Shuttle in order to map the sky completely in the x-spectral range, to identify new binary stars within our galaxy, extra-galactic radiogalaxies, and supernova remnants.

Above: *The configuration model of the Galileo retro-propulsion module in final assembly at MBB. This module will provide for trajectory correction and put the spacecraft in Jupiter orbit.*

France: Venus, Vega

Space in France is synonymous with CNES (Centre National d'Etudes Spatiales), the national space agency formed in 1962. The first satellite launch vehicle, Diamant A, lifted off successfully on 26 November 1965 from Hammaguir, Algeria, and made France the world's third space-faring nation. CNES has advanced the development of its space transportation services, by proposing its 3-stage Ariane rocket as an European launcher. In September 1975, the last Diamant BP-4 vehicle, launched from Kourou, French Guiana, put into Earth orbit a small 234lb (106kg) satellite, D-2B Aura, to return data related to ultra-violet astronomy. Other French astronomy experiments in space, especially for gamma-ray observations, are conducted with the assistance both of ESA and NASA, but mainly in co-operation with the Soviet Academy of Sciences, through the Intercosmos programme. French instruments to detect and locate gamma-ray emissions are flown aboard several types of Soviet spacecraft such as the Prognoz satellites and Venus probes, while the French Signe 3 satellite was launched on 17 June 1977 by a Soviet booster.

France's contribution to the Soviet programme of Venus exploration has been considerable. Since 1978, French scientists have produced experiments for the Venus spacecraft, and French industry has been actively engaged in the design of the atmospheric research payloads. French participation will also be significant when the next two Venus probes are launched in December 1984. These spacecraft, Venera 17 and Venera 18, will fly-by and observe Venus, and attempt to land a scientific module on the surface of the planet in June 1985. Then both will continue on their interplanetary trajectory to encounter Halley's Comet in March 1986, after a flight of some 440 days duration. Specialized

French instruments will be installed in each of the two Venusian soft-landers to study atmospheric composition and phenomena. Because of the dual objective of the Venus 84 programme, it has been renamed the Vega mission (after the Russian for the two targets: VEnera and GAllei).

The two Vega spacecraft will encounter Halley's Comet at distances of 62,000 miles (100,000km) and 6,200 miles (10,000km) respectively at a speed of 48 miles/sec (78km/sec) during March 1986: the first on 8 March, the second about a week later. The Vega probes will pass the nucleus in such a way that the optical instruments will be able to investigate the sunlit side of the comet. The spacecraft will be 3-axis stabilized, and the 275lb (125kg) science payload will be mounted on an automatic pointing platform, so the experiments can be constantly directed at the moving nucleus of Halley's Comet. The French elements of the Vega payload include equipment for the two TV cameras (a telescope for the narrow-angle camera), the 3-channel spectrometer (optics, electronics), the infra-red spectrometer, and one of the two plasma detectors. From a distance of 6,200 miles (10,000km) the resolution of the narrow-angle TV camera will be 590ft (180m) on the surface of the cometary nucleus.

Before the Vega mission, two joint astronomical observatories will be orbited around the Earth. The UFT satellite incorporating an ultraviolet telescope, fitted with a French spectrometer, to study interstellar atmospheres was launched on 23 March 1983 under the name Astron. The 4 ton satellite was placed in an orbit ranging between 1,240 and 124,000 miles (2,000-200,000km). The Gamma 1 telescope will be mounted in an automatic Progress-type vehicle, to map high-energy (50MeV) sources with an angular resolution of the order to 10 arc minutes, in order to ascertain the exact structure of the Milky Way.

Japanese Probes

On 11 February 1970, Japan became the fourth space-faring country in the world with the launch of Ohsumi, a 53lb (24kg) spacecraft, atop a Lambda-4S sounding rocket. This success, after 4 failures, was a spectacular demonstration of the solid propulsion capacity developed by the Institute of Space and Aeronautical Science (ISAS) at the University of Tokyo. ISAS launchers and satellites became more complex and powerful; they were especially used for scientific purposes. ISAS, which in April 1981 became a national inter-university centre (independent from the University of Tokyo) and was reorganized under the new name of Institute of Space and Astronautical Science, has its own laboratories, test and launch facilities. The most important facilities of ISAS are the Kagoshima Space Centre, including the Mu launch area, and the tracking, telemetry and control stations for rockets and satellites.

Today's most important Japanese space organization, the National Space Development Agency of Japan (NASDA), was established in October 1969. NASDA, mostly subsidized by the government, is engaged in the development of powerful launch vehicles, and of satellites for practical and commercial applications, such as communications, television, meteorology, remote sensing, geodesy, and navigation. In order that it might rapidly acquire know-how in space transportation and applications systems, NASDA authorized Japanese industry to co-operate with US firms and to produce certain systems under licence. NASDA operates launch and control facilities on Tanegashima island.

Isas: Tansei 5, Planet A

The Institute of Space and Astronautical Science is unique in the world: it designs, develops, tests and flies its own launchers and scientific satellites. In the 15 year period between 1971 to 1986, ISAS plans to have put ten science spacecraft into Earth orbit and one cometary probe into solar trajectory from its Kagoshima Space Centre. A total of 12 satellites were successfully launched by ISAS Lambda or Mu solid rockets up to 1981: five technological pay-loads, called Tansei in orbit, to test the performance and reliability of the successive

improvements developed for the various Mu vehicles; and seven scientific spacecraft, carrying instruments to study the ionosphere, magnetosphere, exosphere, to observe aurorae, X-ray bursts and sources, and solar flares.

The first astronomy satellite was launched on 21 February 1979: it was a small X-ray observatory, the 198·4lb (90kg) spin-stabilized Hakucho (CORSA-b) spacecraft. Equipped with 11 X-ray detectors, Hakucho surveyed the sky along the galactic plane with a wide spectral coverage (0·1 to 11keV); it studied X-ray bursts thought to emanate from the surface of a neutron star. X-ray observations of the Universe will continue with the ASTRO programme: the first two ASTRO spacecraft, weighing some 408lb (185kg), were launched in February 1981

Below: *A Mu-3S solid-fuel launcher on the pad at the Kagoshima Space Centre in Japan. An improved version of this vehicle is scheduled to launch Japan's first interplanetary probe in 1985.*

and early 1983 respectively; a third (ASTRO C) of 882lb (400kg) weight is planned for launch in 1986 and will observe X-ray sources in the core of active galaxies.

Presently, ISAS is busy with the preparation of its first interplanetary mission. It is working with Nissan Motor on the development of an improved version of the Mu-3S launcher and of a new launch complex at the Kagoshima Space Center. The first Mu-3S II vehicle will be tested in early 1985 by launching into solar orbit an engineering test spacecraft, named Tansei 5. This technological probe, a certification model, is a replica of the Japanese Planet A spacecraft which is destined to encounter Halley's Comet on 8 March 1986. Tansei 5 is identical to Planet A except for its scientific payload which renders it 11lb (5kg) heavier. The 320lb (145kg) Tansei 5 probe is a prototype carrying three experiments to detect plasma wave instability, to measure the solar wind and to analyse the structures of the interplanetary magnetic field. The first Japanese observatory in solar orbit, it will also be the first interplanetary spacecraft to be launched outside the USSR and USA. Used in conjunction with the new 210ft (64m) Deep Space antenna ISAS has established at Usuda, 105 miles (170km) north-west of Tokyo, Tansei 5 will prepare the way for future Japanese probes to the Sun and the planets. In addition, Tansei 5 measurements will supplement the observations of Halley's Comet made by Planet A in March 1986: the two Japanese probes will be located at the same point during the cometary encounter.

Planet A will be launched from the Kagoshima Space Centre on 14 August 1985; a launch window of 20 days until the beginning of September is available. The spin-stabilized probe will weigh at launch about 309lb (140kg), including 26·5lb (12kg) of scientific payload and some 22lb (10kg) of hydrazine propellant for six 3-N thrusters (used for trajectory correction, spin-axis precession, and attitude control). About 2,000 solar cells, installed on the external surface of the cylindrical spacecraft, will supply power of 67 to 104W at a distance form the Sun of 1 to 0·68AU. The main antenna system consists of a high-gain antenna which is an offset-parabolic and mechanically despun 2·62ft (0·80m) reflector.

Two scientific instruments will be mounted on the cylindrical Planet A platform: a vacuum ultraviolet TV camera and a solar wind particle analyzer. Because the ISAS spacecraft has no protection against collision with the cometary dust and has a limited orbital manoeuvring capability, its fly-by distance of Halley's Comet is limited to between 62,000 and 6,200 miles (100,000 and 10,000km). For 10 days during the encounter, the Lyman-alpha TV camera will take pictures of the hydrogen coma in the comet, with a resolution corresponding to 18·6 miles (30km) from 62,000 miles (100,000km). The solar wind particle analyzer, consisting of 2 charged particle detectors, will measure the 3-dimensional distribution of the solar wind plasma within 30 degrees of the ecliptic plane.

For the end of the 1980s, ISAS is planning the development of a Mu-3S III launcher capable of placing a 1-ton spacecraft into low orbit, or sending more important probes into the Solar System. Among these plans, Japanese scientists are proposing both large astronomy satellites and projects for the exploration of Venus.

Nasda: The Polo Proposal

The National Space Development Agency of Japan produced the surprise of the "Space 2000" Congress of the International Astronautical Federation in Paris during September 1982: it described a system study of Moon exploration using a polar orbiter developed in Japan. NASDA activities in orbit are mainly devoted to space applications; its proposal for a Japanese POLO (Polar Orbiting Lunar Observatory) mission is a serious and ambitious project. Following the study made co-operatively by NASDA and NAL (National Aerospace Laboratory), a single lunar orbiter, weighing 1,433lb (650kg), equipped with remote sensing systems, would be launched by a 3-stage H-1A vehicle from the Tanegashima Space Centre in January 1987 and then inserted into a trans-lunar trajectory. After 109 hours of flight, the Japanese spacecraft would use a solid rocket motor for a lunar polar orbit insertion ranging between 62 and 2,485 miles (100 and 4,000km). One month later, when radar tracking had determined the lunar gravitational harmonics, the orbit would be circularized at 62 miles (100km) altitude by firing a bi-propellant thruster. After one year of operation, the orbiter would again reduce its velocity to attain a 31mile (50km) circular trajectory around the poles of the Moon.

The Japanese POLO spacecraft—weighing about 970lb (440kg) at the beginning of lifetime in lunar orbit—would derive electrical power from solar paddles pointing permanently at the Sun. They would deliver some 500W. The payload package would consist of a spectro-stereo imager (for global multi-spectral mapping), a reflectance spectrometer (to detect minerals), a fluorescent X-ray spectrometer (to map elemental composition), a magnetometer, and a radar-altimeter. This original lunar exploratory mission may be realized with foreign co-operation, from NASA and ESA.

China and India

Chinese and Indian activities in space are more modest. The governments of Beijing and of Delhi have made their priority the development of operational Earth satellites for communications, television, and remote sensing observations, in order to accelerate economic growth and social evolution in their respective countries. However, some Chinese and Indian scientists do get opportunities to use rockets to launch scientific payloads for space exploration.

China began its programme of space exploration in 1958 with sounding rockets; many 2-stage vehicles, employing solid propellant first stages and liquid second stages, carried payloads to study cosmic rays and magnetic phenomena. In 1965, a programme for the development of Chinese satellites was drawn up. This led to the successful launch on 24 April 1970 of a new launch vehicle, called CSL-1, Long March 1, which used liquid propulsion in the first two stages and solid in the third, and placed a 382·5lb (173kg) satellite into a near-Earth orbit. It then launched on 2 March 1971 the 485lb (220kg) SKW-2 spacecraft, which was equip-

Above: India's SLV-3 launch vehicle is shown here fully assembled on its transporter at ISRO's Sriharikota Launch Complex in Andra Pradesh State. After only a partially successful test launch in 1979, SLV-3 first demonstrated its full capabilities with the launch of the RS-1 satellite on 18 July 1980. More powerful versions of this rocket are in preparation.

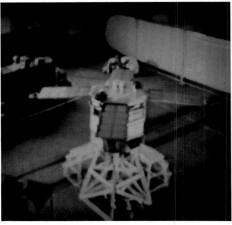

Right: A scene from a Chinese film shown at the Unispace 82 Conference revealing the largest of the three satellites launched by a single FB-1 rocket on 19 September 1981. The satellite is octagonal and is equipped with four solar panels.

ped with solar cells, and carried devices to study cosmic and X-rays, and magnetic fields. A second launcher, the more powerful FB-1, is a 2-stage liquid booster, capable of putting a 2,646lb (1,200kg) payload into low orbit. Two other vehicles, which are improved versions of the first two launchers, are in preparation, with modifications to the third stage: CSL-1A will receive a liquid third stage; while CSL-X3 consists of the FB-1 booster topped with a cryogenic upper stage to launch satellites into geostationary transfer orbit.

Between 1970 and 1982, China successfully launched 12 satellites. The most significant launching for space science was made on 19 September 1981, when three satellites were launched together by the same FB-1 rocket. The Chinese delegation at the Unispace 82 Conference at Vienna, in August 1982, showed an official film detailing the preparation of the main spacecraft. It was a spin-stabilized, scientific satellite with 4 solar panels, equipped to measure charged particles, X-rays, and infra-red and ultraviolet radiation. In the Chinese space report released to UNO, it is interesting to note the following information in the chapter "Future Space Activites":

"In order to meet the needs of space science and enhance our understanding of the Universe and Nature as well as to carry on further tests on different kinds of space technologies, we shall launch some new scientific and technological testing satellites occasionally. A comprehensive testing satellite is also

being developed in order to observe solar activity gamma ray burst and X-ray detection."

India has a long tradition in space exploration and astronomy. A famous astronomer and mathematician of the 5th century, Aryabhata, was commemorated by the naming after him of the first Indian spacecraft which was launched by a Soviet rocket on 19 April 1975: it was a 790lb (358·5kg) spin-stabilized satellite covered with solar cells and equipped with space science instruments for X-ray astronomy, solar physics and aeronomy[2]. The main objective of Aryabhata was to demonstrate India's indigenous ability to design and fabricate complex satellites. Five days after launch, all experiments on board Aryabhata were switched off following the detection of a fault in the power line.

The Government of India, through the Department of Space, promotes national space development and applications for the socio-economic benefits they can confer. Indian space activities are managed by ISRO (Indian Space Research Organization), with the assistance of Indian industry and of foreign space organizations (NASA, ESA, Intercosmos). ISRO is able to launch its own sounding rockets and satellite launchers, all using solid propulsion. It has established on Sriharikota island, on India's east coast, its most important launch complex for the SLV-3 vehicles and subsequent improved ver-

2 Aeronomy: the study of the physics and chemistry of the upper atmosphere.

sions of this rocket. The 75·5ft (22·7m) high SLV-3 is a 4-stage solid propellant vehicle, with an estimated launch weight of 17 tons; in about 8 minutes (2·5 minutes of propulsion phase), it can place an 88lb (40kg) spacecraft into a 186 mile (300km) Earth orbit. The first successful launch of SLV-3 took place on 18 July 1980 when India, with the placing of the technological RS-1 (Rohini Satellite) in orbit, became the seventh nation in space. The SLV-3 rocket will be followed by more powerful models: the ASLV (Augmented Satellite Launch Vehicle) and the PSLV (Polar SLV) which are scheduled respectively for operations in 1985 and 1988 to launch 331lb (150kg) and 1,323lb (600kg) class satellites for scientific, technological and applications purposes. A number of small instruments have been proposed for the next 110lb (50kg) Rohini satellites; they include a transient gamma-ray detector, a langmuir probe, and a solar/ultraviolet radiation monitor.

Private Funds

During 1980 a Californian initiative explored the possibility of privately funding a programme of space exploration. A Citizen's Nonprofit Space Corporation, named Delta Vee (from a rocket formula denoting the energy required to change velocity), was created by a young space enthusiast, Stan Kent, in order to finance by private subscription continued US involvement in interplanetary missions. In its first year Delta Vee collected funds to save the Viking 1 lander still operating from Mars' Chryse Planitia; over 10,000 people dug into their pockets to support a robot lander still active on Mars, and the sum of 100,000 dollars was offered to NASA for Martian data reception and analysis. With its Halley Fund appeal, Delta Vee tried to start a modest US project for Halley's Comet Intercept mission. Now, through its Ferdinand and Isabella Project, it is promoting studies for solar power satellites, asteroid retrieval operations, and explosive propulsion concepts.

To summon up popular support and so obtain private sponsorship is a crucial element for the organization of space exploration projects without government involvement.

Solar sailing in space is considered a very cheap means of sending a spacecraft to explore the Moon, the asteroids and the Solar System. This original technology was studied in 1976 and 1977 by NASA and the Jet Propulsion Laboratory for low-cost interplanetary flights. During these studies, the square sail and the heliogyro system were analysed in depth and specific designs created. However, the efforts were terminated without any fabrication of hardware beyond some demonstration items. The initiative to continue experimentation then passed into private hands.

Sailing on New Oceans

Solar sails in orbit are spacecraft propelled by the pressure of sunlight reflecting off the large, ultra-thin metallized plastic sheets. Photon propulsion has a major advantage for interplanetary exploration: it does not require propellant in pressurized and expensive tanks. The propulsive energy comes directly from the Sun; like its ocean counterpart, a solar sail spacecraft can travel back and forth across the Solar System without refuelling. The problem in solar sailing among the planets is to construct very light, large but strong and controllable structures. Currently two ventures are aiming to advance the development of solar sailing spacecraft.

Firstly, the 1986 World Exposition on Transportation and Communication, to be held in Vancouver (Canada), is sponsoring the test flight of a solar sail between the Earth and the Moon. This first sail is being developed by the privately-financed World Space Foundation, California. The idea of the World Space Foundation was conceived by Robert L. Staehle, an astronautical engineer, and some of his colleagues in the aerospace industry. It is a non-profit organization attempting to provide people with an opportunity of privately supporting space exploration. A dedicated volunteer staff developed a full-size prototype of the solar sail during 1982, and is preparing the engineering development model for a possible flight during the Vancouver Exposition in 1986. The demonstration sail spacecraft will consist of 3 basic elements: the bus forming the core with all systems and payload, the sail and its equipment, and a solid propellant rocket motor to put it on an elliptical trajectory. The sail itself is a square structure, each side being 155ft (47m) long, with tip vanes that provide attitude control. If this Earth orbital test is successful, the World Space Foundation hopes to launch an operational solar sail probe in the 1990s to encounter a comet or observe selected asteroids.

A second stimulus to solar sailing will be provided by an International Space "Transat" race to the Moon, (based on transatlantic sailing races), which is proposed by the French U3P (the Union for the Promotion of Photon Propulsion) for the second half of this decade. This original contest would offer an excellent opportunity to evaluate different concepts of solar sailing spacecraft. U3P is looking for sponsors to support the organization of this "première" in space, and for funds in order to construct its "butterfly" sail.

It seems probable that three or four solar sails will be ready for launch in 1987-1988. They would be packed together in separate modules, placed on top of a common propulsion system which would circularize their orbits after launch. When the modules had been moved close to geostationary orbit, the competing teams would get ready to take the control of their own sails after separation from the common package. The winner would be the first competitor whose solar sail was occulted by the Moon. British, Japanese, Czechoslovak and Soviet engineers and students are considering participation in the race, along with the French U3P team. Launch services can be expected from the European Ariane or Soviet Proton vehicles. It is an intriguing prospect, and further evidence of the exploratory spirit that will be opening the frontiers of space throughout the decade.

Below: *An artist's impression of a solar sail: this spacecraft was studied in 1977 by Jet Propulsion Laboratory scientists for a Halley's Comet fly-by mission.*

Large Launch Vehicles

The progress of Astronautics in the 21st Century will depend, in large measure, upon the economic necessity to expand human interests deeper into the Solar System. Examples of large space ventures responding to this need are:

1 Space factories manufacturing on a large scale materials and products of unique character, difficult or impossible to produce on Earth.

2 Solar power stations in geostationary orbit capable of generating large amounts of electrical energy for transmission to Earth.

3 Exploitation of natural resources on other celestial bodies, the Moon, planets, asteroids, comets, etc.

4 Large space platforms for human occupancy leading to self-sustaining colonies remote from Earth.

Any of these pursuits, rigorously undertaken, by virtue of the immense space transportation systems required, would open gateways to a new Golden Age of space conquest.

It is too early to know how realistic any of these potential developments will be. So far the greatest attention has been paid to the Satellite Power System (SPS). As early as 1978, NASA declared that detailed studies by the Marshall Space Flight Center (MSFC) and industrial partners had found no technical reason for supposing that the SPS could not be built in the 1990s.

Development of space factories will depend partly upon the success of pilot experiments now underway aboard the Soviet Salyut space stations and the NASA Space Shuttle.

Exploitation of extra-terrestrial materials will depend upon the practicability of utilising such materials, and the economics of doing so in competition with traditional materials and processing techniques on Earth. For example, Professor Gerard K. O'Neill has suggested manufacturing Satellite Power Systems in space from processed materials taken from the Moon and asteroids, eliminating the need to lift bulk supplies from Earth's deep gravity pit.

This, however, takes us into the fourth space venture in which manned space stations have already grown to fully fledged colonies.

If we are to expand to this scale of activity, the first requirement will be an efficient space transportation system. This would involve:

1 A space platform in low Earth orbit with facilities for servicing and refuelling large spaceships.

Left: *Space Shuttle* Challenger *lifts off for the first time on 4 April 1983 at the start of Mission STS-6. Modifications to the spacecraft aimed at upgrading its performance included a lightweight External Tank, lighter weight solid rocket boosters and Orbiter, and uprated engines. Follow-on vehicles are now being studied.*

2 Development of reusable boosters of high capacity for delivery of cargo and passengers to the orbiting space platform.

3 Effective vehicle transfer between low Earth orbit and geostationary orbit at 22,300 miles (35,880km).

4 An Earth-Moon inter-orbit transport system with facilities for lunar landing and return.

How can we build on our present space systems to achieve these new goals?

A NASA spokesman has observed,

"As versatile as the NASA Space Shuttle is, we recognize that there are requirements on the horizon that would require some kinds of follow-on vehicles for intra-space use or to lift massive loads up into orbit."

As the Shuttle made its maiden flight into orbit early in 1981, the Marshall Space Flight Center was already considering ways of upgrading it. This included getting more power from the main engines and Solid Rocket Boosters, shaving weight off the External Tank and boosters, using lightweight booster casings, and fitting a Titan III propulsion module under the tank to provide extra boost. Some of these improvements are already underway. If all were embodied, the payload delivered into a close Earth orbit could be increased by 54,000lb (24,494kg) to 119,000lb (53,978kg).

Studies have also been made of ways to improve the performance of the Shuttle Orbiter by replacing the Solid Rocket Boosters (SRBs) with reusable liquid propellant boosters. Such a change could itself increase payload to low Earth orbit by 50 per cent.

The SCLV

Further opportunities stem from the ability to apply Shuttle technology to unmanned launchers. An example is the Shuttle-Derived Cargo Launch Vehicle (SCLV) studied by Boeing Aerospace in conjunction with MSFC. The objective was to minimise development risk, cost and time by utilising proven Space Shuttle flight hardware in a stripped-down, unmanned, cargo lifter. A main aim was to discover how cargo could be split between Shuttle and SCLV.

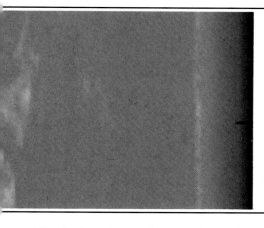

"Let us create vessels and sails adjusted to the heavenly ether, and there will be plenty of people unafraid of the empty wastes."

Johannes Kepler, *Letter to Galileo Galilei, April 1610*

Clearly, there is a wide range of possibilities but a typical vehicle capable of lifting 87,000lb (39,463kg) might consist of a shortened Space Shuttle External Tank with a single SSME at the base.

Attached to the sides of this stage would be shortened Solid Rocket Boosters also derived from Space Shuttle technology. The large payload, attached to an insertion or "kick" stage, would be placed above the core within a jettisonable shroud.

During the ascent from the launch pad, the modified SRBs would separate from the External Tank and payload at a height of some 177,000ft (53,950m), returning by parachute; main engine cut-off would occur at about 184 miles (296km) downrange, the core stage being jettisoned into the ocean.

The "kick" stage provides final insertion into Earth orbit at about 173 miles (278km). It is possible that, with further refinement, the Shuttle engine and "kick" stage could be picked up from low orbit by a Shuttle Orbiter.

To reach geostationary orbit,, an upper stage would replace the "kick" stage. On all missions, the Shuttle-Derived Cargo Launch Vehicle would be guided and controlled by an avionics package in the terminal stage.

Passenger-Carrying Shuttles

Ways of exchanging the cargo compartment of the regular Shuttle for passengers have also been examined. One scheme envisages fitting 28 passengers into the pressure vessel of the ESA Spacelab.

Rockwell International actually devised a passenger transport module which they claimed could accommodate up to 74 people. In this concept the pressure shell of Spacelab, "stretched" to practically the full length of the cargo bay, is fitted with seats on two levels. The upper deck has room for four seats abreast and an aisle 25·2in (64cm) wide running the full length of the module, doors allowing entry and exit at this level. The lower deck has two seats abreast and an aisle of similar length, with stowage space on either side. The decks are linked by two access ladders adjacent to the payload cargo bay exit doors in the side of the compartment, while access to the Orbiter crew compartment is provided by a tunnel adapter and airlock.

Rockwell suggests the accommodation would be suitable for a one or two day flight of the kind that would be involved in transferring personnel to and from an orbiting space platform with minimal g-forces involved in launch and re-entry. Additional toilet facilities would be embodied and passengers would sleep in their seats under weightless conditions.

However, this passenger loading could not be achieved without certain changes to the Orbiter including modifications to the wings, life support system and environmental control system. The estimated cost was $220 million at 1980 prices.

Air-Launched Sortie Vehicle

One of the most unusual concepts for a reusable booster is contained in a study made by Boeing Aerospace for the US Air Force's Rocket Propulsion Laboratory in 1981 in which a 275,000lb (124,740kg) winged spacecraft, called an Air-Launched Sortie Vehicle, leaves the ground on the back of a modified Boeing 747. The virtue of this arrangement is that once the combination is airborne, the spaceplane can be launched at any desired angle to the equator and can fly over any point on Earth within 100 minutes. It could therefore be used for a wide range of military duties including reconnaissance and surveillance and even the interception of satellites in orbit.

It could also, of course, be used to supply space platforms with regular cargo and operate in a space rescue role.

The spaceplane itself, based on NASA Space Shuttle technology, could be either manned or unmanned. It would have the Orbiter's reusable surface insulation and a single disposable tank which stores the liquid oxygen/liquid hydrogen propellants during launch. Nine modified Pratt & Whitney RL-10 engines supply main propulsion. Modifications to the 747 mother include strengthening the structure, fitting propellant tanks and mounting a Space Shuttle Main Engine in the tail.

In a typical mission the 747 mother finally assumes a 60° flight angle, releasing the ALSV spaceplane at an altitude of 37,000ft (11,278m). Two rear outboard engines ignite to control and steer the vehicle. Once the spaceplane has cleared the 747's tail, the remaining seven engines ignite to provide the vehicle's main propulsion. These engines consume propellants in the external tank which the spaceplane jettisons just before going into orbit. On-board propellants are used for the remainder of the flight.

This study, which suggests that such a vehicle could fly before 1990, highlights certain features which may eventually be found in the Soviet "Kosmolyot".

The Russian spaceplane is said to follow techniques recommended by the late Dr. A.I. Mikoyan, co-designer of the famous MiG fighters. A small delta-winged rocket powered spacecraft sits on the back of a large delta-winged air-breathing booster which takes off from a runway. The composite aircraft accelerates to 4,920mph (7,920km/h), approximately six times the speed of sound, at an altitude of 18·6 miles (30km) at which point the rocketplane separates to continue the flight into orbit. The mother circles back to land like a conventional aircraft.

Although one may doubt that the delta mother will achieve this performance in practice, the idea of launching a spaceplane

Below: *The Air-Launched Sortie Vehicle takes off from a Boeing 747. It would be made largely of carbon-fibre polyamide.*

Below: *The Martin X-24B test vehicle flown in 1973; the configuration of the ALSV is based on this earlier design for the USAF.*

in the stratosphere continues to exercise the minds of Soviet designers.

The Kosmolyot will be a good deal smaller than America's Space Shuttle. The Russians are expected to retain big rockets for launching large components of space stations and spaceships. A new space station, still being developed, is expected to have multiple docking ports into which can be plugged scientific laboratories, space tugs and manned and unmanned ferries. Linked to this programme is Russia's Type G booster which, according to an official US Department of Defense document, will have a capability "six or seven times" that of the NASA Space Shuttle.

Although strictly a "mini-shuttle", the Kosmolyot could have duties other than the ability to ferry crews to and from space stations. They might include the servicing of satellites in orbit, space rescue, and military reconnaissance. Inspection and possible destruction of "hostile" satellites could also be within its grasp.

A reliable Russian source claims that the aim is to reduce operating costs to a level one-tenth that of the NASA Space Shuttle. The first flight is expected around 1987 and the project should be discussed openly some two years before that because test flights cannot be kept secret.

The project is expected to develop in four distinct stages.

1 The release of delta-winged test vehicles from a modified Tu-95 Bear bomber. *Aviation Week & Space Technology* revealed in 1977 that the first flight had taken place.

2 The rocket launching of sub-scale test models. One such test took place from Kapustin Yar, near the city of Volgograd, on 3 June 1982 when a 2,200lb (1,000kg) class vehicle made a single orbit of the Earth ending its flight in the Indian Ocean. Soviet ships were waiting in the recovery area some 350 miles (563km) south of the Cocos Islands. It is believed that the launcher was a two-stage C-1 rocket of the type used to launch medium-size satellites in the Cosmos and Intercosmos programmes. A second such test

took place on 15 March 1983; the vehicle again only made one full revolution of the Earth, and was recovered south of the Cocos Islands.

3 Launch of a full-size Kosmolyot prototype—possibly unmanned—on the nose of a large rocket booster of the Proton series.

4 Test flights of a large mother plane which will carry the fully-fledged Kosmolyot to operating altitude. Whether this vehicle will employ turboramjets and auxiliary rockets remains to be seen.

The 2nd edition of *Soviet Military Power*, issued by the US Department of Defense, also cites evidence that the USSR is developing a large reusable vehicle "similar to the US Space Shuttle", adding that reusable systems could be in regular use within a decade. The prototype is reported to have been seen at the large experimental airfield at Ramenskoye, south-east of Moscow, mounted on the back of a modified M-4 Bison bomber. The airfield is associated with the Central Institute of Aero-Hydrodynamics (tsAGI) which has extensive research laboratories and wind tunnels.

The same publication confirms that new launch facilities "are being built" at the Baikonur cosmodrome for the latest generation of Soviet heavy-lift space rockets. Two new expendable launch systems—one capable of lifting 330,750lb (150,000kg) into close Earth orbit, and a medium-lift vehicle able to lift 28,660lb (13,000kg)—are expected to fly in the period 1984-87. New construction at Baikonur can even be seen in photographs obtained by NASA's Landsat satellites. This includes an extensive runway north of the large launch complexes originally built for the Type G "super-booster" which failed in 1969-72.

If development of the smaller air-launched Kosmolyot continues in parallel, the Soviets will be in a position to open up space activities on a routine scale launching spacecraft at any desired inclination. On the 25th anniversary of Sputnik in October 1982, Lt-Gen Vladimir Shatalov, head of cosmonaut training, pointed to the improved living conditions being provided in

existing Salyut space stations. Thanks to regular re-supply missions by Progress cargo ships, the occupants now have a varied diet including fresh vegetables and fruit, hot water, showers, video films and television.
"The main task now is to find an optimum period during which a cosmonaut can live and work with maximum yield."

Then will come bigger space stations—orbiting research institutes and factories—which will be pieced together in orbit.

Shatalov envisages a large complex being put together of "individual blocks". A block is orbited and immediately the station starts to function. Soon it is joined by another block, and so on.

This method of space building was tested on a small scale when the Russians docked Cosmos 1,267 automatically with Salyut 6 in June 1981. Spacecraft designer Dr Konstantin Feoktistov described Cosmos 1,267 as a key step in the Soviet assembly of a major operations centre in Earth orbit. In addition to expanding the size of space vehicles, the system would serve as a launch platform for rockets carrying spacecraft to deeper regions of space. Cosmos 1,267 was subsequently destroyed in the atmosphere still joined to the Salyut 6 space station when tests were completed in July 1982. Experiments of this kind were continued when Cosmos 1,443 was docked automatically with the Salyut 7 space station. The combination was subsequently boarded by the Soyuz T-9 cosmonauts in June 1983.

Using the building block system, says Feoktistov, it would be possible to erect huge generating systems which convert sunlight into electricity and send it to Earth. In a similar way, he continued, orbiting cosmodromes could be put together from which spaceships could be launched towards Mars, Venus and other planets.

The Soviet spacecraft designer also mentioned the possibility "in the near future" of sending unmanned space probes to Mars which would deliver samples of Martian soil from different parts of the planet to Earth. He concluded:
"It is likely that a manned expedition to Mars will begin much earlier than we think. It is almost certain that such an expedition will be an international one."

Space Tugs

The next step in establishing large payloads in geostationary orbit will be to provide an effective inter-orbit transport system compatible with Space Shuttle operations in low Earth orbit. Almost certainly a requirement will arise for large antenna platforms which will take over many of the duties performed by smaller satellites.

NASA and the US Air Force have solicited support for a new technology Space Tug capable of transferring a 10,000lb (4,536kg) payload to 24hr orbit. At first this Shuttle-launched vehicle would be unmanned and telecontrolled but later there was a prospect of adapting it to carry astronauts to geostationary platforms.

Unfortunately, this opportunity was denied by a decision of the Reagan Administration in July 1982 to proceed with a modification of the existing LO_2/LH_2 Centaur stage with markedly reduced performance.

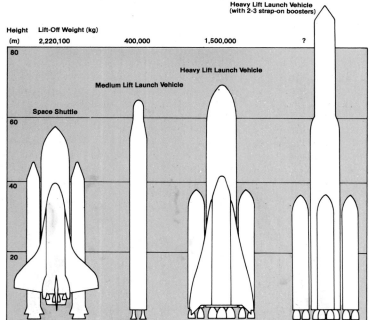

Height | Lift-Off Weight (kg)
(m) | 2,220,100 | 400,000 | 1,500,000 | ?

Space Shuttle
Medium Lift Launch Vehicle
Heavy Lift Launch Vehicle
Heavy Lift Launch Vehicle (with 2-3 strap-on boosters)

New Soviet Launchers
New Soviet launch vehicles are being built on the modular principle, all using liquid propellants. This diagram, adapted from *Soviet Military Power 1983*, shows possible configurations, compared to the US Space Shuttle. Payloads that could be delivered into a 112 miles (180km) circular orbit are: Medium Lift Vehicle: 28,660lb (13,000kg); Heavy Lift Vehicle with spaceplane: 132,000lb (60,000kg); (an optimistic figure according to subsequently released US estimates); Expendable Heavy Lift Vehicle: 286,650lb-330,750lb (130,000kg-150,000kg). Corresponding lift-off thrusts are 1,300,000lb (589,680kg); 4-6 million lb (1,814,400-2,721,600kg); 8-9 million lb (3,629,000-8,082,400kg). The two expendable launchers are expected to fly during 1984-87. Reusable systems could be in regular service within a decade.

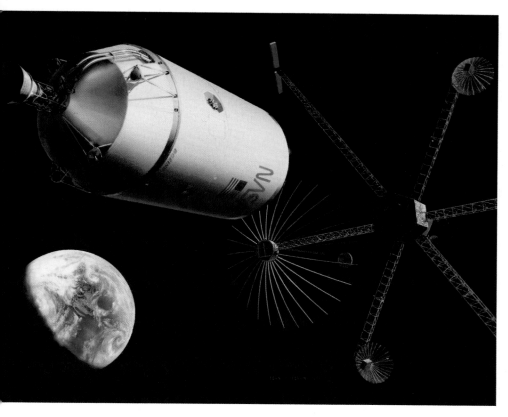

Arguments have ranged back and forth between the advocates of two-stage heavy lift vehicles (HLLVs) with full recovery by wings, to reusable ballistic or semi-ballistic carriers. NASA's original baseline concept for the SPS application was a huge two-staged winged vehicle having a lift-off weight of 11,000 tons and a payload of 420 tons. Later studies by Boeing and Rockwell brought the scale down to 4,000 tons lift-off weight and a payload of 120 tons as this would be more versatile in operation and easier and cheaper to develop.

Advocates of alternative systems emphasise that a reusable ballistic vehicle of similar capability would be cheaper still, assuming that the more limited cross-range capability of the ballistic re-entry vehicle is acceptable.

Boeing, in fact, adopted the ballistic approach in Satellite Power System studies but did not embody the novel plug nozzle/heat shield combination introduced by Bono.

More recent studies by MSFC of the special transportation requirements of the Satellite Power System and other missions of the large space platform era have included dual propellant systems. They include advanced chemical propulsion with liquid oxygen/kerosene first stage and high-energy LO_2/LH_2 second stage. The reason for having mixed propulsion in the same vehicle is because greater stage performance and lower manufactured weight can be achieved. The first stage must have a high propellant density and density impulse, the second a higher specific impulse.

Propellants would be cross-fed from the first stage booster to the second orbiter stage during the boost phase. Launched vertically with reusable flyback landing stages, payload capabilities would range up to a million pounds (453,600kg).

Inter-Orbit Propulsion

Heavy cargo lifters of this type would deliver into low Earth orbit the building block elements of the SPS (or other large orbital construction project) together with necessary factory equipment.

Moving finished structures from low Earth orbit to their operating position in 24 hour geostationary orbit requires a different class of transporter. Conceivably, this would make use of low-thrust Orbital Transfer Vehicles spiralling out gradually to the 24 hour station over periods of months.

Originally, these "lifters" were looked upon as electrical rocket systems deriving their power from nuclear reactors, but more recently a potentially less troublesome system has been advocated.

The concept stems largely from work undertaken by MSFC on the Solar Electric Propulsion Stage (SEPS) which depends upon passing mercury ions through an

---

The aim of this—the "Wide-Body Centaur"—initially is to provide the "kick" stage for Galileo and International Solar Polar Mission replacing the two-stage Inertial Upper Stage (IUS).

The project is being undertaken at a cost of some $250 million and the estimated cost of modifying the *Challenger* and *Discovery* Shuttle Orbiters to carry it, and necessary changes to the KSC launch pads, is around $125 million. Each payload bay door of the Orbiters will include orifices for LO_2 and LH_2 to allow fuelling on the pad; vents through to the rear of the spacecraft will permit propellants to be dumped in the event of an emergency landing.

Heavy-Lift Boosters

Beyond this are ideas for reusable ballistic rockets based on the technology introduced by a NASA patent awarded to Philip Bono of Douglas Aircraft Company (now McDonnell-Douglas) in 1965 and 1967. A good example is the Rombus concept.

Described as a reusable "utility" shuttle, it was aimed at providing the propulsive technology for really large objectives such as lunar base support and interplanetary flight. The vehicle would be capable of delivering many hundreds of tons into close Earth orbit and with a base diameter of 80ft (24·4m) it was essentially a huge ballistic rocket which could take off and land vertically.

Above: *An Orbital Transfer Vehicle has just placed a communications platform in Clarke orbit above the Earth. This Boeing concept envisages the development of a totally reusable, liquid-fuelled spacecraft.*

Its secret was a combined heat shield and plug nozzle with a ring of thrust chambers on the periphery. Used at take off, this engine would operate with a mixture ratio (LO_2/LH_2) of 7:1 and a vacuum expansion ratio of 200:1. Eight hydrogen fuel tanks would be jettisoned on propellant depletion and recovered by parachute.

The plug nozzle engine, which could be throttled over a wide range, could also be used for orbit insertion, de-orbiting (when the vehicle assumed a backward attitude to the path of flight) and retro-thrust for landing.

The vehicle's tail-first re-entry into the atmosphere was possible because the plug nozzle was regeneratively cooled by liquid hydrogen and thus served as an effective heat shield.

The proposed method of landing the Rombus orbital vehicle was by deploying five 61ft (18·6m) parachutes at a height of 30,000ft (9,144m) followed by 12 seconds of retro-thrust beginning at 2,500ft (762m) when the velocity had dropped to 170ft/sec (51·8m/sec). The stroke of the four-legged landing gear was 2ft (0·6m) and the touchdown deceleration approximately 2g.

Rombus Assembly
1 Mate engine to transporter platform.
2 Mate LO_2 tank.
3 Attach 8 LH_2 tanks.
4 Installation/checkout.
5 Mate payload and nose cone.
6 Component and systems checkout.

This reusable spacecraft, conceived in 1965-67, far outstripped in size and

performance any previous launcher. Although a single stage vehicle, it was expected to lift 400-500 ton loads to Earth orbit, and to be re-used 100 times. Variants were envisaged for landing men on the Moon and sending a manned expedition to Mars. Base diameter: 80ft (24·3m). Lift-off thrust: 18 million lb (8·2 million kg).

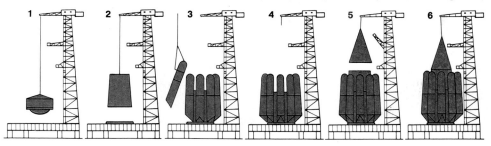

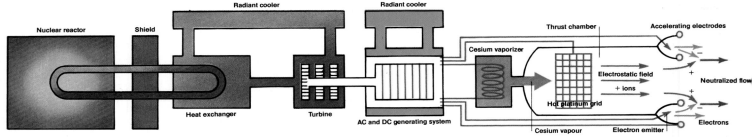

Ion Propulsion
This diagram illustrates the principles of an ion rocket propulsion system. At left a nuclear reactor, coupled to a heat exchanger, heats gas which drives a turbine that generates electrical power. A radiant cooler permits the regenerative recycling of the gas. The ac/dc generator heats a coil, causing cesium propellant to vaporize. The vapour expands into the rocket's thrust chamber where it passes across a hot platinum grid which absorbs the cesium atoms, and re-emits positive ions. These pass across an electrostatic field, and so out of the chamber. The electrons are picked off the grid, preventing it from becoming negatively charged, and routed to two thrusters, out of which they are electrically accelerated. The re-combination of positive and negative ions results in a neutralized flow. The thrust produced by such a vehicle would be very low, but could be continuously produced over very long periods. A Space Electric Rocket Test (SERT 2), launched by a Thrust Augmented Thor-Agena D in February 1970, successfully embodied two such engines in the Agena stage.

electrostatic field to produce thrust. Although frustrated by funding cuts in the late 1970s, the SEPS was evolved as a cost-effective approach to accomplishing a wide variety of missions which could include:

1 High-energy planetary excursions, eg visits to comets, asteroids, the outer planets and the inner planets Venus and Mercury.

2 High-energy or extended operations in Earth orbit, eg satellite servicing, positioning, transfer of large payloads to geostationary orbit and removal of space debris. MSFC had already developed technology for the large deployable solar array that would provide the power for the SEPS electrostatic field. (This solar array incidentally was the basis for a common development programme designed to support not only the SEPS but also to provide power augmentation for the Shuttle and Spacelab missions through the 25kW Power Module, of which it is a major part).

Marshall received the go-ahead for definition and development of the SEPS in August 1978 with the view to launching a dual comet mission: a fly-by of Halley's Comet in 1985, followed by rendezvous with the comet Tempel 2 in 1988. Unfortunately, this project fell victim to budgetary cuts and the entire SEPS programme was put into suspension.

More recently a USAF satellite has been developed for testing mercury-ion propulsion in the shape of small thrusters for station-keeping and attitude control.

In the major league of future development, Marshall believe that the build up of factories in geostationary orbit requiring hundreds of launchings per year, ion solar-electric propulsion could lift two to three times more cargo than chemical rocket stages could manage to do.

Missions to Mars

Another big inducement to the development of large launch vehicles would be a decision to send a manned expedition to Mars. The possibility of using Rombus vehicles for such a mission was investigated by the Douglas project team who saw advantages in refuelling the huge vehicle in Earth orbit before departure.

This would have involved Rombus-type tankers meeting the orbiting expedition ship and replacing the large jettisoned hydrogen tanks with full tanks and pumping across supplies of liquid oxygen.

In this way a 450 day round trip to the Red Planet could be achieved by the Rombus spaceship serving the functions of Earth escape stage; propulsion stage for achieving an orbit about Mars, the Mars escape stage, and the Earth re-entry module.

The United States had begun ambitiously with the development of the NERVA nuclear rocket engine. When this was abandoned in 1972, it seemed that a manned expedition to Mars would be out of the question for a very long time. In the Soviet Union, Academician V.P. Glushko, the veteran rocket engine designer, argued that the ideal would be a combination of chemically fuelled, nuclear and electric propulsion systems.

Since then Rocketdyne and NASA have tested components for an Advanced Space Engine (ASE) fuelled by LH_2 and LO_2 which gives the hint that nuclear engines may not be necessary after all.

Dr R.C. Parkinson has examined the case, based on ASE technology, for a manned Mars expedition beginning in November 1994.

Three vehicles are involved in this expedition and all would be docked together during the transfer orbit to Mars for convenience and safety. Two of the vehicles are intended to remain in orbit about Mars

Above: *An original artist's impression made by the Douglas Aircraft Company showing the Rombus core vehicle being refuelled in Earth orbit, before starting out on a manned mission to the planet Mars.*

while the exploration party lands. These ships embody separate living quarters for the five-person crew, with identical life-support and control centres for greater security should a major systems failure occur. The third vehicle is non-returnable; it comprises the Mars Lander and associated expedition cargo.

At launch each Mars Orbiter vehicle has three propulsive stages, beginning with a Heavy Boost stage the size of Saturn IVB which places the craft en-route for Mars. The second and third stages are based on the proposed Shuttle Orbital Transfer Vehicle using the advanced LO_2/LH_2 engine, and the third stage is used for the return flight. The Lander employs the same first and second stages as the Orbiters but omits stage three.

The expedition plan works out as follows:

1 Arrive Mars orbit 10 June 1995.

2 Spend 45 days in orbit about Mars to survey the ground, release unmanned probes and select the landing site; possibility of a side trip to the Martian moon Phobos.

3 Landing of the Mars Module with surface exploration party.

4 Centre module of Lander returns astronauts and samples to orbiting spaceships.

5 Two spaceships leave Mars orbit 25 July 1995, re-docking for return journey.

6 Swingby of Venus is made 8 December 1995 to save time and delta-V.

7 Expedition ships return to Earth orbit 16 May 1996.

8 Final recovery of exploration party by Space Shuttle.

Electric Rockets and Solar Sails

While these studies were in progress other designers have been reexamining low-thrust techniques of propulsion like the nuclear-ion rocket which, operating in conjunction with chemical boosters, could bring large savings in flight times. Two electron bombardment ion engines were flight tested in an Agena satellite experiment carried out for NASA in 1970.

The MHD (magneto-hydrodynamics) plasma engine is another low thrust candidate which, allied to a nuclear power source, could bring large rewards.

The principle of an MHD rocket engine is as follows: with a current flowing in one direction through the plasma, and a magnetic field at right angles to it, the plasma is expelled in a direction at right angles to both, creating a reactive thrust. Most plasma engines are intermittent in operation, but at a very high frequency, using electronic switching arrangements.

At the other extreme the World Space Foundation has been investigating another low-thrust device, the Solar Sail.

First proposed by the Russian space pioneers K.E. Tsiolkovsky and F.A. Tsander, solar sails operate by bouncing light from highly reflective layers of aluminium only a few Angstroms thick. They obey the principle of reaction (Newton's Third Law) by reversing the momentum of light rays, creating a propulsive force. The force is minute but applied over periods of several months it will produce very high velocities.

Huge square rigged sails of upwards of 8,610ft² (800m²) and giant spinning sails have been examined by the Jet Propulsion Laboratory (JPL) for the study of comets. One of the most interesting is the Heliogyro conceived by two Southern California aerospace engineers, Richard MacNeal and John Hedgepath.

The design, as finally evolved by JPL, took the form of a comet chaser packed into a volume of 70·6ft³ (2m³) and weighing just 1,800lb (816kg). Taken into orbit by the Space Shuttle and boosted to escape velocity by an attached rocket, the sails arranged in two tiers of six would open up slowly as the craft began to spin. Each narrow sail would eventually extend 4·5 miles (7·24km) to catch the maximum radiative power from the Sun.

These sails, which rotate once every three minutes, can be pitch controlled like a helicopter's rotors to provide attitude control and to turn the craft so that the reflective plane can have different orientations with respect to the Sun. Thus the vehicle can fly

Below: *The spinning solar sail, or Heliogyro, as conceived by NASA-JPL scientists for a 1986 Halley's Comet mission. The huge sails would have been pitch controlled, much as a helicopter's rotors are.*

in towards the Sun or out into the Solar System. JPL scientists point out that solar sails are ideal for intercepting high velocity targets like comets because, in theory, they can attain speeds up to some 124,000 mph (200,000km/h).

Translunar Systems

More conventional space tugs refuelled at the space station in Earth orbit would perform shuttle missions to and from lunar orbit, utilising large lunar modules for final letdown onto the Moon's surface. A useful device in the Earth-Moon system would be a swing station equipped with docking facilities for the attachment of cargo. Pursuing a figure-of-eight trajectory, it would require relatively small propulsive adjustments to continue in regular motion as a kind of "space elevator" transferring cargo both ways between Earth-orbit and lunar orbit.

Once this stage has been reached, it will be possible to contemplate routine excursions to the lunar surface and more ambitious explorations of the Solar System in search of extra-terrestrial resources. A key step would be the extraction of oxygen from moonsoil and the development of the Moon as a refuelling base for spaceships (see Chapter 19).

Sampling missions to certain asteroids would be possible to establish their precise chemical composition. Spectroscopic examination suggests that some species contain Earth-like minerals, others carbon compounds and some metallic/carbon combinations. A few years ago roughly 50 per cent of the world's nickel came from a region of Ontario, Canada, and only fairly recently has it been suggested that we are probably mining an asteroid which collided with Earth long ago. The site, a large circular area called the Sudbury astrobleme, is currently being studied by space photography.

Although flight times would be far longer than those required for landing on the Moon, landing on an asteroid should be

comparatively simple because of the body's low gravitation. Having matched speeds the spaceship would drift towards its target, setting down on landing legs with only minor propulsive adjustments.

We should have to choose our target with care, finding a small body of suitable composition which swings in eccentric orbit towards the Sun.

The asteroid may have undergone Nature's own smelting process during the formulative stage of the Solar System, or during the peculiar circumstances of its birth. It may have a nickel-iron composition as do some of the meteorites which fall on Earth. If so, like the cosmic body which apparently founded the nickel mining community in Canada, it would be a valuable property.

On the other hand, if it is of the species known as carbonaceous chondrite it may well be rich in water and carbon both of which are absent on the surface of the Moon.

How could such a body be made more accessible to our planet? Could we install on the body an engine capable of changing its course? The big problem is that very large energies are needed to bring about small changes in the orbits of minor planets. Science fiction abounds with ideas for capturing asteroids, perhaps by installing nuclear-ion drive or even some form of fusion engine. At the other end of the energy spectrum is the suggestion that small asteroids could be fitted with a mass driver. On the surface of the body will be loose soil and dust. Fed into the mass driver—installed like a tower on the surface and directing its thrust through the body's centre of mass— the "reaction engine" would operate by constantly expelling waste material at high velocity.

The technical problems of transforming a small asteroid into a low-efficiency spaceship are considerable, but assuming such things are possible the impulse of the engine would gradually bring the asteroid closer to the Earth-Moon system. On the way use might be made of gravity-assist manoeuvres by taking a course close to one or more of the inner planets. Then, using the Moon's gravity as a "brake" it might finally be deflected into a series of contracting elliptical paths which end with the body being captured as an Earth satellite.

A zero-g refining plant would then rendezvous with the asteroid to begin transforming its raw materials into useful products.

By this time we should be contemplating greater feats of extra-terrestrial mining which could lead to big factory ships leaving the Earth-Moon system to exploit the surfaces and atmospheres of other celestial bodies. Well before the end of the 21st century we should have learned to harness thermonuclear energy both for the propulsion of spaceships and the smelting of ore on a large scale. Using robot techniques, factory ships will undertake the task of constructing space colonies from local materials processed on site.

When that day comes mankind will have established itself as a space-faring community and will be poised for new adventures among the stars.

Energy from Space

The great events that have transformed the way men live, think, and act, ranging from the discovery of fire to the taming of the atom, must now be deemed to include the conquest of space. Our entry into the space age has already had global effects on communications and Earth observations. Success or failure in grasping the opportunities provided by energy and materials in space is likely to have as much influence on the eventual destiny of human society, as the industrial revolution had on the development of the world economy.

Some people view space utilization as a diversion from worthwhile social purposes, as an endeavour primarily of scientific interest, or as a form of entertainment covered by the mass media. Others think it deserves to be recognized as the single, most significant influence on all future human activities. The growth of space utilization could have the most profound effects on the successful resolution of contemporary concerns, ranging from the availability of assured energy resources to meeting Third World nations' economic aspirations.

In the past, government institutions and industrial organizations have concentrated their planning and decision-making on the near-term, considering 5 to 10 years to be long-term. But that view is questionable, even related to strictly terrestrial projects. Space utilization strategies will have to be based on long-term projected consequences, which will involve considering likely developments during the next 50 years. Although such scenarios may have futuristic overtones that might prejudice decisions on necessary research and development programmes, they are required to highlight the goals of near-term space missions and so to ensure that the most promising technology options can be exercised in the 21st Century. Generic space technologies can be developed to satisfy the requirements of a variety of projected space missions, which could in turn lead to step-by-step advances in the broad-based uses of space.

In recent times, profound changes have occurred in the human condition; the undesirable ecological impacts of industrialization have been recognized, and population growth has increased pressures to tap all available natural resources. As a consequence, there are few known but unclaimed terrestrial resources waiting to be exploited. The upsurge in the material aspirations of people worldwide has coincided with wide acceptance of the view that limited resources and environmental constraints inevit-

ably stunt continued economic growth. However, models of social organization accept growth as a prerequisite for progress; no realistic economic system has been proposed which will permit adaptation to a stagnant society. As a result, confidence in the future has been eroded by a pervasive sense of the fragility of civilization.

While space utilization cannot meet all the challenges facing society, its potential benefits are encouraging. The technology is in sight which will provide access to the limitless energy and materials of the Solar System, which could sustain economic growth and improve the living standards of mankind for as far into the future as one may reasonably look.

The Solar Power Satellite Concept

The availability of abundant energy, free of undesirable environmental side effects and produced at an acceptable cost, is a vital element in any realistic plan for future global economic growth. There is a growing consensus that humanity will increasingly rely on renewable energy resources which have their origin in the energy radiated by the Sun.

The major challenge to the effective applications of solar energy is that it is a

Above: *The microwave power transmission and receiver test antenna at Goldstone, Ca. Experiments indicate that a receiving antenna can convert microwaves into direct current with 84% mean efficiency.*

diffuse and distributed resource requiring the use of structures with large surface areas for its conversion into useful forms and, therefore, capital-intensive technology. The successful and widespread introduction of solar energy technology will require considerable development to strike the appropriate balance among the conflicting economic, environmental, and social factors in question.

Although there are many ways of reducing energy supply challenges, especially with effective conservation measures, only a few energy conversion methods have the potential to generate continuous (baseload) power. In addition to known methods based on coal and nuclear fuels and the experimental ocean thermal energy conversion methods, there are two not-yet-demonstrated methods for baseload power generation in the 21st Century: nuclear fusion and the solar power satellite, SPS. Fusion represents a scientific challenge while the SPS concept is based on known technologies many of which have

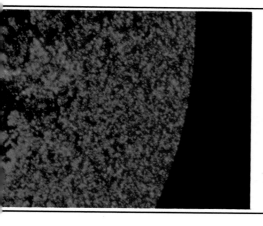

already been demonstrated on a pilot scale, e.g. solar energy conversion, microwave power generation, transmission and rectifications, ion thrusters for attitude control and orbit transfer, and beam builders.

In the SPS concept solar energy would be converted into electricity to power microwave generators forming part of a planar, phased-array transmitting antenna.[1] The antenna would precisely direct a microwave beam of very low power density to one or more receiving antennas at desired locations on Earth. At the receiving antennas, the microwave energy would be safely and efficiently reconverted into electricity and then transmitted to users. An SPS system could consist of many satellites in geosynchronous orbit (GEO), each beaming power to one or more receiving antennas. Alternatively the power could be transmitted from space by lasers and reconverted at terrestrial receiving stations.

The SPS concept challenges the view prevalent in the 1960s that solar energy conversion could not make a significant contribution to the global energy economies, and demonstrates that there are no *a priori* limits to the development of energy resources in space. Although not a panacea for increasingly complex economic, environmental and social problems, the SPS concept represents an alternative direction for developing renewable energy resources and for engaging in sustainable activities in space in the 21st Century.

Energy from space could break open the closed ecological system of planet Earth so that humanity need not be destined to live from generation to generation facing the threats of resource shortages and the resulting social upheavals. There is increasing confidence that, even with present space technology, the resources of the Moon—for example, oxygen, silicon, and aluminum—and possibly those of the asteroids could be the raw materials not only for the construction of the SPS, but also for other orbital industrial complexes.

The SPS concept has the unique advantage of not having to rely on a thermodynamic cycle to generate electricity on Earth, as is the case for fossil fuels and nuclear fission and fusion. It also can provide the impetus for the development of space transportation systems and construction technologies to support a broad variety of industrial programmes in space with useful intermediate and long-term applications. Furthermore, the SPS presents an opportunity for peaceful co-operation among nations in space. Finally, it has the potential to reduce the prospect of conflict between nations by eliminating the need for exploitation of energy resources at the expense of others; energy from space can be supplied on a global scale and thus be of benefit to all people.

Below: *This artist's impression graphically illustrates the relationship between the Solar Power Satellite, the Sun and the Earth.*

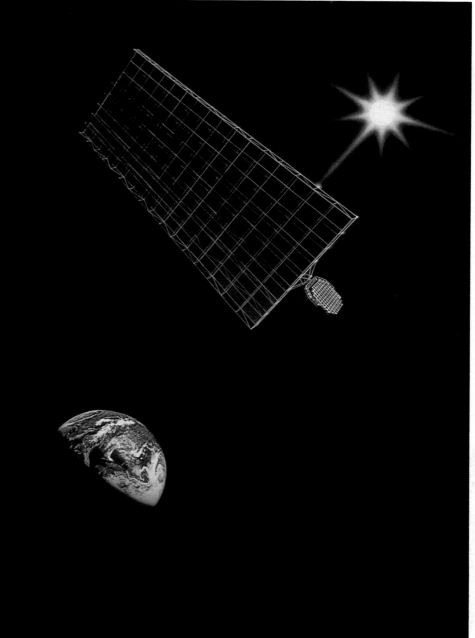

1 In one design the SPS microwave power transmission system employs a 3,280ft (1km) diameter planar phased-array transmitting antenna which is subdivided into 32·8 x 32·8ft (10 x 10m) subarrays. Microwave generators are incorporated on one side and slotted wave guides with a radiating surface on the other side. Phase control is performed at the microwave generator level. Similar transmitting systems are in use in phased-array radar antennas.

SPS Objectives

The SPS concept was conceived with the following objectives in mind:

1 To convert solar energy in space for baseload power generation on Earth.
2 To be of global benefit.
3 To conserve scarce resources.
4 To be economically competitive with alternative power generation methods.
5 To be environmentally benign.
6 To be acceptable to the nations of the world.

The SPS concept is firmly founded on the premise that international participation in all phases of implementation will assure that the power generation and transmission technologies will be used only for peaceful purposes, and that the SPS will contribute to meeting future global energy demands.

The SPS System

As originally conceived, an SPS could utilize various approaches to solar energy conversion, such as photovoltaic and thermal-electric. Among these conversion processes, photovoltaic conversion was selected as a useful starting point because solar cells were already in wide use in communication, Earth observation and meteorological satellites, both in low Earth orbit (LEO) and in geosynchronous orbit (GEO). Since then, an added incentive has been the substantial progress being made in the development of advanced photovoltaic materials and the increasing confidence in the achievement of significant cost reductions.

The SPS Orbit

The most favourable orbit for solar energy conversion would be an orbit around the Sun; however, at this stage of space technology development, GEO represents a reasonable compromise. Solar radiation received in GEO—unlike solar radiation received on Earth—is available 24 hours each day during most of the year. Solar radiation intercepted by a satellite in GEO will be interrupted by the Earth eclipse of the Sun for 22 days before and 22 days after the equinoxes. The maximum period of

interruption, occurring when the Earth as seen from a GEO position is near local midnight, will be 72 minutes a day. Overall, eclipses will reduce the solar energy received in an orbital position in GEO by about 1 per cent of the total available during a year.

With this year-round conversion capability, the SPS could be used to generate baseload power on Earth with virtually no requirement for energy storage. Furthermore, the absence in space of environmental and gravitational constraints on the erection of lightweight, extensive, contiguous structures would permit the deployment of the solar energy conversion system over large areas.

Micrometeoroid impacts are projected to degrade 1 per cent of the solar cell area over a 30-year exposure period. Because of the small probability of impact, large meteoroids are not likely to affect the solar cell arrays, the microwave transmitting antenna, or other structural components in GEO.

Solar Energy Conversion

Several photovoltaic energy conversion processes are applicable to the SPS concept. Both silicon and gallium arsenide solar cells with limited solar concentration have been evaluated. Significant progress is being achieved in the development of thin-film solar cells and multi-bandgap cells so that further performance improvements can be projected.

The solar cells should have as high an efficiency as possible, a low mass per unit area, and be resistant to radiation during transit to, and operation in, GEO. To extend the lifetime of the solar cells, in situ annealing methods have been considered, including heating with solar concentrators and lasers to reduce the degrading effects of accumulated radiation exposure.

Power Transmission

Microwave beams or laser beams could be used to transmit the power generated in the SPS to suitable receivers on Earth. Laser power transmission is an interesting possibi-

lity because of considerable advances in laser technology and the ability to deliver low-power components to receiving sites on Earth.

Microwave power transmission has received more attention, based on considerations of technical feasibility, fail-safe design, and low flux levels. Free space transmission of power by microwaves is not a new technology. The system efficiencies for the interconversion—direct current (d.c.) to microwaves to d.c. at both terminals of the transmission system—have been demonstrated to be 54 per cent; a further improvement to 70 per cent is projected. The general conception of microwave power transmission is that it is an emerging technology which has to rely on fragile and short-lived, as well as expensive, low-power components. In fact, the conversion of d.c to radio frequency power at microwave frequencies has led to the establishment of a major industrial capability to produce devices to meet consumer and industrial requirements. Several microwave generators, including linear beam devices, klystrons, solid-state amplifiers, and cross-field devices, amplitrons and magnetrons, could be used. Magnetron developments indicate that a microwave generation subsystem based on the magnetron would have better performance and a smaller mass.

The microwave generators are incorporated in the transmitting antenna, which is designed as a circular, planar, active, slotted, phased array. Space is an ideal medium for the transmission of microwaves: a transmission efficiency of 99·6 per cent would be achievable after the beam has been launched at the transmitting antenna and before it passes through the upper atmosphere. To generate 5 gigawatts (GW), the transmitting antenna would be about 1km in diameter and the receiving antenna would be an 6x8 mile (10x13km) ellipse at 40° latitude. A peak power density of 23 milliwatts per square centimetre (mWcm $^{-2}$) at the receiving antenna would prevent heating of the ionosphere. The microwave power beam could be shaped so that the power density at the edges of the receiving antenna would be 1mWcm $^{-2}$, and only 0·1mWcm $^{-2}$ at the receiving antenna site perimeter, about 1km beyond the receiving antenna.

The transmitting antenna is divided into a large number of subarrays. A closed-loop retrodirective array with a phase-front control system could achieve the high efficiency, pointing accuracy and safety essential for the microwave beam operation. In the retrodirective array design, a coded reference signal is beamed from the centre of the receiving antenna to the transmitting antenna. With this design, it is physically impossible for the microwave beam to be directed to any other location on Earth but the receiving antenna.

The receiving antenna can be designed to intercept, collect and rectify the microwave beam into d.c. with an efficiency of 85 per cent. The d.c. output interfaces with either high-voltage d.c. transmission networks or is converted into 60 Hertz alternating current (a.c.). The receiving antenna consists of an array of elements which absorb and rectify the incident microwave beam. Each element

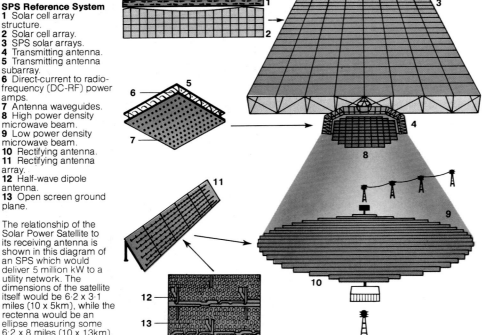

SPS Reference System
1 Solar cell array structure.
2 Solar cell array.
3 SPS solar arrays.
4 Transmitting antenna.
5 Transmitting antenna subarray.
6 Direct-current to radio-frequency (DC-RF) power amps.
7 Antenna waveguides.
8 High power density microwave beam.
9 Low power density microwave beam.
10 Rectifying antenna.
11 Rectifying antenna array.
12 Half-wave dipole antenna.
13 Open screen ground plane.

The relationship of the Solar Power Satellite to its receiving antenna is shown in this diagram of an SPS which would deliver 5 million kW to a utility network. The dimensions of the satellite itself would be 6·2 x 3·1 miles (10 x 5km), while the rectenna would be an ellipse measuring some 6·2 x 8 miles (10 x 13km).

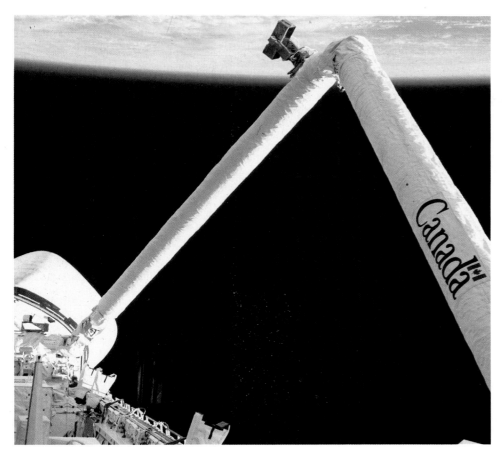

Above: *The early phases of an SPS programme will rely on the Shuttle for space transportation and payload deployment. This is the first test of the Remote Manipulator System arm during STS-2.*

consists of a dipole, an integral low-pass filter, a diode rectifier and a bypass capacitor. The dipoles are d.c.-insulated from the ground plane and appear as radio frequency absorbers to the incoming microwaves.

The collection efficiency of the receiving antenna is insensitive to substantial changes in the direction of the incoming beam. Furthermore, the efficiency is not disturbed by potentially substantial spatial variations in phase and power density of the incoming beam that could be caused by unusual atmospheric conditions. Under normal atmospheric conditions, attenuation and scattering of the microwave beam will result in a loss of about 2 per cent. Under the worst weather conditions the total loss could be as high as 10 per cent.

The amount of microwave power received in local regions of the receiving antenna can be matched to the power-handling capability of the microwave rectifiers. The rectifiers, which could be gallium arsenide Schottky barrier diodes, have a power-handling capability several times that required for this application. Any heat resulting from inefficient rectification in the diode and its circuit can be convected by the receiving antenna to ambient air, producing atmospheric heating which will be only about twice that of the heat release of a typical suburban area. The small increase in air temperature resulting from the microwave power rectification process cannot be equalled by any known thermodynamic conversion process for power generation.

The receiving antenna could be designed to be up to 80 per cent transparent to sunlight, thus permitting the land beneath it to be adapted for agriculture. Microwaves can be excluded from beneath the antenna by a grounded mesh enclosure. With minor design changes, the receiving antenna could provide most of the structure needed for greenhouses and thereby substantially reduce the capital costs involved in implementing large-scale, controlled-environment, high-productivity farming. Previously unproductive land could be prepared for agricultural purposes and cultivated while the receiving antenna is being built.

Design concepts for offshore receiving antennas include floating structures for installation in continental shelf waters and bottom-mounted structures which could be deployed in shallow waters. Offshore receiving antennas could be constructed near major coastal population centres in many countries around the world. They could be designed to permit secondary operations beneath the antenna, for example, mariculture with on-site docking and processing facilities to provide a significant source of fish protein. One such site could meet up to about 5 per cent of the present US demand for fish protein.

Space Transportation

To be commercially competitive, the SPS will require a space transportation system capable of placing payloads into LEO and GEO at the lowest possible cost. The space transportation system which will be available during the early phases of SPS development for technology verification and component functional demonstration will be the Space Shuttle.

Various space transportation systems concepts have been considered, including modified shuttles, launch vehicles utilizing shuttle components and a variety of advanced heavy lift launch vehicles (HLLV), including ballistic single-stage and two-stage vehicles, winged two-stage vehicles for easy recovery, and single-stage-to-orbit vehicles which could take off and land at airports. Such vehicles could transport payloads ranging from 100 to 500 tons into LEO and would be recoverable and reusable. In the two-stage vehicles, the fuel for the lower stage would be liquid oxygen and a hydrocarbon; liquid oxygen and liquid hydrogen would be used for the upper stage.

Both offshore and onshore launch facilities have also been considered. For example, an offshore launch facility con-

Below: *One half of a silicon solar cell array designed to provide supplementary power for the Shuttle. It represents the current state-of-the-art in solar array fabrication.*

structed north of the Galapagos Islands near the Equator would reduce launch costs and eliminate the noise impact of frequent launches in populated regions. In order to achieve the projected cost reduction for launching payloads, turn-around maintenance and mission control procedures similar to those employed in commercial airline operations would be required.

Personnel and cargo would be transported from LEO to GEO by chemically or electrically propelled vehicles which would not need to re-enter the atmosphere. Ion thrusters of high specific impulse would be powered by solar cell arrays. Although the transit time to GEO would be measured in months, ion thrusters would minimize the amount of propellant to lift to LEO.

The development of advanced space transportation systems can be expected to proceed over the next decades as space is used for a variety of experimental and industrial purposes. It is anticipated that the cost of orbiting payloads will drop from thousands of dollars per kilogram for the Saturn-type vehicles used for the Apollo manned lunar landing, to hundreds of dollars per kilogram for the Space Shuttle, to tens of dollars per kilogram for the advanced space transportation system.

Orbital Assembly

The absence of gravity and the forces shaping the terrestrial environment allow a unique freedom for the design of extensive orbiting structures, their fabrication and maintenance in LEO and/or in GEO.

In a selected orbit the function of a structure is to define the position of components rather than to support loads. The loads involved, under the normal operating conditions, are orders of magnitude less than those experienced by structures on the surface of the Earth. The structure will have to be designed to withstand loads imposed on discrete sections during assembly into a continuous structure. Attitude control will be required to direct the solar energy conversion system towards the Sun and the transmitting antenna towards the receiving antenna on Earth. This will require that the transmitting antenna rotate once a day with respect to the solar array system.

The extensive structures envisioned for the solar energy conversion system and the transmitting antenna will undergo large dimensional changes as a result of significant temperature variations imposed during periodic eclipses. Graphite composites are being considered because they have a small coefficient of thermal expansion compared to aluminium alloys.

The contiguous structure necessary for an SPS is of a size which has never been fabricated on Earth. Therefore, unique construction methods will be required to position and support the major components such as the solar arrays forming part of the solar energy conversion system and the microwave subarrays forming the transmitting antenna. One construction method, an automated beam builder, has already been demonstrated on Earth.

Warehousing, logistics and inventory control will be required to manage the flow of material to the SPS construction facilities which will be located in LEO and GEO and designed to handle about 100,000 tons per year. The construction facility might be a rectangular structure which would also provide launch and docking facilities and habitats for about 700 crew members. The work force would return to Earth at regular intervals, as though from remote construction sites on our planet. There may come a time when the space construction facilities will not only serve utilitarian purposes but evolve into habitats where people may wish to stay for extended periods. Whether people will work and live in space habitats for years, decades and even generations is now not possible to predict. What is likely is that humanity will increasingly utilize space to take advantage of the abundant material and energy resources within our Solar System and perhaps, in the distant future, within our Galaxy.

Alternative Energy Concepts

The SPS concept has motivated the consideration of alternative concepts for obtaining energy from space. Several have been proposed which use satellites to generate or transmit energy for use on Earth. While these concepts exhibit considerable differences in specific technologies required for their operation, in unit power output, and in projected costs, they all utilize space as an ideal medium for the transmission of electromagnetic energy in the form of microwaves, laser light, or sunlight.

The technology options which have been explored could use optical reflectors in space to provide continuous insolation at specified points on Earth; reflectors of microwave or laser beams to transmit power from point to point on Earth as an alternative

Below: *Ground test at Langley Research Center of a work station that might be used to construct graphite-epoxy beams in space. It could operate from the Shuttle payload bay, or as a free-flying unit.*

to long transmission lines; and to transmit power from satellites in orbit where either solar energy or nuclear energy is converted and beamed to a receiver at a desired location on Earth.

In the foreseeable future, space systems requiring power supplies with continuous megawatt outputs will be developed. For some space power applications, nuclear reactors will be preferred, but solar energy conversions will also be used extensively. Beamed energy may be useful for supplying power to remote space systems, such as free-flyer carriers, or for laser propulsion. Therefore, it is reasonable to expect that technologies will be developed for generating significant quantities of electrical power in space and for transmitting power over long distances.

There is considerable commonality between the projected space power applications over the nearer term and the conversion of energy in space for use on Earth. Development costs will most likely be spread over several potential applications and technologies which will reduce investment requirements for future space power applications will be preferred.

One of the reasons for confidence in the technical feasibility of the SPS is that alternative technologies have been identified for nearly all components of the system. Most studies have been concerned with the SPS reference system which was evolved to provide a common basis for a broad variety of studies which were subsequently carried out in the US Department of Energy concept development and evaluation programme.

The SPS reference system is a conservative design. It uses only known technologies which require limited development; it does not represent an optimized system. The development of an operational SPS during the next 20 years would use some of the 80 alternative technologies which already have been identified for advanced SPS system designs, and would be quite

different from the SPS reference system. Just as one aircraft design does not meet all of the requirements of the air transportation industry, one SPS design will not suffice: a variety of SPS designs for different purposes will be developed.

The SPS represents a fertile field for innovations. Few of the potentially interesting technological concepts have been analyzed in detail and it would be premature to attempt to choose between them, since the ramifications of the new technologies cannot be evaluated without a vigorous system design study of the impact of technical changes at the system and subsystem levels.

The SPS design objectives based on the use of several alternative technologies include the following:

1 The lowest feasible cost per unit power output.

2 Reduction of environmental and other external costs.

3 Cost-optimum power outputs over a range from 100 megawatts (MW) to 10 gigawatts (GW).

4 Demonstration of performance of preferred system designs at cost low enough to reduce investments needed before returns will be available.

The development of the most effective SPS designs represents a significant challenge. However, it is as inappropriate now to discount the SPS as a major option for the 21st Century as it was for Simon Newcomb, the American astronomer, to state in 1906 that:

"The demonstration that no possible combination of known substances, known forms of machinery and known forms of force can be united

Below: *Several SPS designs have been put forward to meet a variety of projected needs. This NASA concept shows an SPS in geosynchronous orbit; the antennas always face Earth, rotating with respect to the array.*

in a practical machine by which man shall fly long distances through the air seems to the writer as complete as it is possible for the demonstration of any physical fact to be."

Environmental Impacts

While the SPS may be the most benign large-scale energy conversion technology yet conceived, a number of areas of potential environmental concern have been identified, including low level microwave biological effects, heating of the ionosphere, deposition of rocket engine exhaust products in the upper atmosphere, inter-actions of ion engine propellants with the magnetosphere, and interference with optical and radio astronomy.

Several of these effects are not well understood and a few may have long-term consequences; therefore, steps to mitigate them should be explored. Research is needed so that data are available when important decisions have to be made in the SPS programme, and to guide development efforts. No environmental effects have been identified which preclude continued consideration of the SPS.

It is obviously necessary to trade off environmental risks and costs against perceived benefits. The decision not to develop the SPS could also have ecological consequences if the SPS energy option is foreclosed prematurely and intractable problems appear which may stop the large-scale applications of remaining known energy options. If the SPS is not developed, some other souce of energy which is clearly more economically attractive, environmentally benign, and socially desirable must be found.

It must be accepted that risk-free developments of energy conversion technologies are impossible. The best that can be done is to choose a course which maximizes benefits while minimizing undesirable side effects. The environmental impacts of the SPS must

therefore be considered in comparison with those alternative technologies which might be used to meet world energy demands.

Influential Factors

The variability of solar insolation presents serious problems to the exploitation of solar energy on the Earth's surface for generating baseload power. Because of interruptions by inclement weather and the diurnal cycle, terrestrial solar systems require at least four times more area than the SPS solar arrays as well as extensive means for energy storage.

The savings in the cost of solar arrays are likely to be sufficient to offset the cost of transportation to and construction of an SPS in space, and in transmitting power from the satellite to a load centre on Earth. Analyses of the SPS have shown that estimated costs overlap those for competitive power generation technologies, and that an operational SPS can be an economically attractive option for power generation on a global scale. However, for such technologies as fusion and SPS, the cost projections considerably exceed the actual cost differential which will determine their relative competitiveness. Although the SPS and fusion are promising technologies, further research is needed to provide data for economic analyses to justify decisions about their development and deployment.

Worldwide projections indicate that at least 2,500GW and as much as 7,500GW of new electric generating capacity will be needed by the year 2010 to meet projected demand and to replace obsolete plants. There is no alternative to a technological approach to meeting this challenge. The scale of the SPS has to be such that it can meet a significant but not necessarily a major fraction of world demand, because it is unrealistic to assume that any one source of energy will meet all future global demands, or that SPS development would preclude work on alternative energy conversion methods.

Assuming a capital of $3,000 per kilowatt (kW) and a plan for 60 SPSs to generate 300GW implies a capital investment of about $1 trillion over a 30-year period. Although without precedent, this magnitude of investment to supply that amount of power remains much the same whatever type of energy supply technology is selected. The capital cost of any alternative technology, whether based on terrestrial or space resources, would also require an unprecedented level of investment over the extended time period needed to make the transition from non-renewable to renewable energy resources.

An impediment to SPS development is the substantial capital investment which will be required for development and demonstration and the extended time (of the order of 20 years) before returns on investments can be expected. The cost of demonstrating a prototype SPS may reach $25 billion, assuming that space transportation, space station, and assembly and construction technologies have been developed to meet other space mission requirements. The scale of the implementation of an extensive SPS system is such that it may have significant macro-economic effects. Most studies indicate that these effects will be beneficial in stimulating

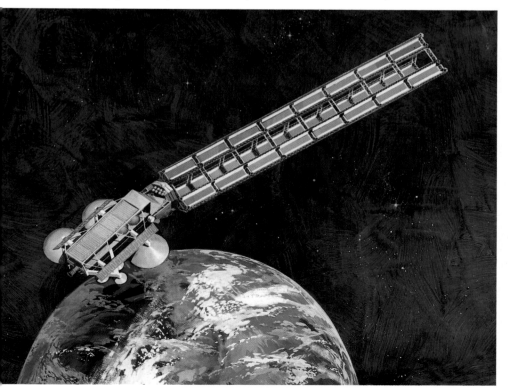

economic growth. However, investment in a global SPS system over a 50-year period may also entail opportunity costs.

The SPS design objective is to minimize the use of rare materials. Although there has not yet been a systematic effort to optimize this aspect of the SPS design, many options are available. For example, argon can be used instead of cesium or mercury as a propellant in ion thruster engines and the heat pipes for cooling the microwave generators can use hydrocarbon compounds instead of mercury.

A study of the industrial infrastructure required to build the SPS has indicated that the only components requiring major increases in present production capability are the solar cell arrays. There are several promising photovoltaic materials suitable to replace the single-crystal silicon now used to supply power for satellites, which lend themselves to mass production at the projected rates to meet SPS requirements.

The energy required for SPS construction, deployment, and orbital assembly is a function of specific design approaches and the materials employed, e.g. photovoltaic materials, structural supports for the receiving antenna arrays, propellants for launch to LEO, and electric propulsion for transfer from LEO to GEO. The energy payback period for the SPS ranges from one to three years, and the energy ratio for the SPS compared with coal and nuclear power plants is positive.

Comparative Assessment

Comparative assessments of the SPS with alternative energy technologies, including coal, nuclear and terrestrial photovoltaic systems, in terms of cost and performance, health and safety, environmental effects, resource requirements, and institutional issues indicate that:

1 The life-cycle cost range for the SPS overlaps the competitive cost ranges of alternative energy technologies.
2 All the technologies considered will have distinct, though different, health and safety impacts.
3 The low-level and delayed impacts of all energy technologies on the environ-

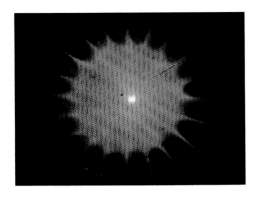

Above: An end-on view of an argon thruster that would maintain SPS attitude control.

ment, public health and safety are difficult to quantify and assess.
4 Each technology has material requirements that could be critical, because of environmental control standards or limited production capability; however these requirements do not appear to rule out the SPS.
5 The total amount of land required for the complete fuel cycle is roughly the same for all energy technologies; however, the SPS and Earth-based centralized photovoltaic systems would require large contiguous land areas.
6 The SPS, fusion and other advanced energy technologies may be difficult to operate within the current regulatory environment; however, the SPS could also be burdened by international regulations that do not appear to limit the other technologies.

The SPS, as a generic concept, can be developed in versions of different power outputs on Earth to match different conditions, based on a broad variety of alternative approaches. Therefore, the SPS presents a potential solution to the energy challenges faced by a large number of

Below: An artist's concept of a large construction base which would produce sections of an SPS. The building process would employ pre-packaged materials and automatic, remotely-controlled machinery.

nations. This should facilitate the obtaining of international agreements in areas such as orbital locations in geosynchronous orbit, frequency assignments for the power beams, and standards to limit environmental effects of the power beam, the space transportation system, and SPS operations.

Institutional Issues

The SPS is an enterprise whose scale compares with the largest engineering programmes ever undertaken. The implications for society could be profound, but whether or not such effects would be beneficial will depend on political, organizational, and institutional factors. Proponents of the SPS believe that it could be a major contributor to solving the global energy supply challenges, that it would stimulate economic growth, and that it would open up space for use by Man. Opponents hold that the SPS is a pernicious example of "megatechnics", the preoccupation with technical feats which they hold responsible for the unsatisfactory predicament of society.

The ideals of a just and rewarding society are more readily attainable by maximizing the options and opportunities available to all people than by curtailing them to coerce the people into adopting a particular (and perhaps less desirable) life style. However, possible social effects should be considered carefully when planning institutional approaches to the development and implementation of the SPS concept and organizational structures for its management.

The most significant aspect of the SPS concept is the global implications of continuous power generation available to all nations. Once the overall feasibility of the SPS concept has been established, and the planned evaluations and ground experiments are concluded with positive results, a broad-based international effort could be mounted during the development and demonstration phases of the SPS programme, including space experiments to be conducted on future space missions.

Already there is significant international awareness of the SPS concept, as witnessed by studies of the United Nations Committee on the Peaceful Uses of Outer Space; discussions of frequency assignment and geosynchronous orbit positions at the World Administration Radio Conference, Geneva, August 1979; and the presentations at United Nations Conferences on Science and Technology for Development, Vienna, August 1979, on New and Renewable Sources of Energy, Nairobi, August 1981, and on the Exploration and Peaceful Uses of Outer Space, Vienna, 1982.

The increasing international interest in the SPS could lead to co-operative efforts among the nations which expect to benefit from the power that would be available to them. International participation in an SPS programme would also provide assurance of the peaceful nature of the SPS, the adherence to agreed-upon environmental standards, and the availability of power from space on a global scale. Furthermore, international involvement in the SPS programme should assure that the SPS will not be controlled by any one industrial organization, sector of industry, or even one nation.

Such international participation in the

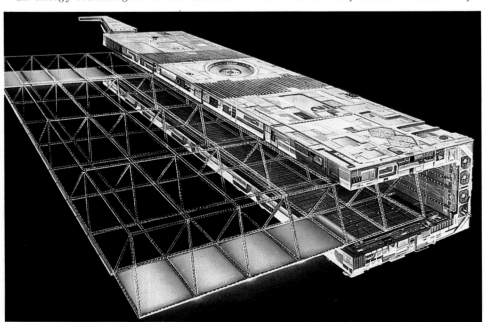

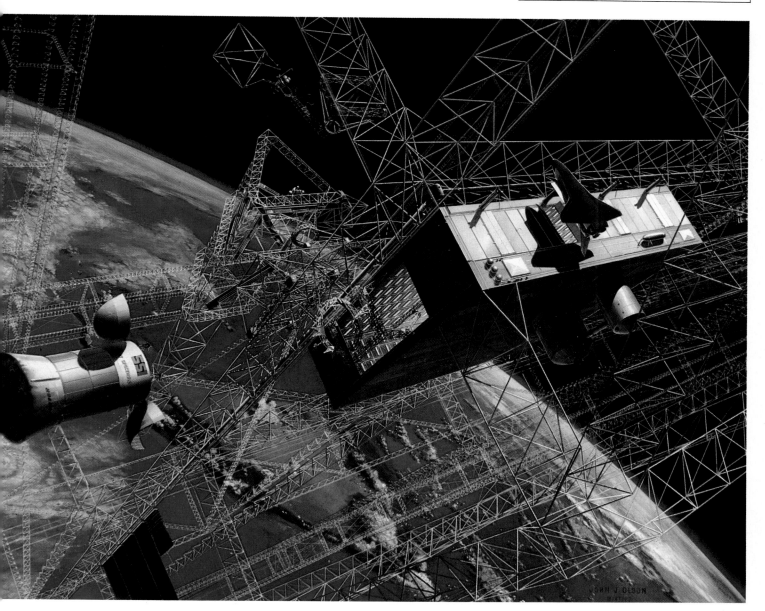

SPS could reduce the vulnerability of the SPS system to overt military action and have a beneficial effect on international relations, because all nations could be assured access to unlimited energy resources in space. Despite diverse and contending interests, a political consensus will need to emerge through widespread realization that humanity is embarked together on a dangerous passage in a world of finite resources, ultimate weapons, and unsatisfied desires.

The SPS may require that new means be developed to manage pluralism from a global perspective. Broad initiatives and declarations of principle will require some sense of participation by all who will be affected by the operation of the SPS. What will be required is the establishment of a consensus regarding the future course of SPS development. To achieve a consensus, a body such as the United Nations may keep the SPS programme under review—not to tell individual nations what to do, but to tell nations collectively what they can bargain about doing together.

Transition

Significant progress has been made as a result of broadly based technical, economic, environmental, and social studies of the SPS

Above: *Tomorrow's space industry? Here an SPS is being constructed in LEO; a Shuttle Orbiter is docked to the facility's assembly bay, while a heavy lift launch vehicle is about to deliver construction materials.*

resulting in the growing consensus that the SPS is one of the promising power-generation options available to meet global energy demands in the 21st Century. Its successful construction, together with energy conservation measures and solar energy applications on Earth, might lead to the elimination of energy-related concerns. The SPS could provide not only the impetus for peaceful co-operation among nations, but help civilization to achieve the inevitable transition from finite to renewable sources of energy.

Contemporary civilization has successfully unlocked the high frontier—space—which promises to lead the extension of human activities beyond the confines of the Earth's surface, opening up new opportunities which today can be perceived only in broad outlines. Space technology brings new options within reach and broadens the limits constraining society. The ultimate limits are as wide as the scope of human creativity and imagination sets them.

RECOMMENDED READING

Bova, Ben. *The High Road*, Houghton Mifflin Co., Boston, 1981.

Freeman, J.W. (Ed.-in-chief), *Space Solar Power Review*, Vols 1,2,3 and 4, Pergamon Press, auspices of the Sunsat Energy Council.

Glaser, P.E. et al, *Feasibility Study of a Satellite Power Station*, NASA CR-2357, Washington, D.C., 1974.

Glaser, P.E., "Solar Power Via Satellite", *Astronautics & Aeronautics*, August 1973.

Glaser, P.E., "Power from the Sun: Its Future", *Science*, Vol 162 (Nov 1968), pp 857-886.

Glaser, P.E., "The Development of Solar Power Satellites", *Advances in Energy Systems and Technology*, Peter Auer (Ed.), Academic Press, New York, 1979.

Final Report, ERDA Task Group on Satellite Power Station, ERDA-76/148, Energy Research and Development Administration, Washington, D.C., 1976.

Solar Power Satellite Concept Evolution Activities Report, Vols 1 and 2, NASA, Johnson Space Center, Houston, Texas, 1976-77.

Space-Based Solar Power Conversion and Delivery Systems Study, Interim Summary Report, Econ Inc., Princeton, N.J., 1976.

"Solar Power Satellites", Congress of the United States Office of Technology Assessment, OTA-E-144, US Govt Printing Office, Washington, D.C., August 1981.

New South Wales, is at the centre. This instrument could resolve the light of a candle at the distance from us of the Moon.

Tomorrow's Moon

With the success of Apollo 11, the first manned landing on the Moon, the expansion of Homo sapiens into the Solar System acquired credibility as a step in human evolution.

The concept had been propounded nearly a century ago by the Russian space pioneer, Konstantin Tsiolkovsky. He wrote the words that are the epigraph to this chapter. They are the credo of the space age.

Apollo 11 seemed to be a beginning, but after the six manned landings, the Moon was abandoned except for robots. A decade after Apollo 17 made the final landfall at Taurus-Littrow, the space-faring powers have not announced any plan to send men back. Instead, they have restricted manned space activity to orbits nearer Earth, preoccupied by their economic and military potential.

What of the promise of human expansion inspired by Apollo 11? If it is to be realized in the next century or beyond, it will start where it left off a decade ago — on the Moon.

That is the belief of one of the West's best known space engineers and scientists. He is Dr Krafft A. Ehricke[1] who heads the consulting firm of Space Global Co in LaJolla, California. In the early 1960s, he developed a far-reaching, philosophical conceptualization of human expansion into space. He called it "The Extraterrestrial Imperative".

In developing this idea, Ehricke has created a scenario based on a broad scientific and engineering background which encompasses the space age from its beginning. Essentially, it deals with the question,

"where do we go from here?" Ehricke has been thinking about it for more than 20 years. The answer is quite straightforward. We go to the Moon and develop it. It is the first step in the evolution of what Ehricke calls a polyglobal civilization, an eventuality which frees mankind from the limits of growth imposed by waning planetary resources and an expanding planetary population.

In the following chapter, based on an extended interview with Ehricke and his subsequent interpolations, the manner in which the Moon could be developed as an economic and industrial annex of terrestrial industrial civilization is described in some detail.

Dr Ehricke was first asked how he related his "Extraterrestrial Imperative" to evolution. He replied,

"This imperative is by no means new. It asserted itself with the rise of photosynthesis when life for the first time began to use an extraterrestrial resource in a controlled manner in order to survive and grow. It is an integral part of the magnificent process of life's evolution that seeks to order and control ever larger regions of planetary size — the Moon, the Solar System and Interstellar Space. Right now, it is the crucible in which the apparently irreconcilable conflict of human growth and environment can be resolved. The industrial revolution is not complete until the substitution of human labour by machines is complemented by enlargement of the environmental base."

In terms of human evolution, Ehricke characterized the Extra-terrestrial Imperative as the onset of the "human Eocene". The Eocene is the second epoch of the Tertiary Period which opened the Cenozoic Era of geologic time about 55,000,000 years ago. It is the era when mammals became dominant on Earth, due to biotechnical advances that allowed animals to roam over all the lands of this planet.

Inasmuch as human civilization evolves at about a million times the rate of biological evolution, he said, the "human Eocene" comprises most of this century. The metaphor suggests that civilization has reached a stage in which new technologies open vast new lands in space and space itself. The Extraterrestrial Imperative asserts itself again — as it did three thousand million years ago when life emerged from sole dependence on Earth.

Ehricke divides the prospective development of the Extraterrestrial Imperative into three phases: space industrialization, space urbanization (the development of space habitats and human occupation of the Moon and other bodies beyond the Earth) and extraterrestrialization (the socio-psychological and anthropological changes in the long-term evolution of independence from Earth). At the turn of 1960s he began publicly to argue for a broad, comprehensive strategy of space industrialization. His strategy was not restricted to near-Earth nor geosynchronous orbits.

In 1972, at the annual International Astronautical Congress in Vienna he presented the first paper on the concept and strategy of comprehensive lunar industrialization as a concrete outgrowth of the Extraterrestrial Imperative. In the intervening decade, he expanded this concept in numerous published papers, and a book appearing in Germany describing the industrialization and settlement of the Moon. He proposed three objectives: full utilization of the potential of cislunar space[2]; utilization of lunar material resources; and creative development of the Moon as the first extraterrestrial partner of Earth in the evolution of a polyglobal civilization. As one technological example of extraterrestrialization, Ehricke described the construction of "Androcells", large, mobile space settlements. These would support a population of up to thousands for exploration, experimentation and, where suitable, industrialization of any part of the Solar System. They would also provide

Above: *Konstantin Tsiolkovsky at work in the study of his home at Kaluga. This great visionary foresaw human expansion into space — the "Extraterrestrial Imperative".*

Above: *An Androcell is constructed in circumlunar orbit; such mobile space settlements would be part of Man's move outwards into the Solar System.*

"The Earth is the cradle of mankind, but one cannot remain in the cradle forever."

Konstantin Tsiolkovsky, *Notebooks*

sociopsychological preparation for life in the outer Solar System and serve as training bases for interstellar flight.

In 1965, Ehricke presented a forerunner of the "Androcell", a habitat for a thousand or more persons he called "Astropolis". However, he did not believe that such structures would be realized before lunar industrialization and settlement for economic and technical reasons.

He envisaged the first step (beyond near-Earth space stations) not as a large space habitat but as the development of our natural sister planet.

In the context of history, Ehricke regards the Apollo expeditions to the Moon as the 20th century recapitulation of the 10th century Norse thrust into North America:

"The briefly visited 'Viking Moon' is history. Today's Moon is ignored by an involute mentality. Tomorrow's Moon, the 'Columbian Moon', rediscovered to stay, can be a source of technological growth, of wealth and the beginning of the age of a polyglobal civilization."

An Extraterrestrial Prospectus

Ehricke belongs to the generation of German university students between the World Wars who helped create the intellectual foundations of space travel. They experimented with rockets in the early 1930s and when Germany re-armed, their work was incorporated into military missile development. The V-2 was the result.

After the war, Ehricke emigrated with his Peenemuende colleagues to the United States. In 1954, he joined a team formed at General Dynamics, Convair Division, in San Diego to develop America's first multi-engine intercontinental ballistic missile, Atlas, later to become the workhorse of the space age and the booster for the Mercury astronauts from John Glenn onwards.

In the late 1950s, Ehricke succeeded in selling to industry a long-cherished concept of an oxygen-hydrogen upper stage atop Atlas. Before World War II, he had studied a proposal for an O_2/H_2 upper stage by his principal mentor, the German space flight pioneer, Prof. Hermann Oberth, and he never lost sight of that concept. He considered this propellant combination the key to the first phase of space flight — the unmanned exploration of Moon and the Solar System at large, and the establishment of large Earth surveillance and commercial information transfer satellites in geosynchronous orbit. It was the key also to the second phase of space flight with nuclear-hydrogen propulsion to other planets. The

Above: *Artist's impression of a Centaur upper stage after deployment from an Orbiter. This reliable high-energy stage still has an important role to fulfil.*

rocket, called Centaur, was developed in the early 1960s.

Centaur became the world's first and most successful high-energy space stage. It was the "father" of the upper stages of Saturn and the "grandfather" of the Space Shuttle main engine propulsion system. Centaur will play an important role in the return to the Moon, Ehricke predicts.

In nearly half a century of thinking about space travel and development, Ehricke has created a detailed prospectus for extraterrestrial expansion. No doubt it reflects a remnant of the German *Verein für Raumschiffahrt* (Society for Space Travel) romanticism of the 1930s, but its rationale expresses a hard-headed pragmatism, attuned to the technological and socioeconomic dynamics of the 1980s and anticipated technical advances of the 21st century. He observes,

"The resources of Earth are limited. They are being administered by a mankind that is still highly parochial and that will no doubt continue to try to exploit these resources at increasing confrontation with environmental concerns.

"In view of this, it is very clear that our civilization must enter a new phase, a polyglobal phase, in which the resources of other worlds can be exploited, and human energy is absorbed in new creative tasks of growth, for there is no limit to growth. But, there has be to a certain economic consideration and a perspective of how this can best be done."

1 Krafft A. Ehricke was born in Berlin, Germany on 24 March 1917. Following graduation from the University of Berlin in 1942 in aeronautical engineering, he worked as a development engineer in the V-2 propulsion system at Peenemuende, 1942-1945. He emigrated to the United States and joined the group of German rocket engineers working for the US Department of the Army at Fort Bliss, Texas in 1947. He became chief of the gas dynamics section, Army Ballistic Missile Agency, Redstone Arsenal, Alabama, 1950; design engineer, Bell Aircraft Corp, 1952; joined Convair Division, General Dynamics Corp, 1954 and became programme director, Centaur space vehicle there in 1958. In 1965, he joined North American Rockwell Corp and became chief scientist, space systems and applications, in 1968. In 1966, Ehricke was named to the International Aerospace Hall of Fame. Following retirement from Rockwell, he organized Space Global Co of LaJolla, California.

2 The region of space between the Earth and the Moon.

In Ehricke's view, Earth is in a fortunate position. It has a "sister planet" nearby, its Moon. The "sister planet" is far more representative of other accessible surfaces in the Solar System than Earth itself, he said.

"Not only have we a good sized world with an abundance of raw materials only two or three flight days away, but we have a strong magnetic field around the Earth, forming a cosmic harbour. It is well protected against most of the radiation of cosmic storms, although not entirely; still, our geomagnetic field is a good breakwater. Once we go beyond the magnetospere of Earth, beyond 10 Earth radii (64,000km) we are on the high seas of interplanetary space. But in the first 500km, inside the belt, we have a harbour, a favourable environment for space stations and space factories supplied from Earth."

The space station, however, is only a trading post on the way to the main market-place, the Moon. Its advantages are so obvious to Ehricke that it is difficult for him to understand how they could be overlooked by "those who want to use it only as a quarry for orbiting installations".

The Moon offers protection against radiation and meteoroids over a large portion of surrounding space and provides materials *in situ* for protection against radiation and meteoroids reaching the surface. In extraction of its resources, only the useful material would be transported into space.

"The slack can be disposed of in the gravitational environment without difficulties. The lunar gravity is strong enough to cause dust and impurities to settle, but weak enough to greatly facilitate mining, transportation and other industrial operations beyond anything imaginable on Earth. Physiologically and psychologically, the low gravity was found to be pleasant by the astronauts (those who landed were in better shape after the mission than the Command Module pilot who remained in a zero-g environment). Plants and animals, too, need gravity, but not as much as the terrestrial level. Yet, the lunar inhabitants are not tied to the lunar gravity level only. Habitats with higher weight levels can readily be built in the surface vacuum in centrifugal arrangements, facilitated, again, by the low outside g-level. At a radius of 1,000 metres, a circumferential velocity of 100 metres a second generates 5m/s², or 3 lunar gravities, 140m/s generates 9·8m/s² or one Earth gravity."

Ehricke has designed such habitats. They are driven electrodynamically by a linear motor without vibration on a magnetic cushion. They can be inhabited continuously for days or much longer, with brief interruptions for supplies, by people who need or desire prolonged periods of higher gravity for medical reasons, for return to Earth after a lunar stay, or who prepare to go to Mars.

True, this could also be done in a space habitat, and "Astropolis" has other-world enclosures, simulating gravity conditions on Mars and other places. On the other end of

the spectrum, a processsing and habitation complex circling the Moon at low altitude provides zero-g.

The high vacuum is of immense importance to industrial operations, Ehricke stresses. It allows ready containment of high temperatures, ready attainment of very low temperatures and ready insulation of given conditions, e.g. for superconducting machines. It facilitates large-scale application of laser and particle beam welding, and of magnetic-field and electrostatic separation processes. The high vacuum environment promises considerable improvement in powder metallurgy and, in the longer run, crucial simplification in the operation of fusion power plants not only for power generation, but for material processing and recycling, and for the production of isotopes, most importantly helium-3.

"Lunar vacuum and absence of meteorological and tectonic activity eliminate the countless terrestrial sources of damage, failures and accidents: storms, floods, hail, snow, earthquakes—even simple rain interrupts power supply, communications, traffic etc—as well as long-term damage due to corrosion, erosion, chemical and biotic influences. The benefits for the lunar industrial economy will be enormous."

Potential Power Sources

Ehricke is convinced that nuclear energy is essential for the development of the Moon despite a "geo-parochial anti-nuclear bias" in the West. Space is the home of nuclear processes (such as power the Sun). Other worlds cannot be cultivated and productively utilized without nuclear energy sources, and distant worlds cannot be reached in practical time spans and economically without nuclear propulsion.

On the Moon, nuclear power (fission and fusion) eliminates the adverse effect of the 354 hours-long lunar night on productivity, if solar energy is the only power source. It also eliminates the cost of establishing solar power stations and their energy storage systems.

Ehricke considers solar power attractive only for complementary purposes for which

Habitat Centrifuge on the Moon
1 Suspended habitats at 1-g-level.
2 Suspended habitats at 0·4-g-level.
3 Suspended habitats at arbitrary g-level.
4 Circular electrodynamic track.
5 Power distribution and control centre.
6 Spokes for provision for suspending habitats at different distances from centre for simultaneous provision of several g-levels.
7 Electrodynamic drive and wheel support on electrodynamic track. Wheel support is needed when speed is not high enough for electrodynamic drive, that is, for initial acceleration and slow-down to stop.

Ehricke's design for habitat centrifuges that can induce higher than lunar gravity levels in specific habitats.

no energy storage is required (i.e. daylight activities). Baseline power, he said, is nuclear power. High vacuum, absence of ground water, tectonic quiescence and the ease of separating nuclear sources from manned facilities make the use of nuclear energy on the Moon a feasible, safe and cost effective solution to the energy problem. He counters the objection that there is neither water nor hydrogen on the Moon with the observation that 89 per cent of water is present on the Moon in the form of oxygen which comprises 42 per cent of lunar rocks. Only the remaining 11 per cent, hydrogen, has to be imported from Earth.

"If there were 42 per cent hydrogen in the lunar rocks instead of 42 per cent oxygen, the barriers to lunar utilization would be formidable!"

Ehricke cited the hypothetical case of an entrepreneur operating in geosynchronous orbit who needs 100 tons of water. He would order 89 tons of oxygen from the Moon at 20 per cent or less of the cost of its delivery from Earth and only the hydrogen from Earth. That, said Ehricke, is business—an example of interworld trade.

Lunar raw materials, in addition to oxygen, include silicon, iron, aluminium and titanium. Lunar products would consist of raw stock from mining and refining, sheet metal and trusses of aluminum, magnesium, titanium, iron or alloys; castings; bars, wires; powders of pure or alloyed materials; glasses and glass wool; ceramics and refractories; fibrous and powdered ceramics; insulation; conductors; anodized metals; coatings, including almost perfectly reflecting sodium coatings; thin film materials; silicon chips; solar cells; entire structures of various metals and alloys for lunar and orbital installations; heat shielding for space ships; insulation and radiation shielding for space ships and stations; lunar liquid oxygen depots and entire spacecraft.

Transportation Costs

Transportation obviously is a key factor. There is comparatively little that can be done to reduce the cost of transportation between surface and near-Earth orbit to a commercially desirable level, at least for passenger traffic and other more sensitive

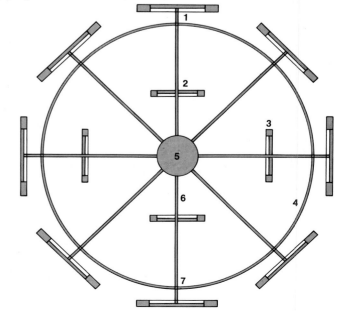

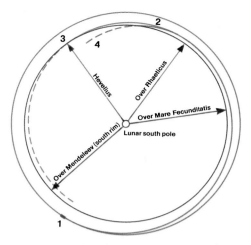

Lunar Slide Lander Descent Profiles (left)
This diagram illustrates a minimum velocity descent profile to a landing strip in the far west Oceanus Procellarum, just east of Hevelius. The LSL decelerates out of circumlunar orbit (**1**) and enters its first descent ellipse. A perilune manoeuvre (**2**)

entails velocity reduction and a small directional correction to put the lander into a second descent ellipse that, after midcourse correction, will bring it to the landing site (**3**). A stronger perilune manoeuvre at **2** allows for a steeper descent and thus an altered second descent ellipse (**4**).

Lunar Slide Lander Approach and Abort Modes (above)
This diagram illustrates the LSL on its elliptic approach path (**1**) towards the landing site. The perilune manoeuvre to reduce velocity and begin the landing approach occurs at **2**, and **3** shows the apolune of the orbit at cut-off. If an

emergency prior to the perilune manoeuvre should require a landing abort, flight path **4** would be adopted. The emergency re-ascent profile when an abort has to be called after perilune manoeuvre is shown by flight path **5**. Otherwise the LSL proceeds to its braked landing on the glass ocean of the mare (**6**).

Above: A view of the Mare Cognitum on the Moon, an example of a region that might be used for braking a Lunar Slide Lander.

freight. However, costs of cislunar inter-orbital transporation, such as the traffic between circumlunar orbit (CLO), geosynchronous orbit (GSO), near-Earth orbit (NEO) and other orbits in cislunar space, can be cut to low levels, in Ehricke's opinion.

"One approach is made possible by lunar industry: the use of lunar oxygen supplied to orbiting filling stations in CLO, GSO, NEO and other frequented orbits for use by O_2/H_2 space vehicles. Not having to transport O_2 from Earth, and being able to take on O_2 at the destination orbits for the return flight, reduces terrestrial supply requirements to those of a hypothetical nuclear spacecraft. It would revolutionize cislunar traffic. The other option is the use of ion or, preferably, magnetoplasmadynamic drives,[3] in most cases solar-powered."

Of special significance to Ehricke, however, is the access to the lunar surface. He points out that the propellant penalty and the ensuing supply costs incurred due to the lunar gravity field are, next to the long lunar night, key reasons given for avoiding the Moon in favour of large space habitats.

"This notion rests on obsolete concepts. It just is not so, even using the Moon Ferry (MF) with conventional vertical descent and ascent technique. With lunar oxygen, the

logical first product of lunar industry, the terrestrial propellant supply per round-trip between CLO at 100km altitude and surface is reduced to about 13 per cent compared to full dependence on Earth."

Lunar traffic requires consideration of what Ehricke believes is the only bona fide environmental issue raised by the industrialization of the Moon—the preservation of its all important high vacuum. This calls for landing and ascent techniques that minimize pollution from exhaust gases.

These considerations have spurred him to take a new approach to the landing problem.

A Glass Ocean

For the lunar industrial age, Ehricke has worked out a technique he calls the Lunar Slide Lander (LSL). The landing vehicle, or ferry, uses the fine sand of the mare surface as a brake. Slide landing, the technique of transferring the momentum of the incoming spacecraft to the lunar sand, is particularly attractive, he said, because it virtually eliminates the descent component of transportation cost (by saving propellant) and preserves the lunar vacuum environment.

LSL, he added, is an example of how extraterrestrial environmental conditions differing from those of Earth need not be a source of frustration, but can be made to harmonize symbiotically with newly conceived technological concepts.

"Again, the lunar environment is helpful. The vacuum allows high speed approach to the surface without

temporary communication blackout due to ionized boundary layer formation. Absence of atmospheric effects, superb sky and ground visibility (including optical signals at night) permit high predictability and automation of approach navigation.

"The LSL body as a whole is not subject to aerodynamic heating which greatly simplifies the design. The LSL lands on flat stretches of mare terrain, on a 'glass ocean' consisting primarily of dust and fines to coarse particles of silica, covering the mare surfaces from a sizeable fraction of a metre (in depth) to several metres. The vehicle's momentum is transferred to the sand by braking surfaces. They do not penetrate the surface more than half a metre; mostly far less. Large rocks need not be cleared below a depth of one metre."

Ehricke is aware of the development problems and has addressed them in various publications. The crucial component is the braking assembly, particularly the brake linings. Their material must resist friction, thermal shock, high temperatures, possibly oxygen, if liberated in the boundary layer, and remain mechanically strong. Moreover, it is highly desirable to manufacture the linings on the Moon from lunar material, such as aluminum oxide, which may meet requirements, except for thermal shock resistance, due to the intrinsic brittleness of refractory ceramics.

However, he cites research presently conducted in Germany which suggests a breakthrough towards combining the resistance of oxide ceramics with the toughness of metals, by doping the ceramics with zirconium oxide particles. The successful

---

3 In an ion propulsion system, thrust is generated by exhaust of atoms (of mercury, xenon sodium etc) from which one electron has been stripped, leaving them with one positive charge, so that they can be accelerated to high exhaust speed in an electrostatic field. In magnetoplasmadynamic drives, a gas (hydrogen) is arc-heated to plasma (ions + electrons) temperature. The plasma is accelerated to high exhaust speed by an electromagnetic force field and by hot-gas expansion. Ions yield higher exhaust velocity, hence less propellant consumption. Plasma yields higher thrust and a more compact, hence lighter system.

experiments conducted so far have greatly enhanced the prospects for a satisfactory solution of the material problem.

Launching payloads from the Moon could be done by catapult, powered chemically or electromagnetically. During early stages of lunar development, Ehricke prefers a chemically powered catapult using a partially enclosed launch track (PELT). The system he proposes consists of a platform on which the freight or the returning vehicle is mounted. The platform is guided on frictionless magnetic cushions. The tracks are mounted on a small tunnel enclosure in which the O_2/H_2 booster is located. The booster is suspended from the platform by a dorsal fin through a slot in the top of the enclosure. As the freight is accelerated to ascent speed, the slot is closed magnetically behind the fin. The exhaust water (with the hydrogen excess burned by oxygen injection behind the nozzle) is captured in the back of the tunnel, condensed and either used as water (in which case the propellant performs double duty) or electrolytically separated to O_2 and H_2, to be re-used as propellant. In the latter case, the propellant can be used many times, at small losses. Because water is particularly convenient to catch and condense, a conservative estimate is that at least 50 launchings can be performed with the same propellant charge. In addition, no gas is released into the environment.

The electromagnetic catapult, considered as an obvious method of payload acceleration on the airless Moon by various researchers in the USSR (first), Europe and the United States during the last 20 years has several shortcomings in the early stages, according to Ehricke. He points out the high electric power requirements, strongly varying acceleration and the need for dedicated equipment such as large condensers for powering the solenoids, whereas electrolytic equipment also serves other functions, such as life support and industrial purposes.

Lunar low gravity makes it economical to service important orbits, such as the geosynchronous orbit, from circumlunar orbit and to supply space stations and factories with oxygen and industrial raw materials. Eventually lunar materials could be provided for constructing space equipment, modules and entire space facilities. Ehricke cites advantages:

"One is cost. Due to less expensive lunar supply, lunar development proceeds with judicious cost effectiveness and with balanced investments and returns. The supplies can be less costly, even to near-Earth orbit. The other advantage is that factories in near-Earth orbits are no longer restricted in competitive pricing by the cost of transport from Earth to the manufacture of low-mass, high-value-added goods, such as pharmaceutical and electronic parts. A third advantage is the reduction in the amount of gases released by terrestrial launch vehicles into the upper and outer atmosphere."

Terrestrial industry itself will, in time, become a market for lunar raw stock, wherever the vagaries of international politics boost prices or cut countries off from supplies. Rarer imports will find steadier

Above: *Krafft Ehricke's impression of a "Macrosoletta" in 48-hour Earth orbit. The primary purpose of such a structure might be to induce beneficial changes in local meteorological conditions.*

markets and produce jobs on Earth. Such imports include special alloys and semi-finished products whose incorporation in terrestrial products enhances quality and value, including toughened ceramics and fine powders of pure or controlled alloyed metals or refractories. These are products that can be delivered cost-effectively in batches of hundreds to thousands of tons.

To Ehricke, this is only one value-generation category: contributions to and related advances in the contemporary industrial sector. Behind it, he sees two more advanced value-generation categories: Space Light, a mirror system that reflects sunlight to areas on the ground, and helium-3 production.

Space Light: Lunetta and Soletta

The general objective of Space Light is to establish orbital reflector systems for the transmission of solar radiation in a controlled manner to selected areas on Earth. In this field too, Ehricke has in the past 15 years carried forward the ideas of Professor Oberth, originator of the space mirror concept.

Ehricke distinguishes between small reflector units ("Lunetta") in swarms for illumination with light levels of one to several dozen times the brightness of the full Moon high in a clear terrestrial sky; and the "Soletta" for solar energy transmission at intensity levels ranging from a sizeable fraction of the solar constant to its full value (about 1·3kw/sq m). Accordingly the reflector units of Soletta clusters must be much larger than their Lunetta counterparts. Lunetta's primary economic value lies in the support of agricultural activities all over the globe, especially in Third World countries in low latitudes; in the support of rescue operations during major catastrophes (floods, typhoons, earthquakes) and in its capacity for emergency lighting of urban areas in case of blackout.

Lunetta units with a light collecting area of 0·04sq miles (0·1sq km) would illuminate an area of 1·15 to 7·7sq miles (3 to 20sq km) on the surface depending on the orbital altitude and inclination, Ehricke said. Soletta units would be much larger, with arrays of 19·3 to 116sq miles (50 to 300sq km) to illuminate surface areas up to 1,544sq miles (4,000sq km) in a 3-hour orbit. They could range up to arrays of 100,000sq miles (260,000sq km) to illuminate an approximately equal area on the ground from a

48-hour orbit at 10·5 Earth radii 41,635 miles, (67,000km).

The primary functions of Soletta would be to increase marine food production by enhancing photosynthesis in suitable ocean regions and to modify local weather conditions. The intensity of the additional sunshine with the largest arrays is relatively small. A 260,000km² "Macrosoletta" produces only 0·1 per cent of the Sun's input—less than the variation due to the elliptical nature of the Earth's orbit. Therefore, to influence local weather, Soletta would have to exert trigger effects in strategic areas. Intervention would range from smog removal by breaking up the inversion layer over a city to moving rain clouds into a drought area (the cleanest form of water transportation over large distances) or out of an area plagued by excessive precipitation. Larger tasks would include modification of the jet stream[4] course by warming ocean areas and ultimately counteracting undesirable global climatic trends.

"There can be no doubt that 'surgical' meteorology and climatology, perhaps the most important planetary engineering project in the long run, will have cost benefits in the hundreds of billions of dollars annually, by enhanced and more assured food production, as well as the saving of many thousands of lives and billions of dollars worth of property."

Looking at the economic aspects of space lighting, Ehricke observes that of the Solettas, only the smallest could be established in orbit from Earth economically.

"It makes far more economic sense to have them put on line and maintained from the Moon."

If built on the Moon, the reflecting surfaces could be made of sodium, one of the most highly reflecting substances known. The manufacture of sodium-coated reflector surfaces is extremely difficult to manage on Earth because of the humidity and the oxygen, while lunar resources contain sodium and there is no free oxygen, no atmosphere and no humidity to interfere with the process. By using sodium, it is possible to achieve 99·9 per cent reflectance. It would save about 1,930sq miles (5,000km²) of area on a 77,220sq miles (200,000km²) reflector system.

Mining the Lunar "Crude"

Turning to the question of how to obtain and process lunar resources, Ehricke explained that the extraction of raw materials will require separation and refining. Mining to great depth does not appear to be required because the lunar surface crude already contains most industrially valuable elements. Present seismic data do not indicate that the composition changes with depth in an industrially favourable way. However, more measurements are desirable to confirm this, particularly in the vicinity of mass concentrations, such as that detected in Mare Imbrium.

Left: Man's first small-scale attempt at mining the lunar "crude": Apollo 11 Lunar Module pilot, Edwin Aldrin, drives a core tube into the lunar soil at the Mare Tranquillitatis landing site.

Above: Our knowledge of the composition of the lunar soil has been immeasurably advanced as a result of spacecraft exploration. This is a photomicrograph of a sample brought back from the Apollo 17 landing site at Taurus-Littrow.

"Lunar crude", as Ehricke calls it, can be obtained by inexpensive strip mining. Inasmuch as there are chemical differences between the mare and highland regions, the mineral or metallic content of surface material is not uniform. There are indications of metallogenic provinces—regions where minerals containing a particular metal are more abundant than elsewhere. One example is the relatively high titanium content at the Apollo 11 landing site in southwestern Mare Tranquillitatis.

If this should be confirmed, Ehricke would establish automated feeder stations in such regions. There the crude would be collected and transported to a crater near the Central Processing Complex (CPC) where it would be picked up and fed to the CPC as needed.

Ehricke recommends ballistic transport of the crude. Velocities would be low and accuracy high on the airless, geographically quiescent Moon. Only one CPC with its expensive equipment would be needed for an industrial zone encompassing millions of square kilometres. The CPC would be an industrial base and settlement. Ehricke has a name for it: "Cynthia", a common poetic term for the Moon, and allusion to the Greek Moon goddess, Artemis.

Separation of metals from the crude is the next step. He has considered magnetic, electric, chemical, mechanical, electrolytic, thermal-centrifugal, fractional distillation and dissociation methods. He would avoid chemical separation as much as possible because of its complexity and high initial investment requirements, at least until lunar industrial capability is more highly developed. Some separation has already been done by nature, however.

"Under the relentless bombardment of solar wind protons, surface material is being deoxidized, saving man some of the energy-intensive process involved in reducing lunar crude."

"Pure iron has been discovered in samples returned by Luna 16 from northeast Mare Fœcunditatis, and probably is present in other samples. From the magnetic susceptibility of surface material it may be concluded that some of it contains 0·15 to 0·2 per cent pure iron by weight and possibly smaller amounts of other metals such as chromium and nickel in pure form. "By passing lunar sand through a magnetic separator, perhaps as much as 1,000 kilograms of pure iron can be extracted from 550,000 to 600,000 kilograms (Earth weight) of sand. Small glass beads, a valuable raw material which is widely distributed in the surface sand, can be extracted by mechanical (a circulating gas flow) or electrostatic separation for further processing to glass products."

Ehricke mentioned other methods as follows: basic or acid leach processes are not attractive for basic separation on a large scale. In electrolytic separation, oxygen and other electronegative nonmetals are collected at the anode, and metals at the cathode. The release of specific metals can be controlled by voltage levels. In the thermal centrifugal method, lunar crude is melted electrically by high processing heat and separated by centrifuge. Distillation can be applied selectively because boiling points vary. This method is facilitated because large, low pressure enclosures can be made readily so that low temperatures can be applied in some cases. The dissociation method requires very high temperatures, but can operate at a larger scale and at higher production rates than the other methods. It can be relatively simple if nuclear energy is used.

In Ehricke's view, nuclear energy is the

---

4 The jet stream is a distinct stream of high velocity winds (several hundred miles per hour) moving from west to east around the planet at altitudes of 8-10 miles (12-16km). Its course varies from year to year (influenced by the location of warm and cold air masses), with significant influence on surface weather.

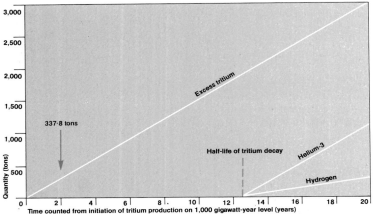

The graph's vertical axis reads "Quantity (tons)" with values 500, 1,000, 1,500, 2,000, 2,500, 3,000. Horizontal axis: "Time counted from initiation of tritium production on 1,000 gigawatt-year level (years)" with markings 0, 2, 4, 6, 8, 10, 12, 14, 16, 18, 20. Labels: "Excess tritium", "337·8 tons", "Half-life of tritium decay", "Helium-3", "Hydrogen".

The Lunar Fusion Energy Industry
The graph illustrates the production chain whereby the isotope of helium, helium-3, is derived from tritium which is in turn produced by the interaction of neutrons with lithium in a reactor. From helium-3 we could obtain quantity production of hydrogen, the key element missing from the Moon. This hydrogen could then be utilized to produce water and rocket propellant on the Moon, and the costly importation of hydrogen from the Earth could be greatly reduced.

There are many more fine points, of course, but that is the general principle."

Hydrogen, Helium-3 and Water

In Ehricke's scenario of the creative technological utilization of the Moon, the *pièce de résistance* is quantity production of the isotope of helium, helium-3, from which hydrogen, the key element missing on the Moon in quantity can be derived. Hydrogen has been found on the Moon only in deposits of the solar wind. With hydrogen, lunar technology could provide water and rocket propellant. Importation of terrestrial hydrogen could then be reduced to the much smaller import of terrestrial deuterium and lithium.

Helium-3 is produced by the decay of tritium, the radioactive isotope of hydrogen which in turn is produced by the interaction of neutrons with lithium in a reactor. Ehricke envisages that, initially, neutron emitters will become available in the form of uranium-233 (U-233), bred in high temperature reactors from thorium-232 and in the form of neutron-rich fusion explosions underground. After deuterium-tritium fusion reactors become operational, another large, high energy neutron flux becomes available.

Although not yet developed on Earth, nuclear fusion, after an initial phase with fission power plants, would be the ultimate wellhead of power on the Moon. Its utilization would be enhanced by the lunar environment. He explains:

"The maintenance of a high vacuum in the plasma region (at least 10^{-6} torr) is a major problem in the high atmospheric pressure on Earth. The larger the volume (of the vacuum region), the more difficult is its maintenance. This limits the size of the reactor chambers and enhances wall erosion by the 14·1 million electron volt electrons. Such problems do not exist on the Moon where a vacuum of 10^{-8} to 10^{-12} torr can readily be maintained without volume restrictions. Moreover, the lunar high vacuum simplifies the use of superconducting magnets for plasma confinement. . ."

sine qua non of lunar development. He would use it to provide electricity and processing heat, supplementing it during the day with solar processing heat. He has designed integrated mining, processing and refining facilities for the Cynthia CPC. They are powered by a nuclear electric central power plant using high temperature gaseous core breeder reactors which would be located some distance away, with adequate shielding constructed of lunar materials.

Sand collected at strip mining sites would be carried by conveyor belts to electrolytic and electrically-powered centrifugal furnaces in which metals and silicon would be produced around the clock. Lunar crude comes as oxidized compounds. By applying intense heat, the oxygen can be separated by dissociation and chemically by combination with hydrogen in furnaces.

Nuclear Detonation

What would be the principal source of the heat? In Ehricke's view, it has to be nuclear, either fission or fusion. The most direct way of providing it is by exploding nuclear devices underground.

"Nuclear underground detonations provide processing heat in its lowest entropy state.[5] They offer the highest level of useful energy per unit mass. The non-covert, peaceful use of nuclear energy including detonation energy underground (on the Moon) is permitted by the International Treaty on Outer Space (1967). Surface conditions are not affected."

Ehricke calculates that the energy released by a series of detonations totalling 75 kilotons (75 x 10^9 kilocalories) would be required to extract at least 10,000 tons (Earth weight) of oxygen and reduce a corresponding mass of silicon, iron, aluminum, titanium, etc., assuming energy utilization at 50 per cent. Having indicated the scale of energy investment, production rates may be inferred. Assuming 285 kiloton detonations in four furnaces, nearly 360 tons of oxygen and 1,000 tons of heavier elements would be produced and extracted every 50 Earth days.

The nuclear devices would be exploded at a depth of 3,200ft (1,000m) in solid lava or rock, well below the loose surface fines and breccia. At that depth, an 85 kiloton detonation would create a cavern 190ft (58m) wide. Subsequent detonations of smaller charges would not increase the radius. These relatively weak explosions would not interfere with astronomical observatories on lunar far side, or at a distance from the processing site.

The walls would be glazed and compacted by the initial explosion to the point where the cavern could hold water without leaking. However, there is no water in the dry lunar crust and, consequently, no steam would develop to shatter the rock and cause the ceiling to collapse, as on Earth. The caverns would serve as stable nuclear furnaces, and in addition they would form cheap, indestructible storage containers for water and gases.

Prior to detonation, the cavern is filled with a thin atmosphere of hydrogen which dampens the seismic shock and binds the oxygen out of the lunar dust mass that is evaporated and melted by the explosion, preventing recombination with the elements from which the oxygen was separated. The de-oxidized elements are washed to the surface as solidified particles with the gas and steam. They are readily filtered out of the condensed steam, from which the oxygen is separated electrolytically as needed.

"Thus, the large-scale underground extraction of oxygen serves as a means to create rich metal ore artificially in a world where none seems to have been provided primordially.

5 Entropy can be viewed as a state of distribution or disorder. A low entropy state of energy means high concentration, rather than a diluted ("lukewarm") condition. Therefore, the lower the entropy state of energy, the higher its ability to perform work, ie, the higher the content of useful or "free" energy.

Lunar Underground Thermonuclear Explosive Facility
1 Compression by soft X-rays.
2 Fusion charge.
3 Fusion igniter.
4 Concentric shells.
5 Shell with breeding material (Th-232).
6 Fission igniter.
7 Automatic valve.
8 Steel plug.
9 Explosive charge.
10 Gas-moondust mixture.
11 Shaft, explosive insertion pipe.
12 Safety valves, pipe supports, expansion joints.

This is a possible configuration for an underground facility for separating oxygen from lunar crude. An explosive charge is dropped to the centre of the gas and moondust-filled cavity, where the igniter is remotely activated.

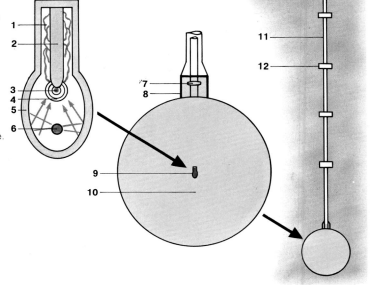

Generally, the lunar environment permits simplification in design, larger units, higher net power yield and improved economy of construction, operation and maintenance. The deuterium-tritium reactor is a tritium breeder. As the excess tritium decays (its half life is only 12·3 years), it emits an electron and turns into helium-3.

Ehricke has looked beyond the deuterium-tritium reactor to a deuterium-helium-3 reaction which has distinct advantages on the Moon, as well as on Earth. The D-He-3 is clean because no radioactive tritium is involved in it, and neutron flux is so small that no radioactive isotopes are generated. The reaction produces protons and alpha particles (helium nuclei) which have electric charges and therefore can be confined magnetically. This plasma is a valuable resource for material extraction processing heat and waste recycling. It is suitable for spacecraft propulsion that will open up the Solar System to human activities. Also, because the reaction products are charged particles, electricity can be generated magnetohydrodynamically at higher efficiency and simplicity than via thermal conversion.

Now, it so happens that the waste product of the D-He-3 reaction is a proton which, when combined with an electron from tritium decay produces hydrogen—which, when combined with oxygen, results in water.

"Does this sound fantastic? There is nothing fantastic about the production of helium-3 and even hydrogen on the Moon, but it is not near term. The nuclear industrial technology I have described will characterize the industrial landscape of the 21st century, much as the chemical, nuclear and electronic industries have put their mark on our century."

Below: *The interior of the continental climate branch of Selenopolis—the culmination of Ehricke's vision of the establishment of lunar civilization.*

Below right: *"Humans have . . . the biotechnology to establish their cosmic niche anywhere in the Solar System . . ." Here an Androcell is seen during manned exploration of the Jovian system.*

Ehricke has calculated that after the initial lead time of 12·3 years (the half life of tritium), one gigawatt (electrical) output from a deuterium-tritium reactor for a decade would produce 1·4 tons of helium-3. The same output of a deuterium-helium-3 reactor would produce enough protons for 0·45 tons of hydrogen, enough for 4 tons of water (Earth weight). And these, he added, are only by-products of the electrical energy and processing heat required by lunar industry.

Cynthia to Selenopolis

Thus, Ehricke's plan for lunar industrial development evolves in five stages: exploration and prospecting; gaining a foothold and experimentation; initial production; diversified production; and advanced utilization and settlements.

In stage 1, synoptic prospecting covering potential mineral deposit sites located from orbital reconnaissance would be carried out. A Lunetta style mirror system could be deployed to illuminate the permanently shadowed polar regions.

Stage 2 would see the establishment of a circumlunar space station. It would serve as an operations centre, laboratory, habitat and ferry station. Most experiments and technology development are carried out there, to save supply costs. But temporary manned surface operations begin, including setting up laboratories that would be soft-landed from Earth.

Stage 3 would set up the first generation Central Lunar Processing Complex in western Oceanus Procellarum. The complex would have nuclear reactors as its power source. The flat surface and small grained sand in the region would make slide landings from orbit feasible. Cynthia 1 evolves.

In this stage, oxygen and metals would be produced. Structural materials, such as building blocks and bricks, using sulphur as a binder, would be developed to make shelters. Ehricke has called these "Ligloos" or lunar igloos, with air-tight liners and airlocks. Structures would include workshops and greenhouses for lunar agriculture. Manufacturing processes would include cold welding in the lunar vacuum, robot and teleoperators, laser and electron beam welding, strip mining, and deep drilling.

In Stage 4, feed stations are set up where particular raw materials (minerals) are comparatively more abundant. The materials are collected and transported, ballistically, to crater storage near the Central Processing Complex. Cynthia 1 grows into Cynthia 2. Population increases.

By Stage 5, with a strong economic foundation and a fusion energy base, it becomes possible to develop a city-state, "Selenopolis", as the seat of lunar civilization. The biosphere would consist of enclosures ranging in size from 1,640ft (500m) to several kilometres in area and 1,640ft (500m) or more in height. It will continue to expand, across (and beneath) the lunar surface.

"Thus the new world is launched and grows into the future according to its own laws. Now, humans are totally independent (on the Moon). They have photosynthesis (lunar greenhouses for food production). They have fusion power. There is no need to change a whole planet, to terraform it. Humans have the materials, the energy and the biotechnology to establish their cosmic niche anywhere in the Solar System and beyond. The dawn of a truly polyglobal civilization has arrived."

RELATED PUBLICATIONS by K.A. EHRICKE

"The Extraterrestrial Imperative", *Bulletin of Atomic Scientists*, Nov 1971.

"The Extraterrestrial Imperative, Part I: Evolutionary Logic", *Journal of the British Interplanetary Society*, 32, 311-317, 1979.

"Lunar Industries and their Value for the Human Environment on Earth", 23rd International Astronautical Congress, Vienna, 1972; *Acta Astronautica, Journal of the International Academy of Astronautics*, 1, 585-622, 1974.

The Seventh Continent—Industrialization and Settlement of the Moon (in German), Verlag Karl Thiemig A.G., Munich, Federal Republic of Germany, 1983.

"Space Light—Space Industrial Enhancement of the Solar Option", *Acta Astronautica*, 6, 1515-1633, 1979.

"Lunetta System Analysis", 31st International Astronautical Congress, Tokyo, 1980; *Advances in Earth Oriented Applications of Space Technology* 1, 123-154, Pergamon Press Ltd. 1981.

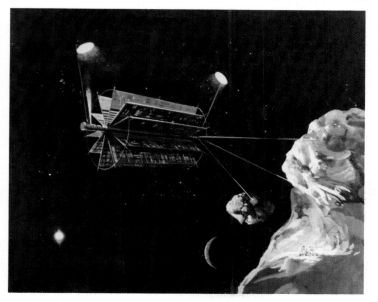

Space exploration by satellites and probes grew out of the International Geophysical Year of 1957-58. Initially considered as an adjunct to the main IGY effort which was focused on the exploration of the oceans, the polar regions and the atmosphere, spaceflight quickly became the most conspicuous scientific activity of the IGY.

Following the launch of Sputnik 1 which inaugurated the Space Age on 4 October 1957, discoveries about the nature of the interplanetary medium came quickly. Data returned by the US Explorers 1, 3 and 4 revealed the existence of zones of high energy radiation trapped high above the Earth in the geomagnetic field. This unexpected discovery was probably the most significant one of the entire IGY.

Three years after Sputnik 1, a new conception of the structure of space was taking shape from satellite data. The US Pioneer 5 confirmed the hypothesis of the solar wind, a stream of particles emanating from the Sun. It was confirmed again by Soviet Luna probes and by the US Mariner 2 en route to Venus in 1962.

In the first half of the 1960s, the structure of the interplanetary magnetic field was defined. The US Interplanetary Monitoring Platform, Explorer 18, depicted in its data the interaction of the solar wind and the Earth's magnetic field generating a "bow shock" as the wind from the Sun broke against the field and flowed around it, streaming out beyond the anti-solar side of the Earth in the geomagnetic tail.

During this period of the 1960s, US Ranger 7 returned the first close-up pictures of the lunar surface with a resolution an order of magnitude greater than had been possible from telescopes on Earth. Craters nested within craters, seemingly ad infinitum, providing a clue to the accretionary process on terrestrial bodies. It was a process to be seen again and again as Mariners 4, 6 and 7 flew past Mars and recorded a cratered surface; as Mariner 10 swept across Mercury three times to reveal a lunar landscape; as Pioneers 10 and 11 and Voyagers 1 and 2 returned images of the Jovian and Saturnian moons.

Yet, one of the most important discoveries about the cosmos was not made by space vehicles but with the horn antenna of the Bell Telephone Laboratories. Two physicists detected radio noise coming from all parts of the sky. It was identified as residue of the primordial explosion from which the Universe began.

By the second half of the 1960s, space exploration was pursued in four categories: measurement of particles and fields and the physics of the interplanetary medium; reconnaissance of the Moon and planets; astronomy and astrophysics; and manned flight.

Lunar reconnaissance by the United States, the diary of the space age shows, was oriented toward preparation for manned landings in Project Apollo. The USSR appeared to be pointing toward an early manned circumlunar flight, but then turned to the use of automatic vehicles to analyze the lunar soil, make photographic surveys and return samples to the Soviet Union.

In planetary exploration, the USSR focused on Venus and was successful there in defining the nature of the Venerian atmosphere, surface temperature and soil composition. The United States was successful in the detailed reconnaissance of Mars by orbiters and in situ exploration of the surface by long-lived landers. Biological experiments by two Viking landers seeking evidence of living organisms in the Martian soil resulted in a strange ambiguity in which the existence of life forms was neither proved nor disproved.

With its Pioneer and Voyager spacecraft, the United States completed detailed surveys of Jupiter, Saturn and their satellite systems. The findings were dramatic. Active volcanoes were seen on the Jovian moon, Io. Saturn's planet-sized moon, Titan, was found to have a nitrogen atmosphere denser than Earth's mainly nitrogen atmosphere.

As Voyager 2 continued beyond Saturn toward an encounter with Uranus, Pioneer 10, the first vehicle to fly by Jupiter, left the Solar System on 13 June 1983 after 11 years in flight.

After the lunar landings, the US Apollo-Saturn transportation system was gradually phased out, to be replaced by the more economical Space Shuttle Transportation System (STS). Apollo-Saturn was used in the 1973-74 Skylab space station demonstration and finally in the 1974 link-up of Apollo and Soviet Soyuz spacecraft in a demonstration of détente in orbit.

During a six-year hiatus in US manned space flight while the Shuttle was built, the USSR continued to maintain a manned presence in orbit aboard Salyut space stations. In 1982, two Soviet cosmonauts established an endurance record of 211 days in space aboard Salyut 7.

The United States resumed manned space flight with the Space Shuttle Columbia in 1981 and began flying its second Orbiter, Challenger, in 1983.

By mid-year 1983, US National Aeronautics and Space Administration officials were preparing to propose construction of a permanent space station to the Reagan administration. The USSR was developing a Shuttle of its own and had dispatched two Venera spacecraft to Venus to map the planet by radar.

Scientists worldwide were analyzing data from the new and powerful Infra-red Astronomical Satellite, orbited early in the year. But many were fretting at a year's delay in the launch of the Space Telescope, rescheduled from 1985 to 1986. It would, its hundreds of users hoped, extend man's perception of the cosmos farther than ever before.

IV

1957

October 4 Sputnik 1, first of three Soviet artificial Earth satellites, launched from Tyuratam during the International Geophysical Year (1957-58), inaugurated the space age. The satellite was an aluminium alloy sphere 22·8in (58cm) in diameter weighing 184·3lb (83·6kg). It carried two radio transmitters and four spring-loaded whip antennas. Scientifically, it was equipped only to measure temperature inside and outside the sphere, but orbital tracking data provided measurements of atmospheric density and electron flux in the ionosphere.

November 3 Sputnik 2, a cone-shaped satellite weighing 1,120lb (508kg), was launched by the USSR (Tyuratam) carrying the first biomedical experiment into space. The subject, a dog named Laika, was monitored to determine physiological responses to free fall until the communications system failed on 10 November. The spacecraft carried instruments to detect cosmic radiation, solar X-ray and ultraviolet radiation, temperature and pressure. Traces of radiation trapped in the Earth's magnetic field were recorded, but not identified as Van Allen radiation.

1958

January 31 Explorer 1, a 31lb (14kg) tube, was launched from Cape Canaveral (ETR : Eastern Test Range) to inaugurate the US Army Ballistic Missile Agency's Project 416 (four satellites for $16 million). It was followed by two more successful launches, Explorer 3 (March 26) and Explorer 4, (July 26). Data from the three satellites processed by Dr James A. Van Allen and his associates at the State University of Iowa, revealed the existence of zones of radiation trapped in the Earth's magnetic field.

March 17 Vanguard 1, a 6·4in (16·3cm) sphere weighing only 3·25lb (1·47kg), was launched from the Eastern Test Range into an oval orbit 403 x 2,448 miles (648 x 3,939km) in altitude. Powered by solar cells, its tiny radio continued to transmit for six years. It enabled scientists to make the first long term measurements of changes in atmospheric height and density with the rise and fall of solar activity, to determine the influence of the Sun's radiation pressure on the orbit of a satellite and to detect gravitational anomalies in the Earth indicating a pear shape with the stem toward the north pole.

May 15 The third Soviet satellite in the Sputnik series, Sputnik 3, was launched into an orbit inclined 65 degrees to the equator (as were its predecessors) from Tyuratam. It carried a scientific payload weighing 2,068lb (938kg), including instruments to measure cosmic and solar radiation, electric fields in space near the Earth, the Earth's magnetic field, micrometeorites and the density and structure of the ionosphere. The spacecraft was equipped with a sophisticated telemetry system which

Assembly of the Soviet Union's third Earth satellite: Sputnik 3.

permitted data to be stored until it could be "dumped" to ground stations as the satellite passed over the Soviet Union. Radio contact persisted for 691 days until the orbit decayed 6 April 1960.

December 6 The United States launched Pioneer 3 (ETR), a 13lb (5·9kg) probe to the Moon, but failed to reach it. En route, spacecraft instruments reported two peaks of trapped radiation at 2,000 and 10,000 miles (3,218 and 16,100km) altitude.

1959

September 14 The Soviet Union succeeded in hitting the Moon with Luna 2, a 860lb (390kg) probe, launched 12 September (Tyuratam). The probe crashed about 268 miles (432km) from the visible centre. En-route the probe detected a stream of low energy protons emanating from the Sun at 40 Earth radii, the first indication by spacecraft of the solar wind.

September 18 Vanguard 3, a 100lb (45·4kg) satellite (payload: 50·7lb, 23kg) was launched (ETR) to make the first reconnaissance of the Earth's magnetic field.

Vanguard SLV-5 which failed to launch; the similar Vanguard 3 was a success.

October 4 On the second anniversary of Sputnik 1, the USSR launched (Tyuratam) Luna 3 to the Moon. The 614lb (278kg) vehicle flew around the Moon and radioed to Earth the first pictures of the far side. It also reported a stream of solar particles beyond 40 Earth radii.

October 13 The US 92lb (41·8kg) Explorer 7 was launched (ETR) into the radiation zones. Its radiation counter reported changes in the inner zone flux during a solar magnetic storm.

1960

March 11 NASA launched (ETR) Pioneer 5, a 95lb (43kg) observatory, into solar orbit. Data from the spacecraft confirmed previous indications of a flow of plasma from the Sun at 22·4 million miles (36 million km) sunward from Earth.

April 1 First Television Infra-red Orbital Satellite (TIROS) was launched (ETR) into 427·5 x 465 miles (688 x 749km) orbit by NASA. The 264·5lb (120kg) weather satellite transmitted the first series of cloud cover photos.

1961

February 12 Venera 1 was launched (Tyuratam) to Venus by the USSR from an A-2-e carrier stage in Earth parking orbit. The 1,419lb (644kg) probe flew past Venus at 62,100 miles (100,000km) on 16 May, but communications failed. Radar showed it had blazed a trail to Venus.

March 9 Sputnik 9, a 10,385lb (4,710kg) animal shelter was launched (Tyuratam) into low Earth orbit to test effects of orbital flight on the dog, Chernuska. The cabin in which the dog survived was recovered.

March 25 The dog experiment was repeated with Sputnik 10 (Tyuratam). Cabin with dog (Zvezdochka) was recovered.

1962

March 7 OSO 1, first Orbiting Solar Observatory, was launched by NASA (ETR) into a 342 x 368 miles (550 x 592km) orbit. The 458·5lb (208kg) observatory was designed to record frequency and intensities of solar flares.

April 26 Ariel 1, the first international satellite launched by NASA (ETR), was placed in a 240 x 749 miles (387 x 1,206km) orbit. The 132lb (60kg) British satellite returned data on ion density and X-ray and cosmic ray intensities.

August 26 NASA launched Mariner 2 (ETR), its first successful inter-planetary spacecraft, to Venus. The 447lb (203kg) probe flew past Venus 14 December at an altitude of 21,520 miles (34,636km) from the cloud-covered surface. Data indicated a dense atmosphere, up to 100 times greater than Earth's atmospheric pressure at the surface, and temperature of about 400°C. En route, Mariner detected a persistent flow of the solar wind beyond the Earth's magnetic field.

September 29 NASA launched its second international satellite, Alouette 1 (ETR), in a co-operative project with Canada. The main mission of the 320lb (145kg) spacecraft was to observe the ionosphere.

1963

Quasi stellar objects (Quasars) which had been discovered by radio astronomers, chiefly Sir Martin Ryle at Cambridge University in the 1950s, were identified as very distant objects emitting radiation with the power of galaxies by Maarten Schmidt at Mount Wilson Observatory.

April 2 Detailed measurements of atmospheric density and pressure were made by Explorer 17, launched by NASA (ETR) on this date. The 408lb (185kg) atmospheric-ionospheric monitor was placed in a 157 x 564 miles (252 x 908km) orbit. Its data revealed a zone of neutral helium surrounding the Earth.

November 26 Explorer 18, Interplanetary Monitoring Platform A, was launched by NASA (ETR) to measure the geomagnetic field's strength from 118 to 121,790 miles (190 to 196,000km) altitude. The small 137lb (62kg) monitor also reported the interaction of solar plasma with the geomagnetic field. The data led to the discovery of the phenomenon called "bow shock" wherein the solar wind "breaks" upon the magnetic field like a surf upon a beach.

1964

January 30 The first Soviet double launching (Tyuratam) was executed successfully, placing Elektron 1 and Elektron 2 into orbits ranging from 250 to 4,386 miles (403 to 7,059km) and 284 to 42,132 miles (457 to 67,803km) respectively. The spacecraft were instrumented to measure intensities of charged particles in the radiation zones. Another pair of Elektron monitors was launched on 11 July.

July 31 The 807lb (366kg) photo probe, Ranger 7, launched on 28 July (ETR), crashed on the Moon, returning 4,316 photographs of the surface in Mare Nubium with the spacecraft's six cameras. Shown close-up for the first time, the lunar surface presented an astonishing array of craters of all sizes, down to centimetre size. These were the first close-up pictures of the surface of an extraterrestrial body.

August 28 NASA launched the first of its series of Nimbus satellites into a 261 x 575 miles (420 x 926km) polar orbit from the Western Test Range (WTR) at Vandenberg Air Force base. The 831lb (377kg) spacecraft carried high resolution television cameras which displayed cloud cover to ground stations in visible and infra-red images. The automatic picture transmission system provided data for forecasters in remote areas minutes after photographs were taken.

September 4 NASA launched (ETR) the first US Orbiting Geophysical Observatory, OGO-1. The 1,074lb (487kg) spacecraft was placed in a 174 x 92,290 miles (280 x 148,523km) orbit with 20 experiments. Loss of power prevented some tests from operating, but the majority returned data on fields and forces in near-Earth and interplanetary space.

OGO-1 is prepared for an integrated systems check at KSC.

1965

Two Bell Telephone Laboratory physicists, Arno A. Penzias and Robert W. Wilson, discovered cosmic, back-ground radio noise at 7·3cm wavelength coming from all directions of the heavens. Their discovery was made while they were measuring radio noise intensities with Bell Laboratory's big horn antenna at Holmdel, N.J., for a communications satellite project. The cosmic background noise is theorized to be the remnant of the primordial "Big Bang," the explosion of the cosmic nucleus from which the Universe began.

May 29 Explorer 28 (Interplanetary Monitoring Platform 3), weighing only 132lb (60kg), was launched (ETR) into a long, looping orbit through the radiation zones ranging from 120 to 162,800 miles (193 to 262,000km). The platform returned data on radiation intensities along its flight path and variations in the strength of the geomagnetic and inter-planetary magnetic fields.

July 14 Mariner 4, a 575lb (261kg) probe launched on 28 November 1964 (ETR), flew past Mars at an altitude of 6,083 miles (9,789km) from the surface and sent back 20 photographs, the first close-up pictures of another planet. The photos revealed a heavily cratered, lunar-like surface, especially in the southern hemisphere where it was winter and crater rims appeared to be covered with ice. No sign of the supposed Martian canals was detected and many observers wrote off Mars as another Moon-like dead body.

1966

February 3 Launched by the USSR on 31 January (Tyuratam), Luna 9 made the first soft landing on the Moon in Oceanus Procellarum. The 3,490lb (1,583kg) bus carried a 220lb (100kg) observatory which separated for the soft landing. The observatory returned photographs showing a rubble-strewn, lava-like field and transmitted radiation data for three days.

Luna 9's shrouded upper stage housed the lunar landing observatory.

February 3 ESSA 1, a 304lb (138kg) advanced weather satellite was launched by NASA (ETR) for the US Environmental Science Services Administration into a 429 x 518 miles (690 x 833km) orbit. It photographed entire sunlit portion of the Earth daily.

March 1 Venera 3, a 2,120lb (960kg) probe, launched by the USSR (Tyuratam 16 November 1965) crashed on Venus, the first man-made machine to land on another planet. It carried the Soviet national emblem and a dead radio.

March 31 Luna 10, a 3,530lb (1,600kg) reconnaissance vehicle (satellite weight: 540lb, 245kg) was launched by the USSR (Tyuratam) into a 217 x 632 miles (350 x 1,017km) orbit of the Moon. It carried a gamma ray spectrometer to identify the chemistry of the surface. No photographs were reported.

June 2 Launched on 30 May by NASA (ETR), Surveyor 1 with a mass of 590lb (270kg) made a soft landing in Oceanus Procellarum and began to photograph the surface. Soil tests and pictures showed the maria surface to be

The shadow of Surveyor 1 on the Moon's surface is prominent in this mosaic.

undulating, with the apparent texture of a freshly ploughed field. Surveyor returned 11,237 photographs of the moonscape, including close-up pictures of its landing gear and its shadowed outline on the surface.

August 10 NASA commenced the systemic photo mapping of the lunar surface with the launch (ETR) of Lunar Orbiter 1, first of five space cameras placed in lunar orbit as a prelude to the manned landings in Project Apollo. The 850lb (386kg) camera craft was injected into a 116 x 1,152 miles (187 x 1,854km) lunar orbit which was later dropped to 25 miles (40km) altitude. A total of 211 high resolution surface photos was radioed to Earth. The vehicle was then crashed into the Moon to avoid conflict with Lunar Orbiter 2, launched the following 6 November.

A Boeing-built Lunar Orbiter as it undergoes pre-flight checks.

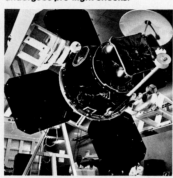

1967

The first pulsating star (pulsar), CP 1919, was discovered by scientists at Cambridge, England, emitting radio energy in precise pulses with a period of 1·337 seconds.

September 10 Surveyor 5, launched on 8 September, (ETR) with a net mass of 617lb (280kg) made a soft landing in southwestern Mare Tranquillitatis. In addition to cameras, it carried a chemical analyzer in a small, gold box. By bombarding the soil with alpha particles, the analyzer could identify the chemical elements from the manner in which the particles were scattered back to a sensor in the box. The data revealed that the mare surface was composed of basalt, an igneous rock found on Earth as the product of volcanism. The

discovery showed for the first time that the Moon was a differentiated, partially evolved planet, and not an undifferentiated, meteoritic body as many eminent scientists had thought.

October 18 Venera 4, a 2,439lb (1,106kg) Venus probe launched by the USSR on 12 June (Tyuratam), arrived at Venus and discharged an 846lb (384kg) capsule into the thick atmosphere. The capsule radioed data as it descended by parachute towards the surface. The final radio transmission reported pressure of 22 (Earth) atmospheres, indicating an altitude of 15 miles (24km). The capsule returned other data showing that the atmosphere was 90 to 95 per cent carbon dioxide.

October 19 The day after Venera 4 reached Venus, NASA's 540lb (245kg) Mariner 5, launched on 14 June toward the planet flew by at a closest approach of 2,440 miles (3,928km) from the surface. Its data confirmed the carbon dioxide atmosphere. Instruments detected an ionosphere, but no magnetic field. A cloud of atomic hydrogen was reported by an ultraviolet photometer at an altitude of 11,800 miles (19,000km).

1968

March 4 OGO-5, the most sophisticated of NASA's orbiting geophysical observatories, was launched (ETR) into a looping orbit of 179 x 90,720 miles (288 x 146,000km) with experiments provided by England, France and the Netherlands as well as by NASA. The 1,350lb (612kg), heavily instrumented satellite detected electric fields in the bow shock region where the solar wind encounters the geomagnetic field.

December 7 OAO 2, a 4,453lb (2,020kg) Orbiting Astronomical Observatory, was launched (ETR) into a 476 x 482 miles (766·4 x 776km) orbit with an array of telescopes. Stars were observed in ultraviolet infra-red, gamma and X-ray portions of the spectrum. This was the heaviest American scientific spacecraft placed in orbit up to that time.

William A. Anders during Apollo 8 intravehicular activity (IVA).

December 21 Apollo 8, the first manned flight of the Saturn V moon rocket, was launched from the Kennedy Space Center (KSC) to the Moon with Frank Borman, James A. Lovell, Jr. and William A. Anders aboard. The Apollo Command and Service Module made 10 revolutions of the Moon on 25 December in an oval orbit 68 x 194·5 miles (110 x 313km) above the lunar surface. Launched without the Lunar Module, the Apollo 8 transport was reduced in weight to 62,240lb (28,231kg). It was the first space voyage in which men journeyed beyond the radiation protection of the Earth's magnetic field. No ill effects were reported although crewmen experienced light flashes when they closed their eyes, a phenomenon presumably caused by the impact of cosmic rays on the optic nerve. Although ostensibly an engineering test, Apollo 8 provided' confirmation that a human crew could

endure flight through cislunar space beyond the geomagnetic field. Crew photos of the Earth from the Moon, showing man's abode as a lone, blue planet in the cosmos, had the effect of reinforcing the environmentalist concept of the singularity of the Earth as the only known habitable planet.

1969

May 16 and 17 Veneras 5 and 6 dropped landing capsules into the atmosphere of Venus, following launch on 5 and 10 January from Tyuratam. Each Soviet vehicle, consisting of a bus and lander, had a launch weight of 2,490lb (1,130kg). Venera 5's capsule transmitted for 53 minutes and Venera 6's capsule, for 51 minutes. Signals were relayed by the main buses as they went on into solar orbit. Surface pressure was reported at 100 atmospheres and temperature, 500°C. Parachutes were used to slow the descent in the high atmosphere and aerodynamic braking was sufficient to retard descent in the dense lower atmosphere after the parachutes were cast off.

"The Eagle has landed . . ." Apollo 11 LM and Buzz Aldrin on the Moon.

July 20 The first men on the Moon, US Astronauts Neil Armstrong and Edwin E. Aldrin, landed the Lunar Module *Eagle* in Mare Tranquillitatis at 20·17pm Greenwich Mean Time. Weighing 96,900lb (43,953kg) at launch on 16 July (KSC), Apollo 11 was the third United States manned spacecraft to fly to the Moon (preceded by Apollo 8 and 10), but first to land. Armstrong and Aldrin spent 2 hours and 13 minutes and 1 hour and 43 minutes respectively on the surface while the third crewman, Michael Collins, remained in the Command Module, *Columbia*, orbiting the Moon at 70 miles (112km) altitude. While Armstrong took photographs of the landing site, Aldrin began setting up the limited scientific experiments taken on the vogage. These were a roll of aluminum foil stretched out on a pole to collect solar wind particles blowing past the site, a 4lb (1·8kg) seismometer to measure moonquakes or meteorite impacts and an 11lb (5kg) laser mirror designed to refine the Earth-Moon distance and make other measurements by reflecting a laser beam from an Earth observatory back to the source. The seismometer and laser reflector remained on the Moon along with the radio transmitter. The aluminum foil was rolled up and brought back to Earth for analysis. Armstrong and Aldrin collected 46·3lb (21kg) of soil and small rocks for laboratory analysis at the Lunar Receiving Laboratory, Houston and at universities. They themselves then became "experimental animals" on their return to Earth (splashdown 24 July) when they were placed in quarantine at Houston for a period of 21 days reckoned from the date of their departure from the Moon. The quarantine was required by the US Public Health Service as precaution against the importation of any alien organisms. The soil turned out to be a mixture of rock fragments and glassy particles in which residues of iron meteorites were found. It proved to be unusually rich in titanium and rare earth elements, but depleted in volatile elements. There was no evidence of water. Apollo 11 set the stage for five more manned expeditions that followed.

July 31 The 910lb (413kg) Mariner 6, launched on 25 February (ETR), flew over the equator of Mars at an altitude of 2,106 miles (3,390km) and radioed back 75 photographs of the mid-latitudes. A new Marscape appeared, less lunar than the views of Mariner 4. Smoother lowland regions were seen, somewhat similar to the lunar maria, but less densely cratered. A chain of huge craters showed up, one about 310 miles (500km) across, with frost on its rims. Investigators called it "Nix Olympica" (Snows of Olympus).

August 5 Mariner 7, a twin of NASA's Mariner 6, flew past Mars and returned 126 photographs of the southern hemisphere. It was launched (ETR) on 27 March. The dark, maria-like areas of Mars were more clearly defined; evidence of extensive volcanism appeared. Passing over the south pole, where it was winter, Mariner 7 revealed that the northward boundary of the ice cap was sharp but irregular. Large circular craters appeared within the ice cap. Because of a haze over the cap, its entire area was not seen. No estimate of depth could be made, although it seemed to be greater than a thin rime of ice predicted by some astronomers. Radio occultation experiments showed the density of the atmosphere was no higher than 5 to 7 millibars or 0·5 to 0·7 per cent of Earth's atmosphere at sea level. Spectrometer data from both spacecraft identified the main constituent of the atmosphere as carbon dioxide.

The Mariner 6/7 design: each craft carried 50lb (22·7kg) of instruments.

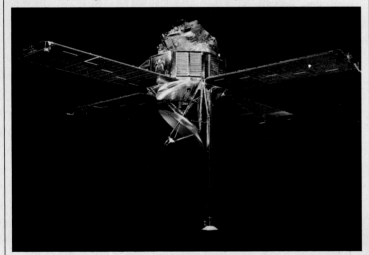

November 19 Apollo 12, weighing 97,000lb (44,000kg) at launch (KSC) on 14 November, brought the second expedition to the Moon. Charles "Pete" Conrad, Jr. and Alan L. Bean landed the Lunar Module *Intrepid* in Oceanus Procellarum, 1,300 miles (2,092km) west of Apollo 11's "Tranquility Base". Astronaut Richard F. Gordon remained in lunar orbit aboard the Command Module, *Yankee Clipper*. Conrad and Bean touched down 790ft (240m) from Surveyor 3, which had made a soft landing in 1967. They hiked to the silent vehicle and found it in good condition, except for a film of dust. They collected 24·25lb (11kg) of glass and metal from Surveyor for analysis on Earth. The surface crew deployed the first Apollo Lunar Surface Experiments Package (ALSEP) which became a standard feature of succeeding missions. These were the aluminum foil solar wind collector, an array of seismometers, a magnetometer, a solar wind spectro-meter, and a gas detector. The instruments were powered by a thermoelectric generator and their data were transmitted by radio from a central station. Conrad and Bean made two extravehicular sorties, extending time outside the LM to 7 hours, 45 minutes and collecting 75·6lb (34·3kg) of soil samples. The seismometer array they emplaced detected the first moon-quakes and the magnetometer reported a remanent magnetic field.

1970

September 20 Luna 16, launched by the USSR (Tyuratam) on 16 September landed on the Moon in Mare Foecunditatis, scooped up 3·63oz (103gr) of soil, deposited it into a

Luna 16 samples being removed from the ampule at the Academy of Sciences.

container, sealed the container, launched itself from the Moon and flew back to Earth, landing in the Soviet Union on 24 September with the sample intact. It was the first automated grab sample from another body in space and fulfilled the goal of Luna 15 which crashed on the Moon on 21 July 1969, the day after Apollo 11 landed. It was the first successful demonstration of the Soviet alternative of exploring the Moon with automata, instead of manned expeditions.

October 14 Intercosmos 4, an international Soviet bloc scientific mission, was launched from Kapustin Yar with East German, Czechoslovakian and Russian scientific experiments. Its mission was to monitor solar X-ray and ultraviolet radiation in a 155 x 388 miles (249 x 624km) orbit.

November 10 Luna 17, a second type of lunar exploration automaton, was launched (Tyuratam) and landed in Mare Imbrium on 17 November, discharging Lunokhod 1, an instru-mented rover. The automatic vehicle was equipped to make soil density and composition tests, televise the topography over a 2·5 miles (4km) range and observe the stars with an X-ray telescope. It was the first wheeled vehicle on the Moon.

December 11 NOAA 1, a 675lb (306kg) advanced weather satellite, was launched by NASA from the Western Test Range into 882 miles (1,420km) polar orbit for the US National Oceanographic and Atmos-pheric Administration. Its camera system was capable of day and night continuous viewing.

December 15 Venera 7, weighing 2,600lb (1,180kg) at launch on 17 August (Tyuratam), dropped an instrumented capsule into the Venerian atmosphere. Radio signals faded after

35 minutes, but another 26 minutes of data were extracted from recordings by computer. The faint signals indicated that the Venera 7 capsule had reached the ground, the first to do so and continue transmitting. Surface tem-perature was reported as 475°C and pressure, 90 atmospheres.

1971

January 30 Explorer 42, launched on 12 December 1970 from Italy's launch site, San Marco (a platform in the Indian Ocean off the coast of Kenya), as a joint NASA-Italian project, detected an apparent black hole in the constellation Cygnus. The 315lb (143kg) small astronomy satellite had been placed in a 322 x 348 miles (518 x 560km) orbit. It detected X-ray and radio sources in the direction of a faint blue star. Spectral changes showed that the blue star has a dark companion, a star so massive that according to theory it cannot be a neutron star and is presumed to be a black hole. Explorer 42 is also known as the "Uhuru" satellite.

January 31 Apollo 14, the third successful manned lunar expedition, was launched (KSC) towards a hilly region of the Moon, the Fra Mauro Formation. The transport had a launch . weight of 111,435lb (50,547kg). Astronauts Alan B. Shepard, Jr. and Edgar Dean Mitchell landed the LM *Antares* in the hills 5 February, 110 miles (178km) east of the Apollo 12 landfall. Astronaut Stuart A. Roosa remained aboard the Command Module *Kitty Hawk* in lunar orbit. Shepard and Mitchell obtained data on sub-soil structure by firing small explosive charges into the ground and recording seismic wave reflections. The results indicated a powdery layer 28ft (8·5m) thick. Seismic waves generated by the impact of the Saturn V third stage on the Moon were recorded by the Apollo 12 seismometer. They indicated a considerable depth of unconsolidated rock. Following quarantine at the Lunar Receiving Laboratory, Houston, the Apollo directorate decided to abandon future quarantine of returning lunar explorers. No micro-organisms were found and the Moon was declared to be sterile, although pre-biotic, organic compounds were present in the soil. The expedition returned 94·4lb (42·8kg) of soil samples.

Edgar Mitchell checks his traverse map during an Apollo 14 EVA.

July 30 Apollo 15, launched 26 July (KSC) weighing 107,407lb (48,720kg), hauled a 4-wheeled, battery-powered "jeep" to the Moon. Astronauts David R. Scott and James B. Irwin drove it along the Apennine Mountain front after landing the LM *Falcon*. Sinking thermal probes into the soil, they made the first measurements of lunar heat flow. A rise in temperature of 1·75°C per metre was calculated, leading analysts to conclude that the interior of the Moon was hot, presumably from the heat of decay of radioactive elements. While Scott and Irwin explored the mountain front and deep canyon, Hadley Rille, Astronaut Alfred M. Worden made spectrometric surveys of the surface aboard the Command Module *Endeavour*. The data resulted in a chemical map of 20 per cent of the surface. In summary, the Apollo 15 expedition confirmed the belief that the Moon is a partially developed planet. The crew brought back 169·1lb (76·7kg) of soil samples.

September 28 The USSR launched Luna 19 (Tyuratam) weighing 9,436lb (4,280kg) into a low orbit of the Moon to photograph the surface, measure lunar gravitational fields (which Lunar Orbiter 5 had found to vary as a result of mass concentrations) and make gamma ray and magnetic surveys.

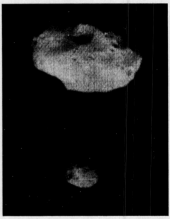

A composite Mariner 9 image of Mars' moons: Phobos and Deimos.

November 13 Mariner 9, a 2,270lb (1,030kg) reconnaissance spacecraft launched on 30 May (ETR), took up an orbit around Mars. A planet-wide dust storm was raging on the surface. As it cleared, Mariner's cameras looked down upon a Mars not seen before—a varied planetscape with extensive plains, gigantic volcanic mountains, larger than any on Earth, and a "grand canyon" stretching along equatorial Mars for a distance of 2,500 miles (4,000km). Detailed photos revealed apparent river and stream beds, indicating vast areas of fluvial erosion in the past. The results of Mariner 9's Martian album of over 7,000 pictures encouraged scientists to believe that life may have evolved on the planet. Interpretation of the fluvial channels as river valleys suggested that the Martian atmosphere was denser in the past.

1972

February 14 Luna 20, the second sample return mission, was launched by the USSR (Tyuratam), weighing 4,012lb (1,820kg). The automated sampler made a soft landing in Mare Crisium and collected 5·3oz (150gr) of sub-surface soil in a hollow drill. The soil was deposited in a container and flown back to the USSR.

April 20 Launched on 16 April (KSC), Apollo 16 flew to a lunar highland region, the Cayley Formation, carrying the second lunar rover and an array of experiments. Astronauts John Young and Charles M. Duke, Jr. landed the LM *Orion* and Astronaut Thomas K. Mattingly remained in the Command Module, *Casper*. Mattingly continued the mineral survey started on Apollo 16. The results of the two orbital surveys demonstrated that the Moon contains the chemical assemblages that would be required to build a technical civilization in space (see also the chapter, "Extraterrestrial Resources"). On the surface, Young and Duke collected 207·8lb (94·3kg) of soil and rocks, including one rock 4·25 billion years old. It was thought to be a piece of the original crust. The magnetometer found a magnetic field of 313 gammas implying a much stronger field in the past. Photographs contributed evidence for a theory that the Moon—possibly the entire inner Solar System—underwent a titanic bombardment of meteors between 3·8 and 3·5 billion years before the present.

July 23 Earth Resources Technology Satellite 1 (ERTS-1), later Landsat 1, was launched into 572 miles (920km) polar orbit (WTR) to make repetitive images of the surface with a vidicon camera and multi-spectral scanner 14 times a day. The imagery recorded changing conditions of croplands, forests, deserts, oceans and urban areas. First of a series of 1,800lb (816kg) global ecology monitors.

The giant OAO 3 is readied for flight. It contained more than 328,000 parts.

August 21 OAO 3, third Orbiting Astronomical Observatory, also known as "Copernicus", was launched into a 460 x 463 miles (740 x 745km) orbit. The 4,860lb (2,204kg) observatory, designed to observe stars in the ultraviolet portion of the spectrum, succeeded OAO 2 as the largest US astronomy satellite.

End of an era: Apollo 17 splashes down southeast of Samoa on 19 December.

December 11 Launched on 7 December, with a mass of 110,230lb (50,000kg), Apollo 17 was the last expedition to the Moon in the Apollo-Saturn series. Astronauts Eugene Cernan and Harrison H. Schmitt landed the LM *Challenger* in the Littrow Valley at the foot of the Taurus Mountains. In the Command Module *America*, Astronaut Ronald E. Evans made infra-red, gamma ray and ultraviolet surveys of the surface from orbit, adding data on lunar surface chemistry to those collected by Apollo 15 and 16. Schmitt, a geologist, believed evidence of volcanism would be found in the valley, but none turned up. Instead, touring the region in their lunar rover, he and Cernan found outcrops of an orange glass, suggesting the presence of volatiles, possibly ice, within the Moon or in permanently shadowed regions of the poles. The expedition brought back 243·4lb (110·4kg) of soil and rocks.

1973

Data from the observatory, Copernicus, showed a low ratio of deuterium (heavy hydrogen) to hydrogen in the interstellar medium, a fact of cosmological significance. It was interpreted as evidence for the "Open Universe" theory that the Universe will continue to expand forever. Other data indicated that heavier elements are less abundant in the interstellar gas than in the stars, suggesting that these elements have condensed into interstellar dust grains.

May 14 Skylab 1, the first US space station, was launched by a Saturn V rocket from KSC into a 262 x 275 miles (422 x 442km) Earth orbit for long-term manned observation of the Earth and experimentation. With its components, the Orbital Workshop, Airlock Module, Multiple Docking Adapter and Apollo Telescope Mount, the station had a launch weight of 220,460lb (100 metric tons).

May 25 Skylab 2 inaugurated the occupation of the station by the first crew. Astronauts Charles Conrad, Jr., Joseph P. Kerwin and Paul J. Weitz were ferried up to the station from KSC by Saturn IB-Apollo. The crewmen worked outside the station making repairs for 5 hours 41 minutes, conducted medical experiments, made scientific observations and set a manned space flight duration record of 28 days, 49 minutes. Data were obtained from 46 scientific experiments.

July 28 Skylab 3: the second crew, Astronauts Alan L. Bean, Owen K. Garriott and Jack R. Lousma, was ferried to the station in Saturn IB-Apollo. They continued space repairs, requiring work outside the station for 13 hours 44 minutes. They

Owen Garriott performing an EVA at the Apollo Telescope Mount.

operated scientific experiments in solar physics, stellar astronomy, space physics, Earth observations, life sciences and materials processing (of alloys and pharmaceuticals). Skylab carried an Earth Resources Experiments Package consisting of a multi-spectral camera, a high resolution terrain camera, a multi-spectral scanner similar to the Landsat instrument and radiometers to measure the Earth's heat budget. The solar telescope photographed a solar flare from start to finish. The crew set a flight record of 59 days 11 hours.

November 16 The third Skylab crew, consisting of Astronauts Gerald Carr, Edward Gibson and William Pogue, was launched to the station on the Skylab 4 mission. They observed the passage of the Comet Kohoutek, the first comet photographed from orbit, and continued operating the Earth resources, astronomy and solar physics experiments. More than 200,000 photographs of the Sun were completed by the solar observatory camera on this tour. The crew conducted physiological experiments to determine the stress of low gravity on physical fitness and the role of exercise. They performed four periods of extravehicular activity totalling 22 hours 21 minutes, and set a flight record of 84 days 1 hour.

This view of Pioneer 10 is dominated by its high-gain antenna dish.

December 3 Pioneer 10, a 570lb (258kg) interplanetary probe, passed Jupiter within 80,530 miles (129,600km) of the clouds of the giant planet following

launch from ETR on 2 March 1972. One of its major discoveries was the low density of debris in the asteroid belt. The belt had been feared as a hazard to navigation to the outer planets. The spacecraft's imaging photopolarimeter took the first close-up pictures of Jupiter. Data showed that the famous Red Spot is a long lasting hurricane. No solid surface was detected and the bulk of the planet appeared to be liquid hydrogen. Tinted cloud bands indicated rising and falling air masses. A huge magnetic field was discovered extending 420 radii from the centre of the planet. Radiation trapped in the field was so intense that, during passage, it interfered with sensors and instruments on the spacecraft. Radiometer data showed Jupiter emits more energy than it receives from the Sun. Solar wind monitor showed that the wind was blowing as energetically at Jupiter as at Earth. After passing Jupiter, Pioneer 10 continued, accelerated by Jovian gravitation, leaving the Solar System in June 1983, to become the first interstellar probe.

1974

Copernicus data support a theory that low density cavities in interstellar space are the result of supernova explosions and are filled with higher temperature gas than surrounding regions, Goddard Space Flight Center reported.

February 5 Mariner 10, launched on 3 November 1973 (ETR), flew past Venus at 2,980 miles (4,800km) from the surface. This was the first double planet reconnaissance mission which used gravity assist at Venus to boost the 1,109lb (503kg) spacecraft on to Mercury. Mariner's cameras took pictures of the clouds of Venus in visible and ultraviolet light, revealing a top layer of clouds rapidly circling the planet. Instruments confirmed earlier US and Soviet findings of a 95 per cent carbon dioxide atmosphere, surface air pressure of 95 to 100 atmospheres and surface temperature of 450°C. The vehicle's ultraviolet spectrometer detected an unexpected abundance of atomic oxygen above the atmosphere. This suggested the dissociation of a large amount of water vapour in the past. It was the first of several indications that Venus at one time had an ocean.

February 12 Mars 5, a 10,250lb (4,650kg) Mars orbiter launched (Tyuratam) on 25 July 1973 was inserted into an orbit of 1,094 x 22,059 miles (1,760 x 35,500km) around Mars. Photographs confirmed the array of huge volcanoes seen by Mariner 9 in near equatorial regions.

March 5 Mars 6, another 10,250lb (4,650kg) vehicle, launched (Tyuratam) on 5 August 1973, dropped a lander. During descent, its radio failed, but initial data indicated that carbon dioxide was the principal constituent of the atmosphere. It reported also a high concentration of argon which was interpreted as residue of a denser atmosphere in the past.

A Mariner 10 picture of Mercury's northern limb, March 1974.

March 29 Mariner 10 made the first of three encounters with Mercury at 437 miles (703km) altitude. Its photographs revealed a heavily cratered, lunar type surface, with one large basin similar to Mare Imbrium on the Moon. Sharp cliffs indicated crustal compression. There was photographic evidence that a planetoid impact which left a large crater in one hemisphere was felt through the planet ball and disrupted the surface in the opposite hemisphere. Temperatures of 510°C on the day side and minus 210°C on the dark side were recorded. Mariner 10 returned to Mercury on 21 September 1974 and 16 March 1975, continuing to transmit data until its power failed.

May 29 Luna 22, a 8,818lb (4,000kg) lunar orbiter, was launched by the USSR (Tyuratam) to continue photo reconnaissance and radiometric scanning of the lunar surface.

May 30 Applications Technology Satellite 6, a 2,050lb (930kg) super communications relay spacecraft, was launched into geostationary orbit (ETR) as an experiment in transmitting educational and informational television and telephone, telegraph and facsimile data to small ground stations in remote areas. Although essentially a techno-logical experiment, ATS 6 served as a communications link for developing countries and relayed scientific data generated by the Apollo-Soyuz Test project in 1975.

December 3 Pioneer 11, twin of Pioneer 10, passed Jupiter at a distance of 67,800 miles (109,100km) from the planet's centre. The spacecraft, launched on 6 April 1973 (ETR), reproduced Pioneer 10's colourful images of the big planet. It also sent back pictures of the large moons Europa, Ganymede and Callisto and confirmed a finding by Pioneer 10 that a powerful electrical current linked the moon Io with Jupiter. Four additional small satellites were identified in

photographs, increasing Jupiter's known retinue to 16 moons. Other data showed that Jupiter not only radiates 1·9 times more heat than it gets from the Sun but also is the strongest emitter of radio signals in the Solar System, next to the Sun.

December 10 Helios 1, an 816lb (370kg) Sun observatory built by West Germany, was launched by NASA (ETR) into solar orbit to make long term studies of solar activity.

MBB technicians at work on one of the German-US Helios solar probes.

December 26 The USSR launched a new space station, Salyut 4, with a mass of 41,666lb (18,900kg) into a 209 x 217 miles (337 x 350km) orbit (Tyuratam).

1975

July 15 Soyuz 19 was launched from Tyuratam by the USSR and Apollo 18 was launched from Kennedy Space Center by NASA for the historic link-up known as the Apollo-Soyuz Test Project (ASTP). The 32,560lb (14,768kg) Apollo carried a crew of three, Astronauts Thomas P. Stafford, Vance D. Brand and Donald K. Slayton, and the 13,630lb (6,182kg) Soyuz a crew of two, Cosmonauts Alexei Leonov and Valery N. Kubasov. Apollo carried the docking module which enabled both vessels to dock at noon Eastern Daylight Time on 17 July so that the crews could visit each other's ships and dine together. Although primarily a political experiment during a period of *detente,* ASTP had practical impli-cations for co-operative manned space projects and emergency rescue. The two vehicles carried an extensive array of scientific equipment, including ultraviolet and X-ray detectors, and

Inside the ASTP Docking Module: Thomas Stafford greets Alexei Leonov.

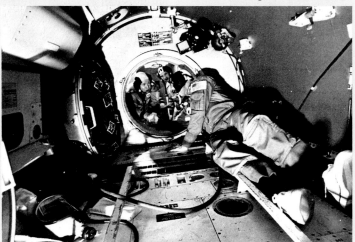

materials processing experiments, including electrophoresis, crystal growth from a vapour phase and multiple materials melting in low gravity. One instrument, an extreme ultraviolet telescope on Apollo, detected white dwarf stars. It also showed low density of gas in the vicinity of the Sun.

October 16 Geostationary Operational Environmental Satellite (GOES) 1, the first weather satellite launched into geosynchronous orbit (ETR), began to transmit cloud photos to ground stations in North America. Launch weight, 650lb (295kg).

October 22 and 25 The USSR's Venera 9 and Venera 10, launched (Tyuratam) on 8 and 14 June, reached Venus and dropped 3,440lb (1,560kg) landers to the surface. Both returned high resolution photographs from the Venerian surface. Instrument data showed the chemistry of a basaltic crust, with Earthlike abundances of potassium, thorium and uranium.

1976

Data from Copernicus (Orbiting Astronomical Observatory 3) revealed that the bulk of the neutral interstellar gas is contained in small dense clouds instead of being uniformly distributed, according to reports from Goddard Space Flight Center.

June 22 The USSR orbited a new space station, Salyut 5, similar to earlier models. Cosmonaut crews operated materials processing experiments including metals smelting, alloy formation and crystal growth.

July 20 Viking 1, a 7,758lb (3,519kg) spacecraft launched to Mars (ETR) on 20 August 1975, released its 2,633lb (1,194kg) lander (with fuel) which came down by parachute in the desert of Chryse Planitia on Mars at 22·4 degrees north latitude, 48 degrees west longitude. The Orbiter section of the Viking bus, weighing 5,125lb (2,325kg), remained in orbit around Mars to photograph and scan the surface. The lander was equipped with organic and inorganic chemical laboratories for soil analysis, a weather station, a seismology station and a complete television "studio" for transmission of surface pictures. The results of its main experiment, the determination of the existence of microbial life in the soil, were ambiguous. The lander's gas chromatograph spectrometer failed to detect any trace of organic compounds which were regarded essential for the rise of biota. The Orbiter photographed the surface, compiling the first photographic map of the planet.

August 18 USSR launched Luna 24 (Tyuratam), the third Soviet soil sampler, to Mare Crisium on the Moon. The automatic drill penetrated 6·6ft (2m) into the regolith, picked up 3·9oz (110gr) of sub-soil, deposited the sample in a sealed container. The flyback module then lifted off the Moon and returned to the Soviet Union.

September 3 Viking 2, launched (ETR) on 9 September 1975, dropped its lander on the Martian plains of Utopia (Utopia Planitia) at 47·6 degrees north latitude, 225·7 degrees west longitude. The Viking 2 orbiter circled the planet, taking photographs and making radiometer scans of the surface. Lander biological experiment results were ambiguous, like those of Viking 1. The Viking biology team concluded that while evidence of life had not been found at either Mars landing site, it could not be ruled out.

1977

Data from two Interplanetary Monitoring Platforms yielded an age of 20 million years for cosmic rays penetrating cislunar space. The two satellites were IMP 7 (Explorer 41), launched (WTR) on 21 June 1969 and IMP 9 (Explorer 47), launched (ETR) on 23 September 1972. The age calculation was made by measurements of the ratio of beryllium 9 and 10 isotopes in cosmic ray particles.

March 10 Cornell University researchers James Elliot, Edward Dunham and Douglas Mink sighted the rings of Uranus while observing a faint star which was intermittently occulted by the planet. Their discovery was made while flying aboard a NASA astronomy aircraft, the Kuiper Airborne Observatory.

August 12 The first High Energy Astronomical Observatory (HEAO 1) was launched (KSC). Its weight of 6,945lb (3,150kg) required an Atlas-Centaur launcher. The satellite was instrumented to map X-ray sources and gamma rays throughout the celestial sphere. It located 1,500 X-ray sources and detected the presence of a universal background gas which appeared to envelop clusters of galaxies and was thought to constitute an important part of the mass of the Universe. The satellite's gamma ray telescope revealed that an unusual galaxy, Centaurus A, emits gamma rays with energies of 1 million electron volts.

August 22 Cosmos 936, Soviet international biology satellite, landed in Siberia after 19 days in orbit with biology experiments from the United States, France, Czechoslovakia, Poland, Romania, Bulgaria, Hungary and East Germany. Satellite launched on 3 August from Plesetsk.

September 29 The USSR launched Salyut 6, its most successful space station, from Tyuratam. The station was improved to provide docking ports at each end so that it could be refuelled by automatic Progress tanker while a Soyuz spacecraft was docked. A radio telescope with a 32·8ft (10m) dish antenna was assembled by crews and deployed.

October 22 International Sun-Earth Explorers A and B (ISEE 1 and 2) were launched by a single Delta rocket (ETR) into looping orbits of 174 x 85,830 miles (280 x 138,124km) and 173 x 85,958 miles (279 x 138,330km) respectively. ISEE 1, managed by the Goddard Space Flight Center, NASA, was the larger of the pair (about 705lb, 320kg). ISEE 2, managed by the European Space Agency, (348lb, 158kg) was manoeuvrable. Both were designed to observe solar activities during the 11 year cycle which began in June 1976 and the effects of these events on the Earth's magnetosphere, ionosphere and upper atmosphere.

1978

January 26 NASA launched the 1,480lb (671kg) International Ultra-violet Explorer (IUE) into geo-stationary orbit (ETR). The satellite

The first star observed by IUE appears on the screen at Goddard SFC.

was developed jointly by the United States, United Kingdom and European Space Agency. Equipped with radio-controlled attitude control engines, the IUE could be pointed to observe specific targets in the cosmos. Control centres at NASA Goddard Space Flight Center, Maryland and ESA's Villafranca Station, Spain, provided dual manoeuvring capability for astronomers on both sides of the Atlantic. IUE detected a hot halo (100,000°C) of oxygen, sulphur, iron, silicon and carbon atoms around the Milky Way. It also showed that the star Capella has a chromosphere, like that of the Sun.

March 16 The US man-in-space record of 84 days set in 1974 aboard the Skylab 4 mission was exceeded by the 96 day tour of Cosmonauts Yuri V. Romanenko and Georgi M. Grechko aboard Salyut 6.

June 27 Seasat 1, 5,070lb (2,300kg) ocean observer, was launched (WTR) into 500 mile (800km) polar orbit carrying a synthetic aperture radar camera. Although malfunctions shortened its mission, the new camera produced exceptionally high resolution photographs, night and day and through clouds.

A Seasat SAR image of the Columbia River basin in Washington State.

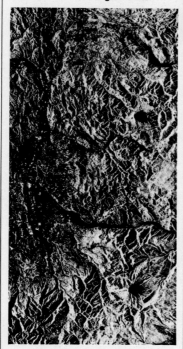

August 12 NASA launched the third International Sun-Earth Explorer (ISEE 3) (ETR) into halo orbit at Earth-Sun libration point (where Earth-Sun gravitational forces equalized) at 1 million miles (1·6 million km) sunward from Earth. ISEE 3 was instrumented to detect solar flares before magnetic disturbances reach vicinity of Earth and monitor events of the solar cycle.

November 13 High Energy Astronomical Observatory 2 (HEAO 2), the "Einstein" observatory, was launched by NASA (ETR) into a 324 x 337 miles (522 x 543km) near circular orbit. The 7,000lb (3,175kg) observatory carried an advanced X-ray telescope, television camera and other imaging systems. Data indicated X-rays were detected from quasars estimated to be billions of light years away. X-ray sources were detected at distances a thousand times greater than those of any previous sources. Nearer Earth, Jupiter was identified as a powerful X-ray emitter.

December 4 NASA's Pioneer-Venus Orbiter, launched on 20 May, reached Venus. The 1,283lb (582kg) spacecraft was inserted into a near orbit of 233 x 41,570 miles (375 x 66,900km). Its survey radar produced images of

Pioneer-Venus Orbiter being assembled at Hughes Aircraft Company's plant.

broad scale topography including two uplifted continental regions, Aphrodite and Ishtar.

December 9 NASA's 1,993lb (904kg) Pioneer-Venus Multi-probe, launched on 8 August (ETR), dropped four atmosphere probes and the bus itself to the Venerian atmosphere. The large "sounder" probe reported enrichment of deuterium relative to hydrogen. The deuterium (heavy hydrogen) "residue" was interpreted as an indication of a former ocean which evaporated with the onset of high temperatures.

December 21 and 25 USSR Veneras 11 and 12, each in the 11,000lb (5,000kg) class, reached the surface of Venus following launch on 9 September and 14 September. Lander 11 operated on the surface for 95 minutes and Lander 12, for 110 minutes. The vehicles tested successfully an aerodynamic braking collar which slowed their descent in the dense atmosphere. Both detected lightning in the clouds and an audio pickup on Lander 11 recorded thunder.

One of Venera 11's instruments is checked prior to installation.

The 617lb (280kg) COS B satellite, launched by NASA in 1975 for the European Space Agency, recorded X-ray emissions during the year from a quasar, OX169. The intensity of the emissions changed every 6 hours. ESA sources suggested that the X-rays emanated from matter falling into a black hole. If so, the rapid changes implied that the hole has a mass a million times greater than the mass of the Sun.

A four picture mosaic of Jupiter's ring, discovered by Voyager 1.

1979

March 5 Voyager 1, NASA's 1,797lb (815kg) outer planet probe, made its closest approach to Jupiter 216,865 miles (349,000km) from the planet centre. The spacecraft was launched (ETR) on 5 September 1977. In addition to photographing the cloud decks in brilliant colour and detecting a ring of particles around Jupiter, Voyager 1 returned the first detailed view of the moons Io, Ganymede and Callisto. Io exhibited an array of volcanoes. It is the first active volcanic celestial body found beyond Earth. Ganymede and Callisto were shown to be scarred by meteor impacts. Ganymede data indicated a mixture of ice and rock.

July 9 Voyager 2, launched (ETR) on 20 August 1977, repeated the photo study of Jupiter's clouds and observed the moons Europa, Callisto and Ganymede as it approached 404,000 miles (650,000km) from the clouds. The photographs showed slow changes in Jovian weather patterns. Jupiter's ring was found to be 4,040 miles (6,500km) wide, with particles descending nearly to the cloud tops. The cameras caught a massive volcano on Io erupting and detected a large impact basin on Callisto.

July 11 The year's most spectacular event in space was the re-entry of the 80 tonne Skylab space station. For months, NASA controllers had attempted to manoeuvre its descent by changing its attitude so that it would not come down in a populated area. The station broke up at a lower altitude than expected (about 18·6 miles, 30 km) near the coast of western Australia. Brilliant flashes were seen from the city of Perth. Pieces rained down over hundreds of miles of the Australian outback, but neither injury nor property damage was reported.

September 1 Pioneer 11 passed Saturn at an altitude of 13,300 miles (21,400km) above the cloud tops. Its imaging photo-polarimeter produced colourful pictures of the ringed planet and discovered two new rings, "F" and "G". The spacecraft also reconnoitred the big moon Titan, photographing it for the first time. Sensors reported that Saturn radiates 2·5 times as much heat as it receives from the Sun.

September 20 NASA launched the third High Energy Astronomical Observatory (HEAO 3) (ETR). The big observatory carried two cosmic ray telescopes, one to study heavy nuclei and the other to identify their isotopes.

1980

February 14 NASA launched its Solar Maximum Mission satellite (SMM) (ETR) into a 352 miles (566km) orbit. The 5,104lb (2,315kg) satellite was the first equipped with latches so that it can be recovered by the Shuttle. Seven instruments observed the peak of the

Sun's 11 year cycle. Flares were observed in the visible, X-ray, ultraviolet and gamma ray portions of the spectrum. The satellite recorded small variations in the solar constant, the intensity of sunlight reaching the top of the Earth's atmosphere. Influence of the variations on the planet's heat budget has remained speculative.

June 2 Once thought to be as dense as Mercury, Pluto, the outermost planet of the Solar System, was reported to have a density of 0·66oz/in³ (1·14g/cm³), (14 per cent higher than water) by Mark J. Lupo and John Lewis of the Massachusetts Institute of Technology, writing in the journal *Icarus*. Pluto's mass was calculated at 1·435 x 10²⁵ grams and its radius, 791·5 miles (1,274km).

June 20 NASA and the Brazilian Institute for Space Research established an informal working group to discuss joint projects in meteorology and space transportation.

October 11 Soyuz 35 crew, Valery Ryumin and Leonid Popov, returned to Earth after setting a new space endurance record of nearly 185 days in Salyut 6.

November 12 Voyager 1 approached within 78,300 miles (126,000km) of the cloud tops of Saturn. Among the 17,500 photographs its cameras sent to the Jet Propulsion Laboratory were those revealing 6 additional moons, raising the total to 18 satellites. Like Pioneer 11, Voyager found that Saturn emits twice as much heat as it gets from the Sun. Detailed cloud studies indicated equatorial wind velocities up to 1,100mph (1,770km/h). The major "A", "B" and "C" rings of Saturn were found to contain ringlets, and "shepherding" moons were noted in the "F" ring system. Four of Saturn's moons, Mimas, Tethys, Dione and Rhea were shown to be densely cratered. The large Moon, Titan, was found to have a nitrogen atmosphere about 1·5 times denser than Earth's atmosphere.

Dark spokes in Saturn's B ring can be seen rotating around the planet in this Voyager 1 sequence of images.

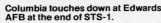
1981

April 12-14 STS-1, first orbital flight test of the Space Shuttle *Columbia,* was launched from KSC before a million spectators. With a length of 122·7ft (37·4m) and weight of 214,445lb (97,272kg), *Columbia* was largest space vehicle ever launched. Its hybrid propulsion system of solid fuel boosters and liquid hydrogen-oxygen engines lifted the winged space ship smoothly into an orbit of 150 x 171·5 miles (240 x 276km) inclined 40·3 degrees to the equator. The crew, John W. Young and Robert L. Crippen, put the ship through a sequence of flight tests. A principal scientific finding was a maximum heat shield temperature of 1510°C during re-entry into the atmosphere on the 37th orbit. The crew landed the ship manually on Rogers Dry Lake at Edwards Air Force Base after a flight of 54 hours 20 minutes. Post flight inspection revealed the loss of 15 heat

Columbia touches down at Edwards AFB at the end of STS-1.

shield tiles (of 31,000), apparently shaken off the rear engine pods by back pressure of the rocket exhaust during launch. The mission was the first of four flight tests of the Shuttle after 10 years of development at an estimated cost of $10 billion.

July 26 Pioneer 10 passed 25 astronomical units (25 times the distance between the Earth and the Sun) as it continued on its journey between Saturn and Uranus out of the Solar System. At 25AU, its tiny radio continued to report the solar wind, indicating that the heliosphere extends throughout the entire planetary system. Scientists at Ames Research Center, California expected that the boundary of the heliosphere, the Sun's extended atmosphere, lies somewhere beyond Pluto. When Pioneer crosses the boundary, its instruments are expected to show it by registering a decrease in particle counts to interstellar levels.

August 26 Voyager 2 encountered Saturn, flying within 62,760 miles (101,000km) of the cloud tops. The sweep enabled the cameras to measure ring thickness. Spoke-like structures seen in rings were surmised to be clouds of micrometeoroids. High resolution photos showed that the moons Mimas, Tethys, Dione and Rhea were heavily cratered. Evidence of crustal motion was seen on Enceladus. Titan's nitrogen atmosphere was calculated as 1·6 times denser than Earth's atmosphere. Titan's surface temperature registered as minus 180°C and its density was calculated at 1·16oz/in³ (2g/cm³), or twice that of water. An abundance of methane was reported. At Titan's low temperature, methane might assume states of liquid, gas or solid, like water on Earth. A methane ocean on Titan was considered possible.

An oblique view of the bright side of Saturn's rings taken by Voyager 2.

September 21 Aureole 3, a powerful ionosphere probe, was launched by the USSR (Plesetsk). The 2,205lb (1,000kg) craft was instrumented to measure the flux of protons and electrons in the region and study the magnetic field.

October 6 NASA launched a Solar Mesosphere Explorer (WTR) into polar orbit to study ozone formation and dissolution in the high atmosphere. The 963lb (437kg) vehicle was placed in a near circular orbit at 333 to 335 miles (536 to 540km). The ozone study was expected to shed light on the effects of chemical contaminants on ozone which plays a role in Earth's heat budget and shields life on the surface from a portion of solar ultraviolet radiation.

October 20 China 9, consisting of three satellites launched by a single rocket, reported to be in orbit observing magnetic fields, charged particles and infra-red and ultraviolet radiation. Launch apparently took place on 19 September from China's East Wind Rocket Development and Launch Complex.

November 12-14 STS-2, second engineering test flight of the Space Shuttle *Columbia,* was launched from KSC and landed Edwards Air Force Base, California. *Columbia* with launch weight of 212,000lb (96,163kg) was boosted into 163 miles (262km) orbit at 38 degrees inclination. It carried a two-man crew, Astronauts Joseph H. Engle and Richard H. Truly. Scientific

Joe Engle shaving in Columbia's middeck area during STS-2.

experiments made remote sensing scans and measurements of the surface. They included the Shuttle Imaging Radar (SIR), an experimental radar camera derived from Seasat; a multi-spectral infra-red radiometer; a feature identification and location experiment, a device which automatically scanned and identified surface features of interest; an air pollution monitor and an ocean colour scanner. In the cabin, the crew attempted to photograph lightning strokes as *Columbia* passed over thunderstorms and tended a bio-

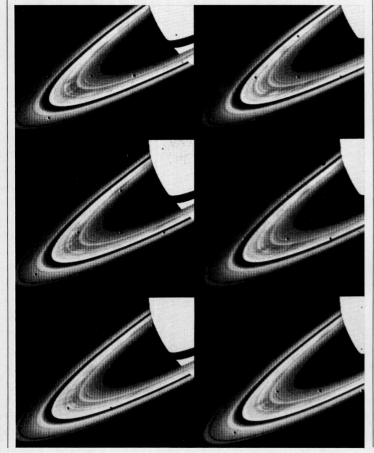

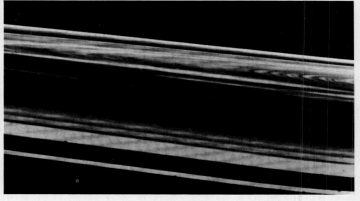

engineering test of plant growth in microgravity. The radar camera produced spectacular results by penetrating the dry sands of the Sahara Desert and recording images of ancient river valleys and stream beds lying 5-6·5ft (1·5-2m) below the featureless sand surface. The main purpose of the experiment array was to demonstrate the Shuttle's utility as an Earth resources reconnaissance platform in addition to its role as a satellite transport to low Earth orbit.

December 15 NASA reported that scientists at the Goddard Space Flight Center and the University of Maryland discovered a natural laser on Mars. The laser process in which atoms are stimulated to release photons was observed as the result of the interaction of sunlight and the carbon dioxide atmosphere. The report estimated that the power output of the Martian laser exceeds a million megawatts. The report was based on observations in 1980, using the McMath solar telescope at Kitt Peak, Arizona and equipment developed at Goddard.

The Salyut 7 space station is prepared for launch at Baikonur Cosmodrome.

1982

March 1 and 5 Veneras 13 and 14 launched by the USSR on 30 October and 4 November 1981 (Tyuratam) landed in the Venerian uplands of Phoebe Regio. Each lander carried a hollow surface drill which extracted a sub-soil sample and dumped it into a miniature laboratory for chemical analysis by X-ray fluorescence. Analysis revealed basalt, a common igneous rock on Earth and Moon. Both landers returned surface colour photos.

March 22-30 STS-3, third engineering flight test of the Space Shuttle ·Columbia, was launched (KSC) with Astronauts Jack R. Lousma and C. Gordon Fullerton as crew into 150 miles (240·8km) orbit at 38 degrees inclination. The mission was extended a day because of unfavourable weather at the California landing site. Landing was diverted to the White Sands Missile Range, New Mexico. Columbia carried 21,293lb (9,658·5kg) of cargo, including an array of NASA Office of Space Science experiments attached to a Spacelab pallet in the cargo bay. These included a solar X-ray polarimeter, a solar ultraviolet irradiance monitor, a photometric contamination analyzer and a plasma diagnostic package which was lifted out of the cargo bay and then replaced by the Canadian-built remote manipulator system (RMS), an electromechanical arm 50·2ft (15·3m) long capable of deploying satellites and retrieving them in orbit. In the Orbiter cabin, a pharmaceutical experiment, a mono-disperse latex reactor, was operated. It sought to determine whether tiny latex spheres which could be injected into the blood-stream to carry radioisotopes to tumour sites could be manufactured in larger diameters in microgravity than on the ground. A second experiment sought to determine whether low gravity affected lignin, the stiffening agent in developing plant seedlings.

Lift-off for STS-3 from Pad-39A at the Kennedy Space Center.

April 19 Salyut 7, an improved version of Salyut 6, was boosted into a 136 x 173 miles (219 x 278km) orbit (Tyuratam) for another round of space station operations by USSR and Soviet block crews. The station was reported to be 95·1ft (29m) long with a Soyuz spacecraft and Progress tanker docked at each end. It carried a powerful X-ray telescope and a complete biomedical diagnostic and examination system.

June 10 A radio signal from Goddard Space Flight Center fired the ISEE-3 rocket engine and moved the solar observatory from its halo orbit a million miles (1·6 million km) sunward to a new orbit around the Earth-Moon system. The manoeuvre had the dual purpose of employing the spacecraft to collect data in the geomagnetic tail, the anti-solar extension of the Earth's magnetic field, and of taking up a position where it could be accelerated by gravitational assist from the Moon on a 59 million mile (95 million km) journey to intercept Comet Giacobini-Zinner in 1985.

June 27-July 4 STS-4, the fourth and final engineering test flight of the Space Shuttle Columbia, was launched (KSC) into 150 miles (240·8km) circular orbit at 28·5 degrees inclination with Astronauts Thomas K. Mattingly and Henry W. Hartsfield. In addition to a classified military experiment and the monodisperse latex reactor, it carried a continuous flow electrophoresis system designed by McDonnell Douglas Astronautics in conjunction with the Ortho Pharmaceutical Division of Johnson & Johnson under a joint endeavour agreement with NASA. The orbiter also carried the first Getaway Special, a small, self-contained payload in the cargo bay with a group of experiments testing microgravity effects on growth of fruitflies, shrimps and algae, and alloying composite materials. The remote manipulator system arm lifted the 800lb (363kg)

contamination monitor above the cargo bay to determine the effect of the orbiter's chemical emissions on the bay's environment. The crew landed Columbia smoothly at Edwards Air Force Base on 4 July with a partial test of the automatic landing system.

June 30 Cosmos 1383 (Cospas 1), a navigation satellite with a search and rescue transponder, launched by the USSR (Plesetsk) as a unit in an international search and rescue satellite facility. Satellite equipped to pick up emergency locator transmissions from downed aircraft and ships in distress and relay their location to ground rescue station. System was devised as a joint venture of the USSR, the United States and Canada. NASA launched its search and rescue unit, Sarsat, aboard a TIROS-N weather satellite on 28 March 1983.

July 16 Landsat 4, NASA's most advanced Earth resources-surface imaging satellite, launched into a 422·5

x 435 miles (680 x 700km) Sun-synchronous, near-polar orbit from Vandenberg Air Force Base, California by a Delta 3920 rocket. The 4,410lb (2,000kg) machine carried dual imaging systems, a multi-spectral scanner (MSS) which imaged the surface in 2 visible and 2 infra-red bands and a new thematic mapper (TM) which imaged in 7 spectral bands at high resolution. Both photo sensing systems produced brilliant surface images showing ground cover, land use, sea states and shallow water features (shoals and reefs). A malfunction in the thematic mapper X-band transmission system halted TM transmissions to ground stations. A second TM transmission system (Ku band) remained operative but required relay to the ground via the Tracking and Data Relay Satellite System projected for 1983. In August 1983 malfunctioning of the solar panel arrays rendered

Landsat-4: MMS units can be seen at the bottom of this spacecraft.

Landsat 4 inoperative. NOAA authorized the launch of the backup craft, Landsat D-prime, in 1984, while consideration was being given to manoeuvring Landsat 4 to a lower orbit, where it could be reached by a possible Shuttle repair mission in 1985 or 1986.

November 11-16 STS-5, the first operational flight of the Space Shuttle *Columbia*, was launched (KSC) into a 185 miles (297·6km) orbit inclined 28·5 degrees to the equator with a crew of four. They were Astronauts Vance Brand and Robert Overmyer, commander and pilot, and mission specialists Dr William B. Lenoir and Dr Joseph Allen. The specialists initiated the launching of two Hughes Aircraft Company communications satellites from the cargo bay: SBS 3, a Satellite Business Systems commercial comsat of 2,337lb (1,060kg), and Anik C, a Canadian comsat, of 1,395lb (632kg). The RMS arm was not used. Instead, the satellites were deployed at 24 hour intervals as *Columbia* passed over the equator by the operation of springs from a revolving turntable that imparted spin to stabilize them in space. When *Columbia* had moved a distance away, each satellite was boosted to synchronous orbit by an attached rocket, a Payload Assist Module (PAM). This new technique of launching satellites to geostationary orbit worked smoothly. The crew landed *Columbia* at Edwards Air Force Base, taking control of the aerospace craft from the automatic landing system on final approach. *Columbia* was then taken out of service for overhaul and refurbishment and in December its sister ship, *Challenger*, was moved to the launch pad at KSC.

STS-5 crew: (clockwise from upper left) Lenoir, Overmyer, Allen and Brand.

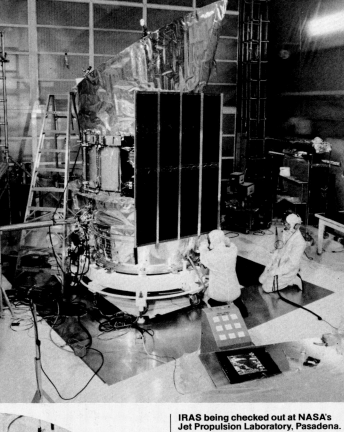

December 10 The USSR announced that Soyuz T-5 Cosmonauts Anatoly Berezovoi and Valentin Lebedev returned safely from 211 days in orbit aboard Salyut 7, a new manned flight record.

December 14 Scientists at NASA's Ames Research Center in California reported that photographs and other data indicate that the Jovian moon, Europa, has a planet wide ocean up to 31 miles (50km) deep, covered by a rind of ice up to 3·1 miles (5km) thick. Heat of radioactive elements decay accounted for keeping the seawater in a liquid state, they surmised. It was speculated that plant life could exist in the ocean, receiving weak sunlight through cracks and fissures in the ice cover.

1983

January 25 NASA launched the International Infra-red Astronomical Satellite (IRAS) into a 560 miles (900km) near-polar orbit with a Delta 3910 rocket from Vandenberg Air Force Base, California. The 2,372lb (1,076kg) observatory is the joint product of NASA, the Netherlands and Great Britain. Its 22·4in (57cm) telescope is capable of detecting celestial objects fainter by 3 orders of magnitude than the limit of balloon or sounding rocket infra-red sensors. Within 12 hours after ejecting its telescope cover on 1 February, IRAS was returning images to the ground station at the Rutherford-Appleton Laboratory, Chilton, England

IRAS being checked out at NASA's Jet Propulsion Laboratory, Pasadena.

from the Large Magellanic Cloud, a galaxy 155,000 light years distant and other galaxies. Scanning the region, it produced one image of a spidery cloud called the "Tarantula" in the nebula 30 Doradus.

March 16 Geographos, a plank-shaped asteroid 0·6 miles (1km) long, was detected passing inside Earth's orbit at 8·3 million miles (13·3 million km). It is one of the smaller Earth-crossing asteroids.

March 30 ISEE-3 in Earth-Moon system orbit was manoeuvred into the first of a sequence of increasingly close swing-bys of the Moon. The tactic positioned it to use lunar gravity assist for a calculated journey toward Comet Giacobini-Zinner. A second lunar swing-by was planned to occur on 23 April, a third on 28 September, a fourth on 22 October and the fifth on 23 December. On the fifth pass, the satellite would graze the lunar surface at an altitude of 62 miles (100km). Lunar gravity was expected to hurl the satellite on a trajectory that would take it through the comet's tail within 1,864 miles (3,000km) of the head on 11 September 1985. ISEE-3 would then fly on to pass 86 million miles (138·4 million km) upstream of Halley's Comet on 31 October 1985 and 19·5 million miles (31·4 million km) upstream of Halley on 28 March 1986.

April 4 STS-6, first flight of the Space Shuttle *Challenger*, was launched at 1·30pm EST from Kennedy Space Center into a 176 miles (283km) orbit inclined 28·5 degrees to the equator. Four crew members were Paul J. Weitz, commander; Karol J. Bobko, pilot and Dr Story Musgrave, a physician, and Donald H. Peterson, mission specialists. The first of three Tracking and Data Relay Satellites (TDRS-A) was deployed by springs from a tilt-table in the cargo bay. The 5,000 pound (2,268kg) machine was the largest communi-cations satellite ever built for NASA. With one other and a spare, it would comprise a space communications relay system linking all US Earth orbiting satellites and the Shuttle with a ground

station at White Sands, New Mexico. The TDRS system was designed to supplant NASA's 20-year-old ground station tracking and data network, except for three Deep Space network Stations equipped for interplanetary-range communication. Following deployment, a two-stage Inertial Upper Stage (IUS) booster attached to TDRS-A fired to lift it to geosynchronous orbit 22,261 miles (35,825km) over Brazil. The second IUS stage malfunctioned, leaving TDRS-A in a lower orbit. After IUS was jettisoned, ground controllers fired TDRS attitude control thrusters to raise the satellite to geosynchronous altitude by 29 June.

TDRS and its IUS in the canister in which they were transported to the pad.

On flight day 4, Dr Musgrave and Peterson donned space suits and spent 3 hours 45 minutes outside the cabin testing support systems, hand holds, footholds and special mechanical devices in the cargo bay. It was the first astronaut EVA in 9 years. Major space processing experiments on board were the Continuous Flow Electrophoresis system, a method of separating biological materials in an electrical field, and a Monodisperse Latex Reactor which made tiny, identical latex beads for medical/surgical use. Crewmen attempted to photograph and take photocell readings of lightning as *Challenger* flew over thunderstorms. Three "Getaway Special" payloads in NASA's programme to carry small, self-contained experiments at nominal cost for researchers in the roomy cargo bay, were flown. One designed by a Tokyo newspaper tested microgravity effect on the structure of snow crystals, another devised by a seed company tested seed germination in orbit and the third, designed by US Air Force Academy cadets, tested metallurgical process and growth of micro-organisms in orbit. *Challenger* landed at Edwards Air Force Base, California at 1·49pm EST on 9 April after a flight of 5 days 19 minutes. Inspection showed that *Challenger* had sustained less wear and tear than had *Columbia* on any of its five missions.

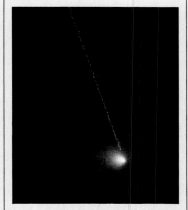

Comet IRAS-Araki-Alcock as seen by an RGO telescope.

April 25 During a search for asteroids, IRAS acquired data revealing a new comet. Subsequent telescopic obser-vation predicted it would pass Earth at 5 million miles (8 million km) on 10 May. The comet was named IRAS-Araki-

Exosat at ESTEC in Holland, where it underwent final functional tests.

Alcock after the satellite, and the Japanese astronomer, Genichi Araki, and the British astronomer, G.E.D. Alcock, who shared the discovery. Scientists at the University of Maryland and Johns Hopkins University later reported diatomic sulphur in the comet, a rare finding.

April 28 GOES 6, a new and more powerful geostationary operational environmental satellite, was launched from Cape Canaveral by a Delta 3914 rocket to geosynchronous orbit at 135 degrees west longitude for the National Oceanic & Atmospheric Administration (NOAA). Its main function was to observe weather in the western half of the United States and Canada and the eastern Pacific Ocean. Images transmitted to ground stations by GOES 6 and its eastern counterpart, GOES 5, provide visual data for commercial forecasting. The satellites sound early warnings of severe storms and hurricanes.

May 9 Pope John Paul II told scientists attending an audience in the Apostolic Palace, Vatican City that the Roman Catholic Church erred in condemning Galileo Galilei in 1633 for his assertion that the Earth was not the centre of the Universe. The Pope expressed the hope that a commission he appointed in 1979 to study the condemnation of Galileo by the Italian Inquisition would make "an important contribution to the examination of the whole matter".

May 13 IRAS found a second comet, much fainter than IRAS-Araki-Alcock. It was sighted moving away from the Sun and was named Comet IRAS.

May 19 NASA's Jet Propulsion Laboratory reported that IRAS had detected protostars in the estimated luminosity range of the Sun forming in dark clouds of dust in our galaxy. They appeared in scans across clouds Barnard 5 and Lynds 1642.

May 22 NASA's Jet Propulsion Laboratory reported failure to elicit a signal from the Viking 1 Lander on Mars after repeated attempts, and concluded that it was dead. The automated scientific laboratory which landed at Chryse Planitia on 20 July 1976 fell silent after a transmission on 13 November 1982. It had radioed thousands of pictures and more than 2 million weather reports.

May 26 Exosat, the European Space Agency's first X-ray observatory satellite, launched by Delta 3914 from Vandenberg Air Force Base, California. Orbit ranges between 217 x 124,274 miles (350 x 200,000km) inclined at 72·5 deg to equator. Exosat will explore cosmic X-ray sources in the energy range 0·04keV to 80keV, parts of the spectrum which are cut off from ground observation by the Earth's atmosphere. It was originally to have been launched by ESA Ariane but mishap to the 5th launch vehicle intervened and it was decided to switch to an American rocket. Exosat weighs approximately 1,124lb (510kg) including 278lb (126kg) of payload and is 10ft (3·3m) high including solar array.

June 2 and 7 The USSR launched Veneras 15 and 16 to Venus from Tyuratam. Due to arrive at Venus in October 1983, the two vehicles were to go into orbit around the planet and survey the surface by means of radar. Each was estimated to have the mass of earlier Veneras (11,023lb or 5,000kg). Unofficially, the reported goal of the double mission is to produce a radar map of the Venus surface, a project also proposed by NASA which is developing a Venus Radar Mapper orbiting satellite.

June 13 After 11 years of flight, Pioneer 10 crossed the orbit of Neptune at 8am EDT to become the first human artifact to leave the known Solar System. The 568lb (257·6kg) spacecraft had crossed the orbit of Pluto, presently inside that of Neptune, on 25 April. Launched from Cape Canaveral on 3 March 1972, Pioneer 10 was the first man-made vehicle to cross the asteroid belt and encounter Jupiter. Jovian gravity accelerated the spacecraft on the trajectory that took it out of the planetary system. The signal that it had finally crossed Neptune's orbit was sent by its 8-watt radio over a range of 2·8 thousand million miles (4·5 thousand million km) to NASA's Deep Space Network. NASA Ames Research Laboratory hopes to track the spacecraft for another 10 years and obtain data on the boundary of the heliosphere and interstellar medium. Trajectory engineers estimated that Pioneer's closest approach to a star will occur 32,610 years hence at a distance of 3·27 light years. The star is Ross 248.

June 18 STS-7, the second *Challenger* mission, was launched at 7·33am EDT from Kennedy Space Center in a 185 miles (298km) orbit at 28·45 degrees inclination. *Challenger* carried a crew of 5, including America's first woman astronaut, 32-year-old physicist Dr Sally K. Ride. Commander was Robert L. Crippen, pilot of STS-1 in 1981, and pilot was Frederick H. Hauck. Mission specialists in addition to Sally Ride were Dr Norman E. Thagard, a physician, and John M. Fabian. Dr Thagard was added to the crew after four members were initially selected, to study causes and relief of space sickness. The disabling malady, medically termed space adaptation syndrome, was prevalent on Skylab in 1973-74 and reappeared on Shuttle.

Sally Ride recording the progress of the CFES experiment on STS-7.

Two communication satellites, Telesat Canada's Anik C and an Indonesian satellite, Palapa B, were deployed early in the mission by spring ejection from rotating turntables and boosted to geosynchronous orbit by Payload Assist Modules. Anik C was established at 112·5 degrees west longitude and Palapa B at 108 degrees east longitude. The 50ft (15·2m) Canadian manipulator arm was used to deploy and then retrieve a Shuttle Pallet Satellite (SPAS-1), a West German prototype of a free flying space platform carrying 10 experiments and a TV camera. NASA's Office of Space Science and Applications (previously Office of Space and Terrestrial Applications) sponsored a payload of 6 experiments (OSTA-2). Three were automated materials processing devices designed by NASA's Marshall Space Flight Center and three were processing tests devised by the German Ministry of Research & Technology. The flight also carried the Continuous Flow Electrophoresis Experiment, the Monodisperse Latex Reactor and seven Getaway Special payloads containing multiple experiments. One included five experiments selected in a nationwide competition among West German high school students. Another devised by Camden, N.J. high school students and teachers sought to study the behaviour of a colony of carpenter ants in microgravity. Other experimenters using the Getaway Special facility were Purdue University, the California Institute of Technology, NASA's Goddard Space Flight Center, the US Air Force and a Van Nuys, California engineering firm. The mission, which lasted 6 days, 2 hours and 24 minutes, missed only one objective: a first Shuttle landing on the 15,000ft (4·57km) runway at Kennedy Space Center. The landing was "waved off" because of poor visibility and diverted to California where *Challenger* touched down smoothly at 9·57am EDT on 24 June at Edwards Air Force Base.

August 10 The Jet Propulsion Laboratory announced that observations of the star Vega by the Infra-red Astronomical Satellite show that the star is encircled by a disc of material in which planetoids appear to be forming. JPL scientists believed they may have found the first evidence of a solar system forming beyond our own. Vega, twice the size of the Sun, is believed to be less than one-fourth the Sun's age. The discovery followed by a few weeks another revelation by the busy infra-red observatory that the supposedly tail-less comet, Tempel 2, actually has a tail 20 million miles (32 million km) long.

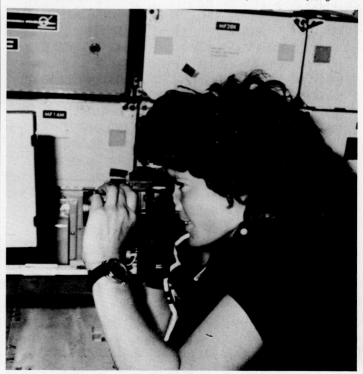

Index

Subjects mentioned in captions
have their page references set in italic numerals.
Those appearing in textual notes have
n appended to page reference.

318

Picture Credits

The publisher wishes to thank all the private individuals and public
institutions who generously supplied photographs, here credited
by page number.

Aérospatiale: 117 left
Anglo-Australian Telescope Board: Endpapers, 34-5, 44-5, 58,
66-7, 84-5, 86-7, 96-7, 200, 237, 238-9, 294-5
AURA (Association of Universities for Research in Astronomy):
44, 46, 69, 81 upper
Big Bear Solar Observatory: 70
Boeing Aerospace: 152-3, 173 upper, 178-9, 281 left, 283, 293, 307
Philip Bono (via K.W. Gatland)
British Museum (Natural History), by courtesy of the Trustees:
246, 247, 248 upper, 249 upper
Brookhaven National Laboratory (Dr Raymond Davis): 68
Catalina Observatory (Dr Bradford Smith): 234, 235
CERGA (Charles Veillet): 236 right
David Dooling: 266
Dornier System: 273 (via SIC)
Dr Krafft Ehricke: 296 right, 297, 299, 300 upper, 303
ESA (European Space Agency): 114-5, 116 lower, 234 lower, 315
ESTEC: 272 (via SIC)
Fairchild Space and Electronics Co: 255 lower
K.W. Gatland: 281 right
Dr Peter Glaser: 286, 287, 289 lower, 292
Hale Observatories: 32
Harris Corporation: 261
Harvard College Observatory/Ball Brothers Research Corp/
Colorado Video: 81 lower (via NASA)
Harvard-Smithsonian Center for Astrophysics: 22, 39, 60 lower, 61
Hasselblad: 104-5, 110-1, 126, 128, 148-9
Dr Rupert Haydn, University of Munich: 118-9
Hughes Aircraft Company: 76 left, 98, 113 top right, 120, 136, 137,
217 upper, 311
ISAS (Institute of Space and Astronautical Science, Japan): 277
ISRO (Indian Space Research Organisation): 278 (via SIC)
JPL (Jet Propulsion Laboratory)—NASA: 38, 40-1, 52-3, 54, 94,
98-9, 99, 122, 123 left, 124-5, 135, 158, 170, 173 lower, 181
upper, 182, 183, 184-5, 185, 191, 192, 192-3, 196, 196-7, 198, 199,
201, 204-5, 210-1, 213, 214, 215, 216, 217 lower, 218-9, 220, 222,
223, 224-5, 226, 227, 228, 229, 242, 242-3, 260 lower right, 279
(via SIC), 285, 308, 311, 312
Kitt Peak National Observatory: 33, 51 middle, 60 upper (H.Y.
Chiu, R. Lynds, S.P. Maran)
Lick Observatory: 47
Lowell Observatory: 241
Lunar and Planetary Laboratory, University of Arizona: 181 lower
Lund Observatory, Sweden: 30-1
McDonnell Douglas Corporation: 265 upper left
Martin Marietta Aerospace: 180
Matra: 267 lower
Messerschmitt-Bölkow-Blohm: 75 lower, 268 middle right, 275 (via
SIC), 276, 310
NASA (National Aeronautics and Space Administration): 9, 22-3,
24, 28, 42, 54 lower (Michael W. Werner), 59, 62, 63, 64, 70-1,
71, 72-3, 75, 76 right, 77, 78-9, 90, 94, 95, 101, 102-3, 106, 108, 109
upper, 110 left, 111 left, 113, 116 upper, 120-1, 127, 128-9, 129,
132-3, 141, 142-3, 144, 145, 146, 147, 150, 151, 154, 156-7, 163,
165, 166-7, 168, 169, 172, 174, 176-7, 184, 187, 188-9, 190, 202
right, 203, 207, 208-9, 209, 232, 233, 240, 250-1, 252 upper
right, 255 upper right, 260 upper left, 262, 263, 264, 265 lower right,
266-7, 267, 268 left, 270-1, 280, 289 upper, 290, 291, 300 lower,
301, 305, 307, 308, 309, 310, 311, 312, 313, 314, 315
NASDA (National Space Development Agency of Japan): 268
lower right
Naval Research Laboratory: 65 (via NASA)
Novosti: 103 right (via SIC), 107, 127 lower (via SIC), 131, 135
right, 138, 140 upper (via SIC), 161 (via SIC), 171 (via SIC), 252 left,
307
NRAO (National Radio Astronomy Observatory): 21, 26-7, 37, 42,
56-7, 230-1
RCA Astro-Electronics: 109 lower, 111 right, 112
Rockwell International: 312
Royal Astronomical Society: 16, 245, 253 right
Royal Greenwich Observatory: 314
Royal Observatory, Edinburgh: 18-9, 48-9, 88-9
Sacramento Peak Observatory: 69
Scala: 244
SERC (Science and Engineering Research Council): 253 left
(Rutherford Appleton Laboratory)
Ronald Sheridan's Photo-Library: 84 upper, 152, 248-9
SIC-Theo Pirard: 103 right (Novosti); 127 lower (Novosti), 131
upper (Novosti), 140 both (upper Novosti), 161 (Novosti), 171
(Novosti), 252 bottom, 272 (ESTEC), 273 (Dornier), 275 (MBB),
278 both (upper ISRO), 279 (JPL)
W.M. Sinton, Institute of Astronomy, University of Hawaii: 236 left
Dr Bradford Smith (Catalina Observatory): 234, 235
Smithsonian Institution: 296 left
Dr Stephen Strom: 32-3
Tass: 110 right, 160-1, 170-1, 306, 308, 311, 313
TRW Inc: 202 left
University of Arizona Press: 260 upper right (from *Rectified Lunar*
Atlas)
US Air Force: 103 left, 153
US Geological Survey, Flagstaff: 123 right, 194-5, 216 upper,
258-9
US Naval Observatory: 20, 36-7, 45, 50, 51, 84 lower, 106-7
Charles Veillet, CERGA: 236 right
Yerkes Observatory, University of Chicago: 248 lower

PRINTED IN BELGIUM BY

proost
INTERNATIONAL BOOK PRODUCTION

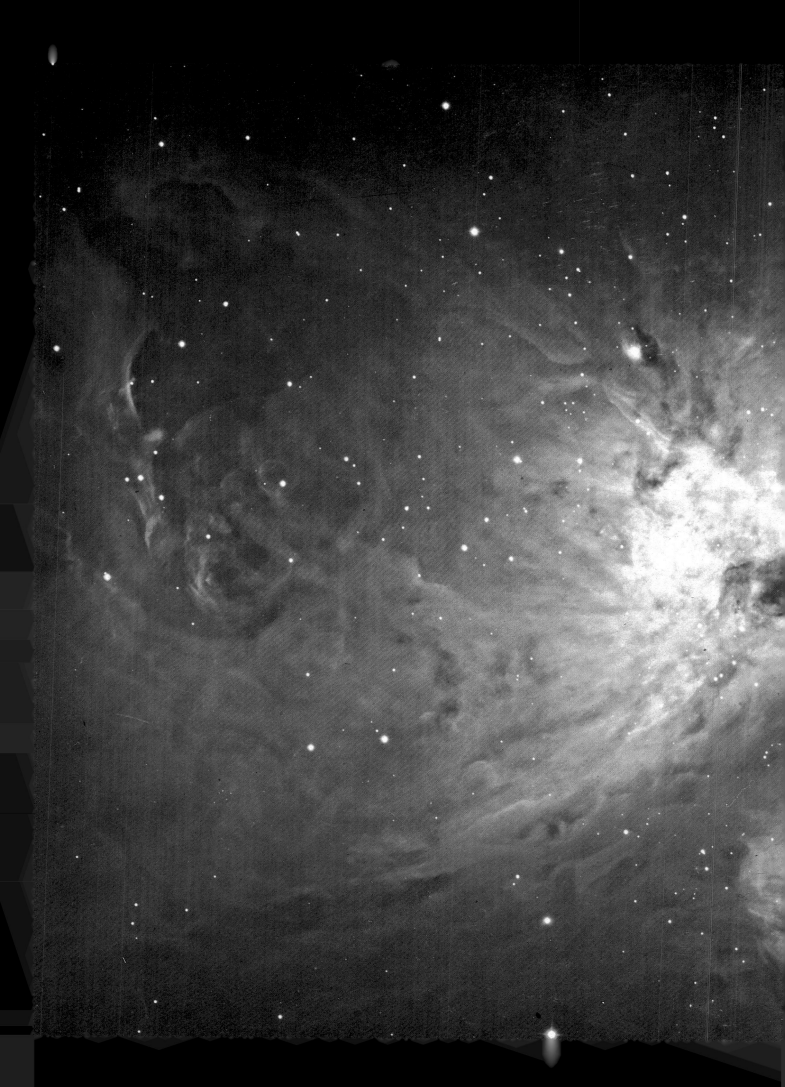